FROM CH
HOCKEY STICKS

MW01515461

THE ACHIEVEMENTS OF
CHINESE CANADIANS

LLOYD SCIBAN

ISBN: 978-0-9784245-0-3 paperback

ISBN: 978-0-9784245-1-0 e-book

Photo of the Dr. Sun Yat-Sen Classical Chinese Garden in Vancouver appears on the front cover.

This work is humbly dedicated to Chinese Canadians who, in their magnanimity, have chosen to disregard the unfair treatment they encountered when they first came to Canada, and instead have contributed immensely to its development.

CONTENTS

AUTHOR'S PREFACE

It was natural for me to be drawn to the achievements of Chinese Canadians. I had studied Chinese culture for nearly ten years in Taiwan and during this time I had developed a deep admiration for and interest in Confucian ethics. After my return to Canada I recognized examples of their practice in these achievements. At first, my observations were serendipitous, noting the enthusiasm with which my Chinese Canadian acquaintances promoted Chinese culture, the diversity and appeal of Chinese restaurants, and the community efforts to establish cultural centres and elder homes. However, as I sought grounding for my teaching of Confucian values, i.e., content that my students could easily relate to, the achievements of Chinese Canadians took on a more utilitarian appeal.

I did not set out to do research on Chinese Canadians once my interest in their achievements became more deliberate. Rather I first sought to gather information that would be of value and interest to my students at the University of Calgary, many of them Chinese Canadians themselves, and as I gathered this information, I came to realize that there was much more happening than I originally anticipated. At this point, one could assume that the path to gathering information would lead directly into that of research, especially as the achievements of Chinese Canadians became more apparent to me. However, instead, the opportunity to immerse my students in experiential learning presented itself.

The Chinese Canadian community in Calgary had not only created outstanding examples of the achievements that I have gone on to document in this book, they were willing to have interested individuals visit and even participate in them. Being presented with the opportunity to have my students gain hands-on experience I launched into the design of courses where students could, through visits to the sites of Chinese Canadian achievements, presentations by the authors of those achievements, and volunteer service, increase their awareness of those achievements and learn from their authors. Of course, in the efforts to design these courses, I was able to gain even deeper understanding of these achievements.

Therefore, when the time came to translate my learning into disseminable research, I already possessed a sizable base from which to proceed. Even more important I was strongly motivated by my admiration and appreciation of the efforts of Chinese Canadians to contribute to a society that originally was unwelcoming to them. Even more admirable was their recognition that contributing was the right thing to do, whether for practical or idealistic reasons. For example, Chinese Canadians had supported Canada's war efforts during WW II even though they were denied many rights, including the right to bring their spouses and children to Canada.

Once I began formal research, Chinese Canadians continued to assist me taking time to hold interviews, providing information, introducing other contacts, reading and signing ethics-approval forms, and even reading through drafts of my work to look for factual errors.

While Chinese Canadian achievements have piqued my interest as localized manifestations of Confucian values, they have also proven attractive to the Canadian population at large. Traditional Chinese Medicine has become popular and practitioners have put in place a system supporting it similar to that of mainstream medicine. The Yee Hong Centre for Geriatric Care in Toronto began by providing culturally sensitive eldercare for Chinese Canadians, then branched into providing similar care for South Asian, Filipino, and Japanese Canadians. Chinatowns, with their array of cultural activities and selection of restaurants, have become magnets for urban dwellers and conduits for novices attempting to understand and participate in Chinese culture. The Chinese language media are viewed by mainstream businesses as ways to reach well-to-do Chinese Canadian consumers, who, as new immigrants require many large ticket items. Chinese cultural activities, such as martial arts classes and New Year celebrations, attract large mainstream participation.

The increased interest on the part of mainstream Canadians in Chinese Canadian culture can also be attributed to the increasing influence of China in the world. On a practical level, understanding China and its culture promises to assist one in sharing in the wealth that China is creating, and for mainstream Canadians understanding Chinese Canadians is a step in that direction. On an ideal level, understanding China and its culture, opens doors to relating harmoniously to the large Chinese population and, again, understanding Chinese Canadians is a step in that direction. It is a gateway, of which visiting Canadian Chinatowns is an example, into Chinese culture. So the rise of China offers further motivation to understand and document the achievements of Chinese Canadians. It conforms to the theory that those outside Chinese culture can learn from it and leads one to think that Chinese Canadian achievements are based in part on Chinese Canadians' inheritance or adoption of that culture.

There is then a myriad of reasons for wanting to document the achievements of Chinese Canadians. One would want to appreciate these achievements as the magnanimous efforts of a previously disadvantaged group to promote themselves to the mainstream community that had one targeted them with prejudice. Canadian readers would want to make amends for past prejudice by acknowledging these achievements. Besides, these achievements also offer significant benefits that Canadians in general would want to be aware if not take advantage of. That awareness also promises assistance in understanding the reasons for the rise of China in the world today. Arguably, China's achievements and those of Chinese Canadians are based at least in part on a long-extant culture knowledge of which may assist others, if not to duplicate these achievements, at least to share in them. This knowledge also offers potential for improving relations with one of the most powerful and populous nations in the world today.

Upon reflection of my reasons for researching the achievements of Chinese Canadians, it seems important to also describe the subjective dimension that has driven this research. Confucius has a phrase "in olden times scholars learned for their own sake" (*gu zhi xuezhe weiji, The Analects* 14:24) that alludes to the significance of the personal value of learning. Of course, the above described reasons will be manifested in one's motivation, which is subjective; however, they will not reflect the degree of duty and privilege felt, nor will they convey the satisfaction that comes with believing that one is making a substantial contribution to other human beings. Of course, dwelling on these feelings may be indulgent, even self-gratifying; however, when combined with the objective reasons that in part produce them and when one realizes that they too can be substantial motivators, this concern seems less important.

Even as one takes satisfaction in describing the achievements of Chinese Canadians, one must also acknowledge the support of others without which the research that informs this book would not have been possible. First and foremost, I should thank my immediate family, my wife Shu-ning, my son Rowan (Yiping), and my daughter Rya (Yijun). They have been my stalwart supporters and I could not have completed this research without them. My colleagues in the Department of Communications (now Communications, Media, and Culture) at the University of Calgary, from which I am recently retired, have also supported me in my research. They allowed and encouraged me to develop and teach a set of courses centered on Chinese Canadians.

I also owe a debt of gratitude to those in Taiwan who assisted me in my nearly ten years of study there. My parents-in-law, Mr. and Mrs. Huang Kuang-yean, and brother and sisters-in-law were most supportive. My thesis director Professor Chang Heng, professors, and classmates at National Taiwan University, especially Yang Rur-bin, all strived to instruct me in spite of my limitations. The family of Wang Chi-ching welcomed me into their home as a visiting student and have maintained contact with me for forty years.

As described earlier, the Chinese Canadian community was highly welcoming of my interest then involvement in their efforts to improve Canadian society. Organizations such as the Calgary Chinese Cultural Centre, the Calgary Chinese Elderly Citizens Association, the Wing Kei Care Centre, the Calgary Chinese Community Services Association, the Avatamsaka Buddhist Monastery, the Calgary Police Service, the Oi Kwan Foundation, the Calgary Sien Lok Society, the Chinese Opera Development Society of Calgary, the Calgary Chinese Merchant's Association, the Calgary Centre for Traditional Chinese Medicine, Sing Tao Daily (Calgary), Fairchild Television and Radio, the Consulate General of the People's Republic of China in Calgary, the Calgary Chinese Private School, the Calgary Chinese Cultural Society, and the merchants of Calgary's Chinatown, all welcomed my students and I and were willing to commit time and personnel to educating us and introducing us to their services.

I was also able to interview members of similar organizations across Canada on the achievements of Chinese Canadians. The following individuals (listed in alphabetic order of surnames) were generous in providing time and information: Joseph Chan, President, Fairchild Media Group, Vancouver; Philip Chang, Executive Secretary, The Winnipeg Chinese Cultural & Community Centre; Philip Chang, Professor, Haskayne School of Management, University of Calgary; Peter Chen, Director, Information Division, Taipei Economic & Cultural Office, Vancouver; Katherine Cheng, Chief Editor, *Sing Tao Daily*, Alberta Edition; Ming-tat Cheung, President, Chinese Cultural Centre Greater Toronto; Julia Ching, Professor, Religious Studies, University of Toronto; Ping J. Chiu, Ottawa; Keo Chong, President, Indochina Chinese Association of Manitoba; Kally Crelly, Calgary Board of Education; Joseph N.H. Du, President, The Winnipeg Chinese Cultural & Community Centre; Ken Fung, General Manager, Sing Tao Newspapers, Vancouver; Joe Khu, Calgary; Boon-Li Lee, Assistant Station Master, Fairchild Radio Calgary; Jack Lee, President, Association of Chinese Restaurants in Quebec; Ray Lee, Founder and Past President, Sien Lok Society of Calgary; Steven Lee, Executive Administrator, Calgary Chinese Cultural Centre; Wayne Lee, Chinese Community T.V., Burnaby; Christine Leung, Regional Manager, Alberta, Fairchild Media Group; Thomas In-sing Leung, Founder and President, Culture Regeneration Research Society, Burnaby; Peter Li, Professor, Sociology, University of Saskatchewan; Xiaoping Li, Professor, Sociology, Okanagan College; Virginia Louie, *The Canadian Chinese Times*, Calgary; Kwok Ngan, Vice President, Indochina Chinese Association of Manitoba; Caroline and Charles Pei, Chinese (Mandarin) Bilingual - Edmonton Public Schools; Eleanor Shia, Chinese Heritage Language School of Saskatoon; Joseph Y.K. Wong, Founder and Chair, Yee Hong Community Wellness Foundation, Toronto; Kileasa C.W. Wong, Principal, Victoria Chinese Public School; Theresa Woo-Paw, Executive Director, Calgary Chinese Community Services Association; and Choon Yong, President, Regina Chinese-Canadian Association.

These organizations and their representatives provided me with insight into their organizations and the Chinese Canadian community in general. I gradually massaged the knowledge I gained from them over several years into a structure that has facilitated a description of the achievements of Chinese Canadians.

Nevertheless, it is common experience among researchers that the deeper they delve into their subject matter, the more they realize its complexity and breadth. My research into the achievements of Chinese Canadians has proved no different. The community is clearly dynamic and evolving. For example, Chinese Canadian youth are creating new forms to identify themselves, ones that place less emphasis on past discrimination and more on their unique identity within the Canadian mosaic. In another example, Chinese Canadians are exploring their historical, but largely unknown relations with Canada's First Nation communities.

This complexity and breadth require that I acknowledge that the research contained in this work cannot be exhaustive. In fact, there are probably many errors and faults in it and for these I assume complete responsibility. I am continuously being made aware of further examples and new areas of achievement. Yet, as I experience the satisfaction that Confucius refers to, I hope and see other scholars take up the cause of uncovering the achievements of Chinese Canadians. There are new areas to explore such as the confluence of the rise of China and Chinese Canadians' achievements. Chinese Canadians are now seen as resource that will assist in building Canada's relations with China. Chinese Canadians' large participation in the medical professions may bring changes in the way care is delivered there. Chinese Canadian efforts to preserve their ethnic identity in the context of Canadian multiculturalism will present a model and encouragement for other ethnic groups. Will a strong interest in physical fitness and being active among Chinese Canadians, notably among the elderly, lead to overall improvements in Canadians' health? Will Chinese Canadian sensitivity to racial prejudice lead to a more just society? These areas are ones that I hope will see further achievements by Chinese Canadians and their subsequent recognition by mainstream society.

2016.01.19
Calgary, Canada

1. INTRODUCTION

This book describes the achievements of Chinese Canadians. These achievements are important because they provide significant benefits and, thereby, not only offer practical lessons for the broader Canadian populace, but also encourage that populace to deepen their perception of an important constituent of the Canadian population. Besides describing these achievements, this book aims to fulfill a secondary purpose, namely, to highlight the role that Chinese culture has had in accomplishing these achievements. Chinese Canadians have drawn on the merits of Chinese culture and their own experiences in Canada to forge an amalgam that offers alternatives to the Canadian mainstream. In doing so, they are bringing to light what is, arguably, the most significant merit of Canada's policy of multiculturalism: to have a selection of alternatives for the many ways Canadians conduct and improve their lives.

This chapter will first touch on the background to these achievements. It will describe the barriers that Chinese Canadians have faced and their later population growth. Then it will outline the lack of academic research on Chinese Canadians, especially in comparison to their counterparts in the United States. Following this the chapter will briefly describe the content of each of the ten chapters that comprise this book. Then the role that the preservation and promotion of Chinese culture has had in assisting Chinese Canadians in overcoming the barriers they faced and in contributing to Canada will be covered. The chapter ends by addressing three considerations that should be kept in mind. The first is the need to be vigilant in preventing racist attitudes. The second is the identity that should be attributed to Chinese Canadians. Third is the diversity among Chinese Canadians that militates against simple description of them.

1. Background

The first known Chinese immigrants to Canada were in 1788 when Captain John Meares established a British outpost on Vancouver Island, which was populated in part by Chinese tradesmen.[1] Later, large numbers came to fill the demand for labour to harvest gold, coal, and lumber, and to build a railway across Canada. However, once these needs were met and no others demanded Chinese labour, their immigration was met by increasingly onerous restrictions in the form of entry taxes and eventually exclusion. It seems more than a coincidence that the decline of slavery in North America, marked by the end of the American Civil War in 1865, saw a need for cheap labour to replace it.[2] Subsequently, when this need diminished, such as with the completion of the transnational railways, prevalent attitudes surfaced, leading to greater opposition to Chinese presence.

The existence of this opposition comprises part of the background of this book. It still existed in an institutionalized form in 1967 prior to the removal of country of origin, and thereby racial characteristics, as a determinant of eligibility to immigrate to Canada. Arguably, systematic opposition still exists and appears periodically in incidents such as the "National Giveaway" episode of the television program W5 in 1979 or the media coverage of the illegal Chinese immigrants who were discovered in 1999 in unsafe ships off the coast of British Columbia.[3] This opposition has constituted a barrier

[1] Li Donghai (David T.H. Lee), *Jianada huaqiao shi (History of the Overseas Chinese in Canada)* (Taipei, Jianada ziyou chubanshi, 1967), 31-35; and John Meares, *Voyages Made in the Years 1788 and 1789 from China to the Northwest Coast of America* (Amsterdam: N. Isreal, 1967), 3, 88-89, and 129.

[2] Rather than see this change as the outcome of improved humanitarian values, Peter Li emphasizes that the development of capitalism caused slavery to become inefficient, thereby creating a need for cheap labour, which Chinese immigrants met. For this reason their working conditions were poor (*The Chinese in Canada* [Toronto: Oxford University Press, 1998], 20-23).

[3] Anthony Chan provides an account of how the program "National Giveaway" portrayed Chinese Canadian students in the University of Toronto's medical school as Chinese nationals, whose training would not benefit Canada (*Gold Mountain: the Chinese in the New World* [Vancouver, (B.C.): New Star Books, 1983], 161-186). Sean Hier and Joshua Greenberg describe "how Canada's press covered the sudden appearance of six hundred Chinese migrants on the coast of British Columbia between July and September 1999" ("News Discourse and the Problematization of Chinese Immigration to Canada" in *Discourses of Domination: Racial Bias in the Canadian English-Language Press*, by Frances Henry and Carol Tator [Toronto: University of Toronto Press, 2002], 15). The authors argue that the news discourse created the perception of a crisis among readers thereby reinforcing the traditionally

that Chinese Canadians and immigrants have had to overcome in order to establish themselves there, making their achievements all that more remarkable.

In order to comprehend fully the achievements of Chinese Canadians, it helps to know figures on their population and language usage. The number of Canadians who reported visible minority status as Chinese was 1,487,580 or 4.4 percent of the Canadian population in 2011.[4] The statistic for 2006 was 1,346,510 (single and multiple origins) or 4.3 percent of the population.[5] The number of Canadians who reported Chinese ethnicity was 1,029,400 or 3.5 percent of the population in 2001, which did not include those who indicated Chinese as part of a multiethnic origin.[6] In 1996, there were 921,585 Chinese Canadians or 3.1 percent of the total population, up 45 percent from 633,933 in 1991 when ethnic Chinese comprised 2.4 percent of the total Canadian population. The 1991 figure was about 2.2 times larger than that of 1981 and five times larger than that of 1971.[7] Of the 2006 population, about 70 percent were living in one of two metropolitan centres, Toronto or Vancouver, indicating a strong preference for urban residency.[8]

The 2011 Census confirmed the position of Chinese as Canada's third most common mother tongue. It reported 1,112,610 individuals using Chinese as their mother tongue

---

marginalized position of the Chinese in Canada.

[4] Statistics Canada, "NHS Profile, Canada, 2011," www12.statcan.gc.ca, accessed 2014.12.21. This figure includes those who reported more than one ethnic origin.

[5] Ibid., "Population by Selected Ethnic Origins, by Province and Territory (2006 Census) (Canada)," accessed 2015.02.05.

[6] Ibid., "Chinese Largest Visible Minority Group, Surpassing 1 Million" ("Ethnocultural Portrait," www.statcan.ca, accessed 2003.01.21). If we assume a 20 percent (2001 percentage increase over the number of single ethnic origin in 1996) increase to the single and multiple ethnic figure of 1996, the corresponding figure would be 1,105,902 Chinese Canadians of single and multiple ethnicity together, a figure quoted in "Ethnocultural Portrait."

[7] Li, The Chinese, 103.

[8] Statistics Canada, "Population by Selected Ethnic Origins, by Census Metropolitan Areas (2006 Census)," www.statcan.gc.ca/tables-tableaux/sum-som/l01/cst01/demo27g-eng.htm, accessed 2014.02.05.

(389,000 Cantonese, 255,000 Mandarin, 441,000 not otherwise specified). Chinese was positioned below English and French (7,298,180) and above Punjabi (460,000).[9] Those whose mother tongue was Chinese were equivalent to 84 percent of Chinese Canadians.[10] The 2006 Census reported 1,012,065 people with Chinese as their mother tongue.[11] These figures indicate that the Chinese Canadian population has reached sufficient numbers and is preserving their culture to the extent that can foster the provision of alternatives to the Canadian mainstream.

2. Research on Chinese Canadians

Although there is enough evidence for the claim that the achievements of Chinese Canadians have been and will be significant, the state of the field, the general state of academic research on Chinese Canadians, does not reflect it. Furthermore, the state of the field has become an arena of contention, a venue within which different parties compete for the authority to define Chinese Canadians. The underdeveloped state of research on Chinese Canadians is seen in comparison to the United States where its counterpart is much more developed even though the history of Chinese Canadians has paralleled that of Chinese Americans to a large degree. The arrival of Chinese in United States was for the purposes of meeting a demand for labour and they subsequently suffered a period of racist treatment including a period of exclusion.[12]

---

[9] *Ibid.*, "Immigrant Languages in Canada," "Table 1: Population of Immigrant Mother Tongue Families, Showing Main Languages Comprising Each Family, Canada, 2011," *www.statcan.c*a, accessed 2013.06.04; and "French and the *francophonie* in Canada," "Table 1, Number of People and Proportion of the Population Reporting French by Selected Language Characteristic, Canada, 2006 and 2011,*" www.statcan.c*a, accessed 2013.06.04.

[10] *Ibid.*, "2011 National Household Survey: Immigration, Place of Birth, Citizenship, Ethnic Origin, Visible Minorities, Language and Religion," *www.statcan.c*a, accessed 2013.06.04.

[11] *Ibid.*, "Population by Mother Tongue, by Province and Territory (2006 Census)," *www.statcan.ca,* accessed 2013.03.26.

[12] The Chinese Exclusion Act, which banned all Chinese immigration to the United States and denied citizenship to those already settled in the country, was implemented in 1882 in the United States and repealed in 1943. The

Adding to this paradox is the fact that ethnic Chinese now compose about 4 percent of the total Canadian population compared to 1.3 percent of the total population in the United States.[13] Furthermore, a 2001 survey of Americans' attitudes indicated that 68 percent of the respondents had somewhat or very negative attitude toward Chinese Americans.[14] This distinction from the U.S. situation highlights even more the underdeveloped state of research on Chinese Canadians as the larger population and more favourable attitudes should support more research there.

In the United States there is, at least, one academic journal, *Chinese America: History and Perspectives* (San Francisco), devoted to Chinese American studies and a number devoted to Asian American studies that have been published for at least the last five years.[15] There is also an association, the Chinese Historical Society of America, that is devoted to Chinese American studies. Also reflecting the relative strength of Chinese American studies is the number of academic publications within the discipline. A search on Google Scholar for articles written between 2005-2014 with the terms "Chinese American" or "Chinese Americans" (indivisible) in the title retrieved 1,373 results. Although there is no post-secondary educational institution with a department of Chinese American studies in the United States; there are many Asian American studies programs, which contain Chinese American studies. In 2007, the directory for the website of the Association of Asian American Studies listed thirty colleges and universities with Asian American Studies Programs, twenty colleges and universities with Asian American studies programs within

---

Chinese Immigration Act implemented in 1923 and repealed in 1947 restricted almost all Chinese immigration to Canada.

[13] United States Census Bureau, "Table 5. Asian Population by Number of Detailed Groups: 2010," *www.census.gov/prod/cen2010/briefs/c2010br-11.pdf*, accessed 2015.02.05.

[14] Yi, Matthew and Ryan Kim, "Asian Americans Seen Negatively: Results of Landmark Survey Called Startling, Disheartening," *San Francisco Chronicle,* 2001.04.27, A-1.

[15] "Asian American Studies in Academia," *asamatprinceton.wordpress.com/what-is-aas/asian-american-studies-in-academia*, accessed 2015.02.05.

departments, and nineteen colleges and universities that offered courses in Asian American studies, for a total of sixty-nine colleges and universities that would support Chinese American studies.[16]

Canada, in contrast, does not have anything near this kind of academic development of Asian Canadian resources, let alone Chinese Canadian resources. A search of major university library catalogues found no journal titles with the terms "Chinese Canadian" or "Asian Canadian"; nor is the author aware of any. There is one academic association, the Chinese Canadian Historical Society of British Columbia, devoted to Chinese Canadian studies. A similar search on Google Scholar for articles written between 2005-2014 with the terms "Chinese Canadian" or "Chinese Canadians" (indivisible) in the title retrieved 244 results, making for a ratio of 5.6 to 1 in favor of the terms "Chinese American" or "Chinese Americans." There are no major programs in Asian Canadian studies in Canada, and similar to the United States, there is no department or program of Chinese Canadian studies.[17] There was the Initiative for Student Teaching and Research in Chinese Canadian Studies at the University of British Columbia, but it was not a department and was largely student driven as indicated by its title.[18] The University of British Columbia, Simon Fraser University, University of Toronto, University of Guelph, and University of Calgary have offered courses on Asian Canadian studies. These efforts, however, pale beside what has been done in the United States.

---

[16] *www.aaastudies.org/index.tpl*, accessed 2007.08.07. A more recent calculation (April 2014) found in *Wikipedia, s.v.* "Asian American Studies" lists twenty-three universities and colleges with major programs. One should also consider the possibility, albeit slim, that there may not be any kind of emphasis on Chinese American studies in these programs; for example, a school may only focus on South Asia. However, the likelihood is that most, if not all, will offer at least a course in Chinese American studies.

[17] The University of Toronto and Simon Fraser University have minor programs in Asian Canadian studies and the University of British Columbia has a minor program pending. The University of Toronto has an endowed chair, the Richard Charles Lee Chair in Chinese Canadian Studies, which is housed in the Canadian Studies program.

[18] *www.instrcc.ubc.ca/INSTRCC/INSTRCC.html*, accessed 2007.08.09.

Furthermore, the field has been complicated by a more politicized approach to producing knowledge about Chinese Canadians. The field is becoming a realm of contention as to whom has the authority to create the knowledge that defines Chinese Canadians. Xiaoping Li in *Voices Rising: Asian Canadian Cultural Activism* (2007) describes a major force that is driving this contention. There is an activism that is targeting racism and prejudice. She compares it to the activism among Asian Americans in the late 1960s that led to the formation of many of the programs of Asian American studies in the universities in United States.[19] Some Asian Canadian activists believe that university research and teaching has failed to reveal the prejudicial forces that are barriers to Chinese Canadians and other minorities; therefore, there is a need to reform Asian Canadian studies including the establishment of departments of Asian Canadian studies as was done in United States.[20]

Li describes the activists' role in this trend:

> . . . there is now a growing awareness among Asian Canadians of the importance of changing education institutions. Claiming the site of knowledge production may then become a main goal of Asian Canadian cultural activism in the new millennium. We see this awareness among both old and young activists. It figures in young Asian activists' concern over school curriculums, in the Vancouver Asian Heritage Month Society's effort to develop education programs, and in the ongoing discussion among some activists regarding the need to establish an institution outside the universities to research and publish materials on Asian Canadians or Asian diasporas.[21]

There is a second trend that is adding to the complexity of the state of the field. Reflecting the movement to have more community involvement in the production of knowledge, universities are establishing alliances with community members. The Initiative for Student Teaching and Research in

---

[19] (Vancouver: UBC Press), 272-73.

[20] *Ibid.*, 274-79.

[21] P. 279.

Chinese Canadian Studies at the University of British Columbia is an example of this trend. The Initiative awarded fellowships to students who were then expected to do research, actively create new knowledge, and teach other students. One type of research project was for students "to record family histories, capturing the stories of parents and grandparents who came before them." By increasing student collaboration in the production of knowledge, UBC was aiding Chinese Canadian students to produce knowledge about themselves.[22]

There are many implications associated with this trend; one of the more significant is the potential it has to expand exponentially the amount of research and information on Chinese Canadians. If this trend were to develop fully, doing research and producing information could become a viable option for many more than a small number of university-appointed researchers.

There is a third trend, closely related to the first two but still slightly different, that is also complicating the field of Chinese Canadian studies. Chinese Canadians are wanting to identify themselves and there is an aspect of the Chinese Canadian efforts to establish an identity for themselves that immediately attracts academic interest. It is the records of early Chinese Canadian organizations that comprise as yet untreated historical material. These records describe how Chinese Canadians adapted to and maintained themselves within Canada, while establishing attributes that would delineate the behaviours of Chinese Canadians that followed them.

In summary, research in the field of Chinese Canadian studies is underdeveloped. However, with greater recognition of the achievements of Chinese Canadians and the benefits these achievements offer, which should lead to increased awareness of the importance of conducting this research, this deficiency should be corrected.

3. Contents of the Book

---

[22] Initiative for Student Teaching and Research in Chinese Canadian Studies, *www.instrcc.ubc.ca/INSTRCC/INSTRCC.html*, accessed 2007.08.12.

Each of the chapters in this book treats a specific topic. The topics have been chosen for their significance and representativeness. The significance derives from the degree of achievement, measured by its extraordinariness, effort required, difficulty, and the value created. The representativeness means that the achievement observed is particular to Chinese Canadians, that it can be recognized as a product of their endeavours.

The book is composed of ten chapters, including an introduction and a conclusion. This introduction is this first chapter. It covers a range of sub-topics from the purpose of this book, through the book's general content, to specific subjects that should be considered in reading it.

The second chapter is a survey, mostly of historical information on Chinese Canadians and some critical analysis of it. While much of this information is available in Canadian archives, libraries, and other collections, some is not.[23] There is also a wide variety in this information. Much of it is localized, such as the records of Chinese Canadian organizations active only in one city. There are also many specific histories, such as the memoirs of a particular individual, that have seen limited circulation. There are also publications to mark important events, such as the anniversary of the opening of a cultural centre. There is also a significant amount of primary material, such as the seventy-seven years of publication of the daily newspaper *Dahan gongbao (Chinese Times,* Vancouver) that are available through the internet or the records of Victoria's Chinese Consolidated Benevolent Association stored in the Archival Library, University of Victoria.[24] Categorizing this information roughly under the headings: organizations, projects, and texts, is more to indicate how the information can

[23] The recent additions to the Historical Chinese Language Materials in British Columbia demonstrate that new sources are being uncovered (*burton.library.ubc.ca/hclmbc/introduction.html*, accessed 2015.02.05).

[24] *Dahan gongbao* was published daily from 1914 until 1992 and maintained coverage of Chinese communities both within and outside British Columbia (Edgar Wickberg, Harry Con, Ronald J. Con, Graham Johnson, and William E. Willmott, *From China to Canada : A History of the Chinese Communities in Canada*, ed. Edgar Wickberg [Toronto: McClelland and Stewart, 1982], p. 335). It was first published as the *Dahan ribao*, and later was named *Dahan gongbao*.

be located rather than to describe it. This categorization is followed by an identification of those sources considered to be most significant.

The third chapter outlines the characteristics of a Chinatown, explores the causes of their origin in Canada, and describes some early examples. This is followed by a description of the achievements shown in their establishment and development. Both Vancouver's and Toronto's Chinatowns are highlighted as outstanding examples. The chapter finishes with a discussion of the future of Chinatowns in face of the challenges now facing them.

The fourth chapter describes the preservation and promotion of Chinese culture within Canada. It emphasizes the role Chinese culture has had in strengthening Chinese Canadians against racial prejudice, but also celebrates the culture as one that has much to offer the Canadian mainstream. Of course, the main manifestation of Chinese culture in Canada is in the use of the language. Chinese Canadians have developed language schools and some of the most sophisticated Chinese language media outside of China. The promotion of culture is also seen in the establishment of cultural centres, Chinese Canadian artistic activity, festivals, and the selling of Chinese food in restaurants and grocery stores.

The fifth chapter describes the economic achievements of Chinese Canadians. One finds examples in their home ownership, larger-reported disposable income and bank accounts, and the creation of large economic organizations, such as H.Y. Louie Company (owns London Drugs) and T & T Supermarkets. These examples direct attention to their past economic achievements in overcoming racial prejudice to establish themselves in Canada. Relatedly, they remain successful in ethnic industries, such as restaurants and grocery stores, and have become generous donors to mainstream causes.

Stepping up from more common economic activity, Chinese Canadians have dominated the Business Immigrant Program established by the federal government both in terms of number of immigrants and the amounts invested. Furthermore, this has led to even greater investments, such as Li Ka-shing's purchase of Husky Oil. Similarly, Chinese Canadians have excelled in residential and commercial property development. From high profile projects, such as the development of the Expo 86 Lands in Vancouver, through the building of numerous shopping centres, to the purchase of marquee hotels, Chinese Canadians have demonstrated this business strength.

In questioning the reasons for this development, a debate pitting proponents of external forces driving Chinese Canadians to succeed and those espousing cultural factors as demanding more attention has arisen. The outcome of this debate may determine how much the Canadian mainstream could learn from the achievements of Chinese Canadians, or more specifically, from the Chinese culture that, arguably, underpins these achievements.

The sixth chapter describes the Chinese language media in Canada. There are now a number of local and international media organizations disseminating information in Chinese, to the point where the Canadian Chinese media is one of the most developed, if not the most developed, outside China. This essay explores the early formation beginning in the early 1900s when Chinese newspapers begin to appear and extending into the present-day where national TV networks, local radio stations, and internet use have augmented the still-popular newspapers. Three main achievements are identified and described: the history and establishment of one of the most advanced Chinese-language media outside China, the Chinese-language advertising industry that has grown along with the media, and the encouragement of Chinese Canadians to involve themselves in the Canadian mainstream. The chapter closes with a critical analysis of whether the Chinese language media is fostering a Canadian identity or not, that is to say whether the continued use of Chinese and exposure to much non-Canadian news is not hampering the integration of Chinese Canadians.

The seventh chapter describes the Culture Regeneration Research Society (CRRS). CRRS is a Canadian organization that is dedicated to promoting the integration of Chinese and Western culture. Established in 1994, and headquartered in Burnaby, British Columbia, it has actively sought to strengthen Chinese culture with Western resources and vice versa. This research examines how CRRS has attempted to increase the interaction between Chinese and Western culture and the difficulties it has faced in doing so. Of particular note is CRRS' promotion of Christianity in China.

The eighth essay describes the development of Chinese Canadian institutional eldercare. It attempts to provide an

exhaustive listing of the providing institutions, while
highlighting the achievements of the Yee Hong Wellness
Foundation. This foundation manages more than eight hundred
beds in nursing homes at four different sites, as well as a broad
network of community-based services for seniors in Toronto.
The essay concludes with an analysis of whether the model of
eldercare developed by Chinese Canadians is sustainable and, if
so, whether it can serve as a model for mainstream Canada.

The ninth chapter describes the basis for, and the status of
Traditional Chinese Medicine (TCM) in Canada. It first
provides background explanation of the underlying concepts
and theories of TCM, then its practices, benefits, detriments,
and its promotion by the Chinese government. This background
facilitates an understanding of the strong presence of TCM in
Canada. It is used in institutions such as hospitals and is
widely commercialized, including testing and selling by private
industry. It is also widely regulated by both governments and
the profession itself. Five provinces and the federal government
all have established laws and bodies for controlling its practice
and the profession has several self-regulatory bodies and
schools to ensure proper practice.

The book concludes in the tenth chapter. Besides reviewing
the achievements described in this book, it summarizes the
claims made. These include the views that Chinese Canadian
achievements present alternatives for the Canadian
mainstream, that Chinese culture has played a significant role
in these achievements, and that Chinese Canadians want to
establish a Canadian identity but face resistance in doing so.

4. Role of Chinese Culture

This book argues that one of the factors contributing to the
achievements of Chinese Canadians is the influence of Chinese
culture and that there is both an increasing and considerable
influence of Chinese culture in Canada. These assumptions are
based on the following premises. First, there is empirical
evidence of Chinese cultural influence in Canada; for example,
the increasing practice of Traditional Chinese Medicine.
Second, there are strong arguments that the material wealth of
China, both past and present, which has motivated much of the
interest in understanding China, is based in great part on the

intrinsic values of its culture.[25] As belief in this claim has
increased, so has the attraction of these values to Canadians.
Third, Chinese Canadians have, until this day, historically
relied upon their culture in order to survive and prosper; for
example, Chinatowns have provided support to Chinese
immigrants.[26] As well, because they are believed to have better
command of Chinese culture, Chinese Canadians are seen as
more able to access China's rapidly growing wealth.[27] Finally,
the increased immigration to Canada by Chinese has increased
the presence of Chinese culture, not only as the way of life of
Chinese immigrants, but also as providing a critical mass of
resources that facilitate the culture's integration with the
mainstream.[28] The Chinese Canadian intention to preserve and
promote its ethnic culture is seen in the rapid construction of
Chinese Canadian commercial space in Canadian cities, the
spreading practice of various forms of Traditional Chinese
Medicine, the proliferation of schools to teach Chinese
language, and the development of national and local media
catering to Chinese Canadians. Furthermore, Chinese culture is

---

[25] Tu Wei-ming, *Confucian Traditions in East Asian Modernity: Moral
Education and Economic Culture in Japan and the Four Mini-dragons*
(Cambridge, Mass.: Harvard University Press, 1996), 10.

[26] Examples of resources provided by early Chinatowns included the shelter
given to the jobless Chinese Canadians during The Depression (1929-1939). In
the absence of work and government assistance, Chinese Canadians drifted
into the cities where Chinese associations provided for them (Brian Dawson,
Moon Cakes in Gold Mountain: From China to the Central Plains [Calgary,
Alberta: Detselig Enterprises, 1991], 153).

[27] Sau-Ling C. Wong, "Denationalization Reconsidered: Asian American
Cultural Criticism at a Theoretical Crossroads," *Amerasia Journal* 21:1 & 2
(1995), 13. As for examples of accessing the wealth of China, most of the
Canadian expatriate community in Hong Kong, which is reported by Industry
Canada to be the second largest expatriate community in Hong Kong, are
ethnic Chinese. They have returned to Hong Kong to work. (Industry Canada,
"Language Industry: Language Training Market in Hong Kong and Macau."
[*strategis.ic.gc.ca*, accessed 2007.07.26] and Asia Pacific Foundation of
Canada. "Value of Canadian Expatriates Ignored, Underutilized, Says New
Report from Asia Pacific Foundation of Canada," news release 2006.03.22
[*www.asiapacific.ca/about/pressreleases/2006/expatriate_22mar06.cfm*,
accessed 2007.07.26]).

[28] For example, Chinese foodstuffs support a healthy diet of more plant and
fewer animal products.

being promoted to the mainstream. This is seen in the comments of Henry Fok, donor of $2,400,000 to the construction of the Calgary Chinese Cultural Centre: "The Cultural Centre not only offers the local Chinese-Canadians a place to get in touch with and to appreciate their heritage and culture, it also allows members of other societies to explore and understand the richness of our culture."[29]

5. Further Considerations

There are some considerations important to the topic of this book. The first of these is the importance of denouncing the claim that race is necessarily linked to culture, that having certain racial characteristics automatically links one to having certain cultural characteristics or behaviour; for example, to claim that if someone has Chinese racial characters, they must be studious.

An important reason for challenging this claim is that, while there are many counter examples, there are none that disprove it entirely. In other words, it is a very difficult claim to disprove absolutely, while, at the same time, it has been used to justify racial discrimination, which, of course, undermines social harmony. One of the main arguments that supported restrictions on Chinese immigration and, eventually, the Chinese Exclusion Act, which severely restricted Chinese immigrants from entering Canada, was that Chinese immigrants were unassimilable. The Royal Commission on Chinese Immigration in 1885 and the Royal Commission on Chinese and Japanese Immigration in 1902 both "came to the same conclusion regarding the Chinese, who were perceived as undesirable and non-assimilable because of alleged cultural and social peculiarities."[30] Indeed, Chinese immigrants were even called the "natural enemies" of the white labour classes.[31]

---

[29] Calgary Chinese Cultural Centre, *The Calgary Chinese Cultural Centre Special Inauguration Publication* (Calgary, Alberta: September 2000).

[30] Peter Li, "Chinese," in *Encyclopedia of Canada's Peoples*, ed. Paul R. Magocsi (Toronto: University of Toronto Press, 1999), 359.

[31] The remark was made in a resolution that was sent to the Secretary of State in Ottawa by a public meeting chaired by the mayor in Victoria, B.C. in 1885 (cited in Ramdeo Sampat-Mehta. *International Barriers* [Ottawa : Harpell's Press, 1973], 34; see also Edgar Wickberg, *et al., From China to*

In contrast to the claim that the early Chinese immigrants had cultural and social peculiarities making them non-assimilable to Canadian society, Chinese Canadians have, in fact, assimilated very well into Canadian society. There have been a Chinese Canadian governor general, three lieutenant governors, and many elected officials at all levels of government. Many of the professionals in Canadian society are racially Chinese and many Chinese Canadians possess few or none of the cultural characteristics that are associated with their race. The claim that certain cultural characteristics are necessarily linked to race, which formed the basis for the claim that Chinese immigrants were non-assimilable into Canadian society, has been severely weakened in Canadian history. Chinese immigrants have assimilated, thereby undermining the claim that they necessarily possessed cultural and social peculiarities that would preclude this. Furthermore, many have taken on cultural characteristics that make them indistinguishable from other Canadians.

Of course, the apparent falsehood of earlier racist claims and the beliefs underlying these claims does not mean that Chinese Canadians do not continue to suffer racist treatment. In 1999 they were the targets of complaints because of their rapid movement into and development of ethnic services within Markham, Ontario. Morikawa Makio has documented the increased movement of Chinese Canadians into Markham, the subsequent development of housing and commercial services suited to them, and the negative reaction to this on the part of earlier residents, including elected officials. What should have been discussed in terms of the suitability of the development took on racial overtones as the Deputy Mayor of Markham and letter writers to the local newspapers criticized Chinese Canadian residents directly for what at worst might have been bad business decisions.[32] Furthermore, Sean Hier and Joshua Greenberg have argued that news discourse surrounding the appearance of six hundred Chinese migrants on the coast of

---

Canada, 56-7).

[32] "When 'Orientals" Are Not Socially Weak: A Conflict Between the Chinese and Canadians in Markham, Ontario," in *Japanese Center for Area Studies (JCAS) Symposium Series 4* (Osaka, Japan: National Museum of Ethnology, 1997), 217-232.

British Columbia between July and September 1999 created the perception of a crisis among readers thereby reinforcing the traditionally marginalized position of the Chinese in Canada.

The claim that race is necessarily linked to certain cultural characteristics is also self-defeating for non-Chinese. It is self-defeating because it gives weight to the possibility that one must be racially Chinese in order to produce the achievements that this book documents. One may be able to validly attribute minor characteristics, such as less susceptibility to sunburn or a greater ability to digest soybeans, as necessarily linked to the Chinese race; however, it would not be logical to make much stronger claims, such as one has to be racially Chinese in order to care enough for one's parents to house them in one's home. However, the necessary linking of cultural characteristics to race would give support to the latter claim. The result would be a discouragement of non-Chinese to learn from Chinese Canadian's achievements. In other words, one should not accept the argument that having certain cultural characteristics are restricted to those having certain racial characteristics because that could preclude one from the accomplishments that are based on these cultural characteristics.

In light of the falsity of the claim that certain cultural characteristics are necessarily linked to certain racial characteristics, another issue that naturally arises is the degree to which Chinese cultural characteristics should be attributed to Chinese Canadians. Although there is no necessary link, there is an apparent affinity of the Chinese race and Chinese culture within Canada. Part of this affinity is due to the fact that many Chinese Canadians have been immigrants. In 2001, 72 per cent of Chinese Canadians had been born outside the country.[33] Many of them would have possessed Chinese cultural characteristics that would have manifested themselves as they integrated with Canadian culture.

At the same time there has been an effort among Chinese Canadians to preserve, recover, or even learn from scratch Chinese culture. Chinese culture forms a part of the daily lives of many Chinese Canadians. Forms of Chinese are spoken and read; community schools further promote these activities. Food

[33] Statistics Canada, "A Chinese Community in Canada," *www.statcan.gc.ca/pub/89-621-x/89-621-x2006001-eng.htm*, accessed 2015.02.05.

is Chinese, with rice and vegetables consumed more than the mainstream and Chinese eating utensils used. Chinese medical concepts and practices are widely known and implemented. The importance of education and structured extracurricular activities is commonplace.

Part of the effort to preserve, recover, or learn from scratch Chinese culture is motivated by the recognition that Chinese culture offers resources that promote individual advancement. An obvious example is the ability to speak Chinese and thus being more able to access economic markets where Chinese is the main form of communication. Surprisingly, these markets include Canadian domestic ones, such as automobile dealerships bordering Chinatowns. Of course, the obvious one is the nation China, which has produced rapid economic growth leading to much foreign interest in both selling to and from its market. Chinese Canadians are natural choices to tap into these markets and, thus, having the skill sets provided by Chinese culture makes the efforts to preserve, recover, or learn the culture worthwhile.

There is, however, a complexity to the identity of Chinese Canadians that should be recognized. The affinity noted between Chinese racial characteristics and Chinese culture is counterbalanced by a desire of Chinese in Canada to forge an identity that is also Canadian. Having characteristics that are Canadian, also provides resources for individual advancement; therefore, Chinese Canadians have made an effort to form a Canadian identity.

The efforts of Chinese Canadians to develop a Canadian identity have their roots in Vancouver during the 1970s. In one milestone of this movement, a tabloid called *Gum Sam Po* called for the ethnic Chinese in Vancouver "to make our concept of a Chinese-Canadian community a viable one."[34] This was followed by the Identity and Awareness Conference at the University of British Columbia in May 1975 that converged on the view that "[i]nstead of nourishing a transplanted and unfamiliar culture from China, ... a Chinese-Canadian consciousness must be rooted in Canada and must be derived from local experience."[35] The new thinking led, in turn, to the

---

[34] Cited in Wing Chung Ng, *The Chinese in Vancouver, 1945-80: The Pursuit of Identity and Power* (Vancouver: UBC Press, 1999), 118.

[35] *Ibid.*, 119.

radio program "Pender Guy." This half-hour weekly program
ran from 1976 to 1981 on Vancouver Cooperative Radio CFRO
FM 102.7 and featured descriptions of Chinese-Canadian
experience. Its focus on promoting a new identity for ethnic
Chinese is seen in one of its articulated goals:

> The goal is not to old-style Chinese-ize the assimilated
> Chinese-Canadian and to make the person say, "I gotta get
> back to my roots, do the kowtow trip, apologize for a couple of
> decades of being Canadian etc." It's not a matter of giving in,
> but more a matter of compromise, understanding that we as
> Chinese-Canadians are different from, yet similar to other
> persons of Chinese descent. We retain some influences from
> old China through our grandparents and, at the same time,
> we are affected by the effects of living in a Western Canadian
> milieu.[36]

This thinking has since then been picked up by Chinese
language media in Canada that have been promoting a new
identity for Chinese Canadians,[37] as well as Chinese Canadian
authors, such as Wayson Choy,[38] who are writing about Chinese
Canadian experiences.

Recognition of the benefit of taking on Canadian
characteristics was not something that the Chinese
automatically possessed upon their birth or arrival in Canada.
However, it did develop and, thus, the identity of Chinese
Canadians has come to possess a complexity that must be taken
into account when considering their achievements.

There is one final issue to consider in this portrayal of the
achievements of Chinese Canadians. Chinese Canadians are
not a homogenous group. There is diversity among them that

---

[36] Quoted in Henry Tsang, ed., *Self Not Whole: Cultural Identity & Chinese-Canadian Artists in Vancouver* (Vancouver: Chinese Cultural Centre, 1991), 50.

[37] Lloyd Sciban, "Chinese Language Media Across the West," in *Challenging Frontiers: The Canadian West*, ed. Lorry Felske and Beverly Rasporich (Calgary: University of Calgary, Press, 2004), 287-89.

[38] *Jade Peony* (Douglas & McIntyre, 1995), *Paper Shadows* (Penguin Group, 1999), and *All that Matters* (Doubleday Canada, 2004) are among Choy's works.

the presence of similar physical characteristics, language, a predominant Confucian ideology, and external forces that have historically forced Chinese Canadians to group together for mutual support have hidden. For this reason one should be cautious in making general claims about Chinese Canadians.

The diversity within the Chinese Canadian population is seen in many ways: the differences in origins, such as being from Hong Kong, the People's Republic of China, or Taiwan; the differences between newcomers and old timers; the differences between foreign born and native born; the differences between those politically active and those politically reserved; and so on. These differences translate into practical consequences. For example, with differences in place of origin, Chinese immigrants from Hong Kong tend to adapt better to Western standards of doing business than those from other parts of China. With differences based on one's historical link to Canada, Chinese Canadians who are second generation or later will probably have better communication skills in English.

Wing Chung Ng has documented manifestations of this diversity. In describing the ability of groups within Vancouver's Chinatown to represent the community's collective interests, he points out the differences in political strategies between a group of immigrant Chinese and a group of local born. The former supported the candidacy of Douglas Jung, the first ethnic Chinese elected to the Canadian Parliament in 1957, while the latter worked to promote the candidacy of a non-Chinese and, according to Ng, were able to challenge the leadership of the former with regard to representing the community's collective interests.[39] Another case of diversity is seen in the elections for the board of directors of the Vancouver Chinese Cultural Centre in 1993. The incumbent board was portrayed as traditionalist with links to the older family and regional associations, Chinatown merchants, and the working class. The challengers were new migrants from Hong Kong and Taiwan, who advocated reform of the board modelled on Western democratic processes. The latter lost their challenge in part because long time Chinatown residents associated them with recent Hong Kong immigrants who were uninterested in the historical

---

[39] *The Chinese in Vancouver, 1945-80*, 96.

memories and spiritual core of Chinatown.[40] These are but two examples of the diversity of perspectives found within Canada's ethnic Chinese.

The presence of diversity among Chinese Canadians, in spite of what one may initially assume, creates a challenge for this book, or, as a matter of fact, for any, general description of Chinese Canadians. In describing the achievements of Chinese Canadians and the reasons for these achievements that are particular to Chinese Canadians, one should be careful not to over-generalize. Moreover, given the tendency to view Chinese culture as monolithic, i.e., a force that has dominated over thousands of years producing arguably the strongest political unit in the world for much of that time, it is easy to make generalizations, and thus the need to keep in mind this precept.

Take the example of Chinatowns in Canada. This author will argue that the establishment and continuing development of housing and services in close proximity so as to form a location, i.e., Chinatown, identifiable as having a predominately Chinese Canadian influence has been an achievement for Chinese Canadians; that it has allowed them to survive in the past and is indicative of their increasing economic strength in the present. However, this claim should be balanced with the facts that most Chinese Canadians do not live within these locations, nor probably would, even if the opportunity were presented to them. Furthermore, some Chinese Canadians do not like patronizing these locations, viewing them as crowded, less sanitary, lacking facilities such as parking, and reminders of the segregation suffered by Chinese Canadians in the past. In light of these opinions, one has to assume that there are diverse views among Chinese Canadians on the value of Chinatowns and similar locations and adjust one's judgments accordingly.

The achievements of Chinese Canadians will be described in the following chapters. In preparation for this, this introduction has presented some of the conditions that have shaped these

---

[40] Katharyne Mitchell, "Hong Kong Immigration and the Question of Democracy: Contemporary Struggles over Urban Politics in Vancouver, B.C.," in *Cosmopolitan Capitalists: Hong Kong and the Chinese Diaspora at the End of the 20th Century,* ed. Gary G. Hamilton (Seattle: University of Washington Press, 1999), 160-165.

achievements. First among these is the opposition to Chinese presence that existed openly in the past and today continues to persist, albeit more clandestinely, even though the targets of this opposition may be people whose ancestors have more than one hundred fifty years of history in Canada. Amid this opposition, Chinese Canadians have not only survived, they have prospered becoming a significant component of Canada's population and society. Their past achievements in overcoming opposition to their presence have been the basis for further achievements in the present day. For one thing, in spite of a period of exclusion, their population has grown, now constituting more than one million or 4 percent of Canada's population.

Accompanying the increasing population, Chinese culture has established itself within Canada. One of the main indications of this is the superior education of Chinese Canadians relative to the population as a whole; another is the common usage of Traditional Chinese Medicine in it various forms. Along with these manifestations of Chinese culture in Canada, there is also a wide range of organizations established to preserve and promote this culture. A clear example is the number of community schools devoted to teaching Chinese language. The culture also offers intrinsic benefits to non-Chinese as well, so one finds many students of Chinese martial arts not Chinese themselves.

One would think with the historical and present achievements of Chinese Canadians, especially in the face of strong opposition, that there would be greater awareness of the achievements of Chinese Canadians. However, there has also been a lack of research on Chinese Canadians, perhaps itself a remnant of early opposition to them. This is changing, though. The desire of Chinese Canadians to redefine their identity, including their role in Canada, is leading to the unearthing of new sources of information on their early presence. Scholars are also taking more critical perspectives of Chinese Canadian presence and thereby producing more analytical and revealing descriptions. It is the hope of the author that this collection of essays on specific achievements by Chinese Canadians will be part of this change.

BIBLIOGRAPHY

"Asian American Studies in Academia."
*asamatprinceton.wordpress.com/what-is-aas/asian-
american-studies-in-academia*, accessed 2015.02.05.

Association of Asian American Studies website,
www.aaastudies.org/index.tpl, accessed 2007.08.07.

Calgary Chinese Cultural Centre. *The Calgary Chinese
Cultural Centre Special Inauguration Publication*. Calgary,
Alberta: September 1992. 84 pages.

Chan, Anthony B. *Gold Mountain: the Chinese in the New
World*. Vancouver, B.C. : New Star Books, 1983.

Dawson, J. Brian. *Moon Cakes in Gold Mountain: From China
to the Central Plains*. Calgary, Alberta: Detselig
Enterprises, 1991.

Hier, Sean and Joshua Greenberg. "News Discourse and the
Problematization of Chinese Immigration to Canada." In
*Discourses of Domination: Racial Bias in the Canadian
English-Language Press,* edited by Frances Henry and
Carol Tator, 138-62. Toronto: University of Toronto Press,
2002.

Historical Chinese Language Materials in British Columbia
website, *burton.library.ubc.ca/hclmbc/introduction.html*,
accessed 2015.02.05.

Initiative for Student Teaching and Research in Chinese
Canadian Studies website,
www.instrcc.ubc.ca/INSTRCC/INSTRCC.html, accessed
2007.08.12.

Li Donghai (David T.H. Lee). *Jianada huaqiao shi* (A History of
the Overseas Chinese in Canada). Taipei: Jianada ziyou
chubanshi, 1967.

Li, Peter. *s.v.* "Chinese." In *Encyclopedia of Canada's Peoples,* edited by Paul R. Magocsi, 355-73. Toronto: University of Toronto Press, 1999.

-------. *The Chinese in Canada.* Second edition. Toronto: Oxford University Press, 1998.

Li, Xiaoping. *Voices Rising: Asian Canadian Cultural Activism.* Vancouver: UBC Press, 2007.

Meares, John. *Voyages Made in the Years 1788 and 1789 from China to the North-west Coast of America.* Amsterdam: N. Israel, 1967.

Mitchell, Katharyne. "Hong Kong Immigration and the Question of Democracy: Contemporary Struggles over Urban Politics in Vancouver, B.C." In *Cosmopolitan Capitalists: Hong Kong and the Chinese Diaspora at the End of the 20th Century.* Edited by Gary G. Hamilton, 152-166. Seattle: University of Washington Press, 1999.

Morikawa Makio. "When 'Orientals' Are Not Socially Weak: A Conflict Between the Chinese and Canadians in Markham, Ontario." In *Japanese Center for Area Studies (JCAS) Symposium Series 4,* 217-232. Osaka, Japan: National Museum of Ethnology, 1997.

Ng, Wing Chung. *The Chinese in Vancouver, 1945-80: The Pursuit of Identity and Power.* Vancouver: UBC Press, 1999.

Sampat-Mehta, Ramdeo. *International Barriers.* Ottawa: Harpell's Press, 1973.

Sciban, Lloyd. "Chinese Language Media Across the West." In *Challenging Frontiers: The Canadian West,* edited by Lorry Felske and Beverly Rasporich, 269-296. Calgary: University of Calgary Press, 2004.

Statistics Canada. "2011 National Household Survey: Immigration, Place of Birth, Citizenship, Ethnic Origin,

Visible Minorities, Language and Religion."
www.statcan.ca, accessed 2013.06.04.

------. "A Chinese Community in Canada."
www.statcan.gc.ca/pub/89-621-x/89-621-x2006001-eng.htm, accessed 2015.02.05.

------. "Chinese Largest Visible Minority Group, Surpassing 1
Million" in "Ethnocultural Portrait." *www.statcan.ca,*
accessed 2003.01.21.

------. "French and the *francophonie* in Canada." "Table 1,
Number of People and Proportion of the Population
Reporting French by Selected Language Characteristic,
Canada, 2006 and 2011." *www.statcan.ca,* accessed
2013.06.04.

------. "Immigrant Languages in Canada." "Table 1: Population
of Immigrant Mother Tongue Families, Showing Main
Languages Comprising Each Family, Canada, 2011."
www.statcan.ca, accessed 2013.06.04.

-----. "NHS Profile, Canada, 2011." *www12.statcan.gc.ca,*
accessed 2014.12.21.

-------. "Population by Mother Tongue, by Province and Territory
(2006 Census)." *www.statcan.ca,* accessed 2013.03.26.

-------. "Population by Selected Ethnic Origins, by Census
Metropolitan Areas (2006 Census)."
www.statcan.gc.ca/tables-tableaux/sum-som/l01/cst01/demo27g-eng.htm, accessed 2014.02.05.

Tsang, Henry, ed. *Self Not Whole: Cultural Identity & Chinese-Canadian Artists in Vancouver*. Vancouver: Chinese
Cultural Centre. 1991.

Tu Wei-ming. *Confucian Traditions in East Asian Modernity:
Moral Education and Economic Culture in Japan and the
Four Mini-dragons*. Cambridge, Mass.: Harvard University
Press, 1996.

United States Census Bureau. "Table 5. Asian Population by
    Number of Detailed Groups: 2010."
    www.census.gov/prod/cen2010/briefs/c2010br-11.pdf,
    accessed 2015.02.05.

Wickberg, Edgar, Harry Con, Ronald J. Con, Graham Johnson,
    and William E. Willmott. *From China to Canada: A History
    of the Chinese Communities in Canada,* edited by Edgar
    Wickberg. Toronto : McClelland and Stewart, 1982.

Wong, Sau-Ling C. "Denationalization Reconsidered: Asian
    American Cultural Criticism at a Theoretical Crossroads."
    Amerasia Journal 21:1 & 2 (1995): 1-27.

Yi, Matthew and Ryan Kim. "Asian Americans Seen Negatively:
    Results of Landmark Survey Called Startling,
    Disheartening." *San Francisco Chronicle,* 2001.04.27, A-1.

2. SIGNIFICANT SOURCES OF INFORMATION ON CHINESE CANADIANS

The venues for understanding Chinese Canadians are be found in many forms, from government supported research projects to the posting of personal histories on the internet. Government agencies, such as Canadian Heritage, reflect the benefit of promoting multiculturalism by funding the scanning of Chinese language newspapers and making them available in digital format. Organizations, such as the Chinese Canadian National Council, have initiated innovative projects, such as the Chinese Canadian Culture Online Project. The Calgary Chinese Cultural Centre maintains a permanent exhibit on the history of the Chinese in Calgary. For a final example, the history behind and pictures of the artifact collection of the Yip Sang family, early Chinese merchants in Vancouver, have been posted on the internet.

The increase in these venues has also fostered awareness of the amount of history Chinese Canadians have preserved themselves. Traditionally, history and writing have been important aspects of Chinese civilization and these traditions have been influential in Canada. One finds collections of histories on Chinese Canadians across the country, in public and university libraries and in archives. Furthermore, special agencies, such as the Chinese Canadian Historical Society of British Columbia and the Chinese Community Library, both situated in Vancouver, have mandates to foster the collection and preservation of these histories. One example of these histories is the personal papers of important figures, such as Alexander Cumyow, an early Chinese Canadian public servant, in the Special Collections Division of University of British Columbia Library.

There have been some scholastic efforts to survey the information on Chinese Canadians that is preserved and collected. Some monographs devoted to Chinese Canadians contain very detailed bibliographies. However, today the efforts are challenged by the fact that information is being discovered and produced faster than it can be catalogued and stored. The creation of the internet has facilitated dissemination and, combined with digitization, has rapidly led to large amounts of related information being posted online.

In the midst of this prolific output, this essay cannot claim comprehensiveness of coverage or categorization with regard to the significant sources of information on Chinese Canadians. At best, it can hope to introduce a few important sources, specific content, and forms of this information. As to what constitutes importance, it is a loose combination of factors such as size, representativeness, recognition, scarcity, and even access. The essay has been organized around subheadings of organizations, projects, texts, most significant sources, and potential sources. The first three subheadings offer a simple scheme by which to introduce sources while indicating some general characteristics of each. An attempt has also been made to compensate for the lack of sophistication in categorization by reviewing the selection of sources from the perspective of functionality and presenting those that are considered the most significant. The essay then looks briefly at untapped sources that have the potential to contribute to one's knowledge of Chinese Canadians.

1. Organizations

Given the history of Chinese Canadians' arrivals in Canada, it is natural that one would find some of the most significant sources of information on the West Coast. One finds important depositories in the University of British Columbia (UBC) Library, *www.library.ubc.ca*. The UBC University Archives contains two large collections donated by Edgar Wickberg, editor of the seminal text *From China to Canada: A History of the Chinese Communities in Canada* (1982). The Chinese Canadian Research Collection, occupying 7.53 meters of shelf space, was the basis for the writing of the text. The Chinese in Canada, 93 cm., documents the history of the Chinese community in Canada and public perceptions, with materials mostly dated from the 1970s and later.

There are also a number of relevant collections of personal papers in Special Collections. One finds the personal papers of Alexander Cumyow, 15 cm., the first Chinese born in Canada;[1]

---

[1] He would later serve as a government interpreter and was active in Chinese Canadian organizations.

those of Fong Sien Wong (8 m.) who was a spokesman for the Chinese Canadian community in Vancouver; the Lee family fonds, 2 m., documenting their business activities; the Thomas Whaun fonds, 46 cm., the personal papers of a newspaper administrator; and the *Dahan gongbao (Chinese Times,* Vancouver), 1915-92.[2] The university's server also contains a list of resources under the term "Chinese Canadians" for researching Chinese Canadians.[3]

The university's server also houses two websites, one "The Chinese Experience in British Columbia: 1850-1950," *www.library.ubc.ca/chineseinbc*, which contains a raft of historical material particularly on social and cultural life and links to more local resources under "Links and Resources." The second website introduces the Chung Collection, *chung.library.ubc.ca/node*, which contains more than twenty-five thousand documents, books, maps, posters, paintings, photographs, and other artifacts. This website contains a subsection "Immigration and Settlement" that introduces Canadian Chinese history, in particular that of the Yip Sang family some of Vancouver's most successful merchants in the early 1900s.

Another organization of importance in the management of information on Chinese Canadians is Library and Archives Canada, *www.collectionscanada.ca*, which is a union of the former National Library of Canada and National Archives of Canada. A search of the catalogue (2014.08.14) using "Chinese Canadian" as a single term produced 713 results: 626 for the library, 67 for the archives, and 19 for the website. A search for the corresponding term in French *"sino-canadien"* turns up 9 results: 7 for the library and 2 for the archives. The library results include not only materials held in the National Library

[2] The *Chinese Times* was published daily from 1914 until 1992 and maintained good coverage of Chinese communities both within and outside British Columbia (Edgar Wickberg, Harry Con, Ronald J. Con, Graham Johnson, and William E. Willmott, *From China to Canada : A History of the Chinese Communities in Canada*, ed. Edgar Wickberg [Toronto: McClelland and Stewart, 1982], p. 335). The Chinese name for the *Chinese Times* was first *Dahan ribao*, and later *Dahan gongbao*.

[3] *guides.library.ubc.ca/content.php?pid=439825&sid=3600746*, accessed 2014.08.14.

of Canada, but also those located in more than 1,300 libraries across Canada. In the library holdings, there are a number of sources that one would be unlikely to find anyway else, particularly sources on Chinese Canadian art, such as *Beyond Borders: Contemporary Chinese-Canadian Art in Manitoba / the Winnipeg Art Gallery* (2000), or those with a limited printing, such as *Evergreen News 15th Anniversary*.[4] The archival records are mostly textual and photographic materials. The website search results link to other related websites.

Library and Archives Canada also maintains the website "The Early Chinese Canadians, 1858-1947" at *www.collectionscanada.gc.ca/chinese-canadians/021022-4000-e.html*. It is developed in detail with major headings "Introduction," "The History," "Historical Photographs and Documents," "Head Tax Records," "Further Research," "Educational Resources," and "About the Early Chinese Canadians." "Research Guide" under "Historical Photographs and Documents" is particularly rich in resources. It links to related government documents such as transcripts of hearings by the Royal Commission to Investigate Chinese and Japanese Immigration into British Columbia (1900–1902) and archival material created by private individuals such as E.C. Mark, former publisher of the *Shing Wah Daily News* (Toronto).

The Asia Pacific Foundation of Canada, *www.asiapacific.ca*, has a mandate to promote understanding of Canada's transpacific relations. As part of its mandate, it commissions the writing of research reports, some of which are important sources of information on Chinese Canadians.[5] The academic quality of these reports makes the foundation exceptional among sources of information.

There are a number of rich sources of information accessible through the server for the David C. Lam Institute for East-West Studies, *www.sfu.ca/davidlamcentre.html*, of Simon

---

[4] This is a publication for Chinese seniors issued by the United Chinese Community Enrichment Services Society (Vancouver), also known by its acronym SUCCESS, in 2000.

[5] Examples include "Multi-stream Flows Reshape Chinese Communities in Canada: A Human Capital Perspective" by Kenny Zhang (2012), "Doing Business at Home and Away: Policy Implications of Chinese-Canadian Entrepreneurship" by Wenhong Chen and Barry Wellman (2007), and "Leveraging Vancouver's Cultural/Ethnic Diversity" by Yuen Pau Woo (2005).

Fraser University. For example, there are links to the histories of five Canadian Chinatowns. Of particular value is the database "Historical Chinese Language Materials in BC" at *burton.library.ubc.ca/hclmbc*, which "comprises over eleven thousand records of Chinese-language items such as manuscripts, newspapers, correspondence, genealogical and family records, business transaction records, association records, certificates, receipts, textbooks, and photographs. The site also provides image galleries on clan associations and pioneer families, a directory of Chinese associations in British Columbia, a directory of religious organizations in British Columbia, links to information websites of various Chinatowns across British Columbia, and other related materials." A link to "Related Materials" leads to further links to individual histories, websites, bibliographies, and twenty-nine organizations preserving Chinese historical materials. The latter list of organizations, mostly archives in British Columbia, is promising because these probably hold unexplored historical records. The database is searchable in Chinese, English, and *Pinyin*, the official phonetic system for transcribing Chinese characters. A downloadable template is available to allow remote users to contribute records and images.

The Chinese Canadian Historical Society of B.C., *www.cchsbc.ca*, is a relatively new organization, having been established in 2004. It is dedicated to promoting the understanding of the history of the Chinese in British Columbia. The society advertises its members' research projects, which are interesting because they reveal many creative perspectives for doing research on Chinese Canadians; for example, the film "Cedar and Bamboo" (2010) created by the society explores the relationships between the early Chinese and the local indigenous people. Under "Resources" on the society's server there are more than seventy links to websites related to Chinese Canadians.

The Chinese Canadian National Council (CNCC), *www.ccnc.ca*, has also been active in managing information on Chinese Canadians, especially about their contemporary situation. Part of its mandate is to promote knowledge of the culture, history, and contributions of Chinese Canadians; the council's various chapters are also active in making information available. One of the council's more notable achievements was the Chinese Canadian Culture Online Project, which included a

special anthology of stories written by or about Chinese
Canadian youth, a collection of short videos by Chinese
Canadians, writings by youth on important events in Chinese
Canadian history, and an introduction to emerging talent
among Chinese Canadians. The Toronto chapter of CCNC
maintains the Chinese Canadian Historical Photo Exhibit
online. To reiterate, the council is active in leading and defining
current events among Chinese Canadians, with a special
emphasis on youth.

The Multicultural Historical Society of Ontario,
www.mhso.ca, has a mandate to increase public awareness of
the multicultural nature of Ontario's history, which includes
collecting, publishing, and disseminating information about
Chinese Canadians. *A Guide to the Collections of the
Multicultural History Society of Ontario* (1992) contains eleven
pages of entries encompassing its Chinese collection. The
materials included in this list are mostly the personal records of
Chinese individuals, though there are also records of Chinese
Canadian organizations such as church groups. The records are
usually narrow in their subject matter, such as personal
photographs or newsletters from a local Chinese-Canadian
association, which means that they probably cannot be found in
other collections.The society has published *Polyphony: The
Bulletin of the Multicultural History Society of Ontario* since
1977. Among its articles, there are about twenty-seven on
Chinese Canadians, many found in a special issue entitled "The
Chinese in Ontario" (no. 15 [2000]). The society also has seven
Chinese Canadian publications on microfilm.[6] The extensive
coverage of these publications gives them high potential value.
Furthermore, there is diversity in the types of information
available; for example, the website "Chinese Canadian Women,
1923-1967" contains more than one thousand items
documenting Chinese Canadian women's history between 1923
and 1967, including oral history interviews and historical
photographs.

---

[6] *Chinese Canadian Community News* (1979-1987), *Chinese Community
Newsletter* (Ottawa, 1979-1984), *Hung Chung She Po* (January-June 1954),
K'uai Pao (Chinese Express) (1971-1989), *Modern Times Weekly* (1985-1987),
National Capital Chinese Community Newsletter (1977-1987), and *Shing Wah
Po* (1923-1990).

The Chinese Community Library, *www.vcn.bc.ca/clibrary*, in downtown Vancouver operates the Chinese Community History Room. Since 1983 it has managed materials documenting the history of Chinese society in Vancouver. These materials include oral histories, books, newspaper clippings, historical photographs, a complete set of *Chinatown Today*, and a complete collection of master tapes of the radio program "Pender Guy."[7] A record of the contents of the History Room can be found at *www.vcn.bc.ca/clibrary/historyroom*.

2. Projects

There are a number of significant projects whose mandate includes the gathering and dissemination of information on Chinese Canadians. The Multicultural Canada Project has been supported by a number of government, academic, and private organizations including the Department of Canadian Heritage, Libraries and Archives Canada, and the Sien Lok Society of Calgary. It has collected newspapers, local histories, speeches, photographs, letters, and oral histories in Chinese and placed them with search engines at *www.multiculturalcanada.ca*. A database and search engine have been established for the *Chinese Times (Dahan gongbao,* Vancouver, 1914-1992), with a total of two hundred fifty thousand pages, approximately six thousand issues including searchable English summaries. With regard to the *Chinese Times* database, in their letter of permission to digitize the *Chinese Times*, the Chinese Freemasons noted, "'The Chinese Freemasons have been in Canada and contributed to the communities since 1864. Therefore we fully appreciate and support your Library's [probably referring to Simon Fraser University Library] commitments to multiculturalism in terms of its services to students, its collections, and its online services."[8]

---

[7] The oral histories are recorded on more than one hundred cassette tapes. Some of the photographs date back to the nineteenth century. *Chinatown Today* is an English magazine on the Chinese community in Vancouver. "Pender Guy" was broadcast once a week between 1976 and 1981 by a group of young Chinese-Canadians concerned with the issues of assimilation and cultural identity.

[8] Cited in "Chinese Canadian Historical Society of B.C. Newsletter" 2.1 (2006), 5.

Other publications available on the Multicultural Canada server include the entire run of the *Ottawa Chinese Community Newsletter*, which was published monthly between 1979 and 1987; all issues of the *Shing Wah Daily News* (Toronto) dating from 29 May 1923 to 29 September 1990, which was once the primary Chinese language newspaper in Canada; and fifty-five documents from the Chinese Consolidated Benevolent Association of Victoria delineating their history, protests against discrimination, and the history of institutions such as Victoria's Chinese Hospital.

The Multicultural Canada Project is noteworthy for its pioneering efforts to provide online access to materials, which, of course, increases the likelihood of their preservation. The effort to digitize a Chinese language newspaper, the *Chinese Times*, with a long history in Canada is a landmark creating a precedent that present-day publishing Chinese language newspapers in Canada have followed.[9] In another online project, Multicultural Alberta, *www.ourfutureourpast.ca/multiab/index.html*, in conjunction with the Sien Lok Society of Calgary, has posted video interviews of nineteen Chinese pioneers in southern Alberta.

The Chinese-Canadian Genealogy Project, *www.vpl.ca/ccg*, an effort of the Vancouver Public Library with support from Library and Archives Canada, provides tools and information for Canadians of Chinese origin who want to explore their personal connection to Chinese-Canadian history. Two sections of the website "History & Pioneers" and "Documents & Records," offer resources for researching Chinese Canadian history. Within "Documents & Records" there is also a link to a site briefly describing the Chinese-language newspapers in Edmonton, Montreal, Ottawa, Toronto, Vancouver, Victoria, and Winnipeg.

3. Texts

Two texts, *From China to Canada: A History of the Chinese Communities in Canada* (1982), edited by Edgar Wickberg, and *The Chinese in Vancouver, 1945-1980: The Pursuit of Identity*

---

[9] The *Mingbao (Ming Pao Daily News)* provides online access to past issues dating back to 2001, *news.mingpao.com*, accessed 2015.02.01.

and Power (1999), written by Wing Chung Ng, have elaborate
bibliographies of sources of information on Chinese Canadians.
From China to Canada contains a bibliographical note that
comments on general sources.[10] The bibliographical note
highlights the *Chinese Times (Dahan gongbao).*[11] The
bibliographical note also stresses the Public Archives of Canada
(probably today's Library and Archives Canada), the United
Church of Canada Archives at Victoria University of the
University of Toronto, and the Vancouver City Archives as most
useful for the book.[12] The note is followed by a selected
bibliography.

The actual bibliography of *From China to Canada* further
identifies two important sources of information: the Special
Collections Division of UBC Library and the journal *B.C.
Studies.* The former contains the personal papers of important
Chinese Canadian figures, such as Alexander Cumyow, the first
Chinese born in Canada, and the latter has served as a forum
for a number of research articles on Chinese Canadians. One
other noteworthy fact about the bibliography is its separate
section on Chinese and Japanese materials with titles and
authors' names given in their original form as well as in
transliteration and translation.

The Chinese in Vancouver contains an extensive
bibliography of sixteen pages. A notable feature of the
bibliography is the detailed categorization of entries. Ng has
separate categories for the special publications and newsletters
of Chinese organizations; for organizational archives, such as
for the Chinese Cultural Centre (Vancouver); for personal
papers and collections of research materials; for public archival
materials; and for published government documents. Most of
the entries under these headings are specific to Chinese
Canadians.

One should also note the article "'White Canada Forever':
Two Generations of Studies" by Patricia Roy. This article,
published in 1979, describes two generations of academic
writing on Chinese Canadians with 1970 a distinguishing point

---

[10] Pp. 334-338.

[11] P. 334.

[12] P. 335.

between them. Roy also discerns that three major themes: political, racial, and economic, are used to explain treatment of Chinese Canadians.

Peter Li's *The Chinese in Canada* (1998) provides one of the best overviews of contemporary Chinese Canadians. The sixteen page bibliography lists several government documents, articles from *The Globe and Mail, The Toronto Star* and *The Vancouver Sun,* and a list of Li's many other publications; all relevant to present day Chinese Canadians.

Building on the Chinese Canadians' emphasis on history and detailed record keeping, there have been a number of local histories that have been produced. These include Jim Wolf and Patricia Owen, *Yi Fao: Speaking Through Memory, A History of New Westminster's Chinese Community 1858-1980* (Surrey, B.C.: Heritage House, 2008); Chad Reimer, *Chilliwack's Chinatowns: A History* (Vancouver, B.C.: Chinese Canadian Historical Society of British Columbia & Initiative for Student Teaching and Research in Chinese Canadian Studies, University of British Columbia, 2011); Wen Lee Soo, *Crossings: A Portrait of the Chinese Community of Moose Jaw* (Moose Jaw Museum & Art Gallery, 2005); C. Millien, E. Woo, and P. Yeh, *Winnipeg Chinese* (Department of the Secretary of State, 1971); Alison R. Marshall, *The Way of the Bachelor: Early Chinese Settlement in Manitoba* (Vancouver: UBC Press, 2011); "Rising Dragon: Chinese Canadians in Windsor" (*www.chineseinwindsor.com*); Arlene Chan, *The Chinese in Toronto from 1878: From Outside to Inside the Circle* (Toronto: Dundurn, 2011); Denise Helly, *Les Chinois á Montréal, 1877-1951* (Ville Saint Laurent, Quebec: Institut québécois de recherche sur la culture, 1987); Chan Kwok Bun, *Smoke and Fire: The Chinese in Montreal* (Hong Kong: The Chinese University Press, 1991); William Seto and Larry N. Shyu, *The Chinese Experience in New Brunswick: A Historical Perspective* (Fredericton, New Brunswick: Chinese Cultural Association, 1985); Hung-Min Chiang, *Chinese Islanders* [Prince Edward Island]: *Making a Home in the New World* (Charlottetown: Island Studies Press, 2006); and John K. Sparrow, "From Sojourning to Citizenship: The Chinese Community in St. John's, Newfoundland, 1895-1967" (*Journal of Chinese Overseas* 6 [2010]).

Two other textual sources of merit are David Chuenyan Lai's *Chinatowns: Towns within Cities in Canada* (1988) and

Chinese Canadian biographies and family histories. Lai's work is important in gathering and preserving information on the historical development of Chinese settlements in Canada. There are also a number of Chinese Canadian biographies and family histories available. The Vancouver Public Library provides a list of some of them at *www.vpl.ca/ccg/Pioneer_Booklist.html.*

4. Most Significant Sources

In an effort to make this chapter more than just a list of significant sources of information on Chinese Canadians, albeit with some description given for each, one should identify which among the list of sources are the most significant. Of the various sources, the UBC Library, the website of the Historical Chinese Language Materials in British Columbia, and Library and Archives Canada stand out among them.

The UBC Library houses many important Chinese Canadian historical records, among them a relatively complete set of the *Chinese Times,* one of the earliest and longest running Chinese language dailies in Canada, along with many of the personal papers of early influential Chinese Canadian figures and two large collections donated by Edgar Wickberg, editor of the seminal text *From China to Canada: A History of the Chinese Communities in Canada* (1982). The list of resources under "Chinese Canadians" on the university's server and the two related websites housed on the library's server "The Chinese Experience in British Columbia: 1850-1950" and "The Chung Collection," add even more to the library's value. These collections alone make UBC Library not only an invaluable source for important information, but also the only source for some.

The resources offered on the website of the Historical Chinese Language Materials in British Columbia of Simon Fraser University challenge previous limitations on what could be conveniently provided as information. First, it has provided Chinese language records in electronic form. This has increased greatly the amount of primary material that is readily available to researchers. Second, it has identified important, but as yet, not deeply investigated sources of information, mostly local archives in British Columbia. Third, it has designed a search engine that uses Chinese characters making the investigation of Chinese language materials much easier. These are all precedent-setting achievements, and, finally, the website provides comprehensive lists of Chinese Canadian associations and religious organizations in British Columbia.

The Library and Archives Canada offers searching of and access to a number of different libraries and archives across Canada, which means remote access to information sometimes not widely available. Their website also provides access to government material related to Chinese Canadians.

Finally, one should mention the Chinese-Canadian Genealogy Project, *ww.vpl.ca/ccg* because of its popular appeal and efforts to educate the public on how to do related research.

5. Potential Sources

There are also significant potential sources of information, ones that have not yet been made publicly available. In spite of a high degree of illiteracy among early Chinese Canadians,[13] one can assume that the importance of history and the tradition of keeping written records led groups like the Chinese Freemasons (Hongmen hui) and the "homeplace" and clan associations to produce them. One sees an example of such records in the fifty-five documents from Chinese Consolidated Benevolent Association of Victoria found on Multicultural Canada's server. Many of these records have not received academic treatment, but as their holders realize the value of receiving such treatment, more of them will become available to the public. When they do, not only will more knowledge of Chinese Canadians be produced, but also alternative perspectives on Canadian history.

6. Conclusion

This article has surveyed some of the important sources of information on Chinese Canadians and even ventured to choose those that are most significant. It has found that there is a wealth of information available on Chinese Canadians and some sophisticated presentations of this information. It has also

---

[13] It is estimated that only 1 percent of the early Chinese immigrants were literate (Li Donghai [David T.H. Lee], *Jianada Huaqiao shi* [A history of Chinese in Canada] [Taipei: Jianada ziyou, 1967], 347).

shown that there is much more that can be done to develop these sources and that efforts are underway to do so.

There are two trends of note that seem to be shaping the development of information sources on Chinese Canadians. First, the more positive perspective on the part of the mainstream toward Chinese Canadians has led to more interest in their achievements, which in turn has required the production of more information about them. For example, there is a broad interest in the reasons for their academic success. Second, Chinese Canadians are taking a greater interest in their own history. On one hand, this has led to the opening of new areas of research; for example, their early relations with the indigenous population. On the other hand, it has led to access to records, such of those of Chinese Benevolent Association in Victoria, that were once inaccessible. Combined with technological developments, such as digitalization, the prospects for doing research on Chinese Canadians have improved immensely.

BIBLIOGRAPHY

"Chinese Canadian Historical Society of B.C. Newsletter" 2.1 (2006).

Li Donghai (David T.H. Lee). *Jianada Huaqiao shi* (A History of Chinese in Canada). Taipei: Jianada ziyou,1967.

Mingbao (Ming Pao Daily News) website, *news.mingpao.com,* accessed 2015.02.01.

UBC website. "Chinese Canadians." *guides.library.ubc.ca/content.php?pid=439825&sid=3600746*, accessed 2014.08.14.

Wickberg, Edgar, Harry Con, Ronald J. Con, Graham Johnson, and William E. Willmott. *From China to Canada: A History of the Chinese Communities in Canada,* edited by Edgar Wickberg. Toronto : McClelland and Stewart, 1982.

3. CANADA'S CHINATOWNS: FROM PRESERVATION TO CELEBRATION

1. Introduction

This chapter details the evolution of Chinatowns from the isolation of Chinese Canadians to the celebration of Chinatowns as offering resources to all Canadians. In doing so the chapter describes the various functions that Chinatowns serve including as platforms for new immigrants to enter into mainstream culture and for mainstream Canadians to experience Chinese culture.

There are various achievements that the existence and growth of Chinatowns are evidence to. Their establishment and continued existence, especially in the face of opposition, are major ones. This opposition was ongoing at least until the 1960s when the merit of their existence gained recognition from the Canadian mainstream. Since then the challenges, and thus their achievements, facing Chinatowns have changed. Now, the challenges to Chinatowns arise from within the Canadian Chinese community itself as their pursuit of convenience has led to the creation of other centres of Chinese Canadian commerce and culture in close proximity to the early, well-established ones and, consequently, undermined their viability.

Chinatowns have served various functions within the Chinese Canadian community. These include the provision of goods and services, protection, mutual support, support for ethnic businesses and workers, and a gateway into mainstream society. Their functions have since evolved to include service to the broader mainstream. They now serve as gateways into and symbols of Chinese culture, thereby allowing all Canadians to appreciate it.

1.1 Concepts of Enclave and Chinatown

The concepts of an enclave and a Chinatown help demonstrate the achievements of Canada's Chinatowns by clarifying what is being observed. An enclave is "any small, distinct area or group enclosed or isolated within a larger one" (*Random House*). The quality that distinguishes an enclave is often the culture of its inhabitants, which is often reflected in its commercial operations. A Chinatown is an enclave that is distinguished on the basis of the strong presence of Chinese Canadian culture, which, of course, contains it a large amount of Chinese culture within it. Toronto's Chinatown around Dundas and Spadina is one of the many examples of an enclave distinguished by the presence of Chinese restaurants and grocery stores, clan and homeland associations with links to China, cultural centres, and services for Chinese Canadian elderly. The majority of residents are culturally distinct and thereby constitute an enclave.

Even though it is the people and their cultural distinctiveness that usually define an enclave, having a physical location or space also seems an important part of the definition. The physical boundaries of an enclave make it easy to identify. In the case of Chinatowns there is a concentration of Chinese Canadians residing, working, and securing goods and services within a defined area, which might only be both sides of a street that is a mere block long, such as in Saskatoon.

Interestingly, a sociologist Min Zhou points out that an enclave need not be "a strict geographical concept as an organizational one." Chinese Canadian businesses exist outside Chinatown but share "ownership patterns, resources, market channels, business performance, management norms, labour control," etc. with Chinese businesses within Chinatown.[1] All of these businesses together could be considered a form of an enclave. Nevertheless, for sake of clearly describing the achievements of Canada's Chinatowns this chapter will limit itself to the Chinatowns that have relatively clear geographical boundaries and even this stipulation needs to be further qualified because the mimicry of a Chinese Canadian commercial centre, such as found within West Edmonton Mall,[2] should not be considered a Chinatown. Clearly, West Edmonton

---

[1] Min Zhou, *Chinatown: the Socioeconomic Potential of an Urban Enclave* (Philadelphia: Temple University Press, 1992), 11-12.

[2] Chinatown West Edmonton Mall combines Chinese architecture, ornaments and specialty shops to create a traditional Chinese market. There are several unique shops and services, some of which have Chinese-speaking staff, including a branch of T & T Supermarket, Canada's largest Asian supermarket chain. (West Edmonton Mall website, *www.wem.ca/#/shop/theme-streets/chinatown*, accessed 2011.02.27)

Mall's Chinatown is purely a commercial operation. As such, it lacks the defining social activities of a Chinatown, for example, services for the elderly, the presence of Chinese language media, the associations, etc., as well as residents.

Assuming that a Chinatown is more than just a concentration of Chinese Canadian businesses begs questions on two fronts: first, what other characteristics are essential to constituting a Chinatown and, second, should the new shopping centres that are being created outside the older Chinatowns be considered Chinatowns. In answer to the first question, two other factors that should be present prior to designating a location as a Chinatown are a substantial number of Chinese Canadian residents within or nearby and the operation of formal social organizations primarily serving Chinese Canadians. The presence of commercial operations in combination with the presence of Chinese Canadian residents and formal social organizations fits closely with the historical identity of Chinatowns in Canada. Therefore, a list of the characteristics of a Chinatown would be

a. a residential population that is racially or culturally Chinese

b. commercial activity that is culturally Chinese

c. a specific and defined location

d. social organizations

e. being an enclave, which means that is perceived differently by the mainstream.

This then constitutes a working definition of a Chinatown. It is an identifiable concentration of Chinese residing, working, and securing goods and services within a defined area. Within this area, one would also find ethnic businesses, that is businesses catering to demand unique to Chinese Canadians, such as Chinese herbalists.[3]

The second question is whether the commercial centres being created outside of the older Chinatowns fit the definition of a Chinatown. For example, the Pacific Mall/Market Village

---

[3] It should also be noted that there are strong arguments supporting the view that Chinatowns are mostly the creations of mainstream efforts and perceptions, that what constitutes a Chinatown is mostly the product of a European way of seeing and acting.

complex, with a total sales area of more than forty-six thousand square meters and more than five hundred stores, is situated in Markham within the Greater Toronto Area. Impressive in its size—said to be the largest Chinese shopping centre in North America[4]—one wonders if it fits the definition of a Chinatown. It seems to for it caters to the many Chinese Canadian residents in Markham and vicinity,[5] thus having a large resident population linked to it. Furthermore, it contains the offices of the Federation of Chinese Canadians in Markham, "a not-for-profit organization dedicated to the provision of services to the Chinese community and the integration of Chinese Canadians into the mainstream of Canada,"[6] and a local branch of the *Sing Tao Daily* newspaper. Lastly, it is clearly identified as distinct by the mainstream population. Therefore, it fits within the definition proposed for a Chinatown.

Including these new Chinese Canadian commercial centres within the category of Chinatowns is justified on the basis of their being new manifestations of the concentration of Chinese Canadian activity. As such observing them has the advantage of revealing trends in Chinese Canadian development. Whereas more historic concentrations, i.e., older Chinatowns, were, in large part, created for protection, the newer forms are more expansionist, in the sense that they are primarily designed to increase their participants' wealth and material comfort.

2. Early Causes of Chinatowns

2.1 Fundamental Causes

Looking at the reasons Chinatowns were established, one has to acknowledge the basic factors of cultural difference

[4] Lucia Lo, "Suburban Housing and Indoor Shopping: The Production of Contemporary Chinese Landscape in Toronto," in *From Urban Enclave to Ethnic Suburb: New Asian Communities in Pacific Rim Countries*, ed. Wei Li (Honolulu: University of Hawaii Press, 2006), 151.

[5] Ethnic Chinese constituted nearly 40 percent of Markham's population, or 118,875 in 2011 (Statistics Canada, "NHS Focus on Geography Series – Markham," accessed 2014.11.20).

[6] Federation of Chinese Canadians in Markham website, *www.fccm.ca/about.html*, accessed 2011.02.27.

and need for protection. Photos of early Chinese arrivals wearing long queues and traditional Chinese dress speak to the cultural differences between them and the local population. Most Chinese migrants spoke their own language, associated with fellow Chinese, ate their own cuisine, worshiped their own gods, and so on, and Chinatowns provided a convenient environment for doing so. Secondly, they created and lived within Chinatowns as protection against the prejudice and persecution perpetrated upon them. Arguably, the need for protection existed soon after their arrival and lasted until they were able to bring their families to Canada starting in 1947. Therefore, even after granting the desire by Chinese Canadians to preserve their own culture—one that continues to exist even after the need for protection has been eliminated—it is apparent that the early enclaves were, in part, the result of mainstream efforts and perceptions, that bias and preconceptions, and the actions that followed from them, led Chinese Canadians to protect themselves within these enclaves.

The question arises if either of these two fundamental causes were sufficient on their own to cause the creation of Chinatowns. Clearly, the need for protection was; in many cases it was the pursuit of basic survival that led Chinese Canadians to group together. Therefore, the more interesting question is whether alone the desire to preserve their culture would have led to creation of Chinatowns. Obviously, it is difficult to abstract this factor from the need for protection. The two existed simultaneously and reinforced one another, but the question has been simplified with the elimination of the need for protection and the desire of the majority of Chinese Canadians to live outside Chinatowns. As this has occurred, the continued desire to preserve Chinatowns, even in the face of strong challenges to their existence, proves very interesting.

2.2 Practical Needs

The general causes for the existence of Canadian Chinatowns have been concretely manifested in the practical needs met by them. In earlier times these needs included the provision of goods and services, self-protection and a response to imposed restrictions, fostering mutual assistance, supporting ethnic businesses and workers, and providing a gateway into mainstream society. With time, as the needs of Chinese

Canadians have evolved with changes in the broader society, the benefits provided by Chinatowns have changed accordingly and taken on contemporary forms.

2.2.1 To Provide Goods and Services (Commercial)

The earliest reason for the creation of Chinatowns was to provide Chinese immigrant labour with goods and services. Victoria's Chinatown came into being primarily to transfer labour sailing from southern China to work projects around British Columbia. These immigrants numbered in the thousands, so there was also a need to provide them with goods and services, such as rice and Traditional Chinese Medicine, and places to stay when they were between jobs or returning to China. These needs were best met by concentrating resources in one location, ideally at the transfer point where goods arriving from China would be taken off ships and put onto smaller vessels for transportation inland, or workers arriving from the inland could board those same ships for return to China.

The particular needs of the Chinese were different from those of the mainstream. They ate different foods, practised a different medical paradigm, consumed opium for relaxation, and were willing to live in more densely populated quarters in exchange for cheaper charges. It made sense to concentrate the means to meet these needs in one location and, because of Chinatowns' uniqueness, and of the Chinese Canadians who utilized them, Chinatowns easily stood apart from other concentrations of population.

2.2.2 Self-protection and Imposed Restrictions

Early Chinese Canadians were forced to create enclaves to protect themselves from the attacks of the general population and to provide the necessities that mainstream denied them. Furthermore, there was added impetus to their creation because mainstream society would sometimes require Chinese Canadians to work or reside in one location in order to keep them isolated from the rest of society.

David Lai gives an overview of the harassment suffered by Chinese Canadians. Landlords would not rent housing to them unless the housing was already unattractive to the White community. Mining companies housed Chinese Canadians in isolated areas. Violence was used to keep them out of gold mining areas. Children would throw stones at them and overturn their vegetable baskets.[7] The worst were the mob attacks, which were also widespread. The attacks on Chinese Canadians and their properties on two separate occasions in Vancouver, in 1887 and then in 1907, and in Calgary in 1892 are well known. Less well known are the attacks in the Slocan Valley, in Atlin, in Salmo, and Penticton. In all these cases the purpose of the attacks was to force the Chinese residents out of the area.[8] There was also an anti-Chinese riot in Halifax in 1919.[9] Under these circumstances, Chinese Canadians were forced to live together for their own protection. Thus, the formation of Chinatowns followed naturally from the actions of mainstream Canadians.

Furthermore, the Chinese were sometimes required by law to keep their activities within specified boundaries. For example, on several occasions the Lethbridge city council restricted Chinese premises to designated areas. In 1910 Calgary city council debated segregating Chinese residents and in 1919 Calgary city commissioners sought to relocate Chinatown.[10] The functionaries of Vancouver's government, the police, the medical officer, the housing and sanitary inspectors, and land use planners, all sought to segregate the Chinese within Chinatown.[11] With the violence perpetrated against them and the opposition of society channeled through the force of the law, early Chinese Canadians had little choice but to

---

[7] David Chuenyan Lai, *Chinatowns: Towns within Cities in Canada* (Vancouver: University of British Columbia Press, 1988), 34-35.

[8] David Lai, *Chinatowns*, 35, citing Peter Ward, *White Canada Forever* (Montreal: McGill-Queen's University Press, 1978), 64.

[9] Judy Torrance, *Public Violence in Canada: 1867-1982* (Kingston, Ont.: McGill-Queen's University Press, 1986), 31.

[10] Brian J. Dawson, *Moon Cakes in Gold Mountain: From China to the Canadian Plains* (Calgary: Detselig Enterprises, 1991), 197 and 48-49.

[11] David Ley, *Millionaire Migrants: Trans-Pacific Life Lines*, (Chichester, U.K.: Wiley-Blackwell, 2010), 34, citing Kay Anderson, *Vancouver's Chinatown: Racial Discourse in Canada, 1875-1980* (Montreal: McGill-Queen's University Press, 1991).

group together. To their credit, they proved that they had the organizational skills to do so.

2.2.3 Mutual Support

The need to support one another naturally followed from the persecution suffered by Chinese Canadians. It was the most effective means to mitigate the violence and restrictions they faced. Needless to say, the prejudice extended far beyond the attacks and attempts to isolate them. In general, Chinese immigrants to Canada did not receive the same kind of support that immigrants from Europe did. They were paid less, often half as much for the same work. They were denied the right to enter certain professions. They were assessed extraordinary fees, such as head taxes to enter the country or municipal taxes to live in a city (e.g., Calgary). During the depression they were first denied relief, then given half that of White Canadians. The police and city inspectors paid extra attention to their behaviours. All of these actions and others served to limit Chinese opportunities within Canada. Under these conditions, it was more than natural that Chinese immigrants would turn to one another for assistance and it was when they were in close proximity that they could most efficiently do so. Thus, enclaves or Chinatowns were formed.

Within Chinatowns there were a number of different types of organizations formed by Chinese Canadians to provide for their needs. Some of the major ones were the locality association called *"tong"* or *"dang,"* the kinship association, and the mutual aid association, called *"huiguan."* These organizations would serve a variety of needs from housing to feeding, to securing employment, to providing credit, and even arranging funeral services.[12]

2.2.4 Support for Ethnic Businesses and Workers

---

[12] A 1971 survey of Chinese residents in Calgary found that more than 70 per cent of them belonged to at least one Chinese organization and that there were nine kinship associations among them and that eight of them had a club hall, which most of them owned (Gunther Baureiss, "The Chinese Community of Calgary," *Canadian Ethnic Studies* 3.1 [June 1971], 49-50).

Canadian Chinatowns have provided a concentration of consumers and workers that have supported ethnic industries while creating employment opportunities for their own inhabitants. The early Chinese landlords rented mostly to fellow Chinese. The restaurants, herbalists, and opium parlours served Chinese Canadians and the employees of these establishments often lived on the premises where they worked. The close quarters of Chinatown made these businesses viable while offering employment to its residents.

These benefits carried forward to the point where the critical mass of workers and economic strength of businesses allowed ethnic businesses and workers to compete more successfully in the broader economic system. Min Zhou, in a study of New York's Chinatown but applicable to Canada as well, shows that ethnic Chinese businesses, such as restaurants and garment factories, rather than compete with better financed companies that are more experienced servicing mainstream clientele, have located within Chinatown and service clientele who share their ethnicity.[13] Zhou also notes that the entrepreneurial immigrants are able to start their careers in America in potentially more rewarding occupations and at higher levels because the opportunities are available within the enclave.[14]

For the workers, New York's Chinatown has also offered a better option. It is not that they are willing to accept low paying jobs and poor working conditions. Rather in Chinatown "they are effectively shielded from deficiencies in language, education, and general knowledge of the larger society. They can obtain first hand information on employment and business opportunities through their family members, kin, and co-ethnics and so avoid the expense in time and effort involved in finding 'good jobs' in the larger market. They are able to work longer hours to accumulate family savings more quickly. They can gain access to rotating credit, clan associations, and the family for financial support and resource mobilization."[15]

---

[13] Zhou, 95-110.

[14] *Ibid.*, 4.

[15] *Ibid.*, 12.

Zhou points out that New York's Chinatown has a large number of Chinese residents and a number of small companies, such as restaurants or garment factories, employing new immigrants who probably do not speak English well if at all. Admittedly, one may be sceptical of applying Zhou's findings to Canadian settings. Although there are restaurants and other small businesses within Canada's Chinatowns and these, no doubt, provide the same support for Chinese Canadian entrepreneurs and workers as New York's does for Chinese Americans, one still does not associate large manufacturing facilities with Canadian Chinatowns, the way that Zhou does with New York City's. In fact, there is, or at least was, a comparable situation in Toronto. Toronto's Chinese Canadian population was 537,060 in 2006.[16] New York's Chinese American population was 660,000 in 2008,[17] about 23 percent larger. Arguably, Toronto's Chinese Canadian population was large enough to provide a workforce similar to New York's. Furthermore, it was reported in 1989 that nearly half of the six thousand garment workers in Toronto were Chinese and that the industry provided work close to Chinatown.[18] Based on data sets from 2000 and 2001, manufacturing facilities still operated within the confines of Toronto's Chinatowns and they comprised nearly 4 percent of Chinese Canadian businesses.[19] Therefore,

---

[16] Statistics Canada, "Population by selected ethnic origins, by census metropolitan areas (2006 Census)," *www.statcan.gc.ca*, accessed 2011.07.16. The number of ethnic Chinese is the sum of those who indicated only a single ethnic origin (462,460) plus those who indicated they had more than one ethnic origin (74,600) of which one was Chinese. The number cited in the text includes the latter figure, those who had more than one ethnic origin of which one was Chinese, because the author assumes that Chinese culture will still be relatively important among them. Chinese Canadian inter-marriage with other ethnic groups has been less common, thus their identification with traditional Chinese culture is still strong. Moreover, Chinese Canadians have preserved their heritage culture well, so it is likely that even among those with partial Chinese origin there will be identification with being Chinese Canadian.

[17] U.S. Census Bureau, "New York-Newark-Bridgeport, NY-NJ-CT-PA Combined Statistical Area," American Community Survey, 2008, accessed 16 July 2011.

[18] Richard H. Thompson, *Toronto's Chinatown: The Changing Social Organization of an Ethnic Community* (New York: AMS Press, 1989), 241.

[19] Eric Fong, Emily E. Anderson, Wenhong Chen, and Chiu Luk, "The Logic of

Canada's Chinatowns have provided support for ethnic businesses and workers, and, arguably, to nearly the same degree as American Chinatowns have done, even with the latter's larger ethnic population and more entrepreneurial attitudes.

2.2.5 Gateway into Mainstream Society

One sees how the functions of Chinatown are linked with conditions in broader society. The hostility directed at Chinese Canadians from the mainstream in early times led to the creation of Chinatowns in order to protect themselves. Ironically, as mainstream society became more open to Chinese Canadian participation, the function of Chinatowns evolved into providing a platform for preparing Chinese Canadians for involvement in the mainstream. When the Sien Lok Society of Calgary convened a national conference on the value of Chinatowns in the face of urban renewal in the 1960s, one of the purposes highlighted was the transition of Chinese immigrants first arriving in Canadian Chinatowns, developing their abilities and adapting, then moving into the mainstream as worthy citizens.[20]

Min Zhou gives a specific example of how this takes place. She points out how ethnic Chinese are able to convert the economic gains of Chinatown employment into acceptance in mainstream society. The gains of employment are turned into housing purchases in better neighbourhoods, which enables their children to assimilate more easily into mainstream society.[21] Other examples include the offering of English classes, the introduction of mainstream culture, and the enrollment in social services provided by various forms of government. Seeing the greatest need for these adaptive measures within Chinatowns, the promoters of greater integration have concentrated their efforts there and

Ethnic Business Distribution in Multiethnic Cities," *Urban Affairs Review* 43.4 (March 2008), 510.

[20] Sien Lok Society of Calgary, "National Conference on Urban Renewal As It Affects Chinatowns" (1969), 86.

[21] P. 225.

Chinatowns have taken on the role of being a gateway for Chinese Canadians wanting to participate more in mainstream society.

3. Later Practical Needs Met by Chinatowns

The progression in Canadian mainstream attitudes has been reflected in changes in Chinatowns, changes that further illustrate the achievements of Chinese Canadians. In general, they have been able to transform Chinatowns to either meet their needs or take advantage of presented opportunities. In the past, Chinatowns could be said to serve a mostly defensive role, protecting Chinese Canadians from the persecution and prejudice targeting them. However, as these diminished, Chinatowns evolved into agencies for promoting integration with mainstream culture.

3.1 Hold Cultural Events

Certain cultural events are important in identifying with Chinese culture, which, in turn, fosters a belief system that unifies Chinese immigrants and promotes their support of one another. A range of events, from the celebration of the Chinese New Year to the group mourning at a funeral, places an individual in a network of ceremonial relationships with elders, fellow kinsmen, the younger generation, ancestors, and so on. Chinatown provides the social network and the physical resources, such as available space and necessary equipment, to hold cultural events. For example, in 1925, when Sun Yat-sen a leader of the 1911 revolution in China died, Chinese gathered in venues in Chinatowns across Canada to honour him.

Overtime, these events have expanded to include the broader population that has been developing an interest in Chinese culture. In 1936 the Chinese community received city approval to produce the "Chinese Village" to coincide with Vancouver's Golden Jubilee celebrations. It included a Chinese tower constructed for the celebrations, a parade, exhibitions of Chinese artistry, and acrobatics. The village was so popular that the city's Jubilee Management Board decided to extend it for two weeks. The board also thanked the Chinese community in a letter stating: "The committee of Chinese residents who raised the funds and supervised the venture did so without trouble or worry to us and displayed a fine cooperative spirit."[22]

Nowadays it is common to see public celebrations of Chinese culture and the events are very much inclusive, allowing Chinese Canadians to celebrate their heritage while introducing their culture to the mainstream. Furthermore, these celebrations are almost always conducted in Chinatown. It offers a sufficiently large venue, such as an auditorium or a street that can be blocked off without incurring detracting complaints, the necessary equipment to stage the event, and contains related services, such as Chinese restaurants that can support it.

3.2 Offer Ethnic Services

As in the past, present day Chinatowns continue to offer ethnic services. These include restaurants, herbalists, martial arts training, and cultural performances. These services have been augmented by professional social services that support Chinatown residents and other Chinese Canadians who reside outside. The elderly have managed residences that range from nursing homes to independent living. They also have recreational and medical centres. For recent immigrants, there are social services that guide them into greater involvement in Canadian society. There are more contemporary commercial services as well, such as firms targeting investment in China and Karaoke bars.

The evolution of ethnic services offered also has involved extending them to other ethnic groups. For example, the Calgary Chinese Community Services Association has offered computer education to the Sikh community and legal advice to Afghan immigrants. T & T, the large Chinese Canadian grocery store chain, stocks South Asian products, and Pacific Place, a Chinese-themed shopping mall in northeast Calgary provides money transfer services for Philippine Canadians. The provision of goods and services continues to be an important function justifying the existence of Chinatowns, and one notes

---

[22] Kay Anderson citing City of Vancouver Archives, Vancouver City, Special Committee Files, No. 1, Vancouver Golden Jubilee Committee, Report of the Managing Board, 1936 (p. 157).

the evolution of these goods and services to meet an even wider clientele and thus maintain the enclaves.

3.3 Conduct Language Schools

One ethnic service, the instruction of the Chinese language, deserves special attention because of its significance in preserving the culture that supports Chinatowns and as a service that has evolved to meet broader needs. In the past, students and teachers often lived in Chinatown. Victoria's Chinese Public School, established in 1899, was the first free Chinese school in Canada. The Chinese Public School was founded in Calgary in 1920 and still operates within Chinatown. Since then the number of schools operating in Chinatowns across Canada has increased and they now teach a broader background of students, including non-Chinese. Chinatown's role in supporting language schools is to offer a location within which to practise one's learning and resources such as a library, bookstores, cultural reinforcement, and recognized language schools that are centrally located. The attraction of these advantages further produces a critical mass of students, whose numbers add to the attractiveness of associating with one's peer group. Group activities, such as choral singing and dance, as well competitions to hone one's heritage language skills, that follow from this association, further enhance the value of this association.

3.4 Gateway

The gateway that Chinatowns have been now goes in two directions. While Chinese immigrants continue to use it to familiarize themselves with and adapt to mainstream culture, Chinatowns have also become a venue for mainstream society to encounter Chinese culture. It is not only to watch the colourful celebrations either. Mainstream children visit Chinatowns in tours organized by the public school system. They also learn Chinese in the language schools and participate in cultural activities, such as martial arts. Adults find alternative medical treatments. Businesses encounter organizations devoted to promoting trade between Canada and China. Governments find representatives for Chinese Canadians and minorities in general. As the importance of

Chinese Canadians increases, so does Chinatown because it contains many means by which to engage them.

3.5 Symbol of Chinese Culture

This is perhaps the most important contemporary function of Chinatowns. It existed in the past in the temples and the ancestral shrines of the kinship associations where homage was paid to spiritual and historical figures. However, this symbolic value was overshadowed by the practical need for the mutual support provided because of cultural beliefs. Overtime, though, as Chinese Canadians were allowed to participate more in mainstream society, the need for mutual support no longer was as great, so as the immediate need to practise the traditional cultural values that promoted mutual assistance decreased, the symbolic value of heritage culture became relatively more important. This was an awareness of the far reaching effects of traditional values beyond the promotion of reciprocal support. For example, the traditional Chinese wedding banquet has no legal status but serves to announce a marriage to family, friends, etc.; to acknowledge the relationship between the families of the bride and groom; and to create dignity (read "face") for all those involved, but especially the bride and groom. The facilities in Chinatown adept in catering to such functions as traditional weddings and funerals know how to amplify the symbolic value contained within, so they are popular choices for conducting them.

In short, Chinatown contains powerful symbols that the community draws upon when it wants to draw psychological resources. It is filled with reminders of the history of its former inhabitants, and the sacrifices they made to establish themselves and others. Perhaps, most important among the symbolic benefits is the reminder of the fundamental values that have led to the success of the ethnic community. In the case of Chinese immigrants to the United States, Min Zhou writes "The success of the Chinese has been built on a collective effort of the family and community that overcame many obstacles along the way. The Chinese are not as ready as expected to give up their culture, language, and values. The majority of them take pride in being Chinese. Even those who have a good command of English speak Chinese at home. They require their children to speak Chinese and to learn Chinese moral teaching, fearing that otherwise their children might become too 'Americanized.' They hold on to their traditional dietary habits. They maintain their own pattern of savings and consumption."[23] In relation, Chinatown is a concrete and significant example of their success and a constant reminder of the benefit of maintaining heritage values.

4. Earliest Examples of Chinatowns

4.1 Victoria

Victoria's Chinatown, which dates to about 1860, is Canada's oldest. It was created to service the flow of immigrant Chinese labourers through its port. Even today, as the population and size of its Chinatown have shrunk and its historical value and attraction to tourists are being promoted, the importance of the commercial sector—restaurants and shops—is still apparent. It is an example of how the commercial sector contributed much to Chinese development within Canada.

David Chuenyan Lai, who has written much on Canada's Chinatowns, particularly on Victoria's, provides a succinct history of Victoria's Chinatown in *Building and Rebuilding Harmony: The Gateway to Victoria's Chinatown* (1997). In it, he and his coauthor Pamela Madoff recount the beginnings of Victoria's Chinatown in 1858 when merchants built wooden shacks close to the harbour in order to service the expected wave of recruited labourers. By 1876 the community was well enough established to warrant the erection of the first temple in Canada, the Tam Kung Temple, which honoured the patron saint of the Hakka people and seafarers in southern China. Between 1881 and 1884, nearly sixteen thousand Chinese landed in Victoria, most on their way to jobs in the interior.[24]

The size and importance of Victoria's Chinatown reached its peak in the early 1910s when it covered six city blocks and housed most of the city's more than three thousand Chinese and nearly all their business concerns. "Chinatown boasted more than one hundred fifty firms, two theatres, a hospital, three

---

[23] P. 227.

[24] P. 45.

Chinese schools, two churches, more than five temples or shrines, and many opium factories, gambling dens and brothels."[25] However, by then Victoria's Chinatown had already begun its decline. Vancouver had become the terminal for the Canadian Pacific Railway and it was attracting more Chinese immigrants. Victoria's Chinese population decreased and by 1971 its area had diminished to two city blocks and the number of residents to one hundred forty-three.[26] In another turn of fortune, Victoria City Council approved a rehabilitation program for Chinatown in 1979. This was followed by the construction of the Chinatown Care Facility for the elderly in 1982, the building of the Chung Wah Mansion in 1984 to provide low cost housing, and Victoria's Chinatown's designation as a national historical district in 1996.

The formation of a Chinatown in Victoria led to the creation of a stable society and the conditions that would increase Chinese Canadians' contributions to their adopted nation. The merchants who supplied labourers, provisions to their job sites, temporary housing, and even the brothels and opium for their diversion were able to establish their families and later the trappings of traditional Chinese culture within Victoria. Traditional organizations such as kinship and locality associations were established as soon as 1893 and even the Chinese Hospital in 1895. The establishment of a stable society able to strengthen their community through the promotion of traditional culture led to two major developments that would have far reaching impact on Chinese Canadians across Canada.

The first development was the creation of the Chinese Consolidated Benevolent Association (CCBA) in 1884 after years of negotiation and compromise among thirty-one local groups.[27] The main reason for the creation of the CCBA was the need "for a representative who would unite the Chinese in British Columbia in their protest against the discriminatory laws passed by the provincial government. The increase of crime, prostitution, gambling and disputes among the Chinese

[25] *Ibid.,* 46.

[26] *Ibid.,* 53.

[27] Robert Amos and Kileasa Wong, *Inside Chinatown: Ancient Culture in a New World* (Victoria, British Columbia: Touchwood Editions, 2009), 13.

had also made it necessary to set up a kind of law-enforcing body which every Chinese in Canada would obey."[28]

While the formation of the CCBA was mainly the result of uniting the Chinese Canadian community to counter the discrimination they were suffering, the need for control over the internal problems also was a factor. Through mandated fees and donations, the CCBA was able to raise thirty thousand dollars to build the CCBA facility and the Chinese Hospital. They also raised funds to assist Chinese in other parts of Canada, such as for the efforts of Chinese Canadians in Regina to oppose proposed legislation prohibiting the hiring of White women in Saskatchewan by Chinese employers, and for Chinese outside Canada, such as those in Cuba suffering under the Spanish colonial government.

The formation of the CCBA contributed to broader achievements among Chinese Canadians. Victoria's organization was duplicated in Chinatowns across Canada. Furthermore, the CCBA and many of its counterparts—often called "Chinese Benevolent Associations"(CBA) --in other cities were still in operation in the early 1990s. David Chuenyan Lai visited twenty cities outside Victoria from 1990 to 1994 and found that seventeen of them still had CBAs in operation in sixteen cities across Canada (Vancouver's Chinatowns had two).[29] These organizations have unified Chinese Canadians at the local level and opened the possibility for nationally unified action, such as when CBAs across the country sponsored an annual Humiliation Day to mark the Chinese Exclusion Act implemented in 1923.[30]

Arguably, the unity among Chinese Canadians produced in the formation of the CCBA enhanced the identity of Chinese Canadians as set apart from that of the mainstream. This is seen in the link the CCBA had with the Chinese government as seen in their calling on that government to sanction their

---

[28] David Chuenyan Lai, "The Chinese Consolidated Benevolent Association in Victoria: Its Origins and Functions," *BC Studies* 15 (Autumn 1972), 55.

[29] David Chuenyan Lai, *Chinese Community Leadership: Case Study of Victoria in Canada* (New Jersey: World Scientific, 2010), 5.

[30] Edgar Wickberg, et al, *From China to Canada: A History of the Chinese Communities in Canada*, ed. Edgar Wickberg (Toronto: McClelland and Stewart, 1982), 174.

organization and communicating the views of local Chinese
Canadians to it. The assertion of an identity distinct from that
of the Canadian mainstream, along with the link to the Chinese
government, highlighted the resources of traditional Chinese
culture available to Chinese Canadians as means to resolve
their problems. Therefore, it is not surprising that one of
Victoria's CCBA's early acts was to establish the Chinese Public
School in 1899.

The founding of Victoria's Chinese Public School was the
second development that had a major impact across Canada. It
was the first free Chinese school in Canada. The idea was
popular and this school was quickly followed by the
establishment of three similar ones run by the Chinese Empire
Reform Association, the Chinese Freemasons, and the Yue
Shan Society in the early 1900s in Victoria.[31] Part of the
mandate of the school was to preserve Chinese culture among
the younger generation by protecting them from assimilation
and Westernization.[32] Twice, in the early 1900s and again in
the 1920s, the school served to mitigate the impact of racial
segregation on Victoria's Chinese Canadian population. In 1902
the Victoria School Board began to segregate Chinese students
and this was followed by a refusal to accept students judged
unable to understand English. In the latter case, it was believed
that students were using school enrollment in order to
circumvent paying the head tax.[33] The Chinese Public School
responded by increasing enrollment and moving into new
premises.[34]

In 1922 the Victoria School Board again decided to
segregate Chinese students, even native born ones, under the
guise that they were retarding the education of other students.
The plan was to segregate Chinese students and place them in
dilapidated facilities. The Chinese community organized a
boycott of public schools in response and the CCBA established

---

[31] *Ibid.*, 87.

[32] Amos and Wong, 32.

[33] Timothy J. Stanley, *Contesting White Supremacy: School Segregation, Anti-Racism, and the Making of Chinese Canadians* (Vancouver: UBC Press, 2011), 98-100.

[34] Amos and Wong, 33.

the Chinese Free School offering a nationalist curriculum in Chinese.[35] This move led the Victoria School Board in 1923 to rescind most of the measures designed to segregate Chinese Canadian students.

Timothy Stanley describes the strategic value of opening a Chinese language school with a nationalist curriculum. He points out that the community could have easily established an English-language school, but that would have absolved the Victoria School Board of its responsibility. Instead, the Chinese language school "was intended as a direct attack on Canadian state formation, in effect a statement that if the strikers were not to be allowed to be Canadian, they would be Chinese instead." While this tact clearly demonstrated that the Victoria School Board was not fulfilling its responsibility, it was also practical in providing competence in written and spoken Chinese, which made possible earning a living dealing with Chinese in and out China.[36]

The founding of the community Chinese school in Victoria led to the founding of similar ones across Canada and they have multiplied to become common fixtures within major Canadian cities, especially within their Chinatowns. Together with the Chinese Benevolent Associations, they are indicative of the far-reaching influence of Canada's first Chinatown. Even as Victoria's Chinese population has assimilated and the portion living with Chinatown has diminished, Chinatown has become a historical symbol. There the CCBA still offers Chinese school and there is a care home equipped to attend to elderly Chinese Canadians. These remain strong reminders of Chinese Canadian presence.

4.2 New Westminster and Others That Have Disappeared

There were many towns in British Columbia that developed flourishing Chinatowns only to see them later disappear. Examples include Cumberland, Lillooet, and Quesnel Forks. Probably the most noteworthy, for its promise and eventual demise was New Westminster. Called *"yifao,"* by

---

[35] Stanley, 37.

[36] *Ibid.*, 190.

Chinese immigrants, the term meant "the second port," after Victoria, and its Chinatown was the largest on the mainland of British Columbia prior to Vancouver's being established.[37] By 1867, New Westminster's approximately one hundred Chinese residents were about one tenth of its total population.

Situated at the mouth of the Fraser River it served as a disembarkation point for workers arriving from China and a major supplier of labour and goods for the mining, fishing, agricultural, and timber industries, and railroad construction along the Fraser River. When the number of Chinese immigrants increased substantially in the early 1880s, New Westminster's Chinatown was quickly transformed. New buildings rose to house workers, stores, restaurants, gambling dens, and joss houses. One prosperous merchant, Kwong On Wo was said to have been the largest Chinese labour contractor in B.C., controlling 75 percent of all the Chinese workers on the C.P.R. line.[38] New Westminster also became a rest over location for workers finished for the winter or in search of new employment.

However, over time the situation changed. Construction of the transnational railroad finished in 1885 substantially decreasing the demand for supplies and labour. Chinatown was continuously monitored for fire hazards after the devastating fire of 1898 that destroyed much of the city including Chinatown. The constant monitoring led to demolition of buildings within Chinatown and reflected a racist mood within the city. Further decline followed after the Exclusion Act of 1923 and by the 1930s only a few of the previous thirty-eight businesses in 1921 remained.[39] The Chinese population also dropped from 792 in 1921 to 561 in 1931.[40] The decline continued until 1979 when New Westminster's Chinatown ceased to be. That year its two remaining organizations, the Chinese Nationalist League and the Chinese Benevolent

---

[37] David Lai, *Chinatowns*, 77.

[38] Jim Wolf and Patricia Owen, *Yi Fao: Speaking Through Memory, A History of New Westminster's Chinese Community 1858-1980* (Surrey, B.C.: Heritage House, 2008), 21.

[39] Lai, *Chinatowns*, 77.

[40] Wolf and Owen, 50.

Association, both disbanded and vacated the buildings they were occupying.

4.3 Calgary`s Chinatown

Calgary's first Chinatown was established in 1890 but it was soon outgrown and a second one became too expensive. Eventually, Chinese Canadians purchased land and started the present-day Chinatown at the corner of Centre Street and Second Avenue S.E. The two-storey building, the Canton Block, erected there still stands today and is the oldest building in Chinatown.

The Calgary community was generally hostile to early Chinese presence. More than three hundred men attacked Chinatown in 1892. Sparked by the outbreak of smallpox among Chinese laundry workers that left three dead among the greater population, the mob ransacked Chinatown and forced some Chinese to flee to the Mounted Police barracks. Opposition continued and in 1911 an alderman lobbied city government to ban Chinese Canadians from building the Canton Block on their newly purchased property. However, the motion was defeated and Calgary's historical Chinatown was established and has remained in the same spot since.

Although Chinese Canadians were met with a general lack of acceptance by most Calgarians, there were notable exceptions, especially among Christian groups. Thomas Underwood, who would later become Calgary's mayor, donated land and built a mission for the Chinese to study English and Christianity. When the building became too small, he erected a larger one on the same spot. After Chinatown moved to its permanent location, Calgary's Chinese joined with Underwood in 1912 to purchase property and build a new mission close by. The Chinese Mission subsequently became an important force in Calgary's Chinatown. It housed the first Chinese Canadian Y.M.C.A. and the first known Chinese Canadian hockey team. Most important, it trained many of the Chinese community's early leaders and has since evolved into an organization that services Chinese Canadian elders, managing two large residences within Chinatown.

Calgary's Chinatown was subject to the same forces of urban renewal as others across Canada in the 1960s, which nearly led to its replacement with an expressway. However, the local community, under the auspices of the Sien Lok Society, was able to mobilize to save not only its own Chinatown but also others across North America. After convincing city government of the merits of preserving Chinatown, the community was able to build a number of large low-cost housing facilities, mostly for seniors, thereby stabilizing Chinatown's population and location. The three-storey Calgary Chinese Cultural Centre was completed in 1992 and has served as a symbol of Chinese Canadian cultural heritage. On Oct. 13, 2011, one hundred years to the day after passing a motion to allow the establishment of Calgary's Chinatown, the City of Calgary declared that date to be Chinatown Day and to be celebrated annually.

4.4 Montreal's Chinatown

The presence of a Chinese in Montreal in 1825, the operation of laundries as early as 1894, and the emergence of a Chinatown between 1890 and 1910 shows that early Chinese immigration to Canada did not only come from the west through British Columbia and follow the transnational railway east. The American transnational railroad was completed in 1869, similarly with extensive use of Chinese labour. This allowed Chinese migrants to move across the American continent and eventually north into Eastern Canada.[41]

Montreal's first and now official Chinatown centred on the intersection of Lagauchetière Street West and St. Urbain Street north of Montreal's business district and close to the St. Lawrence River. It contained about twenty businesses.[42] An influenza epidemic in 1918 led to the founding of the Montreal

---

[41] Rebecca B. Aiken states that 76 percent (54 in number) of the Chinese registered in Montreal in 1900 had arrived in Canada by ship at West Coast ports and 24 percent (17 in number) had arrived by train from the Eastern Seaboard of United States (*Montreal Chinese Property Ownership and Occupational Change, 1881-1981* [New York: AMS Press, 1989], 52). Paul Yee surmises that the earliest Chinese arrivals to Toronto came from United States, which was experiencing a depression in the mid-1870s (*Chinatown: An Illustrated History of the Chinese Communities of Victoria, Vancouver, Calgary, Winnipeg, Toronto, Ottawa, Montreal and Halifax* [Toronto: James Lorimer, 2005], 78).

[42] Lai, *Chinatowns*, 101, citing *Montreal City Directory*, 1910-11.

Chinese Hospital, which still operates today. After the Chinese Exclusion Act of 1923, the Chinese Canadian population shrank across the province of Quebec, the city of Montreal, and within the city's Chinatown.[43] Once the act was rescinded, Montreal saw an influx of new Chinese immigrants. Two major constituents of the new arrivals were refugees from South East Asia that were led to settle in Montreal, in part, because of their ability to speak French, and business investors from Hong Kong.

The provincial government has promoted Quebec as an attractive investment destination with more flexible entry requirements and attractive investment conditions for investors.[44] This has attracted business immigrants to Montreal and investment in Brossard on the south shore of the St. Lawrence River[45] and, probably, to an area close to Concordia University's downtown campus. This investment has, in turn, resulted in Chinatowns developing in these areas giving Montreal three Chinatowns altogether. The one close to Concordia University is referred to as "Chinatown West" and had a population that was 22.9 percent Chinese in 2006.[46]

It is held that part of the reason that investment has flowed into other areas is that the various levels of government have negatively influenced the historical Chinatown on Lagauchetière Street West. In the early 1990s Chan Kwok Bun expressed concern that, unlike in Vancouver and Toronto, where the Chinese Canadian communities have been able to stop government plans that would have led to the destruction of their Chinatowns, Montreal's community had been unable to stop the shrinking of its own Chinatown.[47]

---

[43] Denise Helly, *Les Chinois à Montréal: 1877-1951* (St. Laurent, Québec: Institut québécois de recherche sur la culture, 1987), 122, 218, and 259.

[44] Yee, *Chinatown*, 108-09.

[45] Greater Montreal Sino-Canadian Business Centre, "2007 Sino-Canadian Economic Cooperation Conference," *Business Newsletter,* Edition 04 (July 2007).

[46] Statistics Canada, "Census," "Census tract profile for 0065.01 (CT), Montréal (CMA) and Quebec," *www.statcan.gc.ca*, accessed 2011.08.11.

[47] Chan Kwok Bun, *Smoke and Fire: The Chinese in Montreal* (Hong Kong: Chinese University Press, 1991), 307.

One aspect of note for Montreal's historical Chinatown is the lateness of government support for preserving it. Like Chinatowns across Canada, Montreal's faced the disruptive forces of urban renewal in the 1960s when the provincial government constructed two large buildings along its north side. When other jurisdictions pulled back from continued encroachments into historical Chinatowns, the federal government followed with the Guy Favreau Complex in 1983 that took more than six acres of Chinatown and required the destruction of churches, schools, stores, and residences in order to do so.[48] With construction of Montreal Convention Centre in 1983 and the passing of zoning laws that precluded expansion to the east, Chinatown was virtually boxed in with no way of expanding—except up.

Kwok Bun Chan coined the term "gentrifying Chinatown" to describe the combination of government and commercial forces that began to implement dramatic changes in Montreal's Chinatown[49] and has since been duplicated in Chinatowns across Canada. In 1983, the twenty million dollar condominium-office building Place du Quartier was constructed in Chinatown. The relatively high cost of units within this building and the more affluent residents that it brought into Chinatown led to higher rents, thereby making it difficult for long time occupants to maintain themselves within Chinatown.[50] Another example of change was the Swatow Plaza that opened in 2009 with six floors of offices and shopping.

It is to the credit of Chinese Canadian communities in Montreal and other cities that they have responded to these pressures by establishing alternative Chinatowns, such as Brossard and Chinatown West. However, as Chan points out, "Montreal's Chinatown has been the site of the local Chinese community's institutional structure; it also accommodates and takes care of the disabled, the elderly, the poor, and the disadvantaged." Furthermore, with "its institutional and

---

[48] Kwok B. Chan, "Ethnic Urban Space, Urban Displacement and Forced Relocation: The Case of Chinatown in Montreal," *Canadian Ethnic Studies* 18.2 (1986), 71.

[49] *Ibid.*, 71.

[50] *Ibid.*, 71-75.

cultural infrastructure removed, Chinatown in Montreal as an ethnic neighbourhood will be uprooted from its history and heritage, and will become nothing but a commercial and tourist district catering only to the needs of consumers."[51]

5. Achievements

5.1 Establishment and Development

It may be difficult to conceive of the establishment of Canadian Chinatowns as an achievement. Early Chinese immigrants were often forced to live in them and the term itself was derogatory. However, arguably Canada's Chinatowns are examples of a sow's ear becoming a silk purse for many of them today occupy prime real estate in major city cores. The property values of Canadian Chinatowns are in part an accident of early arrival and occupying locations in what were then smaller communities, which subsequently grew larger around them. However, their continued existence and their ability to meet the needs of their inhabitants and other Chinese Canadians speak to the efforts of Chinese Canadians to establish and develop them, and upon exploring the results of these efforts one finds many notable achievements among them. A large and increasing number of Chinatowns exist across Canada today, the more recent ones taking precedent from the earlier ones. In creating this continuum of concentrated Chinese Canadian social and commercial activity, Chinese Canadians have demonstrated a sophisticated ability to organize themselves. A salient example of this ability is the contribution Sien Lok Society made in saving Chinatowns across North America from the being demolished under the auspices of urban renewal. Because of these past efforts, Vancouver and Toronto today offer examples of thriving Chinatowns that enhance the urban settings they are a part of. Yet in their appeal to the mainstream and in their increasing commercial character, especially among the newer ones, Chinatowns have continued to preserve Chinese cultural traditions. This too constitutes an achievement if only because it has been difficult to do, but also because of the value these traditions have. Today, Chinatowns

---

[51] *Ibid.*, 75 and 73.

across Canada continue to meet the needs of Chinese Canadians, as their predecessors did. It is interesting that preserving cultural traditions has been an important part of doing so, even more interesting in that Chinatowns now provide for mainstream Canadians as well.

5.1.1 Present Day Chinatowns

There are a number of notable Chinatowns in Canada. Most major cities from Montreal west contain at least one. Paul Yee in his book *Chinatown: An Illustrated History of the Chinese Communities of Victoria, Vancouver, Calgary, Winnipeg, Toronto, Ottawa, Montreal and Halifax* (2005) highlights eight, though his list is obviously not exhaustive.[52] If one includes the one in Edmonton and the second in the centre of Toronto, and excludes Halifax, the count rises to nine. However, it still does not include ones formed or forming outside major city centres, so if we add another for Vancouver (Richmond), another for Calgary (surrounding Pacific Place mall in the northeast), one each for both Saskatoon and Regina, include four more for Toronto (Scarborough, Mississauga, Markham, and Richmond Hill), and one more for Montreal (Brossard), the total rises to eighteen functioning Chinatowns in Canada, and the number is likely to grow.

5.1.2 Ability to Organize

Observing the accomplishments seen in the existence of Canada's Chinatowns, an important contributing factor that should also be recognized as an achievement are the organizations that Chinese Canadians have developed since their arrival. Brian Dawson describes their role in the development of Calgary's Chinese community:

> Over the forty-five-year period from 1885 to 1930, the foundations of a vigorous and cohesive ethnic community were laid. Social institutions and political organizations became integral components of everyday activities, and many

---

[52] Arguably, there is no longer a Chinatown in Halifax; however, there is a concentration of Chinese Canadian businesses south of the Halifax Citadel and to the east of it along Quinpool Road.

Chinese concerns were dealt with in an intrinsically independent manner.[53]

Three types of organizations provided for most of their needs, including the need for a physically integrated community. The locality association, the kinship association, and the mutual aid association, called *"huiguan"* all served a variety of needs from housing to feeding, to securing employment, to providing credit, and even arranging funeral services. Edgar Wickberg has detailed the history of Chinese Canadian organizational activities. According to him the earliest organizations were the secret societies in the mining districts and the street associations *(jiefang)* in Victoria.[54] The first secret society was a branch of the Hongmen or Chinese Freemasons, who are still active in Canada today. The Hongmen society originated in the Taiping Rebellion (1850-64) against the Qing Dynasty that contributed to many southern Chinese males leaving China for work in Canada. The first Canadian chapter was in Barkerville, B.C. in 1863. The street association was organized by Chinese Canadian businesses with one in the community taking the lead in organizing around specific issues or projects; for example, the establishment of a Chinese Canadian hospital in Victoria or the collection and return to China for burial of the bones of Chinese railway workers. These two types of organizations were followed by the formation of locality associations in about 1876. Men from the same village or district came together to form co-operative boarding houses. They would also take on other tasks such as transferring remittances or remains after death home.

Kinship associations began to emerge in Victoria and Vancouver between the 1880s and 1911 and eventually became more numerous than locality associations. By 1923 Vancouver had twenty-six kinship associations compared to twelve locality associations. Toronto had ten kinship associations and two locality associations. Calgary had six kinship associations but only one locality association. Nine kinship associations had

---

[53] "The Chinese in Calgary - The Past One Hundred Years," *A Century of the Chinese in Calgary* (Calgary: United Calgary Chinese Association, 1993), 8.

[54] P. 30.

chapters across the nation from Vancouver to Ontario.[55] One kinship association, the Wongs, was said to represent 20 percent of Chinese Canadians.[56] Interestingly, kinship members did not have to be related to one another; rather they only had to have the same surname, which for them indicated possible kinship and also presented a convenient means for forming an association. There were also cases of kinship groups being formed on the basis of having a common radical in one's surname.[57]

Mutual aid associations were different from the other organizations in their efforts to encompass the whole community. The first, the Chinese Consolidated Benevolent Association (CCBA), was formed in 1884 in Victoria. By 1923 similar organizations had been established across Canada as far east as Montreal. Generally referred to as Chinese benevolent associations, these organizations protected members against discrimination, settled disputes, provided aid for those wanting to return to China, housed the sick, poor, and elderly, and arranged burials. They also promoted the learning of traditional Chinese culture; for example, the CCBA established the first free Chinese school in Canada in 1899.

Besides the locality, kinship, and mutual aid associations, there were other organizations that contributed to the development of Canada's Chinatowns while demonstrating the extraordinary ability of Chinese Canadians to organize themselves. The schools promoted Chinese traditions while the churches integrated Chinese Canadians into mainstream society. Wickberg describes how at "the high point of Chinese school development in Canada during the 1930's and early 1940's, there were, according to one survey, twenty-six Chinese part-time schools with forty-seven teachers in eleven locations across the country."[58] It was estimated that 1,500 students were

---

[55] Wickberg, 113.

[56] *Ibid.*, 176.

[57] Bernard P. Wong reports that the Chiu Lung Association united the Tan, Tam, Hsu, and Hsieh families because all of them possessed a common radical in their names (*Chinatown: Economic Adaption and Ethnic Identity of the Chinese* [Fort Worth: Holt, Rinehart and Winston, Inc. 1982], 19).

[58] P. 170.

attending these schools in 1941 and that three were supported in part by the Chinese government. It was within the churches that much of Chinese Canadian leadership was developed. Wickberg notes that in the 1930s many of the ministers were linguistically and culturally equipped to interact with mainstream society and that churches "sometimes served as meeting places for discussions of community problems, involving government officials as well as community leaders and members."[59]

These Chinese Canadian organizations: the locality, kinship, and mutual aid associations, the Chinese churches, and schools, provided the means by which Chinese Canadians would defend and develop themselves. Furthermore, because they were organizations internal to the community, they promoted self-reliance. It was natural that the viability of the Chinatowns that these organizations occupied would be supported by them. In doing so, they highlighted even more the achievements of Canada's Chinatowns.

5.1.3 Efforts of Sien Lok Society

Sien Lok Society is an organization formed in 1968 in Calgary. The name *"sien lok"* means "the greatest happiness lies in being charitable" (*wei shan zui le* in Mandarin and *wai sein tsei lok* in Cantonese). Initially founded to preserve Calgary's Chinatown from demolition in a program of urban renewal, Sien Lok Society has since endeavoured to establish Chinatown as a viable community amid Calgary's encroaching business district and the migration of Chinese merchants and residents to other locations. It has continued to defend and define the physical and cultural boundaries for Calgary's Chinatown while helping to form and articulate a distinctive identity for the Chinese in Calgary and even across Canada. It has an eight to ten-man board of directors elected every two years and its support can he measured from the two hundred people who attend the annual meeting and the approximate seven hundred supporters who attend the annual fund-raising banquet.

---

[59] P. 172.

The issue that led to the founding of Sien Lok Society was the threatened removal of Calgary's Chinatown. During the 1960s the federal government was providing huge funding for urban redevelopment, paying 50 percent of slum clearance costs and 75 percent of redevelopment costs.[60] This, along with added provincial funding, was an encouragement for municipal governments to cheaply acquire property and increase the tax base by redeveloping poorer areas of the city. Canada's Chinatowns, known, and sometimes forced, to be situated in poorer sections of cities, were obvious targets. For example, many of those displaced by Vancouver's redevelopment were Chinese Canadians.[61]

In Calgary's case, the city envisioned tapping into this funding to build a twelve-lane thoroughfare through Chinatown or to reconstruct the Centre Street Bridge. These, among other contemplated projects, probably would have required the demolition of Chinatown. This, of course, created strong concerns among the local Chinese community, so when Ronald Con, regional liaison officer, Citizen Branch, Department of Secretary of State broached the subject of a national conference on the future of Canada's Chinatowns with members of the community, there was a strong response. Businessman Ray Lee took the lead in forming Sien Lok Society and gathering a group of similarly motivated individuals hoping to thwart the threatened destruction of Calgary's Chinatown.

The first major measure taken was to organize the National Conference on Urban Renewal As It Affects Chinatown, which was subsequently held in April 1969. The conference was a huge success. Delegates from across Canada, representing more than one hundred thousand Chinese Canadians,[62] and some from the United States attended the conference. Their exchange of views was subsequently published in conference proceedings that, in turn, prompted action to save Chinatowns in several cities across Canada. The proceedings described the conference as "an attempt to unite Canada's Chinese citizens, for the first

---

[60] Sien Lok Society, 16.

[61] *Ibid.*, 22.

[62] *Ibid.*, 1.

time in history, in a concerted examination of the urban crisis which threatens the existence of Chinatowns everywhere."[63]

The conference explored the significance of Chinatown to new immigrants and the elderly: a refuge for both and a platform for entering into the mainstream for the former, and, more important, the sense of identity provided by its continued existence.[64] It also found that because of the existence of the system of mutual assistance extant within Chinatowns, "Chinese are seldom, if ever, dependent on public or private charities."[65] It was felt that in Vancouver "the whole process of property acquisition and expropriation [had] been carried out in a highly undemocratic manner. Those Chinese residents whose livelihood [was] highly dependent on their small retail establishments and restaurants often were not consulted when the decision was made by the city to expropriate their stores, or when in those cases, they were consulted, they were meagerly compensated for their unwillingly relinquished properties."[66]

During the conference Robert Conway, assistant planner for the City of Calgary, described the contribution of Chinatown to forming a Chinese Canadian identity in these words, "There must be a place people can identify with, and particularly the newcomers that you mentioned, where they can get their feet on the ground, where they can hear a language that they are accustomed to and eat food that they are accustomed to, . . . "[67] The importance in establishing this identity was further recognized in the thoughts expressed in the conference that Chinatown should include residences, schools, churches, as well as commercial entities, in order to ground the community.[68]

In closing, the conference put forward the following resolution:

---

[63] *Ibid.*

[64] *Ibid.*, 18.

[65] *Ibid.*, 21.

[66] *Ibid.*, 22.

[67] *Ibid.*, 61.

[68] *Ibid.*, 66.

Whereas Chinatown is an integral part of the Canadian scene and history; and whereas, Chinatown has made considerable contributions to the growth, progress and development of Canada; and whereas Chinatown is significant social, cultural, economic and physical entity of our community life; and whereas, Chinatown is an outstanding attraction of the tourist industry which is vital to the economy of our country. Therefore, be it resolved that the contributions of Chinatown to the Canadian way of life be accorded full recognition by this conference on redevelopment in Chinatown, and, that it be further resolved, that this conference goes on record in urging the three levels of government to adopt programs favouring and encouraging the continual perpetuation of Chinatown in all major cities of Canada.[69]

The conference received favourable coverage from the Calgary media and led to more in depth reporting on the Calgary Chinese community. A special series of articles appeared in the *Calgary Herald* that were both well-researched and sympathetic to Chinese concerns about Chinatown. Since then, Calgary media have maintained an active and objective interest in Chinese community affairs, particularly the preservation and development of Chinatown.[70]

Ultimately, the National Conference on Urban Renewal As It Affects Chinatown played an important role in preserving Chinatowns across Canada, thereby advancing the opportunity of having a Chinese Canadian identity. Not only was the conference instrumental in preserving Calgary's Chinatown from demolition, delegates from other cities empowered by the conference's message returned to seek the protection of their heritage. The conference also sent a delegation to Ottawa to meet with the pertinent minister, Harvie Andre, adding more weight to arguments for Chinatown's preservation.

Sien Lok has also continued to play a leading role in this cause. It has been collecting and producing exhibits of Chinese-Canadian histories, including placing them on the internet. With this new project, Sien Lok Society is attempting to articulate and support an emerging Chinese identity in Canada. In spite of a background of racist treatment, or perhaps because

---

[69] *Ibid.*, 95.

[70] Dawson, *Moon Cakes,* 156-57.

of, Chinese Canadians are asking that their past and present contributions to Canadian society and culture be acknowledged. At the same time, Chinese Canadian influence is increasing in Canada and this trend creates a need to understand this influence's origin and development. Sien Lok Society is attempting to direct and contribute to this development, as it did in its response to the threats to Chinatowns in the 1960s, and again foster and support a Chinese-Canadian identity.

5.2 Outstanding Examples of Chinatowns

5.2.1 Vancouver's Chinatown

Vancouver offers examples of early and later types of Chinatowns and examples of both types are achievements in their own right. This is not surprising given the city's historical role as the primary gateway for Chinese immigrants to Canada, a role reflected in the presence of 411,475 Chinese Canadians in 2011, 18 percent of its total population.[71] The early Chinatown occupies the east side of the city centre and spreads from the axis of Pender and Main Streets. The commercial section is bordered on the east by the residential area of Strathcona, which is highly populated by Chinese Canadians. This Chinatown is home to the Chinese Cultural Centre, its museum and archives, and the Dr. Sun Yat-sen Classical Garden, as well as the social agency United Chinese Community Enrichment Services Society (S.U.C.C.E.S.S.). Nevertheless, its vitality has diminished considerably from the late 1990s as new arrivals have supported the building of Chinese themed malls and restaurants in the suburbs, particularly in Richmond to the south.

About 45 percent of Richmond's population is ethnic Chinese.[72] Richmond's Chinatown differs from that in other communities because there is an obvious extension from the concentration of commercial facilities into the residential areas surrounding it. The enclave does not seem so much an enclave

---

[71] Statistics Canada, "NHS Focus on Geography Series – Vancouver," accessed 2014.11.20.

[72] City of Richmond website, *www.richmond.ca/home.htm*, accessed 2011.07.04.

because of this; rather the easily identifiable commercial sector seems to amorphously spread into the surrounding area and one is at loss to define where it ends.

In its beginnings, Vancouver's early Chinatown faced formidable challenges, chief among them the sometimes violent opposition to its presence. Vancouver's Chinatown was, as Kaye Anderson describes, the subject of "the first act of concerted physical violence against the Chinese in Canada" when in 1887 it was attacked by a mob of about three hundred men.[73] Anderson describes events leading up to the attack. A week after the great fire of June 13, 1886, which destroyed almost all the buildings in Vancouver, two aldermen held street meetings that passed resolutions aimed at preventing the Chinese who had been forced out from returning. This was followed by a successful effort to renounce former property leases given to Chinese residents and a boycott of businesses that employed, served, or patronized Chinese residents. In November, a committee that included the mayor and two aldermen was appointed to establish a fund for expelling the Chinese. The riot occurred when a contractor was able to secure a court order allowing him to bring in Chinese workers. After they arrived and encamped at Coal Harbour, they were attacked on February 24 by a mob of three hundred men. The attackers burned bedding and beat workers, and a smaller group proceeded to Carrall Street to burn and damage the homes of some ninety Chinese residents.[74]

Twenty years later, in 1907, after a rally of the Asiatic Exclusion League attended by an estimated five thousand, rally participants attacked Chinese and Japanese quarters in Vancouver. As compensation for the damage done, the Chinese were awarded twenty-six thousand dollars and the Japanese nine thousand.[75] As time passed, Vancouver's population recognized the futility of wanting to expel the Chinese, so their strategy turned to containing them. In 1941 a delegation

---

[73] P. 67.

[74] *Ibid.*, 65-67. Raymond Edgar Young describes efforts to deny Chinese access to rental property and cites *The Vancouver Advertiser* of December 27, 1886 as evidence ("Streets of T'ongs: Study of Vancouver's Chinatown" [M.A. diss., University of British Columbia, 1975], 60).

[75] Wickberg, 84-87.

representing West Point Grey property owners urged the City of Vancouver's Zoning Committee to prohibit the sale of a house in their area to a Chinese. They asked "that the City pass special legislation restricting Orientals to certain parts of the city." In response the Zoning Committee "passed a resolution to recommend bylaw changes which, if possible, would restrict orientals to owning and occupying homes in specified localities."[76] If Chinese Canadians could not be forced out or their communities eradicated, at least, their expansion into other areas could be prevented.

The unfavourable views of Vancouver's Chinatown carried on into the 1960s and combined with the forces of urban renewal to threaten its continued existence. Starting in 1959, the City of Vancouver condemned blocks of housing within Strathcona, which was about 50 percent Chinese Canadian occupied, and built public housing in their place. The first two phases cleared eleven blocks and displaced two thousand residents.[77] However, when the city council approved the complete and total removal of the Strathcona neighbourhood for the third phase, the community formed the Strathcona Property Owners and Tenants Association (SPOTA) to fight the decision. SPOTA, together with strong allies, was able to save the community and produce a movement that would preserve Chinatown from the inroads of proposed freeways, and, arguably, downtown Vancouver from being dominated by them.[78]

With the future of Chinatown secure, the community went to work to develop it. From 1974 on SPOTA took control of land the city had originally acquired for urban renewal and

---

[76] Young, 71-2, citing *Vancouver News Herald* of Feb. 04, 1941, p. 4.

[77] Hayne Y. Wai, "Vancouver Chinatown 1960-1980: A Community Perspective," *New Scholars—New Visions in Canadian Studies* (Seattle) 3.1 (1998), 5-6.

[78] It is ironic that in preserving Chinatowns–areas formerly considered blighted but still close to city centres–over the demands of freeway construction, Canadian cities would save some of their most attractive real estate for what would come to be seen as better uses. For example, by rejecting the freeway that was to cut through its Chinatown, Calgary preserved some of its best real estate along the Bow River for pedestrian walkways.

proceeded to build affordable family and senior housing. The Chinese Cultural Centre was opened in 1980 and in 1986 the Dr. Sun Yat-Sen Classical Chinese Garden was laid out adjacent to the cultural centre. The United Chinese Community Enrichment Services Society (S.U.C.C.E.S.S.), an immigrant assistance agency, was founded in Chinatown in 1973 and has grown into an organization managing a budget of more than $35 million.[79] The preservation and development of Vancouver's Chinatown have marked the achievements of its Chinese inhabitants.

In defending and then promoting Vancouver's historical Chinatown, the Chinese community was also able to garner support from the broader community as seen in the government assistance it has received. As early as 1969 SPOTA, together with the three levels of government, was investigating on how to renew rather than demolish Strathcona. Although initially the municipal government was a reluctant participant in negotiations, it later became a major force in the Vancouver Chinatown Revitalization Committee that "was officially formed in January 2001 to bring together more than twenty of the area's social, cultural, resident and business groups to work with the city to develop short-term revitalization plans, and a long-term vision for Chinatown, . . ."[80]
The preservation and development of Vancouver's Chinatown in cooperation with a once-opposed municipal government have marked the achievements of its Chinese inhabitants. Nevertheless, Chinatown faces still more challenges as the attraction of outlying Chinese commercial areas draws patronage and residents away from the historical Chinatown in the city's centre.

Richmond on the southern edge of Vancouver is home to a new flourishing form of Chinatown. Rather than being a sharply defined commercial area, its shops, restaurants, and offices are mostly low-storied premises and they blend into the

[79] "S.U.C.C.E.S.S. Annual Report, 2009-2010," p. 16, www.successbc.ca/eng/images/stories/pdf/AnnualReport_Eng_2010.pdf, accessed 2011.07.09.

[80] City of Vancouver, "Chinatown Revitalization Program: Chinatown Vision," 2002.07.02, vancouver.ca/ctyclerk/cclerk/020723/rr2.htm, accessed 2011.07.10.

surrounding residential areas whose residents are already more than 40 percent Chinese Canadian. Richmond's Chinatown took shape in the late 1980s when investors from Hong Kong developed a number of Asian-themed malls along Number 3 Road.[81]

This development was surprising because Richmond throughout its history had been a predominately European influenced area. As late as 1981 statistics were showing that its ethnic Chinese population was relatively stable as most areas had less than 5 percent Chinese residents.[82] Furthermore, this low number had been preceded in 1885 by objections originating within Richmond to Oriental ways and culture and local government regulations that only White labour would be used in municipal projects as long as they worked for less than 25 percent more than the lowest Chinese tender.[83] With a history of prejudice and a low ethnic population, the establishment of a Chinatown in Richmond was far from inevitable in 1981. However, the commercial area of Richmond's Chinatown, called the "Golden Village," has grown to an area of about 1.6 square kilometers, about 50 percent larger than the Pacific Mall/Market Village complex in Markham, the latter said to be the largest Chinese shopping center in North America.

5.2.2 Toronto's Chinatowns

In many ways the Chinese Canadian community in Toronto has been the most successful in Canada. High participation in Christian churches[84] seems to have linked them

---

[81] Peter Li and Eva Xiaoling Li enumerate that there were sixty-eight Chinese-operated business in Richmond in 1981, and by 1990 the number had increased to one hundred eighty-two (citing Peter Li). Furthermore, the increase was not only in restaurants and grocery stores, but also in professional services and other lines of businesses outside traditional ones. ("Vancouver Chinatown in Transition," *Journal of Chinese Overseas* 7 [2011], 17).

[82] Brian K. Ray, Greg Halseth, and Benjamin Johnson, "The Changing 'Face' of the Suburbs: Issues of Ethnicity and Residential Change in Suburban Vancouver," *International Journal of Urban and Regional Research* 21 (March 1997), 88.

[83] *Ibid.*

[84] Dora Nipp reports that no less than 450 (or 43.6 percent) of Toronto's

to the mainstream population such that professional training and occupations were open to them and, based on their education and experience it was natural for them to take a leading role in Chinese Canadian national activities such as opposition to the Chinese Immigration Act of 1923. This success is reflected in the history and present situation of its Chinatowns. In spite of the fact that it was located far from the west coast gateway of Chinese immigrant arrival, there was a Chinatown in Toronto as early as 1910. As well, prior to any other Canadian city, Toronto saw the development of secondary Chinatowns as complements to the main one. As of 2006 there were more than sixty-five Chinese shopping centers in the Greater Toronto Area with a few more under construction,[85] and two designated Chinatowns.[86] Furthermore, from 1989 to 1996, when Toronto was undergoing periods of deep recession, Chinese Canadians still managed to build more than fifty shopping centres throughout the city.[87] Besides the two designated Chinatowns of Chinatown (Central) (intersection of Dundas and Spadina, 1961)[88] and Chinatown East (Broadview

---

Chinese were attending Sunday school classes in one of the city's churches in 1910 ("The Chinese in Toronto," in *Gathering Places: Peoples and Neighbourhoods of Toronto, 1834-1945*, ed. Robert F. Harney [Toronto: Multicultural History Society of Ontario, 1985], 154) .

[85] Lucia Lo, "Changing Geography of Toronto's Ethnic Economy," in *Landscapes of the Ethnic Economy*, ed. David H. Kaplan and Wei Li (Lanham, Maryland: Rowman & Littlefield, 2006), 86. These centers include the Pacific Mall/Market Village complex, which is the largest Chinese shopping center in North America (*ibid.*, 89).

[86] Lucia Lo, "Suburban Housing and Indoor Shopping: The Production of Contemporary Chinese Landscape in Toronto," in *From Urban Enclave to Ethnic Suburb: New Asian Communities in Pacific Rim Countries*, ed. Wei Li (Honolulu: University of Hawaii Press, 2006), 139. The two Chinatowns were Central Chinatown composed of Old Chinatown and Chinatown Central that were in close enough proximity to be considered as one, and East Chinatown.

[87] Tony Wong, "New Canadians with Global Connections ; What Is the Legacy of Immigration Programs That Drew Many Enterprising Chinese to Canada? Major Canadian Businesses with Links Around the World," *Toronto Star*, 1999.05.10, 1.

[88] Chinatown Central is an extension of what is referred to as "Old Chinatown," which originally centered around York and Queen Streets in 1910 and itself extended north toward Dundas.

and Gerrard, 1972), there are five other locations that are recognized as Chinatowns in the Greater Toronto Area. These include the Agincourt Chinatown in Scarborough (Sheppard near Midland, 1984), Chinatown in Willowdale (Tempo and Victoria Park, 1986), Mississauga (888 Dundas St.), Markham (Steeles and Kennedy), and Richmond Hill (along Highway 7 between Bayview Avenue and Warden Avenue).

The five Chinatowns in the outlying areas of Greater Toronto center around shopping areas that have been built to service the large numbers of Chinese Canadians that have moved into these areas. Their residences are spread throughout the communities and the Chinese malls serve as cores that coalesce and identify their presence and influence. Chinese Canadians are no longer forced, or even encouraged, to live in segregated or concentrated communities; however, they require commercial activities to provide for their material needs while supporting their cultural preferences. The result is that they purchase their homes in the vicinity or their presence encourages the merchants to locate nearby. Cathy Drive in Scarborough has since the 1980s seen a gradual shift from mostly White residents to mostly Chinese, who in 2005 occupied forty-four of the seventy homes on the street. The street is near Chinese malls served by people speaking Cantonese or Mandarin and selling familiar products. A survey of Chinese Canadian residents on the street showed that "the desire to live close to ethnic services" and "the wish to savour familiar products," along with "the need for a bigger lot and larger floor space" were the three main reasons in choosing where they lived.[89] These needs have led to the formation of a type of Chinatown different from the historical ones that remain much more visible yet are limited in some ways in what they can provide for their residents and the broader Chinese Canadian population.

The creation of these new enclaves has had positive effects on the City of Toronto. The malls that are essentially linked to them have made large contributions to the city. It was in Toronto that the building of Chinese shopping centres outside the boundaries of historical Chinatowns began and it has been

---

[89] Sandeep Kumar and Bonica Leung, "Formation of an Ethnic Enclave: Process and Motivations," *Plan*, Summer 2005, 44.

the leader in North America in terms of size and speed of their development.[90] In the early 1980s outlets selling Chinese products began to gather in retail plazas situated in Scarborough. This was followed by speculation that the rising Chinese Canadian population was demanding more ethnic retailing and office space, which in the mid 1980s led to the conversion of existing malls and the construction of enclosed malls and mixed retail/commercial space, all devoted to meeting this demand. Mississauga Chinese Centre, which opened in 1987, was one of the earliest examples, converting a building on an industrial site into a mix of ethnic shops and exhibits of Chinese culture.[91] Most of the developers of these sites were Chinese Canadians; however, with their success, non-Chinese Canadian developers soon followed. Some of the latter's projects had been in danger of failing because of the recession that hit in the 1990s; therefore, they modified them to meet the needs of Chinese Canadians, thereby allowing them to succeed. Capital for new projects was often raised among new and perspective immigrants and, so during "the 1990s, when the rest of the Toronto economy was suffering badly, Chinese shopping mall developments were going full force."[92]

These malls generally range in size from eight hundred eighty to twenty-eight thousand square meters. Of these, the Pacific Mall/Market Village complex, with a total sales area of more than forty-six thousand square meters and more than five hundred stores, the size of a regional shopping center, is the largest indoor Chinese shopping center in North America.[93] These shopping centers are manifestations of both the changing natures of Chinatowns in Canada and of the contributions that

---

[90] Lo, "Suburban Housing," 151.

[91] *Ibid.*, 149; and Mississauga Chinese Centre website, "Founder and History," *mississaugachinesecentre.com/frame2.html*, accessed 07 June 2008.

[92] Lo, "Suburban Housing," 149-150.

[93] *Ibid.*, 150-51. However, the King Square mall, which is under construction in the Greater Toronto Area, is planned to surpass the Pacific Mall/Market Village complex once it is completed (Paul Brent, "With Fresh Funding, Continent's Largest Asian Mall Back on Track," *Real Estate News Exchange*, 2014.06.21, *renx.ca/with-fresh-funding-continents-largest-asian-mall-back-on-track*, accessed 2015.01.21).

these Chinatowns are making to the communities within which they are situated.

5. 3 Commercial, Yet with Cultural Values Maintained

Another achievement of Canadian Chinatowns has been their ability to preserve and promote Chinese culture even as they become more commercial. Arguably, the preservation of Chinese culture was essential to the existence of Canada's Chinatowns, which in turn were essential to the survival of Chinese Canadians. The values of mutual assistance, perseverance, hard work, thrift, occupational flexibility, and economic management that subsequently allowed Chinatowns to function are embedded in Chinese culture. It served the Chinese Canadian population to maintain these values in order to ensure that the settings that provided their protection and mutual support were also maintained.

While preserving Chinese culture contributed to Chinese Canadian survival in the past, it has also contributed to present-day Chinese Canadian success. Therefore, the role of Chinatowns in preserving Chinese culture has not disappeared. One still finds language schools, traditional celebrations, care for the elderly, martial arts studios, facilities for Traditional Chinese Medicine, traditional art forms, mutual aid societies, Chinese foods, and so on primarily within Chinatowns. It is there that Chinese culture has been and continues to be practised.

One also finds examples of the preservation of Chinese culture within Canadian Chinatowns from their early existence to the present day. The Chinese school in Victoria's Chinatown has been in operation over more than three centuries from 1899 to the present day. It was founded to provide Chinese Canadian children with a Chinese education. One finds similar schools in Chinatowns across Canada, often attached to cultural centres. There are Chinese cultural centres, which promote Chinese culture within the Chinatowns of Victoria, Vancouver, Edmonton, Calgary, and Winnipeg. One also finds facilities devoted to housing and serving Chinese Canadian elderly within the Chinatowns of Victoria, Vancouver, Edmonton, Calgary, Winnipeg, Toronto, Ottawa, and Montreal. One can find similar examples for traditional celebrations, Traditional

Chinese Medicine facilities, and so on. Even the newer forms of Chinatowns, the venues that are more commercially oriented than historical Chinatowns, such as the Chinese themed shopping centres, will hold traditional Chinese celebrations, such as for Chinese New Year, or contain offices for Chinese social organizations. Their preservation and promotion of Chinese culture are not as strong as their historical counterparts; however, they do, nevertheless, contribute to the overall achievement of these goals thereby indicating how strong the motivation to do so is.

6. Challenges That Have Made These Achievements Even Greater

The establishment and continued development of Canada's Chinatowns do not require any historical and contemporary background in order to be recognized as an outstanding achievement. However, when their background is considered, these achievements are even more impressive. One becomes more aware of the opposition that Chinese Canadians faced when they first established their communities and how this opposition heightened as they developed. History shows that it was not until the 1960s that the Canadian mainstream began to accept seriously the value of Chinatowns. Once that acceptance was received, the environment for Chinatown development improved immensely; however, a combination of other factors has created another serious challenge to the existence of historical Chinatowns, namely in the form of economic viability.

Chinese Canadians' pursuit of convenience has led to the creation of other centres of Chinese Canadian commerce and culture in close proximity to early ones and this has, consequently, undermined the latters' viability. Two other factors, the rising property values surrounding and within Chinatown and the aging population within, have intensified the challenge. The movement of business out of Chinatown has combined with the pressure to replace older buildings, businesses, and organizations with office towers, condominiums, hotels, and brand name shopping that would provide greater income for property owners. The departure of businesses leaving vacant premises and fewer shoppers within Chinatown is encouraging its business community to promote a model for future development that risks undermining the historical role Chinatowns have had in preserving Chinese culture.

6.1 Early Challenges

While this essay has documented the external pressures, such as the attacks upon Chinese Canadians, that led them to create Chinatowns, more can be told about the opposition to Chinatowns once they were created in order to show how impressive their continued existence has been.

Kay Anderson has documented the application of the term "Chinatown" as it was applied to Canada's Chinese communities. It came loaded with prejudicial preconceptions that identified Chinatowns as unsanitary and immoral. It was being used to describe the Chinese in Vancouver even before they had any substantial settlement there. Usage of the term seems to have begun with American miners in Canada and in the written descriptions of Chinese presence in North America. Government officials described the environs of a Chinese Canadian settlement: "The air is polluted by disgusting offal with which they are surrounded, and vile accumulations are apt to spread fever and sickness in the neighbourhood which in the end may affect extensive districts."[94] Similar perceptions underlay reports by local media of the abuse of sanitation laws and efforts by the municipal government to restrict Chinese businesses and residences for fear of spread of disease. As for immorality, Anderson reports that "Chinatown seems to have signified many of the impulses that Europeans feared and attempted to repress in themselves: gambling, drug addiction, prostitution, slavery in women, licentiousness, and crime."[95]

These views expressed by influential members of the mainstream would have promoted and reinforced negative attitudes toward Chinese Canadians and contributed to the mob attacks on Chinatowns that followed in Vancouver in 1887 and 1907, in Calgary in 1892, and other locales. Given the intensity of these attitudes that would lead to mob attacks, it is

---

[94] P. 81, quoting Commissioner Joseph Chapleau in what is likely a report from the first Royal Commission on Chinese Immigration (1885).

[95] P. 93.

clear that establishing, preserving, and developing Chinatowns was a difficult task for Chinese Canadians. They could have given up their communities, left for China, or made themselves less visible by dispersing across the country. However, they worked to establish their communities, giving rise to even greater future achievement.

Come the 1960s, although mainstream attitudes toward Chinatowns had softened, they could not be described as accepting. Across Canada, Chinatowns were targeted for demolition under urban renewal projects. The federal government was providing huge funding for urban redevelopment, paying 50 percent of slum clearance costs and 75 percent of redevelopment costs.[96] This, along with added provincial funding was an encouragement for municipal governments to acquire property cheaply and increase the tax base by redeveloping poorer areas of the city. Canada's Chinatowns, known, and often forced, to be situated in poorer sections of cities were obvious targets for the wrecking ball. For example, in the 1960s Winnipeg City Council planned to build a highway through Princess Street that would have required the demolition of most of Chinatown.[97] While not openly hostile to Chinese Canadians and their concentration, the efforts to remove Chinatowns, pushing Chinese Canadian residents and businesses from their historical locations still assumed Chinatowns as targets for eradication.

Neither the instigators of the mob attacks and nor the movements to demolish Chinatowns in the name of urban renewal assumed an active role for the Chinese Canadians in defending against the attacks or in opposing urban renewal. It was assumed that the Chinese would passively accept the outcomes envisioned in them. However, in hindsight this assumption seems naive as Chinese Canadians have proven their ability to defend, preserve, and develop their communities. Their achievements cannot be denied.

6.2 New Pressures

---

[96] Sien Lok Society, 16.

[97] *Winnipeg Chinatown: The Revitalization of a Community* (Winnipeg: The Winnipeg Chinatown Development [1981] Corporation, 1988), 27.

Although it is unlikely that Chinatowns would be subjected to the same kind of pressures as in the past, new types of pressures have been affecting Canada's historical Chinatowns adding to the challenges they must meet. As Chinese Canadian populations have grown and their standards of living risen, historical Chinatowns have proven inadequate to meet their needs. As well, property values have risen, making it difficult to maintain the same activities, such as care of the elderly, within Chinatown. Furthermore, the higher age and lower income of Chinatown residents mean that they are less able to support its commercial infrastructure. These pressures are different because, in greater part, they originate within the community itself. However, they still constitute impediments for the continued viability of historical Chinatowns. These challenges are serious enough that one cannot be sure whether Chinatowns will survive. The challenges call for further achievements by Chinese Canadians with regard to the continued existence of their historical Chinatowns.

6.2.1 Historical Chinatowns Inadequate to Meet Chinese Canadian Needs

The strongest pressure facing historical Canadian Chinatowns is that they are simply not large enough to meet the needs of Chinese Canadians. Obviously, the number of Chinese Canadians has increased since Chinatowns first formed, so the overall demand for goods and services from this group has increased and they have become more sophisticated in their values and tastes. For example, many of them find the environment of Chinatown an unsuitable one for habitation. Reflecting this change, 50 percent of Vancouver's Chinese Canadians lived with Chinatown in 1960, but by 1976 that figure had dropped to 10 percent.[98] There have been clear consequences arising from this, such as concentrated populations in expensive neighbourhoods where previously there were few Chinese Canadians.[99]

---

[98] Anderson, 14.

[99] For example, Chinese Canadians comprised over 13 percent of the Vancouver-Point Grey Electoral District in 2006 (*BC Stats, www.bcstats.gov.bc.ca/*, accessed 2011.07.26).

Furthermore, the increased numbers of Chinese living outside Chinatown has created a large customer base that is attractive to ethnic businesses that have then located close to these concentrations. An example is the creation of Pacific Place mall in northeast Calgary away from its historical Chinatown. Also, business premises within Chinatown are often small and simple with limited parking. The result seems to have been that Chinatown has not flourished as much as it could or has even being losing businesses as shops lay empty, likened to a "hollowing out" of Chinatown.

Accompanying the movement of Chinese Canadians to residences outside the historical boundaries of Chinatowns, and sometimes preceding them in anticipation of their move, have been large shopping complexes that have formed the nucleus of newly formed Chinatowns. Areas like Richmond, appealing because of lower house values relative to those in the City of Vancouver and its proximity to the international airport, have seen the growth of Chinese Canadian or Chinese invested businesses, such as the Aberdeen Centre, which opened in 1990 with more than eleven thousand square meters of commercial space housing sixty shops and one cinema.[100] There are similar examples in other Canadian urban centres. Chinatowns have sprung up outside of Toronto's core in suburbs like Mississauga and Scarborough and are anchored by large shopping complexes. In Montreal, a second Chinatown has developed on Boulevard Taschereau in the suburb of Brossard on the South Shore of the St. Lawrence River.

The impact of this change on historical Chinatowns is twofold. There has been a movement of activities, mostly commercial, out of the historical Chinatowns, with replacements showing up in the newly created Chinatowns. Service and good providers in the new Chinatowns are appealing more to clients subsequently drawing more businesses away from the historical ones. The result is the appearance that present-day historical Canadian Chinatowns are being hollowed out as businesses migrate to newer centres in order to retain or regain clients. In Vancouver, by 1999 many diners had abandoned restaurants in Vancouver's historical

---

[100] Peter Li, *The Chinese in Canada* (Toronto: Oxford University Press, 1998), 135.

Chinatown and the best Chinese food was found in the suburbs. In the words of one businessman, "Chinatown used to be the place to go at night; nowadays, after six o'clock, it's like a ghost town."[101] In another example, merchants in downtown Toronto's second Chinatown (Chinatown East) at Broadview and Gerard reported in 2006 that profits had dropped 30 percent. The cause was attributed to residents selling their properties in order to move to the suburbs, leaving the elderly behind.[102]

It is difficult to measure the threat that economic change is creating for historical Chinatowns. In the past, Chinatowns took some strength in the perception that threats originated external to the community; Chinese Canadians could easily unite against such an identified danger. However, the threat in the present form originates much more within the community, as Chinese Canadians once the main, if not sole, defenders of Chinatowns now abandon them for the comfort of homes and the convenience of commercial centres in the suburbs.

6.2.2 Property Values

Another contemporary challenge facing historical Chinatowns is the rise in property values within them. Many of them are located in the centres of major cities where land values have risen much since these Chinatowns were first established there. The resulting rise in property values, while contributing to the hollowing out of Chinatown by forcing less profitable merchants to give up expensive rental space, has also put pressure on Chinatowns to encourage more commercial development. The owners of these properties argue that they should be allowed to maximize the value of their investments. However, there is also strong opposition to intensive commercial development because of concern that it will undermine some of the historical and important functions of

---

[101] Yee, 51, citing Ron Mickleburgh, "After 6, It's Like a Ghost Town," *Globe and Mail*, 1999.02.17, A1 .

[102] Sarah Elton, "Chinatown Blues: Business is Down and For Sale Signs Are Popping Up on a Once-vibrant Strip," *Globe and Mail*, 2006.11. 04, M2. Sandee Wong reported a similar situation in Calgary's historical Chinatown where four restaurants had closed in 2005 and remained empty mainly due to the lack and expense of parking ("Chinatown Gets Down to Business," *Calgary Herald Neighbours*, North Edition, 2006.04.13-19, N1, N4).

Canadian Chinatowns. The presence of the two opposing views
of development makes it difficult to determine what should be
the best strategy for developing Chinatown and to respond to
other challenges. Both views of development seem to have their
merits; however, the consensus that would be required to
support a strong, unified Chinatown response to changing
conditions is difficult to obtain.

The tension and the disunity it created were apparent in
the 1970s in Toronto when local property owners "unveiled
plans for a multimillion dollar commercial/residential complex
consisting of expensive boutiques and high-priced
condominiums to be built in the heart of Chinatown's
commercial district."[103] The plans contravened an earlier plan
that local planners appointed by city government had
tentatively drafted and that had achieved a great deal of
consensus within the Chinatown community. "The consensus
was that the stability (i.e., current character) of the Chinatown
neighbourhood should be maintained at all costs."[104] Efforts by
both sides to have their view of Chinatown development
accepted led to a series of confrontational meetings even
marked by intimidation.[105]

Similar situations can be seen in other Canadian
Chinatowns. In Calgary's case, property on the borders of
Chinatown is zoned for much higher land use density, and thus
is much more valuable. While Chinatown has historically been
legally limited to or enjoyed lower density use, it seems that the
hope that it will be rezoned for greater density use is keeping
some property owners from developing their properties,
allowing them to remain fallow, for example, as parking lots,
awaiting projects of much greater value than would be allowed
under present regulations. This has the effect of taking land out
of circulation and limiting the goods and services that can be
offered to clients in Chinatown. When a development to build
high and low rise condominiums, apartments, and townhouses
with shops on the ground level was approved on property
formerly occupied by the Greyhound bus barn but within the

---

[103] Thompson, 342.

[104] *Ibid.*

[105] *Ibid.*, 355

designated boundaries of Chinatown, the difference of opinions again surfaced. Opponents of the plan said it would destroy Chinatown and that the process had omitted consultation with the families, children, and seniors who would be most impacted. Supporters argued that if Chinatown is to survive, it must have residences such as these to attract young Chinese.[106] Controversy has also revolved around a proposal considered by Vancouver's city council to rezone much of its Chinatown to allow as high as twelve-storey buildings. The proposal was supported by a variety of organizations within Chinatown but opposed by many who saw it making Chinatown unaffordable for its present residents and businesses.[107]

The future development of Canadian Chinatowns is complicated by another issue. In a reversal of past attitudes, local governments across Canada are now protecting Chinatowns as heritage sites. They contain historical buildings and are records of past, especially valuable in highlighting what are now perceived as mistaken prejudices. The policy has its supporters within the community, but in Vancouver as early as the 1990s other community members came to view the policy as limiting development that was necessary for the survival of Chinatown.[108] Local governments have accepted the rationale that development in Chinatowns should be limited in order to preserve the history and in deference to the social agencies that fear development will undermine the traditional functions that Chinatown has had. They have also tried to mitigate any loss to property owners by allowing density transfers. In Vancouver, the purchaser of the Wing Sang building in Chinatown was able to underwrite the cost of purchasing a heritage building by selling the excess density—density that cannot be utilized because it is a heritage building—to a development outside of

---

[106] Canadian Broadcasting Corporation (CBC), "New Housing, Shops to Be Built in Calgary's Chinatown," 2006.07.20, accessed at *myasiancanadian.blogspot.com/2006/07/new-housing-shops-to-be-built-in.html* on 2011.07. 27.

[107] Ian Austin, "Residents Rally Against Chinatown Towers," *The Province*, 2011.03.14.

[108] Chris Wong, "Crossroads for Chinatown," *The Georgia Strait*, 1993.06.18-25, 9, 11-12.

Chinatown.[109] Nevertheless, the city's attempt to mitigate the negative effects of preserving Chinatown's traditional functions brings attention to the problems with doing so and the disagreement among Chinese Canadians over the ideal future for Chinatowns.

Added to this complexity of influences is a trend referred to as "gentrification." As early as 1979, half of the properties and businesses in Victoria's Chinatown were owned and operated by non-Chinese and there were non-Chinese living there as well.[110] This situation indicated a blend of Chinese and mainstream Canadian culture, which is reflected in a vision for Vancouver's Chinatown to become multicultural, to be influenced by artists and art galleries, to be home for band name stores, and to house businesses that appeal to a broader clientele.[111]

The value of diversification was echoed in other descriptions of gentrification taking place in Chinatowns. The real-estate director for the Freemasons in Vancouver explained their decision to rent storefronts to a longboard shop, a German-sausage-and-beer delicatessen, and a vintage shop as bringing people into Chinatown and contributing to its revitalization.[112] A director from the Toronto Chinatown Business Improvement Area described the purpose for holding a summer night market and having local restaurants sponsor the Reel Asian Film Festival was to attract diverse businesses and clientele.[113]

There are also some promising projects that add to the attraction of gentrification. For example, Kelty Miyoshi MacKinnon, a landscape architect, and Inge Roecker, a professor in architecture at the University of British Columbia,

---

[109] Charles Campbell, "The Heart of the City May Be Rising Again After a Long Decline. But Will Chinatown's Rebirth Save It or Destroy It?", *Vancouver Magazine* 38.9 (2009.10), 60.

[110] Lai and Madoff, 3.

[111] Campbell, 65.

[112] Frances Bula, "Behind the Changing Face of Vancouver's Chinatown," *The Globe and Mail*, 2013.01.13.

[113] Matthew Sherwood, "Chinatown BIA Wants to Clean Up Shop," *The Globe and Mail*, 2011.11.11.

under the auspices of Vancouver's Chinatown Revitalization Program, have proposed a number of modifications to buildings within the area that would revitalize it. In doing so they view "heritage as cultural capital, it can be a development asset that can help provide employment, mobilize communities and generate income."[114]

Notably, McKinnon and Roecker are critical of gentrification, seeing it as process that pushes original residents out of an area or turns it into an exotic tourist exhibition. While there are some promising developments that can be grouped under the category of gentrification, it seems to be an outcome of number of different forces including the desire to maintain traditional values, the loss of businesses to suburban commercial centres, and the increase in surrounding property values pressuring Chinatowns to utilize efficiently their spaces. As such it is not a planned outcome nor has it even being fully considered. Nevertheless, it is an effort to promote sustainability within Canada's Chinatowns and as such should be recognized for some positive aspects. Arguably, the vision of Mark Shieh, a Taipei-born, Vancouver-raised developer, to determine what is the essence of Chinatown to be transferred to future generations fits within this rubric. His model envisions residences with access to shared facilities, such as kitchens and laundry, among private apartments, as well as inter-generational living, not only as a way to make accommodations affordable but also as a way to promote cultural vibrancy.[115]

6.2.3 Aging and Lower Income of Chinatown Residents

A third challenge for Canada's Chinatowns is the higher age and lower income of its residents. For example, in 2009, 47.8 percent of Calgary's Chinatown residents were seniors compared to 9.3 percent in the city of a whole, while in 2005, 55 percent of them lived in low income households,

---

[114] Kelty Miyoshi McKinnon and Inge Roecker, "Urban Acupuncture," Canada Mortgage and Housing Corporation, 2006.12.14, 2.

[115] Hadani Ditmars, "How to Harness a Changing Chinatown," *The Globe and Mail*, 2014.01.31.

compared to 14.6 percent for all city seniors.[116] Although not as
remarkable, one finds similar statistics for Vancouver where in
Chinatown there are a higher percentage of seniors and a
household income about 40 percent less than the average in
Metro Vancouver.[117] These statistics reflect the building of
housing and nursing homes for Chinese Canadian seniors
within or close to Chinatown; they also reflect a trend for senior
Chinese Canadians to move out of their children's homes and
into Chinatown, even with minimal income. The higher age and
lower income of Chinatown residents translate into lower
spending and fewer human resources within Chinatown. The
lower spending makes it difficult for Chinatown businesses to
survive. The lack of human resources, due to the higher average
age, means that the community has less talent to draw upon in
order to maintain itself and develop.

7. Future of Chinatowns

Given the achievements of Canada's historical Chinatowns
and the functions they serve, the subject of their future is
relevant enough. Arguably, Canadian society would want to
preserve them and so the question of their future becomes
important. Moreover, the challenges described above add
uncertainty to any answer that affirms their continued
existence. One can claim that Canada's Chinatown should
continue to exist; however, how is that going to take place when
faced with these challenges? Against this concern, one should
weigh positive factors that will influence the future of Canada's
Chinatowns. There are many perceived benefits to preserving
historical Chinatowns; furthermore, an increasing part of the
mainstream, not only Chinese Canadians, are beginning to
share this perception. A second positive factor is the trajectory
or momentum that Chinese Canadians have established in
preserving and developing Chinatowns. This speaks to a will
and ability that are sometime not so easily detected but are still

---

[116] "Calgary Community Statistics on Seniors: Chinatown," 2009 City of
Calgary, Community & Neighbourhood Services, Social Policy & Planning,
2011.07.27.

[117] Vancouver Economic Development Commission, "2009 Chinatown
Neighbourhood Profile," *www.bizmapbc.com/*, accessed 2011.07.28.

present. In other words, Chinatowns faced challenges before, arguably more threatening than the present ones; however, they were still able to survive even when it seemed unlikely at the time. One should not assume the same desire and will are absent in the present day. A third factor is similar to the second in taking a longer view of history, but pushes the scope under consideration back even further. The point can be made that Chinatowns were founded on Chinese cultural values that, because they have proven their worth over time, will continue to endure. Historical Canadian Chinatowns have preserved these values in a critical mass that can be tapped and studied. If traditional Chinese cultural values continue to be ones that should be learned from, Chinatowns should continue to have an important role.

7.1 Perceived Benefits

As newer forms of Chinatowns flourish by providing newer and better services, more choice in goods, indoor malls, and ample parking, leaders in the Chinese community and the municipal governments have become anxious about the vitality of the historical Chinatowns and the downtown core that they often occupy. There are many aspects of the historical centres that are not easily transferred to other locations. There are the cultural centres with all their activities, the Chinese elderly who reside and socialize there, the kinship halls, the temples, the public school groups that tour the facilities, the diversity, tourist attraction, and so on. There is also the symbolic value of the Chinese Canadian ability to provide for themselves in the face of past adversities. Generally, there is concern that the evolving nature of Canadian Chinatowns will contribute to the disappearance of these aspects.

In response to the perceived risks, some organizations have been working to revitalize Canada's historical Chinatowns. There have been two types of organizations with differing motivations but with a similar goal, namely preserving historical Chinatowns as vibrant communities. The first type of organization is comprised mostly of Chinese Canadians who want to preserve the traditional activities in historical Canadian Chinatowns. An example of this type is the Sien Lok Society of Calgary. The second type of organization has been composed of groups representing the interests of municipal governments. Municipal governments see benefits in preserving pockets of ethnic identity, such as Chinatowns, within cities and especially in the inner city.[118] Such areas, beside providing apparent benefits to mainstream society, increase general activity in the vicinity, especially pedestrian traffic, which is conducive to safer streets. Therefore, municipal governments have promoted the viability of Chinatowns by encouraging and supporting grants from private foundations, funding ethnic celebrations, providing advantageous zoning regulations, and by generally cooperating with local Chinese Canadians, such in providing culturally sensitive police services.

With regard to the inability of Chinatowns to meet the needs of their patrons and the subsequent movement to the suburbs of existing and new businesses leading to increased vacancies within Chinatown, leaders in the Chinese Canadian community and the municipal governments have taken steps to ensure the vitality of the historical Chinatowns and the downtown core that they often occupy. For example, the Calgary Chinese Community Services Association, which provides social services out of its office in Chinatown, has been initiating campaigns, such as the Chinatown Safety Project, to improve the attractiveness of Chinatown. Others are articulating the opportunities for businesses within Chinatown to capitalize on their central location by, for example, providing services for the workers in the surrounding office buildings and facilitating trade with the growing economy of China.

The Calgary Chinatown community has also responded creatively with a number of nonprofit organizations that cater to the needs of the elderly. Indeed, instead of seeing the elderly as a problem, they are being seen as a segment of the population that is to be protected. In a way, this has a stabilizing effect on an area that is often frequented by less desirable elements in the city. The Calgary Chinese Elderly Citizens' Association, Wing Kei Care Centre Home, and three

---

[118] Barbara Jenkins states: "In order to draw attention to your cultural renaissance, however, it is necessary to 'brand' your city as a significant international cultural attraction. This 'branding' may focus on cultural attributes such as multiculturalism or on specific cultural icons. For example, cities vie for the honour of having the largest Chinatown . . . " ("Toronto's Cultural Renaissance," *Canadian Journal of Communication* 30.2 [2005], 173).

senior housing projects operate within or close to Chinatown. The housing projects supply two hundred eighty-two units. The presence of the elderly and the Chinese value of filial piety probably leads to a large number of visitors and amount of revenue entering from outside the community. These would increase purchases within the community and thereby balance, to a degree, the lack of spending by, mostly elderly, residents.

The building of cultural centres within Chinatowns is also an example of investing to make them more attractive. For example, the Winnipeg Chinese Cultural and Community Centre was completed in 1987 and supported by municipal, provincial, and federal levels of government, particularly through long term land leases at nominal rates. The rationale provided for the support was "to attract new and privately funded investment back into the area."[119] Aligned with and part of the Winnipeg Core Area Initiative, an overriding goal of the establishment of the Winnipeg Chinese Cultural and Community Centre was to improve Winnipeg's inner city.[120] The Montreal Chinese Community & Cultural Center opened in Montreal's historical Chinatown in 2005, again with large government support. The federal and provincial governments both funded this project; however, the largest commitment, came from the municipal government. From these examples, indications are that municipal governments, which should be most aware of their benefits, are those that most strongly support historical Canadian Chinatowns.

Vancouver's city government has also supported its Chinatown with measures such as grants for facade restoration and property tax relief. Arguably, the most economically advantageous support that municipal governments are now providing for Canadian Chinatowns is density transfer. This allows buildings within Chinatown to sell the right to high density usage that they would have if they were not within the special jurisdiction of Chinatown to developers. Those companies then use the density transfer to increase the size of

---

[119] *Winnipeg Chinatown*, 36.

[120] Judy Layne, "Marked for Success??? The Winnipeg Core Area Initiative's Approach to Urban Regeneration," *Canadian Journal of Regional Science* 23.2 (Summer, 2000).

their projects outside Chinatown. This measure allows
Canadian Chinatowns to maintain their original character by
providing funding from private sources. For example, the
Calgary Chinese Cultural Centre was able to secure land and
funding for its construction from developers that were then
allowed to build bigger office towers than they would under
normal conditions.

The City of Calgary has been especially proactive in
promoting its Chinatown. It is the only one in Canada that has
established official boundaries for its Chinatown and it allows
the residents significant input into decisions affecting the area.
The Chinatown Design Brief in 1976, which provided stimulus
for redevelopment, was followed by the Chinatown Area
Redevelopment Plan in 1986. The latter called for meeting the
special needs of the Chinatown residents, especially the elderly;
providing Chinese motifs on buildings, signage, and
landscaping; and restricting building height in some parts to
45.72 metres (compare this to The Bow on the southern edge of
Chinatown that is 236 metres in height).[121]

7.2 History of Defending, Preserving, and Promoting Chinatowns

Chinatowns were first formed, in part, to defend
Chinese Canadians against violence and prejudice, so it was
natural that the latter would maintain them viable and
functioning. What is notable is the lengthy history of doing so
and within that history the astuteness that Chinese Canadians
have shown in adapting their physically defined communities to
the changing circumstances of Canadian society.

The first Canadian Chinatown was established in Victoria
in about 1860. More than one hundred fifty years later, there
are eighteen or more in various forms and different locations.
They no longer primarily serve to protect Chinese Canadians
against violence and prejudice; instead they have taken on
other functions. Admittedly, they sometimes take on the image
of the exotic, an image promoted even by Chinese Canadians,
whose restaurants place names like "bird's nest soup" and
"eight-treasure hot pot" on their menus. However, apart from

---

[121] The City of Calgary, "Chinatown Area Redevelopment Plan," 1986.

the deliberate emphasis on difference, the practical functions
described above continued to be performed and developed.

One finds an early example of the defense of Chinatowns in
1910 in Calgary when the Chinese Canadian community, forced
from their premises at 10 Avenue and 1 Street Southwest by
landlords wanting to sell into the wave of property buying
brought on by the announced arrival of the Canadian Northern
Railroad, decided that they would have to own their own
property in order to protect themselves and maintain their
community. Amid the public backlash to their doing so, they
were able to join the committee and participate in the decision
that would recommend allowing them to stay, thereby
thwarting any opposition.

The response to threats to their community by Chinese
Canadians in Calgary exemplifies the general Chinese
Canadian ability to organize in order to defend their interests.
Their first mutual aid association was formed in 1884 in
Victoria and similar organizations had been established across
Canada by 1923. These organizations ensured that Chinatowns
remained strong by supporting its residents when in weakened
circumstances, when sick, poor, old, or even young and in need
of education. This mission of supporting the community
demonstrated its importance during the Depression when
unemployed Chinese came to Calgary from outlying areas in
search of relief and some ended up sleeping on the floor of the
Chinese Mission.

Besides providing aid to its weaker members, the residents
of earlier Chinatowns often used legal measures to defend their
interests. For a period starting in 1912, occupants of Calgary's
Chinatown had to contend with a rigorous police campaign
against their illegal social activities of gambling and opium use.
In opposing this campaign, the *Calgary News-Telegram* noted
their determination: ". . . the Chinese will not give in without a
struggle. . . . Every case brought by the chief has been fought by
the Chinamen. The best legal talent obtainable has been
retained by them."[122] There are also many examples of legal
defenses of Vancouver's Chinatown. In 1901, Health Inspector
Robert Marrion in his ongoing campaign to counter what he
perceived was a general lack of sanitation complained that "The

---

[122] Dawson, *Moon Cakes*, 129; citing *Calgary News-Telegram* 1912.04.30.

Chinese appear to be made for litigation.",[123] and in 1915 an editorial in the *Sun* declared that "Chinatown is a dead issue," that civic "efforts to 'tame' it were being contested successfully by its residents in the courts, . . . Chinese residents had resorted increasingly to litigation over police harassment (as they had during Health Inspector Marrion's crusade against buildings), when their protests to city council proved futile."[124]

When Chinatowns faced different pressures from government, namely being targeted for demolition in urban renewal projects during the 1960s, Chinese Canadians responded with organized opposition culminating in the National Conference on Urban Renewal As It Affects Chinatown. Recent efforts to rezone areas in Canadian Chinatowns for other uses and higher density have been dealt with cautiously, both with an eye to maintain valued social services and to garner compensation when such rezoning is permitted, such as the exchange of land and funding for Calgary's Chinese Cultural Centre for support for higher density allowances.

Given the evidence of ongoing Chinese Canadian efforts to defend, preserve, and promote Chinatowns, the present day challenges that they face do not seem so threatening. Take Victoria's Chinatown, for example. It has long outlived its function as a supply and transfer centre for Chinese Canadian labour, but it continues to be viable, arguably thrive, as it evolves. For example, a ceremonial Chinese arch was erected in 1981 for the purposes of memorializing Chinese heritage in the city and to draw tourists into downtown Victoria. It was paid for through community and government funding, of which 25 percent was sourced from the Chinatown community,[125] and later refurbished in 1996 with 50 percent of the three hundred thousand-dollar cost covered by city government and 50 percent by the Chinese and non-Chinese communities.[126] The result is more than the increased number of tourists visiting Victoria's

---

[123] Quoted in Anderson, 88.

[124] *Ibid.*, 103.

[125] Lai and Madoff, 5.

[126] Lai and Madoff, 25.

Chinatown since the arch was erected; it is also that Victoria's Chinatown is now able to draw strong support from government and the broader community. Defending, preserving, and promoting Chinatown is no longer only a Chinese Canadian goal. With this broad-based support the continued existence of Chinatowns is more assured.

7.3 Long Term View of History

Another factor to consider in speculating on the future of Canada's historic Chinatowns is the underlying values that have motivated their preservation and development. It would be easy to view Chinatowns as a contingency that arose to meet a particular need, for example, the protection of Chinese Canadians. The history of Chinatowns demonstrates an evolution of responding to contemporary needs, recently the need to have a gateway by which mainstream society could connect to Chinese culture, for example. Under this paradigm, one can envision a point where there is no practical need for Chinatowns and they would disappear, not quickly, of course, but over time.

There is, however, another perspective that suggests stronger support for the long-term development of Chinatowns. Chinatowns promote fundamental values that are rooted in one of the oldest and most continuous civilizations in the world. These values include concern for others, education and interaction with others, a forum for the practice of ceremony, a sense of responsibility, and acknowledgment of the contribution of one's ancestors. In describing the functional significance of Chinatown Chinese, community leaders have highlighted two main ones: coping with discriminatory treatment and "to safeguard the continuity of Chinese values, beliefs and symbols and to transmit them with dignity and pride to the new generations."[127] The existence of these values justifies the presence of Chinatowns as their promoters within another civilization and for those, such as Chinese Canadians, who rely on them for guidance. It is as Ray Lee, then President of Sien Lok Society, said at the National Conference on Urban Renewal and its Effects on Chinatown: "To the Chinese Canadians like

---

[127] Chan, *Smoke and Fire*, 297-98.

myself who do not reside in the core, we look to Chinatown as a social-psychological well to which we can return to refresh ourselves."[128]

Arguably, it is awareness of these values that allows Chinese Canadians to accept the so-called "gentrification" of Chinatowns. One would think, given the history of Chinatowns as "bastions" of defense against the prejudice and violence perpetrated by mainstream society, that there would be a strong reaction to it. However, gentrification can also be rationalized as mainstream society coming to accept the fundamental values that Chinatowns promote. If one is confident that these values will prevail, one need not worry that much about inroads into the material infrastructure that promotes them; on the contrary, it is an opportunity for these values to receive wider acceptance.

8. Conclusion

In fulfilling various practical functions, Canada's historical Chinatowns have established a record of achievement. They have a long history, more than one hundred fifty years of operation within the country, and they continue to develop taking new forms such as Chinese themed shopping complexes that anchor Chinese Canadian communities. During this history, Chinatowns have exemplified Chinese Canadian ability to organize themselves while promoting Chinese culture. As well, they have faced challenges during this history, opposition from mainstream society in their beginnings, the loss of business to newer commercial centres, and the pressure to maximize property values by replacing traditional businesses and social services with office and condominium towers. However, they are also now supported by mainstream society. This support combined with the tradition that Chinese Canadians have established of preserving and developing their Chinatowns and the underlying values that have motivated their efforts indicates that Canada's historical Chinatowns will continue to develop in face of these challenges.

The fact that Chinatowns are enthusiastic about mainstream participation in their activities and development is cause for reflection. The beginnings and much of the history of

---

[128] Sien Lok Society, 31.

Chinatown are rooted in defending against mainstream prejudice, even violence. That they could make the transition to welcoming mainstream participation speaks to a confidence that will support continued Canadian Chinatown development.

BIBLIOGRAPHY

Aiken, Rebecca B. *Montreal Chinese Property Ownership and Occupational Change, 1881-1981.* New York: AMS Press, 1989.

Amos, Robert and Kileasa Wong. *Inside Chinatown: Ancient Culture in a New World.* Victoria, British Columbia: Touchwood Editions, 2009.

Anderson, Kay. *Vancouver's Chinatown: Racial Discourse in Canada, 1875-1980.* Montreal: McGill-Queen' s University Press, 1991.

Austin, Ian. "Residents Rally Against Chinatown Towers." *The Province*, 2011.03.14.

Baureiss, Gunther. "The Chinese Community of Calgary." *Canadian Ethnic Studies* 3.1 (June 1971): 43-55.

BC Stats. www.bcstats.gov.bc.ca/, accessed 2011.07.26.

Brent, Paul. "With Fresh Funding, Continent's Largest Asian Mall Back on Track. *Real Estate News Exchange,* 2014.06.21. *renx.ca/with-fresh-funding-continents-largest-asian-mall-back-on-track,* accessed 2015.01.21

Bula, Frances. "Behind the Changing Face of Vancouver's Chinatown." *The Globe and Mail*, 2013.01.13.

"Calgary Community Statistics on Seniors: Chinatown." 2009 City of Calgary, Community & Neighbourhood Services, Social Policy & Planning, accessed 2011.07.27.

Campbell, Charles. "The Heart of the City May Be Rising Again After a Long Decline. But Will Chinatown's Rebirth Save It or Destroy It?". *Vancouver Magazine* 38.9 (2009.10): 56-65.

Canadian Broadcasting Corporation (CBC). "New Housing, Shops to Be Built in Calgary's Chinatown," 2006.07.20. *myasiancanadian.blogspot.com/2006/07/new-housing-shops-to-be-built-in.html,* accessed 2011.07.27.

Chan, Anthony. *Gold Mountain: The Chinese in the New World.* New Star Books, c.1983.

Chan, Kwok Bun. "Ethnic Urban Space, Urban Displacement and Forced Relocation: The Case of Chinatown in Montreal." *Canadian Ethnic Studies* 18.2 (1986): 65- 78.

------. *Smoke and Fire: The Chinese in Montreal.* Hong Kong: Chinese University Press, 1991.

City of Calgary. "Chinatown Area Redevelopment Plan." 1986.

City of Richmond website, *www.richmond.ca/home.htm,* accessed 2011.07.04.

City of Vancouver. "Chinatown Revitalization Program: Chinatown Vision," 2002.07.02. *vancouver.ca/ctyclerk/cclerk/020723/rr2.htm,* accessed 2011.07.10.

Dawson, Brian J. "The Chinese in Calgary - The Past One Hundred Years." *A Century of the Chinese in Calgary,* 5-10. Calgary: United Calgary Chinese Association, 1993.

------. *Moon Cakes in Gold Mountain: From China to the Canadian Plains.* Calgary: Detselig Enterprises, 1991.

Ditmars, Hadani. "How to Harness a Changing Chinatown." *The Globe and Mail,* 2014.01.31.

Elton, Sarah. "Chinatown Blues: Business is Down and For Sale Signs Are Popping Up on a Once-vibrant Strip." *Globe and Mail,* 2006.11.04, M2.

Federation of Chinese Canadians in Markham website, *www.fccm.ca/about.html*, accessed 2011.02.07.

Fong, Eric, Emily E. Anderson, Wenhong Chen, and Chiu Luk. "The Logic of Ethnic Business Distribution in Multiethnic Cities." *Urban Affairs Review* 43.4 (March 2008): 497-519.

Greater Montreal Sino-Canadian Business Centre, "2007 Sino-Canadian Economic Cooperation Conference." *Business Newsletter,* Edition 04 (July 2007).

Helly, Denise. *Les Chinois à Montréal: 1877-1951.* St. Laurent, Québec: Institut québécois de recherche sur la culture, 1987.

"Home Turf." CBC Eyeopener, 2006.03.04. Judy Aldous, reporter.

Jenkins, Barbara. "Toronto's Cultural Renaissance." *Canadian Journal of Communication* 30.2 (2005): 169-186.

Kumar, Sandeep and Bonica Leung. "Formation of an Ethnic Enclave: Process and Motivations." *Plan,* Summer 2005: 43-45.

Lai, Chuenyan David. *Chinatowns: Towns within Cities in Canada.* Vancouver: University of British Columbia Press, 1988.

------. *Chinese Community Leadership: Case Study of Victoria in Canada.* New Jersey: World Scientific, 2010.

------. "The Chinese Consolidated Benevolent Association in Victoria: Its Origins and Functions." *BC Studies* 15 (Autumn 1972): 53-67.

Lai, Chuenyan David and Pamela Madoff. *Building and Rebuilding Harmony: The Gateway to Victoria's Chinatown.* Canadian Western Geographical Series, Volume 32. Victoria: University of Victoria, 1997.

Layne, Judy. "Marked for Success??? The Winnipeg Core Area Initiative's Approach to Urban Regeneration." *Canadian Journal of Regional Science* 23.2 (Summer, 2000): 249-78.

Lee, David T. H. (Li Donghai). *Jianada Huaqiao shi* (A History of Chinese in Canada) Taipei, Taiwan: Jianada ziyou chubanshe,1967.

Ley, David. *Millionaire Migrants: Trans-Pacific Life Lines.* Chichester, U.K.: Wiley-Blackwell, 2010.

Li, Peter S. *The Chinese in Canada.* Toronto: Oxford University Press, 1998.

Li, Peter and Eva Xiaoling Li. "Vancouver Chinatown in Transition." *Journal of Chinese Overseas* 7 (2011): 7-23.

Lo, Lucia. "Changing Geography of Toronto's Ethnic Economy." In *Landscapes of the Ethnic Economy*, edited by David H. Kaplan and Wei Li, 83-96. Lanham, Maryland: Rowman & Littlefield, 2006.

------. "Suburban Housing and Indoor Shopping: The Production of Contemporary Chinese Landscape in Toronto." In *From Urban Enclave to Ethnic Suburb: New Asian Communities in Pacific Rim Countries*, edited by Wei Li, 134-154. Honolulu: University of Hawaii Press, 2006.

Sien Lok Society of Calgary. "National Conference on Urban Renewal As It Affects Chinatowns." 1969.

McKinnon, Kelty Miyoshi, and Inge Roecker. "Urban Acupuncture." Canada Mortgage and Housing Corporation, 2006.12.14.

Nipp, Dora. "The Chinese in Toronto." In *Gathering Places: Peoples and Neighbourhoods of Toronto, 1834-1945.* Edited by Robert F. Harney, 147-177. Toronto: Multicultural History Society of Ontario, 1985.

Roy, Patricia. *The Oriental Question: Consolidating a White Man's Province, 1914-41.* Vancouver: UBC Press, 2003.

Roy, Patricia. *A White Man's Province : British Columbia Politicians and Chinese and Japanese Immigrants, 1858-1914.* Vancouver: UBC Press, 1989.

Sherwood, Matthew. "Chinatown BIA Wants to Clean Up Shop." *The Globe and Mail,* 2011.11.11.

Sien Lok Society of Calgary. "National Conference on Urban Renewal As It Affects Chinatowns." 1969.

Stanley, Timothy J. *Contesting White Supremacy: School Segregation, Anti-Racism, and the Making of Chinese Canadians.* Vancouver: UBC Press, 2011.

Statistics Canada. "Census." "Census tract profile for 0065.01 (CT), Montréal (CMA) and Quebec." *www.statcan.gc.ca,* accessed 2011.08.11.

------. "NHS Focus on Geography Series – Markham," accessed 2014.11.20.

------. "NHS Focus on Geography Series – Vancouver," accessed 2014.11.20.

------. "Population by selected ethnic origins, by census metropolitan areas (2006 Census)." *www.statcan.gc.ca,* accessed 2011.07.16.

"S.U.C.C.E.S.S. Annual Report, 2009-2010." *www.successbc.ca/eng/images/stories/pdf/AnnualReport_Eng_2010.pdf,* accessed 2011.07.09.

Thompson, Richard H. *Toronto's Chinatown: The Changing Social Organization of an Ethnic Community.* New York: AMS Press, 1989.

Torrance, Judy. *Public Violence in Canada: 1867-1982.* Kingston, Ont.: McGill-Queen's University Press, 1986.

U.S. Census Bureau. "New York-Newark-Bridgeport, NY-NJ-CT-PA Combined Statistical Area." American Community Survey, 2008, accessed 2011.07.16.

Vancouver Economic Development Commission. "2009 Chinatown Neighbourhood Profile." *www.bizmapbc.com/*, accessed 2011.07.28.

Wai, Hayne Y. "Vancouver Chinatown 1960-1980: A Community Perspective." *New Scholars—New Visions in Canadian Studies* 3.1 (1998): 2-47.

West Edmonton Mall website, *www.wem.ca/#/shop/theme-streets/chinatown*, accessed 2011.02.27.

Wickberg, Edgar, Harry Con, Ronald J. Con, Graham Johnson, and William E. Willmott. *From China to Canada: A History of the Chinese Communities in Canada*, edited by Edgar Wickberg. Toronto: McClelland and Stewart, 1982.

Winnipeg Chinatown: The Revitalization of a Community. Winnipeg: The Winnipeg Chinatown Development (1981) Corporation, 1988.

Wolf, Jim and Patricia Owen. *Yi Fao: Speaking Through Memory, A History of New Westminster's Chinese Community 1858-1980.* Surrey, B.C.: Heritage House, 2008.

Wong, Bernard P. *Chinatown: Economic Adaption and Ethnic Identity of the Chinese.* Fort Worth: Holt, Rinehart and Winston, Inc. 1982

Wong, Chris. "Crossroads for Chinatown." *The Georgia Strait*, 1993.06.18-25, 9, 11-12.

Wong, Sandee. "Chinatown Gets Down to Business." *Calgary Herald Neighbours*, North Edition, 2006.04.13-19, N1, N4.

Wong, Tony. "New Canadians with Global Connections ; What Is the Legacy of Immigration Programs That Drew Many Enterprising Chinese to Canada? Major Canadian Businesses with Links Around the World." *Toronto Star*, 1999.05.10, 1.

Yee, Paul. *Chinatown: An Illustrated History of the Chinese Communities of Victoria, Vancouver, Calgary, Winnipeg, Toronto, Ottawa, Montreal and Halifax.* Toronto: James Lorimer, 2005.

Young, Raymond Edgar. "Street of T'ongs: A Study of Vancouver's Chinatown." M.A. diss., The University of British Columbia, 1975.

Zhou, Min. *Chinatown: the Socioeconomic Potential of an Urban Enclave.* Philadelphia: Temple University Press, 1992.

4. PRESERVATION AND PROMOTION OF CHINESE CULTURE

1. Introduction

Chinese Canadian preservation and promotion of Chinese culture could be likened to a battle line along which Chinese Canadians have defended themselves even today as they pursue greater participation in the Canadian mainstream. However, it would be a mistake to see this activity as purely defensive, holding a "line in the sand" so to speak, that cannot be slackened. The intentions behind the cultural activities are much more complex than this. For one thing, there is the celebration of a culture that has provided much of value to Chinese around the world. There are also the advantages that it offers to the Canadian mainstream and which Chinese Canadians make an effort to promote to other Canadians.

In viewing their efforts as whole, in Canada east to west, from their first arrival until the present day, one could argue that the main achievement of Chinese Canadians in the area of Chinese culture has been to forge a recognition for it within the Canadian mainstream. This recognition is an amalgam of three different processes: both the preservation and promotion of Chinese culture and, third, its establishment within mainstream Canadian culture.

The examples of this achievement vary as much as the locations and occasions of the efforts that produced it. With inferior conditions forced upon them by the public school system at the turn of the twentieth century, Chinese Canadians in Victoria organized their own system using Chinese to teach a curriculum centered on Chinese culture. In a similar fashion, at the turn of the twenty-first century, immigrants from mainland China were relying on traditional values to overcome the perceived prejudices that their children faced in seeking employment. Jun Li's research points out that the success of present-day Chinese Canadian students, although due in part to the pressure to succeed that new immigrants experience in Canada, is also due to the value that traditional Chinese culture places on achievement in formal education and the complementary high expectations of Chinese Canadian parents combined with the acceptance of and desire to fulfill those expectations by their children. These latter qualities are motivated in large part by traditional Chinese cultural values.[1]

The intensity with which Chinese Canadians have promoted their own culture is the first revelation one experiences when exploring the subject. In 1922, Chinese Canadians in Victoria boycotted the inferior facilities provided by Victoria's public school board. At the same time, they set up their own school, teaching a curriculum centred on Chinese culture while refusing to teach the official, public school curriculum. Nearly one hundred years later, Chinese Canadian parents were insistent that their children excel in school and choose careers that would guarantee success rather than personal satisfaction. Even more surprising was that their children were accepting of these demands even though they obviously contravened the freedom of choice that their peers in the mainstream enjoyed.

Xiaoping Li's *Voices Rising: Asian Canadian Cultural Activism* (2007) describes the new intensity with which Asian Canadians, and in particular Chinese Canadians, are promoting their culture. The main goals of this promotion are to build their communities, to reconstruct their identities, and to achieve equality and social justice.[2] Although Li emphasizes artistic culture, other Chinese Canadians see culture in broader terms. A letter sent to New Westminster's mayor and city council and endorsed by a number of Chinese Canadian organizations and individuals asked the city to declare Chinese Heritage Week as a way to acknowledge the city's past historical discrimination against Chinese residents.[3] Chinese heritage or culture is seen as a bulwark against prejudice

---

[1] Jun Li, "Expectations of Chinese Immigrant Parents for Their Children's Education: The Interplay of Chinese Tradition and the Canadian Context," *Canadian Journal of Education* 26.4 (2001). Confucian thinking was emphasized by the parents interviewed as the source of the importance of formal education.

[2] (Vancouver: UBC Press) p. 11.

[3] Charlie Smith, "Chinese Canadians Pressure New Westminster Council in Advance of Anniversary Parade," *Straight.com*, www.straight.com/print/222952, accessed 2010.12.09.

targeting Chinese Canadians and this view is based on a history of Chinese Canadians using culture for this purpose.

The essay that follows will present further examples of Chinese Canadians defending their welfare by preserving and promoting their culture. The examples will also show Chinese Canadians attempting to both celebrate and promote their culture to others.

2. The Concept of Chinese Culture

The term "Chinese culture" is fraught with ambiguity that undermines any clear description of what this essay identifies as the achievements of Chinese Canadians with regard to cultural preservation and promotion. One has to define what one is referring to in using the term in order to specify what exactly those achievements are. Doing so also has the benefit of clarifying what alternatives Chinese Canadians, in their preservation and promotion of Chinese culture, are offering to the Canadian mainstream.

For example, the Chinese Canadian emphasis on formal education is obvious in its presence in Canada. Statistically, their level of education is higher than the mainstream. Young Chinese Canadians study in weekend and evening classes to develop their Chinese language competency and they participate heavily in formal music lessons. While these activities are easily observable, the general emphasis on education also has a direct impact on the mainstream. The increased competition for entrance into universities, particularly professional programs, demonstrates to the mainstream the desirability of post-secondary education and the value of seriously pursuing one's studies there.

2.1 The Concept of Culture

Within the term "Chinese culture," the term "culture" by itself should also be analyzed. This is because the term is very broad in what it encompasses and this essay, for want of length, must be selective in what it describes. There are a variety of definitions for "culture," such as "the characteristics of a particular group of people, defined by everything from language, religion, cuisine, social habits, music and arts."[4] One thing that seems common to these definitions is the broad scope of human behaviour that is included under "culture." The scope of "everything from . . ." immediately impresses upon one that any human activity could be considered culture. Furthermore, there are two other qualities of culture that are apparent in these definitions. One, the characteristics that mark a culture belong to a specific group, such as the Chinese or Canadians; second, the characteristics have a cohesiveness that constitutes the identity of that group.

One thing that is often closely related to culture is artistic activity. It encourages one to express oneself outside the influence of material conditions, an area that is normally seen as a manifestation of culture. This, along with the flexibility in how an art is practised, allows for greater expression of one's culture. Therefore, this activity can contribute much to the preservation and promotion of a culture. Being aware of this helps explain why traditional art forms such as calligraphy and Chinese opera are still popular among Chinese Canadians.

2.2 The Concept of Chinese Culture

The second term to be discussed "Chinese culture" is also complex. Chinese civilization has a long history and, of course, its culture has varied over this time. Therefore, one can easily be confused as to what one is referring to when one uses the term. There is also the variance associated with location. China is a large country with many minorities. One finds different cultures connected to both distinct areas and minorities. Chinese Canadians manifest these differences by distinguishing among Chinese who arrived early, those from Hong Kong, and those from the PRC.

In the context of this essay, the ambiguity of what is referred to as Chinese culture creates further complexity in defining what is meant by the preservation and promotion of Chinese culture. The question arises of what exactly is the "Chinese culture" that is being preserved and promoted. With a number of distinct cultures that could be preserved and promoted, one is justified in asking if the preservation and

---

[4] LiveScience, *www.livescience.com*, accessed 2012.07.21.

promotion do constitute an achievement. Perhaps, what is being preserved and promoted are a number of subcultures, in which case they may not offer promising alternatives to the mainstream. There might not be enough critical mass among any one to do so.

In response to these concerns, one should point out that the use of the term "preservation" in the action of preserving and promoting Chinese culture implies that there is a tradition in place, something is being preserved. This shows that, in spite of the variance of Chinese culture or cultures over space and time, there is also a culture recognized to exist, at least over time, and arguably over space as well.

This description fits with that attributed to Chinese culture by the respected historian Qian Mu (1895-1990). He notes that the Chinese, in the interpretation of their history, have emphasized their commonality, the aspects that they share as a civilization.[5] This explanation supports the view that there is a coherence between what is being referred to as Chinese culture and the culture that Chinese Canadians have preserved and promoted.

The question then becomes how to identity that culture, both so that one can better understand Chinese Canadians and to evaluate the alternatives that they offer to the Canadian mainstream. At the same time, one has to acknowledge the variance that exists across the manifestations of that culture. The best answer to the question then becomes that Chinese culture is a repertoire of values from which Chinese draw to meet practical needs. Specific values need not be identified as essential to Chinese culture; rather, in acknowledging variances in their acceptance, Chinese culture becomes a configuration of values that draws from this repertoire, a configuration not necessarily the same in all instances or manifestations, but still sharing this repertoire.

The answer to this question, if accepted, begs another. What specific values comprise this repertoire. The answer is obviously a matter of debate, but some likely candidates include the importance of the family, education, spiritual contentment,

[5] *Cong Zhongguo lishi laikan Zhongguo minzu xing ji Zhongguo wenhua* (The nature of Chinese people and Chinese culture from the perspective of Chinese history) (Hong Kong: Zhongwen daxue chubanshe, 1979), 75-98, particularly pages 81, 85, 86, and 89.

hard work, thriftiness, the forsaking of personal benefits for the sake of group welfare, respect for age, and reverence for one's cultural legacy. These specific values are themselves based on even more profound principles knowledge of which helps to answer the question. These principles include valuing personal responsibility, which includes responsibility for one's own success, promoting harmony, concern for the welfare of others, unceasing development of the individual, and even the metaphysical meaning of one's own existence.

Culturally, one can draw direct links between the sense of personal responsibility and Confucian thought. The Confucian canon offers several examples of exhorting readers to reflect upon their personal motivations in order to improve themselves. Confucius (551-479 BCE) advised his students to examine themselves when they encountered someone less worthy to make sure that they were not like them.[6] Mencius (371-c.289 BCE) described supreme courage as being able to oppose a force of thousands if one finds oneself in the right, in contrast to being unable to oppose an ordinary opponent if one is in the wrong.[7] *Daxue* (The Great Learning) describes how personal cultivation–learning, strengthening one's intentions, rectifying one's mind–would contribute to order in society.[8] Wang Yangming (1472-1529) advocated the unity of conscience and action.[9]

Another fundamental principle underlying specific Chinese cultural values is the importance of harmony, with other humans, other living beings, and even the physical world. Qian Mu selected this quality as distinguishing the Chinese,

---

[6] *The Analects* 4.17, trans. D.C. Lau (London: Penguin Books Ltd., 1979), 74.

[7] *Mencius* 2a:2, trans. D. C. Lau 3rd ed. (Harmondsworth, Eng.: Penguin Books, 1983), 76-77.

[8] *Daxue* (The Great Learning), in *Source Book in Chinese Philosophy*, trans. Wing-tsit Chan (Princeton, New Jersey: Princeton Univ. Press, 1963), 86-87.

[9] *Wang Yangming quanji* (A complete collection of Wang Yangming's works), ed. Wu Guang, Qian Ming, Dong Ping, and Yao Yanfu (Shanghai: Shanghai guji chubanshe, 1992), Vol. 1, 4. For an English translation see *Instructions for Practical Living and Other Neo-Confucian Writings by Wang Yang-Ming*, trans. Wing-tsit Chan (New York: Columbia University Press, 1963), sec. 5, 10.

particularly in contrast to Westerners.[10] This principle leads
Chinese people to seek a balance in their lives and the broader
matters of the world. For example, it is important for a
businessperson to be artistically aware as well as strategically
astute. This principle also contributes to sustainability,
something that has characterized Chinese civilization since its
beginnings. This is especially seen, albeit not in most recent
times, in the concept of being in harmony with nature.

The principle of seeking harmony with other living beings
and the physical world is closely tied to the principle that one's
welfare is necessarily linked to the welfare of others. It follows
from the famous Confucian precept "The humane man, desiring
to be established himself, seeks to establish others; desiring
himself to succeed, he helps others to succeed."[11] Like the
principle of pursuing harmony, but more apparently, this
principle encourages cooperation and the support of weaker
members of society. It also leads one to consider success more
clearly in terms of the effect of one's actions on others.

Another broad principle that guides the formation of
specific values is the importance of unceasing development to
the individual. Even into old age one is encouraged to learn and
improve oneself. This does not necessarily mean material
development, though that is not precluded. Development is
broadly defined and could include increasing one's contribution
to society, as well as accumulating wealth. This principle
provides the rationale for Chinese seniors continuing to
participate in physically demanding activities, such as *taiji
quan* and line dancing, or their enthusiastic willingness to care
for their grandchildren.

To reiterate, one can debate whether the specific values and
principles outlined above are the ones that identify Chinese
culture, whether as a repertoire from which a configuration is
formed or even as essential to it. However, the debate does not
detract from the assumption, based on the fact that there are
these candidates for identifiers of Chinese culture, that Chinese
culture exists. It has evolved and is not exactly the same
wherever it is found, of course, but the assumption that there is
an entity that fits the definition of culture and is distinctly

---

[10] Pages 22-23, 24-25, 29, and 66.

[11] *The Analects* 6.30, trans. D.C. Lau, 85.

Chinese seems secure. As such, the validity of researching the preservation and promotion of Chinese culture by Chinese Canadians, who, as Chinese, identify with this culture, is assured.

2.3 The Concept of Chinese Canadian Culture

The remainder of this essay will document how Chinese Canadians have attempted to maintain a link to Chinese culture by describing their efforts to preserve and promote their language, their establishment of Chinese cultural centres, their practice of traditional Chinese arts, their holding of traditional festivals, and their promotion of Chinese food. All of these activities are determined in large part by the Chinese culture that one can identify as arising out of the configuration of values described above and historical practices sometimes spanning thousands of years.

Nevertheless, with regard to Chinese Canadian culture, before describing its commonality with Chinese culture, one should acknowledge Chinese Canadian efforts to establish an identity, and thus culture, that is accepted within Canada. Wing Chung Ng documents examples of the awakening within Vancouver's Chinese population of a desire to establish an identity grounded in their Canadian residency. The inception of the term "Chinese Canadian" in 1964 was a key part of the process of forming this identity. This new construct advanced the claim of the Chinese minority to be Canadian.[12] Another key was the enshrining of multiculturalism as official federal policy in 1971, for then being Chinese was no longer irreconcilable with being Canadian.[13]

---

[12] *The Chinese in Vancouver, 1945-1980: The Pursuit of Identity and Power* (Vancouver: UBC Press, 1999), 103. It should also be noted that in 1914 a group of locally born young men from Victoria, British Columbia became the first people to publically call themselves "Chinese Canadians" (Timothy Stanley, "'BY THE SIDE OF OTHER CANADIANS': The Locally Born and the Invention of Chinese Canadians," *BC Studies* 156/157 [Winter 2007], 109; citing Lisa Rose Mar, "From Diaspora to North American Civil Rights: Chinese Canadian Ideas, Identities and Brokers in Vancouver, British Columbia, 1924 to 1960" [Ph.D. dissertation, University of Toronto, 200], 138).

[13] *Ibid.*, 106.

Media also had an early role in awakening among ethnic Chinese the will to establish an identity with a Canadian dimension. In 1974, a tabloid called *Gum Sam Po* challenged ethnic Chinese in Vancouver to "make our concept of a Chinese-Canadian community a viable one."[14] Subsequently, the Identity and Awareness Conference at the University of British Columbia in May 1975 converged on the view that "[i]nstead of nourishing a transplanted and unfamiliar culture from China, . . . a Chinese-Canadian consciousness must be rooted in Canada and must be derived from local experience."[15] The radio program Pender Guy arose out of this new thinking. The half-hour weekly program ran from 1976 to 1981 on Vancouver Cooperative Radio CFRO FM 102.7 and featured descriptions of Chinese-Canadian experience. Its focus was on promoting a new identity for them.[16]

3. Language

3.1 Foundational to Culture

Language is an essential, and arguably the most important characteristic of a culture. To say that it is a basic requirement for the retention and dissemination of culture is an understatement because language has a large constitutive role in forming culture. Even in less obvious areas such as culinary practices, the socialization around a meal and the elegance of the titles for the different dishes cannot be produced without language.

The link between language use and the preservation and promotion of Chinese culture has even been proven. A study of the Chinese community in Toronto through 1981-82 concluded that confidence in using the Chinese language "was associated with a stronger tendency to follow a Chinese lifestyle, as well as Chinese socialization practices and Chinese leisure activities." In contrast, a higher self-confidence in English was related to "a

---

[14] Cited in *ibid.*, 118.

[15] *Ibid.*, 119.

[16] *Ibid.*

weaker sense of self-identity as Chinese and weaker desires to follow Chinese customs . . ."[17]

3.2 Language Use

"The 2001 Census confirmed the position of Chinese as Canada's third most common mother tongue. Almost 872,400 people reported Chinese as their mother tongue, up 136,400 or 18.5% from 1996 [736,000] . . . Italian remained in fourth place . . ."[18]

The 2006 Census reported 1,012,065 people with Chinese as their mother tongue (361,450 Cantonese, 170,950 Mandarin). Again, it was the third most used mother tongue;[19] less than English and French (6,970,405) and more than Italian (455,040) with about 80 percent of Chinese Canadians speaking it.

The 2011 census reported 1,112,610 individuals using Chinese as their mother tongue (389,000 Cantonese, 255,000 Mandarin, 441,000 n.o.s.). It remained the third most used mother tongue behind English and French (7,298,180) and more than Punjabi (460,000).[20] Those whose mother tongue was Chinese were equivalent to 84 percent of Chinese Canadians.[21]

---

[17] Karen K. Dion, Kenneth L. Dion, and Anita Wan-ping Pak, "The Role of Self-Reported Language Proficiencies in the Cultural and Psychosocial Adaption among Members of Toronto, Canada's Chinese Community," *Journal of Asian Pacific Communication* 1.1 (1990), 185. Interestingly, the study also suggested that for Chinese Canadians "cultural assimilation might not be an inevitable correlate of linguistic assimilation" (174). Therefore, even with a minimum command of Chinese language, Chinese culture could still hold some attraction for Chinese Canadians. See also Ai-Lan Chia and Catherine Costigan, "Understanding the Multidimensionality of Acculturation Among Chinese Canadians," *Canadian Journal of Behavioural Science* 38.4 (Oct. 2006), 321.

[18] Statistics Canada, "Languages in Canada," *www.statcan.ca* (2003.01.21).

[19] Statistics Canada, "Population by mother tongue, by province and territory (2006 Census)," *www.statcan.ca*, accessed 2013.03.26.

[20] Statistics Canada, "Immigrant Languages in Canada," "Table 1: Population of immigrant mother tongue families, showing main languages comprising each family, Canada, 2011" ; "French and the *francophonie* in Canada," *www.statcan.c*a, accessed 2013.06.04.

[21] Statistics Canada, "2011 National Household Survey: Immigration, place of

3.3 Language Education

Given that the language is an essential, and arguably the most important characteristic of a culture, education in it that would contribute to the culture's continued existence.[22] Young Chinese Canadians are likely to lose command of Chinese unless they are educated in its use. The Canadian environment and the use of English or French within it are, otherwise, very powerful influences that detract from the use of Chinese language. These influences become even more powerful as the history of the Chinese in Canada lengthens and the numbers in second and later generations increase, consequently, language education will become even more important in the preservation and promotion of Chinese culture.

In the face of these influences, Chinese Canadians have demonstrated the will and ability to preserve their language. In 1998 Canadian-born Chinese spoke Chinese always or mostly with their grandparents more than 77 percent of the time and always or mostly with their mother more than 40 percent of the time.[23] Also, young Chinese in Winnipeg spoke Chinese with their five closest friends 75 to 80 percent of the time, demonstrating that even among young generational peers, Chinese was the most widely used language.[24] The history of promoting language education and the infrastructure and system for doing so that Chinese Canadians have put in place is another testament to their achievements.

---

birth, citizenship, ethnic origin, visible minorities, language and religion," *www.statcan.ca*, accessed 2013.06.04.

[22] Citing Richard L. Warren (*Doing the Ethnography of Schooling: Educational Anthropology in Action* [New York, Holt, Rinehart and Winston, 1982, p. 402), Hilda Mah claims that "[t]he instruction of language has been found to be inseparable from the imparting of cultural knowledge" ("A History of the Education of Chinese Canadians in Alberta, 1885-1947," M. Education thesis [University of Alberta, 1987], 67n.2).

[23] Hong Xiao, "Chinese Language Maintenance in Winnipeg," *Canadian Ethnic Studies* 30.1 (1998), 92.

[24] *Ibid.* 92.

3.3.1 History

The teaching of Chinese culture to Chinese Canadians began early. In the 1880's merchants in Victoria were already importing tutors to teach their children. Once the number of Chinese children increased to about one hundred, the community saw the need for and established a Chinese school. The Lequn Yishu (Sociability Free School) was opened on July 01, 1899 and attended by thirty-nine students. Its opening was followed in the early 1900s by the opening of other schools. The Chinese Empire Reform Association established the Aiguo Xuetang (Patriotic School), the Chinese Freemasons operated the Qinge Xiaoxue (Young Primary School), and the Yue Shan Society opened the Yushan Xiaoxue (Yue Shan Primary School).[25]

These early schools were manifestations of Chinese Canadians' desire and ability to preserve and promote Chinese culture. Teachers employed by the Lequn Yishu were graduates of the Chinese exam system and taught a classical Confucian curriculum including the *Sanzi jing* (Three Character Classic), *The Analects, Mencius, The Great Learning,* and *The Doctrine of the Mean,* along with classics of history and poetry. In many ways Lequn Yishu "set the pattern for subsequent schools in Canada."[26] The intensity of this desire and ability was further revealed in the student strike of 1922. The strike was precipitated by the segregation of Chinese students within Victoria's public school system, and led to the Victoria Chinese community establishing an alternative school rather than a supplement to the public school.

The alternative school established, the Zhonghua Yixue (Chinese Free School), did not attempt to duplicate the curriculum that the striking students were missing. This was the case even though there were Chinese Canadian graduates of the Provincial Normal School who could have taught the school board curriculum, and several Victoria School District

---

[25] David Chuenyan Lai, *Chinese Community Leadership: Case Study of Victoria in Canada* (Singapore: World Scientific, 2010), 87.

[26] Timothy J. Stanley, *Contesting White Supremacy: School Segregation, Anti-Racism, and the Making of Chinese Canadians* (Vancouver: UBC, 2011), 193.

teachers had offered to tutor the striking students.²⁷ Rather, the community persisted in operating a school that "developed knowledge among overseas Chinese of the written language of their ancestral country" and "inspired among overseas Chinese the concept of loving their country and eradicating shame."²⁸ Stanley elaborates on their purpose:

> Chinese-language schools helped to foster a collective identity among Chinese living in British Columbia. . . . By promoting literacy, Chinese-language schools were helping to transcend the restricted local identities of clan and village origin. Being able to read newspapers also connected people to an imagined community, a community that had continuities with China and other places in the diaspora. The creation of a shared identity as Chinese seems to have been a vital factor in the organization of Chinese schools and their Confucian emphasis, in particular.²⁹

The use of education to create a shared identity as Chinese is a characteristic common to Canadian Chinese communities. Research done on the education of Chinese Canadians in Alberta from 1885 to 1947 induced that "[t]he Chinese language schools in Alberta during this period of study . . . ultimately served to maintain the Chinese culture and language."³⁰ A general study of schools in Canada published in 1933 similarly stated that "[o]rganized primarily to afford the Chinese children the opportunity of familiarizing themselves with the rudiments of Chinese culture the schools attempt to conserve the finest elements of that splendid civilization for the Chinese families born in Canada."³¹

---

²⁷ Stanley, 37-8.

²⁸ *"Yuduoli Bu Zhonghua Yixue zhaosheng jianzhang"* (General rules for enrolling students in the Victoria Chinese Free School), reproduced in David Chuenyan Lai "The Issue of Discrimination in Education in Victoria, 1901-1923" (*Canadian Ethnic Studies* 19.3 [1987]), 61.

²⁹ P. 201.

³⁰ Hilda Mah, "Abstract," n.p.

³¹ Gordon R. Taylor, "An Investigation of Chinese Schools in Canada," M. Arts thesis (McGill University, 1933), 88.

The ideals expressed in these claims were also accompanied by a practical dimension. Chinese culture contained material and psychological resources to combat the racism that Chinese Canadians encountered. If they were to be denied opportunities for earning a livelihood in the mainstream community, they still had the option of working within the Chinese Canadian community, i.e., Chinatown, or returning to China because they had retained the language and cultural skills necessary to do so.

As for psychological resources, for example, in turning to their tradition to combat the racism that they encountered, Victoria's Chinese community was able to challenge the Canadian mainstream. To the degree that they were not allowed to participate in Canadian society, they would foster their Chinese identity instead.[32] The near term result was that in August 1923 the Chinese community and the Victoria School Board agreed that all Chinese students would be allowed to return to their original schools, that segregation would not extend beyond elementary school, and that seventeen students required to upgrade their English would be able to study in non-segregated classes once they were proficient in the language.[33] In the long term, the success of the strike contributed to the inclusion of Chinese Canadians within mainstream society.[34]

"[D]uring the 1930's and early 1940's, there were, according to one survey, twenty-six Chinese part-time schools with forty-seven teachers in eleven locations across the country. Approximately one-third of these were in Vancouver . . . By 1941 it was estimated that approximately one thousand five hundred students were attending Chinese schools."[35] Of these, "at least three Canadian Chinese schools were supported in part by the Chinese government."[36] "By 1984 there were fifty

---

[32] Stanley, 190.

[33] Stanley, 44; Lai, "Issue of Discrimination," 63.

[34] Stanley, 244.

[35] Edgar Wickberg, Harry Con, Ronald J. Con, Graham Johnson, and William E. Willmott, *From China to Canada: A History of the Chinese Communities in Canada* (Toronto : McClelland and Stewart, 1982), 170-71.

[36] *Ibid.,* 172.

Chinese language schools in Canada, with the largest number in Vancouver (twelve) and Toronto (ten)."[37]

These dates and numbers demonstrate that there was strong popular support within the Chinese Canadian community for Chinese language instruction at an early point in their history. The first Chinese school was established in 1899 and others followed not long after in cities across Canada. These schools were mostly supported by the resources and efforts of the communities themselves with a small amount of assistance coming from the Chinese government of the time. These efforts were motivated by a strong desire to balance the perceived shortcomings of Western education with a knowledge of Chinese culture and language. Years later this desire saw formal recognition in a survey carried out in 1971 in which 97 percent of each of the Toronto and Hamilton Chinese Canadian communities indicated that they wanted their children to speak and to write Chinese fluently.[38]

The extent of this desire is further seen in the fact that they were Chinese Canadian efforts that led to the establishment of the highly successful Heritage Language Program in Ontario. "In 1973 the parents of children in Ogden and Orde Street schools, where the student population was 90 percent Chinese, formed" an association that petitioned the Toronto Board of Education to include Chinese culture and language in the curriculum. "The board approved a two-year program, for which the parents contributed half the funding. The year 1974, marked the first heritage program even in a Toronto school" and led to official recognition of heritage language programs in 1977 by the Ontario government.[39]

3.3.2 Present State of Language Schools

---

[37] Peter Li, s.v. "Chinese," *Encyclopedia of Canada's Peoples*, ed. Paul Magocsi (Toronto: University of Toronto Press, 1999).

[38] Harold A. Wright, "The Chinese in Toronto - A Personal Appreciation," unpublished, 1976.

[39] Arlene Chan, *The Chinese in Toronto from 1878: From Outside to Inside the Circle* (Toronto: Dundurn, 2011), 123.

The support for Chinese language education has continued as evidenced by *Sing Tao Etel Vancouver* in June 2013 listing nineteen Chinese community language schools.[40] The actual number is probably much higher because there were already twelve Chinese language schools in Vancouver in 1984[41] and Duanduan Li Director of the Chinese Language Program at University of British Columbia estimates there are two hundred Chinese community schools in Vancouver.[42]

Sing Tao Etel Toronto listed sixteen Chinese community language schools as of June 2013,[43] but again the actual number is probably much higher. There were ten Chinese schools in Toronto in 1984,[44] but according to Bernard Luk, *The Chinese Consumer Directory of Toronto, 1997* listed more than one hundred schools.[45]

There is also a national organization of Chinese community schools. The Canadian Association of Chinese Language Schools claims fifty member schools in nine cities across Canada Vancouver, Calgary, Edmonton, Saskatoon, Regina, Winnipeg, Ottawa, Toronto, and Montreal.[46]

3.3.2.1 Particular Examples: Calgary and Edmonton

---

[40] *ww.singtaoetel.ca/VAN/EN/subcategory.php?CategoryID=11&CatalogID=S0 08*, accessed 2013.06.09. *Sing Tao Etel* is a Chinese business directory published by Sing Tao.

[41] Peter Li, *s.v.* "Chinese."

[42] "Chinese as a Heritage Language in Canada," n.d., *crclle.lled.educ.ubc.ca/documents/li.pdf*, accessed 2013.06.09.

[43] *163bbs.servebeer.com/?qbz=ac01CJMsNVllnRlivdQ9P8je1ZAvWpmrKx7rd1 3oV9mfJtmuMRnrXxDvER6cKhm32tQ2a94nclAioF4g6dQ75hQgqAh38RAjj1*, accessed 2013.06.09.

[44] Li, "Chinese."

[45] "The Chinese Communities of Toronto: Their Languages and Mass Media," *Polyphony: The Bulletin of the Multicultural Society of Toronto* 15 (2000), 52.

[46] *cacls.org/About_Us.html*, accessed 2013.06.09.

There are at least nine Chinese community schools in Calgary, from the Calgary Chinese Alliance School to Wah Ying Chinese School. The school with the longest history is the Calgary Chinese Private School (CCPS, formerly Calgary Chinese Public School).[47] It was founded in 1916 and held in a church basement. There were fourteen students and one teacher who was imported from China and lived in the school. In 1989, the school was accredited by the Government of Alberta to offer Language 15, 25, and 35 each having five credits toward a high school diploma. The CCPS was charging $180 a year for tuition in 2001 and offering classes for kindergarten to grade 12 students. Teachers are paid and school is run by volunteers. The textbooks are donated by the Taiwan Overseas Chinese Affairs Commission.[48] The primary purpose of CCPS is to teach students how to speak, read, and write Chinese; however, other instruction--in history, geography, singing and dancing, for example--is also provided. Classes are held daily after regular school hours and on Saturdays. The Chinese Academy is the largest language school in Alberta. It has been in operation in Calgary since 1997 and currently has more than nineteen hundred students.[49]

The Calgary Public School Board offers a Chinese bilingual program in four schools. Highwood offers a K-4 Chinese-English bilingual program, Colonel Irvine offers grades 5-9, Marion Carson offers grades K-1, and Midnapore offers grades K-4. The program began in Sept. 1998 at King Edward, then moved to Langevin in 2001. It began with two grade 4 classes of eighteen students each. The students are taught in English for some subjects (e.g., English and social studies) and Chinese for others

[47] "Kacheng Keshu Chongzheng Hui dishiwu jie jiuzhi dianli ji chunjie jinglao lianhuan wanyan huaxu" (Details of the fifteenth investiture and Chinese New Year banquet honouring the elderly of the Calgary Tsung Tsin Benevolent Association), *Jianada 88 shequbao* (*Canada88 Community News*) (2015.03.26), lists seven not including Calgary Cultural Centre Chinese Learning Academy and Yufeng Chinese School (17).

[48] This information, except for the startup year, which was originally given as 1911, was taken from presentations that Helen Wu, Chairman, Calgary Chinese Public School (Calgary, 2001.09.05) and Helen Wu and Lily Lee (Calgary, 1999.09.08) made to University of Calgary course EAST 321.

[49] The Chinese Academy website, *www.chineseacademy.ca/english/info/e_school.htm*, accessed 2015.01.28.

(e.g., Chinese and math). Some high schools, such as Sir Winston Churchill, Crescent Heights, and Ernest Manning, offer Chinese language courses as options.[50]

Edmonton Public Schools Chinese bilingual program began in 1982. There are twelve public schools offering English-Mandarin bilingual education, from grades K to 12, five elementary, four junior high, and three senior high. The goal is to use 50 percent Mandarin in instruction. Presently, there are almost two thousand students in the program. The Chinese program offered by the Edmonton Public Schools even has an official volunteer organization associated with it that helped initiate the program. The Edmonton Chinese Bilingual Education Association is an organization of volunteers who are dedicated to promoting the learning and understanding of the Chinese language.[51]

3.3.2.2 Content

While language education is one of the main mandates of these schools, it is also significant that language education is accompanied by other content that directly promotes Chinese culture. This is especially true of the community schools that are outside the curricular dictates of the public school systems. For example, the Ai-Cheng Mandarin Chinese School in Toronto offers a course in Chinese history and culture.[52] It is not surprising, but still noteworthy that even public school programs featuring Chinese language education offer instruction in Chinese culture apart from language.[53]

---

[50] Calgary Board of Education (CBE), phone interview with Kally Crelly (2002.08.19), plus CBE website, *www.cbe.ab.ca,* accessed 2015.01.28.

[51] Edmonton Chinese Bilingual Education Association website, *www.ecbea.org*, accessed 2015.01.28.

[52] Ai-Cheng Mandarin Chinese School website, *www.mandarin-school.org/home_ch.htm,* accessed 2014.07.13.

[53] For examples, see p. 25 of "Chinese Language and Culture Program Nine-Year Program Grades 4-5-6" accessible on Alberta Education's' website, *education.alberta.ca/teachers/program/interlang/chinese.aspx,* accessed 2014.07.14.

3.4 Chinese Language Media

The widespread presence of Chinese language media in Canada entails that enough Chinese Canadians can speak or read the language to support their operations. The media are also seen as means of promoting the language because they not only provide widespread usage, they also specifically target promotion through such activities as essay and speech contests, as well as offering services to other organizations within the community that promote Chinese language use. Furthermore, to have this language widely used in public forums indicates that the culture is strong and emboldens those who seek its promotion.

The number of Chinese language media outlets in Canada is something that demands attention. For example, media experts claim "Chinese language television and radio programming in Canada has arguably become the richest and most sophisticated outside China, Hong Kong and Taiwan."[54] Moreover, the number of media outlets reflects this claim. They were estimated to number at least two hundred in 2004.[55] Xu Xinhan and Huang Yunrong estimated the number to be more than one hundred twenty-five in 2010, including more than fifty newspapers and periodicals, more than ten television stations, six to seven radio stations, and more than sixty websites. Further adding to this significance are statistics on consumer demand. A 2007 survey showed that among Chinese Canadians born outside Canada, 81 percent watch Chinese TV programs, 80 percent read Chinese newspapers, and 34 percent listen to Chinese radio programs.[56] Chinese language media are supported by a large audience that justifies their significant presence.

---

[54] Zhou Min, Wenhong Chen, and Guoxuan Cai, "Chinese-language Media and Immigrant Life in the United States and Canada," in *Media and the Chinese Diaspora: Community, Communications, and Commerce,* ed. Wanning Sun (London: Routledge, 2006), 66.

[55] Zhou *et al.,* 51.

[56] IpsosReid and Era Marketing Communications, "IpsosReid 2007 Canadian Chinese Media Monitor: Greater Toronto Area," *www.fairchildtv.com,* accessed 2012.04.08.

3.4.1 History

As one would expect, early Chinese language media were in print form and concentrated in Vancouver and Victoria. Chinese Canadians then did not have the financial or technological resources to establish other types of media and readers were mostly located in those two cities. It is estimated that only 1 percent of the early Chinese immigrants were literate,[57] so one wonders what would motivate the publication of newspapers given the limited readership. Nevertheless, one cannot deny the existence of the early newspapers.

Early Chinese newspapers included the *Dahan gongbao (The Chinese Times)* which began in 1906 in Vancouver and ran for eighty-six years. The *Xinghua ribao (Shing Wah Daily News)* began in Toronto in 1922 and published until the year 2000.The number, longevity, and strength of these publications are impressive. For a poor and largely illiterate population, Chinese Canadians strongly supported a large number of publications. In 1930 there were three major Chinese language dailies in Canada, *Dahan ribao, Xinghua ribao*, and *Xinminguo ribao,* and they claimed a total circulation of 9,250.[58] By 1939, after the Japanese invasion of China, claimed circulation had reached 18,450.[59]

3.4.2 Print

Moving into the latter years of the twentieth century, Chinese Canadians continued to publish newspapers and periodicals catering to their needs. There were two major developments during this period in Chinese language media: the establishment of national newspaper chains and the development of electronic media, namely radio and television stations.

---

[57] Li Donghai (David T.H. Lee), *Jianada Huaqiao shi* (A history of Chinese in Canada) (Taipei: 1967), 347.

[58] Li Yahong, "Market, Capital, and Competition: The Development of Chinese-Language Newspapers in Toronto Since the 1970s" (Ph.D. diss., University of Saskatchewan, 1999), 100; citing A. McKim, *The Canadian Newspaper Directory* (1930) .

[59] *Ibid.*, 103.

Three large Chinese newspaper companies, *Xingdao ribao* (*Sing Tao Daily*), *Shijie ribao* (*World Journal Daily News*), and *Mingbao* (*Ming Pao Daily News*), all started publication in Canada during the latter part of the twentieth century and were well established by the beginning of the twenty-first. During the late 1900s the Toronto edition of *Sing Tao Daily* claimed a daily circulation of about forty thousand copies,[60] and the Vancouver edition's was about thirty-two thousand.[61] The average daily readership for the Alberta edition was fifteen thousand: ten thousand in Calgary and five thousand in Edmonton.[62] *World Journal Daily News*' 1997 estimated daily circulation for Toronto was thirty-one thousand,[63] and in Vancouver it was ten thousand.[64] The estimated circulation for *Ming Pao* in 1997 was thirty-seven thousand in Toronto,[65] and in Vancouver its estimated circulation was twenty-six thousand.[66]

The establishment of large, Chinese language newspapers led to a large increase in daily circulation in Canada. The circulation of Chinese newspapers in Canada in 1980 was six thousand; by 1990 that number had reached thirty-five thousand.[67] At the end of the twentieth century, it was approximately one hundred ninety-one thousand.[68]

---

[60] Peter Li and Yahong Li, "The Consumer Market of the Enclave Economy: A Study of Advertisements in a Chinese Daily Newspaper in Toronto," *Canadian Ethnic Studies* 31.2 (1999), 48n.5; citing *Ethnic Media and Market* ([Winter/Spring], 1997), 11-13. The authors caution that the figures for Toronto were provided by the newspapers themselves.

[61] Ian Haysom, "Newspapers in Hong Kong Are Becoming Increasingly . . . ," *CanWest News*, 1997.04.27, 1.

[62] Katerine Cheung, Chief Editor, *Sing Tao Daily,* Alberta Edition. Interview by author, Calgary, 2000.10.25.

[63] Li and Li, 48n.5; citing *Ethnic Media and Market* (Winter/Spring, 1997), 11-13.

[64] Haysom.

[65] Li and Li, 48 n.5; citing *Ethnic Media and Market* (Winter/Spring, 1997), 11-13.

[66] Haysom.

[67] Peter Li, *The Chinese in Canada,* second edition (Toronto: Oxford, 1998),

Besides the three daily national newspapers, two other national Chinese language newspapers joined them after the year 2000. *Huanqiu huabao* (*Global Chinese Press*) first published in 2000. It has two editions, Canada East and Canada West, and is distributed in British Columbia, Ontario and Alberta twice a week, every Wednesday and Friday. It claims a circulation of sixty thousand for its two editions.[69]

Jianada shangbao (*Today Commercial News*) began in 2005 in Toronto as *Xiandai ribao* (*Today Daily News*). It now issues four editions, one daily in Toronto, and three weekly in Montreal, Ottawa, and Alberta. Its estimated daily circulation in Toronto is fifteen thousand.[70] It was a subsidiary of Media Central, Inc., thus part of a global news corporation. In 2008, the large, Canadian mainstream newspaper publisher, Sun Media Corporation, bought a 50 percent share in the company.

In Toronto there has been a spate of new local papers to replace those that folded prior to 2000. A website accessible in 2012 listed thirty Chinese language newspapers available in the Toronto area.[71]

3.4.3 Television

The first Chinese language television broadcast was in 1982 when Cathay International Television started cable distribution in Vancouver. By the year 2000, Fairchild Television in Vancouver was broadcasting about nineteen hours

---

115; citing statistics compiled from *Canadian Advertising Rates and Data* by George Pigadas (1991, 57).

[68] *Sing Tao* was distributing forty thousand in Toronto, thirty-two thousand in Vancouver, and fifteen thousand in Alberta. *Ming Pao* was publishing thirty-seven thousand copies in Toronto and twenty-six thousand in Vancouver. *World Journal*'s reported daily circulation was thirty-seven thousand in Toronto and twenty-six thousand in Vancouver.

[69] *Huanqiu Huawang* (Global Chinese Press website), *www.gcpnews.com/aboutus_en.html*, accessed 2012.03.26.

[70] "Every Daily Newspaper in Canada," *www.fishwrap.ca*, revised 2011.06.13.

[71] *Qingsong Jianada* (easyca.ca), "*Daduo diqu baozhang guanggao*" (Advertisements for newspapers in the Greater Toronto Area), *easyca.ca/info/list.php?fid=220&city_id=1*, accessed 2012.04.02.

a day in Cantonese and its signal was being transmitted via satellite for direct-to-home reception across Canada and for cable distribution in Saskatchewan and Manitoba. Its Mandarin counterpart, Talentvision TV, was broadcasting in Vancouver about eighteen hours a day and its signal was also being transmitted across the West. Together, the two stations weekly were broadcasting 259 hours of Chinese language programming. In Toronto, Fairchild broadcast a total of 147 hours of TV programming weekly. At the end of the twentieth century, there were five television stations: Fairchild Media operated two in Vancouver, one in Toronto, and a fourth in Calgary; the fifth was CFMT in Toronto. In Toronto Fairchild and CFMT together were broadcasting a total of 161 hours weekly.

Since 2000 the viewing options in Chinese programming have increased immensely. There has been an increase in local broadcasters, even including some mainstream networks that have added Chinese broadcasts to their schedules. On the other hand, the expansion of cable transmission has both extended the reach of broadcasters and enabled the wholesale import of programming from foreign producers.

Omni Television officially began in 2002 when its owner Roger's Broadcasting Ltd. procured a second multicultural TV station in Toronto, namely CJMT. Roger's then won licenses to offer multicultural programs in Edmonton and Calgary. In 2007 it purchased Channel M in Vancouver from Multivan. Presently, its programs are available across most of the country with the amount of Chinese language varying among locales. Until May 2015 OMNI was providing weekly thirty-six hours of Chinese language programming in Toronto, twenty-eight in Vancouver, and fourteen in Calgary. It has since reduced this to eleven hours in Vancouver, including five hours of news in each of Mandarin and Cantonese. Omni also mounts broadcast specials relating to Chinese Canadians, such as on Canadian Chinatowns or biographies of important figures, such as Joseph Wong the founder of Yee Hong Centre for Geriatric Care in Toronto.

This fact leads to another interesting phenomenon in Chinese language media in Canada, one that highlights the importance of Chinese language media to Chinese Canadians. Major Canadian telecommunication companies, such as Rogers Communications, Bell Canada, Telus Communications, and

Shaw Communications, which have large distribution networks, have joined with foreign providers of Chinese language television programming to distribute their programming in Canada. The result has been an abundance of Chinese language television programming available to viewers.

For example, Phoenix TV *(Fenghuang weishi Meizhou tai)* is a popular foreign provider of Chinese language programming. It has been available in Canada since 2006. Based in Hong Kong, it broadcasts a mixture of news and entertainment from China and other areas in the Asian Pacific region, including Canada, in Mandarin. In 2007, 9 percent of those in Toronto self-identified as Chinese or Chinese-Canadian, born outside Canada, and able to speak Mandarin or Cantonese, watched it at least once a week.[72]

Another foreign provider of Chinese language content is Central China Television (CCTV), the predominant state television broadcaster in mainland China. It received approval in 2007 to offer nine Chinese language television channels in Canada. The application was an effort to service the Mandarin speaking population, which was seen as under serviced by Chinese language media largely focused on Cantonese speakers. Shaw, Rogers, Telus, and Bell all offer CCTV channels. The channels are sometimes sold together and offered as the Great Wall Package. Even small stations distribute CCTV content. In 2012 WOW TV in Toronto contracted to carry CCTV's documentary channel.

3.4.4 Radio

The first known Chinese language radio program in Canada was *"Liming zhi sheng"* (Sounds of daybreak) started in 1982 in Vancouver. At the turn of the twentieth century there were eight radio stations in Canada broadcasting Chinese language programming, four in Toronto, three in Vancouver, and one in Calgary. Five of these stations were operated by Fairchild Media Group. They were broadcasting about one hundred fifty-seven hours a week in Toronto,[73] and one hundred

---

[72] IpsosReid and Era Marketing Communications, "IpsosReid 2007 Canadian Chinese Media Monitor, Greater Toronto Area," *www.fairchildtv.com*, accessed 2012.04.08.

[73] "Chinese Media in Toronto," *Toronto Star,* 1999.02.11, 1.

twenty-three in Calgary. Moving into the twenty-first century, one also finds increasing Chinese language radio broadcasting. CHMB AM 1320 in Vancouver, which was broadcasting around fifty hours in 1993, quickly moved to broadcasting one hundred twenty, and presently broadcasts twenty-four hours a day in Chinese. Since Fairchild launched 96.1 FM, CHKG in Vancouver, it has increased its Chinese language broadcast to 70 percent of its total broadcast hours. After Fairchild launched AM 1430 CHKT in 1997 in Toronto, it successfully applied to the Canadian Radio-television and Telecommunications Commission (CRTC) in 2004 to remove the original limitation of being able to broadcast only sixty-six hours a week in Chinese. It presently broadcasts nearly one hundred hours in Chinese.

3.4.5 Internet

The internet is also a revealing medium through which to understand the promotion of Chinese language in Canada. First, it needs to be recognized that the more traditional venues among Chinese language media: the newspapers, radio stations, and TV networks, are using the internet very effectively. For example, *Sing Tao Daily* acquired Ccue Chinese Media in 2007 to develop their online potential. Fairchild Media Group's websites include links to their live radio broadcasts and an archive of television news programs for the watching. The group's entertainment guide, *Popular Lifestyle and Entertainment Magazine,* is also available online.

Besides the websites set up by established Chinese language media companies, there are also many companies that publish only on the internet. *Shijie huaren meiti* (World Chinese media) provides links to twenty Chinese language sources, which can only be found on the internet, of current Canadian news, as well as links to many of the traditional media companies. Xu Xinhan and Huang Yunrong classify the many Chinese language websites based in Canada into four main types 1) those that provide news, 2) those that provide advice and information on matters of daily living, 3) those used for conversation among users (i.e., chat rooms), and 4) those that provide financial services.[74] Among the first type, which is

---

[74] Xu Xinhan and Huang Yunrong, "Jiananda Huawen chuanmei fazhan

the most typical form of media, there are also distinctions between those that are primarily advertising with a small amount of news and those whose content is mostly current news. The websites of the newspapers, such *Sing Tao*'s, are predominantly made up of news, but there are also independent websites, such as *Kuibeike Huaren wang (www.quebecren.com)* that are able to provide current news while keeping advertising to a relatively low level.

There are also some particular developments that are interesting and, perhaps, indicative of trends. The *Vancouver Sun* launched a Chinese language website in 2011 called "Taiyangbao," which translates as "sun newspaper." An administrator of the newspaper explains that Chinese Canadians were one of the fastest growing demographics in Western Canada and the *Vancouver Sun* was targeting households with an income of around seventy-four thousand dollars a year. The *Vancouver Sun* was also able to enlist RBC, four Canadian real estate developers, and an outlet mall in Seattle as sponsors of the site.[75] In early 2012, readership was increasing by 25 percent a month.[76]

4. Chinese Cultural Centres

The Chinese cultural centres that are found in major cities across Canada are the most apparent examples of the achievement of Chinese Canadians in preserving and developing Chinese culture. Centres can be found in Vancouver, Calgary, Edmonton, Regina, Winnipeg, Toronto, Ottawa, and, until recently, Montreal.[77] They are often structures valued at

zongshu" (A general description of the development of Chinese language media in Canada), *blog.udn.com/cwacan/3788974,* accessed 2012.03.11.

[75] Jennifer Horn, "*Vancouver Sun* Launches Chinese-language Website," *Media in Canada,* 2011.12.08, *www.mediaincanada.ca,* accessed 2012.04.13.

[76] United Chinese Community Enrichment Services Society (S.U.C.C.E.S.S.), "New Partnership Launched to Better Serve the Chinese-Canadian Community," 2012.03.07.

[77] The Montreal Chinese Cultural and Community Center officially opened in 2008. It was a four-level facility totaling one thousand square meters. However, because of financial difficulties, it was to be closed at the end of March 2014.

several million dollars that are highly valued and supported by their broader communities for creating diversity. Their functions include offering courses in aspects of Chinese culture such as calligraphy, cooking, theatre, music, dance, and language. They also offer space for cultural performances, establish Chinese language libraries,[78] promote multiculturalism, host school groups, feature visiting artists, organize festivals, and offer leadership to the Chinese Canadian community.

4.1 History and Activities of Particular Centres

4.1.1 Vancouver

The Chinese Cultural Centre of Greater Vancouver opened in 1980. It contains the Dr. David Lam Multipurpose Hall, the Dr. Sun Yat-Sen Classical Chinese Garden, a museum and archives, art exhibits, library, and a commercial complex. A branch office was opened in Richmond in 1991. The Centre offers courses in Chinese language and culture, and organizes lectures and celebrations.[79]

4.1.2 Winnipeg

The Winnipeg Chinese Cultural and Community Centre was completed in 1987 as part of a complex containing housing, offices, shops, and a Chinese gate all within Chinatown. The Centre occupies the second floor of the Dynasty Building. It contains offices, a library, a central hall to be used for cultural exhibits, a multi-purpose room, a recreation room, and a banquet hall.[80]

---

[78] The Edmonton Chinatown Multi-Cultural Centre gives as its mission to introduce Chinese culture to the mainstream. Its Edmonton Chinatown Chinese Library opened on June 06, 2009, one of its purposes being to promote Chinese culture (*Zhongwen caiye, Huaren shequ gongshang nianjian, yashengban* [Chinese Color Pages, Community & Business Guide, Alberta 2000-2010] [Calgary: Eaglestar, 2010], 174).

[79] Chinese Cultural Centre of Greater Vancouver website, *www.cccvan.com*, accessed 2014.07.19.

[80] Winnipeg Chinese Cultural and Community Centre, *www.wcccc.ca*, accessed 2014.07.19.

4.1.3 Toronto

The first phase of the Chinese Cultural Centre of Greater Toronto opened in 1998 in Scarborough. Phase I contains an art gallery, classrooms, and offices. It is more than twenty-one hundred square meters in area. Phase II opened in 2006. It includes a six hundred twenty-six-seat theatre and a seven hundred ninety square meter hall for sports and recreational activities, conventions, exhibitions, and banquets. The Centre claims that the facilities are the largest Chinese cultural centre in North America. The total cost for building both phases was nearly thirty million dollars.[81] The Chairman and President of the Chinese Cultural Centre of Greater Toronto Dr. Ming Tat Cheung has stated that the basic principle of the Centre is to promote traditional Chinese culture to Toronto society in hopes that its cultural and educational activities will strengthen the mutual understanding and interaction of various ethnic groups.[82]

4.2 Efforts to Establish Chinese Cultural Centres: the Example of the Calgary Chinese Cultural Centre

While the existence of these culture centres and the functions they perform are achievements in themselves, the means and efforts that led to their existence also provide impressive examples of the achievements of Chinese Canadians. The consultation, planning, fundraising, and building that led to the establishment of the Calgary Chinese Cultural Centre is a case in point.

The Calgary Chinese Cultural Centre was opened in 1992. It houses an elaborately decorated rotunda modeled after the Hall of Prayer for Good Harvests in Beijing, a library, an auditorium, a museum, classrooms, offices, a restaurant, and

---

[81] Chinese Cultural Centre of Greater Toronto, *www.cccgt.org/index.php/en*, accessed 2014.07.20.

[82] *"Da Duolunduo Zhonghua Wenhua Zhongxin zhengshi qiyong"* (The Chinese Cultural Centre of Greater Toronto begins formal operations), *Shijie Ribao* (World Journal), 1998.05.02.

more commercial space. The total floor area spread over four levels is 7710 m². The Centre holds courses on Chinese culture and physical activities, such as *taiji quan*.

It took ten years of conceptualization, promoting, planning, fundraising, and construction to open the Centre. In reviewing the detailed history of this span, one notes the vision and persistence of the project's leaders. There was also considerable good will on the part of mainstream society as seen in the participation of their elected leaders and their financial support.

The project formally began with the incorporation of the Calgary Chinese Cultural Centre Association in 1985. For the next seven years, until the official opening of the Centre in 1993, the association devoted its efforts to planning and fundraising. Fundraising was ongoing, reflecting the fact that it was a matter of continual concern to the association. There were negotiations with various levels of government leading to the first tranche of government funding in 1986 when the City of Calgary transferred more than $200 thousand to the association. In 1987 the association was approved for and received the first installment of a $2.4 million grant from the City of Calgary. The Wildrose Foundation approved a grant of $50 thousand in 1988; then in 1990 the association received $830 thousand in funding from the Government of Alberta.[83]

Government support was augmented by that of private donors. Dr. Henry Fok, a Hong Kong businessman donated $1 million in 1989, and in 1992, another $200 thousand. Mr. and Mrs. Henry Chow donated $300 thousand in 1990, followed by a donation of $100 thousand in 1991. Of course, the sincerity and efforts that motivated government and private donors to support the association were also reflected in the daily fundraising activities of the association. They held their first casino in 1987, which was followed by a coffee mug sale, walkathons, banquets, telephons, celebrity concerts, radio bingo, movies, and so on.

While all these time-consuming and donor-pressuring activities were being carried out, the association still had to

[83] Information in this and the following paragraphs is sourced from pages 35-50 of the booklet *The Calgary Chinese Cultural Centre Special Inauguration Publication* produced in 1992 by the Calgary Chinese Cultural Centre to commemorate the opening of the centre.

continue to plan the centre's construction. For example, some grants came with the requirement that construction begin by a certain date. Negotiations for the land took place among the city government, private developers, and the association. The architects were hired, exhibits for the museum were procured, association elections were held, donors were updated, friction among personnel was soothed, construction was supervised, and opening ceremonies were arranged. The result was the opening of the impressive Calgary Chinese Cultural Centre on Sept. 27, 1992, the product of much hard work and persistence.

5. Artistic Expression

Another important venue through which Chinese Canadians preserve and promote Chinese culture in Canada is artistic expression. The distinct nature of Chinese culture is often identified by its various forms of artistic expression. Some of the more common forms are calligraphy, painting, literature, and opera. Traditional festivals, such as the Lunar New Year celebrations, also contain forms of artistic expression, such as lion or dragon dances. Even the mundane activity of eating encompasses traditional art forms, such as the names of the dishes or the placement of the ingredients on a dish.

Although these forms of artistic expression are all significant manifestations of Chinese culture, they are widely known in Canada. The reason for this is their preservation and promotion by Chinese Canadians. Even in an age dominated by electronic media, these traditional forms continued to be taught and performed. Among them Chinese Canadian literature, both in English and Chinese, is important.

5.1 Literature

Literature, itself, is important in the preservation and promotion of culture. It allows one of the most direct portrayals of the cultural values that underlie culture, especially when one writes in a language that has historically and literally exhibited those values[84] Chinese Canadian literary expression is

---

[84] Chinese characters, because they are pictographs or ideographs, can directly exhibit a value. For example, the character for "good" is a picture of a woman with an infant.

interesting–and effective in preserving and promoting Chinese culture–because it has developed in two languages: English and Chinese.

5.1.1 In English

There are a number of Chinese Canadian authors such as Wayson Choy (*Jade Peony* 1995), Denise Chong (*The Concubine's Children* 1995), Fred Wah (*Diamond Grill* 1996), Paul Yee (*Tales from Gold Mountain* 1989), Skye Lee (*Disappearing Moon Café* 1990), Judy Fong Bates (*Midnight at the Dragon Café* 2004), Larissa Lai (*Salt Fish Girl* 2002), JJ Lee (*The Measure of a Man* 2011), Jen Sookfong Lee (*The Better Mother* 2011), and Rita Wong (*Forage* 2007). Common to these authors is their exploration of Chinese culture and how it has influenced their values.

While generally these authors do not praise Chinese culture directly, their stories do highlight the merit of retaining the culture. Paul Yee's "Spirits of the Railway" in *Tales from Gold Mountain* is described as performing "a symbolic ritual burial for the Chinese labourers who died in the accidents at the CPR [Canadian Pacific Railway]" and joining "the living with the dead in a continuous life cycle" that "helps contemporary Chinese Canadians reclaim their heroic ancestors."[85] Denise Chong's family memoir *The Concubine's Children* "initiates the dialogue with the older generation, as well as interprets the extant historical data, such as family photographs and letters. Through dialogue, contemporary subjects both reclaim the denied community history and relocate their own worthy, double cultural identity."[86]

In highlighting the importance of retaining Chinese culture, these authors are also promoting it, as Lien Chao describes:

> Contemporary Chinese Canadian literature is community based. Its interior landscapes are emotionally connected with the historical Chinatowns in which the stories and characters

[85] Lien Chao, *Beyond Silence: Chinese Canadian Literature in English* (Toronto: TSAR, 1997), 59.

[86] Chao, 120.

are situated . . . ; also here in the Chinatowns, new
generations were born and raised, including writers, and
traditional Chinese culture was regenerated and circulated
with a Canadian consciousness. Chinese Canadian literature
is characterized by the historical experience of the
community; consistent literary tropes and expressions have
been developed to reclaim the collective community history
and to redefine a collectively shared Chinese Canadian
identity.[87]

Through the efforts of these authors traditional Chinese culture
has been regenerated and circulated with a Canadian
consciousness.

Chao further describes how these efforts have been
transformed into a more permanent venue where Chinese
Canadian authors can preserve and promote their culture. For
example, the literature, culture, and arts magazine *Ricepaper*
features Asian-Canadian work—in English--and has published
quarterly out of Vancouver since 1994. Its monthly distribution
in 2000 was four thousand copies.[88] Chao also describes how in
the 1970s the Chinese Canadian Writers' Workshop gave birth
to Chinese Canadian literature in English and the Workshop
later became the Asian Canadian Writers' Workshop, which
established *Ricepaper*.[89] Chinese Canadian writers have
extended their achievement by creating permanent venues for
the preservation and promotion of their culture.

5.1.2 In Chinese

It has been argued that producing literature in
Chinese in Canada limits an author, "suggesting a self-imposed
silence and isolation in Canadian culture."[90] However, that view
is beginning to change. Chinese Canadians writing in Chinese
have established a niche in Canada where their writing is not

---

[87] *Ibid.*, ix.

[88] Eve Lazarus, "The Road Well Travelled: Can Chinese World Succeed Where
So Many Other Chinese Magazines Have Failed?", *Marketing Magazine*
105.24 (2007.06.19), 17.

[89] P. 186-89.

[90] *Ibid.*, 23.

only accepted but they are gaining recognition for their literary skills. One of the earliest indications of this change was the formation of the Chinese Canadian Writers' Association (*Jianada Huayi zuojia xiehue*) in 1987 in Vancouver. Their first volume of members' works appeared in 1999 and they also published the *Chinese Canadian Writers' Quarterly* for three years, which contained both English and Chinese works. Ten issues of this quarterly were published in the long standing Chinese newspaper *Dahan gongbao (The Chinese Times)*. Then from 2000-2004 members' works appeared in supplements of *Xingdao ribao (Sing Tao Daily)* after which *Huanqiu huabao (Global Chinese Press)* took up publication of their writings.[91] The association even published an anthology of essays, *Fenghua Zheng: Jiahua wenxue pinglun ji (Canadian Maple, Chinese Leaves: Chinese-Canadian Literary Reviews)*, in 2009 critiquing Chinese Canadian literature and actively promoting Chinese cultural events.[92]

This greater recognition of Chinese writing as a medium for manifesting Chinese culture in Canada was also seen with the founding of the Chinese Pen Society of Canada in 1995. Based in Toronto, it claims to have nearly one hundred members whose publications number several hundred, almost all of which are in Chinese.[93]

One Chinese Canadian author Zhang Ling has had considerable success writing in Chinese. Her last book *Yuzhen (Aftershock)* (2009) was made into a 2010 movie that became the biggest box-office hit in Chinese history, taking in more than $100 million. While this novel was set in China, a previous work *Jinshan (Gold Mountain Blues)* (2009) is a historical epic–

---

[91] Information in this paragraph was taken from Lu Yin's essay *"Wenxue Wengehua: jiantan Jianada Huayi zuojia xiehui"* (Literature in Vancouver with an accompanying discussion of the Chinese Canadian Writers' Association), in *Fenghua Zheng: Jiahua wenxue pinglun ji (Canadian Maple, Chinese Leaves: Chinese-Canadian Literary Reviews)*, ed. Chen Haoquan (Burnaby, B.C.: Chinese Canadian Writers' Association, 2009), 2-8.

[92] Chinese Canadian Writers' Association's website, *www.ccwriters.ca*, accessed 2014.08.02.

[93] Jianada Zhongguo bihui (Chinese Pen Society of Canada) website, accessed 2014.07.29. The author was unable to find one non-Chinese title in his survey of members' works.

500 pages in length–about five generations of a Chinese family that came to work and eventually settled in Canada. This text too met with large success in China where it was a bestseller and received a number of awards. Abroad, options on the TV and film rights were sold in twelve countries and an English translation was released in 2014.[94]

Although Zhang Ling is only one author, her success–writing in Chinese about Chinese Canadian subjects–is strong encouragement for other Chinese Canadian authors to explore the values of Chinese culture. The use of Chinese facilitates this exploration, allowing the use of conceptual tools not available outside the language. The result, in Zhang Ling's case, is "a milestone in Chinese-Canadian literature in its scope, depth and characterization."[95]

The recognition of Chinese Canadian literature, in either English or Chinese, is evidence of further Chinese Canadian achievement in preserving and promoting Chinese culture. Presented in English, it opens Chinese culture to the broader Canadian audience; in Chinese it allows for a more direct and essential expression of Chinese values. Furthermore, the two forms mutually reinforce one another. The success of Chinese Canadian authors writing in English encourages deeper exploration of the culture that informs their writing. Writing–or reading–in Chinese is a natural means to conduct this exploration, and with its success, English language writers have access to even more in depth knowledge of the culture.

5.2 Other Forms of Artistic Expression

Apart from their promotion and preservation of Chinese culture through the production of literature, there are many other art forms that are also practised by Chinese Canadians that preserve and promote Chinese culture. Within Canada, one can easily identify the practice of martial arts, calligraphy, opera, dance, *taiji quan*, and orchestral music that are uniquely Chinese. For example, the symbolism of costumes

---

[94] Contents of this paragraph were drawn from "Why Three Prominent Chinese-Canadian Writers Launched a $10-million Plagiarism Suit against Ling Zhang" by Leah McLaren (*Toronto Life* [2014.07.30]).

[95] McLaren cites Professor Xu Xueqing at York University.

and make-up in Chinese opera refer to important features of Chinese culture; the yellow robes are reserved for the emperor and someone who is loyal has a blue face. The practice of these art forms can usually be found in the Chinese cultural centres, but, as one finds with martial arts, there are many other locations where they are practised. Their history and numbers are also surprising. There have been theatrical performances and resident troupes in major Chinese Canadian communities since 1900 or earlier.[96] There were three Cantonese opera groups in Toronto in 1935.[97] It was reported in 1996 that there were nearly twenty Cantonese opera societies in Toronto.[98]

Nor is the artistic presentation of Chinese culture limited to the traditional forms. One can find across Canada Chinese Canadian artists employing contemporary art forms to portray Chinese cultural values. For example, two hundred fifty members of the Chinese Canada Artists Federation in Vancouver use contemporary painting, sculpture, multi-media, film, artistic design, *et cetera* in order to promote the culture of Chinese art.[99]

6. Festivals

The celebration of traditional holidays is another way the Chinese Canadian community preserves and promotes Chinese culture, especially promotes, because these celebrations are largely attended by non-Chinese, which enables Chinese Canadians to reach an audience that is less aware of their culture.

It is interesting to see in the Dragon Boat Festivals that are held across Canada—and the world—each year, that the teams

---

[96] Edgar Wickborg, "Chinese Associations in Canada, 1923-47," in *Visible Minorities and Multiculturalism: Asians in Canada,* ed. K. Victor Ujimoto and Gordon Hirabayashi (Toronto: Butterworths, 1980), 29.

[97] Dora Nipp, "Toronto Chinese Drama Associations," *Polyphony* 5.2 (Fall/Winter 1983), 72.

[98] Bruce DeMara, "A Wave of Good News for the Arts," *Toronto Star* (1996. 11.10), B7.

[99] The Chinese Canada Artists Federation in Vancouver website, *www.ccaf-vancouver.com*, accessed 2015.01.28.

competing are mostly composed of non-Chinese, and even if much of the cultural background to the festival is de-emphasized, the organizers are often Chinese Canadian and the philanthropic character of the festival reflects the Chinese cultural value of supporting others, just as the original boat rowers, in 278 BCE, were said to be racing to save the government official Qu Yuan in 278 BCE from downing or, at least, save his body from being eaten by the fish.[100]

Among the various Chinese festivals, the Chinese New Year is, of course, the most celebrated and widely known. Nor does one need to follow Chinese Canadian events in order to know of its occurrence; the advertisements for related food products in major supermarkets are sufficient. The Calgary Chinese Cultural Centre has held a Chinese New Year celebration since 1992. It is "one of the biggest winter events in the city and attracts more than twenty thousand people each year, including dignitaries from the municipal, provincial, and federal governments."[101] Vancouver's Chinese Benevolent Association has held a parade since 1979 that has been attended by as many as fifty thousand celebrants of Chinese New Year.[102]

Other festivals include the Mid-Autumn Moon Festival when cultural centres put on special events usually involving the mythology surrounding the festival and mooncakes, the iconic food item associated with the festival, are eaten. The Calgary Chinese Merchants Association has organized the Calgary Chinatown Street Festival since 2001. Festival activities include calligraphy demonstrations, Chinese chess (xiangqi) competitions, dragon and lion dances, folk dances, martial arts, and other Chinese cultural activities.

7. Food

---

[100] Legend has it that Qu Yuan drowned himself in the Miluo River in protest of his king's folly in losing the Kingdom of Chu to its enemies.

[101] Amanda Stephenson, "Year of Horse Starts with Celebration; Families and Dignitaries Join in Fun at Festival," *Calgary Herald*, 2014.01. 27, A.5.

[102] Christopher Reynolds, "Thousands Take in Parade's Colourful Mosaic; Festivities to Kick off Year of Snake Celebrate Chinese Culture and Spirit of Multiculturalism," *The Vancouver Sun*, 2013.02.18, A.3.

7.1 Cultural Values Embedded in Concepts of Food and its Distribution

It is obvious that significant cultural values are embedded in any presentation of food and its distribution and this seems even more apparent in the case of Chinese food. Some of the major characteristics of Chinese food, such as the use of chopsticks, the importance of using fresh ingredients, the low quantity of animal products, rice as a staple, the round table, the communal dishes, and their picturesque names, are significantly different from other cuisines and these differences are largely culturally determined. Another formulation of this claim is the statement "People express their cultural identity through their manner of eating and drinking."[103]

One sees the extent of cultural influence on food within Traditional Chinese Medicine (TCM). The link between food and medicine is considered natural for the Chinese because they both come from the same source. Historically, there are references to herbal medicine in China as early as the 1500 BCE.[104] There were hundreds of functional foods and corresponding recipes documented in classical TCM publications running from before the common era until the sixteenth century. The importance and specific uses of food found in TCM are distinct to China. The intricacy of prescriptions and their large number—one hundred thousand or more[105]—are all aspects of the civilization's culture.

Given the obviousness of the claim that cultural values are embedded in Chinese food and its distribution, in the context of this essay it remains to show how Chinese Canadians are, indeed, preserving and promoting Chinese culture through their production of Chinese food. Arguably, it is in the restaurant and grocery store businesses that one finds the clearest and most convincing examples of preservation and promotion of Chinese culture.

---

[103] Josephine Smart, "Negotiating Chinese Immigrant Food Culture in a Global Setting," *IIAS (International Institute for Asian Studies Newsletter)* 1999.06.19, 30.

[104] Daniel P. Reid, *Chinese Herbal Medicine* (Boston: Shambhala, 1987), 19.

[105] Jane Qiu, "Traditional Medicine: a Culture in the Balance," *Nature* 448 (2007.07.12), 127.

7.2 Restaurants

Chinese restaurants have been referred to as "virtual islands of Chinese culture."[106] Their distinct identity as "Chinese" restaurants and not just restaurants speaks to this fact. The experience of the Chinese decor, the Chinese menu, the fish tank, the use of chopsticks, the consumption of rice as the staple, the communal dishes, the shrines with incense and offerings at the entrance, the use of Chinese among the staff, all these experiences reflect Chinese culture.

The presence of Chinese culture in Chinese restaurants has a basis in Canadian history. The restaurant industry has been one of the main venues by which Chinese around the world have contributed to the societies within which they reside and, thereby, earned the right to be supported by those societies. Simply speaking, working in a restaurant has been one of the main ways Chinese have supported themselves. The Chinese in Canada have been no exception. Based on the 1921 Census of Canada, they operated 40 percent of the restaurants in Alberta, 50 percent in Saskatchewan, and about a third of the restaurants in Manitoba and Ontario.[107] In 1931 nearly 9 percent were restaurant keepers and more than 26 percent were waiters, cooks, and servants; arguably more than 30 percent were employed in restaurants.[108] In 1991, still more than 18 percent of Chinese Canadians were working in service occupations and nearly 9 percent in managerial and administrative occupations, some of which would have been in the restaurant industry.[109] Unlike other industries, such as

---

[106] Smart, 30. Although Smart is referring specifically to Chinese restaurants in Britain, the description could also apply to Chinese restaurants around the world. After all, they are identified as "Chinese" restaurants.

[107] Cited in Wickberg, et al., Table 14, "Chinese Occupations, by Province, with percentage of Laundry and Restaurant Businesses," From China to Canada, 311.

[108] Li, The Chinese, 52.

[109] Of note is the fact that Chinese Canadians were 50 percent more likely to be working in service occupations than other Canadians (Peter Li, The Chinese, 120-21).

laundries and small grocers that have become outmoded or replaced by large chain stores, restaurant operation has remained a viable venue by which Chinese Canadians can make a living.

Chinese restaurants are easily identified constituents of the restaurants in major Canadian cities. They are also noticeable by their presence in small towns across the country and, by the fact, that they have historically advertised Chinese food, along with "Western" food, indicating that Chinese food has been popular for some time, even among less cosmopolitan clientele.

However, Chinese Canadian involvement in the restaurant industry has not been limited to simply making a living. They have continued their large scale involvement in the restaurant industry and changed the way they have historically operated in order to avail themselves of new opportunities. Peter Li notes the growth in Chinese restaurant operations that has taken place in Richmond, British Columbia. He describes the transformation between 1981 and 1990 as dramatic and points out that small family operated businesses have been replaced by large and luxurious Chinese restaurants catering to more affluent clienteles.[110]

Today Chinese restaurants in Canada continue to preserve and promote Chinese culture. They are the designated sites for many Chinese Canadian celebrations, such as weddings and New Year's banquets, and some are booked years in advance for these events. The variety of restaurants has also increased dramatically to reflect the different types of food in China. Decor has become more lavish, with traditional ornaments such as bridal palanquins and signage by famous calligraphers; the menus have expanded to include items like birds-nest soup, bean curd dishes, and green vegetables particular to Chinese diet. In this way, the Chinese Canadian restaurant industry continues to be a preserver and promoter of Chinese culture.

7.3 Grocery Stores

Given the importance placed on food, the cultural effect on its distribution, and the history of the Chinese Canadian

---

[110] "Ethnic Enterprise in Transition: Chinese Business in Richmond, B.C., 1980-1990," *Canadian Ethnic Studies* 24.1 (1992), 131.

involvement in the food industry, it is not surprising that Chinese grocery stores would also be preservers and promoters of Chinese culture. Like the restaurants, Chinese grocery stores have an identity clearly distinct from mainstream convenience stores and large supermarket chains. This is due in part to the success of T & T the supermarket chain selling Chinese and Asian food products. Its success has created brand awareness and thus a clearer identity for the Chinese grocery store. Along with the recognition garnered by T & T, is the recognition of the characteristics that are distinctly Chinese.

The difference in products is one of the first things that one notices in a typical Chinese grocery store. There are unusual vegetables such as *gailan, fugua,* and *bokchoy;* and exotic fruits such as durian, sugar cane, dragon fruit, lychee, starfruit (carambola), mangoes, apple-pears, and papaya; varieties of fungi such as mushrooms; and live water animals such as rock cod, lobsters, shrimp, and frogs. Many of the snacks sold are fruit based, or contain unusual ingredients such as seaweed, ginger, or shredded pork. There is also a section selling ceremonial items, such as joss money and incense for honouring the deceased. One other characteristic of note is the freshness of the produce and meats. There is little use of ice to preserve produce and much of the fish is sold live out of tanks.

It is also typical for a number of separately owned businesses to operate in the same space, a characteristic that probably developed early in Chinese Canadian history in order to conserve capital, but also reflects the flexibility of the Chinese. Many different businesses may operate in the same space; for example, a bank, a newsstand, a dry-cleaning outlet, lottery tickets sales, a bakery, a fish monger, a butcher, and a barbeque meat seller.

Even with these differences, Chinese Canadian grocery stores have established a significant presence within Canada. As with restaurants, this is an industry through which Chinese Canadians have been historically known to contribute to the Canadian economy.[111] What were small operations have

---

[111] Brian Dawson provides figures showing that Chinese Canadians operated approximately 6.5 percent of the grocery stores in major cities in Alberta during the early twentieth century (J. Brian Dawson, *Moon Cakes in Gold Mountain: From China to the Central Plains* [Calgary, Alberta: Detselig Enterprises, 1991], 230-32).

developed into major ones with innovations putting them in a position to compete with major supermarket chains, the result being that Canadians are offered a variety of products that were not available before. They can now purchase increased types and amounts of typically Chinese products, such as bean curd, fish, green leafy vegetables, and tropical fruits. It has become commonplace to find large stores, several times the size of the neighbourhood Chinese grocery store, selling mostly Chinese products in many large Canadian cities.

T & T Supermarket is the obvious example of this latter case. T & T is Canada's largest Asian supermarket chain with ten stores in Greater Vancouver, four stores in Alberta, and nine in Ontario, for a total of twenty-three.[112] In terms of sales, it was the sixth largest supermarket in Canada in 2008 with 0.3% of the market.[113] A typical store is between thirty-two and fifty-one hundred square meters in area,[114] which is comparable to stores in major supermarket chains. In other ways, though, T & T stores differ from those of other large chains in containing an Asian deli, a Chinese BBQ department, tanks containing live seafood, and thirty brands of soy sauce.[115] Interestingly, in July 2009 Loblaws announced that it had bought T & T for $225 million, but that it would operate as a separate division.[116]

The various products that Chinese grocery stores offer and their flexible operations are reflective of cultural influences. Chinese Canadians, in their expanding involvement in the grocery business, have preserved and promoted these cultural influences as they continue to offer and add to their distinct products while conducting operations that distinguish them from mainstream grocers. Unquestionably, the remarkable

---

[112] T & T website, "Our Stores," *www.tnt-supermarket.com/en*, accessed 2015.01.19.

[113] Euromonitor International: Local Company Profile, "T & T Supermarket Inc. - Retailing - Canada," February 2008.

[114] Eve Lazarus, "Eastern Star," *Marketing* (Toronto), 112.18 (2007.09.24).

[115] Lorrayne Anthony, "East Meets West: Entrepreneur Marries His Chinese Heritage with Opportunities Offered by His New Canadian Homeland," *Financial Post* 10.40 (1997.10.4/6), T6.

[116] Marina Strauss, "Loblaws Buys Asian Grocery Chain," *The Globe and Mail*, 2009.07.24.

growth and success of the Chinese grocery businesses, which, arguably, has been largely based on Chinese cultural influences, will continue to support the preservation and promotion of Chinese culture.

8. Conclusion

One cannot deny the role that the preservation and promotion of Chinese culture has had in defending Chinese Canadians against racial prejudice. The early establishment of Chinese language and culture education among the Chinese Canadian community in Victoria was a clear example. Faced with segregation, poor facilities, and outright exclusion of their children, they mobilized to form their own schools teaching in Chinese with a curriculum designed to foster an identity based on Chinese culture. The knowledge of the language and culture prepared them for work in a Chinese setting as well as fortified their identity so as to withstand the prejudice directed at them.

The preservation and promotion of Chinese culture continue to serve this latter role even into the present day as described by Xiaoping Li in *Voices Rising: Asian Canadian Cultural Activism*. The book describes the new intensity with which Asian Canadians, and in particular Chinese Canadians, are promoting their culture. The main goals of this promotion are to build their communities, to reconstruct their identities, and to achieve equality and social justice. For example, the film maker Brenda Joy Lem describes how her mother's cultural traditions taught her about human dignity, community, and self-expression, and because of her identification with these, she did not succumb to external forces like peer pressure.[117]

These artists have built on the past role that the preservation and promotion of Chinese culture has had in the Chinese Canadians' struggle to overcome prejudice. The early educators utilized this preservation and promotion to combat the restrictions placed on them by mainstream society, and this strategy is still utilized in the present day. Nevertheless, one would hope that this cause, however noble, would have become less relevant.

---

[117] Cited in Xiaoping Li, 187. It should be noted that Li does not emphasize Chinese culture as a force to resist prejudice and may even object to doing so because it contributes to "essentialism."

Arguably, this is what has happened, as prejudice has diminished, and more and more Canadians of all backgrounds are recognizing the merits of Chinese culture. Nevertheless, Chinese Canadians' have continued to preserve and promote their culture. The number of Chinese speakers continues to increase; the number of schools has as well. There has been growth in the number and sophistication of the media disseminating information in Chinese. These trends are reinforced by the establishment of numerous and large cultural centres across Canada. Within these centres, one finds many actual examples of the practice of Chinese culture. There are courses on Chinese culture, space for cultural performances, and Chinese language libraries. The centres also host visitors, feature visiting artists, and organize festivals.

This essay has also shown that Chinese Canadians are preserving and promoting Chinese culture through artistic expression, the practice of traditional Chinese arts. Of the more common forms, the development of Chinese Canadian literature both in English and Chinese best shows the achievements of Chinese Canadians. There are a number of acclaimed Chinese Canadian authors exploring Chinese culture and how it has affected their lives. The earlier achievements in English have also supported the production of similarly-themed literature written in Chinese. Chinese Canadian authors have two major organizations: the Chinese Canadian Writers' Association in Vancouver and the Chinese Pen Society of Canada in Toronto. Members of these organizations have produced hundreds of works. The recognition of Chinese Canadian literature, written in either English or Chinese, is evidence of Chinese Canadian achievement in preserving and promoting Chinese culture. Presented in English, it opens Chinese culture to the broader Canadian audience; in Chinese it allows for a more direct and essential expression of Chinese values.

The celebration of traditional holidays is another way the Chinese Canadian community preserves and promotes Chinese culture, especially promotes, because these celebrations are largely attended by non-Chinese, which enables Chinese Canadians to reach an audience that is less aware of the culture. Among the various Chinese festivals, the Chinese New Year is, of course, the most celebrated and widely known. Chinese cultural preservation and promotion are also seen in the restaurant and grocery businesses that Chinese Canadians operate in Canada. Historically, both industries were common sources of employment for Chinese Canadians, so it was natural that the strength of Chinese culture would manifest itself within them.

The distinct identity of Chinese restaurants is embodied in the experience of the Chinese decor, the Chinese menu, the fish tank, the use of chopsticks, the consumption of rice as the staple, the communal dishes, the shrines with incense and offerings at the entrance, and the use of Chinese among the staff. They are designated sites for many Chinese Canadian celebrations. Even as other avenues of employment have opened up to Chinese Canadians, their restaurants have not only continued to preserve Chinese culture, they have made extra efforts to do so. Decor has become more lavish and the menus have been expanded to include items more identified with Chinese culture.

The grocery stores too have established an identity distinctly Chinese based on the difference in their products and their business operations. Added to this is the recognition gained by the success of T & T the supermarket chain selling Chinese and Asian food products. Its success has created brand awareness and thus a greater identity for the Chinese grocery store.

In all the areas summarized above Chinese Canadians have established a distinct identity for themselves amid the influence of mainstream culture. As such, their values are preserved for later generations of Chinese Canadians, and more increasingly, for mainstream society. This is yet another achievement.

BIBLIOGRAPHY

Ai-Cheng Mandarin Chinese School website, *www.mandarin-school.org/home_ch.htm*, accessed 2014.07.13.

Alberta Education. "Chinese Language and Culture Program Nine-Year Program Grades 4-5-6." *education.alberta.ca/teachers/program/interlang/chinese.aspx*, accessed 2014.07.14.

Anthony, Lorrayne. "East Meets West: Entrepreneur Marries His Chinese Heritage with Opportunities Offered by His

New Canadian Homeland." *Financial Post* 10.40 (1997.10.4/6): T6.

Calgary Board of Education. Phone interview with Kally Crelly, 2002.08.19.

Calgary Board of Education website, *www.cbe.ab.ca,* accessed 2015.01.28.

Calgary Chinese Cultural Centre. *The Calgary Chinese Cultural Centre Special Inauguration Publication.* Calgary, Alberta: September 1992. 84 pages

Canadian Association of Chinese Language Schools website, *cacls.org/About_Us.html,* accessed 2013.06.09.

Chan, Arlene. *The Chinese in Toronto from 1878: From Outside to Inside the Circle.* Toronto: Dundurn, 2011.

Chao, Lien. *Beyond Silence: Chinese Canadian Literature in English.* Toronto: TSAR, 1997.

Chen, Haoquan, ed. *Fenghua Zheng:Jiahua wenxue pinglun ji (Canadian Maple, Chinese Leaves: Chinese-Canadian Literary Reviews).* Burnaby, B.C.: Chinese Canadian Writers' Association, 2009.

Cheung, Katherine. Chief Editor. *Sing Tao Daily,* Alberta Edition. Interview in Calgary, 2000.10.25.

Chia, Ai-Lan and Catherine Costigan. "Understanding the Multidimensionality of Acculturation Among Chinese Canadians." *Canadian Journal of Behavioural Science* 38.4 (Oct. 2006): 311-324.

Chinese Canadian Writers' Association's website, *www.ccwriters.ca,* accessed 2014.08.02.

Chinese Cultural Centre of Greater Vancouver website, *www.cccvan.com,* accessed 2014.07.19.

The Chinese Academy website,
www.chineseacademy.ca/english/info/e_school.htm,
accessed 2015.01.28.

Chinese Canada Artists Federation in Vancouver website,
www.ccaf-vancouver.com, accessed 2015.01.28.

"Chinese Media in Toronto." *Toronto Star,* 1999.02.11: 1.

Confucius. *The Analects.* Translated by D.C. Lau. London:
Penguin Books Ltd., 1979.

Dawson, J. Brian. *Moon Cakes in Gold Mountain: From China
to the Canadian Plains.* Calgary: Detselig Enterprises Ltd.,
1991.

Daxue (The Great Learning). In *Source Book in Chinese
Philosophy.* Translated by Wing-tsit Chan. Princeton, New
Jersey: Princeton Univ. Press, 1963.

DeMara, Bruce. "A Wave of Good News for the Arts." *Toronto
Star,* 1996.11.10, B7.

Dion, Karen K., Kenneth L. Dion, and Anita Wan-ping Pak.
"The Role of Self-Reported Language Proficiencies in the
Cultural and Psychosocial Adaption among Members of
Toronto, Canada's Chinese Community." *Journal of Asian
Pacific Communication* 1.1 (1990): 173-89.

Edmonton Chinese Bilingual Education Association website,
www.ecbea.org, accessed 2015.01.28.

Euromonitor International: Local Company Profile. "T & T
Supermarket Inc. - Retailing - Canada." February 2008.

"Every Daily Newspaper in Canada." *www.fishwrap.ca,* revised
2011.06.13.

Haysom, Ian. "Newspapers in Hong Kong Are Becoming
Increasingly . . ." *CanWest News,* 1997.04.27, 1.

Horn, Jennifer. "*Vancouver Sun* Launches Chinese-language Website." *Media in Canada*, 2011.12.08. *www.mediaincanada.ca,* accessed 2012.04.13.

Huanqiu Huawang (Global Chinese Press) website, *www.gcpnews.com/aboutus_en.html,* accessed 2012.03.26.

IpsosReid and Era Marketing Communications. "IpsosReid 2007 Canadian Chinese Media Monitor: Greater Toronto Area." *www.fairchildtv.com,* accessed 2012.04.08.

Jianada Zhongguo bihui (Chinese Pen Society of Canada) website, *blog.sina.com.cn/jiazhongbihui,* accessed 2014.07.29.

"Kacheng Keshu Chongzheng Hui dishiwu jie jiuzhi dianli ji chunjie jinglao lianhuan wanyan huaxu" (Details of the fifteenth investiture and Chinese New Year banquet honouring the elderly of the Calgary Tsung Tsin Benevolent Association), *Jianada 88 shequbao (Canada88 Community News),* 2015.03.26, 16-17.

Lai, David Chuenyan. *Chinese Community Leadership: Case Study of Victoria in Canada.* Singapore: World Scientific, 2010.

------. "The Issue of Discrimination in Education in Victoria, 1901-1923." *Canadian Ethnic Studies* 19.3 (1987): 47-67.

Lazarus, Eve. "The Road Well Traveled: Can Chinese World Succeed Where So Many Other Chinese Magazines Have Failed?" *Marketing Magazine* 105.24 (2000.06.19).

------. "Eastern Star. "*Marketing* (Toronto) 112.18 (2007.09.24): 49-52.

Li Donghai (David T.H. Lee). *Jianada Huaqiao shi* (A history of Chinese in Canada). Taipei: 1967.

Li, Duanduan. "Chinese as a Heritage Language in Canada." *crclle.lled.educ.ubc.ca/documents/li.pdf,* accessed 2013.06.09.

Li, Jun. "Expectations of Chinese Immigrant Parents for Their Children's Education: The Interplay of Chinese Tradition and the Canadian Context." *Canadian Journal of Education* 26.4 (2001): 477-494.

Li, Peter. *s.v.* "Chinese," *Encyclopedia of Canada's Peoples,* edited by Paul Magocsi. Toronto: University of Toronto Press, 1999.

------. *The Chinese in Canada.* Second edition. Toronto: Oxford, 1998.

------. "Ethnic Enterprise in Transition: Chinese Business in Richmond, B.C., 1980-1990." *Canadian Ethnic Studies* 24.1 (1992): 120-38.

------ and Yahong Li. "The Consumer Market of the Enclave Economy: A Study of Advertisements in a Chinese Daily Newspaper in Toronto." *Canadian Ethnic Studies* 31.2 (1999): 43-60.

Li, Yahong. "Market, Capital, and Competition: The Development of Chinese-Language Newspapers in Toronto Since the 1970s." Ph.D. diss., University of Saskatchewan, 1999.

Li, Xiaoping. *Voices Rising: Asian Canadian Cultural Activism.* Vancouver: UBC Press, 2007.

LiveScience website, *www.livescience.com,* accessed 2012.07.21.

Lu Yin. *"Wenxue Wengehua: jiantan Jianada Huayi zuojia xiehui"* (Literature in Vancouver with an accompanying discussion of the Chinese Canadian Writers' Association). In *Fenghua Zheng: Jiahua wenxue pinglun ji (Canadian Maple, Chinese Leaves: Chinese-Canadian Literary Reviews),* edited by Chen Haoquan, 2-8. Burnaby, B.C.: Chinese Canadian Writers' Association, 2009.

Luk, Bernard H.K. "The Chinese Communities of Toronto: Their Languages and Mass Media." *Polyphony: The*

Bulletin of the Multicultural Society of Toronto 15 (2000): 46-56.

Mah, Hilda. "A History of the Education of Chinese Canadians in Alberta, 1885-1947." M. Education thesis, University of Alberta, 1987.

McLaren, Leah. "Why Three Prominent Chinese-Canadian Writers Launched a $10-million Plagiarism Suit against Ling Zhang." *Toronto Life,* 2014.07.30.

Mencius. *Mencius.* Translated by D. C. Lau. Third edition. Harmondsworth, Eng.: Penguin Books, 1983.

Nipp, Dora. "Toronto Chinese Drama Associations." *Polyphony* 5.2 (Fall/Winter 1983): 71-73.

Ng, Wing Chung. *The Chinese in Vancouver, 1945-1980: The Pursuit of Identity and Power.* Vancouver: UBC Press, 1999.

Qian Mu. *Cong Zhongguo lishi laikan Zhongguo minzu xing ji Zhongguo wenhua* (The nature of Chinese people and Chinese culture from the perspective of Chinese history). Hong Kong: Zhongwen daxue chubanshe, 1979.

Qingsong Jianada (easyca.ca). "*Daduo diqu baozhang guanggao*" (Advertisements for newspapers in the Greater Toronto Area). *easyca.ca/info/list.php?fid=220&city_id=1,* accessed 2012.04.02.

Qiu, Jane. "China Plans to Modernize Traditional Medicine." *Nature* 446 (2007.04.05): 590-591.

Reid, Daniel P. *Chinese Herbal Medicine.* Boston: Shambhala, 1987.

Reynolds, Christopher. "Thousands Take in Parade's Colourful Mosaic; Festivities to Kick off Year of Snake Celebrate Chinese Culture and Spirit of Multiculturalism." *The Vancouver Sun,* 2013.02.18: A.3.

Shijie Ribao (World Journal). *"Da Duolunduo Zhonghua Wenhua Zhongxin zhengshi qiyong"* (The Chinese Cultural Centre of Greater Toronto begins formal operations), 1998.05.03.

Sing Tao Etel Toronto. *163bbs.servebeer.com/?qbz=ac01CJMsNVllnRlivdQ9P8je1 ZAvWpmrKx7rd13oV9mfJtmuMRnrXxDvER6cKhm32tQ2a 94nclAioF4g6dQ75hQgqAh38RAjj1,* accessed 2013.06.09.

Sing Tao Etel Vancouver. *www.singtaoetel.ca/VAN/EN/subcategory.php?CategoryID =11&CatalogID=S008,* accessed 2013.06.09.

Smart, Josephine. "Negotiating Chinese Immigrant Food Culture in a Global Setting." *IIas (International Institute for Asian Studies Newsletter),* 1999.06.19: 30.

Smith, Charlie. "Chinese Canadians Pressure New Westminster Council in Advance of Anniversary Parade." *Straight.com. www.straight.com/print/222952,* accessed 2010.12.09.

Stanley, Timothy J. *Contesting White Supremacy: School Segregation, Anti-Racism, and the Making of Chinese Canadians.* Vancouver: UBC, 2011.

------. "'BY THE SIDE OF OTHER CANADIANS': The Locally Born and the Invention of Chinese Canadians." *BC Studies* 156/157 (Winter 2007): 109-139, 204.

Statistics Canada. "2011 National Household Survey: Immigration, Place of Birth, Citizenship, Ethnic Origin, Visible Minorities, Language and Religion." *www.statcan.ca,* accessed 2013.06.04.

------. "French and the *Francophonie* in Canada." *www.statcan.ca,* accessed 2013.06.04.

------. "Immigrant Languages in Canada," "Table 1: Population of Immigrant Mother Tongue Families, Showing Main

Languages Comprising Each Family, Canada, 2011."
www.statcan.ca, accessed 2013.06.04.

------. "Languages in Canada." *www.statcan.ca*, accessed
2003.01.21.

------. "Population by mother tongue, by province and territory
(2006 Census)." *www.statcan.ca*, accessed 2013.03.26.

Stephenson, Amanda. "Year of Horse Starts with Celebration;
Families and Dignitaries Join in Fun at Festival."*Calgary
Herald,* 2014.01.27: A.5.

Strauss, Marina. "Loblaws Buys Asian Grocery Chain." *The
Globe and Mail*, 2009.07.24.

T & T website. "Our Stores." *www.tnt-supermarket.com/en*,
accessed 2015.01.19.

Taylor, Gordon R. "An Investigation of Chinese Schools in
Canada." M. Arts thesis, McGill University, 1933.

Wang Yangming. *Instructions for Practical Living and Other
Neo-Confucian Writings by Wang Yang-Ming.* Translated
by Wing-tsit Chan. New York: Columbia University Press,
1963.

------. *Wang Yangming quanji* (A complete collection of Wang
Yangming's works). Edited by Wu Guang, Qian Ming, Dong
Ping, and Yao Yanfu. Shanghai: Shanghai guji chubanshe,
1992.

Wickberg, Edgar, Harry Con, Ronald J. Con, Graham Johnson,
and William E. Willmott. *From China to Canada: A History
of the Chinese Communities in Canada*, edited by Edgar
Wickberg. Toronto : McClelland and Stewart, 1982.

------. "Chinese Associations in Canada, 1923-47." *Visible
Minorities and Multiculturalism: Asians in Canada*, edited
by K. Victor Ujimoto and Gordon Hirabayashi, 23-31.
Toronto: Butterworths, 1980.

United Chinese Community Enrichment Services Society
(S.U.C.C.E.S.S.). "New Partnership Launched to Better
Serve the Chinese-Canadian Community." 2012.03.07.

Wong, Tony. "New Canadians with Global Connections; What Is
the Legacy of Immigration Programs That Drew Many
Enterprising Chinese to Canada? Major Canadian
Businesses with Links around the World." *Toronto Star*,
1999.05.10, 1.

Wright, Harold A. "The Chinese in Toronto - A Personal
Appreciation." Unpublished, 1976.

Wu, Helen. Chairman, Calgary Chinese Public School.
Presentation to University of Calgary course EAST 321
"Introduction to the Calgary Chinese Community."
Calgary, 2001.09.05.

------, and Lily Lee. Calgary Chinese Public School. Presentation
to University of Calgary course EAST 321 "Introduction to
the Calgary Chinese Community." Calgary, 1999.09.08.

Xiao, Hong. "Chinese Language Maintenance in Winnipeg."
Canadian Ethnic Studies 30.1 (1998): 86-96.

Xu Xinhan and Huang Yunrong. *"Jianada Huawen chuanmei
fazhan zongshu"* (A general description of the development
of Chinese language media in Canada).
blog.udn.com/cwacan/3788974, accessed 2012.03.11.

*Zhongwen caiye, Huaren shequ gongshang nianjian,
yashengban* (Chinese Color Pages, Community & Business
Guide, Alberta 2000-2010). Calgary: Eaglestar, 2010.

Zhou, Min, Wenhong Chen, and Guoxuan Cai. "Chinese-
language Media and Immigrant Life in the United States
and Canada." In *Media and the Chinese Diaspora:
Community, Communications, and Commerce*, 42-74,
edited by Wanning Sun. London: Routledge, 2006.

5. ECONOMIC INFLUENCE AND ACHIEVEMENTS

1. Introduction

The economic influence and achievements of Chinese Canadians can be viewed from a number of perspectives and many of them offer surprises. The ethnic industries continue to flourish and support large numbers of the population as they have historically done. At the same time Chinese Canadians are establishing themselves in areas where they have not had a significant impact before. These changes have come quickly as well, for as late as 1947 Chinese were banned from entering Canada and the population was in decline.[1] Speed and surprise also mark the general course of the Chinese Canadians' economic achievements because they have moved from being largely confined to an enclave economy to integrating into the broader economy and now, as Canada develops a much stronger economic link with China, transnationalist Chinese Canadians are leading the country in developing multilateral trading relations, particularly with one of the largest and fastest growing economies in the world. It is indeed ironic that a people whose economic opportunities were among the most limited are becoming leaders within a country that once deliberately restricted them.

Nor should this claim be taken lightly because vestiges of the restrictions still remain. In many ways it remains difficult for Chinese Canadians to fulfill their economic potential, let alone lead in the economy. However, economic forces can often, if not usually, overcome structural barriers and such seems to be the case with Chinese Canadians. This essay will outline some of the general evidence for Chinese Canadian economic achievement, the history of Chinese Canadian participation in the economy, and areas of the economy within which Chinese Canadians have excelled, and describe in depth two particular

---

[1] Peter Li, *The Chinese in Canada* (Toronto: Oxford University Press, 1998) shows population decreasing from 46,519 in 1931 to 34,627 in 1941, p. 55. In 1951, the population was 32,528 (Edgar Wickberg, Harry Con, Ronald J. Con, Graham Johnson, and William E. Willmott, *From China to Canada: A History of the Chinese Communities in Canada,* ed. Edgar Wickberg [Toronto: McClelland and Stewart, 1982], 209).

ones, business investment and property development. These will serve as evidence for and description of the economic influence and achievements of Chinese Canadians.

Following this, the essay will consider the general factors affecting these achievements, including barriers to them. An obvious question that arises is how Chinese Canadians have achieved what they have, a question that is marked by substantial debate. Finally, the essay will consider their future economic achievements. One will see that their achievements have been remarkable and that there are strong reasons that they will continue to surprise.

2. General Evidence of the Economic Strength of Chinese Canadians

2.1 Wealth

Obviously, the wealth of a person or people is a direct indication of their economic strength. Furthermore, although it is difficult to obtain information about private wealth, there are accessible indicators. For example, marketing agencies have been able to develop some estimates of what the wealth of Chinese Canadians is and to show that it is having an influence on the Canadian economy. As early as 1991, indications of their increasing wealth, both in absolute and relative terms, began to appear. The Canadian census that year showed that 78 percent of Chinese Canadians, compared with 70 per cent of other Canadians, lived in a dwelling owned by some member of the household. Moreover, about 60 per cent of Chinese Canadians lived in owner-occupied dwellings worth $200,000 or more, compared with only 23 per cent of other Canadians.[2] In 1994, a survey by DJC Research, a Toronto-market research firm, found that the average personal income of Chinese Canadians was $27,675, compared with $24,329 for non-Chinese Canadians.[3]

These findings are reinforced by more recent ones that 75 percent of heads of Canadian households who were of Chinese

---

[2] *Ibid.*, 127.

[3] Susan Noakes, "Niche Marketing Targets Chinese Consumers," *The Financial Post,* 1994.11.18, C17.

origin in 2001 owned their own homes, compared with 63 percent of those who identified themselves as non immigrants, 67 percent of those of European origin, and 65 percent of those of multiple origin.[4]

Over the years, the evidence of Chinese Canadian wealth has continued to mount. A marketing survey conducted in Vancouver in 1995 and another in Toronto in 1996, again by DJC Research, both found that Chinese Canadians were spending more than the average Canadian.[5] A survey commissioned in 1997 by CFMT International, a Toronto-based multicultural broadcaster, showed that Chinese Canadian households in Toronto, where about 40 percent of Chinese Canadians live, had $5.2 billion to spend annually.[6] Total Chinese Canadian spending in Canada was reported to be $30 billion in 2005,[7] or approximately $25 thousand per person. A survey reported in 2006 by Fairchild Media Group in Vancouver determined that ownership of cars by Chinese Canadian households was at 91 percent compared to 78 percent for what Statistics Canada defines as a "Canadian household."[8] The results of Fairchild's survey are confirmed by the 2006 Canadian Census that showed that third and subsequent generations of Chinese-Canadians surpass the income levels of all other groups.[9]

---

[4] Wendy Leung, "Chinese-Canadians Lead Home-buying Boom," CanWest News, 2006.04.26, 1, citing 2001 Statistics Canada census data.

[5] Li, *The Chinese*, 127.

[6] Showwei Chu, "Welcome to Canada. Please Buy Something," *Canadian Business* (Toronto) 71.9 (1998.05.29).

[7] Don Miller, "Chinese challenge," *Marketing* (Toronto) 111.10 (2006.03.13).

[8] Eve Lazarus, "Vancouver's Driving Force," *Marketing* (Toronto) 111.28 (2006.08.28-2006.09.04).

[9] Reported by David Ley, *Millionaire Migrants: Trans-Pacific Life Lines* (Chichester, U.K.: Wiley-Blackwell, 2010), 238; citing M. Jiménez, "Immigrants Face Growing Economic Mobility Gap," *The Globe and Mail*, 2008.10.08, A1, and Jack Jedwab, *The Changing Vertical Mosaic: Intergenerational Comparisons in Income on the Basis of Visible Minority Status in Canada, 2006* (Montreal: The Association for Canadian Studies, 2008).

The picture that one derives from these statistics is that Chinese Canadians possess significance economic wealth, greater than the average Canadian, which, of course, is surprising given their poor economic situation of earlier times. Information on banking adds to this picture. It seems that in this area too, they are doing well, again even better than average. The most apparent indication from Canadian banks that confirms the significant wealth of Chinese Canadians is the services that are dedicated to them. Peter Li notes the widespread existence of these services as early as 1997 when the Bank of Montreal was already providing Chinese speaking tellers at one hundred twenty-five branches across Canada. Li quotes from an interview with Mr. Tung Chan, vice president of Toronto Dominion's Asian Banking Division, who described the Chinese immigrant community as a "strong, profitable, growing niche" in the financial market and as tending "to have personal accounts with higher deposits than other personal accounts."[10] The claim for larger deposits is also supported by a report that half the twenty thousand clients of the Vancouver Chinatown branch of HSBC Canada (formerly Hongkong Bank of Canada) each had $3 million in deposits in 1994.[11] These deposits would have been augmented by transfers from Hong Kong, which in the case of one bank were reported to average more than ninety thousand dollars in 1995-96 as well as transfers from Taiwan, which in one month–following provocative PRC naval exercises off the coast of Taiwan-were reported to be one hundred million.[12] Also, Chinese Canadians, because of their desire to save for their children's education and the future, have been reported to be big savers, which contributed to the view that the average Asian Canadian's saving account was twice the size of the average Canadian's in 1998.[13]

More than ten years later, Canadian banks were still making strong efforts to attract Chinese Canadian patronage.

[10] Li, *The Chinese*, 128.

[11] The report cites David Bond, the bank's chief economist in Vancouver (Philippe Le Corre, "Culture: Canada's Hong Kong," *Far Eastern Economic Review* [Hong Kong] 157.6 [1994.02.10]).

[12] Ley, *Millionaire Migrants*, 70-71.

[13] Chu.

CIBC was reported to serve more than half a million Chinese-Canadian clients in one hundred ten branches across Canada with Cantonese and Mandarin speaking staff, to have introduced Chinese language capabilities on its network of thirty-eight thousand automated banking machines in January 2008, and to offer a Chinese language website and interactive access system.[14] Moreover, such services were offered by four of Canada's five big banks.

A further indication of Chinese Canadian wealth found in the banking sector is the presence of foreign banks that focus on serving Chinese Canadians. Largest among these and all foreign banks in Canada is HSBC Canada, which has one hundred nine branches and had offered the Immigrant Investor Program to assist those interested in immigrating there.[15] Other examples include the Industrial and Commercial Bank of China (Canada), which took over the Bank of East Asia (Canada) in 2010 and has ten branches and offices in Canada.[16] The Bank of China (Canada) with eleven branches promotes the development and growth of trade and economic relationships between Canada and China where it operates an extensive domestic branch network.[17] CTC Bank of Canada has three branches in Canada. Headquartered in Taiwan, it has a network of more than one hundred branches there.[18] Taiwanese Credit Union in Toronto, which has more than $10 million in assets, has a mandate to serve Ontario residents of Taiwan origin.[19] These banks service those having financial dealings with China, Taiwan, and Hong Kong, which would in great part

[14] Canada Newswire, "CIBC celebrates Chinese New Year with client reception in Toronto," 2008.02.12.

[15] HSBC Canada website, *www.hsbc.ca/1/2/contact-us/atm-branch-locations*, accessed 2015.01.18.

[16] Industrial and Commercial Bank of China (Canada) website, *www.icbk.ca/index_per_con.jsp?screen=menu5.sub7*, accessed 2015.01.18.

[17] Bank Of China (Canada) website, *www.boc.cn/cn/html/canada/en_s1.html*, accessed 2008.04.23.

[18] CTC Bank of Canada website, *www.ctcbank.com/eng.htm*, accessed 2008.04.23.

[19] Taiwan Credit Union website, *www.tctcu.com*, accessed 2008.04.22.

be immigrants to Canada from these places. The fact that the banks believe it profitable to establish branches in Canada is evidence of the economic value of providing these services, and consequently further proof of the wealth of Chinese Canadians. Together with the similar attention given Chinese Canadians by domestic banks and the known facts of Chinese Canadian wealth, they provide strong evidence for confirming the significant wealth of Chinese Canadians, and thus corresponding potential for economic achievement.

2.2 Physical Expansion of Chinese Canadian Commercial Activity

Chinese Canadian commercial activity had historically been limited to the economic enclaves that they have established and ethnic businesses, such as laundries, restaurants, and sundry stores, that offered the best, and sometimes only means to support themselves. In spite of what were often harsh conditions, namely long working hours, low income, and hostility from non-Chinese, establishing commercial operations was obviously an important step in improving Chinese Canadian economic status. It was a source of income, gave Chinese Canadians control of property that could be used for other purposes,[20] and demonstrated the contribution of Chinese Canadians to mainstream society, though many members of the society did not recognize it as such.

Chinese Canadian commercial activity commenced when supply centres for newly arrived Chinese workers were established in urban settings. They became known as Chinatowns and the first was in Victoria, British Columbia around 1860.[21] With the movement of Chinese Canadians eastward, they became an identifiable feature of many Canadian cites and developed examples of ethnic enclave economies. Today, changes in these enclave economies are

---

[20] For example, laundries and grocery stores would double as residences. Some workers would even sleep on top of the washing equipment.

[21] Paul Yee, *Chinatown : an illustrated history of the Chinese communities of Victoria, Vancouver, Calgary, Winnipeg, Toronto, Ottawa, Montreal and Halifax* (Toronto: J. Lorimer, 2005), 26-27.

evidence of increasing Chinese Canadian influence on the nation's economy.

David H. Kaplan and Wei Li have described the ethnic enclave economy as "a parallel economy, less dependent on the mainstream economy, that offers opportunities as rewards to members of a particular ethnic group."[22] As well, they have described the characteristics of "ethnic ownership, [ethnic] employment, [ethnic] customer base, sectoral specialization, and spatial concentration" as the "five primary criteria for identifying an ethnic economy."[23] Canadian Chinatowns have exhibited these characteristics by housing a micro economy that was mainly owned and operated by, and provided services for Chinese Canadians. Moreover, given the restrictions placed on Chinese Canadian placement of business operations and occupations, Chinese Canadian employment became concentrated in a small number of industries and businesses within these areas. These two phenomena are what Kaplan and Li refer to as "sectoral specialization" and "spatial concentration."

Today, these ethnic economic enclaves are changing. Non-traditional businesses are recognizing the value of being situated within or close to Chinatown to meet the needs of its residents and those who work there, and in the process of doing so they are hiring Chinese Canadians into professions that were once denied them. This is especially true of the large Canadian banks that have situated within or near Chinatowns. Furthermore, even with a resident population that is almost completely ethnically Chinese, Chinatown restaurants are still able to attract large numbers of non Chinese from surrounding offices for lunch and supper during the week, so the customer base is diversifying as well, thereby going beyond the ethnic customer base that is one criterion for an economic enclave.

Nevertheless, the aspect that most clearly manifests change and thus evidences the economic influence of Chinese Canadians is the spatial concentration of the ethnic economic enclave. Many of the Chinatowns in Canadian cities have, over the last twenty years, spread beyond their boundaries. Now,

---

[22] "Introduction: The Places of Ethnic Economies," in *Landscapes of the Ethnic Economy,* ed. David H. Kaplan and Wei Li (Lanham, Maryland: Rowman & Littlefield, c.2006), 3.

[23] *Ibid.*

instead of the Chinatown that was relegated to the worse part of town, contained by public pressure, or even legislated to remain in a certain area, Chinatowns are expanding from their present boundaries and establishing new ethnic groupings separate from the earlier locations of Chinatown.

It is ironic, but all the more emphatic because of this, that early Canadian Chinatowns were pressured by various attempts to restrict them. In 1910 a group of angry citizens represented by Alderman James Short asked the city government to move Calgary's Chinatown and proposed setting the Chinese residents apart as one would isolate someone in a hospital.[24] The same year in Lethbridge, following similar public demands to restrict Chinese Canadian businesses, the city government passed a bylaw confining Chinese laundries to a certain section of town.[25]

The physical expansion of Chinatowns is most easily seen in creation of new Chinatowns and the construction of Chinese shopping centers. Vancouver, Toronto, and Montreal have all seen the creation of groupings of residences, shops, and community organizations outside of their original Chinatowns and primarily catering to Chinese Canadians; these new communities have become their second and subsequent Chinatowns. In addition, these cities and Calgary have constructed Chinese shopping centers outside of the older Chinatowns, in neighbourhoods that have large, Chinese Canadian populations. These shopping centers, likewise, cater mainly to Chinese Canadians, offer a large number of products and services that would be identified as Chinese, and are generally operated by Chinese Canadians.

The building of these shopping centers is evidence for the increasing economic influence of Chinese Canadians. For example, as of 2006 there were more than sixty-five Chinese shopping centers in the Greater Toronto Area with a few more

---

[24] J. Brian Dawson, *Moon Cakes in Gold Mountain: From China to the Canadian Plains* (Calgary: Detselig Enterprises Ltd., 1991), 48. The irony is even more profound in that the name of James Short is attached to a park that marks the southern edge of Calgary's Chinatown.

[25] The fact that Chinatown in Lethbridge today exists in name only, as few Chinese Canadians, if any, reside there, puts in relief the expansion of Chinatowns in other cities that were not so extreme in their treatment of them.

under construction,[26] and two designated Chinatowns.[27] Prior to
1972 there was only one Chinatown and no Chinese shopping
centers in Toronto.[28] Similarly in the Vancouver suburb of
Richmond prior to 1990 there were no Chinese shopping
centers, but by 1998 twelve had been constructed.[29]

Interestingly, the creation of subsequent Chinatowns and
construction of large numbers of Chinese shopping centers also
reflects another aspect of the economic development brought
about by Chinese Canadians. They are not only an extension of
Chinese Canadian economic influence; they are also indications
of the integration of Chinese Canadian economic activities into
the Canadian mainstream. Based on a sample of six hundred
thirty-four medium and large Chinese Canadian owned
businesses, Lucia Lo shows that in 2006 in some areas of
Toronto, Chinese Canadian retail establishments were present
in "proportions much higher than what the local population
needs," leading her to conclude that Chinese Canadian
businesses were serving both Chinese and non-Chinese
clients.[30] She further concludes that Chinese Canadian-owned
"businesses are diversifying and the Chinese ethnic economy
has moved away from its traditional focus on consumer goods

---

[26] Lucia Lo, "Changing Geography of Toronto's Ethnic Economy," in
Landscapes of the Ethnic Economy, ed. David H. Kaplan and Wei Li (Lanham,
Maryland: Rowman & Littlefield, 2006), 86. These centers include the Pacific
Mall/Market Village complex, which is the largest Chinese shopping center in
North America (*ibid.*, 89).

[27] Lucia Lo, "Suburban Housing and Indoor Shopping: The Production of
Contemporary Chinese Landscape in Toronto," in *From Urban Enclave to
Ethnic Suburb: New Asian Communities in Pacific Rim Countries*, ed. Wei Li
(Honolulu: University of Hawaii Press, 2006), 139. The two Chinatowns were
Central Chinatown composed of Old and New Chinatown in close enough
proximity to be considered as one, and East Chinatown. Refer to Yee, 81-82.

[28] Yee, 84 and Lo, "Suburban," 147-49.

[29] David W. Edgington, Michael A. Goldberg, and Thomas A. Hutton, "Hong
Kong Business, Money, and Migration in Vancouver, Canada," in *From Urban
Enclave to Ethnic Suburb: New Asian Communities in Pacific Rim Countries*,
ed. Wei Li (Honolulu: University of Hawaii Press, 2006), 171-72.

[30] "Changing," 91-93.

and services to one that covers nearly the whole array of industrial activities."[31]

Consequently, the concept of an economic enclave has become less suitably applied to Chinese Canadian economic activity. Kaplan and Li admit that it was likely that this would take place, granting that what once could be classified as ethnic economic enclaves are now mostly mixed or integrated economies, and have become an "indispensable part of the mainstream economy."[32] In the case of Chinese shopping centers, ownership, employment, customer base, and sectoral specialization have all diversified. Moreover, spatial concentration has changed the most; Chinese economic activity is no longer isolated to Chinatowns or single businesses outside them. This is another clear indication of Chinese Canadian economic strength.

2.3. Marketing to Chinese Canadians

The marketing that targets Chinese Canadians is further evidence of their economic strength. Ad agencies and their clients would not be directing their advertising toward Chinese Canadians if market research did not reveal a potential market. Aware of the statistics on home ownership and household spending, in fact uncovering many of them, they see a likely profit to be made selling to a group that has the wealth and propensity to buy.

Again, the situation was known early; by 1994 there were forty advertising firms in Toronto that were specifically marketing to Chinese Canadians.[33] Peter Li and Yahong Li have estimated that the total advertising revenue for Chinese newspapers in Toronto in 1996 was $34.5 million, a disproportionately large share of which was placed by non-Chinese businesses.[34] They also noted that "about 75 percent of

---

[31] *Ibid.*, 90.

[32] P. 5.

[33] Noakes.

[34] "The Consumer Market of the Enclave Economy: A Study of Advertisements in a Chinese Daily Newspaper in Toronto," *Canadian Ethnic Studies* 31.2 (1999), 43 and 53.

the advertisements had to do with major purchase items or specialized professional services. It is clear that these were targeted to a relatively affluent Chinese consumer market."[35] In describing the general reasons for the large amount of advertising directed at Chinese Canadians, it has been pointed out that in "Canada 'ethnic marketing' most often means Chinese marketing. The Chinese community has the best communications infrastructure and has high concentrations of population within Canada's three biggest urban areas. They also have, on average, fairly highly disposable incomes. And they can be particularly important markets for specific categories."[36]

These markets have led to the creation of individual ad companies. For example, Can-Asian Advertising of Markham, Ontario offered advertising services that targeted Chinese markets in Canada, United States, Hong Kong, China, and Taiwan. Ford Motors of Canada contracted them to change the conceptions that Chinese Canadians have had of North American automobiles.[37] The existence of these markets also supports the existence of the Chinese Canadian Advertising & Media Association (CCAMMA), which was founded in 1987 in Toronto. Originally established to facilitate communications among Chinese Canadian communications professionals, its membership of two hundred now includes non Chinese. CCAMMA continues to focus on Chinese marketing communication and takes as its mission "to serve as a hub between the Canadian businesses and Asian Canadian marketing professionals."[38]

With awareness of the wealth of Chinese Canadians, companies wishing to sell to them and the marketing companies that they have contracted to assist have implemented various measures to promote their products and services. For some, the

---

[35] *Ibid.*, 49.

[36] Patrick Lejtenyi, "The Marketing Report on Multicultural Marketing," *Marketing Magazine* 106.22 (2001.06.04).

[37] *Ibid.*

[38] Chinese Canadian Advertising & Media Association website, *www.ccamma.com/*, accessed 2008.04.23, and *www.ccamma.com/profile.html*, accessed 2015.01.18.

direct approach has been successful. Fields Auto Group, upon
discovering that 45 percent of buyers of the BMWs they sold in
Vancouver were Chinese Canadians, hired salespeople fluent in
Chinese and used a Chinese language ad agency and media.
About forty of their one hundred employees were fluent in
Chinese.[39] Another BMW dealer Brian Jessel, seeing that half
his customers were Chinese Canadian, put 40 percent of his
marketing budget into advertising to Asian Canadians. The
dealership employed the top three salespeople in Canada of
whom two were Chinese.[40]

Volkswagen Canada has used more subtle means to appeal
to Chinese Canadians. After discovering that drivers from Hong
Kong could not maneuver well in snowy conditions, they offered
potential customers appropriate driving clinics in Vancouver
and Toronto with Chinese speaking instructors. It also used
Chinese cultural symbols, red eggs, in its advertisements,
which, according to Volkswagen's district manager for sales in
BC, helped increase Volkswagen sales to Chinese Canadian
consumers by 25 percent in Vancouver and 20 percent in
Toronto.[41]

Another widely used means to appeal to Chinese Canadian
customers is the sponsoring of important cultural events. The
benefits of doing so became apparent early. The Bank of
Montreal has been sponsoring the Yee Hong (an eldercare
provider) Dragon Ball since its inception in 1989.[42] By 1997
Canadian corporations were donating millions of dollars to
support elaborate Chinese New Year festivities when a few
years prior these were limited to parades and fund raisers.[43] By
2000, the Chinese New Year Festival, then sponsored by now
defunct Canadian Airlines, had become the largest trade and

[39] Lindsay Chappell, "Selling Beemers to Chinese: One dealer's lesson,"
Automotive News 6240 (2007.01. 29)

[40] Lazarus, "Vancouver's Driving Force."

[41] Chu.

[42] Discover China Dragon Ball 2008 website, *www.yeehongdragonball.org*,
accessed 2008.04.25.

[43] Paulette Peirol, "Corporate Cash Registers Ring in Chinese New Year," *The
Globe and Mail,* 1997.02.07, A1 and A8.

consumer show in British Columbia. Together with a similar festival in Toronto, they were attracting three hundred fifty thousand visitors and generating reported economic spin offs of twenty million dollars a year. Other major corporate sponsors included Canadian Airlines International, Ford of Canada, United Parcel Service, Telus, Bell Canada, Shoppers Drug Mart, Fairchild Media Group, and Crowne Plaza Hotels. These sponsors were rewarded with direct access to potential customers in a prestigious venue designed to promote and sell their products.[44] Another example of sponsorship is the Chinese New Year reception that the Canadian Imperial Bank of Commerce has held every year in Vancouver and Toronto.[45]

Once one considers the amount of marketing that aims to appeal to Chinese Canadians and the variety of measures employed to earn their patronage, their wealth and economic strength become more apparent. More than thirty-four million dollars in advertising placed in Chinese language newspapers in 1996 in Toronto alone, most of it selling large ticket items; the large number of advertising marketing firms focusing on the Chinese Canadian market; the hiring of Chinese speaking sales staff; and the innovative measures, such as large sponsorships; all of these are evidence of economic strength that large Canadian corporations became aware of as early as 1989.

2.4. Large Chinese Canadian Economic Organizations

The increasing size and diversity of Chinese Canadian economic organizations are also indicative of their increasing economic strength. They evidence increasing business activity and wealth because a business requires a high degree of organization in order to attain optimal performance and utilization of resources. The forms of organization vary and they

---

[44] Wyng Chow, "Vancouver's Chinese New Year Consumer Show Largest in BC," *The Vancouver Sun*, 2000.01. 29, B9.

[45] "CIBC Celebrates Chinese New Year with Client Reception in Toronto," *Canada Newswire*, 2008.02.12. Evidence of the bank's sponsorship of Chinese New Year celebrations could still be found in 2014 and 2015 ("Ring in the Year of the Horse at CIBC LunarFest in British Columbia," *The Globe and Mail*, 2014.01.10, and "CNY Celebrations 2015," *www.cnycelebrations.ca*, accessed 2015.01.18).

are not restricted to bigger more complex businesses; they also include the associations that businesses and entrepreneurs set up among themselves in order to promote business success.

There are already large Chinese Canadian enterprises. These include established firms that were taken over, such as Li Ka-shing's purchase of Husky Oil; joint ventures between foreign and domestic Chinese entrepreneurs, such as T & T Supermarket; and the building of companies purely by Chinese Canadians, such as the H.Y. Louie Company. In fact, research reveals that large Chinese Canadian companies are common. Based on a sample of six hundred thirty-four medium and large Chinese Canadian owned businesses in Toronto, Lucia Lo found that Chinese Canadian firms are expanding. She notes that, although the majority of Chinese Canadian companies "are as small as most other businesses in the general economy, one out of fifty Chinese firms hires more than two hundred workers and one tenth have annual sales of over US$10 million. More significantly, while Chinese firms account for only one thousandth of the Toronto businesses, they account for 1 percent of the largest one thousand Toronto firms."[46]

The example of H.Y. Louie Company is revealing in three ways. For one, the company controls some well known Canadian enterprises; two, it demonstrates that major economic achievements by Chinese Canadian companies can be overlooked; and, three, it shows the potential for even greater economic influence by Chinese Canadian businesses. H.Y. Louie is a wholesale grocer that was formed around 1903. Under the direction of Tong Louie (d. 1998), a son from the second generation of the family in Canada, it has taken control of and built London Drugs, which has seventy-eight stores across the four western Canadian provinces; become the franchiser and distributor for all, and owner of some Market Place Independent Grocers Alliance (IGA) stores in British Columbia; operates one of the largest grocery wholesale and distribution companies in British Columbia; and established London Air Services.[47] In 2002 the family business was ranked as the

---

[46] Lucia Lo, "Changing Geography," 90.

[47] Ken MacQueen, "Louie, Brandt (Profile)," *Maclean's*, 2002.03.25; see also Ernest G. Perrault, *Tong: The Story of Tong Louie, Vancouver's Quiet Titan* (Madeira Park, British Columbia: Harbour Publishing, 2002).

fourth largest corporation with headquarters in British Columbia,[48] and in 2006, Brandt Louie, Tong's older son, was ranked twenty-ninth on the list of Canada's one hundred richest people.[49]

In responding to the claim that most British Columbians had not heard of him, Brandt Louie states that this is his preference, that his aim is to be nondescript.[50] Nevertheless, the vision of his grandfather and founder of the company Hok Yat Louie was hardly moderate. He saw "a time when oriental and occidental trading methods might meet on common ground, and a Pacific Rim economy would present great opportunities."[51] This vision and the teachings that he passed down to his family have formed guidelines that have helped the company to grow. One would also expect that other Chinese Canadian companies will be posting similar achievements based on the farsighted efforts of their founders.

Besides creating large commercial operations, Chinese Canadians have also created large nonprofit organizations that, nevertheless, demonstrate the strength among them, strength that has contributed to their economic achievements. They are often organizations of Chinese Canadians with similar occupations or goals formed to mutually assist one another or contribute to society in more general ways. Examples of these organizations include the Chinese Real Estate Professionals Association of British Columbia that has a membership of approximately three hundred agents,[52] the Hong Kong-Canada Business Association with approximately one thousand three-hundred members,[53] and the Chinese Canadian Advertising &

---

[48] Perrault, 181.

[49] "Association of Chinese Canadian Entrepreneurs," *Canadian Business* (Toronto) 79.8 (2006.04.10-23).

[50] MacQueen.

[51] Perrault, 61.

[52] Chinese Real Estate Professionals Association of British Columbia webpage, *www.crepa.ca/index.php*, accessed 2015.01.18.

[53] The Hong Kong-Canada Business Association, National, website, "About Us/The HKCBA Story," *national.hkcba.com/story.html*, accessed 2015.01.22.

Media Association with two hundred members.[54] Eighty-five
such Chinese Canadian business associations were identified in
a survey published in 2004.[55]

Two of these organizations, the Association of Chinese
Canadian Entrepreneurs (ACCE) and the Chinese Professionals
Association of Canada (CPAC), are particularly active. They not
only exhibit the vitality of Chinese Canadian businesses, they
also show the wealth and potential for greater wealth
generation among them. ACCE was founded in 1995 and its
mission is to encourage entrepreneurship and to strengthen the
competitiveness of Chinese Canadian businesses in the global
market. It has presented the Chinese-Canadian Entrepreneur
Awards since 1997 as a means of achieving this goal. One
initiative has been to assist entrepreneurs to explore and
develop trade potential in the Asian Pacific Region for
Canadian goods and services.[56]

The Chinese Professionals Association of Canada (CPAC)
was founded in 1992 and has more than thirty thousand
members. Among its objectives is to provide opportunities for
interaction among Chinese Canadian professionals and to
facilitate members' career and professional development.[57]
CPAC also has a centre for international exchange and
cooperation. Each year it had been sending several business
delegations to China to visit industry developers and science
parks, participate in high tech expos and trade shows, and
network with government officials there.[58] It now seems to focus

[54] Chinese Canadian Advertising & Media Association website,
www.ccamma.com/, accessed 2015.01.18.

[55] Asia Pacific Foundation of Canada, "The Role of Asian Ethnic Business
Associations in Canada," Canada Asia Commentary 35 (2004), 3.

[56] Association of Chinese Canadian Entrepreneurs website, "About ACCE,"
www.acce.ca/about.html, accessed 2015.01.18.

[57] Chinese Professionals Association of Canada's website, "About Us,"
www.cpac-canada.ca/?page_id=79, accessed 2015.01.19.

[58] Wenhong Chen and Barry Wellman, "Doing Business at Home and Away:
Policy Implications of Chinese-Canadian Entrepreneurship," Canada in Asia
Series, Asia Pacific Foundation of Canada, Apr. 2007, 17.

more on training Chinese Canadian professionals and locating talent in China.[59]

Whether for-profit enterprises, such as London Drugs, or nonprofit organizations, such as the ACCE, the existence of large scale Chinese Canadian organizations is another indication of the potential, if not the actuality, of their economic achievements. Already there are a number of companies, and their number is increasing, with large operations that are having an impact far beyond what has been the historical standard for Chinese Canadian businesses. Furthermore, the nonprofit business associations that Chinese Canadian businesspeople have formed indicate a sophistication in preparing for even greater growth. Within these associations, businesses will be able to develop the appropriate resources that will support this growth.

3. History of Chinese Canadian Economic Activity

Early Chinese arrivals to Canada were directed to filling the needs of a developing country. Canada was establishing a national infrastructure and needed cheap labour to achieve this. Conditions in China aspired to make work in Canada attractive even with the harsh conditions and relatively low wages for Chinese immigrants. Nevertheless, even with these conditions, Chinese Canadians had a significant impact. Their contributions were recognized by Sir Matthew Begbie, British Columbia's Chief Justice, in evidence presented to the 1885 Royal Commission on Chinese Immigration. He stated that the Chinese immigrant had been absolutely indispensable in construction of the transnational railroad, was employed extensively in laborious parts of the coal mines, constituted three quarters of the salmon cannery working force, was a large majority of those employed in the gold mines, and produced the greater part of the vegetables grown in British Columbia.[60]

Furthermore, since their arrival, Chinese Canadians had demonstrated independence in earning their livings. For example, some of the first arrivals worked abandoned gold

---

[59] Chinese Professionals Association of Canada's website, "International Exchange Centre," *www.cpac-canada.ca / ?page_id=49*, accessed 2015.01.19.

[60] Cited in Li, *The Chinese*, 29.

fields. There were enough astute among them to set up businesses catering to the needs of fellow Chinese arriving to work in the various industries, such as the railroad, thereby contributing to the creation in Victoria of Canada's first Chinatown.

Another factor in creating independence among Chinese Canadians was that they had to accept exploitation in operating businesses such as laundries, restaurants, and retail stores. Their operations demanded long hours with low reward. In general, the lack of acceptance of the Chinese immigrant meant that he could not demand market prices for his labour, which had the further consequence of making him even less accepted among his fellow workers or businessmen who saw them as competitors or poor customers. As well, often there were no other alternatives for Chinese Canadians as the lack of acceptance extended to barring them from participating in many occupations. However, in spite of the overall prejudice, early Chinese Canadians continued to provide services to Canadian society.

The period between the early arrival and 1967, the year all restrictions to Chinese immigration to Canada were eliminated, saw the formation of ethnic enclaves, popularly known as Chinatowns. Formed because Chinese Canadians were often segregated, sometimes by law, from other Canadians and to provide mutual assistance in absence of general societal support, these enclaves would become economic enclaves that assisted in the survival of Chinese Canadians and also provided services for the broader society. They spawned the so called ethnic industries, such as Chinese restaurants, grocers, convenience stores, herbalists, and so on that would not only allow Chinese Canadians to survive, but would, over time, develop into major providers of services to other Canadians and contribute to their ethnic enclaves becoming relatively prosperous.

The removal of all racial bias from Canada's immigration laws in 1967 led to the entry of many Chinese immigrants with professional and technical skills, which, in turn, led to more employment of Chinese Canadians in related occupations and relatively fewer Chinese Canadians working in low earning businesses or occupations.[61]

The Business Immigration Program marked the next significant change in Chinese Canadian influence on Canada's economy. Business immigrants from Hong Kong, Taiwan, and The People's Republic of China comprised 53.9 percent of the total number of business immigrants to Canada from 2000-2005 and 51.4 percent of the total from 1986-2005, a period during which all business immigrants invested nearly $8.7 billion in total in Canada.[62] From 1986 to 1996 business immigrants from Hong Kong and Taiwan invested more than $2.7 billion in Canada and created or maintained 38,624 jobs.[63] In 1997, Chinese business immigrants invested more than $1.6 billion in British Columbia alone.[64] The same predominance was reflected in the proportion of Chinese Canadians among immigrant entrepreneurs in Ontario, where in 1986-87 they constituted 58.5 percent of immigrant entrepreneurs, a figure that researchers describe as an extraordinarily large discrepancy.[65]

These immigrations led to major individual investments in Canada. Li Ka-shing purchased and developed the 86 Expo site

---

[61] Lucia Lo, *et al.*, show that in Toronto where approximately 40 percent of Chinese Canadians reside, laundries and cleaners dropped from 32.6 percent in 1966 to zero percent in 1994 of total Chinese Canadian businesses. Food and grocers fell from 18.1 percent to 9.3 percent. Restaurants decreased from 38.8 percent to 13.8 percent. In contrast, financial, real estate, and other business services increased from 1.3 percent to 16.2 percent. Medical and other professional services rose from 0.7 percent to 10.9 percent. ("Immigrants' Economic Status in Toronto: Rethinking Settlement and Integration Strategies," CERIS Working Paper No. 15, 2000.03.29.)

[62] Citizenship and Immigration Canada, "Home/Research and Statistics/Statistics," *www.cic.gc.ca/English/resources/statistics/bus-stats2005.asp#table 6*, accessed 2008.03.24.

[63] Li, *The Chinese*, 132.

[64] David W. Edginton, Michael A. Goldberg, and Thomas A. Hutton, "Hong Kong Business, Money, and Migration in Vancouver, Canada," in *From Urban Enclave to Ethnic Suburb: New Asian Communities in Pacific Rim Countries*, ed. Wei Li (Honolulu: University of Hawai'i Press, 2006),176.

[65] Martin N. Marger and Constance A. Hoffman, "Ethnic Enterprise in Immigrant Participation in the Small Business Sector," *International Migration Review* 26.3 (Autumn 1992), 971 and 977.

in Vancouver and took control of Husky Oil. Thomas Fung of Fairchild Holdings pioneered the development of Chinese shopping malls in Richmond, B.C. and established the national Chinese language TV network, Fairchild TV.[66]

These investments, though well known, are only the tip of the iceberg. Moving into the twenty-first century, Chinese Canadian economic development has produced a number of flourishing industries and not just ones supplying ethnic demand. For example, Chinese Canadians have created a number of highly successful property development and management companies. They are also important participants in the food and high tech industries. At the same time, they have maintained and expanded ethnic industries, such as Traditional Chinese Medicine.

Presently, Chinese Canadians are leading Canada into a diversification of its trading partners. As the economy of China has grown, it has become even more important for Canada to develop its trading relations with it. Chinese Canadians, with a network of contacts, appropriate cultural skills, and their entrepreneurial attitudes, have shown themselves able to foster trade between Canada and China and other parts of Asia. Ironically, the history of the economic influence of Chinese Canadians is one that has run the gamut of being suppressed to becoming leaders. In the passage, though, Chinese Canadians have shown themselves to be economic builders and contributed considerably to Canada through their achievements.

4. Recent Examples of Economic Achievement

There are a number of examples of recent economic achievements of Chinese Canadians. This essay will briefly describe three: the restaurant industry, the food distribution business, and philanthropy; then move on to detail areas where the economic achievements of Chinese Canadians are most pronounced.

---

[66] Edgington et al., 175, 177. Including his son Victor's share, the family of Li Ka-shing took control of 95 percent of Husky Oil in 1991 (Cathryn Motherwell, The Globe and Mail, "Li Ka-shing Rescues Husky with $600-million Bailout. Sale Will Help Ease Nova's Long-awaited Restructuring," 1991.10.24, B1).

4.1 Restaurant Industry

Historically, the restaurant industry has been one of the main venues by which Chinese around the world have contributed to the societies within which they reside and, thereby, earned the right to be supported by those societies. Simply speaking, working in a restaurant has been one of the main ways ethnic Chinese have supported themselves. The Chinese in Canada have been no exception. In 1931 nearly 9 percent were restaurant keepers and more than 26 percent were waiters, cooks, and servants; arguably more than 30 percent were employed in restaurants.[67] In 1991, more than 18 percent were still working in service occupations and nearly 9 percent in managerial and administrative occupations some of which would have been in the restaurant industry.[68] Unlike other industries, such as laundries and small grocers that have become outmoded or replaced by large chain stores, restaurant operation has remained a viable venue by which Chinese Canadians could make a living.

Chinese restaurants are an easily identified component of the restaurants of major Canadian cities. They are also noticeable by their presence in small towns across the country and, by the fact, that they have historically advertised Chinese food, along with "Western" food, indicating that Chinese food has been popular for some time, even among less cosmopolitan clientele. Furthermore, this presence has produced an economic impact. The Ontario Chinese Restaurant Association for example, estimated that more than ten thousand people were directly employed in more than one thousand two hundred Chinese restaurants in Toronto in 1999.[69]

However, Chinese Canadian involvement in the restaurant industry has not been limited to making a living. They have continued their large scale involvement in the restaurant industry and changed the way they have historically operated in order to avail themselves of new opportunities. Peter Li notes

---

[67] Li, *The Chinese*, 52.

[68] Of note is the fact that Chinese Canadians were 50 percent more likely to be working in service occupations than other Canadians (*ibid.*, 120-21).

[69] Cited in Tony Wong, "New Canadians."

the growth in Chinese restaurant operations that has taken place in Richmond, British Columbia. He describes the transformation between 1981 and 1990 as dramatic and points out that small family operated businesses were replaced by large and luxurious Chinese restaurants catering to more affluent clienteles.[70]

An example of how Chinese Canadians have evolved in their restaurant operations is Mandarin Restaurant Franchise Corporation. Founded by a Taiwan immigrant, it has twenty-two restaurants and has created two thousand jobs across Ontario.[71] The restaurant has been honoured a number of times, receiving the *Toronto Sun* Reader's Choice Award for the best Chinese restaurant and buffet many times and been placed among the top hundred food companies in Canada by *Foodservice and Hospitality Magazine*. Mandarin is also careful to preserve its reputation. In order to become a franchisee, one must have worked in one of the existing restaurants for at least a year.[72]

4.2. Grocery stores

Another area within which Chinese Canadian economic influence has grown is in the operation of grocery stores. As with restaurants, this is an industry through which Chinese Canadians have contributed to the Canadian economy.[73] What has changed is that, although early Chinese Canadian operations were generally small, they are now developing into major ones with innovations putting them in a position to compete with major supermarket chains. One result of this is that Canadians are offered a variety of products that were not

---

[70] "Ethnic Enterprise in Transition: Chinese Business in Richmond, B.C., 1980-1990," *Canadian Ethnic Studies* 24.1 (1992), 131.

[71] Brian McKechnie, "Mandarin Celebrates Canada Day with Free Buffet in Ontario," Global News, 2014.07.01.

[72] Mandarin Restaurant Franchise Corporation website, *www.mandarinbuffet.com*, accessed 2008.05.11

[73] Brian Dawson provides figures showing that Chinese Canadians operated approximately 6.5 percent of the grocery stores in major cities in Alberta during the early twentieth century (230-32).

available before. Tan Louie became a pioneer in this evolution after becoming the owner of several and distributor for all IGA stores in British Columbia. He and others who followed him increased types and amounts of typically Chinese products, such as bean curd, frozen Chinese processed foods, fish, green leafy vegetables, and tropical fruits. It subsequently became commonplace to find large stores, several times the size of the neighbourhood Chinese grocery store, selling mostly Chinese products in many large Canadian cities. Today, Chinese grocery stores are benefitting from fact that Chinese Canadians, together with South Asian Canadians, have accounted for about one third—or $5.7 million—of grocery spending in Toronto and Vancouver and spend about $136 weekly, 9 percent higher than an average household for groceries.[74]

As quickly as they have progressed, it did not take long for the large Chinese grocery stores to be eclipsed by an even newer development, the Chinese supermarket chain. T & T Supermarket was founded and is headed by a Chinese Canadian Cindy Lee.[75] The first "T" stands for Tawa Supermarket Inc., a California-based Asian supermarket chain, the second "T" for Uni-President Enterprises Corp., the largest food group in Taiwan. Both are major shareholders in T & T Supermarket Inc. T & T is Canada's largest Asian supermarket chain with ten stores in Greater Vancouver, four stores in Alberta, and nine in Ontario, for a total of twenty-three.[76] In terms of sales, in 2008 it was the sixth largest supermarket chain in Canada with 0.3% of the total Canadian market.[77] A typical store is between thirty-two and fifty-one hundred square meters,[78] which is comparable to stores in major supermarket

---

[74] Marina Strauss, "Grocers Target Big-spending South Asian, Chinese Shoppers," *The Globe and Mail*, 2008.05.19.

[75] Michael Scott, "100 Influential Chinese-Canadians in B.C.," *Vancouver Sun*, 2006.10.21, C7.

[76] T & T website, "Our Stores," *www.tnt-supermarket.com/en*, accessed 2015.01.19.

[77] Euromonitor International: Local Company Profile, "T & T Supermarket Inc. - Retailing - Canada," Feb. 2008.

[78] Eve Lazarus, "Eastern Star," *Marketing* (Toronto), 112.18 (2007.09.24).

chains. In other ways, though, the stores differ from those of other large chains in containing an Asian deli, a Chinese BBQ department, tanks containing live seafood,[79] and thirty brands of soy sauce.[80] The mix of products varies according to the ethnic makeup of the area served by a T & T store. In order to appeal to South Asian and Filipino Canadians who have been shopping at T & T, the stores have been stocking more of their ethnic products.[81]

Even with stores reaching across the country, T & T could still have a much larger impact in Canada. Seventy percent of the grocery products sold in the T & T chain have been imported from Asia, a huge amount, estimated to be worth billions of dollars, which Canadian suppliers could be providing. T & T is willing to purchase from Canadian companies; however, most have been unwilling to adapt to Chinese Canadian standards, such as developing bilingual labels (Chinese/English), creating Chinese language posters, advertising in the Chinese media, and supporting events in the Chinese Canadian community.[82] The size of T & T is an achievement in itself, but the possibility of becoming a medium to persuade mainstream food suppliers to cater to Chinese Canadian clientele seems even more significant. John Scott, president of the Canadian Federation of Independent Grocers has stated that Asian Canadian customers "weren't being serviced by any cohesive organization" and that T & T has "done something unique and high quality."[83]

4.3. Philanthropy

---

[79] T & T website.

[80] Anthony Lorrayne, "East Meets West: Entrepreneur Marries His Chinese Heritage with Opportunities Offered by His New Canadian Homeland," *Financial Post* 10.40 (1997.10.4-6), T6.

[81] Strauss.

[82] Don Miller, "Chinese Challenge," *Marketing* (Toronto), 111.10 (2006.03.13): 24-26.

[83] Lazarus, "Eastern Star."

Interestingly, Chinese Canadian generous charitable contributions were some of the earliest indications of Chinese Canadians' economic achievements. For example, in "an action verging on sainthood, Lethbridge Chinese gave money for the construction of a clubhouse for the Great War Veterans' Association (precursor to the Royal Canadian Legion), despite that organization's virulent anti-Asian stance."[84] During World War II, when they were being denied many avenues to improve themselves and their own resources were limited, Chinese Canadians made surprisingly large donations to Canada's war effort. They bought a total of ten million dollars worth of Canadian Victory Bonds, the Chinese Canadian community in Victory being cited four times by the government for its extraordinary efforts.[85]

In fact, the spirit of giving was already well developed within the Chinese Canadian community. They had been donating to China's war effort, to an estimated sum of five million dollars,[86] prior to donating to Canada's. After the war, charitable efforts continued in support of Chinese Canadian community needs, such as the construction of cultural centres and the operation of social service agencies, and the relief of natural disasters in China. However, Chinese Canadians also began supporting non-Chinese causes. For example, in 1979, Victoria's Chinese Consolidated Benevolent Association donated nearly five thousand dollars for Vietnamese relief and sponsored a Vietnamese family of six to come to Victoria. In 1988 and 1989, it donated about three thousand dollars to the Handicapped Children's Clinic, Cancer Society, United Way, and other organizations.[87] The Chinese language media group

---

[84] Brian L. Evans, *The Other Side of Gold Mountain: Glimpses of Chinese Pioneer Life on the Prairies from the Wallace B. Chung and Madeline H. Chung Collection* (Edmonton: University of Alberta Libraries, 2010), 59.

[85] Wickberg, *et al.*, 200. It should be noted that Chinese Canadian generosity was not limited to financial donations. In spite of being denied many of the rights of average Canadians, over five hundred Chinese Canadians served in the Canadian armed forces, some as commissioned officers.

[86] *Ibid.*, 188-89.

[87] David Chuenyan Lai, *Chinese Community Leadership: Case Study of Victoria in Canada* (Singapore: World Scientific Publishing, 2010), 202.

Fairchild Media Group has been successful in securing Chinese Canadian support for mainstream causes including donations to children's hospitals in both Vancouver and Calgary, the Cancer Society, and Toys for Tots.[88]

Following Fairchild's example, other Chinese Canadian businesses have begun to contribute to mainstream charitable causes. Mandarin Restaurant Franchise Corporation donated fifty thousand dollars in 2007 to begin the CNIB's (Canadian National Institute for the Blind) Diversity program.[89] Milton Wong led a one hundred million-dollar campaign for the B.C. Cancer Foundation and was one of the first major business leaders in British Columbia to support negotiating land claims with First Nations.[90] Johnny Gon, chairman of Canasia Toys and Gifts Inc., has raised large amounts of money for cancer research and health care initiatives and was instrumental in setting up a relief campaign for families hurt by the Kamloops forest fire in 2003.[91] Besides making individual contributions, some Chinese Canadians have established foundations solely devoted to philanthropic work. The Chan Foundation of Canada was founded by two brothers who own GolfBC. This foundation largely funded the University of British Columbia's Chan Centre for the Performing Arts through a ten million-dollar gift.[92] David See-Chai Lam created the David and Dorothy Lam Foundation that has donated millions of dollars a year to causes

---

[88] Lloyd Sciban, "Chinese Language Media Across the West," in *Challenging Frontiers: The Canadian West*, ed. Lorry Felske and Beverly Rasporich (Calgary: University of Calgary Press, 2004), 285. For example, Fairchild in 2000 raised one hundred thousand dollars for the Alberta Children's Hospital (*Popular Lifestyle & Entertainment* 2000, 2-3).

[89] CNIB's website, "Support Us/Partnerships," *www.cnib.ca/en/support/companies/mandarin/Default.aspx*, accessed 2008.05.12.

[90] Charlie Smith, "Vancouver's Canadian-born Chinese in their 30s and 40s Make their Mark, No Small Thanks to Milton Wong," *straight.com*, 2012.01.18.

[91] Scott, C6.

[92] *Ibid.*, C1. The David Lam Management Research Library and the Choi Building (Asian Studies) are two other buildings donated to U.B.C. by Chinese Canadians.

in Vancouver, including the Sun Yat-Sen Gardens.[93] Gary Ho headed the Canadian arm of the Tzu Chi Foundation, which had two thousand one hundred active volunteers in British Columbia. Alongside donations totaling six million dollars to Canadian charities, the foundation provided nearly two million dollars to create the Tzu Chi Institute for Complementary Medicine at Vancouver General Hospital.[94] Annually, for twenty-six years, Chinese Canadians have donated to the BC Children's Hospital Foundation through the Chinese-Canadian Miracle Weekend. More than nine hundred thousand dollars was raised in 2014.[95] Not only do Chinese Canadians have a long history of philanthropy in Canada, they have become major donors contributing as individuals and through the foundations that they have founded. This record is a testimony to their economic achievement.

5. Areas of Obvious Economic Achievement

There are at least four areas where the economic achievements of Chinese Canadians are more obvious; not necessarily because the amounts of money circulating in these areas are huge, though that is true in some cases, but also because Chinese Canadians have a high profile in these areas. The four areas are Traditional Chinese Medicine (TCM), Chinese language media, business investment, and property development. The first two are described in chapters devoted to them within this book, so they will only be touched on briefly here. The latter two will be discussed in more detail.

At first glance, one may not recognize the economic impact of TCM. The premises operated by practitioners tend to be small and concentrated in Chinatowns, which are only found in larger cities. However, one should keep in mind that this is a completely different medical system that, until recently, operated outside of highly regulated, mainstream medicine.

---

[93] *The Canadian Encyclopedia, s.v.* "Lam, David See-Chai."

[94] Scott, C6. The Tzu Chi Institute for Complementary Medicine ceased operations in 2003.

[95] BC Children's Hospital Foundation website, "Chinese-Canadian Miracle Weekend," *www.bcchf.ca/events/event-calendar/chinese-canadian-miracle-weekend*, accessed 2015.01.19.

Therefore, the establishment of any presence is still a major accomplishment. Furthermore, in the case of TCM that presence is substantial. For example, a passing search of the Yellow Pages directories for Toronto, Vancouver, and Calgary in 2014 uncovered, respectively, 495, 276, and 94 practitioners of acupuncture, for a total of 865. The same search for herbalist turns up 25, 20, and 8 in the respective cities, for a total of 53. A 2005 report estimated that 650 stores in Canada featured traditional Chinese medicines.[96]

The institutionalization of TCM in commercial endeavours is more evidence. Afexa Life Sciences was a large scale TCM manufacturer with headquarters in Calgary, Alberta until it was bought out by Valeant Pharmaceuticals International in 2011. It was capitalized for about fifty million dollars and its flagship product Cold-FX was said to be the top selling cold and flu remedy in Canada since 2004.[97] Other Afexa products are said to strengthen the immune system and improve memory and concentration. These functions, and the company's mission to discover, develop, and commercialize natural therapeuticals that prevent disease and maintain good health, fit with the emphasis in TCM to maintain human physical and mental capacities.

Chinese language media is another system that lies outside the mainstream and is surprising in its impact. There are national networks of television and daily newspapers, along with local radio stations, broadcasters, and publishers, that all disseminate information in Chinese. As for the economic impact, the investment to build and costs to operate these different media, added to the charges for advertising that is done within them, are already impressive, and that is without

---

[96] "Healthy Choices Impact Food Product Sales," *Plant* (Willowdale, Ontario), 64.11 (2005.11.14), 35; citing a study sponsored by the Canadian Health Food Association, in cooperation with the Canadian Natural Products Association and the Canadian Homeopathic Pharmaceutical Association.

[97] "Cold-fx® Chosen Canada's # 1 Pharmacist Recommended Natural Cold Remedy for Fourth Straight Year. Recommended by 73% of Pharmacists Nationally According to Leading Pharmacy Magazine Survey," news release on COLD-FX website, citing AC Nielsen's MarketTrack Drug Service for Cold Remedies, natural Supplements & Vitamins categories, *www.cold-fx.ca/news_may5_09.htm*, accessed 2010.05.25.

considering other economic effects of being able to communicate among a large population, such as encouraging philanthropy.

In the following text, this chapter attempts to describe in more detail how Chinese Canadians have had and are having an economic impact in Canada. It investigates two areas, business investment and property development, that have large Chinese Canadian influence.

5.1. Business Investment

The topic of business investment provides a general perspective on Chinese Canadian economic impact that helps us better understand its size and character, and thus what Chinese Canadians have achieved in this area.

5.1.1 Business Immigrants

Canada has been accepting business immigrants since 1978. Business immigrants are provided expedited immigrant processing if, generally speaking, they can demonstrate that they will invest a certain amount of money or conduct a certain amount of business in Canada. The Business Immigration Program was expanded in 1985 and since then has attracted large numbers of foreign investors, who have contributed financially to the country. Chinese business immigrants from Hong Kong, Taiwan, and the People's Republic of China have dominated this program.[98] The criteria for qualifying have varied over the history of and categories within the program. The general criterion as of 2008 was to make a four hundred thousand dollar investment or to own and manage a business in Canada.[99]

Although the program is open to emigrants from any country without restriction, Chinese business immigrants have by far outweighed other immigrants in terms of total numbers and investment. In the years 1986 through 2005, Hong Kong (24,945; 28 percent), Taiwan (12,601; 14.1 percent), and the

---

[98] Li, *The Chinese*, 132,

[99] Citizenship and Immigration Canada website, "Home/Immigrating to Canada/Investors, entrepreneurs and self-employed persons," *www.cic.gc.ca/english/immigrate/business/index.asp*, accessed 2008.05.20.

People's Republic of China (8,282; 9.3 percent) have comprised 51.4 percent of the total number (89,114) of business immigrants to Canada.[100] This weighting was even more pronounced in later years; business immigrants from the People's Republic of China (1,665; 45.7 percent), Taiwan (310; 8.5 percent), and Hong Kong (86; 2.4 percent) comprised 56.6 percent of the total number of (3,642) business immigrants to Canada in 2005.[101]

The program created substantial investment in Canada. From 1986 to 2005 business immigrants in the investor category officially subscribed nearly $8.7 billion in Canada.[102] In 2005 alone, total subscriptions by immigrants in the investor category were $940 million; for the entrepreneur category more than $65.5 million was invested and 570 full time and 397 part time jobs were created.[103] It is also estimated that over the

---

[100] *Ibid.*, "Home/Research and Statistics/Statistics/Top Ten Source Countries for Business Immigrants Landings by Country of Last Permanent Residence (Principal Applicants Only) 1986-2005," *www.cic.gc.ca/English/resources/statistics/bus-stats2005.asp#table-3*, accessed 2008.05.20.

[101] *Ibid.*, "Home/Research and Statistics/Statistics/Top Ten Source Countries for Business Immigrants Landings by Country of Last Permanent Residence (Principal Applicants Only) 2005," *www.cic.gc.ca/English/resources/statistics/bus-stats2005.asp#table-1*, accessed 2008.05.20.

[102] Citizenship and Immigration Canada website, "Home/Research and Statistics/Statistics/Immigrant Investor Program, Fully Paid Subscriptions by Province, 1986-2005," *www.cic.gc.ca/English/resources/statistics/bus-stats2005.asp#table-6*, accessed 2008.05.20. There were three categories in the Business Immigration Program: investor, entrepreneur, and self employed. The numbers and total investment by the self employed were very small and of the two remaining, total subscriptions through the investor category were nearly five times higher than those through the entrepreneur category. Through the years 2000-2005, immigrants in the investor category subscribed over $3.6 billion to Canada and those in the entrepreneur category invested approximately $758.1 million (various tables found on the Citizenship and Immigration Canada website, "Home/Research and Statistics/Statistics"). The investor and entrepreneur programs were terminated in 2014 and a "start-up" program replaced them (Citizen and Immigration Canada website, "Business Immigration Program," *www.cic.gc.ca/english/helpcentre/results-by-topic.asp?st=6.3*, accessed 2014.01.19).

[103] *Ibid.*, "Home/Research and Statistics/Statistics/Immigrant Investor Program, Fully Paid Subscriptions by Province, 2005," *www.cic.gc.ca/English/resources/statistics/bus-stats2005.asp#table-5*; and

decade from 1988 to 1997, there was at least $35-$40 billion available to business immigrants in Vancouver.[104]

Mirroring their domination in numbers of successful applicants, Chinese business immigrants also dominated in the amounts invested into Canada. For example, of the $3.7 billion in capital brought to Canada between 1986 and 1996 by investor immigrants through the subscription of investment funds, about $1.5 billion can be attributed to Hong Kong investors and $364 million to Taiwan investors. Their investment is also estimated to have created or maintained 18,624 jobs.[105] The strength of Chinese Canadian investment is also apparent when one considers the relative wealth that Chinese business immigrants have had. When they entered Canada in the year 1986 through 1995, they had a net worth of $39.9 billion, which was more than 44 percent of the total wealth of all immigrants combined.[106]

Their investments were especially effective because they were concentrated in Ontario and British Columbia. Seventy-one million dollars was invested in Ontario in 1997, creating 2,264 jobs from just one of the business immigration programs that targeted entrepreneurs. Over half of that money came from Chinese immigrants.[107] It is further estimated that $331 million was transferred from Hong Kong to personal bank accounts in central Ontario and Greater Toronto in 1995-96, and $505 million to such accounts in British Columbia in the same year.[108]

---

ibid., "Home/Research and Statistics/Entrepreneur Program, Dollars Invested and Jobs Created, by Province, 2005," *www.cic.gc.ca/English/resources/statistics/bus-stats2005.asp#table-7*; both accessed 2008.05.20.

[104] Ley, *Millionaire Migrants*, 70.

[105] Li, *The Chinese,* 132.

[106] Lloyd Wong, "Globalization and Transnational Migration: A Study of Recent Chinese Capitalist Migration from the Asian Pacific to Canada," *International Society* 12.3 (Sept. 1997), 340.

[107] Tony Wong, "New Canadians."

[108] Li, *The Chinese,* 139.

Commenting on the effect of Chinese Canadian investment in Canada, Don Myatt, director of business immigration for the federal department of citizenship and immigration, recognized that it has been a saviour for the country, "You just have to look at how British Columbia survived the Canadian recession of the [early] '90s. They were protected largely because of the money flowing in from Asia."[109] Furthermore, from 1989 to 1996, when Toronto was undergoing periods of deep recession, the Chinese still managed to build more than fifty shopping centres throughout the city.[110]

Given the initial strength of Chinese Canadian investment, one would have thought that Canadians could have anticipated what was to follow. However, the growth of Chinese Canadian influence on the Canadian economy that the Business Immigration Program has led to does not seem to have been foreseen, and one wonders why not.

5.1.2 Individual Investments

Arising out the Business Immigration Program and running parallel to it, further Chinese Canadian investment has dwarfed the amounts required by the program. Much of the continued Chinese Canadian investment has been business immigrant capital joining forces with offshore capital to form syndicates for large projects. For example, Li Ka-shing and other Hong Kong investors purchased and developed the former Expo 86 site in Vancouver into Concord Pacific Place for a sum of $3 billion. President Asian Enterprises of Taiwan combined with President Canada Syndicated Incorporated, a Vancouver-based company that employed immigrant investor funds, to develop a large shopping and hotel complex in Richmond.[111]

---

[109] Quoted in Tony Wong, "New Canadians."

[110] Tony Wong, "New Canadians."

[111] Li, *s.v.* "Chinese," in *Encyclopedia of Canada's Peoples*, ed. Paul R. Magocsi, 364.

Li Ka-shing also purchased a majority shareholding in Calgary-based Husky Oil, a stake that was worth $12 billion.[112] Li was also invested in Canadian Imperial Bank of Commerce (CIBC) until he sold his $1.2 billion stake in 2005 and deposited the proceeds into Li's existing charities and the new Li Ka-shing (Canada) Foundation, which was to become Canada's second-biggest foundation.[113] His son, Victor Li, also made a near successful bid of $650 million in 2004 to control about one third of Air Canada.

Thomas Fung's investments are also having a large influence in Canada and far surpassing anything that would be required to immigrate. Fung is founder and chairman of Fairchild Group. His father, the late Fung King Hei, owned Hong Kong's largest securities brokerage, Sun Hung Kai.[114] Fairchild Group pioneered the development of Chinese shopping malls in Richmond, British Columbia among which Aberdeen Centre was worth one hundred fifty million.[115] It also owns a national media network that made a profit of $6.5 million in 2004.[116]

Phoebus Wong, another immigrant from Hong Kong, has set up a clothing and textile export business in Canada including two companies, Able Clothing Gear and Artex Sportswear, that have about two hundred employees. He is also president of the Chinese Canadian Textile and Garment Manufacturers and Marketers Association.[117] Able Clothing

---

[112] "Li Ka-shing," *Forbes.com*, *www.forbes.com/lists/2008/10/billionaires08_Li-Ka-shing_SO0W.html*, accessed 2008.05.21.

[113] Virginia Citrano, "Li Ka-shing: Hong Kong Billionaire Sells CIBC Stake, Sets Up Huge Charity," *Forbes.com*, 01.13.05, *www.forbes.com/2005/01/13/0113uutofacescan01.html*, accessed 2008.05.21.

[114] Edgington, *et al.*, 177.

[115] *Ibid.* and Thomas Boddy, " The Compelling Trajectory of Thomas Fung," *BC Business,* Mar. 2005, 24.

[116] Boddy, 26.

[117] Government of Ontario website, "Business Immigration Home/Success Stories/Phoebus Wong," *"www.2ontario.com/bi/s_PhoebusWong.asp*, accessed 2008.05.22.

invested about $3.5 million to open a factory in 2001 in
Yarmouth, Nova Scotia, with the provincial government
providing assistance of $350 thousand as a payroll rebate.[118]
Artex Sportswear produces the outerwear portion of uniforms
for the Canadian Armed Forces, Correctional Services, and
various government departments.[119]

Besides investments in property and textiles, Chinese
Canadians have also heavily promoted technology. A survey of
computer wholesale and manufacturing firms in Toronto
showed a 33 percent Chinese Canadian ownership in 1998.[120]
One example is the success story of Kwok Yuan Ho, cofounder
and former CEO of Markham-based ATI Technologies Inc. Ho
came to Canada as a business immigrant in the 1980s. With
$300 thousand, he started a company making computer graphic
chips. In 1997 ATI was Canada's third largest computer firm,
surpassing the $1.1 billion mark in revenues.[121] It was
purchased by AMD, a US semiconductor producer, in 2006 for
$5.4 billion.[122]

Canadian Solar is one of the largest solar energy-system
manufacturers in the world. It was founded in 2001 by Shawn
Qu a Chinese immigrant to Canada. It is capitalized at more
than one billion dollars and has more than seven thousand
employees.[123] VTech Electronics Canada, a branch of VTech
Holdings, the worldwide educational electronics company, was
established by its chairman Allan Wong who landed in Canada

[118] Government of Nova Scotia website, "News Releases," "Clothing
Manufacturer Attracted to Yarmouth," 2001.10.29,
www.gov.ns.ca/news/details.asp?id=20011029001, 2008.05.22.

[119] Artex Sportswear website, "Our Services,"
"www.artexsportswear.com/Homepage/HP_all.htm, accessed 2008.05.22.

[120] Lo, *et al.,* "Immigrants' Economic Status in Toronto," 22; citing research
done by Fairchild Group in 1998.

[121] Tony Wong, "New Canadians."

[122] Ed Oswald, "AMD, ATI Merge in $5.4 Billion Deal," *betanews,* 2006.07.24,
betanews.com/2006/07/24/amd-ati-merge-in-5-4-billion-deal, accessed
2015.01.20.

[123] MarketWatch, "Canadian Solar Inc.,"
www.marketwatch.com/investing/stock/csiq, accessed 2015.01.22.

under the Business Immigration Program. In four years, from 1985-89, VTech's Canadian operation, which is based in Richmond, grew from three employees with $3 million in sales to 143 employees with an expected $50 million in sales.[124]

While the strength and resulting achievements of Chinese Canadian businesspeople are apparent when one considers large investors, this strong economic growth is also found among small and medium sized Chinese Canadian companies. These companies do not necessarily receive the publicity; however, their growth demonstrates that Chinese Canadian economic achievements occur in all sizes of companies and are, therefore, likely present in all Chinese Canadian economic activities. It was found in a study conducted in 1998 of Chinese Canadian business development in Toronto that there has been significant development across a number of areas. First, Chinese Canadian businesses were no longer confined to the retail sector. Out of sixty-five industrial sectors, Chinese Canadian businesses were represented in fifty-two. Second, the locations of Chinese businesses are shifting; many were located outside of Chinatown and were instead linked to industrial areas. Third, Chinese firms are expanding. Multiplant establishments have surfaced. While 57 percent of Chinese businesses still employ less than 20 employees, 41 percent have a workforce between 20 and 199 people, and the remaining 2 percent, covering a range of business types in wholesale, manufacturing, realty, and accommodation, employ 200 to 750 workers. In terms of sales volume, while 26 percent made less than $1 million in 1997, slightly over 10 percent of the Chinese firms exceed the $10 million mark. The study also noted that Chinese firms, while representing 0.1 percent of the total in Toronto, account for 1 percent of the top 1000 Toronto firms in both employment and sales.[125]

The achievements that one finds among the stellar investors are mirrored among the more ordinary ones. They are

---

[124] Daniel Stoffman, "Asia Comes to Lotusland," *Report on Business Magazine* 6.5 (Nov. 1989).

[125] Lo, *et al.*, "Immigrants' Economic Status in Toronto," 29; summarizing a study reported on in Lucia Lo and Shuguang Wang, "Immigration, Ethnic Economies and Integration: a Case Study of Chinese in the Greater Toronto Area. Research Report to the Toronto Joint Centre of Excellence for Research on Immigration and Settlement" (1998).

casting off the stereotype of what it means to be a Chinese Canadian entrepreneur by moving into new types of business and areas outside Chinatowns; in addition they are expanding their operations, employing more workers, and earning more revenue.

In spite of what is broad growth in Chinese Canadian economic strength, it seems that many Canadians have been taken by surprise and are not psychologically prepared for it. The result has been negative reactions to some consequences of Chinese Canadian investment. Probably, the most publicized opposition to Chinese Canadian investment was from the mid 1980s to the mid 1990s in the Vancouver area. During this time, coincident with large scale immigration from Hong Kong, a steep rise in housing prices and the apparent building of so called "monster houses" took place. Opposition to these changes was vented in public meetings, letters to editors of local publications, television coverage, and city council meetings, which assumed harsh and hostile tones.[126] Another related response to the building of shopping centers catering to Chinese Canadians in Vancouver and Toronto was also characterized by strong opposition. This response consisted of complaints about traffic congestion, lack of parking, noise, late hours of restaurants, lack of management control over strata title owners, lack of English signs, and even odors.[127]

Probably the earliest indication that the populace was unprepared for a display of Chinese Canadian economic strength was the criticism leveled at Concord Pacific Group for

---

[126] Edgington, et al., 169. For a detailed description of this opposition see Edgington, et al., 165,167-171; Peter Li, "Unneighbourly Houses or Unwelcome Chinese: the Social Construction of Race in the Battle over 'Monster Homes' in Vancouver Canada," *International Journal of Comparative Race and Ethnic Studies* 1-2 (1994): 47-66; and Katharyne Mitchell, "Transnational Subjects: Constituting the Cultural Citizen in the Era of Pacific Rim Capital (Hong Kong Chinese Immigrants in Vancouver, British Columbia)," in *Ungrounded Empires: the Cultural Politics of Modern Chinese Transnationalism,* ed. Aihwa Ong and Donald Nonini (New York: Routledge, 1997), 228-256.

[127] Valerie Preston and Lucia Lo, "Canadian Urban Landscape Examples - 21 'Asian Theme' Malls in Suburban Toronto: Land Use Conflict in Richmond Hill," *Canadian Geographer* 44.2 (Summer 2000), 186-88. For further description of opposition to Chinese Canadian shopping malls, see Edgington, et al., 171-74.

selling apartments in 1988 on the former Expo 86 site to buyers in Hong Kong before they were offered for sale in Vancouver. The issue became sensitive enough that politicians were commenting on the size of advertisements in Hong Kong compared to those in Vancouver.[128] These displays of economic strength were surprising to Canadians, as seen in the negative response and publicity that they have received. However, the response of surprise is itself surprising; one would have expected both a broader awareness of the positive consequences arising out of Chinese Canadian investments and a psychological readiness for the display of Chinese Canadians economic strength. The existence of either of these would have mitigated the opposition that occurred.

5.1.3 Investment in Equities

Before turning to a detailed description of how Chinese Canadians have had a large impact in the specific area of property development, it would further increase our awareness of Chinese Canadian economic achievement to consider how these achievements have also occurred in more common ways. Coinciding with the implementation of the Canadian Business Immigration Program, Chinese Canadians increasingly began investing in various forms of investment instruments, including stocks and mutual funds. Admittedly, some of these instruments were designed specifically to meet the requirements of participants in the Business Immigration Program; however, investment companies also recognized that opportunities existed across the spectrum of Chinese Canadians.

Traditionally, Chinese Canadians have been conservative investors putting their money into guaranteed interest-bearing investments or property, which are seen to hold their value, or even keeping large amounts of money within bank accounts. For companies such as Trimark, Mackenzie Financial, and Fidelity, this attitude presented an opportunity. In 1995, Trimark launched a national program designed to educate the Asian community about mutual funds. In the three years that

---

[128] Gordon Hamilton, "Flashy Ads in Hong Kong Market Pacific Place Condos," *The Vancouver Sun*, 1990.11. 27, B1.

followed, sales to Asian Canadian customers became the fastest
growing segment within the mutual fund industry and almost
all the major Canadian mutual fund companies followed
Trimark's example by implementing similar campaigns. The
result was that the growth rate in holding mutual funds for
Chinese Canadians was almost double that of the market in
general.[129]

Mackenzie Financial noted the same trend in 1996. The
segment of the Canadian population that was attracting most
attention among mutual fund companies was Chinese
Canadians from the PRC and Hong Kong. This interest was
reflected in the increasing portions of advertising budgets
devoted to Chinese print and broadcast media. Mandarin and
Cantonese speaking representatives were placed on toll free
lines and the companies offered seminars targeting Chinese
Canadians.[130] Equity investment had become another avenue
for demonstrating Chinese Canadian economic strength.

5.2 Property Development: Residential and Commercial

Another obvious area of Chinese Canadian economic
achievement is the development of residential and commercial
property. Most Canadians probably first noticed Chinese
Canadian economic strength in the shopping centers that had
been built to cater to them. This strength has been supported
by the high percentage of home ownership among Chinese
Canadians and includes the development of residential, as well
as commercial property.

5.2.1 Home Ownership

One could have anticipated the otherwise
surprising development of residential and commercial property
by Chinese Canadians if one had been paying close attention to
the pattern of Chinese Canadian home ownership. Census

---

[129] Chu, quoting John Yuen, vice president of sales for Trimark.

[130] Andrew Trimble, "Courting New Fund Customers," *Toronto Star*,
1996.09.15, C4; in part quoting Laurie Munroe, Vice President of Marketing
at Mackenzie Financial Corp.

results from as early as 1991 showed that 78 percent of Chinese Canadians lived in an abode owned by some member of their household, compared to 70 percent for other Canadians. At the same time, about 60 percent of Chinese Canadians lived in owner-occupied homes worth $200,000 or more, which compared to only 23 per cent for other Canadians.[131] Furthermore, large ownership of expensive homes by Chinese Canadians seemed to be a growing trend. A survey of title transfers in 1996 showed that people with Asian names, mostly Chinese, bought 62 percent of the property in Richmond, 61 percent in East Vancouver, 50 percent in Burnaby, 44 percent on Vancouver's west side, and 37 percent in Coquitlam.[132] Not only were these high percentages, the purchases were also made in Vancouver, one of Canada's most expensive property markets. This trend in home buying by Chinese Canadians was probably the largest factor in the immigration that shaped the Greater Vancouver housing market.[133] This shaping included those selling the homes; in 1995 the top three realtors by MLS sales were Chinese Canadian.[134]

5.2.2 Residential Development

With such an interest and influence in home owning and, thus, the housing market, it is natural that the entrepreneurial abilities that Chinese Canadians possess would have been demonstrated in residential development. For those whose home had been Hong Kong, where property values were so much higher, the opportunities for arbitrage would have been obvious.

Reflecting conditions in Hong Kong, where many of the earlier buyers originated, Chinese Canadian development of

---

[131] Li, *The Chinese*, 127, citing Statistics Canada.

[132] *Ibid.*, citing *Vancouver Sun*.

[133] David Ley, "The Rhetoric of Racism and the Politics of Explanation in the Vancouver Housing Market," in *The Silent Debate: Asian Immigration and Racism in Canada*, ed. by Eleanor Laquian, Aprodicio Laquian, and Terry McGee (Institute of Asian Research, University of British Columbia, 1997), 333.

[134] Ley, *Migrant Millionaires*, 139.

large scale residential housing began with multistoried
structures containing many individual dwellings. These were
sold as condominiums. It was not until afterwards that Chinese
Canadians' strength expanded to include the development of
the more typical, smaller structures, including detached single
family dwellings.

Chinese Canadian residential development was first
noticed when what was described as "the biggest urban
development on the continent" took place. In 1988 Concord
Pacific Group Inc. (then Concord Pacific Developments Ltd.)
purchased the 82.5 hectares that comprised the former Expo 86
lands in downtown Vancouver for one hundred twenty-five
million dollars and proceeded to commit three billion dollars to
building eight thousand five hundred housing units along with
schools, daycare centres, hotels, parks, and theaters for twenty
thousand residents.[135] Li Ka-shing, the main investor, was
joined by K.M. Hui and Cheng Yu-tung in the project called
Concord Pacific Place.[136] The project has since grown and when
completed will have approximately ten thousand residential
units and more than two hundred thirty thousand square
meters of retail and commercial space.[137] Not only has the
project grown, but the company had other ongoing large scale,
residential developments as of 2008: fourteen in Vancouver, one
in the Okanagan, one in Calgary, and two in Toronto.[138]
Concord CityPlace, on eighteen hectares of former railway lands
in downtown Toronto, was said to be "the largest master
planned community in Toronto with some six thousand
residential units and is an integrated neighbourhood of
residences, retail and commercial establishments, a school, and
urban park, and public spaces."[139]

---

[135] David Thomas, "Vancouver's Pacific Place to Transform the City," *The Financial Post*, 1994.11.18, C18.

[136] *Ibid.*, and Li, *The Chinese*, 135.

[137] Canada NewsWire, "Concord Pacific Announces Closing of Sale of North York Site," 2006.12.07.

[138] Concord Pacific webpage, *www.concordpacific.com/*, accessed 2008.06.03.

[139] Canada NewsWire, "Concord Pacific."

In 2003 Chinese K.M. Hui's son Terry Hui and his family purchased Concord Pacific and took it private. Terry Hui had previously taken control of the property assets of Marathon realty the real estate arm of Canadian Pacific Railway. The Concord Pacific property was valued at $5 billion in 2005.[140]

Notwithstanding the interest that the development of Concord Pacific Place created, Chinese Canadians had been active in land development for years prior to this. David Lam, who would go onto become lieutenant governor of British Columbia, had in the 1970s, became one of Vancouver's leading land developers and was instrumental in bringing Hong Kong investors to Vancouver while amassing a fortune that would exceed $100 million.[141] Stanley Kwok, another early Chinese Canadian residential developer, was a partner in Canadian Freehold Properties during the 1970s. The company developed property from Halifax to Vancouver owned by chemical and explosives producer Canadian Industries Ltd. It started with $10 million in assets and then was sold to Marathon Realty for $280 million. Kwok then headed Pendboro Development, which initiated development of Douglasdale Estates, a five hundred twenty-six-hectare property in 1981 in Calgary. In 1984 Kwok became president of BC Place, which was charged with developing the 1986 Expo lands and Whistler Village.[142]

The integration of Chinese Canadian strength, initially influenced by Hong Kong standards, with residential development in Canada is also seen in the results of the Hopewell Group of Companies. Hopewell is headed by Sanders Lee, who immigrated from Hong Kong in 1991. Founded by his family, under his administration the company has grown to five primary operating divisions headquartered in Calgary and employs three hundred in locations across Canada. One division focuses on residential development, two on commercial development, one on product distribution, and one on finance. Building residences under the brand Sabal Homes, it has

---

140 Ley, *Migrant Millionaires*, 136-38.

141 *The Canadian Encyclopedia*, s.v. "Lam, David See-Chai," *www.thecanadianencyclopedia.com/index.cfm?PgNm=TCE&Params=A1ART A0009013*, accessed 2008.05.16.

142 John Schreiner, "A Capital Deal-Maker," *The Financial Post* (Toronto), 1997.08.23, 29.

constructed three thousand homes and five times has been named "Developer of the Year."[143] It also had over $60 million in revenues in 2005.[144]

The Swan Group, operated by Richard Li, has been building homes since 1990 in Calgary and Canmore. It began building single family houses and has since expanded to other housing options, such as condominiums and assisted living facilities. The company is composed of two divisions: Swan Homes and Calvanna Developments. Swan Homes builds and sells single and multifamily residences while Calvanna caters to the fifty-plus market. The Lodge at Valley Ridge Estates in Calgary was their inaugural project for those over sixty-five. After construction was finished, ownership and management were turned over to a long term care provider.[145] The company now specializes in building condominiums.

Trico Homes is also headquartered in Calgary. It was formed in 1993 by Wayne Chiu, who was originally from Hong Kong. Since its inception it has built over eight thousand single and multifamily homes. Chiu and his employees have been active philanthropists and volunteers and the company has been named one of "Canada's Best 50 Managed Companies."[146] In fact, Chiu began donations even before Trico started to be profitable, committing $100 thousand annually to the Kids Cancer Care Foundation. The importance of community values is reflected in the company name: **Trust, Respect, Integrity,**

---

[143] Hopewell Group of Companies website, "Hopewell Residential," *www.hopewell.com/companies/hrm*, accessed 2015.01.20.

[144] "My Best Mistake," *Alberta Venture* 9.10 (Dec. 2005), 15.

[145] "The Swan Group," *The Calgary Sun*, 1999.04.10-11, 24-25.

[146] Trico Homes website, "Trico Corporate/Why Choose Trico/Trico Homes Accolades," *www.tricohomes.com/about-trico.html*, accessed 2008.06.05. The "Canada's Best Managed Companies" awards recognize excellence in Canadian-owned and managed companies with revenues over $10 million. They are sponsored by Deloitte, CIBC Commercial Banking, National Post, and Queen's School of Business. (Canada's 50 Best Managed Companies website, *www.canadas50best.com/en/about/pages/home.aspx*, accessed 2015.01.20)

Community, and Opportunity.[147] The company has since
increased the number of charities that it supports.[148]

One sees further evidence of the ability and evolution
among Chinese Canadian residential developers in the
achievements of Yee Hong Centre for Geriatric Care in
Toronto,[149] which has been very innovative in designing housing
for seniors. It provides housing in proximity to nursing home
facilities so that seniors can live independently while being able
to partake in the services offered by their centre.[150] Yee Hong
also owns and directly manages a housing complex, the Yee
Hong Aw Chan Kam Chee Evergreen Manor, in order to provide
affordable housing for seniors. The philosophy underlying this
complex is to provide a "continuum of health and social services
which enable seniors to live independently in their own homes
for as long as possible."[151] Yee Hong is also involved in private
initiatives. Villa Elegance, a condominium project designed for
seniors jointly by Tridel, a large builder of condominiums in
Toronto, and Yee Hong, is an example of how a charitable
organization and a private business can work together in order
to meet the housing needs of seniors.[152]

5.2.3 Commercial Property

It is probably the development of commercial
property that has received the most attention among Chinese
Canadian achievements. One cannot deny the daring and
economic strength shown in building the Chinese shopping

---

[147] Julia Howell, "The Business of Community," *Maclean's* 121.12
(2008.03.31).

[148] Trico Homes website, "About Us/Partners,"
www.tricohomes.com/goodwill/partners.bpsx, accessed 2015.01.20.

[149] Described in chapter eight, "Chinese Canadian Institutional Eldercare," of
this book.

[150] Yee Hong Garden Terrace,
www.yeehong.com/centre/gardenterrace/index.html, accessed 2007.10.19.

[151] Yee Hong website, "Centre/Programs and Services/Subsidized Housing,"
www.yeehong.com/centre/subsidized_housing.php, accessed 2008.07.04.

[152] Yee Hong website, *www.yeehong.com*, accessed 2003.09.27.

centres to the size and numbers as seen in Canada. One can, of course, argue that the business immigrants from Hong Kong, brought with them a surfeit of capital that has supported the capital costs; still, there had to be customers with funds to buy the products sold in these commercial venues, especially in the midst of recessions in Vancouver and Toronto. Also, there had to be entrepreneurs clever and brave enough to design the properties, such as with strata titles, so they would appeal to the business immigrants with capital to invest. In other words, the shopping centres are indicative of much more than Chinese Canadians with the capital to build them.

Although some reactions to the shopping centres has been negative, complaints about traffic, etc., there has also been recognition of the vitality and diversity brought to the communities where property was developed.

5.2.3.1 Shopping Centres

New shopping centres offer the most notable examples of Chinese Canadian development of commercial property. Their large numbers, the fact that most of them are being built outside the historical boundaries of Chinatowns, and the changes that they have created, have not and could not have been missed. They have been built mostly in greater Vancouver and Toronto, and, as the number of local Chinese Canadians has increased, they have also emerged in Calgary and Montreal as well.

The building of Chinese shopping centres outside the boundaries of Chinatown began in Toronto and it has been the leader in North America in terms of size and speed of their development.[153] Lucia Lo provides a brief history of this beginning and the events that followed it. In the early 1980s outlets selling Chinese products began to gather in retail plazas situated on the intersection of Sheppard and Glen Watford in Scarborough. This created speculation that the rising Chinese Canadian population would demand more ethnic retailing and office space, which in the mid 1980s led to the conversion of existing malls and the construction of enclosed malls and mixed retail/commercial space, all devoted to meeting this demand.

---

[153] Lo, "Suburban Housing," 151.

Mississauga Chinese Centre, which opened in 1987, was one of the earliest examples, converting a building on an industrial site into a mix of ethnic shops and exhibits of Chinese culture.[154] Others followed in Scarborough. Most of the developers of these sites were Chinese Canadians; however, with their success, non-Chinese Canadian developers soon followed. Some of the latter's projects had been in danger of failing because of the recession that hit in the 1990s; therefore, they modified them to meet the needs of Chinese Canadians, thereby allowing them to succeed. One of the modifications they made was to sell retail store units within their malls instead of leasing them, which was common practice in Hong Kong and came to be known as "selling strata titles." With the success of the initial ventures to sell strata titles in the midst of a recession, jurisdictions around Toronto soon passed laws allowing the sale of strata titles and the building of retail condominiums. Capital for new projects was often raised among new and perspective immigrants and, so during "the 1990s, when the rest of the Toronto economy was suffering badly, Chinese shopping mall developments were going full force."[155]

There are now more than sixty-five Chinese Canadian shopping malls in the Greater Toronto Area, ranging from eight hundred eighty to twenty-eight hundred square meters. Of these, the largest is the Pacific Mall/Market Village complex. It has a total sales area of over 46.5 thousand square meters and over five hundred stores, the size of a regional shopping center. As such, it is the largest indoor Chinese shopping center in North America and a designated tourist destination.[156] Some newer additions to Chinese shopping malls include Splendid China Tower in Scarborough with eighty-four hundred square meters, with plans to expand to twenty-eight thousand.[157] The King Square mall, which is under construction, is planned to

[154] *Ibid.*, 149; and Mississauga Chinese Centre website, "Founder and History," *mississaugachinesecentre.com/frame2.html*, accessed 2008.06.07.

[155] Lo, "Suburban Housing," 149-150.

[156] *Ibid.*, 150-51.

[157] Splendid China Mall website, *www.splendidchinamall.com/en/home.php*, accessed 2015.01.21.

surpass the Pacific Mall/Market Village complex in size once it is completed.[158]

David Edgington, *et al.*, provide a similar history of the development of Chinese shopping centres in the Vancouver area. The first large Chinese shopping centers opened in 1990 in Richmond. The Aberdeen Centre, constructed by Thomas Fung was eleven thousand square meters in area and contained Chinese Canadian owned shops, cinemas, restaurants, and professional services, all catering to Chinese Canadian customers. The Aberdeen Centre was quickly followed by nine other shopping complexes: Parker Place (1992), President Plaza (1993), Yaohan Centre (1995), Central Square (1996), Continental Centre (1997), Pacific Plaza (1997), Cosmo Plaza (1997), Admiralty Centre (1997), and Union Square (1998), all over the space of the next eight years. As with Aberdeen Centre, these malls catered mainly to Chinese Canadians, and all of them, except for the Aberdeen Centre, sold strata titles of shop and office units to investors.[159] For example, about 10 percent of the owners of Parker Place Plaza Shopping Center, said to have offered the first strata titles in North America, were estimated to be new business immigrants who were using their investments to meet the conditions of their immigrant status.[160]

The number of Chinese Canadian shopping centers in Vancouver has given investors a base upon which to grow, which has included renovation of existing sites. In 2004 Thomas Fung spent sixty-three million dollars to renew Aberdeen Centre a mere fourteen years after it had been completed.[161] He

---

[158] Paul Brent, "With Fresh Funding, Continent's Largest Asian Mall Back on Track," *Real Estate News Exchange*, 2014.06.21, *renx.ca/with-fresh-funding-continents-largest-asian-mall-back-on-track*, accessed 2015.01.21.

[159] 171-72.

[160] *Ibid.*, 178, quoting J. Nan, "Immigration and Integration: Development of 'Chinese' Shopping Centres in the Suburbs of Vancouver"(Master of Science thesis, University of British Columbia,1999), 64; and Peter Li, "Chinese Investment and Business in Canada: Ethnic Entrepreneurship Reconsidered," *Pacific Affairs* 66.2 (Summer 1993), 230.

[161] "Diversity and Quality Abound: Projects and Personalities Honoured at VRCA Annual Awards," *Journal of Commerce* (Vancouver) 91.1 (2004.11.15), 1.

had been dissatisfied with the results in the previous center but still had the confidence and funding to add twenty-eight hundred square meters and an eight-story condominium building.[162]

Chinese shopping malls have also developed in Calgary and Montreal demonstrating that the demand goes beyond Toronto and Vancouver. In Calgary, Chinese Canadian developers erected the Central Landmark Mall in 1996 not far from the expanding Chinatown. It is fifty-six hundred square meters and cost eight million dollars to build.[163] Calgary's first suburban Chinese shopping center, Pacific Place Mall, opened in 1999 in Calgary's northeast, which is said to be where most of the city's Asia immigrants reside. The mall is anchored by a thirty-seven hundred square meter T & T supermarket. Interestingly, the developers were able to demand a premium over market prices from tenants after the mall converted to its Chinese Asian theme.[164] In Montreal, Chinese malls were being put in place as early as 1995 in Brossard on the South Shore,[165] again in order to meet the demands of the growing Chinese Canadian population.

Chinese shopping centers were developed quickly in Toronto and Vancouver once the demand for them was known. The speed and size of the developments were remarkable especially amid the poor economic environments. The continuing development and spread to cities besides Toronto and Vancouver indicates that more achievements are to come.

5.2.3.2 Hotels

Investment in hotels by Chinese Canadians is another form of Chinese Canadian participation in the development of commercial property. Henry Wu, a member of the family that controls Hopewell Holdings Ltd., one of Hong

---

[162] Boddy, 26-27.

[163] Gordon Jaremko, "Cultural Crossroads: Central Landmark Mall Adds Cosmopolitan Flavor," *Calgary Herald*, 1996.06.15, final edition, D1.

[164] Anne Crawford, "Franklin Mall to Add Flavor of Asia," *Calgary Herald*, 1999.05.14, E1.

[165] Harvey Shepard, *The Gazette* (Montreal), 1995.11.23, G1.

Kong's largest companies, is a Canadian citizen. He purchased
the five hundred-room Metropolitan in Toronto in 1993 and the
two hundred-room Metropolitan in Vancouver in 1995, each for
twenty-eight million dollars,[166] and built the eighty-eight-room
SoHo Metropolitan in Toronto in 2003.[167] Jack Lee heads a
multimillion-dollar conglomerate that includes the eighty
million dollar, four-star Radisson President Hotel and Suites
complex in the Vancouver suburb of Richmond.[168] Si Wai Lai
bought Queen's Landing Inn in Niagara-on-the-Lake for twenty
three million dollars in 1996.[169]

Besides these Chinese Canadians, there are Chinese who
may not have immigrant status or citizenship in Canada but at
least have residences there and have made large investments
into the Canadian hotel industry. The well-known Sutton Place
in Toronto was purchased in 1995 by Stanley Ho, the former
casino mogul who has had his family and a house in Toronto.[170]
The investments in hotels by Chinese Canadians and Chinese
who have family and residential links to Canada are part of a
bigger trend of investment in commercial property by Chinese
Canadians. The high visibility of this trend makes it a clear
example of the economic achievement of Chinese Canadians.

5.2.4 Summary and Innovation

Property development has probably provided the
clearest example of Chinese Canadians' economic achievements.
Indications of this achievement were first seen in the high
percentage of expensive home ownership among them. They
viewed property investment as important. Nevertheless, even
with these signs, the purchase of Expo 86 lands in Vancouver

[166] Tony Wong, "Hong Kong Money Likes GTA," *The Toronto Star*, 1996.11.10,
A1, A10.

[167] John Barber, "Worlds Apart," *The Globe and Mail*, 2004.10.23, M1.

[168] Lorrayne.

[169] Bertrand Marotte, "Si Wai Lai has been pouring millions... " CanWest
News, 1996.08.15, 1.

[170] *Ibid.* and Tony Wong, "Stanley Ho, Hong Kong's Most Flamboyant
Multimillionaire, Loves a Bargain," *Toronto Star*, 1990.02.11, D1.

and the proposal to build a residential area of eight thousand five hundred housing units was certainly not expected. While continuing to build multifamily structures across Canada, Chinese Canadian property development companies have also joined in building the more common single family structures.

Chinese Canadian development of commercial property has also been surprising. Begun in the mid 1980s in Toronto, it led to the building of over sixty-five Chinese shopping malls, including the Pacific Mall/Market Village complex, the largest indoor Chinese shopping center in North America. In Vancouver, ten major Chinese shopping malls were built during the 1990s. When one also considers Chinese Canadian investments in the hotel industry, the achievements are all that more remarkable. One even sees development in Canadian farmland. There are Chinese Canadian realtors in Saskatoon and Regina dedicated to purchasing farmland for Chinese immigrants. Purchasers hope to open new markets in Asia and ship agricultural products directly to them.[171]

Part of this achievement has been the innovation that Chinese Canadians have promoted. This innovation has had three notable aspects. Firstly, it has contributed to the diversity of product choice for Canadian consumers, the diversity in shopping experience, and diversity in the ethnic makeup of Canadian communities. Secondly, it has vitalized Canadian communities by encouraging a diversity of shoppers and, most important, pedestrian traffic. Thirdly, it has introduced economic innovations that have strengthened the Canadian economy and promise to continue doing so.

Examples of unusual products found in Chinese malls include ginseng tea perfumed with rose petals, green tea cake topped with white chocolate, products spun off from Japanese animation, medicinal herbs, and Asian designed glass frames. Of course, one will find a wide selection of Chinese and Asian foods in the food courts.[172] There are also malls dedicated to specific geographic areas of China; for example, Metro Square in Greater Toronto is occupied exclusively by Taiwanese

---

[171] Paul Waldie, "Seed Capital: How Immigrants Are Reshaping Saskatchewan's Farmland," *The Globe and Mail*, 2012.10.12.

[172] Olivia Stern, "Pacific Mall," *Toronto Life* 40.3 (Mar. 2006), 69.

immigrants and provides Taiwanese-style products.[173] The
shopping experience varies as well because there are fewer of
the big brand retailers in Chinese malls. Instead, the malls
reflect the lifestyles, trends, brands, and even groceries of
modern societies in China and Asia.[174] The overall result is that
Chinese shopping centers "introduce a diversity of functions
and aesthetics and ambiance to the relatively standardized city
scape of modern suburbia."[175]

The malls also encourage diversity in the ethnic makeup of
the communities surrounding them. Some of the malls were
developed to attract more Chinese Canadians into the
surrounding areas. As pointed out earlier the number of and
size of the malls was disproportional to the relative size of the
Chinese Canadian population. However, it was thought that the
malls would attract them to move into the area and thereby
correct the imbalance. A similar strategy, to attract residents,
was used in North American shopping centre development in
North American cities in the 1970s, but it was the first time
that an ethnic group had adopted it.[176] In the case of the
Chinese shopping centers, the drawing of Chinese Canadians
into the area as residents has increased the area's ethnic
diversity.

The difference in Chinese shopping malls also encourages a
diversity of shoppers and more pedestrian traffic, thereby
adding to the vitality of a community. This is especially
valuable in the suburbs where there is little in the way of street
level retail activity and most transportation is in automobiles.

---

[173] Shuguang Wang and Lucia Lo, "Chinese Immigrants in Canada: Their
Changing Composition and Economic Performance," CERIS Working Paper
No. 30 (Mar. 2004), 3.

[174] Doug Ward, "The New Chinatown: Mall Style: for Some of Us Shopping at
an Asian-style Mall Is a Cross-cultural Experience. It's like Being a Tourist in
Your Hometown," *The Vancouver Sun*, 2000.02. 26 (Final Edition), F1.

[175] Mohammad Qadeer, "Ethnic Malls and Plazas: Chinese Commercial
Developments in Scarborough, Ontario," CERIS Working Paper No. 3
(Toronto: Joint Centre of Excellence for Research on Immigration and
Settlement, 1998), 13.

[176] Shuguang Wang, "Chinese Commercial Activity in Toronto CMA: New
Development Patterns and Impacts," *Canadian Geographer* 43.1 (Spring
1999), 28.

It has been observed that Chinese malls help create lively
commercial zones, similar to the pedestrian walkways in the
downtown cores of major cities. It seems that the strata titles
and flexible opening hours available in Chinese malls make it
easier for small business to operate in them. This is in contrast
to the major malls that are too expensive and too restrictive for
most small businesses.[177] More small businesses mean more
diversity, which attracts window shoppers. Furthermore, the
Chinese malls encourage a market like atmosphere, e.g.,
moving their products into the common passageways to
encourage shoppers to browse.[178] Once one adds the various
celebrations of Chinese holidays, such as the Mid Autumn
Festival, the result is increased pedestrian traffic moving from
one store to another. This increased pedestrian traffic creates
increased human interaction, which fosters vitality in the
community.

A third notable aspect of Chinese malls is the economic
innovations that have benefitted the Canadian economy and
promise to continue doing so. The sale of strata titles fostered
large scale building of malls in the 1980s in Vancouver and
Toronto allowing their respective economies to weather
recessions. Thomas Fung invented ten new-to-Canada retail
businesses in Aberdeen Centre. These included North American
tests of Thai furniture sellers, Smart Living and Flash
Living.[179] Other additions include Chef Hung's, a Taiwanese
noodle shop, a Japanese *izakaya* (a casual after-work bar), and
the "100 Yen" discount retailer Daiso.[180]

5.3 Areas of Obvious Economic Achievement: Conclusion

Business investment and property development are
two areas where the economic achievements of Chinese
Canadians have been most obvious. Canada has encouraged

---

[177] John Lorinc, "How Bazaar," *The Globe and Mail*, 2003.12.20, M7.

[178] It is interesting that major malls have also adopted this strategy.

[179] Boddy, 24 and 28.

[180] Iain Marlow, "B.C.'s Transpacific Pioneer Thomas Fung Is a Uniquely
Canadian Success Story," *The Globe and Mail*, 2014.08.31.

business immigrants since 1978 and in the time since, Chinese applicants have dominated the program, comprising over 50 percent of the total number of successful applicants through the program from 1986-2005. This initial strength was a portent of increasing economic influence in Canada and, subsequently, the country saw major investments outside the program, not only by individual investors, such as Li Ka-shing and Thomas Fung, but also by the average Chinese Canadian. In a parallel to the large percentage of expensive home ownership noted earlier, small Chinese Canadian businesses were exhibiting signs of growth and leaving the ethnic enclave leading to the average Chinese Canadian becoming a target for the promotion of equities.

Property development has provided the most visible examples of Chinese Canadian economic achievement. The building of Concord Pacific Place was the first and it has been followed by other major residential and commercial property developments. Of these, the construction of over sixty-five Chinese shopping malls in Toronto and ten in Vancouver have been the main examples of Chinese Canadian economic achievement. Many of them were built under recessionary conditions and Chinese Canadians have exhibited the entrepreneurship and the strong demand to create and maintain the shopping centers catering to them.[181]

6. Overview of Economic Achievements

In making a claim for Chinese Canadian economic achievements, this essay has first provided general evidence for Chinese Canadian economic strength, the assumption being that the latter is a required condition for economic achievement. Chinese Canadians have demonstrated adequate wealth to exert economic strength. They have a higher percentage of home ownership and their homes are more expensive. Market surveys have shown them to have more disposal income than average and reliable reports say they have larger bank deposits. In fact, there are banks in Canada whose main function is to serve them.

---

[181] Qadeer, 4-5.

The economic strength of Chinese Canadians is also seen in the physical expansion of Chinese Canadian commercial activity. The establishment of new Chinatowns and the development of Chinese shopping centers indicates that Chinese Canadians have both the buying power to support the new businesses occupying these locales and the capital to construct them. Furthermore, two aspects seen in the growth of commercial activity are that Chinese Canadians are no longer restricted to ethnic economic enclaves, such as Chinatowns, and they are working in occupations that are outside ethnic industries. Both of these aspects are indicative of increased economic strength.

Marketing that targets Chinese Canadians also reveals their economic strength. There are a large number of advertising firms targeting the Chinese Canadian market and sellers take direct measures, such as hiring of Chinese speaking sales staff and sponsoring ethnic festivals, to target Chinese Canadians directly. Chinese Canadians have also established large economic organizations that reflect their economic strength. Some were purchased, such as Husky Oil by Li Ka-shing, some were joint ventures between foreign and domestic Chinese entrepreneurs, such as T & T Supermarket, and others were built purely by Chinese Canadians, such as H.Y. Louie Company. Nonprofit organizations include the Association of Chinese Canadian Entrepreneurs and the Chinese Professionals Association of Canada. The apparent need for and ability to form large economic organizations both indicate economic strength.

The signs of economic strength apparent today have a history that led to their appearance and also gave reason to expect the achievements of Chinese Canadians. These signs include a people who worked to build the early infrastructure that Canada needed. In doing so and also in face of exploitation, they were able to establish their own economic enclaves and ethnic industries. Then after racial bias was removed from Canada's immigration laws in 1967, many Chinese immigrants with professional and technical skills arrived to bolster the economic strength of Chinese Canadians. They were followed by applicants to the Business Immigration Program, who dominated the numbers accepted, and likewise the funds subscribed.

There are number of areas where Chinese Canadians' economic achievements have been apparent. The restaurant industry has historically provided a means of living and under Chinese Canadian guidance has evolved to include franchises and high class establishments. Grocery stores, also a common employment venue, have likewise evolved to the point where Chinese Canadians have a strong position among mainstream supermarkets, e.g., IGA in British Columbia, and have created a supermarket chain, T & T, catering to their and other ethnic groups' needs. Chinese Canadians have also built a history of philanthropy. They were noted for supporting Canada's war efforts through purchase of Victory Bonds and since then have helped fulfill Canada's needs through foundations designed to do so.

Among the apparent areas of Chinese Canadian economic success, there are two, business investment and property development, that have been most obvious. Chinese Canadians have dominated the Business Immigration Program from 1986 till the present day, comprising over 50 percent of the total number of successful applicants through the program from 1986-2005. Large investments outside the program, such as by Li Ka-shing, have come as well. In addition to these large investors, small Chinese Canadian businesses have been exhibiting signs of growth and leaving the ethnic enclave. As for property development, Chinese Canadians have been the architects of major residential and commercial property developments, such as Concord Pacific Place and many shopping malls across Canada. These developments have been impressive in their own right; nevertheless, they form but a part of the many economic achievements of Chinese Canadians that continue to appear.

7. Consideration of General Factors Affecting Achievements

7.1 Importance of Culture

If one were to question the significance of Chinese Canadian economic influence, there seems to be an obvious answer. These achievements have created obvious material benefits for both Chinese Canadians and the broader society. Nevertheless, there also seems to be practical knowledge that can be garnered from the economic achievements of Chinese Canadians especially given that they have had to overcome huge barriers in achieving what they have. This and the fact that these barriers were put in place from the time of their early arrival indicate that the ability of Chinese Canadians to overcome them offers possible lessons for other Canadians.

The promise of practical knowledge does not come without complexity, however, because there is an ongoing debate as to how Chinese Canadians have been able to achieve what they have. It seems that this debate could apply to all of the achievements described in this book: eldercare, media, promotion of Chinese culture, Traditional Chinese Medicine, etc.; however, it has mostly developed in the context of economic accomplishments. Roughly speaking, the debate has revolved around the issue of how much weight to give to cultural factors and how much to give to external factors as determinants of Chinese Canadian economic achievements. An approximate evaluation of the debate is that arguments favouring greater weight being given to external factors as determinants of Chinese Canadian economic achievements have been stronger, if only, for their frequency of appearance and depth of development. In contrast, arguments supporting cultural factors have been weaker, the result being that a reading of much of the related literature will emphasize the external factors including their sometimes unjustified existence. What follows in this section will outline some of the arguments emphasizing external factors; however, it will also offer rebuttal that cultural factors have been underestimated and that, in searching for practical knowledge from the history of Chinese Canadian achievements, one may find more of value in the cultural factors.

7.1.1 Arguments for External Factors Being More Important in the Economic Achievement of Chinese Canadians

Broadly speaking, there are two dimensions to the argument that external factors have been more important in producing the economic achievements of Chinese Canadians. The first is that external factors can account for the economic achievements of Chinese Canadians. The second argues that external factors by default offer the best explanation because cultural factors cannot offer an adequate explanation. This section describes the first dimension.

External factors are those that occur mostly outside the control of Chinese Canadians. The physical environment, the character of mainstream society, the broad historical situation, are all factors that Chinese Canadians can or could have done little to change. External factors are sometimes referred to metaphorically as "structural," meaning that they constitute the broad framework within which Chinese Canadians make their lives. In the past, legal restrictions on Chinese Canadians were structural factors affecting them. Today, Chinese Canadians' ascribed status as a minority would be a structural factor, providing them certain privileges under Canada's policy of multiculturalism, but also designating them as different from the norm, which makes perception of them open to a number of indefinite observations.

External factors contrast with ethnicity or cultural factors, such as language or main traditions, that are largely controllable by the group possessing them. They constitute part of the group's identity and as such they could be referred to as internal or intrinsic factors.

One theory that emphasizes the role of external factors in determining the achievements of minority groups is the blocked mobility thesis. This theory holds that an ethnic group may be limited by structural factors from developing their potential in one area; therefore, they will attempt to and may succeed in another that is open to them. Peter Li claims its usefulness in "understanding the emergence of Chinese business in Canada in the historical period prior to the Second World War."[182] Because Chinese Canadians were restricted then from participation in the mainstream labour market, they turned to establishing private businesses, such as laundries and restaurants, in order to make a living. Despite the restrictions they faced, large numbers of Chinese Canadians were able to form their own business, which is rightly considered an achievement.

Nevertheless, the blocked mobility thesis holds that this "achievement" should be seen as forced upon Chinese Canadians. They had little choice, as opening a private business

---

[182] "Ethnic Enterprise," 135.

was one of the few viable options they had. Therefore, the large numbers of Chinese Canadians participating in private business prior to the Second World War are more accurately viewed as the result of desperation in the face of restrictions on one's livelihood.[183] They are not an example of the commendable act of trying to improve oneself; they are, instead, examples of trying to survive.

As for other examples of Chinese Canadian economic achievement, Peter Li again offers external factors. The economic strength exhibited by Chinese Canadians in the 1980s and 1990s was the result of the fact that "many recent Chinese immigrants [had] come to Canada with previously acquired qualifications and capital that [enabled] them to do well in Canadian society."[184] According to Li, the large investment and heightened economic status of Chinese Canadians seen during this time were more due to the capital and entrepreneurial skills that they brought with them, mostly from Hong Kong. While offering these external factors as the main reasons for the economic achievement, in the same vein, he dismisses cultural factors as possible explanations by asking why those factors have remained dormant for most of the history of Chinese Canadians only to play an effect in the 1980s and 1990s.[185]

In another example, Li attributes the expansion of Chinese Canadian business in Richmond from 1980 to 1990 to the "growth of the ethnic consumer market, the emergence of the Chinese professional class, and the increase in investment

---

[183] 20.4 percent and 14.7 percent of Chinese Canadians were self employed in 1921 and 1931, respectively (Li, *The Chinese*, 52). It is important to keep in mind that Chinese Canadians were able to attain these high rates even though they had few economic, linguistic, and managerial resources with which to operate their businesses in these years. In comparison, in 1991, when they were much more capable, only 10.9 percent of Chinese Canadians (compared to 9.7 percent of other Canadians) were self employed (*ibid.*, 126, citing Statistics Canada, 1991, *Census of Canada, Public Use Microdata File on Individuals [1994]*). The diminished percentage of Chinese Canadians self employed in 1991, in spite of more favourable circumstances, can be interpreted as indicating that Chinese Canadians were not originally inclined to operating a private business but were forced to.

[184] *The Chinese*, 9-10.

[185] *Ibid.*

218

capital which is influenced by the state's policy toward immigration and the economy." In Li's opinion, none of these are closely linked to Chinese culture, but rather are better explained by a link to "specific historical economic and social conditions."[186]

According to proponents of external factors as the main causes of Chinese Canadian economic achievements, these factors provide a sufficient explanation with examples for these achievements. In addition, they can also support arguments showing how cultural factors are insufficient for the same purposes.

7.1.2 Arguments Against Culture as a Factor

The second dimension of the argument that external factors have been more important in producing the economic achievements of Chinese Canadians takes the indirect approach of reasoning that cultural factors do not offer an adequate explanation for their achievements. The reasoning is diverse, offering views that it would have been irrational to rely on Chinese cultural resources, that Chinese Canadians have established their own culture in Canada distinct from that in China, that there were no economic achievements until long after the arrival of Chinese Canadians, and that there is no such thing as core Chinese culture to serve as a resource.

The argument that it would have been irrational to rely on Chinese culture as resource for economic success is itself complex. Superficially, one would think that promotion of common cultural values would have led to group solidarity and mutual assistance. However, Peter Li points out that this kind of solidarity actually reduces one's "opportunities in the open job market due to lack of connections and contacts in mainstream society, as well as in terms of accentuating social distinctiveness. Ethnic distinctiveness also becomes grounds for economic penalty in a society that reinforces and rewards conformity and assimilation."[187] He argues that there is a

---

[186] "Ethnic Enterprise," 135.

[187] "Social Capital and Economic Outcomes for Immigrants and Ethnic Minorities," *Journal of International Migration and Integration* 5.2 (Spring 2004), 178.

penalty for embracing ethnic identity and that, because of this penalty, ethnic groups would not have rationally embraced difference from the mainstream.

Chan Kwok-bun concurs that reliance on ethnic resources in order to succeed economically may, in fact, be irrational. The restrictions imposed by mainstream society lead to the creation of an ethnic economy within which entrepreneurs compete fiercely with one another thereby further undermining their own ability to succeed while isolating themselves from participation in the more lucrative mainstream economy.[188] Lloyd Wong and Michelle Ng documented evidence of this phenomenon in their survey of sixty-four Chinese business immigrants to Canada. They found that many of them were forced into the ethnic economy even though they had originally wanted to establish themselves in the mainstream economy. The result was that they faced greater competition in the ethnic economy and had to endure longer working hours and lower rates of return.[189] Therefore, it seems illogical that Chinese Canadian entrepreneurs would want to rely on cultural resources in order to succeed economically.

The risks may even go beyond reduced opportunity and self exploitation. Thomas Menkhoff and Solvay Gerke hold that a tendency among Chinese businessmen toward what Edward Said called "self-orientalization" could "provide certain interest groups with opportune arguments to blame the Chinese minority for economic crises or the lack of development progress and/or to justify their political, cultural, socioeconomic and physical subordination."[190] According to Menkhoff and Gerke, this is what occurred in Indonesia. Chinese Indonesians distinguished themselves by their different culture and this distinction served as a means to identify and subject them to persecution.[191]

---

[188] *Migration, Ethnic Relations and Chinese Business* (London: Routledge, 2005), 119.

[189] "Chinese Immigration Entrepreneurs in Vancouver: A Case Study of Ethnic Business Development," *Canadian Ethnic Studies* 30.1 (1998).

[190] "Introduction: Asia' s Transformation and the Role of the Ethnic Chinese," in *Chinese Entrepreneurship and Asian Business Networks*, ed. Thomas Menkhoff and Solvay Gerke (London: RoutledgeCurzon, 2003), 6.

[191] *Ibid.*

Apart from arguing that it is irrational and, therefore, unlikely that Chinese Canadians have mainly relied on cultural resources to achieve economic success, it is also held that there were few cultural resources available to begin with, which is another reason why they could not be a determinant factor. This argument also takes various forms. It is held that Chinese Canadians have developed their own culture distinct from that of the country from which they or their ancestors emigrated. Therefore, given the short history of Chinese in Canada, there would be few cultural resources developed and ready for use.

Chan Kwok-bun takes the debate to an extreme by arguing that there is no such thing as a core Chinese culture anywhere in the world, even in China.[192] While Chan may not be claiming that there never was a core culture, his implication is that, if there was, it certainly could not have been much of an influence given the differences one finds among Chinese in the world today. For example, the Chinese of Hong Kong, Macau, and Taiwan have long been exposed to foreign influences, the Chinese of Southeast Asia have similarly been exposed to a variety of influences. He notes that some ethnic Chinese have started to adopt traits and practices associated with China now that its economic status has risen; however, in this case they are creating an image for themselves rather than tapping into an ethnic core.[193] Chan then goes on to argue that some of the characteristics that one would associate with Chinese economic achievement, such as flexibility in preserving one's business, a desire to embark on a business career, and a reliance on personal relations, are not, in fact, Chinese.[194] The underlying claim in this argument is that there is no common culture that Chinese can tap as a resource in business; therefore, one cannot make the claim for cultural factors being important in their economic achievements, which would include, of course, Chinese Canadians.

---

[192] *Migration*, 140.

[193] *Ibid.*, 141-42.

[194] *Ibid.*, 142-46.

7.1.3 Arguments for Cultural Factors Being More Important in the Economic Achievements of Chinese Canadians

Turning to the other side of the debate, one thing required is to reflect upon the nature of the debate that has been conducted. There are a number of things about it that should be highlighted in order to aid one in judging the merit of both sides. Firstly, Chinese Canadian achievements have not been limited to the economic. Achievements in other areas do not seem to be as easily explained by external factors; for example, in eldercare, Chinese Canadian elders would have been treated according to standards widely practised in Canada and any incompatibilities easily overcome. Certainly, overcoming language barriers only requires interpreters, not the completely separate facilities that Chinese Canadians have created. When one sees these facilities being expanded to include non-Chinese,[195] one has to ask not only what external factors are at play in this situation, but also, are Chinese Canadians being controlled or are they doing the controlling.

Another example that does not seem easily explained by reference to external factors is Traditional Chinese Medicine (TCM). It has proliferated when arguably there was a superior system in place, which constituted an external factor. If one argues that the external factor is weaknesses in the Western medical system, one also has to ask which are more significant, the weaknesses or the specific responses to those weaknesses that are part of TCM. It seems to be the latter because these responses have produced a fairly complex medical system offering a range of alternatives to the Western system.

A second aspect of the nature of the debate is the seemingly ad hoc nature of explanations from the side supporting external factors. To explain the ability of Chinese Canadians to establish private businesses early in their history the blocked mobility thesis is employed. The formation of capital and business expertise in Asia that was later encouraged to enter Canada explains large scale Chinese Canadian investment. While it has not appeared yet, one can anticipate the economic rise of China

---

[195] Refers to Yee Hong; see chapter VIII "Chinese Canadian Institutional Eldercare" of this book.

will be used to explain the economic contributions of Chinese
Canadians in fostering trade between Canada and China.

Although these explanations of how external factors have
contributed to the economic achievements of Chinese
Canadians are informative, one has to wonder whether there is
not some more intrinsic factor, such as their culture, that is a
more important determinant of these achievements. Otherwise,
it seems mostly fortuitous that Chinese Canadians have so
often encountered external factors conducive to accomplishing
what they have, and this reasoning seems strained because it is
unusual to have such good fortune.

In analyzing the economic growth in East Asia, the World
Bank published a major study on East Asia in 1993 and
concluded that there was only one chance in ten thousand that
so many miracle economies would randomly be located so close
to one another.[196] In other words, it was almost impossible that
the economic growth in those countries was fortuitous, not due
to properties or a situation commonly possessed or experienced
by them all. The World Bank effectively challenged the
assumption that the growth in these countries was merely
coincidental.

In the case of Chinese Canadians, one has to also ask if it
was just good fortune that Chinese Canadians had to deal with
the circumstances they did, that this was the main determinant
of their economic achievements. When compared to the case of
East Asia, an affirmative answer to this question does not seem
so obvious. In the case of East Asia, because there is no other
obvious set of external circumstances common to all of the
countries but also unique to them alone that explains their
growth, a commonly offered explanation is their shared
culture.[197]

Of course, that debate is not settled, but its present form
does offer insight for the one being conducted around Chinese
Canadians. Just as a common culture is cited more insistently

---

[196] World Bank, *The East Asian Miracle: Economic Growth and Public Policy,*
(New York: Oxford, 1993), 2.

[197] Nathan Glazer's essay "Two Cheers for Asian Values" (*China in the
National Interest,* ed. Owen Harries [New Brunswick, N.J. : Transaction
Publishers, 2003]) gives a balanced overview of the debate surrounding East
Asian culture's role in fostering economic growth. Page 177, which contains a
list of books arguing for its importance to this growth, is of particular interest.

as the most important factor for economic growth in East Asia, it increases the validity of raising the same factor–a factor that is similar in content, for the culture of Chinese Canadians is strongly influenced by that in East Asia–as a consideration in the debate on Chinese Canadian economic achievement.

A third aspect to consider about the nature of the debate as to whether external or intrinsic factors have been more important influences in Chinese Canadian economic achievements is the use of the term "achievement." This essay has taken the position that many of the highlights of Chinese Canadian history are the result of Chinese Canadian efforts, that Chinese Canadians are responsible for their existence so to speak. Use of the term "achievement" assumes this position and, therefore, weighs the debate in favour of cultural factors being more important. This having been acknowledged, a reverse position should also be considered: is "achievement" a correct description. Nevertheless, if upon reflection the term "achievement" does, in fact, seem appropriate, one has to grant intuitive evidence to the argument that cultural factors have been important in determining the record of Chinese Canadians.

A fourth notable aspect in the nature of the debate is the need to choose carefully the cultural characteristics that one investigates as possibly having an impact on Chinese Canadian achievements. Research on the business cooperation among Chinese in Southeast Asia has shown that the cooperation was only an expediency to overcome the lack of systemic support for Chinese entrepreneurs, indicating that the willingness to cooperate was only a rational decision to defend one's interest and not a deeper cultural characteristic. Otherwise, the rotating credit associations and voluntary associations that typified this cooperation would not have become almost irrelevant for Chinese doing business in Canada and United States where they had legal rights.[198]

While this shows that the tendency to form business associations may not be a Chinese cultural characteristic, it does not show that cultural characteristics do not play a role in

---

[198] Peter S. Li, "Overseas Chinese Networks: A Reassessment," in *Chinese Business Networks: State, Economy and Culture* , ed. Chan Kwok Bun (Singapore: Prentice Hall, 2000), 271-72.

the economic achievements of Chinese Canadians and even among Chinese across time and space.

This fourth aspect leads to a fifth and final aspect of the nature of the debate. Arguably, the underlying motivation for the debate is or should be practical and not theoretical; therefore, the scepticism of some scholars is inappropriate. In a Canadian context, what is or should be taking place is a search for alternatives to rectify weaknesses in Canadian culture. This is one of the purposes of Canadian multiculturalism, as the author understands it, and it is being intensified by a variety of serious problems that affect not only Canada but many of the world's main cultures. In this case, what is being searched for is not a definitive answer that eliminates all other possibilities or even that tells us what is not the case. We are searching for solutions rather than truth. Of course, truth is important, but not as important in this case.

In researching the role of culture in the Chinese Canadian economic achievements, given the practical nature of the quest, one would be best to focus on Chinese culture, which one can duplicate to a certain degree. An investigation of the historical circumstances in Canada that have surrounded Chinese Canadian achievements might be able to inform one that it was entirely these circumstances and not the culture of Chinese Canadians that resulted in their economic achievements. In this way, a researcher would be saved the effort of exploring the culture for resources to duplicate these achievements. On the other hand, if the investigation did not at some early point demonstrate that the historical circumstances were entirely the cause, it would be more in conformance with one's purposes if one switched their research to Chinese Canadian culture. One could not practically, nor does it seem that one would want to,[199] duplicate the historical circumstances that supposedly led to their economic achievements. However, it is possible, as the ideal underlying multiculturalism holds, to learn about and adopt cultural characteristics of other groups, especially if they can be shown to produce benefits.

Given that aspects of the debate indicate that the cultural characteristics of Chinese Canadians do, in fact, contribute to

---

[199] In principle, one should not want to block the constructive development of any group in Canada.

their economic achievement and even if this is not immediately apparent, these characteristics seem to offer the more practical avenue of research, the question that naturally arises is what cultural characteristics contribute to the economic achievements in question. While it is beyond the scope of this essay, and even this book, to attempt a full answer to this question, an attempt to point out the effect of some characteristics could indicate the potential merit and benefit of deeper research in this area.

Consider the value of personal responsibility, that is responsibility for one's own success, health, impact on others, and even the metaphysical meaning of one's own existence. Arguably, if one has a stronger sense of personal responsibility, one is going to be more successful in many ways, including economically. One is going to work harder and persevere longer when they believe that one's economic success depends upon one's own efforts. Reflecting this greater sense of personal responsibility, Chinese Canadians have a greater propensity to save, to own their homes, to pursue education, to care for their own health, and to support their elderly.

Culturally, one can draw direct links between this sense of personal responsibility and Confucian thought. The Confucian canon offers several examples to exhorting readers to reflect upon their personal motivations in order to improve oneself. Confucius (551-479 BCE) advised his students to examine themselves when they encountered someone less worthy to make sure that they were not like them.[200] Mencius (371-c.289 BCE) described supreme courage as being able to oppose a force of thousands if one finds oneself in the right, but, in contrast, being unable to oppose an ordinary opponent if one is in the wrong.[201] *Daxue* (The Great Learning) describes how personal cultivation–learning, strengthening one's intentions, rectifying one's mind–would contribute to order in society.[202] Wang

[200] *The Analects* 4.17, trans. D.C. Lau (London: Penguin Books Ltd., 1979), 74.

[201] *Mencius* 2a:2, trans. D. C. Lau, third ed. (Harmondsworth, Eng.: Penguin Books, 1983), 76-77.

[202] *Daxue* (The Great Learning), in *Source Book in Chinese Philosophy,* trans. Wing-tsit Chan (Princeton, New Jersey: Princeton Univ. Press, 1963), 86-87.

Yangming (1472-1529) advocated the unity of conscience and action.[203]

As representatives of Confucian thought, these beliefs were widely disseminated and became norms for common behaviour in China and even East Asia. Because they became part of the ordinary person's belief system, they had important influence on ensuring one's economic success. The respected thinker Herman Kahn argues that "both aspects of the Confucian ethic—the creation of dedicated, motivated, responsible, and educated individuals and the enhanced sense of commitment, organizational identity, and loyalty to various institutions—will result in all the neo-Confucian societies having at least potentially higher growth rates than other cultures."[204] Furthermore, Confucian thinking promotes sobriety, a high value on education, a desire for accomplishment in various skills, and seriousness about tasks, job, family, and obligations in the individual.[205] All of these qualities, arguably, can be derived from a strong sense of personal responsibility.

Turning to Chinese Canadians, the case could be made that, despite the barriers pitted against them, the cultural resources available to them, such as a strong sense of personal responsibility, meant that they were less likely to blame others for their impediments, but instead believe that they themselves were mainly responsible for finding a solution. This attitude would allow them to succeed where others might have failed, and produce some of the characteristics and results that Kahn observed.

There are other qualities, besides a strong sense of personal responsibility, that are more profound and, therefore, offer

---

[203] *Wang Yangming quanji* (A complete collection of Wang Yangming's works), ed. Wu Guang, Qian Ming, Dong Ping, and Yao Yanfu (Shanghai: Shanghai guji chubanshe, 1992), Vol. 1, 4. For an English translation see *Instructions for Practical Living and Other Neo-Confucian Writings by Wang Yang-Ming*, trans. Wing-tsit Chan (New York: Columbia University Press, 1963), sec. 5, 10.

[204] *World Economic Development: 1979 and Beyond* (Boulder, Colorado: Westview Press, 1979), 122. Kahn does not explain his use of the prefix "neo" with "Confucian," but seems to be referring to Confucian culture as practised in modern nation states with a greater adaptability than before (see pages 121-123).

[205] *Ibid.*, 121.

greater potential if investigated as cultural resources that contribute to Chinese Canadian economic achievement. Chinese people value harmony and the company of others. The famous Chinese historian Qian Mu (1895-1990) selected this quality as distinguishing the Chinese, particularly in contrast to Westerners.[206]

Again, in Kahn's view practising harmony is conducive to economic success: it promotes efficiency.[207] One could add that it helps one empathize with those of different perspectives, including those with whom one is doing business and even competing. As such, one's perspective on doing business is more farsighted and comprehending of the variety of factors that make for successful business. As well, an appreciation of the company of others allows one to function easily in a group setting, which again furthers cooperation and is conducive to creating synergies with others.

In short, there are characteristics found within Chinese culture that are more profound and which could have contributed to the economic accomplishments of both the Chinese and Chinese Canadians. One should consider these well in attempting to understand these accomplishments. Moreover, if one's search has a practical motivation, even more careful consideration should be given because these cultural characteristics offer the potential for improving one's own economic performance.

There is another reason why it would be practical to attempt to understand any cultural factors that have contributed to the economic achievements of Chinese Canadians. This reason is more apparent if one considers all the achievements described in this book; however, even if one considers just the economic achievements, the point is still clear. Many economic achievements come with cultural concomitants and in many ways are culturally supportive. The establishment of TCM as a parallel medical system is an economic achievement because it required a substantial

---

[206] *Cong Zhongguo lishi laikan Zhongguo minzu xing ji Zhongguo wenhua* (The nature of Chinese people and Chinese culture from the perspective of Chinese history) (Hong Kong: Zhongwen daxue chubanshe, 1979), particularly pages 22-23, 24-25, 29, and 66.

[207] P. 121.

economic outlay. At the same time, it is also a cultural achievement; it supports a practice that is distinctly Chinese. Similarly, Chinese language media promotes even greater use of the language. The large Chinese grocery stores, like the T & T Supermarket chain, are not only economically successful, they promote Chinese culture by supplying its material manifestations: the iconic foods (e.g., the thousand-year-old eggs), the holiday decorations (e.g., red envelopes used to distribute money during the Chinese New Year), the basic constituents (e.g., soy products and fresh green vegetables), and so on. In establishing themselves economically, these industries and companies also promote Chinese culture. As they do, it becomes potentially more beneficial for one to understand this culture if only for the simple purpose of making a living by also supporting it; for example, as a supplier, replacing some of the 70 percent of T & T's merchandise that originates outside Canada with Canadian products.

Therefore, there are two practical aspects embedded in the claim that more importance should be given to cultural characteristics when investigating the reasons for Chinese economic success. On one hand, there is the potential for benefit that could be derived from adopting relevant cultural characteristics. On the other, there will be cultural consequences of these economic achievements that can also provide opportunities for material gain. Chinese culture could be so intrinsically connected to the economic achievements of Chinese Canadians that any effort to extract greater benefit from those achievements will necessitate some understanding of the culture.

7.2 Ongoing Barriers to Achievement

If openness to Chinese Canadians and their culture offers greater access to the benefits that can be derived from their achievements, it is likely that a lack of openness to them, in the various forms that it can take, creates less access to those same benefits. However, it seems that Canadian society is not aware of these potential benefits and losses because as a society it has not reflected deeply on the existence of barriers to even greater Chinese Canadian achievements. Not only are newly arriving Chinese immigrants finding it difficult to make an adequate living in spite of the high levels of education and expertise they possess, they also seem to be encountering racial discrimination in their efforts to improve themselves. One would think that, given Canada's past history of racial discrimination, the country would be sensitive to the presence of its remnants and even recurrences.

The presence of barriers to Chinese Canadian economic achievements may be difficult to discern because they are hidden to a certain degree by the magnitude of the achievements themselves. Chinese Canadians, in general, seem to be prospering as evidenced by figures on home ownership and income, for example. Against a background of this strength, the areas of underachievement are not readily seen. However, the low incomes of the newest Chinese Canadians indicate the existence of impediments, and when their incomes are considered in the context of expressed frustration and subsequent departure from Canada by Chinese Canadians, the detriments to Canadian society that occur because of these should make one alert to the existence of these impediments.

A number of studies have confirmed the economic difficulties that recent Chinese immigrants have been encountering in Canada. Individual incomes for Hong Kong immigrants to Canada were very low in 1996 with 45 percent earning less than $1000 a month and mean income below half that of those who had returned to Hong Kong to work.[208] In 1999, the average income of Chinese immigrants was slightly less than fifteen thousand dollars, which was only half of that of the general population.[209] A 2004-2005 survey of three hundred twenty-two recently arrived and economically active Chinese households, mostly from the PRC, recorded that for 60 percent of them the employment situation had been worse in Canada than it had been in China. The same survey revealed that 60 percent of these households had earnings of less than thirty-one thousand dollars a year, including 44 percent who had earned less than twenty thousand dollars.[210] Finally, a 1995 survey of

---

[208] D.J. DeVoretz, J. Ma, and K. Zhang, ""Triangular Human Capital Flows: Some Empirical Evidence from Hong Kong," in *Host Societies and the Reception of Immigrants*, ed. J.G. Reitz, (San Diego: Center for U.S. Mexican Studies, Univ. of California, 2003), 482-3, 489.

[209] Wang and Lo, "Chinese Immigrants in Canada," 18.

[210] Shibao Guo and Don J. DeVoretz, "Chinese Immigrants in Vancouver: Quo Vadis?", Vancouver Centre of Excellence, Research on Immigration and

twenty-two Chinese entrepreneur immigrants who originally had plans to operate businesses in the Canadian mainstream economy found that about eleven of them were forced into the ethnic market where conditions were more competitive and less rewarding. The results were interpreted as indicating that Chinese business immigrants were blocked from operating in the mainstream economy by systemic constraints.[211]

Although there is evidence to support it, the claim that Chinese Canadians have been systemically blocked from reaching their potential remains difficult to prove. There are so many factors that impact their efforts that it seems nigh impossible to prove that a particular one is more influential than another. However, what cannot be questioned are the reactions of Chinese Canadians to the barriers they face. They claim the existence of unfairness and other forms of injustice in their lives and describe their dissatisfaction with having come to Canada.

Many of the entrepreneur immigrants surveyed in 1995 claimed that racism was a factor in blocking their entrance into the mainstream Canadian economy.[212] Another survey conducted between 1997 and 1999 of one thousand one hundred eighty PRC immigrants to Canada found that 73 percent of respondents believed that their entry into professional occupations was blocked because of unequal opportunities for visible minority immigrants. Furthermore, 44 percent of them perceived discrimination on the basis of skin colour and 43 percent on the basis of national or ethnic origin.[213] In yet another survey, 50 percent of the respondents felt they were worse off in Vancouver than in China.[214]

Integration in the Metropolis, Working Paper Series No. 05-20 (Oct. 2005–updated Feb. 2006), 13, 14.

[211] Wong and Ng, 72, 74, 83.

[212] *Ibid.*, 73.

[213] Li Zong, "International Transference of Human Capital and Occupational Attainment of Recent Chinese Professional Immigrants in Canada," Prairie Centre of Excellence for Research on Immigration and Integration Working Paper Series, Working Paper No. WP03-04, Mar. 2004, 9.

[214] Guo and DeVoretz, 23.

The disaffection among Chinese Canadians was so strong that they allowed their cases to be featured on the former website *NotCanada.com*. This website, run by former Canadian citizens who had permanently departed from Canada, sought to reveal the difficulties and deception involved in immigrating to Canada. Much of the criticism of Canada's immigrant policies found on the website reflected the experiences of Chinese immigrants. Many immigrants had been unable to find employment commensurate with their qualifications in spite of claimed promises that they would be able to. The result was that they had been forced to live substandard lives in Canada.[215]

Anecdotes of the underutilization and resulting dissatisfaction of Chinese Canadian immigrants abound. Mary Yang, host of a popular current-events show on Chinese-language Fairchild Radio in 2004 related how acquaintances that were professors worked in bakeries or as labourers in the underground economy. She reported that everybody else in the local Chinese community had similar stories about friends and relatives. Kristyn Wong-Tam, president of the Toronto chapter of the Chinese Canadian National Council, described why these recent Chinese Canadian immigrants suffered from alienation and isolation. "'They have three degrees from Shanghai, they're dentists, they're doctors, they're engineers or chemists and now they're washing dishes in Chinatown,' she says. 'They feel they've been sold this bill of goods.' Promising human lives are being wasted in Toronto; non-English-speaking professionals, Ms. Wong-Tam says frankly, are 'a failed class.'"[216]

Arguably, the difficulties that Chinese immigrants to Canada have encountered could be due to reasons apart from prejudices against them. One 1993 study noted that 58 percent of Chinese immigrants did not possess the required language skills at the time of immigration.[217] Furthermore, statistics showing the percentage of average Toronto income made by Chinese immigrants in 1996 indicated that immigrants born in Hong Kong had 20 percent more income (81.2 percent compared

---

[215] NotCanada.com, accessed 2008.06.27.

[216] Cited in Barber.

[217] Wang and Lo, "Chinese Immigrants in Canada," 16.

to 60 percent) than those born in the PRC.[218] Therefore, the
incomes for Chinese immigrants seemed to vary based on place
of origin, which would further indicate that prejudices are only
part, if any, of the reason for the difficulties encountered.
Otherwise, incomes would be more similar for all groups
because prejudice would not distinguish among them.

Nevertheless, the high level of education possessed by
Chinese immigrants has to create suspicion that the reason for
their difficulties was more than their own limitations;[219]
otherwise, with their high level of education they should be able
to overcome them. Indeed, studies indicate that their own
limitations cannot account for all the difficulties they
encounter. In a comparison of three hundred two foreign
trained professionals, one hundred twenty-eight from China
and one hundred seventy-four from Poland, in 1998 in Toronto,
it was found that only 23 percent of the Chinese Canadian
professionals had ever worked in Canada as professionals in
contrast to 43 percent for the Polish Canadians. The 50 percent
lower participation rate in professional work by the surveyed
Chinese Canadians is all the more surprising in light of their
seeming to have had higher levels of occupational attainment in
their country of origin than Polish Canadians in theirs.[220]
Moreover, this drop in occupational attainment and lower
achievement rates relative to Polish Canadians occurred even
when Chinese Canadians reported commands of English and
Western culture equivalent to them.[221]

---

[218] Lucia Lo and Lu Wang, "A Political Economy Approach to Understanding
the Economic Incorporation of Chinese Sub-ethnic Groups," *Journal of
International Migration and Integration / Revue de l integration et de la
migration internationale* 5.1 (2004), 131.

[219] Of Chinese immigrants arriving between 1980 and 2000, 36.2 percent had,
at least, some post secondary education (Shuguang Wang and Lucia Lo,
"Chinese Immigrants in Canada," 15).

[220] Li Zong, "Language, Education, and Occupational Attainment of Foreign-
Trained Chinese and Polish Professional Immigrants in Toronto, Canada," in
*Chinese Migrants Abroad: Cultural, Educational, and Social Dimensions of
the Chinese Diaspora*, ed. Michael W. Charney, Brenda S. A. Yeoh, and Tong
Chee Kiong (Singapore: Singapore University Press, 2003), 168.

[221] *Ibid.*, 173.

The large differential in occupational attainment by Chinese Canadians compared to Polish Canadians adds evidence to the suspicion that the difficulties encountered by Chinese Canadians are much more than the result of their own limitations. It further strengthens the argument that Chinese Canadians are still being victimized by racism. Even though all determining factors--except for race--were approximately equivalent, Chinese Canadian's occupational attainment measured in the survey was substantially lower. This leaves race as the main determinant of the discrepancy and, thus, supports the charge of racism.

Another example shows how barriers to Chinese Canadian achievement directly harm Canada. In 2002, Vancouver's largest Chinese community group, the United Chinese Community Enrichment Services Society (S.U.C.C.E.S.S.) initiated a program called Gateway to Asia for the purpose of assisting Canadian companies to do business in China. S.U.C.C.E.S.S. collected a list of six hundred fifty recently immigrated Chinese businesspeople, 40 percent of whom had or continued to own a business in China. These businesspeople were trained on how to do business in Canada and taken to trade fairs in order to promote their connections in China. They also took the initiative to contact Canadian companies to do the same. However, most of the Canadian companies they contacted did not return their telephone calls or respond to their emails.[222]

The decision not to respond to an offer of assistance to do business in China by itself does not imply racism. However, when considered together with the ignorance of the abilities of Chinese Canadians demonstrated in the study comparing them to Polish Canadians, one detects a pattern of neglect that would seem to be the product of irrational factors such as racism. The Chinese Canadians with professional experience were in a position to assist Canadian companies and organizations as

---

[222] Andrea Mandel-Campbell, *Rescuing Canadian Business from the Suds of Global Obscurity: Why Mexicans Don't Drink Molson* (Vancouver: Douglas & McIntyre, 2007), 220. S.U.C.C.E.S.S.' report on the project is much more positive; for example, they report twenty-five million dollars in new export sales ("Gateway to Asia: Linking Chinese Entrepreneurs with Canadian Suppliers," Asia Pacific Foundation of Canada website, www.asiapacificgateway.net/pdf/success.pdf, accessed 2008.07.04.

were the businesspeople with contacts in China. However, their abilities and efforts to help were largely ignored to the detriment of those who were the recipients of their offers. The more logical explanation for this rejection seems to be a prejudice among the recipients rather than the limitations among the Chinese Canadians offering their services.

There is further evidence for the claim of prejudice. In 2008, 59 percent of Canadians regarded the power of China and other emerging Asian nations as an opportunity and as important to Canada's prosperity. When the Asia Pacific Foundation of Canada asked the same question in 2011, a mere three years later, the percentage that still thought so had dropped to 44 percent, even though more Canadians believed that the country should be diversifying its trade to become less dependent upon the U.S.[223]

The presence of possible prejudice has significant practical implications. If an educated population, such as Chinese Canadians, perceives that they are targets of injustice, they have the resources to respond. In the case of Chinese Canadian immigrants many are choosing to leave rather than suffer the perceived degradation. "An internet survey conducted in 2002 of recent Chinese immigrants by the Toronto-based North Chinese Community of Canada found that only 20 percent of the one thousand three hundred forty-five participants indicated that they would remain in Canada after obtaining Canadian citizenship."[224] Studies have also documented large numbers of immigrants returning to Hong Kong from Canada.[225] One study showed that those who did return outperformed stayers in several important categories, such as income earned,

---

[223] Brian Milner, "Asia: From Opportunity to Crisis in the Eyes of Canadians," *The Globe and Mail,* 2011.04.13.

[224] Wang and Lo, "Chinese Immigrants," 30; citing *World Journal [Shijie ri bao],* 2003.01.10.

[225] Don J. Devoretz and Kangqing Zhang, "Citizenship, Passports and the Brain Exchange Triangle," *Journal of Comparative Policy Analysis* 6.2 (Aug. 2004), 205, 207; and Abdurrahman Aydemir and Chris Robinson, "Return and Onward Migration among Working Age Men," Analytical Studies Branch Research Paper Series, Catalogue no. 11F0019MIE — No. 27321 (Statistics Canada, Mar. 2006), 21.

educational attainment, and occupational distribution.[226] Therefore, dual forces–a lack of success in Canada and the attraction of doing better in Hong Kong–were at work, leading Chinese Canadians to return.

7.3 Consequences of Barriers

There are many ramifications to Canada's weakness in retaining its immigrants, particularly Chinese. Two of the more practical ones are the loss of investment Canada makes in immigrants who later leave and the inability to meet the country's need for skilled immigrants. There are a number of expenditures involved with assimilating immigrants into a country. These include language training, higher education, education for children, and a commitment to provide benefits such as medical care, pensions, and a healthy environment. If immigrants are only present in the country to receive the benefits provided by these expenditures, whether early in their stay or later in old age when they have greater need for some of them, it will be difficult for that country to recover the expenditures required to provide them the benefits. A specific example of an expenditure that may be difficult to recover is the estimated $2.7 billion subsidy paid to provide post-secondary education to immigrants who later returned to Hong Kong.[227]

It has been predicted that one million Canadian jobs could go unfilled by 2020. For this reason, immigration is being seen as necessary for economic growth and well-being.[228] Canada has had a target of admitting 50 percent of its immigrants from the independent class. The reasoning is that immigrants from this class make a net economic contribution to Canada. Moreover, it has been because of the arrival of immigrants from China that it has been able to meet this target.[229] However, factors are

---

226 Don J. DeVoretz, "Asian Skilled-Immigration Flows to Canada: A Supply-Side Analysis," Foreign Policy Dialogue Series (Asian Pacific Foundation of Canada, 2003), 9.

227 Devoretz and Zhang, "Citizenship, Passports," 208.

228 Erin Tolley, "The Skilled Worker Class," Policy Brief (The Metropolis Project) 1 (January 2003), 1.

229 DeVoretz, "Asian Skilled-Immigration," 3-6.

starting to jeopardize the inflow. The age groups from which the most desirable immigrants are drawn are shrinking in China, one of Canada's largest source of immigrants. As well, Canada is facing greater competition from Australia, the European Union, and the USA for these immigrants.[230] This increases the chances that Canada will not be able to meet its target of attracting more immigrants who can contribute economically the most to the country. When these two ramifications, the loss of investment in and the competition for the most attractive immigrants, are taken into consideration, the presence of barriers to Chinese Canadian development seems self-defeating on Canada's part.

In summary, even though Chinese Canadians have achieved much economically, they are still encountering difficulties in reaching their full potential. Many recent immigrants are unable to find employment and earn wages commensurate with their qualifications. This is creating much disaffection among them and is leading many of them to return or want to return to their place of origin or move onto another country. This creates tremendous cost for Canada both in the lost investment in their assimilation into Canadian society and the lost opportunity of attracting and retaining immigrants who are more likely to contribute economically to the country. Furthermore, the potential opportunity loss is increasing as the pool of these immigrants shrinks and Canada faces increased competition for their loyalty. One could, perhaps, rationalize Canada's position by saying that the country has made a sincere effort to attract and retain new immigrants, and that the country offers benefits that should appeal to them. However, the truth seems that Canadian society still harbours prejudice against Chinese and this bias is a major factor in limiting Chinese Canadian achievement. If this is the case, Canada is hurting itself; not only because it is limiting the achievements of Chinese Canadians that could benefit the country, but also because the existence of prejudice ultimately has negative effects far beyond its target.

8. Future Economic Achievements

---

[230] *Ibid.*, 10-11.

Nevertheless, it is likely that Chinese Canadians will continue to develop economic strength. Their continued immigration into the country, their demonstrated ability to handle their finances well–investing in homes and accumulating large bank accounts–and their pursuit of education are all factors that should support them in this endeavour. This increasing economic strength will lead to greater demand for products and services to meet their needs and these products will in large part, if not mostly, be provided by Chinese Canadian businesspeople. At the same time, non-Chinese will become more aware of the advantages to these products and services, and will not only add to the demand but also attempt to profit from meeting it. These developments will be manifested in incremental changes in Canadian society: more Chinese shopping centers, greater use of TCM, greater use of Chinese script in promotion and information, etc.

There are likely to be major changes brought about by Chinese Canadian strength. Canada should see an increase in the number of large, capital intensive Chinese Canadian businesses. There are already a number of these, most of which have been supported by foreign investment. However, the cultural characteristics, such as the ability to handle one's finances well and the pursuit of education, and the increasing population will contribute to the establishment of domestically invested companies.

Chinese Canadians will also take the lead in developing economic relations with China. China's economy is developing quickly and they have large needs for the resources, services, and technology that Canada can provide. Chinese Canadians, who have made large efforts to preserve their culture,[231] are in a position to and, in fact, are helping to foster business relations between Canada and China. There is a potential for Chinese Canadians to become important players in Canada's international trade.

A third major change that Chinese Canadians will probably create in the Canadian economy is the development of the material and intellectual infrastructure necessary for Canada to conduct trade with Asia and, in particular, China. The Asia

---

[231] See chapter four "Preservation and Promotion of Chinese Culture" in this book.

Pacific Foundation of Canada has been spearheading a plan called the Asia Pacific Gateway Strategy. It envisions a framework of policies, investments, and initiatives that will make Canada the most competitive exit and entry point in North America for Asian and Canadian goods, services, and investment. Just as Chinese Canadians are taking a transnationalist role in promoting trade between Canada and China, they would also take a role in developing the broader strategy and infrastructure for Asia.

8.1 Organic Growth of Large Chinese Canadian Businesses

The formation of large Chinese Canadian companies, such as Husky Oil, indicates a trend that will probably continue because Chinese Canadians are demonstrating the ability to grow their companies organically, that is to say using resources that they can harness within the company. This means that growth is more within their control and, therefore, more likely to continue. Chinese Canadian companies can still benefit from infusions of outside capital or purchases of large assets from other companies; however, they now also possess the ability to grow themselves, without these infusions or purchases.

It was noted that many Chinese Canadian companies have surpassed their historical size. One out of fifty Chinese Canadian firms in the Toronto area employs more than two hundred workers and one tenth have annual sales of over US$10 million. They have also moved beyond traditional sector boundaries. Chinese Canadian businesses are no longer confined to the retail sector and they are starting to develop knowledge-based companies.[232]

One fact that should be garnered from this situation is that Chinese Canadian economic achievement no longer depends on an influx of investment from Chinese business immigrants. Based on the large investment by Chinese immigrants, the rise in house prices in Vancouver from 1986 to 1996, and the subsequent building of Chinese Canadian shopping centers in Toronto and Vancouver, one might believe that it was mostly investment dollars from abroad that has been driving the

---

[232] Lo, *et al.*, "Immigrants' Economic Status," 29, 30.

growth of Chinese Canadian business. Certainly, early examples, such as the capital for development of Concord Pacific Place seemed to be sourced in Hong Kong. However, later companies have grown on the basis of creating capital or generating revenue using resources already possessed by the company. K.Y. Ho used $300 thousand of capital to start up ATI Technologies Inc. in the 1980s. In 1997 ATI was Canada's third largest computer firm surpassing the $1.1 billion mark in revenues. The Louie family began as grocers in Vancouver's Chinatown. Yet, under the direction of Tong Louie, a member of the second generation, the family's business operations were expanded to include London Drugs, which has seventy-eight stores across the four western Canadian provinces; and franchiser and distributor for all, and owner of some Market Place Independent Grocers Alliance (IGA) stores in British Columbia. In 2002 the family business was ranked as the fourth largest corporation with headquarters in British Columbia, and in 2006, Brandt Louie, Tong's older son, was ranked twenty-ninth on the list of Canada's one hundred richest people.

These examples demonstrate that Chinese Canadians can grow their businesses organically. Ho and the Louies relied on effective business plans and execution within their companies in order to grow them.[233] They started relatively small and they did not need large investments from outside the company in order to become large companies. They realized the skill to generate huge economic value within their companies. If these companies have been able to develop these skills, it is likely that other Chinese Canadian companies will be able to as well. The increasing number of large size Chinese Canadian companies seems to be evidence of this. Furthermore, Chinese Canadian organizations, such as the Association of Chinese Canadian Entrepreneurs, exist for the purposes of disseminating the knowledge required to develop these skills.

The ability to grow organically is evidence of maturation of Chinese Canadian businesspeople. They are able to grow their companies without having to rely heavily on external investments; rather they can utilize already present resources to create and take advantage of market opportunities. There

---

[233] The Louies did have access to local loans, but even this was under less favourable conditions than other businesspeople with similar assets (Perrault, 129).

are companies, such as the Hopewell Group of Companies and T & T, that seem to be growing by accretion and have the potential to become even larger than they already have. There are also areas, such as in TCM, that could produce major Chinese Canadian companies. There seems to be large potential for consolidation in TCM that could see the formation of a large Chinese Canadian company or companies. There are many small practitioners of TCM while regulation is increasing within the industry. Those companies that are able to meet new regulations could take over market share from those that are not, leading to the formation of larger firms. Another possibility is that a company will be able to synthesize the advantages of TCM and Western medicine. For example, CV Technologies, headed by a Chinese Canadian, Jacqueline Shan, used a pharmaceutical model to develop natural therapeutics for health maintenance. Its lead product, a cold and flu preventive Cold-FX, is derived from the root of North American ginseng, which is widely used in TCM.

The ability of Chinese Canadian companies to grow organically gives them yet another means to achieve economically. Furthermore, the companies that have already succeeded in doing so, such as H.Y. Louie, provide models that can instill confidence in other Chinese Canadian companies so that they too can break through the historical barriers that have limited their growth. Therefore, one is likely to see Chinese Canadians create more large companies in the future.

8.2 Taking Canada Across the Pacific: Transnationalism

Another potential economic achievement for Chinese Canadians lies in developing trade with China. Canada is undergoing a shift in its trading relations, moving toward stronger economic ties with China. Chinese Canadians have become leaders in promoting this trend, but they could be achieving more. The economic opportunity that China presents is readily apparent. Asia is the fastest growing region of the world. It produces one quarter of global exports and accounts for over 35 percent of the world's GDP. This figure is expected to increase to 43 percent by 2020.[234] As the major contributor to Asia's growth, China's economic might has made it Canada's second largest trading partner since 2003.[235]

Although Asia, and China in particular, are booming, Canada's portion of the total Asian market in 2012 was .93 percent, down from 1.72 percent in 1995 and 2.51 percent in 1984.[236] Canada has fallen behind key competitors such as Australia in the Chinese market. Canada's share of China' imports and exports has been stagnant at about 1 percent in the midst of a commodity boom.[237] Specifically, Canada's share of China's market went from a peak of 1.67 percent (2000) to 1.25 percent (2012), its share of Hong Kong's market fell from a peak of .65 percent (2000) to .34 percent (2012), and similarly its share of Taiwan's market dropped from a peak of 1.46 percent (1994) to .6 percent (2012).[238] As to why the decline, BMO Financial Group has observed that there is a lack of Canadian business in China because of the lack of links between the two countries.[239] This is further reflected in the fact that only 0.6 percent of total Canadian outward investment in 2012 was destined for China.[240]

---

[234] Asia Pacific Foundation of Canada, "Leading the Way: Canadian Business Strategies in Asia," Oct. 2007 (*www.asiapacificgateway.net/pdf/summary.pdf*, accessed 2008.04.16).

[235] Jafar Khondaker, "Canada's Trade with China: 1997 to 2006," Statistics Canada, *www.statcan.ca/english/freepub/65-508-XIE/65-508-XIE2007001.htm*, accessed 2008.07.01.

[236] Asia Pacific Foundation of Canada, "Canada's Market Share in Asia," *www.asiapacific.ca/statistics/trade/market-share/canadas-market-share-asia*, accessed 2015.01.21; and Asia Pacific Foundation of Canada, "Leading the Way."

[237] Chen and Wellman, 21.

[238] Asia Pacific Foundation of Canada, "Canada Asia Agenda 2006," 50; and Asia Pacific Foundation of Canada, "Canada's Market Share in Asia."

[239] Asia Pacific Foundation of Canada website, "Asia Pacific Gateway/Gateway Convenings/Toronto," *www.asiapacificgateway.net/convenings/ontario_summary.cfm*, accessed 2008.07.02.

[240] $4, 239 million of Canada's $711 billion foreign direct investment went to China (Canadian International Development Platform, "Canadian Foreign

Given Canada's poor competitive record in China, there is strong motivation to take remedial measures, and it is natural that Chinese Canadians would be seen as key players in these efforts to take advantage of China's growth.[241] The term "transnationalism" describes Chinese Canadian involvement in this trade. The term refers to their influence, which usually consists of personal connections and practical knowledge, and physical presence in two or more different parts of the world, usually Canada and China. They utilize this influence in an effort to promote deeper contact among these different parts of the world, for example, by importing Chinese products for Canadian consumption.

Research done in 1995 showed that Chinese immigrant entrepreneurs were already conducting transnational business. They continued to maintain and operate their businesses in Asia after migrating to Canada and attempted to integrate them into their Canadian operations.[242] Some examples of transnational business included having factories in China and using Vancouver as a wholesale centre for their products, exporting Canadian products to China, and using professionals to design products that were then manufactured in China and sold to North American distributors.[243] A 2008 report documented a more sophisticated arrangement. A team of Chinese transnationalists developed the means to commercialize Canadian drug inventions in China. The transnationalists where able to save on labour costs—about 70 percent of the cost of research and development for pharmaceuticals—obtain large numbers of test participants, and

---

Direct Investment Abroad," cidpnsi.ca/blog/portfolio/canadian-foreign-direct-investment-overseas-quick-review, accessed 2015.01.21).

[241] Chen and Wellman ask how increasing transnational entrepreneurship among Canada's immigrant population can be translated into economic competitiveness (22).

[242] Wong and Ng, 81.

[243] *Ibid.*

receive generous resource commitments from eager collaborators in China.[244]

The strength and potential significance of transnational commerce between Canada and China is seen in the growth of organizations to meet its structural needs. The largest foreign bank in Canada HSBC specializes in providing banking services for those wanting to do financial transactions in China. Formerly named The Hongkong and Shanghai Banking Corporation Limited, it was founded in 1865 in Hong Kong.[245] Its headquarters remained there until 1993 prior to the return of Hong Kong to the People's Republic of China in 1997.[246] It was one of the first foreign banks to incorporate in China where it has one hundred seventy-nine branches,[247] not including the fifty that its subsidiary, Hang Seng Bank has.[248] Together with this subsidiary, HSBC has over six hundred seventy service locations in Hong Kong.[249] Currently, it is pursuing growth in China to add to the considerable assets it already holds there.[250] HSBC was established in Canada in 1981 under the name Hong Kong Bank of Canada. It has one hundred nine branches there and was offering the Immigrant Investor Program to assist

---

[244] Xiaohua Lin, Jian Guan, and Mary Jo Nicholson, "Transnational Entrepreneurs as Agents of International Innovation Linkages," Asia Pacific Foundation of Canada, December 2008, 5.

[245] HSBC Holdings website, "The HSBC Group, A Brief History," *www.hsbc.com/1/2/about-hsbc/group-history*, accessed 2008.04.20.

[246] *Ibid.*

[247] HSBC website, "About HSBC," *www.hsbc.com.cn/1/2/hsbc-china*, accessed 2015.01.22.

[248] Hang Seng Bank website, "Bank Profile and History," *bank.hangseng.com/1/2/about-us/corporate-info/bank-profile*, accessed 2015.01.22.

[249] *Ibid.*; and HSBC Holdings website, "The HSBC Group in the Hong Kong Special Administrative Region (SAR) fact sheet," *www.hsbc.com/1/PA_1_1_S5/content/assets/newsroom/media_kit/fact_shee ts/hong_kong_sar_fact_sheet_en_april_2007.pdf*, accessed 2008.04.20.

[250] Vidya Ram, "HSBC Gets Back In Touch With Its Roots," *Forbes.com*, 2008.03.10, *www.forbes.com/2008/03/10/hsbc-bocom-china-markets-equity-cx_vr_0310markets13.html*, accessed 2008.04.17.

those interested in immigrating there. The presence of HSBC in Canada provides Chinese Canadian transnational entrepreneurs with the structural and familiar means to promote trade and business between China and Canada, thereby better linking Canada to one of the largest and fastest growing economies in the world.

Another organization that has been established to foster trade between Canada and China and likewise harness the abilities and motivation of Chinese Canadians is the Hong Kong-Canada Business Association (HKCBA). Its main missions are to encourage two-way trade between Canada and Hong Kong, to provide a forum for discussion of trade issues involving the two, and to promote government policies that will lead to expanded trade and closer ties between the two. It was established in 1984 as a nonprofit organization and has become one of the largest bi-lateral trade associations in Canada. It has approximately one thousand three-hundred members in eight major Canadian cities. Typically, the members are owners or managers of small or medium sized businesses trading with Hong Kong, China, and South East Asia; trade related enterprises; and professionals who are involved in international trade.[251]

The existence of these organizations demonstrates a number of points with regard to Chinese Canadians and their efforts to foster this trade. For one, a large number of these organizations' supporters are Chinese Canadian.[252] Two, there is strong recognition of the actual and potential benefits of developing business relations with China. Three, Canada is in an improved position to foster trade with greater China. Four, there are important structural elements in place that will allow Chinese Canadian entrepreneurs to move beyond the typically small scale retail businesses and to develop businesses that will have significant influence on Canada's economy. Five, Canada will continue to benefit from the achievements of Chinese Canadians.

---

[251] The Hong Kong-Canada Business Association, National, website, "About Us/The HKCBA Story," *national.hkcba.com/story.html*, accessed 2015.01.22.

[252] The participation of many Chinese Canadians is ascertained by the surnames of members and personal contact with them.

Further evidence for these points is seen in the actuality of having Chinese Canadians in place to realize them. This is seen in the number of Canadian citizens living in Hong Kong. The transnationalist activities of Chinese Canadians have led to almost three hundred thousand of them in Hong Kong in 2010 and the figure could be as many as nearly five hundred and fifty thousand. Furthermore, more than 50 percent had received their education in Canada.[253] A number of community groups, such as twenty-four Canadian university alumni associations and the Chinese Canadian Association of Hong Kong with three thousand active members, have been promoting Chinese-Canadian relations.[254] It was this group of transnationalists that Dalton McGuinty, then Premier of Ontario, addressed in 2005 when he referred to the quarter million Canadians living in Hong Kong and the five hundred thousand Chinese Canadians living in Ontario and the potential for developing a "passageway to the world economy."[255]

A 2007 study in Canada confirmed that Chinese Canadians are developing this kind of passageway for Canada. It showed that 42 percent of Chinese Canadian entrepreneurs are transnational, which is a huge figure. Their transnational enterprises trade goods, services, technology, knowledge, and culture between Canada and their countries of origin. On average, international trade makes up 30 percent of their annual revenue. This passageway building extends to nearly three quarters of Chinese Canadian transnational entrepreneurs helping Canadian firms to do business in their home countries or home country firms to do business in Canada. The Chinese government has even recognized the

[253] Asia Pacific Foundation of Canada, "Close to 300,000 Canadian Citizens Estimated to be Living in Hong Kong," 2011.02.24, *www.asiapacific.ca/media/press-releases/28323*, accessed 2015.01.22. These figures jibe with the results of a survey conducted in British Columbia and reported in 2007 showing that "two-thirds of males of Hong Kong origin, and between the ages of 25 and 44, live and work outside Canada" (Ley, *Migrant Millionaires,* 92; citing M. Cernitig, "Chinese Vancouver: A Decade of Change," *Vancouver Sun,* 2007.06.30, A1).

[254] Geoffrey York, "Canadians by Choice, Hong Kongers by Nature," *The Globe and Mail,* 2005.09.29, H4.

[255] Canada Newswire, "Premier Talks Trade and Investment in Hong Kong," 2005.11.14.

merit of utilizing them and it has designed a set of policies to encourage them to return to China, the result being that enterprises launched by transnational entrepreneurs have grown exponentially in China.[256]

The study goes on to describe the benefits to Canada and Chinese Canadians alike. "Transnational enterprises comprise the more dynamic part of the ethnic economy. They tend to be larger in terms of revenue and employment than their domestic counterparts. Furthermore, transnational enterprises have expanded into the manufacturing and wholesale sectors, while domestic ethnic enterprises are more concentrated in the retail and service sectors."[257] It also noted the correspondence between immigration from China and Canada's increasing trade with that country, that "between 1995 and 2004, each thousand increase in the number of immigrants from China was associated with about a seven hundred million-dollar increase in Canada's trade with China."[258]

The rapid growth in China has created an opportunity for Chinese Canadians to further demonstrate their economic influence in Canada. They have established structures, and are working to support them, that will help Canada tap into the rapid growth and the size of the Chinese economy. This is more than an example of Chinese Canadians casting off the image of a controlled minority; they are now taking on the role of economic leaders.

8.3 Asia Pacific Gateway

Canada's hope that Chinese Canadians will help create avenues of trade with China is being accompanied by the conceptualization and construction of an infrastructure that will facilitate their efforts. Canada has been attempting to articulate and realize the goal of establishing the facilities, services, and mindset that will link it with the expanding China and other areas of Asia. Present articulators of this vision see a major role for Chinese Canadians in realizing it.

---

[256] Chen and Wellman, 6.

[257] *Ibid.*, 10.

[258] *Ibid.*

One of the earliest and most significant formations of this vision was the creation of the Asia Pacific Foundation of Canada (APE) in 1984. The foundation "is an independent, not-for-profit think-tank on Canada's relations with Asia. APF functions as a knowledge broker, bringing together people and knowledge to provide current and comprehensive research, analysis, and information on Canada's transpacific relations."[259]

Other earlier steps in realizing this vision included Vancouver's trade missions to Asian business centers in the late 1980s. The joint federal-provincial Asia Pacific Initiative from 1987 to 1990 led to about sixty projects in transportation, tourism, finance, and education. Canada's Year of the Asia Pacific culminated in the Asia-Pacific Economic Cooperation (APEC) summit in Vancouver in 1997. The British Columbia government started a $1.1 billion transportation plan in 2003 called "Opening Up BC" to expand local infrastructure in order to position the province as a gateway to global markets. The government followed this in 2005 with a proposal, Asia Pacific Gateway Initiative, to have $12.1 billion spent on infrastructure. Likewise in 2005 the federal government proposed the Pacific Gateway Act, which was later modified in 2007 to become the Asia Pacific Gateway and Corridor Initiative, with $1 billion in funding.[260] In September of that year Prince Rupert's Fairview Container Terminal opened and offered reduced sailing times for vessels travelling to North America from East Asia.[261]

Much of the work that has been done to realize this vision has coalesced around the title "Asia Pacific Gateway," which has been described as "a burgeoning national strategy that is responding to the rise of Asian economies and the challenges

---

[259] Asia Pacific Foundation of Canada website, "About Us," *www.asiapacific.ca/about/index.cfm*, accessed 2008.07.04.

[260] *Ibid.*, "Asia Pacific Gateway/About Canada's Asia Pacific Gateway/A Brief History of Canada's Pacific Gateway," www.asiapacificgateway.net/about/a_brief_history_of_canadas_asia_pacific_gateway.cfm, accessed 2007.10.16.

[261] Yuen Pau Woo, "Building the Asia Pacific Gateway Economy," Sept. 2007, Asia Pacific Foundation of Canada website, www.asiapacific.ca/editorials/canada-asia-viewpoints/editorials/building-asia-pacific-gateway-economy, accessed 2015.01.10.

and opportunities Asia now poses for Canada. The strategy
provides a framework for policies, investments, and initiatives
that seek to make Canada the most competitive exit and entry
point in North America for Asian and Canadian goods, services,
and investment."[262]

APF has been leading the efforts to articulate this vision by
conducting research projects and convening consultations
across the nation. The foundation makes the point that the
vision is no way limited to the building of physical
infrastructure and to believe so would be an abuse. The vision
entails creating a broad environment that includes such areas
as education, cultural awareness, and an enlightened
immigration policy.[263] Based on this broadened vision of the
Asia Pacific Gateway, APF emphasizes Asian immigration and
developing a greater understanding of Asia as means toward
realizing it. APF holds that immigration is one of the main
factors that have allowed Vancouver to develop into a gateway
to Asia.[264]

The emphasis on Asian immigration and cultural
awareness is evidence of the role APF sees for Chinese
Canadians in realizing the Asia Pacific Gateway. They are one
of Canada's largest group of Asian immigrants and have
cultural affinity to China. An APF survey of top-tier accounting
and legal firms in Vancouver found the presence of Asia Pacific
expertise and networks in all but one of the firms and that this
expertise and these networks were supporting a services export
industry.[265] In other words, Vancouver is developing as a
gateway on the basis of persons who possess Asia Pacific

[262] Asia Pacific Foundation of Canada website, "Asia Pacific Gateway/About
Canada's Asia Pacific," *www.asiapacificgateway.net/about/index.cfm*,
accessed 2008.04.07.

[263] *Ibid.*, "Asia Pacific Gateway/Gateway Convenings/Vancouver,"
www.asiapacificgateway.net/convenings/vancouver_summary.cfm, accessed
2008.07.02.

[264] *Ibid.*, "Asia Pacific Gateway/About Canada's Asia Pacific Gateway/Human
Dimensions of the Pacific Gateway,"
*www.asiapacificgateway.net/about/human_dimensions_of_the_pacific_gatew
ay.cfm*, accessed 2008.07.02.

[265] Woo, "Building the Asia Pacific Gateway Economy."

expertise and networks, which is most likely to be Chinese Canadians.

Many Chinese Canadians have experience, connections, and cultural awareness of China that few Canadians possess. They have also developed organizations that will facilitate economic links to China. Therefore, when Canadian governments and the private sector envision a strategic plan to allow Canada to benefit from the economic growth in China, it is natural that Chinese Canadians would be an integral part of it. Chinese Canadians are being asked to take and are accepting a leading role in this strategy.

9. Conclusion

Chinese Canadians have demonstrated general economic strength. Mainly, they have amassed considerable wealth in their assets and bank accounts. This has enabled them to increase their commercial activities beyond what has historically been the case, as seen in the building of Chinese shopping centers in areas not known for having many Chinese Canadian residents. The marketing that targets Chinese Canadians is an indirect indication of their wealth. It supports a bevy of Chinese language media. There are also marketing firms whose main or sole purpose is to sell to Chinese Canadians and big corporations that find it rewarding to sponsor Chinese Canadian community events. The large scale of Chinese Canadian economic activity, seen in their economic organizations, is also evidence for Chinese Canadian economic strength. Examples include the Louie family's holdings in IGA and London Drugs and the nonprofit Association of Chinese Canadian Entrepreneurs. The existence of these organizations is not only a huge departure from the small size that used to be standard for Chinese Canadian economic organizations, they are also an indication that the growth will continue and even quicken.

These indicators of economic strength are better viewed against the history of Chinese Canadian economic activity. Chinese Canadians first came to help build the national infrastructure. In doing so, they showed themselves to be independent and able to survive in the face of exploitation. When the opportunity arose, and sometimes out of necessity, Chinese Canadians turned to commercial activities and in doing so spawned the so-called ethnic industries of laundries, restaurants, grocers, and herbalists. Their economic strength increased rapidly after 1967 with the removal of racial bias in Canada's immigration laws. More professionals arrived, and then, starting in the 1980s Chinese Canadians dominated Canada's Business Immigration Program. Li Ka-shing and his family's investments in Concord Pacific Place and Husky Oil are examples of what Chinese Canadians could accomplish when encouraged. Now Chinese Canadians are posed to lead Canada in diversifying its trading partners. They have progressed from being suppressed to being on the verge of leading in the Canadian economy.

Chinese Canadians are highly successful in a number of areas. They continue to do well in the restaurant and grocery industries, evolving and expanding as success in the industry demands. T & T Supermarket is an example of a niche market provider that is increasingly appealing to a larger clientele. From an early point, Chinese Canadians have also shown themselves to be generous supporters of the broader community, for example, buying large amounts of war bonds during WW II. Today their charitable contributions are most noticeable in the efforts by companies such as Fairchild Media Group, and in the foundations established by wealthy individuals, such as David Lam.

Among these areas of economic achievement, two stand out, business investment and property development. Chinese applicants have dominated Canada's Business Immigration Program. Furthermore, their acceptance has been followed by a wave of investments far outstripping those required by the program, such as Li Ka-shing's purchase of Husky Oil. Chinese Canadian builders have developed residential communities across the nation. They have also constructed a large number of ethnic shopping centers and purchased high scale hotels.

There are two broad issues relevant to the economic achievements of Chinese Canadians and how Canada may benefit from them. The first is the role of Chinese culture in these achievements and the second is the barriers that exist to even greater achievements. The role of culture is significant because, if one wants to duplicate or learn from these achievements, one may have to study it. This essay holds that cultural factors should be given more weight than external factors in understanding Chinese Canadian success; however, there are strong views that argue for external factors, and not culture, being more important. Although Chinese Canadians have achieved much economically, there seem to be systemic barriers hindering them from doing even better, which is discouraging newer immigrants from remaining in Canada, resulting in a serious loss for the country.

In spite of these barriers, there are reasons to be optimistic about the future economic achievements of Chinese Canadians. They have built large companies and business associations demonstrating that they have the skills and resources to continue their unprecedented growth. Moreover, their links to China are allowing them to take a transnational role in the Canadian economy while contributing to the government's Asia Pacific Gateway plan, thus creating conditions for even greater achievements.

In closing, readers may be asking themselves what practical lesson they can take from this description of Chinese Canadian economic achievements. There are, of course, many and even these may be inadequate when one also considers that economic achievements are but one sort, among the many, that are described in this book. After all, would one want to consider only the economic achievements and ignore the medical achievements when the latter may offer large benefits as well?

Faced with a myriad of possible lessons, it might be helpful to consider the claim that "among the world economies, the Chinese diaspora ranks in the top five in wealth and economic clout."[266] Then consider why the APF emphasizes that educating the Canadian population in order to attain a greater understanding of Asia is an integral part of realizing the Asia Pacific Gateway strategy.[267] A common thread that links these considerations and the other achievements described in this book is Chinese culture. In other words, the practical lessons that one can draw are linked to Chinese culture. This may seem to be expanding the realm of the reader's consideration even further, rather than providing an easy choice. However, it does alert one to an important dimension of the search for significance among the economic achievements of Chinese

[266] Peter Newman, "David Ho," *Maclean's* 118.48 (2005.11.28), 53.

[267] Asia Pacific Foundation of Canada, "Canada's Asia Challenge: Creating Competence for the Next Generation of Canadians," 2013.11.04, 54 pages.

Canadians. The cultural aspect promises to reveal how one can most benefit from what Chinese Canadians have achieved, economically or otherwise.

Even if attention to the cultural aspect does not promise the immediate benefit that one often seeks in practical considerations, it does offer the opportunity to reduce one's limitations, which should only be beneficial. In light of the benefits offered in understanding Chinese culture, Canadians should reflect on the fact that their society penalizes the Chinese Canadian for retention of their culture.[268] The tension that the Chinese Canadian must feel in the choice of retaining aspects of their culture or not should be something that the mainstream Canadian shares; not only for the sake of opening him or herself to more choice, but also so as to know not to limit the choice of others, especially when more choice for them may bring greater benefit for all.

BIBLIOGRAPHY

Anthony, Lorrayne. "East Meets West: Entrepreneur Marries His Chinese Heritage with Opportunities Offered by His New Canadian Homeland." *Financial Post* 10.40 (1997.10.4-6), T6.

Artex Sportswear website, *www.artexsportswear.com*, accessed 2008.05.22.

Asia Pacific Foundation of Canada. "Canada Asia Agenda 2006." 54 pages.

------. "Canada's Asia Challenge: Creating Competence for the Next Generation of Canadians," 2013.11.04. 54 pages.

------. "Canada's Market Share in Asia." *www.asiapacific.ca/statistics/trade/market-share/canadas-market-share-asia*, accessed 2015.01.21.

---

[268] Peter Li "The Economics of Minority Language Identity," *Canadian Ethnic Studies*, 33.3 (2001): 134-154.

------. "Close to 300,000 Canadian Citizens Estimated to be Living in Hong Kong," 2011.02.24. *www.asiapacific.ca/media/press-releases/28323*, accessed 2015.01.22.

------. "Leading the Way: Canadian Business Strategies in Asia." Oct. 2007. 14 pages.

------. "The Role of Asian Ethnic Business Associations in Canada." Canada Asia Commentary 35 (2004). 8 pages.

Asia Pacific Foundation of Canada website. "About Us." *www.asiapacific.ca*, accessed 2008.07.04.

------. "Asia Pacific Gateway/About Canada's Asia Pacific Gateway." *www.asiapacific.ca*, accessed 2008.07.04.

------. "Asia Pacific Gateway/About Canada's Asia Pacific Gateway/A Brief History of Canada's Pacific Gateway." *www.asiapacific.ca*, accessed 2007.10.16.

------. "Asia Pacific Gateway/About Canada's Asia Pacific Gateway/Human Dimensions of the Pacific Gateway." *www.asiapacific,ca*, accessed 2008.07.02.

------. "Asia Pacific Gateway/Gateway Convenings/Toronto." *www.asiapacific.ca*, accessed 2008.07.02.

------. "Asia Pacific Gateway/Gateway Convenings/Vancouver." *www.asiapacific.ca*, accessed 2008.07.02.

"Association of Chinese Canadian Entrepreneurs." *Canadian Business* (Toronto) 79.8 (2006.04.10-23): 47-50.

Association of Chinese Canadian Entrepreneurs website. "About ACCE." *www.acce.ca/about.html*, accessed 2015.01.18.

Aydemir, Abdurrahman and Chris Robinson. "Return and Onward Migration among Working Age Men." Analytical Studies Branch Research Paper Series, Catalogue no.

11F0019MIE — No. 27321. Statistics Canada, Mar. 2006. 49 pages.

Bank of China (Canada) website, *www.boc.cn/cn/html/canada/en_s1.html*, accessed 2008.04.23.

Bank of East Asia (Canada) website, *ca.hkbea.com/index/index.html*, accessed 2008.04.22.

Barber, John. "Worlds Apart." *The Globe and Mail*, 2004.10.23, M1.

BC Children's Hospital Foundation website. "Chinese-Canadian Miracle Weekend." *www.bcchf.ca/events/event-calendar/chinese-canadian-miracle-weekend*, accessed 2015.01.19.

Boddy, Thomas. " The Compelling Trajectory of Thomas Fung." *BC Business,* Mar. 2005: 22-29.

Brent, Paul. "With Fresh Funding, Continent's Largest Asian Mall Back on Track. *Real Estate News Exchange,* 2014.06.21. *renx.ca/with-fresh-funding-continents-largest-asian-mall-back-on-track*, accessed 2015.01.21.

Canada's 50 Best Managed Companies website, *www.canadas50best.com/en/about/pages/home.aspx,* accessed 2015.01.20.

Canadian International Development Platform. "Canadian Foreign Direct Investment Abroad." *cidpnsi.ca/blog/portfolio/canadian-foreign-direct-investment-overseas-quick-review*, accessed 2015.01.21.

Chan, Anthony B. *Li Ka-shing : Hong Kong's Elusive Billionaire.* Toronto: Macmillan Canada, 1997.

Chan Kwok-bun. *Migration, Ethnic Relations and Chinese Business.* London: Routledge, 2005.

Chappell, Lindsay. "Selling Beemers to Chinese: One Dealer's Lesson." *Automotive News* 6240 (2007.01.29).

Chen, Wenhong and Barry Wellman. "Doing Business at Home and Away: Policy Implications of Chinese-Canadian Entrepreneurship, Apr. 2007." Canada in Asia Series. Asia Pacific Foundation of Canada. 30 pages

Chinese Canadian Advertising & Media Association website, *www.ccamma.com*, accessed 2008.04.24, and *www.ccamma.com/profile.html*, accessed 2015.01.18.

"Chinese Medicine; Registration a Must in BC." *Canadian Medical Association Journal*, 169.1 (2003.07.08): 54.

Chinese Professionals Association of Canada's website, *www.chineseprofessionals.ca*, accessed 2015.01.19.

Chinese Real Estate Professionals Association of British Columbia webpage, *www.crepa.ca/index.php*, accessed 2015.01.18.

Chow, Wyng. "Vancouver's Chinese New Year Consumer Show Largest in BC." *The Vancouver Sun*, 2000.01.29, B9.

Chu, Showwei. "Welcome to Canada. Please Buy Something." *Canadian Business* (Toronto) 71.9 (1998.05.29): 72-73.

"CIBC Celebrates Chinese New Year with Client Reception in Toronto." Canada Newswire, 2008.02.12.

Citrano, Virginia. "Li Ka-shing: Hong Kong Billionaire Sells CIBC Stake, Sets Up Huge Charity." *Forbes.com*, 2005.01.13. *www.forbes.com/2005/01/13/0113autofacescan01.html*, accessed 2008.05.22.

Citizenship and Immigration Canada website, *www.cic.gc.ca*, accessed 2008.03.24 and 2008.05.20.

------. "Business Immigration Program." *www.cic.gc.ca/english/helpcentre/results-by-topic.asp?st=6.3*, accessed 2014.01.19.

CNIB's website, *www.cnib.ca/en/Default.aspx*, accessed 2008.05.12.

"CNY Celebrations 2015." *www.cnycelebrations.ca*, accessed 2015.01.18.

"Concord Pacific Announces Closing of Sale of North York Site." Canada NewsWire, 2006.12.07.

Concord Pacific website, *www.concordpacific.com*, accessed 2008.06.03.

Confucius. *The Analects*. Translated by D.C. Lau. London: Penguin Books Ltd., 1979.

Crawford, Anne. "Franklin Mall to Add Flavor of Asia." *Calgary Herald*, 1999.05.14: E1.

CTC Bank of Canada website, *www.ctcbank.com/eng.htm*, accessed 2008.04.23.

Daxue (The Great Learning). In *Source Book in Chinese Philosophy,* 84-94. Translated by Wing-tsit Chan. Princeton, New Jersey: Princeton Univ. Press, 1963.

Dawson, J. Brian. *Moon Cakes in Gold Mountain: From China to the Canadian Plains*. Calgary: Detselig Enterprises Ltd., 1991.

DeVoretz, Don J. "Asian Skilled-Immigration Flows to Canada: A Supply-Side Analysis, 2003." Foreign Policy Dialogue Series. Asian Pacific Foundation of Canada. 20 pages.

------, J. Ma, and K. Zhang. "Triangular Human Capital Flows: Some Empirical Evidence from Hong Kong." In *Host Societies and the Reception of Immigrants,* edited by J.G. Reitz, 469-92. San Diego: Center for U.S. Mexican Studies, Univ. of California, 2003.

------ and Kangqing Zhang. "Citizenship, Passports and the Brain Exchange Triangle." *Journal of Comparative Policy Analysis* 6.2 (Aug. 2004): 199-212.

Discover China Dragon Ball 2008 website, *www.yeehongdragonball.org*, accessed 2008.04.25.

"Diversity and Quality Abound: Projects and Personalities Honoured at VRCA Annual Awards." *Journal of Commerce* (Vancouver) 91.1 (2004.11.15): 1.

Edgington, David W., Michael A. Goldberg, and Thomas A. Hutton. "Hong Kong Business, Money, and Migration in Vancouver, Canada." In *From Urban Enclave to Ethnic Suburb: New Asian Communities in Pacific Rim Countries.* Edited by Wei Li, 155-183. Honolulu: University of Hawaii Press, 2006.

Evans, Brian L. *The Other Side of Gold Mountain: Glimpses of Chinese Pioneer Life on the Prairies from the Wallace B. Chung and Madeline H. Chung Collection.* Edmonton: University of Alberta Libraries, 2010.

Euromonitor International: Local Company Profile. "T & T Supermarket Inc. - Retailing - Canada." Feb. 2008.

Glazer, Nathan. "Two Cheers for Asian Values." In *China in the National Interest,* edited by Owen Harries, 175-85. New Brunswick, N.J. : Transaction Publishers, 2003.

Government of Nova Scotia website. "News Releases," "Clothing Manufacturer Attracted to Yarmouth," 2001.10.29. *www.gov.ns.ca/news/details.asp?id=20011029001,* 2008.05.22.

Government of Ontario website. "Business Immigration Home/Success Stories/Phoebus Wong." *www.2ontario.com/bi/s_PhoebusWong.asp,* accessed 2008.05.22.

Guo, Shibao and Don J. DeVoretz. "Chinese Immigrants in Vancouver: Quo Vadis?" Vancouver Centre of Excellence, Research on Immigration and Integration in the Metropolis, Working Paper Series No. 05-20 (Oct. 2005– updated Feb. 2006). 25 pages.

Hamilton, Gordon. "Flashy Ads in Hong Kong Market Pacific Place Condos." *The Vancouver Sun*, 1990.11.27: B1.

Hang Seng Bank website. "Bank Profile and History." *bank.hangseng.com/1/2/about-us/corporate-info/bank-profile*, accessed 2015.01.22.

"Healthy Choices Impact Food Product Sales." *Plant* (Willowdale, Ontario) 64.11 (2005.11.14): 35.

The Hong Kong-Canada Business Association, National, website. "About Us/The HKCBA Story." *national.hkcba.com/story.html*, accessed 2015.01.22.

Hopewell Group of Companies website. "Hopewell Residential." *www.hopewell.com/companies/hrm*, accessed 2015.01.20.

Howell, Julia. "The Business of Community." *Maclean's* 121.12 (2008.03.31): 43-47.

HSBC Canada website, *www.hsbc.ca/1/2/contact-us/atm-branch-locations*, accessed 2015.01.18.

HSBC website. "About HSBC." *www.hsbc.com.cn/1/2/hsbc-china*, accessed 2015.01.22.

HSBC Group Holdings website. "The HSBC Group, A Brief History." *www.hsbc.com/1/2/about-hsbc/group-history*, accessed 2008.04.20.

------. "The HSBC Group in the Hong Kong Special Administrative Region (SAR) Fact Sheet." *www.hsbc.com/1/PA_1_1_S5/content/assets/newsroom/media_kit/fact_sheets/hong_kong_sar_fact_sheet_en_april_2007.pdf,* accessed 2008.04.20.

Industrial and Commercial Bank of China (Canada) website, *www.icbk.ca/index_per_con.jsp?screen=menu5.sub7*, accessed 2015.01.18.

Irastorza, Nahikari. "The Liability of Foreignness: Survival Differences Between Foreign-and Native-owned Firms in the Basque Country." Vancouver Centre of Excellence: Research on Immigration and Integration in the Metropolis. Working Paper Series No. 06-18, Dec. 2006.

Jaremko, Gordon. "Cultural Crossroads: Central Landmark Mall Adds Cosmopolitan Flavor." *Calgary Herald*, 1996.06.15, final edition: D1.

Kahn, Herman. *World Economic Development: 1979 and Beyond*. Boulder, Colorado: Westview Press, 1979.

Kaplan, David H. and Wei Li. "Introduction: The Places of Ethnic Economies." In *Landscapes of the Ethnic Economy*, edited by David H. Kaplan and Wei Li, 1-16. Lanham, Maryland: Rowman & Littlefield, c.2006.

Keating, John. "Taiwanese View Canada as a Land of Opportunity." *Financial Post*, 1994.11.18.

Khondaker, Jafar. "Canada's Trade with China: 1997 to 2006." Statistics Canada. *www.statcan.ca/english/*, accessed 2008.07.01.

Lai, David Chuenyan. *Chinese Community Leadership: Case Study of Victoria in Canada*. Singapore: World Scientific Publishing, 2010.

Lau, Andrea. "Duelling Malls." *The Globe and Mail*, 2007.04.14, M4.

Lazarus, Eve. "Eastern Star. "*Marketing* (Toronto) 112.18 (2007.09.24): 49-52.

------. "Vancouver's Driving Force." *Marketing* (Toronto) 111.28 (2006.08.28-2006.09.04): 19-21.

Le Corre, Philippe. "Culture: Canada's Hong Kong." *Far Eastern Economic Review* (Hong Kong) 157.6 (1994.02.10).

Lejtenyi, Patrick. "The Marketing Report on Multicultural Marketing." *Marketing Magazine* 106.22 (2001.06.04): 19-29.

Leung, Wendy. "Chinese-Canadians Lead Home-buying Boom." CanWest News, 2006.04.26: 1.

Ley, David. *Millionaire Migrants: Trans-Pacific Life Lines.* Chichester, U.K.: Wiley-Blackwell, 2010.

------. "The Rhetoric of Racism and the Politics of Explanation in the Vancouver Housing Market." In *The Silent Debate and Asian Immigration: Racism in Canada*, edited by Eleanor Laquian, Aprodicio Laquian, and Terry McGee, 331-348. Vancouver: Institute of Asian Research, University of British Columbia, 1997.

"Li Ka-shing." *Forbes.com*, *www.forbes.com*, accessed 2008.05.21.

Li, Peter S. *s.v.* "Chinese." In *Encyclopedia of Canada's Peoples*, edited by Paul R. Magocsi, 355-73. Toronto: University of Toronto Press, 1999.

------. *The Chinese in Canada.* Second edition. Toronto: Oxford University Press, 1998.

------. "Chinese Investment and Business in Canada: Ethnic Entrepreneurship Reconsidered." *Pacific Affairs* 66.2 (Summer 1993): 219-43.

------. "The Economics of Minority Language Identity." *Canadian Ethnic Studies* 33.3 (2001): 134-154.

------. "Ethnic Enterprise in Transition: Chinese Business in Richmond, B.C., 1980-1990." *Canadian Ethnic Studies* 24.1 (1992): 120-38.

------. "Overseas Chinese Networks: A Reassessment." In *Chinese Business Networks: State, Economy and Culture,* edited by Chan Kwok Bun, 261-84. Singapore: Prentice Hall, 2000.

------. "Race and Ethnicity." In *Race and Relations in Canada,* edited by Peter S. Li, 3-20. Second edition. Don Mills, Ontario: Oxford, 1999.

------. "Social Capital and Economic Outcomes for Immigrants and Ethnic Minorities." *Journal of International Migration and Integration* 5.2 [Spring 2004]: 171-90.

Li, Peter S., and Yahong Li. "The Consumer Market of the Enclave Economy: A Study of Advertisements in a Chinese Daily Newspaper in Toronto." *Canadian Ethnic Studies* 31.2 (1999): 43-60.

Lin, Xiaohua, Jian Guan, and Mary Jo Nicholson. "Transnational Entrepreneurs as Agents of International Innovation Linkages." Asia Pacific Foundation of Canada, December 2008. 28 pages.

Lo, Lucia. "Changing Geography of Toronto's Ethnic Economy." In *Landscapes of the Ethnic Economy,* edited by David H. Kaplan and Wei Li, 83-96. Lanham, Maryland: Rowman & Littlefield, 2006.

------. "Suburban Housing and Indoor Shopping: The Production of Contemporary Chinese Landscape in Toronto." In *From Urban Enclave to Ethnic Suburb: New Asian Communities in Pacific Rim Countries,* edited by Wei Li, 134-154. Honolulu: University of Hawaii Press, 2006.

------ and Lu Wang. "A Political Economy Approach to Understanding the Economic Incorporation of Chinese Sub-ethnic Groups." *Journal of International Migration and Integration / Revue de l integration et de la migration internationale* 5.1 (2004): 107-140.

------ and Shuguang Wang. "Immigration, Ethnic Economies and Integration: a Case Study of Chinese in the Greater

Toronto Area. " Research Report to the Toronto Joint Centre of Excellence for Research on Immigration and Settlement. 1998.

-------, Valerie Preston, Shuguang Wang, Katherine Reil, Edward Harvey, and Bobby Siu. "Immigrants' Economic Status in Toronto: Rethinking Settlement and Integration Strategies." CERIS Working Paper No. 15, Mar. 2000. 78 pages.

Lorinc, John. "How Bazaar." *The Globe and Mail*, 2003.12.20: M7.

McKechnie, Brian. "Mandarin Celebrates Canada Day with Free Buffet in Ontario." Global News, 2014.07.01.

MacQueen, Ken. "Louie, Brandt (Profile)." *Maclean's*, 2002.03.25.

Mandarin Restaurant Franchise Corporation website, *www.mandarinbuffet.com*, accessed 2008.05.11.

Mandel-Campbell, Andrea. *Rescuing Canadian Business from the Suds of Global Obscurity: Why Mexicans Don't Drink Molson*. Vancouver: Douglas & McIntyre, 2007.

Marger, Martin N. and Constance A. Hoffman. "Ethnic Enterprise in Immigrant Participation in the Small Business Sector." *International Migration Review* 26.3 (Autumn 1992): 965-81.

MarketWatch. "Canadian Solar Inc." www.marketwatch.com/investing/stock/csiq, accessed 2015.01.22.

Marlow, Iain. "B.C.'s Transpacific Pioneer Thomas Fung Is a Uniquely Canadian Success Story." *The Globe and Mail*, 2014.08.31.

Marotte, Bertrand. "Si Wai Lai has been pouring millions...." CanWest News, 1996.08.15: 1.

Mencius. *Mencius.* Translated by D. C. Lau. Third edition.
Harmondsworth, Eng.: Penguin Books, 1983.

Menkhoff, Thomas and Solvay Gerke. "Introduction: Asia's
Transformation and the Role of the Ethnic Chinese." In
Chinese Entrepreneurship and Asian Business Networks,
edited by Thomas Menkhoff and Solvay Gerke, 1-19.
London: RoutledgeCurzon, 2003.

Miller, Don."Chinese Challenge." *Marketing* (Toronto) 111.10
(2006.03.13): 24-25.

Milner, Brian. "Asia: From Opportunity to Crisis in the Eyes of
Canadians. *The Globe and Mail,* 2011.04.13.

Mississauga Chinese Centre website,
mississaugachinesecentre.com, accessed 2008.06.07.

Motherwell, Cathryn. "Li Ka-shing Rescues Husky with $600-
million Bailout. Sale Will Help Ease Nova's Long-awaited
Restructuring." *The Globe and Mail,* 1991.10.24, B1.

"My Best Mistake." *Alberta Venture* 9.10 (Dec. 2005): 15.

Newman, Peter. "David Ho," *Maclean's* 118.48 (2005.11.28): 53-
57.

------."Ultra-Secretive, and Ultra -Rich." *Maclean's* (Toronto),
118.48 (2005.11. 28).

Noakes, Susan. "Niche Marketing Targets Chinese Consumers."
The Financial Post. 1994.11.18.

Oswald, Ed. "AMD, ATI Merge in $5.4 Billion Deal." *betanews,*
2006.07.24. *betanews.com/2006/07/24/amd-ati-merge-in-
5-4-billion-deal,* accessed 2015.01.20.

Peirol, Paulette. "Corporate Cash Registers Ring in Chinese
New Year." *The Globe and Mail,* 1997.02.07: A1 and A8.

Perrault, Ernest G. *Tong: The Story of Tong Louie, Vancouver's Quiet Titan*. Madeira Park, British Columbia: Harbour Publishing, 2002.

Popular Lifestyle and Entertainment (Yule shenghuo) (Richmond, B.C.). Alberta edition. Dec. 2000.

Preston, Valerie and Lucia Lo. "Canadian Urban Landscape Examples - 21 'Asian Theme' Malls in Suburban Toronto: Land Use Conflict in Richmond Hill." *Canadian Geographer* 44.2 (Summer 2000): 182-90.

"Premier Talks Trade and Investment in Hong Kong." Canada Newswire, 2005.11.14.

Province of Ontario website, "Business Immigration Home/Success Stories/Phoebus Wong." *www.2ontario.com/bi/s_PhoebusWong.asp*, accessed 2008.05.22.

Qian Mu. *Cong Zhongguo lishi laikan Zhongguo minzu xing ji Zhongguo wenhua* (The nature of Chinese people and Chinese culture from the perspective of Chinese history). Hong Kong: Zhongwen daxue chubanshe, 1979.

Qadeer, Mohammed. "Ethnic Malls and Plazas: Chinese Commercial Developments in Scarborough, Ontario." CERIS Working Paper No. 3. Toronto: Joint Centre of Excellence for Research on Immigration and Settlement, 1998.

Ram, Vidya. "HSBC Gets Back in Touch With Its Roots." *Forbes.com*, 2008.03.10. *www.forbes.com*, accessed 2008.04.17.

"Ring in the Year of the Horse at CIBC LunarFest in British Columbia." *The Globe and Mail*, 2014.01.10.

Schreiner, John. "A Capital Deal-Maker." *The Financial Post* (Toronto), 1997.08.23, 29.

------. "Investor Lin Aims to Prove High Tech Good Investment."
   The Financial Post, 1994.11.18, C16.

Sciban, Lloyd. "Chinese Language Media Across the West." In
   Challenging Frontiers: The Canadian West, edited by Lorry
   Felske and Beverly Rasporich, 269-296. Calgary:
   University of Calgary Press, 2004.

Scott, Michael. "100 Influential Chinese-Canadians in B.C."
   Vancouver Sun, 2006.10.21: C7.

Shepard, Harvey. *The Gazette* (Montreal), 1995.11.23: G1.

Smith, Charlie. "Vancouver's Canadian-born Chinese in their
   30s and 40s Make their Mark, No Small Thanks to Milton
   Wong." *straight.com*, 2012.01.18.

Splendid China Mall website,
   www.splendidchinamall.com/en/home.php, accessed
   2015.01.21.

Stern, Olivia. "Pacific Mall." *Toronto Life* 40.3 (Mar. 2006): 69.

Stoffman, Daniel. "Asia Comes to Lotusland." *Report on
   Business Magazine* 6.5 (Nov. 1989).

Strauss, Marina. "Grocers Target Big-spending South Asian,
   Chinese Shoppers." *The Globe and Mail,* 2008.05.19.

S.U.C.C.E.S.S. "Gateway to Asia: Linking Chinese
   Entrepreneurs with Canadian Suppliers." Asia Pacific
   Foundation of Canada website,
   www.asiapacificgateway.net/pdf/success.pdf, accessed
   2008.07.04.

T & T website. "Our Stores." *www.tnt-supermarket.com/en*,
   accessed 2015.01.19.

Taiwan Credit Union website, *www.tctcu.com*, accessed
   2008.04. 22.

Thomas, David. "Vancouver's Pacific Place to Transform the City." *The Financial Post,* 1994.11.18: C18.

Tolley, Erin. "The Skilled Worker Class." *Policy Brief* (The Metropolis Project) 1 (Jan. 2003). 8 pages.

Trico Homes website. "About Us/Partners." *www.tricohomes.com/goodwill/partners.bpsx,* accessed 2015.01.20.

------. "Trico Corporate/Why Choose Trico/Trico Home Accolades." *www.tricohomes.com/about-trico.html,* accessed 2008.06.05.

Trimble, Andrew. "Courting New Fund Customers." *Toronto Star,* 1996.09.15: C4.

Waldie, Paul. "Seed Capital: How Immigrants Are Reshaping Saskatchewan's Farmland." *The Globe and Mail,* 2012.10.12.

Ward, Doug. "The New Chinatown: Mall Style: for Some of Us Shopping at an Asian-style Mall Is a Cross-cultural Experience. It's like Being a Tourist in Your Hometown." *The Vancouver Sun,* 2000.02.26 (Final Edition), F1.

Wang, Shuguang. "Chinese Commercial Activity in the Toronto CMA: New Development Patterns and Impacts." *The Canadian Geographer* 43.1 (Spring 1999): 19-35.

------ and Lucia Lo. "Chinese Immigrants in Canada: Their Changing Composition and Economic Performance." CERIS Working Paper No. 30, Mar. 2004. 37 pages.

Wang Yangming. *Instructions for Practical Living and Other Neo-Confucian Writings by Wang Yang-Ming.* Translated by Wing-tsit Chan. New York: Columbia University Press, 1963.

------. *Wang Yangming quanji* (A complete collection of Wang Yangming's works), edited by Wu Guang, Qian Ming, Dong

Ping, and Yao Yanfu. Shanghai: Shanghai guji chubanshe, 1992.

Wickberg, Edgar, Harry Con, Ronald J. Con, Graham Johnson, and William E. Willmott. *From China to Canada: A History of the Chinese Communities in Canada*, edited by Edgar Wickberg. Toronto: McClelland and Stewart, 1982.

Wong, Lloyd. "Globalization and Transnational Migration: A Study of Recent Chinese Capitalist Migration from the Asian Pacific to Canada." *International Society* 12.3 (Sept. 1997): 329-351.

------ and Michelle Ng. "Chinese Immigration Entrepreneurs in Vancouver: A Case Study of Ethnic Business Development." *Canadian Ethnic Studies* 30.1 (1998): 64-85.

Wong, Tony. "Hong Kong Money Likes GTA." *The Toronto Star*, 1996.11.10: Al, A10.

------. "Stanley Ho, Hong Kong's Most Flamboyant Multimillionaire, Loves a Bargain." *Toronto Star*, 1990.02.11: D1.

Woo, Yuen Pau. "Building the Asia Pacific Gateway Economy," 2007.09.17. Asia Pacific Foundation of Canada website, *www.asiapacific.ca/editorials/canada-asia-viewpoints/editorials/building-asia-pacific-gateway-economy*, accessed 2015.01.10.

World Bank. *The East Asian Miracle: Economic Growth and Public Policy.* New York: Oxford, 1993.

Yee, Paul. *Chinatown: An Illustrated History of the Chinese Communities of Victoria, Vancouver, Calgary, Winnipeg, Toronto, Ottawa, Montreal, and Halifax.* Toronto: J. Lorimer, 2005.

Yee Hong Garden Terrace. *www.yeehong.com/centre/gardenterrace/index.html*, accessed 2007.10.19.

Yee Hong website, *www.yeehong.com*, accessed 2003.09.27.

------. "Centre/Programs and Services/Subsidized Housing." *www.yeehong.com*, accessed 2008.07.04.

York, Geoffrey. "Canadians by Choice, Hong Kongers by Nature." *The Globe and Mail,* 2005.09.29: H4.

Zong, Li. ""International Transference of Human Capital and Occupational Attainment of Recent Chinese Professional Immigrants in Canada." Prairie Centre of Excellence for Research on Immigration and Integration Working Paper Series, Working Paper No. WP03-04, Mar. 2004. 12 pages.

------. "Language, Education, and Occupational Attainment of Foreign-Trained Chinese and Polish Professional Immigrants in Toronto, Canada." In *Chinese Migrants Abroad: Cultural, Educational, and Social Dimensions of the Chinese Diaspora*, edited by Michael W. Charney, Brenda S. A. Yeoh, and Tong Chee Kiong, 163-178. Singapore: Singapore University Press, 2003.

6. CHINESE LANGUAGE MEDIA: ESTABLISHING AN IDENTITY[1]

1. Introduction

The presence of Chinese language media in Canada is impressive even with a cursory awareness of it. There are national television and newspaper networks, many local newspapers, local radio and TV stations, and extensive internet publication; all done in Chinese in its variations of Cantonese, Mandarin, and traditional and simplified characters. Mainstream media, like the Canadian Broadcasting Corporation, have even begun posting online news in Chinese.

Acknowledging this presence leads to the following question: How did it come to be and what significant implications does it have for Chinese Canadian identity. The question of Chinese language media development naturally extends to the role Chinese Canadians had in establishing this presence. Early Chinese Canadians were a disadvantaged minority denied many of the resources required to develop communications among themselves. Moreover, even though they were able to develop means of communication, these should have been limited to local productions. What further should be noted is the development of Chinese language community schools that have preserved the Chinese language and fostered the talent for creating and managing Chinese language media and an audience capable of appreciating it that at the same time had the buying power to support it. The production of media was also marked by a large degree of volunteer labour as community members were willing to devote their time to promoting communications. The increasing number of immigrants from China after 1967 and the investment from business immigrants during the 1980s and 1990s also gave a large boost to Chinese language media. The

---

[1] A small number of claims in this chapter, particularly related to the state of Chinese language media at the end of the twentieth century, are not documented because the media managers who provided them have chosen to remain anonymous. Even the interviews are not cited because the managers could easily be identified if they were. In spite of the initial concern that this may create, the coherence of the undocumented claims with the documented ones should mitigate it.

business immigrants invested in national networks and reflected the growing wealth of Chinese Canadians, which in turn stimulated more advertising revenues for the media that serviced them.

Since then, disseminating information to minorities in Canada has attracted the interest of mainstream organizations and companies such as Rogers Broadcasting, Toronto Star, and Sun Media have invested in or created media catering to Chinese Canadians. It seems that Chinese language media are now producing profits that make them attractive to mainstream businesses.

In spite of this success, one salient criticism leveled at Chinese language media is that much of it does not truly reflect Chinese Canadians, rather it is composed of reporting and programming produced by large media companies in China, Hong Kong, and Taiwan. This is a cost-effective way to provide content, less expensive than producing local content. Nevertheless, under the influence of its location of origin, non-Canadian production does little to foster a unique Chinese Canadian identity and may be seen as continuing to deter Chinese Canadians from participation in the mainstream.

The response to this criticism is that Chinese Canadians need to find an appropriate balance between maintenance (sometimes recovery) of their heritage culture and involving themselves in the mainstream. Arguably, this is taking place as one finds Chinese language media focusing more on Canadian content while encouraging Chinese Canadians to become involved in the mainstream. At the same time, the traditional ethnic values, which multiculturalism is willing to protect, are at least being reflected upon prior to their possible discard.

In short, Chinese language media's role in establishing a Chinese Canadian identity is a valuable one, allowing them to compare the advantages of retention of heritage values with greater participation in the mainstream and on the basis of this comparison establish a measured identity for themselves.

2. History of Chinese Language Media Development

2.1 Early Need and Want

The creation of media among early Chinese immigrants to Canada was motivated by both need and want. The need arose because the treatment of Chinese workers who traveled early to Canada in order to meet its requirement for cheap labor was very harsh. Their wages were about half those of other workers, governments legislated limits specifically to their rights, mobs attacked their homes and businesses, politicians rallied voters against them, and labor unions sought their exclusion from the country. By 1923, the country had implemented the Chinese Immigration Act that banned all but a few new Chinese immigrants from entering Canada. In the face of this opposition, it was hardly surprising that Chinese immigrants found little support in Canada.

As a consequence, Chinese immigrants were forced to rely on themselves in order to provide for their needs. In doing so they created a variety of organizations whose purpose was meeting these needs. They included kinship associations, locality associations, mutual aid societies, and even political parties. They provided lodging, assistance in finding work, loans, legal advice, recreation facilities, a means to deliver remittances to family in China, and financial assistance for burial. The kinship associations were among the more numerous of the Chinese Canadian organizations. For example, in 1923 Vancouver had twenty-six kinship associations, Toronto ten, and Calgary six. Nine of these kinship associations had chapters in cities from Vancouver to Ontario.[2] The Wong Association, which was one of the largest Chinese groups and said to represent 20 percent of the Chinese in Canada, convened its first national convention in 1922.[3]

Efficient communication was crucial for supporting these organizations, which were often very complex. This need, in turn, led to the creation of media, which was one of the most efficient means to communicate. For example, the newspaper *Dahan gongbao (The Chinese Times)* was published daily from 1914 to 1992 in Vancouver. It was the official organ of the Chee Kung Tong, a political party that later became the Hongmen Association or Chinese Freemasons Society of Canada. It was transported daily from Vancouver to Chilliwack where:

---

[2] Edgar Wickberg, Harry Con, Ronald J. Con, Graham Johnson, and William E. Willmott, *From China to Canada: A History of the Chinese Communities in Canada,* ed. Edgar Wickberg (Toronto: McClelland and Stewart, 1982), 113.

[3] Wickberg *et al.*, 176, 167.

272

This voice gave expression to the pent-up feelings of
grievance, resentment and suspicion that local Chinese
mostly stifled. If Whites had been able to read the Chinese
language daily, they would have been surprised, for what
they were used to seeing was the façade of meekness and
agreeableness adopted as a defense mechanism by their
Chinese neighbours. The *Chinese Times* also provided some
comfort to relatively isolated Chinatowns like those in
Chilliwack, that they were not alone, that Chinese in the rest
of the province struggled through the same trials and
tribulations. For instance, the *Times* kept its readers
informed of the seemingly endless series of campaigns waged
against the province's Chinese residents. It thereby created a
sense of shared community, even if that sense was a
community besieged.[4]

Media enabled Chinese Canadians to promote communication
among themselves, which fostered a basis for uniting in various
forms of organization in order to meet their needs.

There was also a political purpose that motivated the
creation of Chinese language media. The early newspapers were
mostly published by political parties with strong interest in
contemporary developments in China.[5] During this period
China experienced a momentous change in government, the
elimination of the dynastical system that had been in place for
thousands of years. This change gave rise to a myriad of
political views many of which had their own organized
representatives. There were parties that supported the status
quo. There were parties that promoted a constitutional
monarchy. Others, ultimately victorious, advocated wholesale
adoption of Western forms of government, such as the

[4] Chad Reimer, *Chilliwack's Chinatowns: A History* (Vancouver, B.C.: Chinese
Canadian Historical Society of British Columbia & Initiative for Student
Teaching and Research in Chinese Canadian Studies, University of British
Columbia, 2011), 174.

[5] Karl Lo and H.M. Lai note the early influence of Western missionaries on
Chinese-American journalism, but also point out that this influence had
dwindled by the early twentieth century when Chinese language newspapers
began to be established in Canada (*Chinese Newspapers Published in North
America, 1854-1975* [Washington, D.C.: Center for Chinese Research
Materials, Association of Research Libraries, 1977], ix).

Nationalists (also named KMT or Kuomintang), who advocated creating a republic in China.

These political parties had strong support in North America as well, to the extent that their advocates would tour there in order to solicit donations for their causes. In fact, they had their own local headquarters, collected dues, and were often the largest organizations among the Chinese Canadian community. Furthermore, they produced most of the early Chinese language newspapers.

2.2 Early Formation

As stated, early Chinese language media were in print form and concentrated in Vancouver and Victoria. Chinese Canadians then did not have the financial or technological resources to establish other types of media and readers were mostly located in those two cities. What is surprising was the large number of newspapers that were set up and the strong link between print media and political goals. It is estimated that only 1 percent of the early Chinese immigrants were literate,[6] so one wonders what would motivate the publication of newspapers given the limited readership. Nevertheless, one cannot deny the existence of the early newspapers. At the same time, one should keep in mind the strong motivation to create them given the need to communicate and the interest in political developments in China. Furthermore, Chinese Canadians would soon take steps to improve and maintain their literacy by establishing Chinese schools.

Li Haidong details the early creation of newspapers by Chinese Canadians in *Jianada Huaqiao shi* (A history of Chinese in Canada).[7] Karl Lo and Him Mark Lai also do this in a more focused work, *Chinese Newspapers Published in North America, 1854-1975*. The Vancouver Public Library has continued in this vein with a website that provides an overview

---

[6] Li Donghai (David T.H. Lee), *Jianada Huaqiao shi* (A history of Chinese in Canada) (Taipei: 1967), 347.

[7] P. 347-354.

of Chinese language newspapers in Edmonton, Montreal, Ottawa, Toronto, Vancouver, Victoria, and Winnipeg.[8]

The first Chinese newspapers in Canada were imported, the *Huayang ribao* from San Francisco, and the *Zhixin bao* from Macau. The latter included news of Chinese in Canada and was distributed in Vancouver and Victoria. The first domestic Chinese language newspaper was the *Rixin bao (China Reform Gazette)*; it was published in Vancouver by the Chinese Reform Association, and later the Chinese Constitutionalist Party. It lasted from 1903 to 1911 or 1918.[9] The *Huaying bao (Chinese-English Daily News)* began in 1906 in Vancouver and closed in 1910. It supported revolution in China and would later become the *Dahan ribao*. The *Dahan ribao (The Chinese Daily News)* started in 1910 and became *Dahan gongbao (The Chinese Times)* in 1914. It was an organ of the Chinese Freemasons and lasted until 1992. Including its years as *Huaying bao*, it had a history of eighty-six years, which with *Xinghua ribao (Shing Wah Daily News)*, made it one of the longest running Chinese language newspapers in Canada.[10] The *Dalu bao* also promoted revolution in China. It was published in Vancouver but only for a few months in 1909.

The *Xinminguo ribao (The New Republic)* was an organ of the KMT, the Chinese Nationalist Party. It was issued daily after 1911, moved from Victoria to Vancouver in 1957, and stopped publishing in 1984. *Jianada chenbao (Canada Morning News)* was published in Vancouver from approximately 1921 to 1929. It also was an organ of the KMT. The *Xinghua zhoubao (Shing Wah)* began in 1916 in Toronto and became the *Xinghua ribao (Shing Wah Daily News)* in 1922. It was also an organ of the KMT and in 1967 it was the only Chinese language newspaper in Eastern Canada. In various forms it carried on until the year 2000. *Hongzhong shibao (The Chinese Times)* was published in Toronto from 1928 until 1956 and began as a joint effort of the Freemasons and the Constitutionalist Party. It

---

[8] "Newspapers-Chinese," *www.vpl.ca/ccg/Newspapers_Chinese.html*, accessed 05 Mar. 2012.

[9] Yahong Li, "Market, Capital, and Competition: The Development of Chinese-Language Newspapers in Toronto Since the 1970s" (Ph.D. diss., University of Saskatchewan, 1999), 110-11, n.14.

[10] *The Chinese Times* is described in depth in chapter two "Significant Sources of Information on Chinese Canadians."

started as a weekly but became a daily in about 1929. The
Sanmin ribao began in Winnipeg during the Sino-Japanese
War (1937-45); however, it only lasted a few months. *Xinji
minbao (New Citizen)* started in 1949 in Vancouver, and moved
to Toronto in 1951. The *Qiaosheng ribao (The Chinese Voice)*
began publishing in Vancouver in 1953 and lasted until 1987.
The *Zhongxing ribao (The Chinese Free Press)* began in 1954 in
Vancouver, but it only lasted a few months.

Besides the newspapers, there were also a number of
magazines published by early Chinese Canadians. *Guangzhi
congcan* began publication in 1961 in Vancouver but only lasted
a few months. *Rensheng mantan (Life Mirror Weekly)* was
published every five days in Vancouver. *Chinatown News
(Huafu zazhi)* was an English-language publication catering to
Canadian born Chinese that appeared in Vancouver twice a
month from 1953 to 1996. *Dazhong bao (The Masses)* was
published by left-leaning youth in Vancouver. It started in
1960. The *Huaqiao jingji daobao* appeared irregularly. *Gongdao
shehui* began in 1966. *Longgang jikan* was published by the
headquarters of the Longgang kinship association in San
Francisco. The *Lizu yuekan* based in Vancouver was the only
publication by a Chinese-Canadian kinship association. By
1967 it had already been circulating news of the Lee
Association for many years.

Apart from these magazines, there were others that
appeared irregularly including the *Dongfeng* (1959) in
Montreal, *Kaiming* in Toronto, *Xinchao* in Calgary, and *Ziyou
daobao* (1961), *Chinese Citizen*, and *Chinese Lumber Worker*--
the latter published from 1948 to 1953–in Vancouver.

The number, longevity, and strength of these publications
are impressive. For a poor and largely illiterate population, the
Chinese Canadians supported a large number of publications.
In 1930 there were three major Chinese language dailies in
Canada, *Dahan ribao, Xinghua ribao*, and *Xinminguo ribao*,
with a claimed total circulation of 9,250.[11] By 1939, after the
Japanese invasion of China, claimed circulation had reached
18,450.[12] Although some publications were short-lived, others

---

[11] Yahong Li, 100; citing A. McKim, *The Canadian Newspaper Directory*
(1930).

[12] *Ibid.*, 103.

were in operation for more than twenty years. They also seem to have been versatile, evolving into different forms--probably to meet changing needs--spreading across the country, and utilizing English to reach those who could not read Chinese.

2.3 Later Twentieth Century

With the abolishment of the Chinese Immigration Act in 1947 and the gradual loosening of restrictions on Chinese immigration that followed in 1967, Chinese language media developed quickly and in many directions. New immigrants, particularly from Hong Kong and later Taiwan, had both the capital and talent to invest in and create media organizations. Other factors came into play as well. The augmenting numbers of Chinese immigrants created large potential audiences. Their increased wealth and need to establish households in Canada made them attractive targets for advertising. Added to these was the easier access to the technology used to create media. The combination of these factors has led to remarkable achievements that one sees in the present.

The period from the 1960s to the present has been a dynamic one. There has been diversification as the number and sophistication of media outlets have increased in the cities that historically housed them, and similar outlets have been established in urban centres that did not originally possess them. At the same time, national brands have established themselves with newspapers that are available in most large urban areas and TV networks that broadcast across the country. The remarkable growth of Chinese language media is seen in the simultaneous proliferation of media outlets while strong media organizations create easily recognized brand names.

2.3.1 Print Media

In the first twenty-five years of the latter half of the twentieth century, printed media remained the main form of mass communication among Chinese Canadians. Papers from the early 1900s continued to publish; however, all of them had ceased by the end to the century. The *Dahan gongbao (The Chinese Times)* finished in 1992. *Xinminguo ribao (The New Republic)* stopped in 1984. *Xinghua bao (Shing Wah)* carried on until the year 2000. *Qiaosheng ribao (The Chinese Voice)* lasted until 1987 and *Chinatown News* stopped in 1996. Arguably, the attachment of these early publications to political parties in China undermined their appeal to a Chinese-Canadian population that was developing a more Canadian-focused identity.

Nevertheless, there were many new entrants into the newspaper publishing business. In Vancouver, the *Chinese Bulletin (Huaqiao daobao)* began publishing in English and Chinese in 1960 and carried on under various names containing "Chinese-Canadian Bulletin" until 1979 and then again for a few years in the 1980s. Also in Vancouver, the United Chinese Community Enrichment Services Society (S.U.C.C.E.S.S.), an influential organization in the Vancouver Chinese community, began publishing *Evergreen News (Songhe tiandi)* in 1985 and presently claims a distribution of about eight thousand copies a month.[13] *Shenzhou shibao (China Journal)* published weekly from 1997 until 2008. There was even a Chinese version of *Buy and Sell* in Vancouver, but it seems to have stopped publishing after 2010. In Toronto, the *Jiahua ribao (Chinese Canadian Daily)* was published daily from 1984-89, the *Kuaibao (Chinese Express)* appeared with varying frequency from 1971 to 1989, the *Duolunduo shangbao (Chinatown Commercial News)* was issued biweekly from about 1966 to 1986, and the *Dazhong bao (Chinese News)* published three times weekly from 1993 to about 2011. *Jiahua bao (Canadian Chinese Times)* has appeared weekly in Calgary since 1981 until the present, and in Edmonton, since 1982. Similarly, *Dongfang bao (Oriental Weekly*, previously *Oriental News)* has been published in Calgary since 1983 until the present. In Saskatchewan, *Shasheng Huabao (Overseas Chinese Times)* has been published monthly since 1994 until the present. In Winnipeg, the *Miansheng Huabao (Manitoba Chinese Post)* published monthly starting in 1978 until it stopped between 2005 and 2008. *Miansheng Yue Mian Liao Huabao (Manitoba Indochina Chinese News)* has been publishing and distributing eighteen hundred to two thousand copies, each about thirty-two pages in length, monthly since 1984 until the present.

---

[13] United Chinese Community Enrichment Services Society (S.U.C.C.E.S.S.), "New Partnership Launched to Better Serve the Chinese-Canadian Community," 2012.03.07.

In Ottawa, *Jiajing huabao (The Capital Chinese News)* appeared monthly from 1977 to about 1987, *Jiahua qiaobao (Chinese-Canadian Community News)* was published monthly from 1979 to 1989, *Zhonghua daobao (Canada China News)* has published weekly from 1991 to the present, and *Wojing (The Ottawa Weekend)* has published weekly from 1994 until the present. This is a large presence for a Chinese Canadian population that is about 3 percent of the total Ottawa-Gatineau population of 1.2 million.[14] In Montreal, *Huaqiao shibao (La Presse Chinoise)* has been publishing weekly from 1981 till the present, *Huaqiao xinbao (Les Nouvelles Chinoises)* first appeared in 1991 and is still been published weekly, and *Lubi Huaxun* has been published weekly from 1992 until the present.

2.3.1.1 New Developments in the Later Twentieth Century

Moving into the latter years of the twentieth century, Chinese Canadians continued to publish newspapers and periodicals catering to their needs. These evolved, though, from publications that were closely aligned with political interests in China or Taiwan, into ones that attempted to cater more directly to the interests of their readers, which were more aligned with the situation in Canada. Furthermore, Chinese Canadians were able to develop new types of media by entering into the field of electronic broadcasting. There were two major developments during this period in Chinese language media: the establishment of national newspaper chains and the development of electronic media, namely radio and television stations.

Three large Chinese newspaper companies, *Sing Tao Daily (Xindao ribao), World Journal Daily News (Shijie ribao),* and *Ming Pao Daily News (Mingbao),* all started publication in Canada during the latter part of the twentieth century and were well established by the beginning of the twenty-first. Successful operations in Hong Kong and Taiwan provided expertise and capital for establishing their Canadian operations. Large numbers of educated Chinese immigrants,

---

[14] Statistics Canada, "Population by selected ethnic origins, by census metropolitan areas (2006 Census)," *www.statcan.gc*, released 2009.08.14.

mainly from Hong Kong, were able and willing to read their publications and to purchase the products and services advertised therein.

Sing Tao Daily first arrived in Canada in the early 1970s when it was printed in San Francisco and shipped north to Vancouver. Its owner, then Sally Aw, thought that overseas Chinese should have reading material on China. The first Canadian edition was established in Toronto in 1978 and was followed by a British Columbia edition in 1983 and an Alberta edition in 1988. During the late 1900s the Toronto edition had a daily circulation of about forty thousand copies,[15] and the Vancouver edition's was about thirty-two thousand.[16] The average daily readership for the Alberta edition was fifteen thousand: ten thousand in Calgary and five thousand in Edmonton.[17] At that time, *Sing Tao's* Vancouver edition was as long as seventy-two to eighty pages in length. Forty per cent of content was news or commentary and the other 60 per cent was advertising. About one-half of the news and commentary was about Hong Kong, China, and Taiwan.

World Journal Daily News is a subsidiary of *United Daily News* in Taiwan. The Eastern Canadian edition began in 1987 in Toronto and the Western Canadian edition in 1991 in Vancouver. In 1997, its estimated daily circulation for Toronto was thirty-one thousand,[18] and in Vancouver it was ten thousand.[19] The Western and Eastern Canadian editions of *Ming Pao* both began in 1993. In 1997, circulation for *Ming Pao*

---

[15] Peter Li and Yahong Li, "The Consumer Market of the Enclave Economy: A Study of Advertisements in a Chinese Daily Newspaper in Toronto," *Canadian Ethnic Studies* 31.2 (1999), 48 n.5; citing *Ethnic Media and Market* (Winter/Spring) 1997, 11-13. The authors caution that the figures for Toronto were provided by the newspapers themselves.

[16] Ian Haysom, "Newspapers in Hong Kong Are Becoming Increasingly . . . ," *CanWest News*, 1997.05.27, 1.

[17] Katerine Cheung, Chief Editor, *Sing Tao Daily,* Alberta Edition, interview by author, Calgary, 2000.04.25.

[18] Li and Li, 48 n.5; citing *Ethnic Media and Market,* Winter/Spring 1997, 11-13.

[19] Haysom. The *World Journal Daily News* ceased publication on 2015.12.31.

in Toronto was estimated at thirty-seven thousand,[20] and in Vancouver the estimate was twenty-six thousand.[21]

Besides the large, well-established newspapers, *Sing Tao, World Journal,* and *Ming Pao*, there were also a number of national newspapers that were not dailies that appeared before the end of the century. Two promoted Christian views: *Haojiao yuebao (Herald Monthly)* and *Zhenli bao (Truth Monthly). Haojiao yuebao* was first published in 1992 in Toronto and a western edition appeared in 1995 in Vancouver. It printed fifty-five thousand copies monthly, thirty thousand distributed in the east and twenty-five thousand in the west.[22] Similar to *Haojiao yuebao, Zhenli bao* began publishing monthly in Vancouver in 1994 and would later become a national newspaper. Also, national in scope was *Jiankang shibao (Health Times),* which began publishing weekly in 1997 in Toronto and Vancouver. It later expanded to Ottawa in 2002 and Montreal in 2006. Presently, only the weekly Ottawa edition seems to be available.[23] Fairchild Media Group, a television and radio conglomerate, was also distributing forty-five thousand issues monthly of its television and lifestyle guide *Yule shenghuo zazhi (Popular Lifestyle & Entertainment Magazine)* in three editions across British Columbia, Alberta, and Ontario at the end of the century. The number of editions would be reduced to two after the year 2000; however, reported circulation would reach eighty-two thousand, five hundred.[24]

The establishment of large, Chinese language newspapers led to a large increase in daily circulation in Canada. The circulation of Chinese newspapers in Canada in 1980 was six thousand; by 1990 that number had reached thirty-five

---

[20] Li and Li, 48 n.5; citing *Ethnic Media and Market,* Winter/Spring 1997, 11-13.

[21] Haysom.

[22] Lloyd Sciban, "Chinese Language Media Across the West," *Challenging Frontiers: The Canadian West*, ed. Lorry Felske and Beverly Rasporich (Calgary: University of Calgary Press, 2004), 274.

[23] *Jiankang shibao (Health Times), http://www.healthtimes.ca,* accessed 2012.04.02.

[24] *Popular Lifestyle & Entertainment Magazine,* Fairchild Group website, *http://www.fairchildgroup.com/plem.php,* accessed 2012.03.27.

thousand.[25] At the end of the century, it was estimated at one hundred ninety-one thousand.[26] This thirty-two-fold increase over twenty years is another clear example of the achievements of Chinese Canadians. Granted one can question the accuracy of the circulation figures, but then one risks overlooking the overall phenomenal growth in Chinese newspaper circulation that is demonstrated in other ways such as the large amounts of advertising revenues being generated.

This large and rapid increase in Chinese language newspaper readership, no doubt, was an influential factor in leading mainstream publications to attempt to attract Chinese Canadian readers. Although the creation of Chinese publications by mainstream Canadian publishers should not necessarily be indicative of Chinese Canadian achievement, these creations show that the numbers and buying power of Chinese Canadians had reached sufficient size to support them and that Chinese Canadians had suitable talents to contribute to their creation. For example, *Maclean's* and *Toronto Life*, two influential magazines, launched Chinese editions in 1995. Before their termination in 1998, *Toronto Life* was being distributed by *Ming Pao* ten times a year with a circulation of thirty-eight thousand. *Maclean's* was distributed by *Sing Tao* and had a bimonthly circulation of eighty thousand.[27]

The decision to create these Chinese language venues would have been a business one, which relied on market surveys. Those surveys would have shown that Chinese Canadians had acquired the economic strength to support the advertisers that would buy space in *Toronto Life* and *Maclean's* and the educational level to appreciate the content. As well, the

---

[25] Peter Li, *The Chinese in Canada,* second edition (Toronto: Oxford, 1998), 115; citing statistics compiled from *Canadian Advertising Rates and Data* by George Pigadas (1991, 57).

[26] *Sing Tao* was distributing forty thousand in Toronto, thirty-two thousand in Vancouver, and fifteen thousand in Alberta. *Ming Pao* was publishing thirty-seven thousand copies in Toronto and twenty-six thousand in Vancouver. *World Journal's* reported daily circulation was thirty-seven thousand in Toronto and twenty-six in Vancouver.

[27] Eve Lazarus, "The Road Well Travelled: Can Chinese World Succeed Where So Many Other Chinese Magazines Have Failed?", *Marketing Magazine* 105.24 (2000.06.19), 17.

expertise–writers, translators, etc.–to produce these publications would have had to come, at least in part, from the Chinese Canadian community. An even greater recognition of these achievements came from Torstar, parent company of the *Toronto Star*, which purchased 55 percent of *Sing Tao's* Canadian operations for twenty million dollars in 1998. The investments by *Maclean's, Toronto Life*, and Torstar are examples of mainstream recognition of Chinese Canadian achievements with regard to the establishment of Chinese language media. The mainstream publishing companies that have invested in Chinese language publications have acknowledged that their Chinese counterparts are value creating entities.

2.3.2 Electronic Media

The second major development in Chinese language media by the end of the twentieth century was the establishment of electronic media, namely radio and television stations. The first known Chinese language radio program was *"Liming zhi sheng"* (Sounds of daybreak) that ran on the ethnic broadcaster New Generation Broadcasting, Radio CFRO FM 102.7 in Vancouver. It broadcast a mixture of music, information, and news every morning from 1982 to 1995. Toronto's CHIN AM 1540 started broadcasting in Chinese forty-four hours a week in 1985 and was jointly managed with Sing Tao in 1998. Sing Tao and Fairchild Group assumed control of Chinese language broadcasting at the station in 2008 broadcasting under the name "A1 Chinese Radio." In Montreal, Radio Centreville 102.3 FM has had Chinese-language programming since 1983. It presently broadcasts five hours a week of this programming. Also in Montreal, CFMB AM 1280, as Canada's first multilingual broadcaster,[28] probably has had Chinese language broadcasting since before the turn of the century. Presently it broadcasts one hour a week of Chinese programming.

Canadian (Ont.) Chinese Broadcast *(Duolunduo Meijia Huayu diantai)* started broadcasting in Toronto in 1988 as a

---

[28] Canadian Communications Foundation, "CFMB," *www.broadcasting-history.ca*, accessed 2012.04.06.

member of North American Chinese Broadcasters, then as
Toronto Chinese Radio in 2003. It became Canadian (Ont.)
Chinese Broadcast in 2007 and presently broadcasts in Chinese
twenty-four hours a day on the subsidiary communications
operating channel of CKFM-FM. In Vancouver, CHMB AM
1320 began broadcasting over fifty hours of Chinese language
programming in 1993 under the call letters CHQM. The
number of hours increased to one hundred twenty a week when
CHQM was sold to Chinese Canadian investors and changed its
call letters to CHMB later that same year. It presently
broadcasts almost completely in Chinese.

The first Chinese language television broadcast was in
1982 when Cathay International Television (then named
"World View Television") started cable distribution in
Vancouver. In 1985 Chinese Community TV also started
distributing Chinese language programs via cable in British
Columbia's lower mainland. The same year, further east, in
Metro Toronto and Calgary, Chinavision started transmission
of Chinese language programs and later expanded to Edmonton
and Vancouver. As early as 1989, multicultural station CFMT
in Toronto was broadcasting 12 hours of Chinese programming.
In 1990, AATV Productions began distributing programs from
Hong Kong, Taiwan, and China in Calgary.

Chinese language electronic media also saw the
development of national networks, paralleling the earlier
establishment of national newspapers. The development began
when Thomas Fung, who had immigrated from Hong Kong, and
other investors began to purchase and create a number of
media outlets under the Fairchild *(Xin shidai)* brand. These
outlets would eventually be gathered under the umbrella of the
Fairchild Media Group.

In 1993, Fairchild acquired Vancouver's original
multicultural radio station AM1470 CJVB and in 1997, it
launched 96.1 FM, CHKG in the same city. In Toronto, the
company began broadcasting on 88.9 FM CIRV in 1995 and
launched AM 1430 CHKT in 1997. 94.7 FM, CHKF was
launched in Calgary in 1998. With the Calgary launch Fairchild
Radio stations' broadcasts were able to reach nearly 80 percent
of the Chinese Canadian population. By the year 2000, Chinese

language radio stations were broadcasting about 157 hours a week in Toronto,[29] and 123 in Calgary.

Fairchild Media also expanded into television. In 1993 it acquired a nationally licensed television network from Chinavision and turned it into Fairchild TV with stations in Vancouver, Calgary, and Toronto. The same year it also acquired Cathay TV in Vancouver, giving it two stations there and changing its name to "Talentvision."

By the year 2000, Fairchild Television in Vancouver was broadcasting about nineteen hours a day in Cantonese and its signal was being transmitted via satellite for direct-to-home reception across Canada and for cable distribution in Saskatchewan and Manitoba. Its Mandarin counterpart, Talentvision TV, was broadcasting in Vancouver about eighteen hours a day and its signal was also being transmitted across the West. Together, the two stations weekly were broadcasting 259 hours of Chinese language programming and reaching 74 per cent of Vancouver adults, or one hundred sixty thousand individuals, who spoke Chinese at home. The Vancouver radio stations were reaching 23-33 per cent of this population in the same week.[30] In Toronto, Fairchild broadcast a total of 147 hours of TV programming weekly. Furthermore, the scope of Fairchild's electronic media coverage made it a standout among Chinese language media organizations outside China.

Reflecting these accomplishments, the Chinese Language Media Index conducted by ACNielsen in 1999, determined that about 80 percent of Chinese in Toronto were reading at least one newspaper in Chinese a week, while more than 50 per cent read three or more issues per week. In addition, 87 percent of them watched Chinese television, averaging 12.4 hours of viewing per week. They were also listening to an average of 8.5 hours a week of Chinese language radio programming.[31]

---

[29] "Chinese Media in Toronto," *Toronto Star*, 1999.02.11, 1.

[30] Fairchild Media Group, Fairchild Television website, *www.fairchildtv.com/english*, accessed 2000.12.04; citing *ACNielsen Vancouver Chinese Media Index* 2000.

[31] Cited by Zhou Min, Wenhong Chen, and Guoxuan Cai, "Chinese-language Media and Immigrant Life in the United States and Canada," in *Media and the Chinese Diaspora: Community, Communications, and Commerce*, ed. Wanning Sun (London: Routledge, 2006), 52.

Chinese language media were effectively reaching a large part of their targeted audience.

3. Heritage Language Retention

It is important to consider the relation of Chinese language media in Canada to the degree of heritage language retention among Chinese Canadians. The retention of the Chinese language is a necessary condition for the existence of Chinese language media and Chinese Canadians have clearly fulfilled this condition. Furthermore, the way that they have done so is highly supportive of Chinese language media. This is seen not only in the absolute numbers of Chinese listeners and readers, but also in the deliberate efforts to preserve the language through establishing formal programs to instruct it, especially to the younger generations. Also to be considered is the synergy between language instruction and fostering the skills to operate the media.

The widespread presence of Chinese language media in Canada entails that enough Chinese Canadians can speak or read the language to support their operation. In 2006, Chinese, in its various forms, was the third most common mother tongue in Canada with 1,012,065 speakers,[32] an increase of more than 140,000 from 2001 when almost 872,000 people reported Chinese as their mother tongue, which itself was an increase of 136,000 over the 1996 figure of 736,000.[33] The 2011 census reported 1,112,610 individuals using Chinese as their mother tongue (389,000 Cantonese, 255,000 Mandarin, 441,000 n.o.s.). It remained the third most used mother tongue behind English and French (7,298,180) and more than Punjabi (460,000).[34]

---

[32] Statistics Canada, "Population by mother tongue, by province and territory (2006 Census)," *www.statcan.gc.ca*, released 2007.12.11.

[33] Statistics Canada, "Languages in Canada: 2001 Census," Catalogue no. 96-326-XIE, *www.statcan.gc.ca*, released 2004.12.13.

[34] Statistics Canada, "Immigrant Languages in Canada," "Table 1: Population of immigrant mother tongue families, showing main languages comprising each family, Canada, 2011" ; "French and the *francophonie* in Canada," *www.statcan.ca*, accessed 2013.06.04.

Those whose mother tongue was Chinese were equivalent to 84 percent of Chinese Canadians (1,324,700).[35]

The increasing absolute numbers of Chinese Canadians whose mother tongue is Chinese not only fulfill a necessary condition for the existence of Chinese language media; they also represent significant support for them. Readers, listeners, and watchers not only consume the media catering to them, they also buy the products and services that are advertised within them. Moreover, they are a pool from which to draw talent to create and manage these media. Herein is the synergy between Chinese language media and its consumers. The large numbers of consumers provide talent for the creation and maintenance of the media and the media provide opportunities for developing and using this talent. What also should be noted is that Chinese Canadians have been active, even from an early point, in creating schools and programs to ensure that younger generations raised in Canada are able to master the Chinese language.

3.1 Chinese Language Schools

The first known Chinese language school in Canada was Victoria's Lequn Yishu (Sociability Free School), which was established in 1899, over one hundred years ago. Other schools followed shortly after in cities across Canada. "[D]uring the 1930's and early 1940's, there were, according to one survey, twenty-six Chinese part-time schools with forty-seven teachers in eleven locations across the country. Approximately one-third of these were in Vancouver . . . By 1941 it was estimated that approximately 1,500 students were attending Chinese schools."[36] Language training was an important part of the curriculum in these schools. Research done on the education of Chinese Canadians in Alberta from 1885 to 1947 induced that "[t]he Chinese language schools in Alberta during this period of

---

[35] Statistics Canada, "2011 National Household Survey: Immigration, place of birth, citizenship, ethnic origin, visible minorities, language and religion," *www.statcan.ca*, accessed 2013.06.04.

[36] Wickberg *et al.*, 170-71.

study . . . ultimately served to maintain the Chinese culture and language."[37]

This same goal was seen in a survey carried out in 1971 in which 97 percent of each of the Toronto and Hamilton Chinese Canadian communities indicated that they wanted their children to speak and to write Chinese fluently.[38] This desire led to the establishment of the Heritage Language Program in Ontario. "In 1973 the parents of children in Ogden and Orde Street schools, where the student population was 90 percent Chinese, formed" an association that petitioned the Toronto Board of Education to include Chinese culture and language in the curriculum. "The board approved a two-year program, for which the parents contributed half the funding. The year 1974 marked the first heritage program ever in a Toronto school" and led to official recognition of heritage language programs in 1977 by the Ontario government.[39]

The support for Chinese language education has continued as evidenced by *Sing Tao Etel Vancouver* in June 2013 listing nineteen Chinese community language schools.[40] The actual number is probably much higher because there were already twelve Chinese language schools in Vancouver in 1984[41] and Duanduan Li Director of the Chinese Language Program at University of British Columbia estimates there are two hundred Chinese community schools in Vancouver.[42]

---

[37] Hilda Mah, "Abstract," "A History of the Education of Chinese Canadians in Alberta, 1885-1947" (M. Education thesis, University of Alberta, 1987), 67n.2.

[38] Harold A. Wright, "The Chinese in Toronto - A Personal Appreciation," unpublished, 1976.

[39] Arlene Chan, *The Chinese in Toronto from 1878: From Outside to Inside the Circle* (Toronto: Dundurn, 2011), 123.

[40] www.singtaoetel.ca/VAN/EN/subcategory.php?CategoryID=11&CatalogID=S008, accessed 2013.06.09. *Sing Tao Etel* is a Chinese business directory published by Sing Tao.

[41] Peter Li, "Chinese," in *The Encyclopedia of Canada's Peoples*, ed. Paul Magocsi (Toronto: University of Toronto Press, 1999).

[42] "Chinese as a Heritage Language in Canada," n.d., crclle.lled.educ.ubc.ca/documents/li.pdf, accessed 2013.06.09.

Sing Tao Etel Toronto lists sixteen Chinese community language schools as of June 2013,[43] but again the actual number is probably much higher. There were ten Chinese schools in Toronto in 1984,[44] but according to Bernard Luk, *The Chinese Consumer Directory of Toronto, 1997* listed more than one hundred schools.[45]

There is also a national organization of Chinese community schools. The Canadian Association of Chinese Language Schools claims fifty member schools in nine cities across Canada: Vancouver, Calgary, Edmonton, Saskatoon, Regina, Winnipeg, Ottawa, Toronto, and Montreal.[46]

These schools and organizations and the history that has led to them indicate that there has been and will continue to be a strong foundation in place to support Chinese language media and its continued development.

4. Recent State of Chinese Language Media

The twenty-first century has seen continued growth and sophistication in Chinese language media. While the number of outlets has continued to increase and media are developing on the internet, the large organizations, such as Sing Tao, Ming Pao, World Journal, and Fairchild have also been able to grow as well and consolidate their strong positions within the field. They have created the phenomenon of marquee brands and their success has motivated mainstream media organizations to increase their audiences by attempting to attract Chinese Canadians.

The continued and increasing success of Chinese language media also focuses attention on potential issues in their development; i.e., whether Chinese language media accurately

---

[43]

163bbs.servebeer.com/?qbz=ac01CJMsNVllnRlivdQ9P8je1ZAvWpmrKx7rd13o V9mfJtmuMRnrXxDvER6cKhm32tQ2a94nclAioF4g6dQ75hQgqAh38RAjj1, (2013.06.09).

[44] Li, "Chinese."

[45] "The Chinese Communities of Toronto: Their Languages and Mass Media," *Polyphony: The Bulletin of the Multicultural Society of Toronto* 15 (2000), 52.

[46] *cacls.org/About_Us.html*, accessed 2013.06.09.

reflects the identity of its users and whether they contribute to the integration of its users and mainstream society.

Despite this being the case, the number of Chinese language media outlets is still something that commands attention. Zhou *et al.* estimated them to number at least two hundred in 2004.[47] Xu Xinhan and Huang Yunrong have estimated the number to be more than one hundred twenty-five in 2010, including more than fifty newspapers and periodicals, more than ten television stations, six to seven radio stations, and more than sixty websites.[48] Further adding to this significance are statistics on consumer demand. A 2007 survey shows that among Chinese Canadians born outside Canada, 81 percent watch Chinese TV programs, 80 percent read Chinese newspapers, and 34 percent listen to Chinese radio programs.[49] Chinese language media are supported by a large audience that justifies their numbers.

4.1 Newspapers

4.1.1 National Newspapers

While it has been only a few years since the end of the last century, already there have been significant developments in the make-up of national Chinese language newspapers. The three major dailies still compete for readership; however, readership has increased and so has the number of newspapers that can be considered national.

Earlier this chapter reported the increasing daily circulation of large, Chinese language newspapers in Canada. Circulation in 1980 was six thousand, by 1990 it was thirty-five thousand, and it was approximately one hundred ninety-one thousand at the end of the century. In 2011, the estimated daily circulation of all three Chinese language dailies was two

---

[47] P. 51.

[48] Xu Xinhan and Huang Yunrong, "Jiananda Huawen chuanmei fazhan zongshu" (A general description of the development of Chinese language media in Canada), *blog.udn.com/cwacan/3788974*, accessed 2012.03.11.

[49] IpsosReid and Era Marketing Communications, "IpsosReid 2007 Canadian Chinese Media Monitor: Greater Toronto Area," *www.fairchildtv.com*, accessed 2012.04.08.

hundred twenty-three thousand, an increase of more than 17 percent over eleven years.[50] Furthermore, a number of non-daily, yet national newspapers, have joined the three main dailies.

The dailies have also added supplements, creating a number of specialized features to attract more readership. *Sing Tao* publishes the *Sing Tao Weekly (Xingdao zhoukan)* focusing on entertainment; the *Xing zhoukan (Star Magazine)* featuring current events in Hong Kong; the *Xingdao dichan zhoukan (Real Estate Guide)*; *Meishi (Gourmet)*; and *Chao (Trend)*, which contains lifestyle and fashion content. It also publishes *Dushi bao (Canadian City Post)* in Vancouver and Toronto, a free weekly catering to new immigrants from mainland China. Add to these supplements for festivals and seasonal needs, such as for the Chinese Lunar New Year, the Dragon Boat Festival, and new homes, and one has a wide variety to attract reader interest. Sing Tao also produces annual directories for Chinese Canadian businesses in Toronto, Vancouver, Calgary, and Edmonton. These latter are substantial; for example, the 2012 Calgary edition was three hundred sixty-six pages in length.

Ming Pao also publishes weekly and special supplements. Among its weekly supplements are *Le zai mingchu (Gourmet Supplement)*; *Ming bao xingqi liu zhoukan (Saturday Magazine)*, a lifestyle-and-news magazine; *Xingqi ri Mingbao zhoukan (Ming Pao Sunday Magazine)*, with a focus on Hong Kong entertainment; *Mingsheng bao (Canadian Chinese Express)*, targeting immigrants from mainland China; *Mingbao dichan jinye (Ming Pao Property Gold Pages)*; and *Zhonghua tansuo (Exploring China)*, containing political criticism from Hong Kong. Special annual supplements include ones on weddings in March and one in August on going back to school.

The *World Journal* has one known supplement, *Shijie zhoukan (World Journal Sunday Magazine)*, which is a news and entertainment magazine.

---

[50] "Every Daily Newspaper in Canada," *www.fishwrap.ca*, revised 2011.06.13. One wonders about the credibility of the website that does not document the source of its numbers; however, the circulation numbers provided seem to correspond to those found in other sources, such as *Wikipedia*, for the most part and, if anything, are slightly lower. Verified circulation numbers are not readily available.

Joining the three daily and three monthly *(Haojiao yuebao, Zhenli bao, and Yule shenghuo zazhi (Jiankang shibao* would probably cease publication in 2011) national newspapers after the year 2000 were three other national Chinese language newspapers. *Huanqiu huabao (Global Chinese Press)* first published in 2000. It has two editions, Canada East and Canada West, and is distributed in British Columbia, Ontario and Alberta twice a week, every Wednesday and Friday. It claims a circulation of sixty thousand for its two editions[51] and targets immigrants from mainland China with news from there and through some use of simplified Chinese characters. A single issue contains about forty pages.

Jianada shangbao (Today Commercial News) began in 2005 in Toronto as *Xiandai ribao (Today Daily News)*. It now issues four editions, one daily in Toronto, and three weekly in Montreal, Ottawa, and Alberta; and two weekly supplements *Dichan shangbao (Property Weekly)* and *701 zhoukan (701 Magazine)*. Its estimated daily circulation in Toronto is fifteen thousand.[52] It was a subsidiary of Media Central, Inc. part of a global news corporation. In 2008, the large, Canadian mainstream newspaper publisher, Sun Media Corporation, bought a 50 percent share in the company.

Another national newspaper that began publishing in 2000 was *Dajiyuan shibao (The Epoch Times)*. It is the organ of *Falun Gong*, a religious group with a strong following in China but also officially banned there. It publishes two editions, one in Vancouver and the other in Toronto, and has a total weekly circulation of forty-one thousand.[53]

Also in this century, *Zhenli bao (Truth Monthly)* expanded its coverage from Vancouver to include Western Canada and western United States with a reported circulation of twenty-eight thousand; and in 2003 an Eastern Canada edition was

---

[51] *Huanqiu Huawang (Global Chinese Press* website), *www.gcpnews.com/aboutus_en.html*, accessed 2012.03.26.

[52] "Every Daily Newspaper in Canada."

[53] Canadian Newspaper Association, "Circulation Data Report 2009," accessed 2012.03.26.

established with a reported circulation of twenty-two thousand.[54]

In summary, the three Chinese language daily newspapers distributed across Canada have continued to do well, indeed expanding on their circulation. Anecdotally, one is also made aware of their vitality; Jan Wong, when reporting for *The Globe and Mail,* noted that the size and amount of advertising in the Toronto editions often outflanked Toronto's mainstream press.[55] Besides these national dailies, two new national Chinese language newspapers have begun publishing, one twice a week, the other on a weekly basis. Add to these, the four monthly national publications and one becomes aware of the publishing plenty of Chinese language newspapers in Canada.

4.1.2 Local Newspapers

Although many of the early local Chinese language newspapers have ceased publication, some still continue to do so and they have been joined by new ones that bring new ideas to the industry and demonstrate its vitality.

4.1.2.1 British Columbia

Evergreen News (Songhe tiandi) the organ of the United Chinese Community Enrichment Services Society (S.U.C.C.E.S.S.) in Vancouver has been published since 1985. It has been joined by *Dahua shangbao (Dawa Business Press),* which commenced in 2001 and is published three times a week, and is also distributed in Victoria, Edmonton, and Calgary. It claims to be the only Chinese Canadian business magazine.[56]

4.1.2.2 Prairie Provinces

---

[54] *Zhenli bao (Truth Monthly), www.truth-monthly.com/misc/tru_info.htm,* accessed 2012.03.26.

[55] "The Other Newspaper War," *The Globe and Mail,* 2004.12.18, M3.

[56] *Dahua wang* (Dawa website), *www.dawanews.com,* accessed 27 March 2012.

On the prairies, *Jiahua bao (Canadian
Chinese Times)* continues to be published in Calgary and
Edmonton. Similarly, *Dongfang bao (Oriental Weekly)* is still
published in Calgary. The *Guanghua bao (The Chinese Journal)*
began publishing weekly in Edmonton in 2002. In
Saskatchewan, *Shasheng Huabao (Overseas Chinese Times)* has
been published monthly since 1994 until the present. In
Winnipeg, *Miansheng Yue Mian Liao Huabao* (Manitoba
Indochina Chinese News) has been publishing and distributing
eighteen hundred to two thousand copies, each about thirty-two
pages in length, monthly since 1984. Also in Winnipeg, *Fenghua
zhi sheng (The Manitoba Chinese Tribune)* has been publishing
every two months since early 2002.

4.1.2.3 Ontario

In Toronto there has been a spate of new local
papers to replace those that folded prior to the year 2000. A
website accessible in 2012 listed thirty Chinese-language
newspapers available in the Toronto area.[57] The *Xinxing
shenghuo (New Star Times)* has been published weekly since
2001. The *Jiazhong shibao (Chinese Canadian Times)* has been
published weekly in Toronto since 2002. It claims a circulation
of thirteen thousand[58] and from 2007-09 also published an
edition in Vancouver. *Jinri Zhongguo wenhuibao (China Today
Wen Wei Bo)* began as a semiweekly in 2002. It seems to have
ceased publication; however, may still have been publishing in
2009. The *Dichan zhoukan (Chinese Real Estate Weekly)* began
publishing in 2005 and continues to this day. Starting with
Huabao (Very Good News) in 2004, *Jianada Huabao (Very Good
News)* has also published *Wenzhai bao (Chinese Readers)*
(2005), *Jiankang zhoukan (Health Guide)* (2006), and *Renwu
zhoukan (People Weekly)* (2008). All of Very Good News'
publications are weeklies and they each claim a distribution of

---

[57] *Qingsong Jianada* (easyca.ca), *"Daduo diqu baozhang guanggao"*
(Advertisements for newspapers in the Greater Toronto Area),
easyca.ca/info/list.php?fid=220&city_id=1, accessed 2012.04.02.

[58] "About Us," *Jiazhong shibao (Chinese Canadian Times)* website,
www.cctimes.ca, accessed 31 March 2012.

eleven thousand.[59] Norstar Media Group *(Beichen xinwen meiti jituan)* has also published a number of newspapers in the Toronto area. *Beichen shibao (Norstar Times)* has been published weekly since 2008. *Beichen dichan zhoukan (Norstar Realty Weekly)* and *Beichen caifu (Fortune Weekly)* began publishing in 2010. Norstar Media Group's sister company Estar Media Group *(Dongfang chuanmei jituan)* has published *Anju zhoukan (Home Weekly) and Caijing zhoukan (Finance Weekly)* both since 2011. 401BZ INC has published *Xinbao caijing zhoucan (Ads Guide . Fortune Smart) weekly* since 2006, *Xinbao yishi wangju (MyHomeGuide)* weekly since 2008, and *Xinbao dichan zhoukan (Chinese Real Estate Magazine)* weekly since 2011. It claims that the monthly circulation for *Ads Guide . Fortune Smart* is fifty thousand and forty thousand for *MyHomeGuide.*[60] *Duolundou zhoubao (WJToronto Chinese News)* is distributed free weekly by *World Journal* in order to compete with the large number of free Chinese newspapers available in Toronto. It began publication in 2010 and has a circulation of thirty-two thousand.[61] *Luse shenghuo (Green Life)* began publishing weekly early in 2011. It claims to be the only publisher dedicated to "green" messaging in Chinese.[62] *Mingren mingshang zhoukan (Fame Weekly)* has published weekly since 2010.

In Ottawa the *Zhonghua daobao (Canada China News)* has been published weekly since 1991, and *Wojing (The Ottawa Weekend)* has published weekly from 1994 until the present. The *Hong fenglin (Red Maple)* began publishing every two weeks in London, Ontario in 2011. The *Jiahua shibao (CCL Chinese Journal)* based in the Mississauga-Hamilton region started in 2005 and publishes twice a week.

---

[59] Very Good News website, *www.verygoodnews.ca*, accessed 2012.04.22.

[60] AdsGuide.ca, "Guanyu women" (About us), *www.adsguide.ca/siteinfo.php?t=1*, accessed 2012.04.02.

[61] Toronto's Online Chinese Community, *"Duolunduo zuida Zhongwen mianfei bao"* (Toronto's largest free Chinese newspaper), *www.torcn.com/bbs/deal/4983.html*, accessed 2012.04.02.

[62] *Luse shenghuo* (Green Life) website, *www.greenlifeweekly.com*, accessed 2012.04.02.

The proliferation of newspapers in Ontario, especially in Toronto, is indicative of not only a thriving economic environment that can support publication of free and paid newspapers, some nearly two hundred pages long, but also of the expertise to produce them and of the creativity to identify the niches that some of them fill.

4.1.2.4 Quebec

In Montreal, *Huaqiao shibao* (La Presse Chinoise) has been publishing weekly from 1981 till the present, *Huaqiao xinbao* (Les Nouvelles Chinoises) first appeared in 1991 and is still being published weekly, and *Lubi Huaxun* (Luby Chinese Weekly Newspaper) has been published weekly since 1992.

Since the year 2000, Montreal has also added Chinese language newspapers. The *Mengcheng Huaren bao (Journal Chinois Sinoquébec)* has been published weekly since 2001. It claims to be the only Chinese newspaper distributed in Quebec City and Trois-Rivières.[63] The fact that it is distributed in these two cities is important as it demonstrates that they have a sufficient readership to support delivery. *Qitian (Sept Days)* has published weekly since 2006. *Xinjia yuan (Éventual)* has published weekly since 2010. It claims to be the first bilingual Chinese-French newspaper in Quebec.[64]

4.1.2.5 Maritimes

Even the Maritimes had its own Chinese language newspaper called *"Ni Hao PEI"* for about a year. It started in 2011 and claimed a circulation of two to three thousand copies for each quarterly issue.[65]

4.2 Magazines

---

[63] *Mengcheng Huaren bao,* *www.sinoquebec.com/sinoquebecmedia/sinoquebecnewspaper_e.htm,* accessed 2012.04.03.

[64] *Xinjia yuan (Eventual), www.greader.ca,* accessed 2012.04.12.

[65] *Ni Hao PEI, nihaopei.com,* accessed 2012.04.03.

In strong contrast to the proliferation of Chinese language newspapers in Canada, there have not been many Chinese language magazines published. Arguably, the higher cost of production and higher standards for content have hindered the publishing of magazines in Chinese. Also of interest is how efforts to produce magazines have favoured the use of English. *Chinatown News* (1953-1996), described earlier as a newspaper, could also be classified as a magazine, with smaller sized pages, and relatively more photographs. The literature, culture, and arts magazine *Ricepaper* features Asian-Canadian work–in English--and has published quarterly out of Vancouver since 1994. Its distribution in 2000 was four thousand copies.[66] *Maclean's* and *Toronto Life* published Chinese versions of their English magazines, both from 1995 to 1998. A commendable effort is *AsianWave (Yazhou langchao),* which has been published in Toronto every two months since 2003. It is a bilingual publication, English and Chinese, and claims a readership of fifteen thousand.[67]

4.3 Radio

In review, at the turn of the twentieth century there were eight radio stations in Canada broadcasting Chinese language programming, four in Toronto, three in Vancouver, and one in Calgary. Five of these stations were operated by Fairchild Media Group.

While at first glance it seems that Chinese language radio broadcasting has not seen the growth that newspaper publishing has experienced, there still have been some changes. Sing Tao took a share in the broadcasting operations of CHIN AM 1540 in 1998 in Toronto, and was later joined by Fairchild Group in 2008 under the name "A1 Chinese Radio." Moving into the twenty-first century, one also finds increasing Chinese language radio broadcasting. CHMB AM 1320 in Vancouver was broadcasting around fifty hours in 1993, quickly moved to broadcasting one hundred twenty, and presently broadcasts twenty-four hours a day in Chinese. Since Fairchild launched

---

[66] Lazarus.

[67] *AsianWave,* "About Us," *asianwavemag.com,* accessed 2012.04.04.

96.1 FM, CHKG in Vancouver, it has increased its Chinese
language broadcast to 70 percent of the total broadcast hours.
After Fairchild launched AM 1430 CHKT in 1997 in Toronto, it
successfully applied to the Canadian Radio-television and
Telecommunications Commission (CRTC) in 2004 to remove the
original limitation of only being able to broadcast sixty-six
hours a week in Chinese. It presently broadcasts nearly one
hundred hours in Chinese.

4.4 Television

        The growth in Chinese language television
broadcasting has been much more dynamic than that of radio
broadcasting. Of course, one reason for this is the greater
attraction that television imagery offers; another is the
technology that allows the delivery of television, literally, across
the world so that a consumer can now choose from hundreds of
different channels. At the end of the twentieth century, there
were five television stations: Fairchild Media operated two in
Vancouver, one in Toronto, and a fourth in Calgary; the fifth
was CFMT in Toronto. Fairchild's two Vancouver stations were
broadcasting two hundred fifty-nine hours of Chinese
programming per week and in Toronto Fairchild and CFMT
together were broadcasting a total of one hundred sixty-one
hours.
        Fairchild Television continued to retain its popularity
among Chinese Canadians. In 2007, 53 percent of those in
Toronto self-identified as Chinese or Chinese-Canadian, born
outside Canada, and able to speak Mandarin or Cantonese
viewed Fairchild TV (Cantonese) at least once a week and 40
percent of them every day. Seventeen percent of them viewed
TalentVision (Mandarin) at least once a week and 10 percent
every day; therefore, the percentage of them viewing some form
of Chinese language television is probably higher, especially
given that they may also have been watching OMNI TV's
programming. For Chinese Canadians in Vancouver, 55 percent
of them viewed Fairchild TV at least once a week and 39
percent of them every day. Forty-nine percent of them viewed
TalentVision (Mandarin) at least once a week and 29 percent
every day. Again, the percentage of them viewing some form of

Chinese language television is probably higher, especially given that 30 percent viewed OMNI TV at least once a week.[68]

Since the year 2000, the viewing options in Chinese programming have increased immensely. There has been an increase in local broadcasters and even mainstream networks have added Chinese programming to their schedules. On the other hand, the expansion of cable transmission has both extended the reach of broadcasters, both domestic and foreign, and enabled the wholesale import of programming from foreign producers.

In 2003 in Vancouver, Multivan started a multicultural station broadcasting on what would be called "Channel M." Ownership included Chinese Canadians and their studios were in Vancouver's downtown Chinatown. Eventually the station became part of Omni Television's network.

Omni Television officially began in 2002 in Toronto when its owner Roger's Broadcasting Ltd. procured a second multicultural TV station in Toronto, namely CJMT. Roger's then won licenses to offer multicultural programs in Edmonton and Calgary. In 2007 it purchased Channel M in Vancouver from Multivan. Presently, its programs are available across most of the country with the amount of Chinese language varying among locales. Until May 2015 OMNI was providing thirty-six hours of Chinese language programming weekly in Toronto, twenty-eight in Vancouver, and fourteen in Calgary. It has since reduced this to eleven hours in Vancouver, including five hours of news in each of Mandarin and Cantonese. Omni also broadcasts specials relating to Chinese Canadians, such as on Canadian Chinatowns or biographies of important figures, such as Joseph Wong the founder of Yee Hong Centre for Geriatric Care.

More mainstream broadcasters are also developing an interest in Chinese language broadcasting. The Canadian Broadcasting Corporation (CBC) through its international broadcast arm Radio Canada International set up a website,

---

[68] IpsosReid and Era Marketing Communications, "IpsosReid 2007 Canadian Chinese Media Monitor, Greater Toronto Area"; and "IpsosReid 2007 Canadian Chinese Media Monitor, Greater Vancouver Area," *www.fairchildtv.com*, accessed 2012.04.08.

www.rcinet.ca/chinese/, to broadcast news in Chinese.[69] As
well, a major television network in Canada, Global Television
Network, produces a thirty-minute, nightly newscast "Global
National Mandarin" that is broadcast on Shaw Multicultural
Channel in Vancouver and Calgary.

With the involvement of mainstream media producers,
another aspect of the achievements of Chinese Canadians
comes to light. Based on the evidence presented to this point,
one could argue that the Chinese Canadians have shown
perseverance, devotion to their ethnic culture, and the ability to
produce a highly-developed ethnic media. The early Chinese
Canadians probably were hardly literate, yet they established
newspapers and schools as a means to communicate and
preserve traditional values. This has led to a well developed
Chinese language media in Canada.

The efforts of the mainstream media producers to create
Chinese language programming builds on this development, but
it also recognizes another dimension of Chinese Canadian
achievement and that is their economic achievement. Their
economic status has become such that they are now an
attractive market for mainstream media producers. Of course,
the mainstream producers will rely on Chinese Canadians to
produce and present their products, which is recognition of the
latter's abilities; however, the profit motive is a greater
determinant of this programming and as such recognizes even
more Chinese Canadian economic achievement.

This fact leads to another interesting phenomenon in
Chinese language media in Canada, one that highlights even
further the economic strength of Chinese Canadians as well as
indicating further the importance of Chinese language media to
Chinese Canadians. Major Canadian telecommunication
companies, such as Rogers Communications, Bell Canada,
Telus Communications, and Shaw Communications, that have
large distribution networks within Canada have joined with
foreign providers of Chinese language television programming

---

[69] Interestingly, the site is partially aimed at attracting viewers in China. It is
one example of Canadian producers of Chinese language broadcasts
attempting to promote their products outside of Canada. Another example is
Rogers Communications joint venture with Sun Wah Media of Hong Kong to
produce a documentary series for sale to China (Paul Brent, "Rogers Tackles
Chinese TV Market," *National Post,* 2004.04.27, p. FP.6).

to distribute their programming in Canada. One result has been further abundance of Chinese language television programming available to viewers.

Phoenix TV *(Fenghuang weishi Meizhou tai)* is a popular foreign provider of Chinese language programming. It has been available in Canada since 2006. Based in Hong Kong, it broadcasts a mixture of news and entertainment from China and other areas in the Asian Pacific region, including Canada, in Mandarin. In 2007, 9 percent of those in Toronto self-identified as Chinese or Chinese-Canadian, born outside Canada, and able to speak Mandarin or Cantonese watched it at least once a week.[70]

Another foreign provider of Chinese language content is Central China Television (CCTV), the predominant state television broadcaster in mainland China. It received approval in 2007 to offer nine Chinese language television channels in Canada. The application was seen as an effort to service the Mandarin speaking population, which was under serviced by the Chinese language media largely focused on Cantonese speakers. Shaw, Rogers, Telus, and Bell all offer CCTV channels. The channels are sometimes sold together and offered as the Great Wall Package. Even small stations distribute CCTV content. In 2012 WOW TV in Toronto contracted to carry CCTV's documentary channel.

New Tang Dynasty TV *(Xin Tangren dianshi tai),* based in New York since 2002, has reporters stationed around the world, including four in Canada. It broadcasts in Mandarin, Cantonese, English, and French. It also has strong connections to the religious group *Falun Gong* that is banned in China.

Channel V Taiwan *(Xingkong chuanmei jituan),* offered under the name "Star Channel," offers a variety of entertainment from Taiwan, with an emphasis on popular music. It has been available in Canada since 2008. Star Chinese *(Weishi Zhongwen tai)* has its headquarters in Hong Kong. It has provided a general entertainment channel originating in Taiwan since the latest 2010. It broadcasts in Mandarin. Its movie channel Star Movies *(Weishi dianying tai)* is also available in Canada.

---

[70] IpsosReid and Era Marketing Communications, "IpsosReid 2007 Canadian Chinese Media Monitor, Greater Toronto Area," *www.fairchildtv.com,* accessed 2012.04.08.

LS Times TV *(Longxiang pindao)* has provided a mix of popular movies from China, Taiwan, Japan, South Korea and other Asian countries, along with some news programs, since 2009. It is a Canadian subsidiary of the Long Shong Group, a film distributor in Taiwan. Seventy percent of its programming is to be in Cantonese. ETTV *(Dongsen weishi)* is a general entertainment channel broadcasting in Mandarin. It is a subsidiary of Eastern Broadcasting Group *(Dongsen dianshi shiye)* in Taiwan, which operates around the world. It has been available in Canada since 2006.

Beside the foreign providers described above, there is also a single channel whose programming is broadcast in Canada. A Cantonese television channel from Hong Kong, ATV Home Channel (America) (Asia Television Limited *[Yazhou dianshi]*).[71] It has been available in Canada since 2007.

In summary, the number of Chinese language television viewing options has increased immensely since the beginning of the century. This is not only a testament to the desire of Chinese-Canadians to create the Chinese language media present in Canada. It also is evidence of the economic strength that has been required for building and support of the television programming that serves them.

4.5 Internet

The internet is also a medium through which to understand the achievements of Chinese Canadians. Granted it is relatively inexpensive and easy to set up a website, which also makes it difficult to discern and measure the achievements of Chinese Canadians in this area. However, research in the area does show that Chinese Canadians have adopted the new medium both quickly and effectively. At the same time, they are creatively utilizing the internet to expand their activities.

First, it should be recognized that the more traditional venues among Chinese language media: the newspapers, radio stations, and TV networks, are using the internet very

---

[71] Guangdong Southern TV (TVS) *(Nanfang weishi),* a news and entertainment channel broadcast in Cantonese from Guangzhou, also seems to fit into this category. However, it can also be seen as one of the channels provided by Central China Television. It has been available in Canada since 2007.

effectively. For example, *Sing Tao Daily* acquired Ccue Chinese Media in 2007 to develop their online potential. *Sing Tao* now places much of their hard print content online, including excerpts from each of three for-pay and their two free editions. There is also a large amount of commercial linkage and advertising. There are links to Sing Tao`s radio station, to a chat room, to a blog, and to community news. As well, there are English translations for their news stories, the capacity to switch between simplified and traditional characters, and links to *Sing Tao's* various supplements. Fairchild Media Group's websites include links to their live radio broadcasts and an archive of television news programs for the watching. The group's entertainment guide, *Popular Lifestyle and Entertainment Magazine,* is also available.

Besides the websites set up by established Chinese language media companies, there are also many companies that publish only on the internet. *Shijie huaren meiti (World Chinese media)* provides links to twenty Chinese language sources, which can only be found on the internet, of current Canadian news, as well as links to many of the traditional media companies. Xu Xinhan and Huang Yunrong classify the many Chinese language websites based in Canada into four main types 1) those that provide news, 2) those that provide advice and information on matters of daily living, 3) those used for conversation among users (i.e., chat rooms), and 4) those that provide financial services. Among the first type, which is the most typical form, there are also distinctions between those that are primarily advertise with a small amount of news and those whose content is mostly current news. The websites of the newspapers, such *Sing Tao's,* are predominantly made up of news, but there are also independent websites, such as *Kuibeike Huaren wang (www.quebecren.com)* that are able to provide current news while keeping advertising to a relatively low level.

There are other characteristics of Chinese language websites. There is a distinction between websites that feature items of gossip and titillating photos and those that feature news of greater significance. A rough comparison shows that the amount of significant news found in newspapers is proportionally much greater than that found on Chinese language news websites. There are also websites that are devoted to specific Canadian locations, such as

calgarychina.net, www.torcn.com (Toronto Chinese),
ottawachinese.com, and *windsorchinese.net.*

There are also some particular developments that are
interesting and, perhaps, indicative of trends. The *Vancouver
Sun* launched a Chinese language website in 2011 called
Taiyangbao, which translates as "sun newspaper." An
administrator of the newspaper explains that Chinese
Canadians were one of the fastest growing demographics in
Western Canada and the *Vancouver Sun* was targeting
households with an income of around seventy-four thousand
dollars a year. The *Vancouver Sun* was also able to enlist RBC,
four Canadian real estate developers, and an outlet mall in
Seattle as sponsors of the site.[72] In early 2012, readership was
increasing by 25 percent a month.[73]

This development indicates that mainstream media still
have strong interest in attracting a Chinese-Canadian
audience. In the past, the publication of Chinese issues of
Maclean's and *Toronto Life,* and the purchase of a 50 percent
ownership in Sing Tao's Canadian operations by Torstar were
examples of this interest. The *Vancouver Sun's* creation of a
Chinese language website is a more recent one. To add to its
attractiveness, the *Vancouver Sun* has even added content from
S.U.C.C.E.S.S.'s *Evergreen News.*

A second particular development that seems indicative of a
new trend is a Vancouver company's website specifically
devoted to connecting companies and institutions in North
America to strategic partners in the Greater China region and
Chinese-speaking communities abroad. ChineseWorldNet.com
of Vancouver has established online financial information and
service platforms for this purpose. These platforms are
examples of the creativity that the internet fosters among
Chinese language media in Canada.

5. Achievements

The history and present state of Chinese language media in
Canada reveal the achievements of Chinese Canadians in this

[72] Jennifer Horn, "*Vancouver Sun* Launches Chinese-language Website,"
Media in Canada, 2011.12.08, *www.mediaincanada.ca,* accessed 2012.04.13.

[73] United Chinese Community Enrichment Services Society (S.U.C.C.E.S.S.).

area. The history shows a course of development that has led to the establishment of a widespread and sophisticated media. Chinese Canadians have demonstrated foresight, skill, and idealism in creating this media. Their media produce large advertising revenues and they encourage mainstream involvement on the part of Chinese Canadians. Chinese language media stand as further examples of what Chinese Canadians have achieved.

5.1 Development of Media

The development of Chinese language media stands out as a remarkable achievement. From the first Chinese language medium created in Canada, the newspaper *Rixin bao (China Reform Gazette)* that began publishing in 1903, to Sing Tao's national media group, Chinese Canadians, in a little more than one hundred years, have created and are operating vast and complex media that cater to their cultural values. The result is that "Chinese language television and radio programming in Canada has arguably become the richest and most sophisticated outside China, Hong Kong and Taiwan,"[74] and the same argument could be made for the print media as well.

The early Chinese immigrants to Canada faced many hurdles in attempting to establish themselves in Canada not the least of which was the racial discrimination that generally saw them paid half of what other workers were making. They were largely uneducated. Yet, they found the means to establish newspapers. They needed to acquire Chinese printing type, purchase paper and ink, obtain and write news, distribute the papers, sometimes on a daily basis. This took place across the nation even as the population shrank and Canada went through the Great Depression, and two world wars.

These early immigrants had the foresight, in spite of their common illiteracy, to establish schools to teach themselves and later generations the Chinese language, thereby enabling them to create the media and utilize the advantages that media offered. These efforts were precursors to the many community schools that have taught the language skills and cultural

---

[74] Zhou *et al.*, 66.

awareness required to appreciate and draw practical value from
Chinese language media. Of particular significance were the
abilities to read and write, which would sustain the media into
the twentieth-first century by fostering a vibrant print media,
and which is no easy feat if only because of the difficulty of
mastering Chinese characters.

After 1947 when Chinese immigrants were once again
permitted to enter Canada, there was already a solid base upon
which the future media builders could work and which would
encourage Chinese Canadians to foster media dedicated to their
cultural preferences. Investors, such as Thomas Fung, one of
the founders of Fairchild Group, created major media networks
and countless volunteers worked to publish local newspapers.
As a result of this hundred years of development, there are
were major dailies with an estimated circulation of two hundred
twenty-three thousand. A circulation that met the demands of a
population of approximately 1.5 million in 2011,[75] which means
that approximately one in six Chinese Canadians was reading a
Chinese language newspaper daily and this does not take into
account the other daily, *Jianada shangbao (Today Commercial
News)*, and the many weekly and monthly Chinese language
newspapers published in Canada.

In short, the Chinese Canadian population has developed
from a highly illiterate population into a highly literate one. As
Jan Wong a reporter for *The Globe and Mail* pointed out in
2004, there are many ethnic newspapers in Toronto, but "only
the highly literate Chinese community of 550,000 can sustain
three dailies, not to mention a dozen free weeklies, three radio
stations (including a 24-hour one) and two television stations."
Moreover, the Chinese language media has developed hand-in-
hand with the growth of Chinese Canadian literacy.

A further achievement of note in the development of
Chinese language media has been their versatility as seen in
their ability to develop niche markets within which to prosper.
There are newspapers devoted to each of business, human
health, and entertainment, among other areas. As well, Chinese
media operators have been willing to cooperate and promote the

---

[75] The exact figure is 1,487,580, which includes those who reported more than
one ethnic origin (Statistics Canada, "NHS Profile, Canada, 2011,"
www12.statcan.gc.ca, accessed 2014.12.21).

media of other ethnic groups by operating multicultural radio and television stations.

5.2 Advertising

The ability to attract advertising demonstrates a multitude of achievements that have been realized in Chinese language media. Chinese language media have been able to attract major and minor advertisers in large numbers as well as earn substantial income in doing so. These achievements, besides being further testaments to the economic strength of Chinese Canadians, also cast light on their high level of literacy. They are not only large consumers of media in general,[76] they are also avid readers, supporting a number of national, local, and web-based newspapers.

5.2.1 Content

The remarkable aspect of advertising in Chinese language media is the amount that is devoted to large ticket items, such as homes, cars, and appliances. Many Chinese Canadians are new comers to Canada, so they often need to purchase such items as part of the process of settling in the country. Furthermore, they buy more expensive homes and are anecdotally known for driving high-end automobiles.

In 2000, about half of Fairchild's advertisers were national companies, such as major banks and automobile manufacturers. In their research on advertisements placed in Chinese daily newspapers in 1996 in Toronto, Peter Li and Yahong Li found that

---

[76] IpsosReid and Era Marketing Communications points out that 40 percent of those in Toronto self-identified as Chinese or Chinese-Canadian, born outside Canada, and able to speak Mandarin or Cantonese viewed Fairchild TV (Cantonese) on a daily basis, 15 percent read *Sing Tao Daily*, 11 percent read *Ming Pao*, and 12 percent listened to Fairchild Radio. For the same group in Vancouver, 39 percent viewed Fairchild TV (Cantonese) on a daily basis, 29 percent viewed Talentvision TV, 16 percent read *Sing Tao Daily*, and 18 percent listened to Fairchild Radio ("IpsosReid 2007 Canadian Chinese Media Monitor: Greater Toronto Area" and "IpsosReid 2007 Canadian Chinese Media Monitor: Greater Vancouver Area").

Among the different types of product and services being advertised, professional services related to finance, banking, real estate, law, instruction, communication and travelling accounted for about 42 percent of all advertisements, while advertising for cars, building materials and appliances, home decorating and furniture made up another 33 percent. In short, about 75 percent of the advertisements had to do with major purchase items or specialized professional services. It is clear that these were targeted to a relatively affluent Chinese consumer market.[77]

5.2.2 Quantity and Revenue

The quantity of advertising and revenue derived from it are further proof of the accomplishments of Chinese Canadians in the area of Chinese language media. Many media outlets disseminate mostly advertising and not news, indicating both that they are recognized for being able to access a large number of potential customers or clients for the advertising organizations, and that Chinese Canadians have considerable buying power. Add to this the fact that many of the advertisers are major mainstream companies, which would have researched the effectiveness of their advertising. Therefore, their advertising in the Chinese language media would be confirming these indications. Even more affirming of these indications is the substantial advertising revenue that Chinese language media commands.

A perusal of some of the publications shows just how much advertising can be found in Chinese language media. More than 80 percent of the contents of Calgary's *Jiahua bao (Canadian Chinese Times, calgary.2010cctimes.com)* is advertising. *Zhonghua daobao (Canada China News, www.canadachinanews.com)* contains more than 50 percent advertising. Seventy-five percent of the website *Jiaguo wuyou www.51.ca* is composed of advertisements. Furthermore, these proportions of advertising are common in Chinese language media. Free newspapers composed primarily of advertisements are often found on stands in commercial centres. A survey of twenty issues of *Ming Pao* selected randomly during 1996

[77] P. 49.

showed that advertising occupied on average fifty-one of eighty-eight pages.[78]

Another telling example is that there are four Chinese language publications promoting real estate sales in Toronto. The contents are very similar to the English equivalents that are distributed in supermarkets, except that there is much more colour in them and pictures of agents figure prominently in the display. What is unusual is the number. A casual online search reveals the same number in English for the Toronto market. The English publications are glossier; however, it is surprising that Chinese Torontonians, who form 8.5 percent of its population, are catered to with the same number of publications promoting real estate. This phenomenon is more than an indication of Chinese Canadian wealth; it is also evidence of the ability of Chinese Canadians to develop the media by which to tap into this wealth.

Mainstream advertisers have become aware of this accomplishment so are now advertising in the Chinese language media. Non-Chinese advertisers occupy a significant percent of the total. Fifty percent of the advertising revenues for Fairchild's Vancouver TV broadcasts came from non-Chinese companies in the late twentieth century. Research on *Ming Pao* determined that 31 percent of the advertisements in 1996 were placed by non-Chinese businesses.[79]

Advertising revenues in Chinese language media are equally impressive. The estimated advertising revenue for Toronto's three main Chinese dailies in 1996 was a total of $34.4 million: *Ming Pao* $10.7 million, *Sing Tao* $17.9 million, and *World Journal* $5.9 million.[80] The impressiveness of the total of 34.4 million dollars in advertising revenues can be seen when comparing it to the advertising revenues for the *Toronto Star*, the Canadian newspaper with the largest circulation. Based on its "2001 Annual Report," its advertising revenues for 1996 can be roughly estimated to have been 215 million dollars,[81] and the daily circulation for the *Toronto Star* was in

---

[78] Li and Li, 48.

[79] *Ibid.*, 49.

[80] *Ibid.*, 56.

[81] Torstar, "2001 Annual Report," www.torstar.com, accessed 2012.04.25.

excess of 700 thousand.[82] Yet, compared to the three Chinese
dailies that were targeting about 8.5 percent of Toronto's
population and whose circulation was about 109 thousand,[83]
with about one-twelfth the target audience and one-seventh the
circulation, advertising revenues were about one-sixth those of
the *Toronto Star*. In short, advertising revenues for the Chinese
language dailies were proportionally greater than those of the
Toronto Star.

One finds a further example of the achievement of Chinese
Canadians as seen in the revenues for Chinese language media.
It was reported in 2004 that Fairchild's radio station CHMB
AM 1320 in Vancouver had the third highest advertising
revenue in the city.[84] The revenues and quantity of advertising
accrued by Chinese language media, and the recognition of the
value of advertising in them are all indicators of the
accomplishments in Chinese language media.

5.2.3 Advertising Agencies

Another aspect of advertising that evidences the
achievements of Chinese Canadians in the area of Chinese
language media is the existence of numerous advertising
agencies, many of them operated by Chinese Canadians. The
existence of these agencies is clearly a testament to the
economic strength of Chinese Canadians. In 1994 in Toronto
alone there were forty marketing firms targeting Chinese
Canadians.[85] Moreover, the operation of these agencies by
Chinese Canadians shows their ability to build on the wealth
developed by their fellow ethnic members, and their likely use
of Chinese Canadian media to do so is a further indicator of the

---

[82] Ian G. Masters, "Bringing Surround Sound Home," *SurroundView '96*,
www.torontoaes.org/surroundview96/masters.html, accessed 2012.04.28.

[83] Li and Li, 48.

[84] Zhou, *et al.*, 60; citing Clifford Kraus, "Vancouver Journal: Chinese Prosper
in Canada, and Eagerly Read about It," *New York Times*, 2004.04.01, 4.

[85] Susan Noakes, "Niche Marketing Targets Chinese Consumers," *Financial
Post*, 1994.11.18, C17.

effectiveness of these media in reaching the Chinese Canadian consumer.

The organization underlying Chinese Canadian operation of advertising agencies is impressive as well. Founded in 1987, the Chinese Canadian Advertising Marketing & Media Association was formed by a group of professionals in marketing, advertising, public relations, media, promotion, research, and production to meet and share Canadian business and social experience. It has an executive committee comprising fourteen Chinese Canadians and more than two hundred members with experience in Chinese marketing communications.

5.3 Encourage Mainstream Involvement

A third achievement for which Chinese Canadian media should be acknowledged is their effort to encourage Chinese Canadians to involve themselves in mainstream Canadian activities. This is even more the case because from the earliest point Chinese language media was either defensive, for just reasons, of mainstream actions against Chinese Canadians or focused on developments in China.

The concept of involvement in the mainstream was generally remote to Chinese Canadian thinking. This state continued into the 1960s at which point there seemed to be greater welcoming of Chinese immigration; however, the focus on China continued as media found it inexpensive to import large amounts of content from China and forego significant investment in local production. However, eventually, opportunities to participate in the mainstream became available and Chinese Canadians showed themselves willing to take advantage of them.

The most obvious area of Chinese Canadian participation in the Canadian mainstream has to be in charitable giving. One of the easiest ways to participate and therefore overcome general mainstream barriers to doing so, Chinese Canadians early on made a name for themselves by aiding causes outside their own community. For example, during the Second World War the "Chinese community oversubscribed every Victory Loan Drive, and in Vancouver contributed more per person than any other group in Canada."[86] In 1994, Chinese Canadians were influential in Vancouver's United Way campaign.[87]

By the year 2000, the Chinese language media had become involved in promoting charitable giving by Chinese Canadians. Fairchild Media Group was collecting donations for the Children's Hospital and Cancer Society in Vancouver, while Fairchild in Calgary was introducing Chinese residents to the needs of the Alberta Children's Hospital, Alberta Ballet, and Calgary Philharmonic Orchestra. It used to be that the large need and limited resources within the Chinese Canadian community precluded assistance to anyone outside it; however, that changed when Chinese Canadians, encouraged by their media, began involving themselves in causes outside their own ethnic group.

This trend has continued as seen in the telephons that Fairchild Media Group organized in 2005 to raise funds among its audience for relief after the 2004 tsunami in Southeast Asia. In the first telephon, Chinese Canadian viewers donated five hundred thousand dollars.[88] Fairchild, along with other Chinese language media, also donated air time and print space to allow its audience to donate to the victims of the Haitian earthquake in 2010. Together, the donations pledged to the Chinese language media amounted to more than two hundred thousand dollars.[89]

There are other areas that Chinese language media encourage Chinese Canadians to participate in. The November 2000 Canadian federal election was an example. The October 25, 2000 Alberta edition of *Sing Tao Daily* featured Chinese Canadian candidates in its front page reporting. Fairchild Media Group carried special programs on the election, and of particular note was a simulcast of election results and analysis

---

[86] Peter Li, 90; citing Carol Lee, "The Road to Enfranchisement: Chinese and Japanese in British Columbia," *BC Studies* 30 (1976): 44-76.

[87] Susan Noakes, "Chinese Immigrants Bring Wealth, Jobs," *Financial Post*, 1994.11.18, C3.

[88] "Jackie Chan, Jet Li Joining Chinese Canadian Tsunami Relief Efforts," Canada NewsWire, 2005.01.07, 1.

[89] "Fairchild Media Group Answers the Call by Donating Airtime to Help Haitian Earthquake Victims," Canada NewsWire, 2010.01.25.

by all broadcasting units. This type of media activity creates interest among their audiences leading to their greater participation in the publicized events. Fairchild Television has even been awarded three times for its efforts to encourage Chinese Canadians to join a police force. In April 2005, it was for publicizing the need for Chinese-speaking police officers in the Peel region.[90]

Apart from these specific examples, scholars have also noted the general effects that Chinese language media have on ethnic Chinese. Zhou *et al.* have argued "that Chinese language media not only connect immigrants to their places of origin, but also serve as a roadmap for the first generation to integrate into their new homelands by promoting home-ownership, entrepreneurship and second-generation education."[91] They offer two examples of value shifts promoted by Chinese language media, the acceptance of take-out food and the practice of democracy,[92] that lead to further integration of Chinese Canadians with the mainstream.

6. Developing a Chinese Canadian Identity?

Whether from the perspective of a Chinese Canadian or of the mainstream, it is reasonable to assume that there should be some degree of integration between the two. Of course, that was not the case in the early history of Chinese Canadians when many non-Chinese believed that they were unassimilable. However, such a belief in the present age is unacceptable for many reasons. Media, which have tremendous influence on public opinion, therefore, have an important role in promoting integration. In the case of Chinese language media, though, there is some question as to whether they have fulfilled this role well. It is reasonable to ask, both from the perspective of Chinese Canadians and the mainstream whether Chinese language media have fostered a Chinese Canadian identity;

---

[90] "Fairchild Awarded Best Ethnic News by Peel Regional Police," *Canada NewsWire,* 2005.04.28, 1.

[91] P. 44.

[92] *Ibid.,* 69.

that is to say the identity of a people, or even of their individual members, that reflects their history and presence in Canada.

6.1 Barriers

There are three barriers to Chinese language media playing a larger role in the establishment of a Chinese Canadian identity. First, the media have a history of directing their audience's attention to the situation in China. Two, there seems to have been a lack of interest among Chinese Canadians in developing a Canadian identity. Three, the recent content of media has largely comprised material imported from Hong Kong, China, and Taiwan..

The earliest media, newspapers in Vancouver, Victoria, and Toronto, were closely aligned with the political parties that were competing for influence in China. As such, their readers' attention was drawn to events in China and away from those in Canada. As Yahong Li states, "The review of the history of Chinese press in Canada before the early 1970s suggests that the politics of China played a major role in the nature and development of Chinese newspapers in the first 70 years of the twentieth century. With few exceptions, most Chinese newspapers were published as party organs and their main mission was to mobilize Canadian Chinese to support their political cause in China."[93]

This historical trend has been reinforced by the seeming lack of interest on the part of Chinese Canadians in Canadian subject matter. A study has shown that their media consumption is heavily inclined to the Chinese language. The Chinese Language Media Index conducted by ACNielsen in 1999 found that "about 80 percent of Chinese Torontonians read at least one newspaper in their own language a week, while more than 50 per cent read three or more issues per week. In addition, 87 per cent of Chinese in Toronto watched Chinese television. They spent on average 12.4 hours per week watching Chinese television in 1999, an increase of 27 per cent from 1996. The average hours they tuned into Chinese language radio programming had increased by 21 per cent since 1996 to 8.5 hours a week in 1999. While the consumption of Chinese

---

[93] P. 107.

language media does not mean that the Chinese do not consume mainstream media, only 42 per cent of Chinese in Toronto read an English newspaper on a weekly basis."[94]

Some scholars are extremely critical of this trend. Anthony Chan takes immigrants from Hong Kong to task for what he refers to as "Hong Kong Chinese ethnocentricism."[95] His study of the daily fare of Chinavision broadcast in September and October 1987 showed that its programming remained closely structured to a Hong Kong format, which encouraged Hong Kong Chinese to continue their lives as if they were extensions of their lives in Hong Kong:

> Hong Kong television is but one aspect of the ready vehicles used by Hong Kong Chinese immigrants to continue their socialization process as the ultimate sojourner, the ultimate transient in Canadian society. Because of this, they look more to Hong Kong for their socio-cultural times and values than to Canadian culture.[96]

In short, Chinese Canadians were not seen as making an effort to access mainstream media, which would have facilitated their integration with the Canadian mainstream.

While one can explore whether Chinese Canadians should be making more effort to access mainstream content in the media, it seems also that there should be an onus on Chinese language media to also provide this content even though this may involve translating or interpreting local content or even producing their own. While it seems that should have been the case, the fact was that at the end of the twentieth century, most of the content in Chinese language media was originating in Hong Kong, Taiwan, and China. *Sing Tao's* British Columbia edition was about 50 percent, and its Alberta edition 80 percent. Fairchild Media was importing about 50 percent of its programming, and Chinese Community TV in Vancouver and AATV Productions in Calgary were importing all of theirs.

---

[94] Zhou *et al.*, 52.

[95] "Citizen Aliens: Television and the Hong Kong Chinese as Sojourner," *Asian Profile* 18.2 (April 1990), 123.

[96] P. 125.

Reusing or purchasing China-sourced content was probably less expensive than producing one's own and at the same time it satisfied the demand of ethnic Chinese consumers for reinforcement of their culture. *Ming Pao (Mingbao)* provided a salient example of this. A typical issue at the end of the twentieth century contained eighty-eight pages, but only five pages of these were dedicated to Canadian news, two for news and sports and three for entertainment. A manager for *Ming Pao* explained their reasoning: "We come from Hong Kong and our base is in Hong Kong. We have our base format and we don't want to lose our current readers."[97]

Similar criticism has cropped up on other occasions. Yahong Li pointed out that when *World Journal (Shijie ribao)* began publishing in Canada there was no news about the country or Canadian Chinese communities.[98] Gabriel Yu, a reporter for the *Vancouver Sun,* in an article entitled "More Grist for the Chinese Readers: The Newcomer on the Chinese-Canadian Media Scene Is the Taiwan Daily–But Where's the Local News?" states that while *World Journal (Shijie ribao)* had improved, their newspaper was still the only one that included a daily editorial written by North American staff. All the other Chinese papers only carried opinion pieces from Hong Kong and Taiwan parent papers.[99] Joyce Yip describes the scanty content of local news presented on Chinese language television. It is mostly taken second hand from other stations and translated poorly with little analysis. The product, thus, lacks information on the reported issue's impact on the Chinese Canadian community.[100]

---

[97] Quoted in Michael Szonyi, "Paper Tigers: for the past Decade, Three Chinese-language Nowspapers Have Battled it out for Market Dominance," *National Post Business,* July 2002, 34.

[98] P. 215.

[99] 2000.02.24, A 15.

[100] "State of Disarray: Chinese Stations in Canada Well Serve their Audience with Popular Fare from Hong Kong the People's Republic. Why the Same Can't Be Said of their Amateur News Shows," *Ryerson Review of Journalism* Summer 2010; citing Tam Goosen, Vice President of Toronto's Urban Alliance on Race Relations.

316

Commentators have uncovered even more serious consequences arising from these weaknesses in Chinese language media. The Chinese Canadian National Council (CCNC) and the United Chinese Community Enrichment Services Society (SUCCESS) voiced the opinion to the Canadian Radio-television and Telecommunications Commission's (CRTC) 1999 hearing on ethnic broadcast that existing Chinese language television services were not providing content that reflected the identity of Chinese Canadian audiences; rather the content was about the "homeland" (i.e., Hong Kong, China, or Taiwan), not Canada.[101] For this reason, the content did not cater to the diverse interests of Chinese Canadians, but, in fact, tended to isolate them linguistically and culturally.[102]

Chinese language television was not educating its audience about the reality of the diversity one experienced living within Canada. If it were, the content of the media would have encouraged Chinese Canadians to become more involved in this environment and fostered their development as Canadians. Instead, the media were directing their attention to a culture and environment that was unshared by the majority of Canadians and, for this reason, this guidance was contributing to Chinese Canadians setting themselves apart from the rest of Canada. Some commentators even see Chinese Canadian attitudes extending to the point of disrespect and intolerance for other cultures.[103]

The seriousness of the situation sometimes even broaches on being sinister when local Chinese language media is viewed as propagating the political views of the government of the People's Republic of China. Nicholas Hune-Brown gives the example of an article on protests in Tibet that originally appeared in *Toronto Star* in April 2008 and was then translated and reprinted in its affiliate *Sing Tao*. According to Hune-Brown the criticisms by local commentators were removed from the translated copy. Similarly, facts and comments critical of China were removed from other articles that were reprinted in

---

[101] Sharon Mah, "Inclusive and Exclusive Spaces: A Look at Ethnic Television in Canada" (Master thesis, Carleton University, 2001), 94-95, 111.

[102] *Ibid.*, 97.

[103] Yip; citing Gloria Fung, a Toronto-based independent media commentator.

Sing Tao from *Toronto Star* during that period.[104] The acting
editor of *Sing Tao* was reported to have been dismissed for
these omissions; however, concern still remained that *Sing
Tao*'s Canadian publications had been unduly influenced,
possibly by the minority ownership of Charles Ho, a member of
the Standing Committee of the Chinese People's Political
Consultative Conference.[105]

These concerns were further supported by claims from the
former Chief of Asia Pacific of the Canadian Intelligence
Security Service that the Chinese government was attempting
to influence Chinese language newspapers in Canada by
pressuring their writers and editors.[106] In another example, in
2008 *Xiandai ribao (Today Daily News)*, which is 50 percent
owned by Sun Media, published twenty-four stories taken from
the newspaper *Wen Wet Po,* which was said to be controlled by
the Chinese government.[107] In yet another seeming example, in
2006 Jack Jia the editor of *Dazhong bao (Chinese News)* became
the target of some coordinated invectives after he published a
number of pieces critical of a group of Chinese language media
for lobbying Canadian regulators to approve the broadcast of
China Central Television within the country.[108]

Obviously, if the government of China is interfering in the
broadcasts of Chinese language media in Canada, it is
detrimental to Chinese Canadians developing their own
identity. Furthermore, it adds to the other barriers to authentic
identity formation: the history of Chinese language media
concentrating on events and organizations in China, the lack of
reliance on English or French language media by Chinese
Canadians, and the present day heavy use of news and

[104] "Lost in Translation," *Toronto Life* 42.8 (Aug. 2008), 29-34

[105] Jason Lofthus, "Editor Dismissed Over Pro-Beijing Edits, Say Sources,"
The Epoch Times, 2009.04.09.

[106] Hune-Brown.

[107] *Ibid.*

[108] Charlie Gillis, "A Question of Influence: As Beijing Ramps Up Attempts to
Use Chinese-Canadian Media to Promote its Own Propaganda, New
Questions Arise about How Free the Press Really Is," *Maclean's* 123.27
(2010.07.19), 38.

programming produced in Hong Kong, China, or Taiwan by Chinese language media. Given the existence of these barriers, the question of whether Chinese language media in Canada truly contribute to the formation of a Chinese Canadian identity becomes a valid one.

6.2 Establishing a Course

Given their treatment, it is not surprising to find that early ethnic Chinese were unable or unwilling to establish an identity built on their presence within Canada. From their arrival, they were excluded from participation in mainstream society and pressured to live in defined communities called "Chinatowns." Instead, the identity of being Chinese was based on traditions imported from China that created unity and led to mutual support, which, in turn, provided a means of survival. One of the roles of media was to strengthen this identity by promoting Chinese culture.

At the same time, China was experiencing momentous political change and the attention of overseas Chinese was easily captured by the events taking place. The various parties involved in the change also saw overseas Chinese media as a means by which to garner support for their causes. Therefore, most early Chinese language media in Canada, i.e., the newspapers, were affiliated with political parties with headquarters in China. The result was that large portions of their contents originated in or were about events there.

However, beginning in the 1960s there was a noticeable change in Chinese Canadian thinking. They began to identify more with the Canadian mainstream and to establish a self-image distinct from one derived from the culture of their hometowns or ancestral places in China. Reflecting and fostering this shift, Chinese-language media have been adapting their role to present the image of ethnic Chinese involved in mainstream Canadian society.

Wing Chung Ng has documented the awakening in Vancouver's ethnic Chinese of the desire to establish an identity grounded in their Canadian residency. The inception of the term "Chinese Canadian" in 1964 was a key part of the process of forming this identity: "This new construct advanced the claim of the Chinese minority to be Canadian."[109] Another key was the enshrining of multiculturalism as official federal policy, for being Chinese was no longer irreconcilable with being Canadian.[110]

Media had an early role in awakening the will to establish an identity with a Canadian dimension among ethnic Chinese. *Chinatown News* sometimes used the term "Chinese Canadian" to describe all Chinese residents in Canada and sometimes to refer specifically to local born Chinese. In doing so, it "often emphasized the professed identification with Canada, whereas the ethnic half of the label remained largely muted." Its reporting responded to the appointment of the Royal Commission on Bilingualism and Biculturalism in 1963 by linking "an incipient belief in Canadian pluralism and the forging of a Chinese-Canadian identity."[111]

In 1974, the tabloid *Gum Sam Po* challenged ethnic Chinese in Vancouver "to make our concept of a Chinese-Canadian community a viable one."[112] Subsequently, the Identity and Awareness Conference at the University of British Columbia in May 1975 converged on the view that "[i]nstead of nourishing a transplanted and unfamiliar culture from China, . . . a Chinese-Canadian consciousness must be rooted in Canada and must be derived from local experience."[113]

The radio program "Pender Guy" arose out of this new thinking. The half-hour weekly program ran from 1976 to 1981 on Vancouver Cooperative Radio CFRO FM 102.7 and featured descriptions of Chinese-Canadian experience. Its focus on promoting a new identity for ethnic Chinese is seen in one of its articulated goals:

> The goal is not to old-style Chinese-ize the assimilated Chinese-Canadian and to make the person say, "I gotta get

---

[109] Wing Chung Ng, *The Chinese in Canada, 1945-80: The Pursuit of Identity and Power* (Vancouver: UBC Press, 1999), 103-5.

[110] *Ibid.*, 106.

[111] *Ibid.*, 104.

[112] *Ibid.*, 118.

[113] *Ibid.*, 119.

back to my roots, do the kowtow trip, apologize for a couple of
decades of being Canadian etc." It's not a matter of giving in,
but more a matter of compromise, understanding that we as
Chinese-Canadians are different from, yet similar to other
persons of Chinese descent. We retain some influences from
old China through our grandparents and, at the same time,
we are affected by the effects of living in a Western Canadian
milieu.[114]

6.3 Media's Role

The goal of defining a new identity for Chinese in
Canada is still relevant, as the latest reported figures from the
Canadian census in 2006 showed about 58 percent were born
outside the country.[115] They would want to adjust to their new
environment, naturally taking on some of the attributes of
mainstream members. Various Chinese language media have
recognized and fostered this desire. The Fairchild Media Group
perceives their mandate to be to foster a local identity for ethnic
Chinese, and they do this by encouraging them to participate in
mainstream society. The group pictures itself as a bridge
between ethnic Chinese and the Canadian mainstream. The
Miansheng Yue Mian Liao Huabao (Manitoba Indochina
Chinese News) has a similar mandate: to display China from
the perspective of Canadians and not from the perspective of
Chinese.[116] These media organizations reflect the trend that has
been developing among the ethnic Chinese community toward
constructing their identity within a Canadian context, and as
this trend develops, the media will continue to promote it.

This is precisely what *Ming Pao* did when it entered the
Toronto market in 1993. Yahong Li explains that prior to its
arrival in 1993, local editorial content in the three daily
Chinese language newspapers, including local news, business,

---

[114] Quoted in Henry Tsang, ed., *Self Not Whole: Cultural Identity & Chinese-Canadian Artists in Vancouver* (Vancouver: Chinese Cultural Centre, 1991), 50.

[115] Calculation based on Statistics Canada document "Lunar New Year... by the numbers Chinese New Year: 2012 is the Year of the Dragon!", 2012.01.11, *www.statcan.gc.ca*, accessed 2012.05.16.

[116] Keo Chong, editor, interview by author in Winnipeg, 2000.10.31.

and sports constituted of only about two to four pages on average. After Ming Pao's arrival, local news became an area of competition and increased to ten to twelve pages in all three newspapers. Furthermore, *Ming Pao* took the precedent of reporting on the larger society while *Sing Tao's* and *World Journal's* local coverage was mostly about the activities of local Chinese associations. In 1993, *Ming Pao* sent a correspondent to the Parliamentary Press Gallery in Ottawa to report news of the federal government. Another reporter was sent to cover city news and was later transferred to the Provincial Legislative Assembly of Ontario. Li believes that this was probably the first time the ethnic press had dispatched reporters to these government locations, let alone the Chinese press.[117]

Ming Pao also pioneered in depth and serial reporting among Chinese newspapers in Toronto. For example, it utilized thirty-one pages to report on the 1995 Ontario provincial election. Furthermore, much of the reporting was "analytical and produced through direct contact with politicians." Prime Minister Jean Chretien's visit to China in 1994 garnered similar, in depth reporting as did the 1995 referendum in Quebec.[118]

Ming Pao set a precedent in another way: it maintained a critical attitude toward English language media. Where other Chinese language newspapers were relying on English language newspapers as major news sources and accepted their reporting as authoritative, *Ming Pao* would question their findings, especially with regard to the Canadian Chinese community. For example, in response to the Deputy Mayor of Markham Carole Bell's criticism of Chinese Canadian funded commercial development in 1995, the *Globe and Mail, Toronto Star,* and *Toronto Sun* published long reports on her actions. *Ming Pao* responded by saying that the mainstream media "focused on social conflict resulting from the development of Chinese malls, but hardly mentioned the positive contributions of Chinese investments to Markham economy."[119] *Ming Pao* was also the first Chinese language newspaper in Toronto to shift

---

[117] P. 276-79.

[118] Yalong Li, 278.

[119] *Ibid.*

its advertising focus from local Chinese businesses to non-Chinese businesses in the broader society.[120]

In short, even as media companies from Hong Kong and Taiwan began to establish subsidiaries in Canada, they also took up the trend of moving away from a focus on homeland news and affairs. Instead, like the media already established in Canada, the newcomers began to contribute to the cause of developing a Chinese Canadian identity.

6.4 More Domestic Content

An important aspect of *Ming Pao's* ground breaking strategy was the goal of publishing more local or domestic content. It marked the transition of Chinese Canadian perceptions to being mostly focused on events in China to being concerned with affairs in Canada, and not just affairs within the Chinese Canadian community but also affairs within the broader mainstream. This refocusing of Chinese Canadian interests was a major step in the development of an identity grounded in Canada, a Chinese Canadian identity. Three years after the arrival of *Ming Pao* it partnered with a local magazine *Toronto Life* to translate and distribute a Chinese version of the latter in 1996. Similarly, *Sing Tao* partnered with *Maclean's* to publish and distribute a Chinese version of the latter in the same year. Chinese language media were making major efforts to publish Canadian content.

At the same time that the media were including more local and domestic content in their publications and productions, their audience, i.e., Chinese Canadians, were commending them for doing so. For example, in Toronto, the *Dazhong bao (Chinese News),* which concentrated on informing new Chinese immigrants how to adapt within Canada, was ranked second, behind *Sing Tao Daily* as the most liked newspaper by immigrants from mainland China.[121]

The importance of providing local and domestic content was also echoed in the claims by the Chinese language media. Fairchild Media Group was claiming that in 2000, 50 percent of

---

[120] *Ibid.*, 283.

[121] Zhou, *et al.*, 64; citing Li Xiao, "Taking Off: Canadian Chinese Language Newspaper in a New Era," *Sinoquebec Chinese Newspaper,* 2002.12.20.

their television programming and as high as 80 percent of their radio programming was produced domestically. When it began to publish in Canada, *Sing Tao Daily's* local content consisted of translations of a few columns from the local newspapers. By 2002, however, an editorial staff of thirty-five was producing twelve pages of Toronto news each day and accessing material from its partner paper *The Toronto Star*.[122] In Vancouver the paper had a half-page of Canadian news in 1985, but by 1997 it had increased to as many as fifteen pages.[123]

A noteworthy example of Chinese language media's efforts to introduce local content was Fairchild Television's 2007 production "A Century of Vicissitudes." It documented the hardships that Chinese immigrants overcame in helping to build Canada. Fairchild described itself as "proud of its accomplishment in producing this documentary–it is an important contribution to the documentation of Canadian history and it is relevant to our viewers' understanding of themselves within society."[124]

6.5 Independence

Along with acknowledging Chinese language media's efforts to provide more Canadian content, one should also recognize their desire to remain independent and, therefore, objective. In other words, they are aware of the risk of being influenced unduly by political powers and aware of the importance of independence and objectivity within news dissemination. Therefore, it is not surprising to find examples of Chinese language media within Canada attempting to uphold these ideals.

In the run-up to China's recovery of Hong Kong in the 1997, newspapers there, particularly *Ming Pao*, became increasingly conciliatory toward the Chinese government. *Ming Pao* even dropped a columnist Canadian-based Tony Cheung, who had been highly critical of China. However, the Vancouver edition

---

[122] Szonyi.

[123] Haysom.

[124] "Fairchild Putting the Canadian Chinese Head Tax in Context," Canada NewsWire, 2007.04.02.

continued to publish his column and had no plans to discontinue it. The editor-in-chief of Vancouver's *Sing Tao Daily* also emphasized the independence of their newspaper stating that it had a high degree of independence from its parent company and implying that the other Canadian editions did as well.[125]

7. Conclusion

The overview of the history of Chinese language media in Canada is one of achievement and promise. During the early part of this history during the early 1900s, Chinese Canadians were able to develop local newspapers that published as often as daily even though only a small part of the population was literate and they were denied many of the resources that mainstream Canadians enjoyed. The denial of these resources made it all the more important for Chinese Canadians to develop the media that would promote communications among themselves and unite them. At the same time, the media kept them in touch with events in China during a time of momentous political change there. For this reason, the early media, i.e., newspapers, were mostly associated with political parties active in China. In the years that followed, Chinese Canadians did well to maintain their media amid their falling population in Canada and the occupation of China by foreign countries, mainly Japan. There were three major dailies and a number of other periodicals published in Canada's major cities, primarily Vancouver and Toronto.

The strength of Chinese language media and the language preservation that supported it established a basis for the rapid growth that followed the end of World War II and the opening up of Chinese immigration. The new immigrants came in large numbers and brought capital and expertise to Canada. This led to a strengthening and diversification of Chinese language media. Three large Chinese newspaper companies, *Sing Tao Daily (Xindao ribao)*, *World Journal Daily News (Shijie ribao)*, and *Ming Pao Daily News (Mingbao)*, all started publication in Canada during this time. By the end of the twentieth century, their circulation had reached about one hundred ninety-one

---

[125] Haysom.

thousand. Chinese language media had also diversified with Fairchild Media Group, among others, operating five radio stations and a national television network of four stations.

Into the twenty-first century, scholars were estimating that there were between one hundred twenty-five and two hundred Chinese language media outlets in Canada, ranging from newspapers, through radio and television stations and websites. In 2011, there were nine national Chinese language newspapers being published in Canada and the estimated daily circulation of the three major newspapers was two hundred twenty-three thousand.

Chinese language media in Canada were making a mark outside of Canada as well. Min Zhou, *et al.*, were pointing out "that Chinese language television and radio programming in Canada has arguably become the richest and most sophisticated outside China, Hong Kong, and Taiwan."[126] They were also pointing out that as "a subsidiary of the Hong Kong-based Sing Tao Newspaper Group, *Sing Tao Daily* has twenty-two branch offices globally and has arguably the second largest international coverage in the world, following the international *Herald Tribune*."[127]

Moreover, along with its past and present accomplishments, the future of Chinese language media in Canada is promising. Chinese Canadians have a tradition of preserving and promoting the use of Chinese as seen in their highly developed and popular community schools. This tradition should be easily maintained especially with the extra onus placed on preservation and promotion by the continual arrival of new Chinese immigrants and China's economic growth. The new immigrants will require and demand services in their native tongue. Their addition to the numbers of ethnic Chinese will add to the already large numbers that function in varying degree in Chinese and, therefore, create even greater demand for its preservation and promotion. Similarly, China's economic growth will encourage the practical learning of Chinese even among non ethnic Chinese. This latter attraction can also lead Chinese who have never learned the language to do so, in part

---

[126] P. 66.

[127] *Ibid.*, 52; citing *s.v.* *"Sing Tao Daily,"* in *BrainyEncyclopedia*, 2004.

because of the expectation that learning the language can create material benefits for them.

The material benefits of learning Chinese are also highlighted in the proliferation of Chinese language around the globe. On one hand, the learner can see the increasing use of Chinese around the world, not just in China. This, of course, increases the potential benefits of learning Chinese. Sing Tao's newspaper network stretches across four continents. Until the end of the 1980s there were no locally produced Chinese language newspapers in New Zealand. This situation changed quickly and by 2004 there were twenty, including two dailies. There were also three television stations broadcasting Chinese language programs, four radio stations, and three magazines.[128] All these to service a population of about one hundred thousand, one tenth that of Canada's. Most recently it was reported that China's biggest English language newspaper would publish a weekly African edition, with offices in South Africa and Kenya.[129] Although this is an English language publication, its purpose is to present a Chinese perspective. Furthermore, there are an estimated one million Chinese in Africa and the publication could easily be adapted to appeal to them as well. In other words, the market for Chinese language media content is expanding in Africa as well, something that would offer opportunities for Chinese language media in Canada, which has already developed abilities in providing content, advice, management, and capital.

There is another interesting example of the development of Chinese language media, which also points to the increasing international importance of Chinese language communication. Similar to the way that *Maclean's* and *Toronto Life* once offered Chinese language versions, other English publications are offering Chinese language versions, except not specifically to Chinese Canadians, but to Chinese readers in general. The *Financial Times* publishes content on a Chinese language

---

[128] Manying Ip, "Chinese Media in New Zealand: Transnational Outpost or Unchecked Floodtide?", in *Media and the Chinese Diaspora: Community, Communications, and Commerce,* ed. Wanning Sun (London: Routledge, 2006), 187-90.

[129] David Smith, *"China Daily* to Publish African Edition as Beijing Strengthens Voice Abroad," *The Guardian,* 2012.05.14.

website (*www.ftchinese.com*) five days a week for which it claims 2.2 million registered readers.[130] In a similar example, *Harvard Business Review is* translated into Chinese and published online *(www.hbrchina.org/).*

The implications of these examples for Chinese language media in Canada can be seen more clearly in an example that occurred there. The magazine *Jianada shiyou (Energy Bridge)* introduced Canada's energy sector to China's petroleum industry and institutional investment communities. Written in Chinese, launched in 2011, and published in Calgary, the plan was to distribute the magazine three times a year in China, both digitally and in print.

In other words, Canada's Chinese language media will have further opportunity to add to their achievements. While meeting the needs of Chinese Canadians, they are also developing and maintaining the use of a language that is already used by one fifth of the world's population and is increasingly being used around the globe. In doing so, it will also be contributing to the internationalization of Canada. In their efforts to serve Chinese Canadians, Chinese language media in Canada have developed the capacity to serve a much larger Chinese population, and at the same time provide benefits for Canadians in general.

BIBLIOGRAPHY

AsianWave. "About Us." *asianwavemag.com*, accessed 2012.04.04.

Brent, Paul. "Rogers Tackles Chinese TV Market." *National Post,* 2004.04.27.

Canadian Association of Chinese Language Schools. *cacls.org/About_Us.html,* accessed 2013.06.09.

Canadian Communications Foundation. "CFMB." *www.broadcasting-history.ca*, accessed 2012.04.06.

---

[130] *"Guanyu women"* (About us), *FTZhongwen wang* (Chinese *Financial Times* website), *www.ftchinese.com/m/corp/aboutus.html*, accessed 2014.12.17.

33

Canadian Newspaper Association. "Circulation Data Report 2009," accessed 2012.03.26.

Chan, Anthony. "Citizen Aliens: Television and the Hong Kong Chinese as Sojourner." *Asian Profile* 18.2 (April 1990): 117-126.

Chan, Arlene. *The Chinese in Toronto from 1878: From Outside to Inside the Circle*. Toronto: Dundurn, 2011.

Cheung, Katherine. Chief Editor. *Sing Tao Daily,* Alberta Edition. Interview by author. Calgary, 2000.10.25.

The Chinese Academy. *www.chineseacademy.ca/english/info/e_school.htm*, accessed 2011.08.23.

"Chinese Media in Toronto." *Toronto Star,* 1999.02.11, 1.

Chong, Keo. Editor *Miansheng Yue Mian Liao Huabao* (Manitoba Indochina Chinese News). Interview by author, 2000.10.31.

"Dahua wang" (Dawa website). *www.dawanews.com,* accessed 2012.03.27.

"Every Daily Newspaper in Canada." *www.fishwrap.ca*. Revised 2011.06.13.

"Fairchild Awarded Best Ethnic News by Peel Regional Police." *Canada NewsWire,* 2005.04.28, 1.

Fairchild Media Group. Fairchild Television website, *www.fairchildtv.com/english*, accessed 2000.12.04.

"Fairchild Media Group Answers the Call by Donating Airtime to Help Haitian Earthquake Victims." Canada NewsWire, 2010.01.25.
"Fairchild Putting the Canadian Chinese Head Tax in Context." Canada NewsWire, 2007.04.02.

Gillis, Charlie. "A Question of Influence: As Beijing Ramps Up Attempts to Use Chinese-Canadian Media to Promote its Own Propaganda, New Questions Arise about How Free the Press Really Is." *Maclean's* 123.27 (2010.07.19): 38.

"Guanyu women" (About us). *FTZhongwen wang (*Chinese *Financial Times* website), *www.ftchinese.com/m/corp/aboutus.html*, accessed 2014.12.17.

Haysom, Ian. "Newspapers in Hong Kong Are Becoming Increasingly . . ." *CanWest News*, 1997.04.27, 1.

Horn, Jennifer. "*Vancouver Sun* Launches Chinese-language Website." *Media in Canada*, 2011.12.08. *www.mediaincanada.ca*, accessed 2012.04.13.

Huanqiu Huawang (Global Chinese Press website). *www.gcpnews.com/aboutus_en.html*, accessed 2012.03.26.

Hune-Brown, Nicholas. "Lost in Translation." *Toronto Life* 42.8 (Aug. 2008): 29-34.

Ip, Manying. "Chinese Media in New Zealand: Transnational Outpost or Unchecked Floodtide?" In *Media and the Chinese Diaspora: Community, Communications, and Commerce,* 178-99, ed. Wanning Sun. London: Routledge, 2006.

IpsosReid and Era Marketing Communications, "IpsosReid 2007 Canadian Chinese Media Monitor: Greater Toronto Area," *www.fairchildtv.com,* accessed 2012.04.08.

IpsosReid and Era Marketing Communications. "IpsosReid 2007 Canadian Chinese Media Monitor: Greater Vancouver Area." *www.fairchildtv.com*, accessed 2012.04.08.

"Jackie Chan, Jet Li Joining Chinese Canadian Tsunami Relief Efforts." Canada NewsWire, 2005.01.07, 1.

Jiankang shibao (Health Times). www.healthtimes.ca, accessed 2012.04.02.

"About Us." *Jiazhong shibao (Chinese Canadian Times)* website, *www.cctimes.ca*, accessed 2012.03.31.

Lazarus, Eve "The Road Well Travelled: Can Chinese World Succeed Where So Many Other Chinese Magazines Have Failed?" *Marketing Magazine* 105.24 (2000.06.19).

Li, Duanduan. "Chinese as a Heritage Language in Canada." *crclle.lled.educ.ubc.ca/documents/li.pdf*, accessed 2013.06.09.

Li, Peter. "Chinese," *Encyclopedia of Canada's Peoples*, ed. Paul Magocsi. Toronto: University of Toronto Press, 1999.

------. *The Chinese in Canada.* Second edition. Toronto: Oxford, 1998.

------ and Yahong Li. "The Consumer Market of the Enclave Economy: A Study of Advertisements in a Chinese Daily Newspaper in Toronto." *Canadian Ethnic Studies* 31.2 (1999): 43-60.

Li, Yahong. "Market, Capital, and Competition: The Development of Chinese-Language Newspapers in Toronto Since the 1970s." Ph.D. diss., University of Saskatchewan, 1999.

Lo, Karl, and Him Mark Lai. *Chinese Newspapers Published in North America, 1854-1975.* Washington, D.C.: Center for Chinese Research Materials, Association of Research Libraries, 1977.

Lofthus, Jason. "Editor Dismissed Over Pro-Beijing Edits, Say Sources." *The Epoch Times,* 2009.04.09.

Luk, Bernard H.K. "The Chinese Communities of Toronto: Their Languages and Mass Media." *Polyphony: The Bulletin of the Multicultural Society of Toronto* 15 (2000), 46-56.

Luse shenghuo (Green Life) website, *www.greenlifeweekly.com*, accessed 2012.04.02.

Mah, Hilda. "A History of the Education of Chinese Canadians in Alberta, 1885-1947." M. Education thesis, University of Alberta, 1987.

Mah, Sharon. "Inclusive and Exclusive Spaces: A Look at Ethnic Television in Canada." Master thesis, Carleton University, 2001.

Masters, Ian G. "Bringing Surround Sound Home." *SurroundView '96*. *www.torontoaes.org/surroundview96/masters.html*, accessed 2012.04.28.

Mengcheng Huaren bao website, *www.sinoquebec.com/sinoquebecmedia/sinoquebecnewspap er_e.htm*, accessed 2012.04.03.

Ng, Wing Chung. *The Chinese in Canada, 1945-80: The Pursuit of Identity and Power*. Vancouver: UBC Press, 1999.

"Niche Marketing Targets Chinese Consumers," *Financial Post*, 1994.11.18, C17.

Ni Hao PEI. *nihaopei.com*, accessed 2012.04.03.

Noakes, Susan. "Chinese Immigrants Bring Wealth, Jobs." *Financial Post*, 1994.11.18, C3.

------. "Papers Battle to Attract Chinese Readers in Canada." *Financial Post*, 1994.11.18, C11.

------. "Niche Marketing Targets Chinese Consumers." *Financial Post*, 1994.11.18, C17.

Omni Television website. "Cantonese News Team Bios." *www.omnitv.ca/on/yue-can/bios*, accessed 2015.01.30.

------. "Mandarin News Team Bios." *www.omnitv.ca/bc/cmn/bios*, accessed 2015.01.30.

Popular Lifestyle & Entertainment Magazine. Fairchild Group. *www.fairchildgroup.com/plem.php*, accessed 2012.03.27.

Qingsong Jianada (easyca.ca). *"Daduo diqu baozhang guanggao"* (Advertisements for newspapers in the Greater Toronto Area). *easyca.ca/info/list.php?fid=220&city_id=1*, accessed 2012.04.02.

Reimer, Chad. *Chilliwack's Chinatowns: A History.* Vancouver, B.C.: Chinese Canadian Historical Society of British Columbia & Initiative for Student Teaching and Research in Chinese Canadian Studies, University of British Columbia, 2011.

Sciban, Lloyd. "Chinese Language Media Across the West." In *Challenging Frontiers: The Canadian West*, edited by Lorry Felske and Beverly Rasporich, 269-296. Calgary: University of Calgary Press, 2004.

Shijie huaren meiti (World Chinese media). *www.worldchinesemedia.com*, accessed 2012.04.11.

Sing Tao Etel Toronto. *163bbs.servebeer.com/?qbz=ac01CJMsNVllnRlivdQ9P8je1 ZAvWpmrKx7rd13oV9mfJtmuMRnrXxDvER6cKhm32tQ2a 94nclAioF4g6dQ75hQgqAh38RAjj1*, accessed 2013.06.09.

Sing Tao Etel Vancouver. *www.singtaoetel.ca/VAN/EN/subcategory.php?CategoryID =11&CatalogID=S008*, accessed 2013.06.09.

Smith, David. *"China Daily* to Publish African Edition as Beijing Strengthens Voice Abroad." *The Guardian*, 2012.05.14.

Statistics Canada. "2011 National Household Survey: Immigration, place of birth, citizenship, ethnic origin, visible minorities, language and religion." *www.statcan.ca*, accessed 2013.06.04.

------. "French and the *francophonie* in Canada." *www.statcan.ca*, accessed 2013.06.04.

------. "Immigrant Languages in Canada," "Table 1: Population of immigrant mother tongue families, showing main languages comprising each family, Canada, 2011." *www.statcan.ca*, accessed 2013.06.04.

------. "Languages in Canada: 2001 Census." Catalogue no. 96-326-XIE. *www.statcan.gc.ca,* released 2004.12.13.

------. "Lunar New Year... by the numbers Chinese New Year: 2012 is the Year of the Dragon!", 2012.01.11. *www.statcan.gc.ca*, accessed 2012.05.16.

-------. "NHS Profile, Canada, 2011." www12.statcan.gc.ca, accessed 2014.12.21

------. "Population by mother tongue, by province and territory (2006 Census)." *www.statcan.gc.ca*, released 2007.12.11.

------. "Population by selected ethnic origins, by census metropolitan areas (2006 Census)." *www.statcan.gc.ca*, released 2009.08.14.

Szonyi, Michael. "Paper Tigers: for the past Decade, Three Chinese-language Newspapers Have Battled it out for Market Dominance." *National Post Business,* July 2002: 34-44.

Toronto's Online Chinese Community. *"Duolunduo zuida Zhongwen mianfei bao"* (Toronto's largest free Chinese newspaper). *www.torcn.com/bbs/deal/4983.html*, accessed 2012.04.02.

Tsang, Henry, ed. *Self Not Whole: Cultural Identity & Chinese-Canadian Artists in Vancouver*. Vancouver: Chinese Cultural Centre, 1991.

United Chinese Community Enrichment Services Society (S.U.C.C.E.S.S.). "New Partnership Launched to Better Serve the Chinese-Canadian Community." 2012.03.07.

Vancouver Public Library. "Newspapers--Chinese."
www.vpl.ca/ccg/Newspapers_Chinese.html, accessed
2012.03.05.

Very Good News website, *www.verygoodnews.ca*, accessed
2012.04.22.

Wickberg, Edgar, Harry Con, Ronald J. Con, Graham Johnson,
and William E. Willmott. *From China to Canada: A History
of the Chinese Communities in Canada*, edited by Edgar
Wickberg. Toronto: McClelland and Stewart, 1982.

Wong, Jan. "The Other Newspaper War." *The Globe and Mail*,
2004.12.18, M3.

Wright, Harold A. "The Chinese in Toronto - A Personal
Appreciation." Unpublished, 1976.

Xinjia yuan (Éventual). *www.greader.ca*, accessed 2012.04.12.

Xu Xinhan and Huang Yunrong. "*Jiananda Huawen chuanmei
fazhan zongshu*" (A general description of the development
of Chinese language media in Canada).
blog.udn.com/cwacan/3788974, accessed 2012.03.11.

Yip, Joyce. "State of Disarray: Chinese Stations in Canada Well
Serve their Audience with Popular Fare from Hong Kong
the People's Republic. Why the Same Can't Be Said of their
Amateur News Shows." *Ryerson Review of Journalism*,
Summer 2010.

Yu, Gabriel. "More Grist for the Chinese Readers: The
Newcomer on the Chinese-Canadian Media Scene Is the
Taiwan Daily–But Where's the Local News?". *Vancouver
Sun* 2000.02.24, A 15.

Zhenli bao (Truth Monthly). *www.truth-
monthly.com/misc/tru_info.htm*, accessed 2012.03.26.

Zhou Min, Wenhong Chen, and Guoxuan Cai. "Chinese-
language Media and Immigrant Life in the United States

and Canada." In *Media and the Chinese Diaspora: Community, Communications, and Commerce*, edited by Wanning Sun, 42-74. London: Routledge, 2006.

7. THE CULTURE REGENERATION RESEARCH SOCIETY: INTEGRATING WESTERN AND CHINESE CULTURES

1. Introduction

From a certain perspective it seems natural that an organization such as Culture Regeneration Research Society (CRRS) would appear. There are a number of factors that would lead one to think that an organization dedicated to promoting the exchange between and mutual enhancement of Chinese and Western cultures would inevitably develop within Canada. There is a large population of ethnic Chinese that continues to be added to by immigration. Chinese Canadians have promoted Chinese culture in Canada[1] and Western culture in China. These factors would be enough to prompt the appearance of CRRS, and when combined with the idealism of traditional Chinese thinking,[2] the motivation is even greater and infuses the efforts of this organization.

Yet CRRS has also developed its own identity outside of the external factors leading to its creation and has grown because of strong ideals and leadership. CRRS seeks to foster the melding of Chinese and Western cultures for the purpose of producing benefits for both and new resources for the world. Led by an active scholar, Thomas Leung, and headquartered in Burnaby, British Columbia, CRRS has actively pursued the fulfilment of its purpose since its founding in 1994.

This chapter describes how CRRS has attempted to fulfill this purpose and the results that it has achieved. It also shows that CRRS has gained the support of a broad section of the Chinese Canadian community. It has also been able to transform this support into actions that assume the benefits of utilizing aspects of Western culture in order to improve the

---

[1] See chapter four "Preservation and Promotion of Chinese Culture" for examples.

[2] Examples of this idealism include core beliefs in the goodness of human nature as seen in Mencius' arguments (e.g., *Mencius* 6a:2) and that a strong will can overcome any obstacle as seen in the legend of Yu Gong moving a mountain.

future of China and in doing so it has become an agent of change in China. Two defining aspects of CRRS' agency are the philanthropic nature of its activities and its strong embracement of Christianity.

CRRS ranks as a notable achievement of Chinese Canadians for the reason that it began merely as an ideal in 1994, yet it has come to channel the efforts of many Chinese Canadians and ethnic Chinese in other countries to the aid of China while having an increasingly positive influence there.

2. Purpose and Principles

CRRS describes itself as "a non-profit, non-political, non-denominational, academic organization."[3] Its purpose is "to influence the emergence of a new Chinese consciousness--firmly rooted in China's proud heritage and open to limitless possibilities offered by a world rich in diversity of culture, knowledge, thought, and creativity," and "to seed China's future generation with visions of its own potential and to give it the fundamental tools to enable every child to live out his/her aspirations."[4] CRRS' vision shows an emphasis on China, including its traditional culture and its emergence as an importance influence on the world.

In order to achieve its purpose the society has established "four strategic directions: 1. achieve an understanding of the latest developments in contemporary Chinese culture and possible future direction through academic dialogue and interchange, 2. promote mutual understanding and harmonization with Western culture, spiritual disciplines, religious thoughts, and contemporary philosophies so that amalgamated resources and synergies can be tapped like wellsprings for self-growth, 3. encourage this new Chinese consciousness to be a force for positive world change and renewal," and "4. exemplify the foregoing by practical and measurable actions."[5]

---

[3] "Home/About Culture Regeneration Research Society," CRRS website, *crrs.org/en/*, accessed 2014.08.23.

[4] *Ibid.*

[5] *Ibid.*

These strategies are to be implemented through six main ministries: "1. encourage and enable (through subsidization) scholars from mainland China to study contemporary Western thought, moral and spiritual disciplines, 2. promote and enable (through subsidization) overseas scholars to study the development of contemporary Chinese culture, 3. support research specific to the social and cultural reform processes unfolding in contemporary China, 4. publish research findings and academic perspectives, 5. organize forums to enable academic discussion and exchange," and "6. initiate the 'Basic Education Program' in underserved rural areas of China and Christian study programs in universities and research institutes."[6]

Leung later elaborated on CRRS' mission. In 2012 he emphasized that the term "cultural China" meant "a global Chinese culture," "a culture that transcends geographic and political boundaries, that contributes to and becomes a spiritual resource for humanity."[7] He states that if China could renew its foundational value of benevolence *(renai)* and absorb the better values of the West, such as the rationality, science, equality, justice, rule of law, self-respect, and so on of Christianity, it would create a new age of Chinese culture, one that could counter the egoism developing in the West.[8] In practice, CRRS should educate the disadvantaged youth of rural and urban areas with a spirit of love. It should also encourage intellectual and cultural exchange between China and other cultures. As well, it should respect the needs of the people and present petitions to the central government.[9]

---

[6] *Ibid.*

[7] Liang Yancheng (Thomas In-sing Leung, note: this latter is Leung's official English name, partially transcribed from the Cantonese pronunciation), *"Wenhua gaige yu Wenhua Zhongguo"* (Cultural reform and *Cultural China*), *Tianqing tongxun* (Heaven's sentiment newsletter) 55 (2012), CRRS website, *crrs.org/w/wp-content/uploads/2012/08/425201223847PM.pdf*, accessed 2014.09.19.

[8] *Ibid.*

[9] *"Jianada Wengehua ganen yixiang fenxiang"* (Sharing our appreciation for the unusual event in Vancouver, Canada), *Tianqing tongxun* (Heaven's sentiment newsletter) 62 (2013), CRRS website, *crrs.org/w/wp-content/uploads/2014/01/TienQing-62-p8-9.pdf*, accessed 2014.09.18.

Summarizing this manifesto, CRRS aims to revitalize Chinese culture with an integration of values from the West, and based on the resulting integration, create a new Chinese culture that will be a resource for the rest of the world.

3. Early History

The founder of CRRS, Thomas In-sing Leung, came to Canada in 1984 at the invitation of a well-to-do businessman David Lam, who would later become lieutenant governor of British Columbia (1988-1995) and an honorary patron of CRRS.[10] Lam had heard one of Leung's tapes on Chinese culture and asked him to come to Canada to do research. Lam's hope was that Leung's deep understanding of Chinese culture would contribute to Canadian multiculturalism.

Leung returned to his native home of Hong Kong in 1986 to teach in a college and promote the establishment of a reformed Chinese culture and a new form of democracy that is suitable for Hong Kong. Hong Kong was facing decolonization and return to Chinese governance. With the signing of the Basic Law (1989) that formalized Chinese rule in Hong Kong, Leung felt his goal had been, at least, partially achieved and that he should return to Canada for the purpose of mobilizing overseas Chinese to help China develop, which he did in 1990.

Canada's attempt to harmonize different cultures attracted Leung. He sensed that the Canadian government was friendlier to China than other Western governments, making it easier to acquire resources there that could be helpful for the reform program run by the Chinese government. As his residency in Canada lengthened, Leung realized that he could also contribute to Western culture; that the emphasis Chinese culture placed on the family and ethical relations would be of service in the West. It was this thinking that would lead to the founding of the Culture Regeneration Research Society in 1994. His hope was that both Chinese and Western cultures could be regenerated and that CRRS could play a role in the process.

---

[10] David Lam has been one of Vancouver's leading land developers and the first person of Asian ancestry to hold a vice-regal post in Canada (*The 1999 Canadian Encyclopaedia, World Edition*, s.v. "Lam, David"). He has also given strong spiritual and financial support to CRRS.

Leung left a position as Academic Director of the Chinese Studies Program at Regent College at the University of British Columbia in 1994. This was a crossroads in his career. A number of friends had been encouraging him to establish a venue whereby he could more directly assist China, which was in the process of dramatic change. A meeting in 1993 of thirty friends to discuss this possibility established strong momentum toward this goal. The banquet that followed in 1994 was a major test of broad interest and demonstrated strong support for the idea by raising $60,000.

After the banquet, CRRS was able to secure one room of office space in a community centre in Richmond. As finances improved, they moved to their present address, #202-6960 Royal Oak Avenue, in Burnaby, British Columbia, which is well located, next to a rapid transit station.[11]

To a certain degree, the choice of Canada to house the headquarters of CRRS was the product of circumstance. Leung had established himself there and could direct local resources toward fulfilling CRRS' mission. Beginning with the inaugural meeting and the following fund-raising efforts, the Canadian setting provided resources that Leung and his supporters could shape into CRRS.

The fact that Canada would provide these resources is evidence of Canadian characteristics that have been conducive to the creation of CRRS. Apart from the presence and strength of Chinese Canadians, a main characteristic is the good relations that Canada has had with China. Historically, Canada has never invaded the country nor sent troops to occupy its territory. For this reason, China trusts the Canadian government more so than those of other states. China would be suspicious of an organization like the CRRS if it were housed in the United States, for example, because of the strong pro-Taiwan and anti-Chinese sentiments among the government and its elected representatives. In comparison, a majority of Chinese in Canada have Hong Kong roots and tend to be supportive of the Chinese government.

Since its founding, CRRS has struggled to achieve its mandate, burdened by a limited budget. This burden lightened

---

[11] They have moved once within the building to larger quarters, part of their requirements being the need to display a collection of cultural artifacts that Leung has gathered in his travels.

in 1999 when CRRS received funding from the Canadian
International Development Agency (CIDA) to do development
work in China and in 2000 when CRRS began to receive large
funding from various foundations, such as the Chan Foundation
in Canada and the Kwok Foundation in Hong Kong.[12]

4. Structure

CRRS is a non-profit organization that began with three
full-time employees, which increased to six full-time and three
part-time project employees by 2000. Full-time employees
included Leung as president, a managing director, a
development director, an office manager, a typist, and an editor.
The part-time employees included a public relations director
and fund-raiser, a translator, and a computer specialist. CRRS
could also mobilize a force of 20 to 50 volunteers.[13] More recent
figures, as of 2012, had five paid employees in the Canadian
office, five in the Hong Kong office, and one in the U.S.A.
office.[14]

CRRS has six offices across three continents. There is a
number of sub-units within CRRS, including the CRRS Board of
Directors, CRRS Worldwide Foundation, CRRS Production
Association, and a group of nearly sixty academic advisors that
provides direction for *Cultural China*, the society's journal.[15]
The CRRS Worldwide Foundation coordinates all the activities

---

[12] Most of the contents of this section were taken from interviews conducted
with Thomas Leung, President of Culture Regeneration Research Society on
2000.03.21 in Burnaby, British Columbia and 2001.10.21 in Vancouver,
British Columbia.

[13] *Ibid.*

[14] Liang Yancheng (Thomas In-sing Leung), "*Wenhua gaige yu Wenhua
Zhongguo*" (Cultural reform and *Cultural China*), *Tianqing tongxun* (Heaven's
sentiment newsletter) 55 (2012), CRRS website, crrs.org/w/wp-
content/uploads/2012/08/425201223847PM.pdf, accessed 2014.09.19; and
Melvin W. Wong, "Culture Regeneration Research Society U.S., report on
2011 activities," *Tianqing tongxun* (Heaven's sentiment newsletter) 55 (2012),
CRRS website, *crrs.org/w/wp-
content/uploads/2012/08/425201223847PM.pdf*, accessed 2014.09.18.

[15] List of advisors is given in "*Wenhua gengxin*" (Culture regeneration) an
introductory pamphlet (n.d.) produced by CRRS.

related to the Basic Education Program for Rural China, including those of separate offices. The CRRS Production Association is responsible for publishing and promotion.[16]

Besides the head office in Burnaby, CRRS has branches in Toronto; in Torrance, in the Los Angeles area; in Hong Kong; in Australia; and in Singapore. Each branch had a board of directors as of 2001, one member of which is a member of the international board of directors. Leung is a member of all local boards. Apart from the offices in Canada, Hong Kong, and the U.S.A. that are managed by paid employees, volunteers administer the other branches and run them out of facilities mainly devoted to other purposes.[17]

The Burnaby head office does not attempt to direct the affairs of CRRS branches, nor does there seem to be a strong effort to actively establish branches. There is a common code of principles that each branch is supposed to follow; however, it mainly pertains to business matters. Some of the funding received by the branches is transferred to head office; however, the large part seems to stay with them to support their own activities. Some funding used to come to the head office through a Singapore affiliate and the head office used to receive $US100,000 annually from the U.S. Now, funding originating in the U.S. stays to support the U.S. branch. The head office also sometimes supports the activities of its branches and also arranges visits by Leung to present lectures, which are usually significant fund-raisers. As well, the head office supplies information materials, such as DVDs, that the branches sell to fund themselves.[18]

It is common for the branches to have been founded by persons who were already familiar with Leung before the founding. The head of the Singapore chapter was a former student of Leung's and had started a successful organization to educate children in Singapore. At one point there was a Calgary

---

[16] Wei Liu Guojing, "Shenghuo-Shenghuo: <<Wenhua Zhongguo>> yu Wenhua gengxin" (Life-life: <<Cultural China>> and Culture Regeneration Research Society)," *Zhenli bao* (Truth monthly) 145 (October 2005), *www.truth-monthly.com/simp/issue145/0510ex04.htm,* accessed 2008.01.28.

[17] Contents of this paragraph taken from Thomas Leung, interview, 2000.03.21.

[18] *Ibid.*

affiliate and the sponsor was a successful businessman. Having done well in business, he wanted to support cultural activities. He decided to donate $100,000, which was placed in an endowment the interest from which paid the costs of visiting lecturers. The head of the Australian branch is a friend of Leung's from Hong Kong. He is also the leader of an anti-discrimination movement in Queensland, a Christian pastor, and was a doctoral candidate.[19]

5. Leadership

The founder Thomas In-Sing Leung has led CRRS since 1994. He was born in 1951 in Hong Kong, coming to Canada in 1984. His career has always been connected to academia and public service. He completed a doctoral degree in Confucian philosophy at the University of Hawaii in 1986. He has held teaching positions at a number of post-secondary institutions including present adjunct professorships at a number of universities such as Sichuan University, Zhongshan University, Shandong University, and Lanzhou University.[20] As for public service, besides founding CRRS and serving as its president since 1994, Leung has served in a number of philanthropic organizations, such as World Vision. He has also published extensively, more than twenty books and seventy academic papers as of 2014.[21] Two of his representative works are *Houxiandai Zhongguo zhexue de chonggou* (Post-modern reconstruction of Chinese philosophy) (1999) and *Shiji zhi bian de fansi* (Reflections on the changing of the times) (2007).

Leung has harnessed a history of idealism and activism in the creation of CRRS. He had long embraced the ideals of wanting to help China and the West regenerate their respective cultures. He became sensitive to his underlying concern for others through tours with aid agencies in Africa, India, South East Asia, China, and the indigenous reservations of Canada. The poverty and suffering he had seen in those places moved

---

[19] *Ibid.*

[20] "Dr. Leung In-sing, Thomas," CRRS Hong Kong website, *www.crrshk.org/en/node/283*, accessed 2014.09.01.

[21] *Ibid.*

him to compassion and fostered in him a desire to help. Earlier, he had found an outlet for this compassion in the establishment of organizations such as Hong Kong Green Power, Concern for Homeless People in Hong Kong, and Love One Another Healing Centre for Drug Addicts in Hong Kong, and administration of the Chinese Ministry in the West Coast of World Vision Canada. He has also utilized his position in the media--radio commentator and newspaper columnist--to promote the causes of the disadvantaged. Leung's compassion for the needs of others and his ability to transform this compassion into concrete action were forged into the creation of CRRS.

Leung travels extensively, lecturing on Chinese philosophy and culture and soliciting support for CRRS' activities. CRRS has a network of offices and membership groups throughout the world, which Leung visits even while increasingly involved in activities in China.[22]

Leung's passion for his mission to aid China is seen in the following quotation:

> As I peer at China in the distance, I see the misty dawning of a new era. China is changing rapidly and marching toward prosperity. But what concerns me the most is that, while the economy is gathering strength and people are feverishly making money, corruption in Chinese society has almost become the norm. The traditional moral disciplines of goodness, integrity, and justice have possibly come to the stage of utter disintegration. China's crisis is no longer the occupation by foreign invaders, but the self-destruction of the nation's soul![23]

Leung follows this quotation with a plea for overseas Chinese to transfer beneficial elements of traditional Chinese wisdom and Western civilization to China in order to rebuild its spiritual foundation. There is a strong sense of urgency in his statement of purpose because Leung fears that Chinese culture has seriously degenerated. However, he hopes to reinvigorate Chinese culture by integrating traditional wisdom with

---

[22] Most of the contents of this section "Leadership" are to this point taken from Thomas Leung, interview, 2000.03.21.

[23] Culture Research Regeneration Society, "Wenhua gengxin" (Culture regeneration), introductory pamphlet, n.d.

philosophical resources from the West. An ultimate goal is that a reinvigorated Chinese culture will serve as resource for all mankind, including the West.

6. Funding

CRRS started in 1994 with seed money of $3,000, the sum of thirty $100 donations, contributed by each attendee at a founding meeting. This seed money paid for a fund-raising banquet, which in turn produced $60,000 for CRRS start up. The first year, 1994, CRRS operated on a budget of $200,000 and this increased to $430,000 in 2000.

For the first five years of its existence CRRS survived on smaller donations from all over the world. The sale of Leung's recordings also added to the budget. One third of its support has come from Canadian Chinese, one-third from Asian Chinese, and one third from Chinese in the U.S. It was not until 2000 that CRRS started to receive large grants from major institutions, such as an important family foundation in Vancouver,[24] CIDA, and a leading real estate company in Hong Kong. Even though CRRS is, in part, an academic organization, it is not associated with any university and so cannot count on the support that would be available from one.

Support from an important family foundation in Vancouver came after the foundation founder traveled with Leung to China and observed first-hand the desire of the Chinese people to develop. At that time, the founder noted the lack of modern thinking and knowledge that would allow Chinese to progress. These observations led him to support CRRS as an organization that could help remedy this situation by transferring such thinking and knowledge to China. As a result, the foundation made a commitment to contribute fifty thousand a year for five years starting in 2000 and challenged the owner of the leading real estate company in Hong Kong to do the same, which the latter subsequently agreed to.

---

[24] CRRS' "Annual Report 2006" mentions the Chan Sisters Foundation and the David and Dorothy Lam Foundation as supporting the training of teachers within China as part of the Basic Education Program for Rural China ("About Us/Fund Designation," CRRS website, *www.crrstoronto.org/funddesignation.html*, accessed 2008.01.19).

Support has primarily come from Chinese and not Western institutions, such as the one hundred thousand U.S. dollars donated by a leading courier company in Hong Kong. It was through the intercession of Raymond Chan, then Canadian Secretary of State for Asia, that CIDA became aware of CRRS. Leung admits that, due to his lack of time, CRRS has been unable to establish sources of funding among mainstream Canadian foundations.

Some costs are saved by having employees who work for less than what they could earn in the marketplace. At one point, the managing director resigned her post as personnel director for a big hospital and took a 50 percent cut in salary to join CRRS because of the love contained in its vision. The development director was earning two thousand dollars monthly, but could have made much more as a chartered accountant. CRRS also utilizes volunteer services to keep costs under control.

Interestingly, Chinese middle class Christians have become major contributors to the work of CRRS. Leung, himself, has been active in Christian related activities since 1979. Christian congregations, especially Chinese Canadian ones, view China's needs as fitting with the compassionate mission of Christian churches. Even though CRRS is not expected to promote Christianity in China, the work that it does do there appeals to the Christian value of caring for fellow human beings.

CRRS employed a fund-raiser since 1997 when CRRS tried to muster resources to support the anti-corruption project, which was eventually supported by CIDA. Prior to soliciting CIDA, CRRS had no experience fund-raising with mainstream Canadian foundations. Part of the reason for this, which remains to a certain extent, is that Leung has had to spend most of his time travelling, writing, and ascertaining needs, so he has been unable to devote time to soliciting domestic mainstream organizations. However, he remains the force behind the organization, as it is his influence that leads to the establishment of and further contact with contributors.[25]

The "Annual Report 2006" reported total income for CRRS of $673,957, including general donations of $392,452.00 and

---

[25] Contents of this section "Funding" are to this point mostly taken from Thomas Leung, interviews, 2000.03.21 and 2001.10.21.

fundraising of $275,514.00. Expenses were a total of
$615,403.00, including $336,801.00 for the Basic Education
Program for Rural China and $103,649.00 for university
scholarships.[26] More recent financial reports indicate a large
increase in revenue. The head office in Vancouver reported
revenue/donations of $908,127 in 2011 for educational purposes
alone.[27] The Hong Kong office reported income of $C551,525 in
2012[28] and the U.S. office reported income of $C330,841 in
2013.[29] Assuming that the Hong Kong or U.S.A. offices had no
income in 2006, CRRS income for each of the years 2011-13
increased approximately $1,116,536 from 2006, an increase of
approximately 166 percent in five to seven years.

7. Activities

CRRS' activities revolve around its six main ministries: "1.
encourage and enable (through subsidization) scholars from
mainland China to study contemporary Western thought, moral
and spiritual disciplines; 2. promote and enable (through
subsidization) overseas scholars to study the development of
contemporary Chinese culture; 3. support research specific to
the social and cultural reform processes unfolding in
contemporary China; 4. publish research findings and academic
perspectives; 5. organize forums to enable academic discussion
and exchange"; and "6. initiate the 'Basic Education Program
[for Rural China]' in underserved rural areas of China and

---

[26] "About Us/Fund Designation," CRRS website,
www.crrstoronto.org/funddesignation.html, accessed 2008.01.19. It is odd
that the expense for administration is only $26,283.00 and there are no office
expenses or costs for the publication of *Cultural China*.

[27] "CRRS Education Fund 2011 Financial Highlights," CRRS website,
crrs.org/education/finance/, accessed 2014.09.02. This amount likely does
not include donations for non-educational projects or income from sale of
publications.

[28] "Financial Status–2012 Income & Expenditure Report and 2013 Budget,"
CRRS Hong Kong website, *www.crrshk.org/en/content/financial-status*,
accessed 2014.09.03.

[29] "Culture Regeneration Research Society USA 2013 Financial Report,"
CRRS USA website, *www.crrsusa.org/DispSPE.asp?uID=344*, accessed
2014.09.03.

Christian study programs in universities and research institutes."[30] The first five of these have not changed since 2005, but the last one, the Basic Education Program, is newer and seems to have been given priority by CRRS.

The Basic Education Program for Rural China was conceived when Leung was travelling in rural areas of Gansu, Guangxi, Hebei, and Shaanxi during 2001 hoping to find ways to improve primary and secondary education in those regions. A subsequent application to Canadian International Development Agency (CIDA) led to a provisional award of $600,000 toward this cause on the condition that CRRS was able to raise $300,000 in matching funds.[31] Seemingly without CIDA aid, CRRS has been able to carry on the project.[32] The project began in two counties, Jinxiu and Ziyuan, in Guangxi in 2002 with the goals of training teachers and assisting with students' education. The original plan was to work with Zhongguo Cishan Zonghui (Charities of China, Head Office) to provide certification fees, teaching materials, transportation, lodging, and salaries for substitutes for two hundred teachers in Jinxiu and Ziyuan for more than three years.[33] The project has been expanded and CRRS reported that as of 2008 it had aided more than one thousand Guangxi teachers to complete university training and more than 1420 students from six Guangxi

[30] "English/Introduction," CRRS website, *www.crrs.org/index_en.asp*, accessed 2008.01.19.

[31] *Xunbao (Calgary Trend Weekly)* 213 (2002.1.4), 9-10.

[32] It seems that CRRS was unsuccessful in raising the $300.000 because the only project described as receiving CIDA support under the list "Culture Regeneration Research Society Partners and Support Network" was the Chinese and Western Anti-Corruption Cultural Research Study ("English/Introduction," CRRS website *www.crrs.org/index_en.asp*, accessed 2008.01.19).

[33] *"Zhongxin jianjie"/"Jichu jiaoyu"/"Zhuhuan nongcun jiaoshi xiangmu gongzuo baogao"* (Brief introduction to Culture Regeneration Research Society/Basic education/Report on aid to rural teachers), CRRS website, *www.crrs.org,* accessed 2005.04.07. CRRS was also to work with the Guangxi Cishan Conghui (Charities of Guangxi Head Office) *("Jianada 'Wenhua gengxin yanjiu zhongxin' zai Guilin juan zhuxue zhujiao"* [Canada's Culture Regeneration Research Society donates learning and teaching aids in Guilin], *Zhonghua Fujiao xinxi wang* [Chinese Buddhist news network], 2005 .09.10, *www.fjnet.com/cssy/cssynr/t20050910_13528.htm*, accessed 2008.01.28).

counties and one Yunnan county to continue their education.[34] Moreover, they have established university scholarships to assist further students in these regions and have helped rebuild schools in danger of collapsing.[35] More recently it was reported that 139 high school students and 11 teachers had received assistance in 2013.[36]

In a related project, the establishment of schools for migrant workers in major Chinese urban centres, CRRS has demonstrated its leadership in meeting the needs of China's underprivileged. China's cities are attracting many millions of migrant workers into the cities to earn higher incomes than what they could in their native rural areas. Often, this has led to separation of families where parents leave their children in the care of others or even to fend for themselves. Part of the reason for this is that China's social services have not been designed to meet the needs of a mobile population, thereby preventing children from accompanying their parents into the cities. Subsequently, in a family-orientated society like China's, this has created many problems.

CRRS is attempting to mitigate these problems by establishing schools for the children in the cities where their parents work. In September 2007 CRRS established Shanghai Migrant Workers High School, the first of its kind. The project paid the tuition for sixty students within an already established high school. Another class of sixty was added in 2008 and again in 2009. As a result thirty-four graduated in 2010 and seventeen were successful in entering university. In 2011 fifty graduated and twenty-two entered university. In total, as of 2013 CRRS has had occasion to assist the students and teachers of Guangxi and the children of Shanghai migrant workers about seven thousand times.[37]

[34] "About Us/Organization/President's Message." CRRS website, *www.crrstoronto.org/presidentmessage.html*, accessed 2008.01.19.

[35] "About Us/Fund Designation," CRRS website, *www.crrstoronto.org/funddesignation.html*, accessed 2008.01.19.

[36] *"2013 Xianggang Wengeng shigong huigu"* (Culture Regeneration Research Society Hong Kong: A look back on work in 2013), *Tianqing tongxun* (Heaven's sentiment newsletter) 62 (2013), CRRS website, *crrs.org/w/wp-content/uploads/2014/01/TienQing-62-p10-11.pdf*, accessed 2014.09.18.

[37] *"2013 Xianggang Wengeng shigong huigu"* (Culture Regeneration Research

CRRS has continued to add educational projects to its agenda. In 2008 it began a three-year project funding twenty-five students a year at Lanzhou University in Gansu.[38] The project was renewed for another three years in 2011.[39] In addition, a project to assist with high school education in Tibet was established in 2012.[40] CRRS offices in Canada, the United States and Hong Kong estimate that as of 2014 CRRS has, altogether, assisted a total of twelve thousand economically disadvantaged students in completing their studies,[41] and it has rebuilt seven schools in Guangxi.[42]

CRRS has also taken up educating Canadian youth about the needs of China and in doing so foster mutual understanding among Canadian and Chinese youth along with contributing to China's material development. Through 2008-13 CRRS has led more than one hundred North American youth and adults to teach English to underprivileged students in rural areas of China. As a result, more than one thousand two hundred

---

Society Hong Kong: A look back on work in 2013), *Tianqing tongxun* (Heaven's sentiment newsletter) 62 (2013), CRRS website, *crrs.org/w/wp-content/uploads/2014/01/TienQing-62-p10-11.pdf*, accessed 2014.09.18.

[38] Li Jingyi, *"'Wenhua Zhongguo' jiangzhu jihua" (Cultural China's* Scholarship Project), *Tianqing tongxun* (Heaven's sentiment newsletter) 37 (2011), CRRS website, *crrs.org/newsletters/n51/*, accessed 2014.09.12.

[39] *"Lanzhou Daxue 'Wenhua Zhongguo' jiangzhu jihua neirong"* (The content of *Cultural China's* plan to scholastically assist Lanzhou University), CRRS Hong Kong website, *www.crrshk.org/node/528,* accessed 2014.09.12.

[40] *"Wengeng shibazai gongzuo chengguo"* (Eighteen achievements of the Culture Regeneration Research Society), CRRS website, *crrs.org/about-crrs/achievement/*, accessed 2014.09.12.

[41] Liang Yancheng (Thomas *Leung), "Jianchi lixiang 20 nian"* (Upholding one's ideals 20 years), *Tianqing tongxun* (Heaven's sentiment newsletter) 61 (2013), CRRS website, *crrs.org/w/wp-content/uploads/2013/10/TienQing-61-p8-9-Project-Shine-2013.pdf*, accessed 2014.09.13. Note: the article states that a total of eight thousand students had been assisted; however, personal communication from the CRRS Vancouver office stated that twelve thousand is the more accurate figure.

[42] *"Jiaoyu gongcheng gongzuo baogao 2012"* (2012 report on education development), *Tianqing tongxun* (Heaven's sentiment newsletter) 58 (2012), CRRS website, *crrs.org/w/wp-content/uploads/2012/12/TienQing58-C-p4-5-web.pdf*, accessed 2014.09.17.

Chinese senior high school students experienced cross-cultural contact and received free English lessons.[43] CRRS implemented a similar project "Salt and Light" in 2013 when it sent a class of grade 11 students from Carver Christian High School in Burnaby to serve the needy in Hong Kong over the spring break.[44]

CRRS also donates directly. It donated $80,200 to flood relief in Guangdong Province in 2006.[45] In 2008 CRRS collected 1.1 million dollars for earthquake relief in Sichuan and one hundred ten thousand dollars for winter disaster relief. Since then it has sent delegations to Sichuan annually in order to develop counseling services for earthquake victims.[46]

CRRS also takes an academic approach to realizing its mission. It publishes the journal *Cultural China,* organizes conferences, and produces a large number of books and video and audio recordings. One of CRRS' more widely known activities is the publication of *Cultural China,* an academic journal written in Chinese. The purpose of the journal is "to research Chinese culture and to compare it to Western culture." The title "Cultural China" (*Wenhua Zhongguo)* was chosen as one that Chinese around the world could accept, thereby overcoming political differences, such as those between Chinese from the People's Republic of China and those from Taiwan.[47]

---

[43] *"Project Shine 2013," Tianqing tongxun* (Heaven's sentiment newsletter) 61 (2013), CRRS website, *crrs.org/w/wp-content/uploads/2013/10/TienQing-61-p8-9-Project-Shine-2013.pdf*, accessed 2014.09.13.

[44] "Project Salt & Light 2013," *Tianqing tongxun* (Heaven's sentiment newsletter) 61 (2013), CRRS website, *crrs.org/w/wp-content/uploads/2013/06/TienQing60-p10-11-web.pdf*, accessed 2014.09.13.

[45] "About Us/Fund Designation," CRRS website, *www.crrstoronto.org/funddesignation.html*, accessed 2008.01.19.

[46] *"Wengeng shibazai gongzuo chengguo"* (Eighteen achievements of the Culture Regeneration Research Society), CRRS website, *crrs.org/about-crrs/achievement/*, accessed 2014.09.12.; and Guo Yushuang, *"Sichuan guanai zhi lu 2013"* (The compassionate path to Sichuan in 2013), *Tianqing tongxun* (Heaven's sentiment newsletter) 61 (2013), CRRS website, *crrs.org/w/wp-content/uploads/2013/10/TienQing-61-p8-9-Project-Shine-2013.pdf*, accessed 2014.09.13.

[47] Culture Regeneration Research Society, editorial division, *"Wenhua Zhongguo xueshu dongtai"* (Academic developments in *Cultural China*) 15 (June 2002), 3.

The journal serves as a forum for dialogue among differing groups. For example, the journal has published dialogues between representatives of Christianity and Daoism (e.g., second quarter, 2004) and articles supporting both Marxism and liberalism, even though their views would likely be in opposition. That the supporters of each view are still willing to publish in *Cultural China* signals an acceptance of the journal as a medium for discussion among them. The journal is also one of only sixteen foreign Chinese publications that are included in the Chinese Social Sciences Citation Index in 2008.[48]

The journal is a slick production printed in Hong Kong and has been published quarterly since 1994. Each issue contains a glossy cover and a colored reproduction of original Chinese art, as well as several illustrations accompanying the various articles. Common sections in the journal are "Special Feature," "China Study," "Cultural Critique," and "Philosophical Forum." CRRS has been distributing two to three thousand issues quarterly and about seven hundred of these are distributed free of charge to readers in mainland China. A board of about sixty academic advisors provides guidance for the journal.

Besides the journal, CRRS has organized and participated in a number of projects. An important one was a set of conferences on anti-corruption. Under the title of "A Pure Heart Culture--Experience and Culture of Anti-Corruption: Canada and China" *(Zhong Jia lianzheng wenhua yanjiu ji jingyan jiaoliu)*, CRRS secured funding from CIDA to hold a series of public meetings of high ranking government officials, academics, and lawyers from both China and Canada. The first meeting was held in Shanghai in September 1999 and was followed by another in Vancouver at the end of the following February. The meetings focused on promoting anti-corruption measures and the rule of law in society.[49]

---

[48] "English/Achievements," CRRS website, *www.crrs.org/achievements.asp*, accessed 2008.01.19.

[49] Commenting on their financial support, the Canadian government noted the significance of a Chinese Canadian group helping in the development of their ancestral home (*"Jia Zhong jiaoliu lianzheng fazhi, liu xuezhe jiang pu yi chuxi"* [Canada and China exchange views on anti-corruption in government, six academics travel to Shanghai], Chinese newspaper article reprint, no source or date given).

CRRS has also organized a number of conferences all around themes of developing Chinese culture and thereby assisting in China's contemporary reconstruction. These conferences have included "Cultural Conflict and Cultural China" (1995), "Urban Development and Cultural Preservation" (2009), "Religion and Disaster" (2009), "Religion and Disaster: the May 12 Earthquake in Wenchuan, Sichuan" "Religious Dialogue and Social Harmony" (2011), "Urban and Cultural Preservation" (2012), "The Outlook for Reform in the Xi Jinping Era" (2013), and "Cultural Dissemination and Societal Ethics" (2013).

CRRS also produces a number of video and audio video recordings, as well as books for overseas Chinese, narrated or written by its president Thomas Leung. The books are mainly about culture and philosophy of life. Religion and the search for the meaning in life are common themes in the videos. The audio recordings cover a range of themes, but philosophy of life, understanding of Chinese culture, and religion are common. The audience for these recordings and books has usually comprised overseas Chinese who desire to know more about their native culture. According to Leung, they discover that Western culture is different from their native one and then wish to reestablish an understanding of Chinese culture, as well as deepen their understanding of Western culture.[50]

Besides directing CRRS' formal projects, Leung also has been going on lecture tours for about one hundred eighty-six days a year, including two to three months in China. These tours have attracted large audiences and are important means of fund-raising for local branches. In Brisbane, Australia more than five hundred people attended one of Leung's lectures. This was a record for the Brisbane Chinese community for previously no more than four hundred fifty had attended a single meeting in the community. Leung's lectures have also attracted crowds of a thousand in Sydney, Melbourne, and Malaysia. Sometimes, Leung's lectures are very topical. Two weeks after the bombing of the World Trade Centre in New York, he gave a lecture in Vancouver on the conflict in the Middle East, which was attended by about twelve hundred people.[51] In a more recent

[50] Thomas Leung, interviews, 2000.03.21 and 2001.10.21.

[51] Contents of the preceding paragraph were based on interviews conducted with Thomas Leung on 2000.03.21 and 2001.10.21.

example, in 2013 Leung did a lecture tour in Hong Kong which involved forty-five different meetings and a total attendance of over five thousand.[52]

8. Achievements

It is difficult to gauge what constitutes an achievement for CRRS because so much about it could be highlighted. It has obviously been innovative in its mission to introduce the strengths of Western culture to China and, if possible, to do the same with Chinese culture for the West. Furthermore, CRRS' activities are certainly commendable. Just the creation and continued existence alone of CRRS seem to be achievements of note. One approach would be to present an internal view of what CRRS believes to have been its own achievements.

In the opinion of Leung, one foundational achievement CRRS takes pride in has been its ability to garner support from a wide variety of sources. For the first five years of its existence it survived on smaller donations from all over the world. It was not until 2000 that it started to receive large grants from major institutions.

Another accomplishment, in Leung's opinion, is the neutrality of CRRS. This neutrality has allowed CRRS more flexibility in attempting to deal with China's problems. For example, its image of not promoting a political agenda that could contribute to overturning the Chinese Communist government allows it to be active in China; on the other hand, more liberal and conservative advocates, who often oppose communism, view CRRS' efforts as laying a foundation for a Chinese style of democracy and, consequently, are willing to support its activities. One result is that both Chinese-government and anti-government proponents support the work of CRRS. A similar situation exists for those intellectuals who sympathize with Christianity in China and those supporters of Chinese culture who are less sympathetic to it. Both groups find it acceptable to serve in CRRS. The obvious advantage to this,

---

[52] *"2013 Xianggang Wengeng shigong huigu"* (Culture Regeneration Research Society Hong Kong: A look back on work in 2013), *Tianqing tongxun* (Heaven's sentiment newsletter) 62 (2013), CRRS website, *crrs.org/w/wp-content/uploads/2014/01/TienQing-62-p10-11.pdf*, accessed 2014.09.18.

and thus an achievement, is the reduction of barriers among competing groups and, thus the creation of a broader basis for working with one another to advance China.

A third achievement has been gaining access to high-ranking officials in China, such as in the State Department, the United Front Work Department, and the Central Committee of the Communist Party of China. It took CRRS seven years to gain the trust of Chinese authorities; however, it can now comment directly on government policy and sends commentaries to China for response. The two sides have been discussing matters of mutual interest, such as how to conduct humanitarian work in other countries, how to deal with Taiwan, and a concept of humanitarian rights suitable for China.[53]

If one reviews CRRS' achievements since the president and founder Thomas Leung provided the interviews cited above, one would have to add the development of education, especially in rural China. As stated above, CRRS offices in Canada, the U.S., and Hong Kong estimate that as of 2014 it had assisted a total of twelve thousand economically disadvantaged students in completing their studies—most of whom were in rural areas of Guangxi and Yunnan—and it had rebuilt seven schools in Guangxi and Yunnan. While these numbers pale in comparison to the approximate six hundred and fifty million rural residents in China, one should not underestimate the influence of a small stimulus in a country with a culture of deeply valuing education. CRRS has chosen some of the poorest and most isolated areas within China to promote basic education and has even focused on females and minorities, groups that are most challenged in pursuing education. In demonstrating that even the poorest and most challenged can have the opportunity to receive an education in China CRRS is offering hope that should resonate in the grass-roots population and encourage them.

9. Distinctive Characteristics

---

[53] Contents of the preceding two pages are based on interviews conducted with Thomas Leung on 2000.03.21 and 2001.10.21.

There are two characteristics that form a significant part of CRRS' identity: the increasingly philanthropic nature of its activities and its belief in a Christian spirit that is rooted in Chinese culture and society. The presence of both these characteristics in what is described as a research organization is surprising though one has to acknowledge that CRRS obviously does more than research and is active in applying its research findings.

CRRS' interest in philanthropy is seen in its mission statement and the goals that it sets for itself. The mission statement exhorts CRRS members "to seed China's future generation with visions of its own potential and to give it the fundamental tools to enable every child to live out his/her aspirations,"[54] and includes the ambitious goal of providing adequate resources for every single Chinese child.

This philanthropic spirit is fortified by the strong idealism found within CRRS. One of its objectives is to advance "the interaction of the Chinese values and wisdom with the highest ideals of ethics, spiritual disciplines, and contemporary philosophy of the West."[55] To unify overseas Chinese in the regeneration of Chinese culture is another of CRRS' idealistic goals.[56] President Leung also talks of sharing love with fellow Chinese and rebuilding sincerity.[57] The idealism espoused in these statements is exemplified in the actions of two young men who walked from St. John's, Newfoundland to Toronto in order to raise funds for CRRS.[58]

---

[54] "Introduction," CRRS website, *www.crrs.org/index_en.asp*, accessed 2008.01.19.

[55] "New Scholarship Available at TWU," Trinity Western University website, *www.twu.ca/about/news/general/2007/new-scholarship-available-at-twu.html*, accessed 2008.01.19.

[56] *"Wengeng chengguo"* (Culture Regeneration Research Society achievements), CRRS website, *www.crrs.org/achievement.asp*, accessed 2008.01.19.

[57] *"Yuanchang jieshao"* (Introduction of Culture Regeneration Research Society's President), CRRS website, *www.crrs.org/introduce.asp*, accessed 2008.01.19.

[58] "ET COME HOME," CRRS website, *www.crrstoronto.org/et.html*, accessed 2008.01.19.

CRRS' idealism is significant because it enthuses CRRS' efforts and encourages it to adopt far reaching goals, which feeds into its philanthropy. The idealism and philanthropy seem to build on one another. The idealism produces enthusiasm and the philanthropy reinforces it; the philanthropy reinforces the attractive values that are intrinsic to it. Furthermore, CRRS seems to have been able to combine these two qualities in a way that avoids the dangers of extremism and delusion.

Christianity that takes root in Chinese culture is a resource that Leung wants to use to influence China because he believes that the Christian spirit of unconditional love, self-sacrifice, and forgiveness fused with the Chinese humanistic philosophy of interpersonal relationships could have a strong, positive impact there. Leung started to study and practice Chinese culture when he was only thirteen, and converted to Christianity when he was twenty-two years old. In his own words "I accepted the redemption of Jesus and immediately I sensed the power of the sacred spirit from the divine world flow into me. My body and mind were bright and I was in ecstasy."[59]

Christian churches and Chinese Canadian Christians are also major supporters of CRRS, both financially and as volunteers, but this support is not tied to conditions, such as doing missionary work in China. There seems to be a natural fit between a Christian desire to help those in need and the recognized needs of China. Nevertheless, Christianity would have to be "Sinocized" before introducing it widely into China. If this could take place, Leung believes that the Christian concepts of a transcendent truth and a transcendent god, which relate to the development of a rational civil society, could help China to develop a more balanced social and political system and reduce tyranny, which is linked to the traditional political culture. In Leung's opinion, given the new profound reform movements by the government in China, an understanding of reason, moral principle, and love would create conditions for a better society.

---

[59] Liang Yancheng (Thomas *Leung*), *"Jianchi lixiang 20 nian"* (Upholding one's ideals 20 years), *Tianqing tongxun* (Heaven's sentiment newsletter) 61 (2013), CRRS website, *crrs.org/w/wp-content/uploads/2013/10/TienQing-61-p8-9-Project-Shine-2013.pdf*, accessed 2014.09.13.

CRRS' promotion of of a Chinese form of Christianity with a respect for Chinese values can be seen in the views of its directors and in the activities it conducts in China. The first two projects for which the Chinese donation form requested support contained goals such as the amalgamation of Christianity with Chinese culture, the contributing of Christians to Chinese popular culture, and providing evidence of the value of sharing beliefs. In the same form, the journal *Cultural China* is described as establishing a dialogue with traditional Chinese knowledge from a basis of Christian beliefs.[60] Leung speaks of God yearning "to heal China's wounds and to restore China's strength and spirit."[61] The founder and director of the CRRS' San Francisco branch Melvin Wong (Huang Weikang) describes CSSR as providing service based on Christian principles.[62]

Wong's belief in Christianity is also quite strong. He claims that the opportunities for Christians to express their love and practice their faith to serve the Chinese people were created by God: "When the Lord opened ministries opportunities in China fifteen years ago, CRRS USA was founded to facilitate this process of transforming lives one at a time through educational advancement."[63] CRRS' Australian branch has organized Christian research sessions and art exhibits.[64] Also, a former head of CRRS' Hong Kong branch Clara Cheng Wanling

---

[60] *"Juankuan biao"* (Donation form), CRRS website, *www.crrs.org/down/donation_form.pdf,* accessed 2008.02.07.

[61] "About Us/Organization/President's Message," CRRS website, *www.crrstoronto.org/presidentmessage.html,* accessed 2008.01.19.

[62] *"Chengchang zhong de fushi"* (Serving while growing), *Tianqing tongxun* (Heaven's sentiment newsletter) 37 (2006), CRRS website, *crrs.org/cchinalist.asp?id=120&news_kind=%E5%A4%A9%E6%83%85%E9% 80%9A%E8%A8%8A,* accessed 2008.01.19.

[63] "Pushing New Service Frontiers after Fifteen Years," *Tianqing tongxun* (Heaven's sentiment newsletter) 55 (2012), CRRS website, crrs.org/w/wp-content/uploads/2012/08/425201224249PM.pdf, accessed 2014.09.23.

[64] *"Aozhou Wengeng huodong"* (Activities of Culture Regeneration Research Society's Australian branch), *Tianqing tongxun* (Heaven's sentiment newsletter) 36 (n.d.), CRRS website, *www.crrs.org/cchinalist.asp?id=134&news_kind=%E5%A4%A9%E6%83%85% E9%80%9A%E8%A8%8A,* accessed 2008.01.19.

reported that in 2007 CRRS secured the support of religious
organizations to do work in China.[65]

In addition, CRRS is working with research centres to
promote a kind of Christianity that respects and takes root in
Chinese culture and society; for example, in 2005 CRRS
partnered with Lanzhou University to establish the Research
Centre for Christianity Studies and assisted Sichuan
University in launching the first doctoral programme in
Christian studies in China. Leung sees these centres as
important channels through which to supply Christian related
resources to scholars in China in order to increase their
understanding of the true meaning of a Christian faith that is
not from the West and to find examples of the positive influence
of the Chinese Christian church in history. This will further
result in "the integration of Christian faith with Chinese
philosophies, so that a unique contribution can be made to the
regeneration of Chinese culture."[66] In a further step to realize
this goal CRRS collaborated in the publication of three tomes in
the series "Christianity and Chinese Culture." They are *Ru,
Dao, Yi yu Zhongguo Jidu xinyang* (Confucianism, Daoism, and
The Book of Change and Chinese Christian beliefs) by Thomas
Leung; *Jidu jiao yu Zhongguo wenhua chujing* (Christianity
and the plight of Chinese culture) by Zhuo Xinping Chair of the
World Religions Research Centre of the Chinese Academy of
Social Sciences; and *Jidu jiao Zhongguo hua yanjiu–diyi ji*
(Research on the Sinification of Christianity–volume one) edited
by Beijing University professor Zhang Zhigang and Tang
Xiaofeng Vice-director of the Christianity Research Section of
the World Religions Research Centre of the Chinese Academy of
Social Sciences. The three books were all published in 2013.

CRRS' promotion of a Chinese mode of Christianity is
significant because it brings into question CRRS' ability to be
effective in China. Religion has been criticized by the
Communist government in power since 1949 to the extent that

---

[65] *"Xueshu wenhua' cong Xi wang Dong, Lanzhou dao Shanghai"* ("Academic
culture" from West to East, from Lanzhou to Shanghai), *Tianqing tongxun*
(Heaven's sentiment newsletter) 40 (2007), CRRS website,
*www.crrs.org/cchinalist.asp?id=143&news_kind=%E5%A4%A9%E6%83%85%
E9%80%9A%E8%A8%8A,* accessed 2008.01.19.

[66] Leung, Thomas, "Message from the President," 2013, CRRS Hong Kong
website, *www.crrshk.org/en/content/message-president,* accessed 2014.09.22.

some religions are still banned and their followers arrested. There is, of course, an ideologically-based opposition to religion within communism, but the anti-religious stance of the government has also been justified by describing religion as containing elements of superstition and limiting critical thought. Further impeding the acceptance of Christianity in China is its association with Western imperialism of the eighteenth and nineteenth centuries, during a period of much suffering in China. This association was seen in the attacks of the Boxers against Christian missionaries during the uprising of 1899-1901.

From 1979 to the present, the Chinese government has been in the process of reforming its religious policy and Leung's views have found support among academics within China. Zhuo Xinping Chair of the World Religions Research Centre of the Chinese Academy of Social Sciences holds that "contemporary Chinese society requires unconditional love, the willingness to serve, and the spirit of sacrifice that are emphasized in Christianity. His hope is that Christianity will take roots in China, make a contribution, and exist harmoniously with Chinese society and culture."[67] Zhou also holds that the Chinese government is no longer opposed to religion; rather its approach is more complex and proactive. China no longer interacts with the rest of the world solely on the basis of political and economic interests; there are also strong cultural and religious dimensions to its relations.[68]

Notwithstanding the basis and history of opposition to Christianity, there seem to be a new and open policy for Christianity in China. In 2008 then President Hu Jintao announced that the government should recognize the role of religion in promoting economic and social development and reach out to believers.[69] Furthermore, a recent estimate placed

[67] Liang Yancheng (Thomas In-sing Leung), *"Ningjing de weixiao: tan Zhuo Xinping"* (A quiet smile: about Zhuo Xinping), *Tianqing tongxun* (Heaven's sentiment newsletter) 50 (2010), CRRS website, *crrs.org/w/wp-content/uploads/2012/08/1015201031755PM.pdf*, accessed 2014.09.18.

[68] *"Zongjiao zhengce jian kuanrong, tsujin shehui hexie* (Policy on religion gradually loosens, promoting social harmony), *Tianqing tongxun* (Heaven's sentiment newsletter) 50 (2010), CRRS website, *crrs.org/w/wp-content/uploads/2012/08/1015201031755PM.pdf*, accessed 2014.09.18.

[69] Edward Cody, "China's Leaders Puts Faith in Religious," *Washington Post,*

the number of Christians in China at forty-eight million (2010)[70] compared to the official figure of sixteen million in 2005.[71] This reported shift has been accompanied by academic predictions that China would become the largest Christian country in the world by 2030.[72]

Nevertheless, there is also a cornucopia of indigenous resources within China that provide for its needs and because of these resources, China's circumstances and needs may not be as dire or in need of Christianity as CRRS would claim. Given the past opposition to religion, particularly Christianity, in China and the growing education of the Chinese people, it would seem better for CRRS to promote the principles of Christianity that it sees most worthwhile without promoting the religion itself.

10. Future Issues

Given the trends within Canada and CRRS' record of diversified growth, CRRS should play an increasing role in developing China and relations between it and Canada. As Canada continues to attract skilled and educated immigrants from China and as Chinese Canadians improve their status within Canada, there will be increased recognition of what Canada has to offer China and desire to contribute to its development. On the other hand, as China's economy develops, the attraction of participating in its development will also increase. CRRS has situated itself geographically and organizationally in a position to participate in this development and has a track record of doing so. It seems likely that its activities in China will continue and even increase.

2008.20.01, (www.washingtonpost.com/wp-dyn/content/article/2008/01/19/AR2008011902465_pf.html, accessed 2008.02.09).

[70] Tom Phillips, "China on Course to Become 'World's Most Christian Nation' within 15 Years," The Telegraph, 2014.04.19.

[71] "Survey Finds 300m China Believers," BBC News, International Version, 2007.02.07 (news.bbc.co.uk/2/hi/asia-pacific/6337627.stm, accessed 2009.02.09). The survey of 4,500 people was conducted by Shanghai university professors.

[72] Phillips, "China on Course."

While the future for CRRS is bright, there are two issues that may affect that future: the imbalance in the implementation of CRRS' mandate–its resources are overwhelmingly devoted to promoting the development of China, compared to the development of the West, particularly Canada, where it is resident and securing major support–and the heavy reliance upon Leung's leadership.

CRRS seems unable to make the general Canadian public aware of the advantages of learning from Chinese culture. Nor does CRRS have formal measures to introduce Chinese values to Westerners because it finds that there is little interest in them. Leung is also apologetic about his ability to speak English, thinking that it is inadequate to persuade Westerners of the merits of what is to them an unknown culture. However, in large, the difficulty in communicating with the Canadian public seems to be due to the lack of recognition of Chinese culture and its potential importance.

This has had a direct impact on how CRRS perceives its capacity to work in a Canadian setting. Leung feels that CRRS is being kept outside the Western mainstream even though they recognize problems in the West. Leung is worried about generations that have grown up accustomed to violence because of its prevalence in the media and that have lost their intellectual abilities because of their intensive involvement with computer games. He also worries about the total secularization of life in the West. He believes that Chinese culture and people could contribute to solving these problems; however, although Westerners are willing to offer advice to China and its people, a certain amount of arrogance makes them unwilling to accept help from China and its people. Leung feels powerless in the West. He is disappointed in the lack of attention given by Canadian mainstream media to CRRS, indicated by the fact that even letters to newspaper editors do not get published.

For this reason, Leung believes that he has little to say in the West, so does not speak out against secular liberalism, which he believes contributes to an excessively permissive environment. Leung believes Chinese Canadians typically think that the education system in Canada should deal more directly with moral issues. Leung holds that the values of the Chinese community are correctly characterized as right wing and conservative. However, the majority of those with similar values in Canada have little interest in the Chinese Canadian community. Left wing thinkers are willing to listen to the Chinese Canadian community; however, their values are different.

Another issue for CRRS is its reliance on Leung. Although, to this point, Leung seems to have been able to handle the extra work that has accompanied the success of CRRS, the demands on his time are significant. He is invited to lecture all over the world and is away from home for much of the time promoting and implementing CRRS' various projects. Furthermore, he would like to spend more time in China, directly assisting in its development. In the future, he would like to live in Hong Kong or China and teach and lecture there.

From 2013 to 2014, through Leung's dialogue with Members of Parliament for Canada and Members of the Legislative Assembly of British Columbia, Canadian governments have noticed that CRRS has worked in and helped to develop China for 20 years. Canadian governments now often consult with Leung for more understanding of China. In 2014, Prime Minister Stephen Harper extended an invitation to Leung to join the Canadian delegation to APEC in Beijing. This invitation showed that the Canadian Government had finally recognized Leung's work and expertise in the field of Chinese culture and relations.

A number of factors make the question of leadership an important one for CRRS. Leung, personally, would like to devote less time to fund-raising and public relations, and more time to his research and writing. However, organizational needs demand the majority of his time, evidenced by the one hundred eighty-six days a year that Leung was spending away from Vancouver on visits to other CRRS offices, in fund-raising, and lecture tours. Leung hopes that in the future CRRS will not be so dependent upon his reputation and efforts. In order to meet this goal, CRRS is working toward the establishment of an efficient structure manned by talented personnel.[73]

11. Conclusion

---

[73] Contents of this section are based on interviews conducted with Thomas Leung on 2000.03.21 and 2001.10.21.

From a critical perspective the growth of CRRS is quite amazing. In an era of decentralization, when people are becoming more sensitive to local identities, CRRS has been successful in drawing the attention and support of Chinese outside China to development within the country. At the same time, CRRS has been resistant to the secular liberalism that seems to be prevalent in the West. In its place it would like to promote discussion leading to a common set of moral values that would have their foundation in religious belief. At the same time one cannot deny the success of CRRS. The increase in the operation budget, from two hundred thousand dollars to more than one million in twenty years since its founding, understates the achievements that have their origin in the dedication of CRRS staff and volunteers and the accumulated support of many others around the globe. The amazement persists because it does not seem reasonable to attribute this success to the standard motivations that one could use to explain it. There are much better candidates for charity than China and a foreign-based, non-government organization that is highlighting China's deficiencies can hardly harness nationalism.

So what gives rise to the dedication of CRRS staff and the support of so many others? The most likely answer is that there is a complexity of incentives that motivate the supporters of CRRS, including degrees of charity and idealism. Another incentive that should not be underestimated is the inherent value of Chinese culture, which supporters of CRRS recognize the value of maintaining as a choice amid cultural diversity. Granted, they also recognize the need to infuse this culture with new dimensions imported from the West; however, the infusion is a judged supplementation, not an overall substitution. The core of Chinese culture is still seen as worth preserving, even regenerating.

As for what CRRS' achievements can tell us about those of Chinese Canadians, one should note foremost that CRRS' achievements are primarily Canadian. Most of the administrators live in Canada, the head office is there, and most of the fundraising takes place there. There are reasons why CRRS can operate most effectively in a Canadian environment: the relative lack of bias, the surplus wealth that can be distributed to needy Chinese, a relatively large Chinese Canadian population, the widespread acceptance of multiculturalism, the lack of past aggression against China, among other things. These factors combine to create the general situation where Chinese Canadians are both able and proud to support CRRS' efforts in China.

It is important to note the balance in the perspective of CRRS and the donors who provide its resources. They are aware of the values of Western culture as embodied in Canada and their potential benefit to China. This is evidence of their Canadian identity as well as their generosity in wanting to provide aid where it can be most effective. In providing this aid, CRRS and its supporters have established precedents in both China and Canada. In China, CRRS has established the first migrant workers high school, its journal *Cultural China* is one of only sixteen foreign Chinese publications that are included in the Chinese Social Sciences Citation Index, and it has partnered with Lanzhou University to establish the Research Centre for Christianity Studies. In Canada, CRRS was the country's only Chinese Canadian managed, non-governmental organization (NGO) when it achieved NGO status in 1997 and it was the first overseas Chinese organization made eligible for support by CIDA.[74]

From 2012 to 2014, Dr. Leung has continued his involvement in Chinese and Canadian affairs. In the span of less than a year the governments of both China and Canada have recognized him for his unstinting work. In China, where he and CRRS spend the bulk of their time and resources, he has been accepted into the Chinese People's Political Consultative Conference,[75] a political advisory body. This shows just how much China values his contributions to both academia and philanthropy within China over the past 20 years. Leung's efforts within Canada have not been in vain either, as he received a Diamond Jubilee medal from the Queen of England through the Government of Canada identifying him as one of the Canadians who have contributed significantly to Canada

---

[74] These latter two claims are found in CRRS' list of ministries and achievements ("Achievements," CRRS website, *www.crrs.org/achievements.asp,* accessed 2008.01.19).

[75] This claim based on email communication of 2015.01.12 with Leung's daughter Esther Leung-Kong, Executive Officer of CRRS.

and its communities.[76] Finally, China saw his record in helping ethnic minorities within China and appointed him to a committee devoted to promoting philanthropy in Tibet, which is significant given China's usual wariness about Western influence in Tibet. In short, both the Chinese and Canadian governments have formally recognized Dr. Leung as someone they can trust and work with, so the future of CRRS shines a little brighter.

In spite of its focus on China, it is CRRS' hope and goal to contribute more in Canada. It recognizes the benefits that Canada would gain in learning from China and has taken on the mission of fostering this learning. Once the benefits of doing so are more widely recognized, it is likely that CRRS' achievements will grow and CRRS' Canadian identity will be even more defined.

BIBLIOGRAPHY

"2013 Xianggang Wengeng shigong huigu" (Culture Regeneration Research Society Hong Kong: A look back on work in 2013). *Tianqing tongxun* (Heaven's sentiment newsletter) 62 (2013). CRRS website, *crrs.org/w/wp-content/uploads/2014/01/TienQing-62-p10-11.pdf*, accessed 2014.09.18.

"About Us/Fund Designation." CRRS website, *www.crrstoronto.org/funddesignation.html*, accessed 2008.01.19.

"About Us/Organization/President's Message." CRRS website, *www.crrstoronto.org/presidentmessage.html*, accessed 2008.01.19.

"About Us/Fund Designation." CRRS website, *www.crrstoronto.org/funddesignation.html*, accessed 2008.01.19.

---

[76] "Burnaby Residents to Get Queen's Diamond Jubilee Medals," *Burnaby NewsLeader*, 2011.12.11, *www.burnabynewsleader.com/community/183031081.html*, accessed 2015.01.09.

"Achievements." CRRS website, *www.crrs.org/achievements.asp,* accessed 2008.01.19.

"Aozhou Wengeng huodong" (Activities of Culture Regeneration Research Society's Australian branch). *Tianqing tongxun* (Heaven's sentiment newsletter) 36 (n.d.). CRRS website, *www.crrs.org/cchinalist.asp?id=134&news_kind=%E5%A4 %A9%E6%83%85%E9%80%9A%E8%A8%8A,* accessed 2008.01.19.

"Burnaby Residents to Get Queen's Diamond Jubilee Medals." *Burnaby NewsLeader,* 2012.12.11. *www.burnabynewsleader.com/community/183031081.html* , accessed 2015.01.09.

"Chengchang zhong de fushi" (Serving while growing). *Tianqing tongxun* (Heaven's sentiment newsletter) 37 (n.d.). CRRS website, *www.crrs.org/cchinalist.asp?id=120&news_kind=%E5%A4 %A9%E6%83%85%E9%80%9A%E8%A8%8A,* accessed 2008.01.19.

Cody, Edward. "China's Leaders Puts Faith in Religious." *Washington Post,* 2008.20.01. *www.washingtonpost.com/wp-dyn/content/article/2008/01/19/AR2008011902465_pf.ht ml,* accessed 2008.02.09.

"CRRS Education Fund 2011 Financial Highlights." CRRS website, *crrs.org/education/finance/,* accessed 2014.09.02.

Culture Regeneration Research Society. "Wenhua gengxin" (Culture regeneration), introductory pamphlet, n.d.

Culture Regeneration Research Society, editorial division. "Wenhua Zhongguo xueshu dongtai" (Academic developments in *Cultural China*) 15 (June 2002), and 21 (June 2004).

"Culture Regeneration Research Society USA 2013 Financial Report." CRRS USA website, *www.crrsusa.org/DispSPE.asp?uID=344*, accessed 2014.09.03.

"Dr. Leung In-sing, Thomas." CRRS Hong Kong website, *www.crrshk.org/en/node/283*, accessed 2014.09.01.

"English/Introduction." CRRS website, *www.crrs.org/index_en.asp*, accessed 2008.01.19.

"ET COME HOME." CRRS website, *www.crrstoronto.org/et.html*, accessed 2008.01.19.

"Financial Status–2012 Income & Expenditure Report and 2013 Budget." CRRS Hong Kong website, www.crrshk.org/en/content/financial-status, accessed 2014.09.03.

Guo Yushuang. *"Sichuan guanai zhi lu 2013"* (The compassionate path to Sichuan in 2013). *Tianqing tongxun* (Heaven's sentiment newsletter) 61 (2013), CRRS website, *crrs.org/w/wp-content/uploads/2013/10/TienQing-61-p8-9-Project-Shine-2013.pdf*, accessed 2014.09.13.

"Home/About Culture Regeneration Research Society." CRRS website, *crrs.org/en/*, accessed 2014.08.23.

"Introduction." CRRS website, *www.crrs.org/index_en.asp,* accessed 2008.01.19.

"Jia Zhong jiaoliu lianzheng fazhi, liu xuezhe jiang pu yi chuxi" (Canada and China exchange views on anti-corruption in government, six academics travel to Shanghai). Chinese newspaper article reprint, no source, n.d.

"Jianada Wengehua ganen yixiang fenxiang" (Sharing our appreciation for the unusual event in Vancouver, Canada). *Tianqing tongxun* (Heaven's sentiment newsletter) 62 (2013). CRRS website, *crrs.org/w/wp-content/uploads/2014/01/TienQing-62-p8-9.pdf*, accessed 2014.09.18.

370

*"Jianada 'Wenhua gengxin yanjiu zhongxin' zai Guilin juan
zhuxue zhujiao"* (Canada's Culture Regeneration Research
Society donates learning and teaching aids in Guilin).
Zhonghua Fujiao xinxi wang (Chinese Buddhist news
network), 2005.09.10.
www.fjnet.com/cssy/cssynr/t20050910_13528.htm,
accessed 2008.01.28.

"Jiaoyu gongcheng gongzuo baogao 2012" (2012 report on
education development). *Tianqing tongxun* (Heaven's
sentiment newsletter) 58 (2012). CRRS website,
*crrs.org/w/wp-content/uploads/2012/12/TienQing58-C-
p4-5-web.pdf,* accessed 2014.09.17.

"Juankuan biao" (Donation form). CRRS website,
www.crrs.org/down/donation_form.pdf, accessed
2008.02.07.

"Lanzhou Daxue 'Wenhua Zhongguo' jiangzhu jihua neirong"
(The content of *Cultural China's* plan to scholastically
assist Lanzhou University). CRRS Hong Kong website,
www.crrshk.org/node/528, accessed 2014.09.12.

Leung, Thomas In-sing. President, Culture Regeneration
Research Society. Interviewed 2000.03.21 in Burnaby,
British Columbia and 2001.10.21 in Vancouver, British
Columbia.

-----. *"Jianchi lixiang 20 nian"* (Upholding one's ideals 20 years).
Tianqing tongxun (Heaven's sentiment newsletter) 61
(2013). CRRS website, *crrs.org/w/wp-
content/uploads/2013/10/TienQing-61-p8-9-Project-
Shine-2013.pdf,* accessed 2014.09.13.

-----. "Message from the President," 2013. CRRS Hong Kong
website, *www.crrshk.org/en/content/message-president,*
accessed 2014.09.22.

-----. *"Ningjing de weixiao: tan Zhuo Xinping"* (A quiet smile:
about Zhuo Xinping). *Tianqing tongxun* (Heaven's
sentiment newsletter) 50 (2010), CRRS website,
crrs.org/w/wp-

content/uploads/2012/08/1015201031755PM.pdf, accessed
2014.09.18.

------. *"Wenhua gaige yu Wenhua Zhongguo"* (Cultural reform
and *Cultural China)*. *Tianqing tongxun* (Heaven's
sentiment newsletter) 55 (2012), crrs.org/w/wp-
content/uploads/2012/08/425201223847PM.pdf, accessed
2014.09.19.

Leung-Kong, Esther, Executive Officer of CRRS. Email
communication of 2015.01.12.

Li Jingyi. *"'Wenhua Zhongguo'jiangzhu jihua"* *(Cultural
China*'s Scholarship Project). *Tianqing tongxun* (Heaven's
sentiment newsletter) 51 (2011), CRRS website,
crrs.org/newsletters/n51/, accessed 2014.09.12.

Mencius. Trans. D.C. Lau. Harmondsworth, England: Penguin,
1970.

"New Scholarship Available at TWU." Trinity Western
University website,
*www.twu.ca/about/news/general/2007/new-scholarship-
available-at-twu.html*, accessed 2008.01.19.

Phillips, Tom. "China on Course to Become 'World's Most
Christian Nation' within 15 Years." *The Telegraph,* 2014.04

"Project Salt & Light 2013." *Tianqing tongxun* (Heaven's
sentiment newsletter) 60 (2013). CRRS website,
*crrs.org/w/wp-content/uploads/2013/06/TienQing60-
p10-11-web.pdf*, accessed 2014.09.13.

"Project Shine." CRRS website,
www.crrs.org/projectshine_en.asp, accessed 2008.01.19.

"Project Shine 2013" (Project Shine 2013). *Tianqing tongxun*
(Heaven's sentiment newsletter) 61 (2013). CRRS website,
*crrs.org/w/wp-content/uploads/2013/10/TienQing-61-p8-
9-Project-Shine-2013.pdf*, accessed 2014.09.13.

"Shanghai mingong zinuu zhuxue gongcheng" (Academic support for migrant workers' children in Shanghai). *crrs.org/control%20panel/tiny_mce/upimages/201107110 1326205.pdf*, accessed 2014.09.10.

"Survey Finds 300m China Believers." *BBC News*, International Version, 2007.02.07. *news.bbc.co.uk/2/hi/asia-pacific/6337627.stm*, accessed 2009.02.09.

Wei Liu Guojing. *"Shenghuo–Shenghuo: <<Wenhua Zhongguo>> yu Wenhua gengxin"* (Life-life: <<Cultural China>> and Culture Regeneration Research Society). *Zhenli bao* (Truth monthly) 145 (October 2005), *www.truth-monthly.com/simp/issue145/0510ex04.htm,* accessed 2008.01.28.

"Wengeng huodong" (Culture Regeneration Research Society activities). CRRS website, *www.crrs.org/event.asp,* accessed 2008.02.07.

"Wengeng shibazai gongzuo chengguo" (Eighteen achievements of the Culture Regeneration Research Society). CRRS website, *crrs.org/about-crrs/achievement/*, accessed 2014.09.12.

"*Wengeng chengguo"* (CRRS' achievements). CRRS website, *www.crrs.org/achievement.asp*, accessed 2008.01.19.

Wong, Melvin W. "Culture Regeneration Research Society U.S., report on 2011 activities." *Tianqing tongxun* (Heaven's sentiment newsletter) 55 (2012). CRRS website, *crrs.org/w/wp-content/uploads/2012/08/425201224249PM.pdfcrrs.org/w/wp-content/uploads/2012/08/425201224249PM.pdf,* accessed 2014.09.18.

-----. "Pushing New Service Frontiers after Fifteen Years." *Tianqing tongxun* (Heaven's sentiment newsletter) 55 (2012), CRRS website, *crrs.org/w/wp-content/uploads/2012/08/425201224249PM.pdf,* accessed 2014.09.23.

"'Xueshu wenhua' cong Xi wang Dong: Lanzhou dao Shanghai" ("Academic culture" from West to East, from Lanzhou to Shanghai). *Tianqing tongxun* (Heaven's sentiment newsletter) 40 (2007). CRRS website, *www.crrs.org/cchinalist.asp?id=143&news_kind=%E5%A4 %A9%E6%83%85%E9%80%9A%E8%A8%8A,* accessed 2008.01.19.

Xunbao (Calgary Trend Weekly) 213 (2002.1.4).

"Yuanchang jieshao" (Introduction of CRRS' President). CRRS website, *www.crrs.org/introduce.asp,* accessed 2008.01.19.

"Zhongxin jianjie"/"Jichu jiaoyu"/"Zhuhuan nongcun jiaoshi xiangmu gongzuo baogao" (Brief introduction to CRRS/Basic education/Report on aid to rural teachers). CRRS website, *www.crrs.org,* accessed 2005.04.07.

"Zongjiao zhengce jian kuanrong, tsujin shehui hexie (Policy on religion gradually loosens, promoting social harmony). *Tianqing tongxun* (Heaven's sentiment newsletter) 50 (2010), CRRS website, *crrs.org/w/wp-content/uploads/2012/08/1015201031755PM.pdf,* accessed 2014.09.18.

8. CHINESE CANADIAN INSTITUTIONAL ELDERCARE

1. Introduction

Chinese Canadian achievements in the area of eldercare are some of their most obvious. These achievements have appeared in most cities where there are sizeable Chinese Canadian populations. Traditionally, Chinese Canadians have cared for their elders within the family and still do. Nevertheless, this tradition is now complemented by community services and facilities that offer alternatives to traditional care. These developments demonstrate even more clearly the accomplishments of Chinese Canadians, in part because they constitute alternative models for study and imitation by mainstream eldercare.

Over the past thirty years, Chinese Canadians have created several examples of culturally-orientated eldercare. These examples are noteworthy for various reasons, perhaps most importantly because of the models they have become; and also because they are examples of Chinese Canadians overcoming severe financial limitations and a lack of acceptance by government, while establishing new standards for eldercare.

A number of factors inform the environment within which Chinese Canadian institutional eldercare has developed. There are the cultural values of Chinese Canadians, the perceived need to develop forms of eldercare more suitable to themselves, and the availability of resources to support this development. Based on these defining factors, Chinese Canadians have produced the planning, donors, volunteers, and expertise to support the building and operating of institutions to care for their elders. One organization, Yee Hong, has been especially successful in this regard. It manages more than eight hundred long term care beds at four sites in the Toronto area. In its inception, planning, and implementation, it has shown itself to be innovative and able to offer new models of eldercare and now enjoys large demand for its services.

2. Background

2.1 General State of Eldercare in Canada

The institutional eldercare that Chinese Canadians have developed offers different models at the same time as providers of care, eldercare experts, and Canadian governments are searching for alternatives to care for the elderly. Major drivers of this search include the fact that Canada faces rapid aging of its population as the proportion of seniors increases more quickly than for all other age groups. In 2001, one Canadian in eight was aged 65 years or over. By 2026, one Canadian in five will have reached age 65.[1] A government report states: "seniors constitute the fastest growing population group in Canada. In 2001, it was estimated that 3.92 million Canadians were 65 years of age or older, a figure that is two thirds more than in 1981. During the same period, the overall Canadian population increased by only one quarter. . . . the seniors population is expected to reach 6.7 million in 2021 and 9.2 million in 2041 (nearly one in four Canadians)."[2] Added to this, health expenditures for seniors are substantial; they represented 43 percent of total health expenditures in Canada in 2000-01, which in 2000 were an estimated ninety-five billion dollars.[3] This meant that the expenditures on seniors' health were nearly forty-one billion dollars. Total health expenditures doubled to more than two hundred billion by 2011, but health expenditures for seniors seemed to remain relatively the same, constituting 45 percent of provincial and territorial health expenditures.[4] At the same time many provinces were reducing funding for the construction and operation of new nursing home beds.[5] Therefore, in light of increasing demand and reduced

[1] Health Canada, *Canada's Aging Population* (Minister of Public Works and Government Services Canada, 2002), 1.

[2] *Ibid.*, 3. More recent government reports confirm that seniors will comprise nearly 25 percent of the Canadian population in 2041 (Rohan Kembhavi, "Research Note – Canadian Seniors: A Demographic Profile," Elections Canada, Nov. 2012, *www.elections.ca/content.aspx?section=res&dir=rec/part/sen&document=ind ex&lang=e*, accessed 2014.11.11).

[3] *Ibid.*, 28.

[4] Canadian Institute for Health Information, *National Health Expenditure Trends, 1975 to 2013* (Ottawa, Ont.: CIHI; 2013), 3 and 56.

[5] Various sources cited in Sherry Ann Chapman, Norah Keating, and Jacquie

funding, providers of care are searching for alternatives in order to maintain standards.

In responding to these challenges, two models of eldercare, client-centred and community-based, have sparked interest and have led to government trials and scholarly research.[6] Client-centred care is care that emphasizes the values, preferences, and needs of care users.[7] It contrasts with a provider-driven, medical model in which decision making is less in the hands of the client.[8] Community-based care is care provided in the community close to family, friends, and others who know the client. Because it is usually provided in the client's home where there is more familial support, it is thought to be less costly than institutional care.[9] Reflecting a change in thinking, new programs in Canada have assumed that institutional care could be considered community-based if boundaries to the community were open and if a social rather than a medical model were used.[10] Although these models present intuitive value, research has shown that they face three thematic challenges: (1) engaging with others in a care partnership, (2) responding to residents' preferences and care needs with limited resources, and (3) maintaining residents' connections with the community.[11]

2.2 Traditional Chinese Cultural Values and Their Manifestation in Canada

One of the main determinants of Chinese Canadian institutional eldercare has been the increasing influence of

---

Eales, "Client centred, community-based care for frail seniors," *Health and Social Care in the Community* 11.3 (May 2003), 254.

[6] *Ibid.*, 253-54.

[7] Jacquie Eales, Norah Keating, and Annita Damsma, "Seniors' Experiences of Client centred Residential Care," *Ageing and Society* 21.3 (May 2001), 279.

[8] Eales et al, 281.

[9] Chapman et al, 253.

[10] *Ibid.*, 254.

[11] *Ibid.*

Chinese culture within Canada. This increasing influence emerges from three factors: China's increased wealth encourages its study, the increased immigration of Chinese to Canada, and the significant economic and social influence of Chinese Canadians. The values uncovered in the study of the culture, in turn, strongly support care of elders. Embedded within these values, and therefore fostered by their increasing influence within Canada, is a respect for the elderly. Chinese elders are given high status in society and are recipients of a large amount of resources. This status and material benefits are part of a long Chinese tradition, epitomized in the core component of filial piety, that has honoured the elderly. The main environment for practising this tradition has been the family where children pay great respect to the wants and needs of their parents, especially in their old age.

The high respect that the Chinese have traditionally held for the elderly is exemplified in once widely read and still often cited texts, such as the *Classic of Filial Piety, Biographical Accounts of Filial Piety*, and *Twenty-Four Stories of Filial Piety*, that have encouraged acts of filial piety. It had such social importance that during the Han dynasty (220 BCE - CE) it was officially promoted, "systematically making unfilial conduct a punishable crime and rewarding acts of filial piety."[12] It was also important to give one's parents an elaborate funeral as a sign of filial devotion and families were expected to spare no expense and felt they had to incur debt in paying for it.[13]

Today in Canada, thousands of years and kilometres away from China then, filial piety has become and is still important. Chan Kwok Bun reports that among the Chinese who moved to Quebec in the early 1900s, "It was not unusual for parents to write long letters to the elders overseas asking for their assistance in monitoring the moral conduct of their children,

---

[12] Alan K.L. Chan and Sor-Hoon Tan, "Introduction," *Filial Piety in Chinese Thought and History,* ed. Alan K.L. Chan and Sor-Hoon Tan (New York: RoutledgeCurzon, 2004), 2.

[13] Susan Naquin, "Funerals in North China: Uniformity and Variation," *Death Ritual in Late Imperial and Modern China,* ed. James L. Watson and Evelyn S. Rawski (Berkeley: University of California Press, 1988), 49. Also, Martin K. Whyte, "Death in the People's Republic of China," *Death Ritual in Late Imperial and Modern China,* ed. James L. Watson and Evelyn S. Rawski (Berkeley: University of California Press, 1988), 294.

and, under other circumstances, in punishing them for delinquencies and misdeeds. One such misdeed was failure on the part of the young migrant to send remittances home. Parents in China were often quick in prompting elders overseas to remind the young migrants of the importance of such old Chinese values as filial piety, obligations to ancestors, parental authority, and the primacy of the family over the individual."[14]

Further indications of the importance of filial piety to Chinese Canadians appeared in the 1960s when an organization called Gee How Oak Tin Benevolent Association was established in cities across Canada.[15] It is a clan association of three families with chapters in United States as well. The meaning of their name is "most filial association" and indicates the importance of filial piety in establishing moral values.[16][17] This name use was indicative of something greater because the first nursing home devoted to Chinese Canadian elderly was built in 1975, less than fifteen years later.

A number of recent studies have found that today filial piety remains an important value for Chinese Canadians. Daniel Lai and Shireen Surood found that in a sample collected in 2003 of 339 Chinese Canadian caregivers for elderly relatives that the traditional cultural value of filial piety is present among them. They scored a mean of 27.2 (SD=3.2) out of the possible range of 6 to 30 indicating a relatively high level of

---

[14] Chan Kwok Bun, *Smoke and Fire: The Chinese in Montreal* (Hong Kong, The Chinese University Press, 1991), 30.

[15] The website of Historical Chinese Language Materials in British Columbia lists semi-annual publications of the Vancouver chapter from the 1960s [*www.ofu.ca/davidlumcentre/hclmbc/*, accessed 2007.10.07]. The Calgary chapter was established in 1962 (*A Century of the Chinese of the Chinese in Calgary* [n.p.: United Calgary Chinese Association, 1993], 60).

[16] The Gee How Oak Tin Benevolent Association of America (*www.ghot.org/history.html*, accessed 2007.10.07).

[17] "Youzi said, 'It is rare for a man whose character is such that he is filial as a son and obedient as a young man to have the inclination to transgress against his superiors; . . . Being filial as a son and obedient as a young man is, perhaps, the root of a man's character'" (Confucius, *The Analects*, 1.2, translation, with slight modification, by D.C. Lau, 59).

acceptance among Chinese Canadian family caregivers of the value of filial piety.[18]

While Chinese culture contains strong traditions of respecting and caring for its elderly and Chinese Canadians, in general, are influenced by these traditions, there is a more personal dimension to the motivation that has led Chinese Canadians to produce the achievements they have in eldercare. Lai and Surood attribute the motivation to affection: "Chinese children tend to express love by taking care of their parent's needs."[19] Researchers Ho Hon Leung and Lynn McDonald cite examples of needing to express filial responsibility and wanting to live with one's parents in order to do so.[20] The personal dimension indicates the strength of the tradition in that it is aligned with strong affective forces.

One could argue that this tradition would be even more salient had Chinese Canadians not been discriminated against in Canada. The lateness of indications of this tradition relative to the arrival of Chinese immigrants in Canada in the late 1800s can be attributed to the inability of Chinese Canadians to form the family units within which filial piety would be practised. Because of the onerous head tax starting in 1885 and later the Chinese Exclusion Act (1923), first women, then any family members were highly restricted from joining the Chinese men already in Canada; thus, there was no way that a parent-child relationship could be created.

This changed in 1947; once Chinese Canadians could bring their spouses to Canada, they could produce the children who would be taught the values of filial piety. Later, starting in the 1960s, they would be able to bring their own parents and the conditions for practising filial piety improved even more. Then starting in the 1970s and on, Chinese Canadians became more

[18] "Filial Piety in Chinese Canadian Family Caregivers," version of paper presented to Western Social Science Association Conference 49th Annual, 2007.04.13, in Calgary, Canada.

[19] Ibid., 5.

[20] "Chinese Immigrant Women Who Care for Aging Parents," Joint Centre of Excellence on Immigration and Settlement, 2001, www.ceris.metropolis.net/Virtual%20Library/RFPReports/RFPReports.htm, accessed 2007.11.17.

assimilated into the mainstream Canadian economy.[21] The result of their assimilation into the Canadian economy has been twofold. Chinese Canadians now have at their command greater resources with which to promote their traditional values. At the same time, they have had to modify these values so as to accommodate themselves to the demands of the Canadian economy. The main change that has impacted eldercare is that increasingly there is no family member available to provide for those elders that require intensive care. There is increasing pressure for both members of the middle generation (i.e., the child of the elders with his or her spouse) to work and for older grandchildren, who could care for grandparents, to go to school and work as well.

Although this assimilation may have weakened some standard manifestations of the tradition, it does not mean that the influence of the tradition has disappeared, or even weakened. Chinese Canadian elderly still, more than the average Canadian elder, live with their children even when their spouses are alive. Nana Chappell and Karen Kusch interviewed 2,272 Chinese seniors aged fifty-five and older living in seven Canadian cities in 2001 and 2002.[22] Of these 73.8 percent reported living with their children in a multigenerational household.[23] The figure compares to the only 9 percent of Canadian older adults estimated to be living with their adult children or with other relatives.[24]

---

[21] It was not until 1967 that the universal point system that placed significant emphasis on immigrant applicant's training and occupation was instituted. Chinese Canadians had become more evenly distributed across the various economic occupations in Canada by 1971. Whereas 69 percent of Chinese Canadians were employed in the service sector in 1931, the figure had reduced to 28 percent in 1971. "In contrast, less than half of one percent of the Chinese work force in 1921 and 1931 were in professional occupations. In the census years of 1971, 1981, and 1991, professional and technical occupations constituted 18 to 19 percent of all employed Chinese." (Peter Li, *The Chinese in Canada*, second edition [Toronto: Oxford, 1998], 119-20).

[22] Neena L. Chappell and Karen Kusch, "The Gendered Nature of Filial Piety: A Study among Chinese Canadians," *Journal of Cross-Cultural Gerontology*, 22 (2007), 33.

[23] *Ibid.*, 35.

[24] *Ibid.*, 41; citing N.L. Chappell, E. Gee, L. MacDonald, and A. Stones, Aging in Contemporary Canada (Toronto: Prentice-Hall, 2003).

On the other hand, the state of eldercare is complex and one notes that many Chinese Canadian elders would also prefer other living arrangements. There are reports that many Chinese Canadian seniors who are living with their adult children would prefer not to.[25] Doman Lum *et al.* in 1980 pointed out that the American born Chinese were moving out of central city enclaves but that the elderly within their households were choosing to stay in Chinatowns where their sociocultural needs could be better met.[26]

Chan Kwok Bun has noted that some elderly Chinese Canadian women move out of intergenerational living arrangements in order to live by themselves in apartments in Montreal's Chinatown. Some of the reasons that he cites for this unconventional behaviour are intense intergenerational conflicts, particularly value differences between the more traditional grandmothers and their grandchildren. Isolation is another reason. Chan describes sons working long hours; therefore, having little time to spend with their elderly mothers, and language barriers when the elderly cannot communicate with grandchildren and neighbours. In contrast to the isolation that living in an intergenerational relationship surprisingly can create, residence in Chinatown offers "ease of communication with other residents; meeting people of same culture and background; proximity to many Chinese friends and neighbours; cheap rent; and proximity to church, community, and social services."[27] [28]

---

[25] Neena L. Chappell, "Correcting Cross-Cultural Stereotypes: Aging in Shanghai and Canada," *Journal of Cross-Cultural Gerontology* 18 (2003), 130. Chappell's reference to E.M. Gee's research findings that are reported in "Living Arrangements and Quality of Life among Chinese Canadian Elders" (*Social Indicators Research*, 51.3 (2000): 309-329) is puzzling. Gee's results show an equivalence of satisfaction and well-being for Chinese Canadian elderly whether living solely with a spouse or intergenerationally (320). However, those living intergenerationally have much higher satisfaction and greater well-being compared to those living alone (321).

[26] Doman Lum, Lucia Yim-San Cheung, Eric Ray Cho, Tze-Yee Tang, and How Bao Yau, "The Psychological Needs of the Chinese Elderly," *Social Casework: The Journal of Contemporary Social Work* 61.2 (1980), 102.

[27] *Smoke and Fire: The Chinese in Montreal*, 242-46. See also See also Kwok B. Chan, "Coping with Aging and Managing Self-Identity: The Social World of the Elderly Chinese Women," *Canadian Ethnic Studies* 15.3 (1983), 45-48.

One can see why Chinese Canadians would consider breaking with tradition and seeking out mainstream institutional care for their elderly. Unable, because of the demands of the economy and society, to provide adequate care for their elderly at home, Chinese Canadian families have been searching for means outside the family to do so. One would think that this would translate into a simple increased use of facilities, such as nursing homes, already present in the greater community. However, such is not the case. Instead, in what probably manifests a response to discrimination and dissatisfaction with prevalent eldercare standards, but is not articulated as such--at least not in an obvious manner--Chinese Canadians have been creating new and modifying old institutions in order to meet their eldercare needs.

The work of researchers supports and elaborates on the claim that the creation of new and modification of old eldercare institutions by Chinese Canadians has been motivated by a response to discrimination and dissatisfaction with prevalent eldercare standards. Ho Hon Leung and Lynn McDonald conclude from in-depth interviews with eighteen Chinese Canadian caregivers to the elderly that the "mobility, independence, and the life circle of these elderly Chinese immigrants were largely curtailed by a set of social factors such as language barriers, transportation, isolated social environments, lack of culturally and linguistically sensitive health and social services, and so on."[29] Jik-Joen Lee describes five reasons for what he sees is the underutilization of services by Asian American elderly: culturally inappropriate services, Asian values, a history of officially tolerated discrimination, organizational barriers, and social alienation.[30] Chappell, building on the research of others, induces two reasons why

[28] Chapter three of this book, "Canada's Chinatowns: From Preservation to Celebration," also discusses the attraction of Chinatowns to Chinese Canadian elderly.

[29] "Chinese Immigrant Women Who Care for Aging Parents" (Joint Centre of Excellence on Immigration and Settlement, 2001, *www.ceris.metropolis.net/Virtual%20Library/RFPReports/RFPReports.htm*, accessed 2007.11.17).

[30] Jik-Joen Lee, "Asian American Elderly: A Neglected Minority Group," *Journal of Gerontological Social Work* 9.4 (1986), 107-109.

Chinese elders do not find mainstream services suitable. One, they have been excluded from using mainstream services, and two, they prefer services that reflect their culture.[31] The views of these scholars support the general conclusion that the main reasons why Chinese Canadians would want to reform eldercare institutions relate to discrimination within these institutions and their culturally insensitive standards.

These views are further supported by specific examples. The exclusion of Chinese elderly from common social services was officially noted already in 1971. Doman Lum *et al.* state that special agencies in the United States had "identified the problem of exclusion [of Asian American elderly] from public, social, and health services that [were] presumably available to all older persons."[32] A 1987 study of provincially funded community, social, and health services in Montreal suggested to Michael J. MacLean *et al.* "that there is institutional discrimination against elderly Chinese people."[33] Sheila Cruikshank documents how language barriers and food differences create difficulties for the family caregivers of elderly Chinese in hospitals.[34]

Therefore, one finds sufficient motivation for Chinese Canadians to want to create and improve on eldercare. This motivation is complex and is seen at first blush to be a response to discrimination and inappropriate care toward Chinese Canadian elderly within the mainstream eldercare system. However, in the description of the achievements produced by Chinese Canadians that follows, one sees that traditional Chinese values toward the care of the elderly are asserting themselves as well, taking the result far beyond what would be

---

[31] Neena L. Chappell and David Lai, "Health Care Service by Chinese Seniors in British Columbia, Canada," *Journal of Cross-Cultural Gerontology*, 13 (1998), 23.

[32] P. 101, citing *Special Concerns Reports: The Asian-American Elderly* from the 1971 White House Conference on Aging.

[33] Michael J. MacLean, Nancy Siew, Dawn Fowler, and Ian Graham, "Institutional Racism in Old Age: Theoretical Perspectives and a Case Study about Access to Social Services," *Canadian Journal on Aging* 6.2 (1987), 137.

[34] Sheila Cruikshank, *Chinese Families in Supportive Care* (Master of Science dissertation, University of British Columbia, 1990), 135.

a response to discrimination and inappropriate treatment. The institutions that Chinese Canadians have consequently created are remarkable enough that one could describe them as a transition in Chinese Canadian norms and a challenge to mainstream eldercare.

3. Types of Institutions

Institutional care differs from the traditional and more common form of caring for the elderly within the family by Chinese Canadians. Its degrees of organization, professionalism, scale, self-sustenance, and ability to individualize treatment are all significantly different. There is a large amount of planning, preparation, and building required to create and operate an institution, unlike the situation in the family where the decision to care for an elder member may be spontaneous or one that occurs naturally as the children take over the upkeep of the family property leaving their parents and themselves in place. Once this situation occurs, adjustments to allow the elderly to live comfortably may be made on an *ad hoc* basis with little reference to long term planning. In the former situation there is great deal of thought that goes into the decision to provide care and what follows while in the latter it may stimulate no reflection whatsoever.

An institution requires professionals in nearly all aspects of its creation and operation. There are builders, medical experts, managers, accountants, dieticians, fund raisers, and so on. In contrast, for the family, required skills are acquired by family members in practice or in *ad hoc* efforts, and these skills normally would not reach professional caliber. There is obviously a difference of scale of operation between institutional care and care within the family. An institution is designed to care for large numbers in an ongoing operation while eldercare within the family focuses on the needs of usually one or two individuals, for a limited period of time.

Care of the elderly is the primary function of the institution, so it derives its livelihood from this activity. Fees are paid directly to the institution in exchange for the service it provides to the elderly. Within the family, in contrast, there is no direct exchange of resources in the provision of the care. The care providers may inherit property from the care recipients, but not as a necessary condition for providing the care.

Furthermore, the family does not rely on eldercare as a means to continue in existence. Finally, the institution in its goal to provide standardized care, in order to ensure both quality and profit, is limited in its ability to individualize this care. The family, on the other hand, assumes individualized care as a given. One is caring for an individual who has particular needs and abilities that should be catered to.

Needless to say, the creation, and even the use of institutional eldercare within the Chinese Canadian community is a novel development. Given its novelty and the large differences between what has been their tradition and norm, i.e., family-based eldercare, and their amazing accomplishments in creating institutional eldercare, there is the potential for developing promising forms of eldercare that not only serve their own community well, but also offer alternatives to mainstream care providers. In an effort to bridge the large gap between what has been and is the norm and the criteria that an institution must meet, one is seeing the development of institutions with Chinese Canadian characteristics, characteristics that as of yet have not had prominent presence in Canada.

The institutions that Chinese Canadians are developing can be roughly grouped into two types. First, there are those that provide direct support to seniors in order to allow them to remain independent longer and to their families in order to facilitate care for them within the home. Their focus on preserving independence is what mostly distinguishes them from the second type, nursing homes whose mandate is more to make the elderly comfortable once they are no longer able to be independent. The former institution, for example the Calgary Chinese Elderly Citizens' Association, offers a wide range of services such as outreach, medical checkups, daycare, education, and reading rooms. These programs are usually limited to day programs and often are run by clients themselves. Subsequently, the number of salaried staff in this type of institution is much smaller than in nursing homes. The second type of institution, long-term nursing homes, is exemplified in facilities built and managed by Yee Hong. However, the latter differs from mainstream nursing homes in having defining Chinese characteristics.

Earlier examples of institutions serving senior Chinese appeared in the United States. In 1969 an evening clinic for

Chinese American patients was set up in Tufts-New England Medical Center in Boston.[35] In 1972 the Boston Chinese Community Health Center was opened.[36] A Chinese American senior day health center was opened in San Francisco in 1973.[37] About this time, meals, including home delivery of such, were provided, as was an adult daycare center, for Chinese American seniors in Boston.[38] These examples would have been studied by Chinese Canadians who were planning to launch similar programs.

As it was, Chinese Canadians established institutional facilities for their elderly not long after the Americans. The first Chinese Canadian nursing home was built by the Mon Sheong Foundation in 1975. It started with 65 long-term care beds and offered staff, environment, and culinary service catering to Chinese Canadians in Toronto. Since then Mon Sheong has added two other sites and 392 beds for a total of 457 long term care beds.[39] It was the beginning of achievements in providing both types of care.

4. Yee Hong: Improving Eldercare for Chinese Canadians

4.1 Overview and Founder

Yee Hong is an impressive example of what Chinese Canadians have been able to accomplish in the field of eldercare. This organization was founded in 1987 in order to create culturally and linguistically sensitive eldercare for Chinese seniors in Toronto who were not receiving this kind of treatment in the facilities that existed for them then. The

---

[35] Charlotte Ikels, *Aging and Adaption: Chinese in Hong Kong and the United States* (Hamden, Connecticut: Archon, 1983), 236.

[36] *Ibid.*

[37] *Ibid.*, 236.

[38] *Ibid.*, 233-34 and 237.

[39] "Mon Sheong Long-term Care Centres," Mon Sheong website, *www.monsheong.org/msf2/eng/index.php/27-ltc/27-homeforaged*, accessed 2014.09.29.

organization has since developed into one that manages more than eight hundred beds in nursing homes at four different sites, as well a broad network of community-based services for seniors. The Chinese characters that "Yee Hong" stands for separately mean "to cultivate" and "healthy." Together they mean "to cultivate health." Yee Hong's mission is to enable seniors to live their lives to the fullest.

Yee Hong's founding chairman is Joseph Wong. Wong was born in Hong Kong in 1948. He began practising family medicine in Toronto in late 1982. His community service work began in 1979 when he was serving refugees from Vietnam. Motivated by the pleas of elderly Chinese Canadians whose institutional care was not alleviating their suffering, he founded Yee Hong. He has since received numerous awards, such as the Order of Canada in 1993 and an honorary Doctorate of Science degree from the University of Toronto in 1992, for his efforts.

4.2 History of Yee Hong

The Yee Hong Centre for Geriatric Care, formerly known as the Chinese Community Nursing Home for Greater Toronto, was conceived after Wong noticed the lack of emotional support for and communication between Chinese seniors and staff within mainstream medical facilities. In 1987 he gathered thirty Chinese Canadian friends to develop his vision of establishing a nursing home that would cater to the specific needs of their parents and grandparents. These efforts came to fruition in 1994 when the Yee Hong Centre for Geriatric Care was officially opened in Scarborough, part of Metropolitan Toronto. This centre, subsequently, embarked on an eight million dollar expansion in November 1996 that added two floors and sixty-five long term care beds.[40] The facility presently has one hundred fifty-five beds.[41]

Another milestone was reached when in December 1999 the Canadian Council on Health Services Accreditation, a national body that scrutinizes and gives accreditation to health facilities

---

[40] "About Us/Our Story," Yee Hong website, *www.yeehong.com/foundation/index.php*, accessed 2007.10.10.

[41] "How it All Started," Yee Hong website, *www.yeehong.com/centre/story.php*, accessed 2014.09.29.

all over Canada, authorized another three-year license to the just expanded facility. In awarding this accreditation, the council praised Yee Hong for providing "stellar care" to elderly members of the Chinese population in Scarborough.[42]

Between 1998 and 2001, the Ministry of Health awarded Yee Hong Centre a total of seven hundred fifteen bed licences, which was the largest allocation of its kind to a nonprofit organization in the history of Ontario. The Yee Hong Centre Capital Campaign began 1999 with the goal of soliciting support to build three new Yee Hong Centres housing two hundred beds in each of Markham and Mississauga and two hundred fifty in Scarborough. Originally designed to meet the needs of Chinese Canadian seniors, their services have now been extended to non-Chinese seniors, particularly those of the South Asian, Filipino, and Japanese communities.[43] The Markham centre was completed in 2002, the Mississauga centre in 2004, and the second Scarborough centre in 2004.

All four Yee Hong Centres were awarded full accreditation for 2007-09 by the Canadian Council on Health Services Accreditation and since 2004 Yee Hong has been operating a total of eight hundred five long term care beds and servicing more than ten thousand individuals from different ethnic communities in Greater Toronto and the surrounding areas.[44]

4.3 Yee Hong's Services

Yee Hong offers a number of services that together are comprehensive in meeting seniors' needs. Yee Hong's main function is to provide long term nursing care. This service includes twenty-four hour nursing, personal care, and access to an attending physician. There are also daily social, recreational, therapeutic, and religious programs.[45]

---

[42] "About Us/Our Story," Yee Hong website.

[43] "Yee Hong Centre for Geriatric Care: A Special Marketing Supplement Prepared for the Yee Hong Community Wellness Foundation," *The Globe and Mail*, 2001.04.23, Y2.

[44] "Yee Hong Centre for Geriatric Care," Yee Hong website, *www.yeehong.com/foundation/index.php*, accessed 2007.10.10.

[45] "Long Term Care," Yee Hong website, *www.yeehong.com/centre/long-term_care.php*, accessed 2014.09.29.

Another major function of Yee Hong, especially in meeting the needs of seniors residing outside of their nursing homes, is providing community services. These include an adult day program, social dining, transportation, visitation, caregiver support, client intervention, and support for independent living. They take a client-centered and a holistic approach to care.[46]

There is much more demand for Yee Hong's services than what the four nursing homes can provide, which is evidenced in the long waiting lists for admittance.[47] The provision of community services is a way of meeting this need. An example of the latter is Congregate Dining; it is designed to bring seniors living outside nursing homes, who would otherwise be isolated, together for meals and activities. Yee Hong utilizes the occasion of a meal to provide for other more complex needs as well.

Yee Hong also provides medical services. Besides the obvious needs of nursing home residents and the local communities, Yee Hong meets special medical needs through the Memory Program and Cancer and Palliative Care Services. The Memory Program is claimed to be "the first and only memory program offering Chinese and English cognitive tests in the Greater Toronto Region."[48] At one time Yee Hong was offering a cancer and palliative care program claimed to be the first-of-its-kind and innovative in allowing home hospice,

---

[46] "Community Services," Yee Hong website, *www.yeehong.com/centre/community_services.php*, accessed 2014.09.29.

[47] In February 2006, Joseph Wong reported to the Legislative Assembly of Ontario that "The waiting list now for the four Yee Hong centres totals more than 1,000 people. Although we have less than 1 percent of the total beds in the province, our waiting lists consist of more than 30 percent of the total waiting list of the whole province" (Legislative Assembly of Ontario, "Standing Committee on Social Policy, Local Health System Integration Act, 2006," *Official Report of Debates [Hansard]*, 2006.02.06, p. 350). More recently, the waiting period to enter the Yee Hong Geriatric Care Centre in Mississauga has been more than five years and for Yee Hong's Scarborough-McNicoll location, ten years (Dakshana Bascaramurty, "Ethnic-focused Nursing Homes Put a Canadian Face on Filial Piety," *The Globe* and *Mail*, 2012.01.27).

[48] "Medical Services," Yee Hong website, *www.yeehong.com/centre/medical_services.php#1*, accessed 2014.09.29.

delivering "care to terminally ill patients and their families in their own homes."[49]

Yee Hong also provides rehabilitation services. In keeping with its policy of being client-centered, besides the common treatments of physiotherapy and occupational therapy, services include culturally specific techniques, such as acupuncture and shiatsu.[50]

There are also housing services. The Yee Hong Garden Terrace with three hundred eight residential units promotes independent living while allowing access to the facilities of the Yee Hong Scarborough Finch Centre, a long term care facility.[51] The Aw Chan Kam Chee Evergreen Manor meets an economic need with a supply of subsidized housing. Of the one hundred thirty units of seniors apartments and twenty-six units of three-bedroom townhouses, one hundred twenty-two apartments and twenty-two townhouse units are offered to people who meet the requirements for Rent-Geared-to-Income assistance.[52]

4.4 Achievements

Yee Hong has been able to produce a number of noteworthy achievements out of its years of mobilization, planning, and operation. Firstly, they have proven the merit of and put into practice the value of culturally and linguistically sensitive care for the elderly, particularly for Chinese Canadians. Originally, the Ontario government had been unwilling to fund this type of eldercare. It took the founder Joseph Wong years of effort to persuade them to do so. Now the

---

[49] "About Us/Our Story," Yee Hong website.

[50] "Yee Hong Centre for Geriatric Care" (pamphlet), post 2012, www.yeehong.com/centre/pdf/YHGenBro%28E%29.pdf, accessed 2014.09.29.

[51] "Yee Hong Garden Terrace - Harmonious Living in Balance with Nature," Yee Hong website, *www.yeehong.com/centre/lifelease_housing.php*, accessed 2014.09, 29.

[52] "Subsidized Housing - Aw Chan Kam Chee Evergreen Manor," Yee Hong website, www.yeehong.com/centre/subsidized_housing.php, accessed 2014.09.29. Rent-Geared-to-Income is an Ontario government program whereby financial assistance given to a housing provider so that a qualified household can pay rent based on their income.

service is offered to not only Chinese Canadians, but also to South Asian, Japanese, Filipino, and Portuguese Canadians.[53]

A second achievement of note are the physical facilities that have been put been put in place. There are the four centres with more than eight hundred long term nursing care beds. Besides the property and buildings that have been developed and constructed to house these beds, Yee Hong has built two major residential complexes with a total of four hundred sixty-four units. There are also the offices, equipment, and communications that have set up to support community, rehabilitation, and medical services.

Also noteworthy is Yee Hong's ability to motivate community support. The Yee Hong Community Wellness Foundation is Yee Hong's fundraising, communications, and public relations arm. Yee Hong is required to raise 2.5 million dollars a year to cover its operation expenses and to accumulate capital to construct new centres.[54] As for volunteers, it is estimated that Yee Hong has benefitted from the contribution of more than one thousand service volunteers each year. Between 1995 and 2010, they contributed more than one million hours of service.[55]

A fourth noteworthy achievement is the large number of awards and amount of recognition that Yee Hong has garnered. These are too numerous to list, many of them volunteer awards, but some of the more exceptional ones include the Ontario Non-Profit Housing Association's Award for Excellence (1997) and recognition by The Toronto Commandery of the Order of St. Lazarus for Dr. Stanley Zheng, Director of Cancer and Palliative Care Services for the Yee Hong Centre in Scarborough.[56] "Florence Wong, retired CEO of the Yee Hong Centre for Geriatric Care, was one of the two civilians who received the inaugural 2008 International Women's Day Award

---

[53] Legislative Assembly of Ontario, 350.

[54] "Yee Hong Community Wellness Foundation," Yee Hong website, *www.yeehong.com/foundation/index.php*, accessed 2014.09.29.

[55] "Volunteer and Make a Difference," *www.yeehong.com/centre/volunteer.php*, accessed 2014.09.29.

[56] "Awards and Accreditation," Yee Hong website, *www.yeehong.com/foundation/index.php*, accessed 2007.10.10.

presented by the Toronto Police Service." As well, the Indo-Canada Chamber of Commerce, representing 1,000 business and professional members across Canada, honoured Ben Sennik, member of Yee Hong Foundation's Board of Directors, with the Lifetime Achievement Award on June 10, 2006. Among other achievements, Mr. Sennik was instrumental in helping establish the South Asian wing at the Yee Hong Ho Lai Oi Wan Centre. Nevertheless, the main accolade earned by Yee Hong is the continued accreditation that it has received from the Canadian Council on Health Services Accreditation. In 2012 "all four Yee Hong Centres and Social Services received Accreditation with Exemplary Standing for 2012-2016—the highest honour and recognition awarded by Accreditation Canada for an organization's commitment to Quality and Excellence. This has been the sixth consecutive time that the Yee Hong Centre received full accreditation since it began operation in 1994."[57]

4.5 Broader Influences

The achievements of Yee Hong have created impacts that go far beyond the walls and functioning of Yee Hong's facilities and services. Firstly, Yee Hong has become a model for other eldercare facilities in cities across Canada, even the world. It was reported in 2001 that Yee Hong Centre was visited on a weekly basis by various delegations wanting to learn from Yee Hong's achievements.[58] Chinese Canadian populations in other cities facing the same situation that the founders of Yee Hong had, have learned from them. Subsequent to Yee Hong's initial success in 1994, facilities designed for Chinese Canadian elders were opened in Vancouver (Simon KY Lee Senior Care Home, 2001), Calgary (Wing Kei Care Centre, 2005), and Edmonton (Edmonton Chinatown Care Centre, 2004). Yee Hong's model has also been adopted in Hong Kong where the Hong Kong Rehabilitation Society and the Hong Kong Jockey Club have established Yee Hong Heights Charity,

---

[57] "Awards and Accreditation," Yee Hong website, *www.yeehong.com/centre/awards.php*, accessed 2014.09.29.

[58] "Yee Hong Provides Model for Other Groups," *The Globe and Mail*, 2001.04.23, Y2.

a care home for the elderly that is modeled on the Yee Hong
Centre of Geriatric Care in Canada.[59]

Second, the concepts, standards, and goals established by
Yee Hong have challenged accepted thinking, thereby fostering
progress in the development of standards of care for elders. As
Joseph Wong reported to the Standing Committee on Social
Policy of the Legislative Assembly of Ontario: "It took me more
than three years, from 1987 to 1990, to convince the Ministry of
Health and Long-Term Care that the needs of seniors of
different cultural diversity in Ontario really do require special
treatment."[60] Initially, the Ontario government opposed
granting bed licenses to Yee Hong on the grounds that it would
be discriminatory against non-Chinese Canadians; however,
Yee Hong appealed to the Human Rights Commission and was,
subsequently, allowed to proceed. Ironically, one of the results
of Yee Hong's success in providing culturally-sensitive eldercare
was that the Ontario government asked Yee Hong to open three
other similar care facilities.[61] Part of the reason for the
government changing its policy would have been the improved
conditions in Yee Hong's care. It routinely scores "lower rates of
depression, falls, skin ulcers, and hospitalizations among its
residents, compared with those living in mainstream homes."
For example, "25.1 percent of Ontario nursing home residents
reported worsened mood from symptoms of depression after
admission. At Yee Hong, the average is 3.35 percent."[62]

A third broad influence sparked by Yee Hong is the spread
of culturally-sensitive eldercare beyond the Chinese Canadian
community. Yee Hong's centres provide this kind of care to
South Asian, Filipino, and Japanese Canadians. The value of
culturally-sensitive eldercare is shared by these communities.
Furthermore, while Chinese Canadians use 50 percent of the
services provided by Yee Hong, they contribute 85 percent of

[59] *Ibid.* and "Yee Hong Heights/Long Term Care/Our Services/Introduction to
HKSR," Yee Hong website, *www.rehabsociety.org.hk/english.html*, accessed
2007.10.19.

[60] Legislative Assembly of Ontario, 350.

[61] Joseph Wong, public lecture, 2001.05.05 at the Calgary Chinatown Senior's
Centre in Calgary, Alberta.

[62] Bascaramurty, "Ethnic-focused Nursing Homes."

the funding and 95 percent of the time.[63] This includes raising thirty million of the one hundred ten million dollars required to fund the construction of the care centres.[64] Their goal is not only to provide care for Chinese Canadian elders, but also to make this care available for other ethnic groups.

The fourth major influence that Yee Hong is having is through the innovations that it has created and implemented in its operations, besides the development of culturally-sensitive eldercare. The first innovation is in the unique services that it offers. These include daycare for seniors, home visitations for shut-ins, and culturally orientated food services. A specific example is the Hospice Care Services (formerly known as Cancer and Palliative Care Services). Inaugurated in 1997, physicians were delivering care to terminally ill patients and their families in their own homes.[65] Another innovation is intensive fundraising for seniors, which has increased the acceptability of fundraising for them. Prior to these efforts by Yee Hong, seniors were under represented in this area.[66] An even further innovation is allowing couples who may not both be suitable for nursing home care to live close together, one in a nursing home and another is a senior's apartment.[67]

Yee Hong has also been very innovative in designing housing for seniors. At one point it provided senior housing in proximity to nursing home facilities so that seniors could live independently while being able to partake in the services offered by Yee Hong Centre for Geriatric Care.[68] Yee Hong still owns and manages senior housing complexes in the vicinity of its nursing homes in order to provide both affordable housing for seniors and a continuum of health and social services that

---

[63] Joseph Wong, interview, 2001.06.01, Toronto, Canada. The author assumes that Wong is referring to non-governmental funding and volunteer time.

[64] *Ibid.*

[65] "About Us/Our Story," Yee Hong website.

[66] Joseph Wong, interview, 2003.06.27, Calgary, Canada.

[67] Judy Creighton, "Chinese Geriatric Centre Keeps Spouses Together," Canadian Press NewsWire, 1997.09.16.

[68] Yee Hong Garden Terrace, *www.yeehong.com/centre/gardenterrace/index.html*, accessed 2007.10.19.

enables seniors to live independently in their own homes for as long as possible.[69] Yee Hong is also involved in private initiatives. Villa Elegance, a condominium designed for seniors jointly by Tridel, a large builder of condominiums, and Yee Hong is an example of how a charitable organization and a private business can work together in order to meet the housing needs of seniors.[70]

Another innovation is seen in the variety of methods that Yee Hong utilizes to fundraise. It has set the precedent of having eBay host a charity auction for a condominium suite.[71] It also offers endowment funds and affinity credit cards.[72]

Yee Hong has been a pioneer in the development of services for Chinese Canadian seniors. In this role, it has raised the standards of eldercare for Chinese Canadian seniors, and in doing so should be having a widespread impact on mainstream eldercare.

5. Other Institutions

While Yee Hong has produced the most notable achievement by Chinese Canadians in the area of eldercare, there are smaller institutions that are also noteworthy. Chinese eldercare is very much tied to the local community and to the elderly of that community. Therefore, its scale of operations is often relatively small. The institutions that offer this care are likewise small, and it is the needs of their community, composed of family, friends, neighbours, and those of a similar background with which they are most familiar. These organizations are also, almost without exception, nonprofit, so their purpose is solely to assist others and often this can be accomplished satisfactorily enough within the local community.

---

[69] "Subsidized Housing - Aw Chan Kam Chee Evergreen Manor," Yee Hong website, *www.yeehong.com/centre/subsidized_housing.php*, 2014.09.29.

[70] "Our Story," Yee Hong website, *www.yeehong.com/centre/story.php*, accessed 2014.09.30.

[71] "eBay Canada helps Yee Hong build caring," *communitypages.ebay.ca/community/aboutebay/releases/0303.html#2Ibid*, accessed 2014.09.30.

[72] "Yee Hong Community Wellness Foundation."

Even Yee Hong, with its worldwide influence, is an organization that caters to the needs of elderly in only the Toronto area. It is because Chinese Canadian eldercare is determined so much by local circumstances--the needs of the elderly and the resources available there--that one finds institutions that have very much a local identity,

One sees the connection to the local community in the description of various institutions that follows. The institutions that will be described include the Hôpital Chinois de Montréal Pavillon Sung Pai; the Mon Sheong Foundation and the Carefirst Seniors & Community Services Association Centre, both in Toronto; the Sek On Toi in Winnipeg; the Chinese Elders' Mansion, the Edmonton Chinese Seniors Lodge, and the Edmonton Chinatown Care Centre, all in Edmonton; the Calgary Chinese Elderly Citizens Association and Wing Kei Care Centre of Calgary; the Simon KY Lee Senior Care Home, the Austin Harris Residence, Chieng's Adult Day Care Centre, Harmony House, Villa Cathay Care Home, all of Vancouver; and the most westerly, the Victoria Chinatown Care Centre. These will be described along with various housing projects.

5.1 Hôpital Chinois de Montréal Pavillon Sung Pai (Montreal Chinese Hospital)

The Montreal Chinese Hospital was opened in 1920 after the Chinese community acquired a synagogue and converted it to a hospital. Between 1922-45, the Hospital was entirely financed by donations from the Chinese community.[73] The present building was constructed in 1999 in Montreal's Chinatown and contains one hundred twenty-eight beds.[74] The hospital's goal is to accommodate elderly patients and its services are particularly adapted to those with Chinese or Southeast Asian backgrounds.[75]

---

[73] Huguette Turcotte, "Hospitals for Chinese in Canada: Montreal (1918) and Vancouver (1921)," *Canadian Catholic Historical Association Historical Studies*, 70 (2004), 133.

[74] "History," Montreal Chinese Hospital website, *www.montrealchinesehospital.ca/history.html*, accessed 2014.10.01.

[75] "Our Mission," Montreal Chinese Hospital website, www.montrealchinesehospital.ca/ourmission.html, accessed 2014.10.01.

5.2 Mon Sheong Foundation[76]

Mon Sheong Foundation built the first Chinese Canadian nursing home in Canada in 1975. Since then, it too, like Yee Hong, has achieved much in the area Chinese Canadian eldercare. The original facility is downtown Toronto has been expanded from sixty-five beds to the present one hundred five beds. In 2000, Mon Sheong Foundation obtained permission from the Ontario Ministry of Health to open long-term care beds within the Greater Toronto area. Since then the foundation has built two new long-term care centers with one hundred ninety-two beds in Richmond Hill (2003) and one hundred sixty beds in Scarborough (2004). In total the foundation is operating four hundred fifty-seven long term care beds.

Since then, Mon Sheong has branched into building and operation of senior housing. Scarborough Mon Sheong Court was completed in 2008 and contains two hundred forty two suites. Richmond Hill Mon Sheong Court, which commenced occupancy in 2010, will have more than three hundred senior apartments upon completion. Markham Mon Sheong Court will provide four hundred fifty suites and is expecting to be completed in 2016.[77]

5.3 Carefirst Seniors & Community Services Association

The Carefirst Seniors & Community Services Association began in 1976, so ranks as one of the longest operating agencies providing for Chinese Canadian seniors. It is situated in Toronto. It began with delivering meals and

---

[76] According to the Mon Sheong Foundation website, Mon Sheong was a man of legendary generosity who lived in China around 300 B.C.E. ("Mon Sheong Foundation–Profile," Mon Sheong Foundation website, *wwww.monsheong.org/msf2/eng/index.php/1-foundation/2-history*, accessed 2014.10.01).

[77] Contents of this section are taken from "Mon Sheong Foundation–Profile," Mon Sheong Foundation website, *wwww.monsheong.org/msf2/eng/index.php/1-foundation/2-history*, accessed 2014.10.01.

expanded to assist more than six thousand elders and disabled annually. It now has three hundred fifty employees and twelve hundred volunteers and serves sixty-five hundred clients a year.[78] It offers home care, housing services, adult daycare, health education, transportation, meals, interpretation, and so on out of nine service centres across the Greater Toronto Area.[79]

5.4 Sek On Toi Senior Citizens' Home

As part of efforts to rebuild Winnipeg's inner city, including Chinatown, the Chinese United Church erected the Sek On Toi Senior Citizens' Home in 1978. It is an eleven-story, eighty-eight unit building that cost $2.5 million to build.[80]

5.5 Chinese Elders' Mansion and Edmonton Chinatown Care Centre

The Chinese Elders' Mansion was constructed to provide housing and support for Chinese elders in Edmonton. The first tower was completed in 1977 in Edmonton's Chinatown. It cost $2.5 million to build, is twelve stories high, and contains ninety-two suites. It included a wing for recreational activities, a library, four recreation halls, and a landscaped inner court.[81] The second tower was ten-stories, cost $7.2 million to build, and was completed in 1991.[82]

This two-tower complex has been managed by the China Benevolent Association (CBA) who have taken the leading role in providing eldercare for Edmonton's Chinese. They also built

[78] "About us," Carefirst Seniors & Community Services Association website, www.carefirstseniors.com/websites/content.php?id=1, accessed 2014.10.01.

[79] "Carefirst's Services," Carefirst Seniors & Community Services Association website, *www.carefirstseniors.com/websites/content.php?id=2*, accessed 2014.10.01.

[80] Paul Yee, *Chinatown: An Illustrated History of the Chinese Communities of Victoria, Vancouver, Calgary, Winnipeg, Toronto, Ottawa, Montreal and Halifax* (Toronto: James Lorimer, 2005), 75.
[81] Brian Dawson, *Mooncakes in Gold Mountain: From China to the Canadian Plains* (Calgary: Detselig, 1991), 181.

[82] David Chuenyan Lai, "Three Chinatowns" in *Edmonton the Life of a City*, ed. Bob Hesketh and Frances Swyripa (Edmonton: NuWest Press, 1995), 262.

the Edmonton Chinese Seniors' Lodge in 1993 and it provides weekly housekeeping services, three Chinese meals per day, recreation programs, and Chinese-English speaking staff twenty-fours a day for eighty clients.[83] Then in 2004 they built the Edmonton Chinatown Care Centre that provides assisted living and continuing care to seventy-five long-term care and fifteen assisted-living residents. In 2006, there were one hundred twenty-seven staff and eighty-one volunteers who contributed 7,747 hours of time.[84] Presently CBA is planning to replace the three-story Edmonton Chinese Seniors' Lodge with a twenty-eight story, three-hundred-sixty-unit, mixed use condominium that would continue to serve Chinese elders as well as encourage young professionals into the area.[85]

5.6 Calgary Chinese Elderly Citizens' Association (CCECA)

CCECA is one of those institutions whose main purpose is to promote the independence of Chinese Canadian elderly. This purpose is seen in their strong outreach and educational programs. It began in 1985 with twenty-four members and a plan to construct what would become the Calgary Chinatown Seniors' Centre. The centre was subsequently opened in 1995.[86]

The Calgary Chinatown Seniors' Centre is said to be the only facility of its kind in Canada, that is a stand-alone structure catering solely to the elderly and primarily serving Chinese Canadians. The area of the building is fourteen hundred square meters. The construction costs were 7.7 million

---

[83] "Our Story," China Benevolent Association website, www.edmccc.net/aboutus.htm, accessed 2014.10.03; and "Edmonton Chinese Seniors Lodge (Seniors Lodge)," China Benevolent Association website, *www.edmccc.net/seniorslodge.htm*, accessed 2014.10.03.

[84] Edmonton Chinatown Care Centre website, *www.edmccc.net/*, accessed 2007.11.29.

[85] Kristin Annable, "Chinese Seniors Lodge Residents 'Unsettled' by Condo Proposal," *Edmonton Journal*, 2013.05.28.

[86] "Looking Back the Twenty Unforgettable Years . . . .," in *Calgary Chinese Elderly Citizens' Association 20th Anniversary Supplement* (Calgary, Calgary Chinese Elderly Citizens' Association, 1996), 49-57.

dollars. Except for twenty-five thousand dollars, it all was raised within the Chinese community.[87] Li Ka Shing, Chairman of Hutchison Whampoa Limited and Cheung Kong Holdings in Hong Kong, donated four hundred thousand dollars in 1991.[88] The City of Calgary donated land for the building. Sixty percent of the maintenance costs are paid for by the community. Services provided include outreach programs, education, health maintenance, social activities, daycare for special-need clients, and meals.[89] There were more than one hundred twenty-thousand client contacts in 2012.[90]

The outreach programs are well developed. They include home and hospital visitations, intra-community support groups, transportation, interpretation, and meal delivery.[91] Education programs include English, computer literacy, cooking, and Chinese culture. There is also a library in the centre. Health services, such as blood and urine tests, mammograms, and blood pressure monitoring are very popular. Social activities include choir, travel, birthday parties, and gardening. The daycare program brings in groups of ten special need seniors at a time; a group will usually come twice a week. One on one contact is provided as well as a hot lunch. Meals are also provided through Meals on Wheels to Chinese elders throughout Calgary.[92] As is the case with Yee Hong, CCECA is

---

[87] Liza Chan, Program Director, Calgary Chinese Elderly Citizens' Association (presentation 2007.02.07, Calgary, Alberta).

[88] "A Review of Five Years Work of F.E.E.C.S.R." in *Kaimu tekan, Jianada Yaboda sheng, Kacheng Huafu Laoying Zongxin* (Special Inauguration Publication, Grand Opening of the Calgary Chinatown Seniors' Centre, Alberta, Canada) (Calgary, Calgary Chinese Elderly Citizens' Association, 1996), 31.

[89] Liza Chan.

[90] "2012 Programs Statistics," Calgary Chinese Elderly Citizens' Association website, *www.cceca.ca/english/report.html*, accessed 2014.10.02.

[91] *Ibid.* The cost in 2014 was $5.25 a meal, which included rice, meat, and vegetables.

[92] Contents of this paragraph based on presentation by Liza Chan, Program Director, Calgary Chinese Elderly Citizens' Association (2007.02.07, Calgary, Alberta) and CCECA website (*www3.telus.net/cceca*, accessed 2007.11.27).

able to rely on a large bevy of volunteers who contributed 34,159 hours of effort in 2006.[93]

5.7 Wing Kei Care Centre

The Wing Kei Care Centre is an aesthetically pleasing facility that was opened in 2005 in Calgary and is situated in the Calgary core close to Chinatown. It has an area of ninety-three hundred square meters spread over more than five floors. The cost for construction of the building was eighteen million dollars.[94] It has 135 beds and in 2006 there were 160 staff.[95] In 2011, 313 individuals and 11 groups contributed 16,359 volunteer hours to Wing Kei.[96]

Wing Kei started providing care in a partnership arrangement with Bethany Care Society in 1996 when a section of thirty-beds was designated the Wing Kei Villa for Chinese seniors then residing in Bethany Care Centre.[97] This was the first attempt to serve the Chinese seniors of Bethany centre with Chinese programs and food.[98] After its opening, Wing Kei received approval from Calgary Health Region to function as an independent care provider in March 2006.[99] Wing Kei has since

---

[93] *Calgary Chinese Elderly Citizens' Association Annual Report* (Calgary, CCECA, 2007), 5.

[94] *Wing Kei Care Centre Grand Opening Publication* (Calgary: Chinese Christian Wing Kei Nursing Home Association, 2005), 19.

[95] *Chinese Christian Wing Kei Nursing Home Association 2006 Annual Report,* Wing Kei website, *www.wingkeicarecentre.org/aboutus.htm,* accessed 2007.11.28.

[96] *Chinese Christian Wing Kei Nursing Home Association 2012 Annual Report,* Wing Kei website, *www.wingkeicarecentre.org/images/AnnualReports/WingKei-AnnualReport2012.pdf,* accessed 2014.10.02.

[97] *Wing Kei Care Centre Grand Opening Publication,* 31. Chinese Canadian elderly continue to use this wing in Bethany Care Centre because Wing Kei's new facility is full.

[98] *Ibid.,* 31.

[99] *Chinese Christian Wing Kei Nursing Home Association 2005 Annual Report,* 5.

added an adult day program where elders living at home visit the centre to participate in a variety of activities. Wing Kei also opened a ninety-five-bed, supported living facility called Wing Kei Greenview in October 2014. Much of the total cost of twenty-four million dollars for building the facility will come from donations.[100]

5.8 Simon KY Lee Senior Care Home

The Simon K.Y. Lee Seniors Care Home in Vancouver is a multi-level care facility that admitted its first residents in September 2001. Its area of sixty-five hundred square meters is distributed over three stories. There are one hundred three beds in ninety-eight private rooms. Twenty-one beds are designated for cognitively impaired residents who require special environmental adaptations. The other beds are for complex care residents. The home is located in the area of Vancouver's downtown Chinatown.[101]

The home is one of a number of facilities, including Austin Harris Residence, Chieng's Adult Day Care Centre, and Harmony House, that are managed by S.U.C.C.E.S.S. in Vancouver.[102] S.U.C.C.E.S.S. also publishes a monthly Chinese newsletter *Evergreen News* (*Songhe tiandi*) that used to target Chinese elderly and now targets Chinese immigrants in

---

[100] "Programs and Services," Wing Kei website, *www.wingkeicarecentre.org/programs-services*, accessed 2014.10.02.

[101] Contents of this paragraph taken from "Simon K.Y. Lee Seniors Care Home," S.U.C.C.E.S.S. website, *www.successbc.ca/eng/services/multi-level-care-society/simon-k-y-lee-seniors-care-home*, accessed 2014.10.03

[102] S.U.C.C.E.S.S. stands for the United Chinese Community Enrichment Services Society and is a multi-service agency in British Columbia, Canada. It was established in 1973 to promote the well being of all Canadians and immigrants. Its services include to assist "new immigrants with settlement; provide counseling and support to families and individuals with personal issues; promote personal development of children and youth; facilitate social participation of parents and seniors in the community; help the unemployed in job and career development; facilitate entrepreneurs in business development; deliver education and employment related training; and promote social change through community development and advocacy." (S.U.C.C.E.S.S. website, *www.successbc.ca/eng/*, accessed 2014.10.03).

general, though the affairs of the Chinese elderly remain an important concern.[103]

5.9 Austin Harris Residence

The Austin Harris Residence is a fifty-unit subsidized, assisted living facility opened in 2007 in Richmond, a suburb of Vancouver. Each unit is self-contained with a kitchen and so on, and within the complex there is a common dining room, a library, a spa, and a laundry. Total usable floor area is about forty-nine hundred square meters in a two-storey building. Outdoors there is a landscaped garden of about eighteen hundred and fifty square meters. The estimated cost of the residence was $15.5 million.[104]

5.10 Chieng's Adult Day Care Centre

The Chieng's Adult Day Care Centre started operation in January 2003 in Vancouver. The centre provides respite care for medically frail seniors or those with dementia and chronic disease who are being cared for at home by family members. Its program also offers lunch, recreational activities, health monitoring, and health education for seniors. Twenty or more seniors are served each weekday. Its physical facilities include a lounge, an activity area, a kitchen, a dining room, a meeting room, and a quiet room. It is attached to the Simon KY Lee Senior Care Home in the area of Vancouver's downtown Chinatown.[105]

5.11 Harmony House

---

[103] *Evergreen News* has published monthly since 1985. Its circulation is about eight thousand copies ("Services/Publications," S.U.C.C.E.S.S. website, *www.successbc.ca/eng/services/publications/evergreen-news*, accessed 2014.10.03).

[104] Contents of this paragraph taken from "Austin Harris Residence," S.U.C.C.E.S.S. website, *www.successbc.ca/eng/services/multi-level-care-society/austin-harris-residence*, accessed 2014.10.04.

[105] Contents of this paragraph taken from "Chieng's Adult Day Centre," *www.successbc.ca/eng/services/multi-level-care-society/chieng-s-adult-day-centre*, accessed 2014.10.04.

Harmony House, which opened in 2006, is a subsidized assisted living facility in the first four stories of a newly built high rise condominium in Vancouver. There are nineteen studios and fourteen one bedroom suites containing kitchen and laundry appliances. Chinese meals are served regularly. It is located next to Simon KY Lee Senior Care Home in the area of Vancouver's downtown Chinatown.[106]

5.12 Villa Cathay Care Home

Villa Cathay Care Home in Vancouver was opened in 1978 and claims to be the largest full service Chinese care home in North America with more than four thousand square meters of space, one hundred eighty-eight beds, and one hundred twenty-five staff. Staff refer to residents with titles such as "Uncle Wong" and "Auntie Chow," reflecting the respect they are given.[107]

5.13 Victoria Chinatown Care Centre

The Victoria Chinatown Care Centre, built by Victoria's Chinese community on a site of the old Chinese hospital,[108] was opened in 1982 on a site where there had been over a century of medical care for the Chinese Canadian community. It is home to thirty-one residents with a long waiting list, so there are plans for expansion. It is unique in offering multicultural, language-sensitive services in Greater Victoria.[109]

---

[106] Contents of this paragraph taken from "Harmony House," S.U.C.C.E.S.S. website," *www.successbc.ca/eng/services/multi-level-care-society/harmony-house-assisted-living*, accessed 2014.10.04.

[107] Villa Cathay Care Home website, *www.villacathay.ca/*, accessed 2008.06.06.

[108] "Victoria Chinatown Care Centre," Victoria Chinatown Care Foundation, *chinatowncarefoundation.com/component/content/article/21-featured-news/236-victoria-chinatown-care-centre*, accessed 2014.10.04.

[109] Debates of the Legislative Assembly (Hansard), Province of British Columbia, Fourth Session, 38th Parliament, 2008.02.19, Afternoon Sitting, 26.8.

5.14 Housing Societies

Besides the formal institutions established by Chinese Canadians to care for their elderly, there is another form of eldercare, the housing society, created by Chinese Canadians to supply residences for the elderly. The elderly who benefit directly from this institution, i.e., the residents of the housing that is built and managed by these societies, are usually independent, therefore, requiring less support.

Two examples of such housing societies, Sek On Toi Senior Citizens' Home and Chinese Elders' Mansion were described above. Reflecting the desire of Chinese Canadian elderly to live in a location that offers ease of communication with other residents, neighbours with similar cultural background, and proximity to friends, and community and social services, many of these societies operate within the Chinatowns of Canadian cities. For example, there are three senior housing complexes in Calgary's Chinatown. The Oi Foundation Wai Kwan Manor was built in 1985 and has one hundred twenty-two, one-bedroom units. In 2007 there were one hundred sixty tenants whose average age was seventy-nine. Oi Kwan Place was built in 1976 and in 2007 contained thirty-six single and twenty double units. There were sixty-four tenants, whose average age was eighty-one.[110] Oi Kwan has since expanded by building an adjacent sixteen-storey tower with one hundred twenty-nine units, forty-four of which are one-bedroom and the remainder being bachelor suites.[111]

The third housing complex is Wah Ying Mansions, built in 1988. There are one hundred four units and in 2006 the average age of the residents was eighty-four years old. Rent varied from four hundred ten to six hundred fifty dollars a month depending on income; however, there was a long waiting period of about

---

[110] Figures for number of units, residents, and average age were taken from the Calgary Health Region's website (*www.calgaryhealthregion.ca/hecomm/diversity/reaching_populations/reaching_senior_apartments.pdf*, accessed 2007.12.02).

[111] David Parker, "Facility Operates for the Love of Seniors," *Calgary Herald*, 2012.06.29, E.2.

two years. Wah Ying Mansions is managed by Calgary Chinatown Seniors Housing Society.[112]

Nor is Calgary an exception in having housing projects devoted to Chinese Canadian seniors. One finds examples across the country of Chinese Canadian communities that have established similar institutions. In Winnipeg, City Oasis, a six-storey apartment complex, contains forty-two units and caters to Indochina Chinese seniors. Its construction is the result of a partnership between the Winnipeg Housing and Homelessness Initiative and the Indochina Chinese Association of Manitoba. The association manages the complex and also contributed three hundred forty thousand dollars in equity toward the estimated four million dollar cost of the project. The association also manages the Indochina Gardens, a twenty-six-unit, nonprofit housing complex in downtown Winnipeg.[113]

In Ottawa the Chinese Community Building was built in 1982 for a cost of 1.9 million dollars. It is eight stories high and has forty-six self-contained units that were renting for four hundred sixty to six hundred eighty-eight dollars. There are fifteen bachelor apartments, twenty-seven one-bedroom apartments, and four two-bedroom apartments. It is run by a board of twenty-seven directors elected from the Chinese Canadian community.[114] Similarly, the Montreal Chinese Community and United Centre built and manage a building at the corner of the streets St-Dominique and De la Gauchetière

---

[112] Information on Wah Ying Mansions was provided by building manager, Mr. Christopher Yip, in a personal interview on 2006.09.08 in Calgary, Alberta.

[113] Information in this paragraph was taken from postings on the Canada Housing and Mortgage Corporation (Corporate Information > Newsroom > News Releases > 2006 > City Oasis Apartment Complex Opens in Downtown Winnipeg Will Benefit Seniors Needing Affordable, Rental Housing, *www.cmhc-schl.gc.ca/en/corp/nero/nere/2006/2006-08-05-1300.cfm*, accessed 2007.12.12; and Corporate Information > Newsroom > Speeches > 2006 Speeches > Opening Event for City Oasis, *www.cmhc-schl.gc.ca/en/corp/nero/sp/2006/2006-08-05-1330.cfm*, accessed 2007.12.12).

[114] Ottawa Seniors website, www.ottawaseniors.com/resview.php?srchqry=&query_id=10&offset=5, accessed 2007.12.06; and Jeff Keshen, *Construire Une Capitale: Ottawa* (Ottawa: University of Ottawa Press, 2001), 297.

close to amenities in Montreal's Chinatown; the building provides housing for low-income Chinese seniors, families, and individuals.[115]

As one investigates the institutions that are devoted to Chinese Canadian eldercare, one finds that there are a large number of these and that many of them have only limited information available about themselves. It seems that they do not need to do broad promotion, that awareness of their existence is sufficient within the communities they serve in order to meet the need for which they were created. Often any information that is available is provided by the government organizations with which these institutions work, such as Canada Housing and Mortgage Corporation. The lack of self-promotion undermines an accurate awareness of their numbers. The institutions described above are probably a fraction of the total number. When one searches the internet, one comes across institutional names like "Chinese Elders Mansion," "Chinese Alliance Manor," and "Chinese Seniors Highrise," which are not usually accompanied by a detailed description.[116] The lack of self-promotion done by these institutions is in strong contrast to some, like Yee Hong, whose heavy reliance on donations leads them to make strong public relation efforts.

6. Conclusion

6.1 Summary

This paper has described the general state of Chinese Canadian institutional eldercare. Traditional Chinese cultural values, such as filial piety, have had a large influence on this state and the institutions described are obvious manifestations of this influence. Other forces that have influenced the establishment of Chinese Canadian institutional eldercare

---

[115] Stephanie O'Hanley, "Kicked to curb," *Hour,* 2005.12.01, *www.hour.ca/news/news.aspx?iIDArticle=7879*, accessed 2007.12.11.

[116] Chinese Elders Mansion and Chinese Alliance Manor are found in the "Seniors Housing Guide 2007" published by the Senior Association of Greater Edmonton (*www.mysage.ca/housingguide.cfm*, accessed 2007.12.12). The Chinese Seniors Highrise in Saskatoon is listed on the Robb Kullman Engineering website, *www.robb-kullman.com/Residential.htm* (accessed 2007.12.12).

include the increased assimilation of Chinese Canadians into the mainstream economy, which has placed demands on their time while also giving them access to greater resources by which to support their needs. This has led to a number of initiatives in the establishment of culturally-sensitive eldercare, some of which, such as Yee Hong care centers, have been remarkable successes.

From a practical and academic perspective this development has proved potentially rewarding and very interesting. Canada's population is aging; health costs, which are disproportionately–not meaning "inappropriately"–spent on the elderly, are rising; and governments and caregivers are searching for different ways to deal with the difficulties created because of these changes. Two principles, of providing community-based and client-centered eldercare, have attracted much attention. By coincidence, and perhaps not, the institutions established by Chinese Canadians have exemplified these principles and, therefore, merit the increased attention that they are receiving. With this increased attention, it is worthwhile to delve into some important issues surrounding Chinese Canadian eldercare, as well as speculate about its future.

6.2 Issues

There are four significant issues closely connected to Chinese Canadian eldercare. The first, more academic issue, is whether the value of filial piety will continue to be held in such high regard. A more practical issue is whether the Chinese Canadian elderly are in need of, or even want the resources that have been provided for their care. Another practical issue is why Chinese Canadians had to make such a tremendous effort in order to obtain adequate care for their elderly. This issue speaks to the discrimination, or at least insensitivity, that has existed in the Canadian eldercare system. A last issue is the continued viability of the institutions that Chinese Canadians have established in the area of eldercare given the attractiveness of the facilities and their services to non-Chinese Canadians.

6.2.1 Retention of Filial Piety

It is relevant to ask whether the underlying factors that have contributed to the achievements of Chinese Canadians in the field of eldercare will continue to be drivers in maintaining these achievements. If not, one would be correct to suspect that Chinese Canadian eldercare will not continue to develop and may even decline from the levels now seen. Chief among these factors is the value of filial piety. One can envision this basic value being weakened, and thereby the impetus it gives to providing the facilities and services that constitute Chinese eldercare being undermined. The potential causes of this weakening are its absence among new Chinese immigrants and the assimilation of future generations of Chinese Canadians into the Canadian mainstream.

There is reason to suspect that the value of filial piety may diminish within the Chinese Canadian community in the years to come. Approximately 11.5 percent of Canada's new immigrants are presently arriving from the People's Republic of China (PRC). This amounts to an annual total of approximately twenty-nine thousand immigrants of PRC origin,[117] which, in turn, adds about 2 percent to the total Chinese Canadian population. As the number of immigrants from the PRC accumulates, their influence on Chinese Canadian values increases.

The effect of new immigrants on traditional Chinese Canadian values is unknown because China has undergone radical change in the past fifty to sixty years. For a period of time Chinese traditional values, including filial piety, were officially criticized in China as "feudal." The state now promotes the virtue especially in light of the increasing need for eldercare there; however, the state's support is qualified in emphasizing support for aged parents rather than obeying them or producing descendants. Nevertheless, the strength of filial piety cannot be easily dismissed. Neena Chappell and Karen Kusch, with the cited support of other scholars, conclude that "filial piety continues as an ideology, defining a hierarchical relationship between the generations despite China's tumultuous political

---

[117] "Facts and figures 2011 – Immigration overview: Permanent and temporary residents," Government of Canada, *www.cic.gc.ca/english/resources/statistics/facts2011/permanent/10.asp*, accessed 2014.11.06.

shifts and rapid social and cultural change since the middle of the 20th century."[118]

It makes common sense to think that a traditional value with over two thousand years of strong promotion could not be eradicated or even seriously diminished in a period as short as sixty years. This conjecture is confirmed by evidence that residents of Hong Kong, a place of origin for a large number of immigrants to Canada, still place great value on filial piety. Sheung-Tak Cheng and Alfred C.M. Chan's research has shown "support for the continuing importance of filial piety in the Chinese society of Hong Kong."[119] Hong Kong was a British colony for over one hundred fifty years and has a relatively small population of about six million; therefore, the value of filial piety would have weakened substantially under the influence of Western culture if it were not deeply rooted.

In defending the claim that the value of filial piety will not diminish within the Chinese Canadian community in the years to come, one can also point out that the importance of filial piety among Chinese Canadians has not been affected even though the PRC has been one of the largest sources of new immigrants since 2002.[120] This would seem to be the case because, as pointed out earlier, Chinese Canadian elders much more so than other elders, in the mainstream live with their children, which is a typical characteristic of filial practice. This claim is further supported by a report in 2003 that Chinese Canadian caregivers for elderly relatives retained the traditional cultural value of filial piety.[121]

Moreover, if assimilation were leading to a loss of traditional values, one would expect to see this loss most likely among Chinese Canadian youth who, if they were not born in Canada had spent formative time there. However, the McCreary Centre Society, a non government, nonprofit organization committed to improving the health of BC youth,

---

[118] "The Gendered Nature of Filial Piety - A Study among Chinese Canadians," *Journal of Cross Cultural Gerontology*, 22 (2007), *30-31.*

[119] "Filial Piety and Psychological Well-Being in Well Older Chinese," in *Journal of Gerontology: PSYCHOLOGICAL SCIENCES 2006*, 61B.5, 267.

[120] "Facts and figures 2011."

[121] Lai and Surood, 1 and 13.

conducted the province-wide Adolescent Health Survey of 25,838 students in grades 7 through 12 in 1998. Their findings were that Chinese Canadian youth have different values than their peers in the mainstream. Although the survey did not ask about filial piety, it did show that Chinese Canadian youth placed greater importance on education, another traditional Chinese value, and were more conservative in their lifestyle.[122] This indicates not only less assimilation, but also an affinity for traditional Chinese values.

The acceptance of the value of filial piety by Chinese Canadian youth is further seen in the large numbers seen in photographs of volunteers serving at various Chinese Canadian eldercare institutions.[123] This, plus the continued acceptance of the value of filial piety in China and the results of research done in Canada, seems to indicate that the value of filial piety will continue to be important for Chinese Canadians and, in turn, drive their efforts to provide exceptional care for their elders.

6.2.2 Questionable Need, Even Desire, for Resources Provided

Another reason to question whether the traditional value of filial piety will continue to be appreciated is the increasing financial and physical independence of the elderly and intuitive appeal of wanting to be so. In other words, as more Chinese Canadians age within a Canadian setting they are going to be able to accumulate the cultural and economic resources to remain independent longer, that is not having to rely on their children as has been the case. Furthermore, it seems natural that one would want to be independent as long as possible. The result of these factors would be the diminishing importance of filial piety because there would be less demand for its practice.

In fact, at first glance, that may seem to be what is happening in China as the standard of living rises. Chappell and Kusch cite studies that show the numbers of Chinese elderly not wanting to live with their children increasing, and

---

[122] "Silk Road to Health: A Journey to Understanding Chinese Youth in BC."

[123] For example, *Wing Kei Care Centre Grand Opening Publication.*

the numbers who actually do not increasing as well.[124] These observations conform to the movement of Chinese Canadian elderly in Montreal out of their children's homes and into Chinatown.[125] One of the reasons cited for this included intense intergenerational conflicts, which indicates a desire to retain an independent perspective rather than accept the views of others.

Juxtaposing this trend with the ability of Chinese Canadian elderly to make use of mainstream services, one can see the potential for undermining of the value of filial piety. There seems to be a desire on the part of Chinese Canadian elders to be more independent but as yet they lack the cultural resources to be able to. [126] Furthermore, there may be some pressure for them to acquire these cultural resources sooner rather than later as those who may not recognize the need for culturally-sensitive eldercare criticize the use of public funds to provide it. The trend of Chinese Canadians becoming more independent, and therefore, less in need of the resources created by the importance of filial piety, would lead to less importance being placed on it.

The opposing side to this argument is that even if improved health and finances allow for a longer period of independence, eventually one will have to rely on others, and having the family seen as the main providers of this necessary assistance seems to be a good thing. Furthermore, promotion of the value of filial piety, reinforces the value of traditional Chinese culture, which, in turn, has been shown to be beneficial to Chinese Canadian elders. Another consideration is that the assumed benefits of independence are not as great as believed and that Chinese have cultivated a different type of parent-

---

[124] "The Gendered Nature of Filial Piety - A Study among Chinese Canadians," 32.

[125] Chan Kwok Bun, *Smoke and Fire: The Chinese in Montreal*, 242-46; and Kwok B. Chan, "Coping with Aging and Managing Self-Identity: The Social World of the Elderly Chinese Women," 45-48.

[126] Neena Chappell and David Lai reported that of eight hundred thirty Chinese elders in Vancouver and Victoria chosen to participate in interviews on health care service use by Chinese seniors in British Columbia, 43.2 percent could not speak English ("Health Care Service by Chinese Seniors in British Columbia, Canada," *Journal of Cross-Cultural Gerontology*, 13 [1998], 25, 31).

child relationship that offers value for them and possibly other cultures. After all, the practice of filial piety is in keeping with the policy of community-based eldercare, which is presently been promoted in Canada.

Again, it seems common sense that persons would want to be taken care of in the latter stages of their lives and that, ideally, the primary caregivers would be the family. The increased independence in a Chinese setting has been welcomed;[127] however, not to the degree that filial piety has lost its importance. Neena Chappell offers proof for this when she cites research showing that, in contrast to the negative correlation perceived by German elderly (1993), elderly in China (2002) note no significant effect on perceived happiness by age.[128] It would seem that the value of filial piety as a main determinant of the treatment of Chinese elderly contributes to the continuing wellbeing of Chinese elders and, therefore, has not lost its importance.

Within Canada, research has shown that Chinese traditions also contribute to the wellbeing of Chinese Canadian elderly; those "who involve themselves more in traditional Chinese culture view life as better."[129] The same holds true for other countries where Chinese have emigrated in large numbers; for example, Chappell and Kursch report a correlation between a good quality of life and strong ties to the ethnic community for Chinese in Australia.[130]

The benefits of involvement in traditional culture, and thus the importance of filial piety, seem to go beyond what independence and the ability to function in mainstream culture can provide. In other words, while independence does seem

---

[127] Chappell and Kusch cite research that shows a new pattern emerging in China where "elderly parents live on their own but geographically near several grown children who provide assistance as needed which is replacing the traditional pattern of parents living with at least one married son . . ." (32).

[128] "Perceived Change in Quality of Life among Chinese Canadian Seniors: The Role of Involvement in Chinese Culture," *Journal of Happiness Studies* 6 (2005), 71.

[129] *Ibid.*, 82.

[130] "The Gendered Nature of Filial Piety–A Study among Chinese Canadians," 32.

attractive and to offer benefits for the elderly, it is limited in
what it can provide and Chinese elderly are demonstrating an
awareness of this when they involve themselves in Chinese
culture. Chappell has noted that for the elderly, greater
involvement in Chinese culture leads to improved family
relationships, social relationships, improved attitude toward
life, and improved religion/spirituality.[131]

That involvement in Chinese culture, which in great part
encourages reliance on one's children in upper ages by
promoting the value of filial piety, actually contributes to the
happiness of Chinese Canadian elders, as Chappell and others
have shown, creates a question. There is perhaps reason to
question the assumption that independence contributes to the
happiness of the elderly, or at least the degree of independence
that is considered optimum in North America. The apparent
qualities that support independence, i.e., the possession of
sufficient economic and intellectual resources, do not seem to
produce the psychological benefits of involvement in Chinese
culture, e.g., better family relationships and improved attitude
toward life, etc. In other words, there may be benefits from
practising filial piety that being independent does not account
for and may even be reduced if independence is promoted.

This assumption conforms to the research findings of
Cheng and Chan who report the surprising result that there "is
no evidence that in the Chinese context of filial devotion,
overmeeting parental expectations brings adverse psychological
effects to the parents."[132] This is to say children acting in such a
way as to decrease their parents' independence and thus
jeopardize their physical well being may, in fact, be
psychologically beneficial. This research suggests a likely
possibility, that there is a distinction between physical and
psychological well being such that what is detrimental to the
former might promote the latter. While this is a likely
possibility, it is also undermined by the fact that one's culture is
a determinant factor. Cheng and Chan note that their findings
in Hong Kong are the opposite of "the Western finding that

---

[131] "Perceived Change," 84.

[132] "Filial Piety and Psychological Well-Being in Well Older Chinese," 268.

overmeeting the expectations of the parents was detrimental to their well-being."[133]

In the face of this logical conundrum let us suppose that for Chinese Canadians the need for independence of their elders will be given less emphasis as they attempt to determine the best configuration of care for their elders. This assumption seems reasonable because there seem to be more cases where elderly well-being is co-related with decreasing their independence. It may be that the underlying philosophy views the value of independence differently and that it leads to better treatment when the need for independence is not given such high priority within the general concept of care for the elderly. There may also be a basis for this supposition in the general observations "that traditional Chinese culture provides a much more positive role for seniors than does Western society, . . ."[134] and that the filial piety practised by Chinese in United States contrasts strongly with the ageism prevalent in North American work culture.[135]

The description above, besides explaining the preferences of Chinese Canadians, also indicates a further dimension in the achievement of Chinese Canadian eldercare. This eldercare offers an alternative model to that practised in the mainstream. This essay has noted some of its special characteristics. One should also take note of its viability. Not only does it have a number of institutions in place implementing these special characteristics, it also has an underlying set of values that motivate the implementation and help define an integrated and holistic policy of operation.

6.2.3 Why Such Effort in the First Place?

A third issue that should be raised in the context of Chinese Canadian eldercare is why Chinese Canadians would have had to expend such a large effort to obtain adequate

---

[133] *Ibid.*, citing research from M. Silverstein, X. Chen, and K. Heller ("Too much of a good thing? Intergenerational social support and the psychological well-being of older parents," *Journal of Marriage and Family* 58 [1996]: 970-982).

[134] Chappell, "Perceived Change," 86.

[135] *Ibid.*, 75.

eldercare. One would have thought that the Canadian health system would have been more sensitive to the needs of the elderly no matter what their ethnic background. Yet, for more than twenty years scholars and practitioners alike have been pointing out the efforts that Chinese Canadians were having to make to care for their elderly and the need for the institutions and governments to help. A researcher stated in 1989:

> Chinese families appear to provide a substantial quantity of services and care for their aging parents/in laws. The need to be acknowledged for this and considered in the formulation of policies governing social services and health agencies is great. The relationship among the elderly, family caregivers and formal systems, government agencies, can be an important factor in influencing the effectiveness of these families. Problem areas in caregiving have been identified by caregivers. These areas need to be addressed and attempts made to problem solve and support these families. There is much mutual sharing that could be done between cultures so that the positives from both the Chinese and Western cultures can be utilized in helping caregiving families.[136]

Likewise, Joseph Wong, founder of Yee Hong, spent more than three years to convince the Ontario Ministry of Health and Long-Term Care that the needs of seniors of different cultural diversity in Ontario required special treatment.[137]

Now that Chinese Canadians have through much their own efforts put in place forms of institutional eldercare that one can admire and even learn from, the question becomes even more important: Why did it take so long and why did Chinese Canadians have to expend such effort to produce a system that not only serves their elderly well, but even has lessons for mainstream eldercare.

6.2.4 Viability in Face of Broad Demand

The issue of viability in face of potential broad demand arises largely because of the degree of success Chinese

---

[136] Mary Wilson, "Family Caregiving to the Elderly in the Chinese Community" (M.S.W. thesis, University of British Columbia, 1989), 84.

[137] Legislative Assembly of Ontario, 350.

Canadians have had in establishing eldercare, and it is complicated by the question of how resources coming from various Canadian governments are to be used. There should no question about the attractiveness of the facilities and services that Chinese Canadians have established, not only for Chinese Canadian elderly, but increasingly for non Chinese Canadians. There are already waiting lists of five to ten years for Yee Hong's long term care facilities.[138] Also, who would not want to rent a decent apartment for $410-$650 in downtown Calgary where the average rent for a two-bedroom apartment is more than one thousand dollars in 2006 prices. In another example, the range of services from medical to travel to education and a Chinese meal delivered for $5.25 inclusive (not much more than what you would pay for just delivery charges from a Chinese restaurant) offered at a location like the Calgary Chinatown Seniors' Centre seem to be attractive whatever the linguistic challenges one might meet.

Of course, services are geared to Chinese Canadians, which would discourage non Chinese Canadians, but these facilities are already having to adapt to other ethnic groups in the case of Yee Hong and for all the facilities to the different dialects spoken among Chinese Canadians. Furthermore, the large amount of volunteer input means that one can receive more individualized attention.

The Canadian Chinese community no doubt is primarily concerned with meeting the needs of its own elderly, especially when those needs have not been met by mainstream services. However, often the community relies on government and the broader community funding to provide these services, so it would be difficult to deny them to non community members. The argument would be that government funding and broad community resources are supporting these services, so they should be open to all. This reasoning, indeed, seems to be the basis for initial objections on the part of the Ontario government to Yee Hong's request for government support for culturally-sensitive eldercare: it would be discriminatory

---

[138] More recently, the waiting period to enter the Yee Hong Geriatric Care Centre in Mississauga has been more than five years and for Yee Hong's Scarborough-McNicoll location, ten years (Dakshana Bascaramurty, "Ethnic-focused Nursing Homes Put a Canadian Face on Filial Piety," *The Globe* and *Mail*, 2012.01.27).

against non-Chinese Canadians. In fact, this question—should the services be restricted to Chinese Canadians—is implied in the descriptions of the individual senior housing projects for Chinese Canadians. The building titles, organizers, and management, and often much of the funding is clearly connected to Chinese sounding organizations and individuals; however, in joint communiques with the supporting government agencies, it is difficult to find language restricting access to Chinese Canadians.[139]

The problem may be that the principle of providing culturally-sensitive eldercare has not been widely accepted enough to become a rationale for allowing restriction to only those that require it, like the restriction of admission to a children's hospital only to those under a certain age. Until this principle is accepted, it will be difficult to refuse non-Chinese Canadians once they start requesting access to the facilities and resources that Chinese Canadians have established.

6.3 Future

6.3.1 Increased Demand

It is likely that there will be increased demand for the services that Chinese Canadians are providing for the elderly. Two facts lead to this conclusion. In 2011, foreign-born residents comprised 20.6% of Canada's total population, which was the highest proportion of foreign-born since 1931.[140] Furthermore, China, including the People's Republic of China, Taiwan, and Hong Kong, has been one of the biggest sources of newcomers to Canada.[141] With an increasing foreign born and

---

[139] It is important to be clear that this paper does not question the right of Chinese Canadians to the resources that they have received from Canadian governments; in fact, it supports an argument that these resources should have been sooner in coming.

[140] Statistics Canada, "2011 National Household Survey: Immigration, Place of Birth, Citizenship, Ethnic Origin, Visible Minorities, Language and Religion," *www.statcan.gc.ca/daily-quotidien/130508/dq130508b-eng.htm*, accessed 2014.11.09.

[141] The total was 35,349 in 2011, which was both the largest source and nearly 14 percent of Canada's immigrants that year (Government of Canada, "Facts and Figures 2012 – Immigration Overview: Permanent and Temporary

thus ethnic population, the demand for culturally-sensitive eldercare will increase in Canada. Second, Chinese Canadians are pioneering the establishment of culturally-sensitive eldercare, so they will be the obvious choice to provide this care.

6.3.2 Model for Mainstream

The care that Chinese Canadians have developed for their elderly offers promising options just at a time when eldercare experts and Canadian governments are searching for alternative models of eldercare. An example of a promising alternative is client-centered, community-based eldercare. As noted earlier, client-centered care is care that emphasizes the values, preferences, and needs of care recipient. It contrasts with a provider-driven, medical model in which decision making is less in the hands of the client. Community-based care is care provided in the community close to family, friends, and others who know the client.

Chapman *et al.* have documented the interest there is in this form of eldercare. They describe three residential care models that were part of a larger initiative to increase "the scope of community care to encompass residential care to frail seniors needing nursing-home-level support."[142] These new programmes have been implemented in Alberta and their main criteria were being client-centred, community-based, and less expensive than nursing homes. The fact that the Alberta government has been willing to devote considerable funding, such as the capital costs of buildings, to the establishment of client-centred, community-based eldercare and the number of related academic publications are evidence of the interest that exists in this type of eldercare.

The two main values underlying this interest are that this type of eldercare is both preferable to the user and less expensive. User preference derives from being recognized as an

---

Residents,"
www.cic.gc.ca/english/resources/statistics/facts2012/permanent/10.asp, accessed 2014.11.08).

[142] "Client-centred, Community-based Care for Frail Seniors," 255. Chapman *et al.* also list a number of publications that address directly client-centred and community-based eldercare in their article's bibliography.

individual, remaining connected to the community, viewing staff as family rather than experts, and having family members provide a large part of the care. With recognition of the interest in and value of community-based and client-centred eldercare it becomes worthwhile to present a credible argument that Chinese Canadian eldercare meets the criteria of being client-centred and community-based.

Community-based care is also viewed as less costly than institutional care because familial support is assumed in addition to institutional.[143] There is also the elimination of unwanted or unused institutional services that would otherwise be provided in a generic package. In fact, the Alberta programmes in client-centred, community-based eldercare, were implemented with operations budgets as much as 39 percent below nursing home operating budgets.[144]

The study of community-based, client-centred eldercare benefits from the experiences of Chinese Canadians because they have already established programmes with these attributes. Chinese Canadian eldercare has developed along the lines envisioned in client-centred eldercare. Joseph Wong was motivated to found Yee Hong when he encountered under-served Chinese Canadian elderly within nursing homes and it was Yee Hong that fought years of provincial government resistance in its efforts to prove the value of culturally-sensitive eldercare. The special needs of Chinese Canadian elderly for minority linguistic services, for contact with those of a similar culture, and even for the basic services when Chinese Canadians were once excluded from them are ones whose fulfillment is justified under a policy of client-centred eldercare. The myriad of programs offered by the Chinese Canadian organizations also support a client-centred policy. Clients can choose among these programs to meet their individual needs.

Furthermore, the organizations and measures that Chinese Canadians have developed to care for their elders have in large part taken as reference family-based care, attempting to

---

[143] Chapman et al. citing C., "A Key Piece of the Integration Puzzle: Managing the Chronic Care Needs of the Frail Elderly in Residential Care Settings" (*Generations* 23 [1999], 51-55), 253.

[144] Chapman et al. citing C. Schalm and D. Lier, *The Public Costs of Three New Models of Continuing Care* (Edmonton, 1998), 260.

complement and supplement what is provided in the home. Community-based eldercare assumes a large component of family-provided care, which is already a given in Chinese traditional eldercare. It has been relatively easy for Chinese Canadians to extend care that has been provided in the home to those who are institutionalized, even non family members. Members of the community are mobilized to perform visitations and services. Therefore, Chinese Canadian eldercare primarily developed within their communities, i.e., Chinatowns, rather than being directed by government policies. As would be the case with a grassroots model, the social needs are emphasized more than medical ones, in contrast to a more centralized, expert-administrated model.

As well, Chinese Canadians have made large efforts through outreach, daycare, and respite programs to provide community-based care to those who would otherwise be institutionalized, thus leading and reinforcing this emerging trend in mainstream care. Needless to say, much of this has been accomplished with minimal government support, again allowing it to reflect the nature of the community within which it arises.

As a practical model, relatively independent of mainstream eldercare, but still challenged by similar problems, Chinese Canadian eldercare can offer insight into how models such as client-centred, community-based eldercare could be modified in order to be more successful. Chapman et al, while identifying the endorsement of client-centred care by family and staff, also note its challenges. Three themes illustrate these challenges: "(1) engaging with others in a care partnership; (2) responding to residents' preferences and care needs within limited resources; and (3) maintaining residents' connections with the community."[145]

Looking at how Chinese Canadian eldercare has responded to these challenges, one finds that they have implemented extraordinary measures to surmount them. With regard to the first one, they have been able to secure huge donations and

---

[145] *Ibid.*, 256. The immediate context of these challenges only refers to a client-centred approach, without mentioning community-based; however, the broader context and the nature of the challenges, particularly (1) and (3) demonstrate that Chapman *et al.* are also referring to challenges to a community-based approach.

mobilize large numbers of volunteers for the sake of the elderly. This is, no doubt, due in great part to the importance of filial piety within traditional Chinese thinking. Leveraging this value allows them to solicit funds even from foreign donors and to establish the elderly as legitimate benefactors of fundraising. Of course, one has to wonder how much mainstream eldercare can gain from this example because it seems the main factor is one of fundamental belief, i.e., the value of filial piety, which is not easily changed.

On the other hand, the example of Yee Hong's willingness to provide its services to other ethnic communities, such as Indo-Canadians, is telling. It demonstrates an unusual openness and generosity especially when compared to the initial reception that they themselves received from the Ontario government when it denied them bed licenses. If we accept the value of engaging with others in a care partnership, then the Yee Hong example offers mainstream organizations the opportunity to reflect on whether they are actually meeting this challenge to the best of their abilities.

Chinese Canadians seem to have also met the second challenge, responding to residents' preferences and care needs within limited resources, well. Chinese Canadian eldercare has come into existence to meet the specific needs of its users, i.e., Chinese Canadian elderly. Surprisingly they have done this when, originally, Chinese Canadian welfare was given a low priority by society and governments, so they did not have access to the kind of resources that most Canadians had. However, they were able to overcome this limitation and still achieve what they have in eldercare. This is evidence of their ability to meet needs within limited resources.

Apart from the lesson that it is possible to provide for residents' preferences with limited resources, the Chinese Canadian example also demonstrates that an eldercare organization should be flexible if it wants to raise funds. Yee Hong has demonstrated this with the variety of measures–from affinity credit cards, galas, to e-Bay auctions of condominiums– it has pioneered in fundraising for seniors. The success of these efforts should provide models to mainstream organizations to follow in securing financial stability.

Perhaps, even more important is the different philosophical perspective. Chinese Canadian eldercare is viewed much more as a community responsibility rather than overwhelmingly a government one. Of course, this meshes well with providing community-based care. It also points to the importance of education if Canadians are going to establish community-based eldercare, which may be easier than it sounds given that it is part of what it means to be a human being, to have elderly family members, and to age oneself, and that there is Chinese Canadian eldercare that shows that it can be done.

The third challenge seems also to have been met well by Chinese Canadian eldercare. The population base of Chinatowns is largely composed of seniors who reside in homes specially built and operated for them by the community. One of the purposes of maintaining Chinatown long after Chinese Canadians have been accepted into the broader community has been to provide the elderly with a familiar community within which they can function. The attraction of doing so is seen in the example described earlier of Chinese Canadian elderly in Montreal leaving the homes of their children to live within Chinatown. The fact that Chinatowns in Canada still maintain their identities is due in part to the community environment they provide for Chinese Canadian elderly.

As for the lessons that mainstream eldercare can take from Chinese Canadian's efforts to provide client-centred, community-based eldercare, again there is the simple one that it can be done, and done well given the richness of activities provided for seniors in Chinatown, e.g., diversity of housing, shopping, peer groups, senior centres, recreation opportunities, restaurants, reading rooms, etc. Apart from this, one should note the degree to which Chinese Canadian seniors are organized to help one another. For example, the community social groups that the Calgary Chinese Elderly Citizens' Association organizes are conducted for seniors in the homes of other seniors. It makes sense for seniors who are capable of helping other seniors to preserve and promote a system and value that they may have need of themselves soon. This may be more apparent to Chinese Canadian elderly, but should not be difficult to promote among non-Chinese Canadian seniors.

In closing, Chinese Canadian achievements in the area of eldercare have been exceptional and notable for the lessons that they provide for mainstream eldercare providers. Chinese Canadians have shown that high quality care can be provided even when resources are limited.

BIBLIOGRAPHY

"About Us." Carefirst Seniors & Community Services Association website, *www.carefirstseniors.com/websites/content.php?id=1*, accessed 2014.10.01,

"About Us/Our Story." Yee Hong website, *www.yeehong.com/foundation/index.php*, accessed 2007.10.10.

Annable, Kristin. "Chinese Seniors Lodge Residents 'Unsettled' by Condo Proposal." *Edmonton Journal*, 2013.05.28.

"Austin Harris Residence." S.U.C.C.E.S.S. website, *www.successbc.ca/eng/services/multi-level-care-society/austin-harris-residence*, accessed 2014.10.04.

"Awards and Accreditation." Yee Hong website, *www.yeehong.com/foundation/index.php*, accessed 2007.10.10.

"Awards and Accreditation." Yee Hong website, *www.yeehong.com/centre/awards.php*, accessed 2014.09.29.

Bascaramurty, Dakshana. "Ethnic-focused Nursing Homes Put a Canadian Face on Filial Piety." *The Globe* and *Mail,* 2012.01.27.

Calgary Chinese Elderly Citizens' Association *www3.telus.net/cceca*, accessed 2007.11.27.

Calgary Chinese Elderly Citizens' Association Annual Report. Calgary, CCECA, 2007.

Calgary Health Region website, *www.calgaryhealthregion.ca/hecomm/diversity/reaching_populations/reaching_senior_apartments.pdf*, accessed 2007.12.02.

Canada Housing and Mortgage Corporation website, *www.cmhc-schl.gc.ca*, accessed 2007.12.12.

Canadian Institute for Health Information. *National Health Expenditure Trends, 1975 to 2013.* Ottawa, Ont.: CIHI; 2013.

"Carefirst's Services." Carefirst Seniors & Community Services Association website, *www.carefirstseniors.com/websites/content.php?id=2*, accessed 2014.10.01.

Chan, Alan K.L. and Sor-hoon Tan, ed. "Introduction." In *Filial Piety in Chinese Thought and History,* edited by Alan K.L. Chan and Sor-hoon Tan, 1-11. New York: RoutledgeCurzon, 2004.

Chan, Liza, Program Director, Calgary Chinese Elderly Citizens' Association. Presentation, 2007.02.07, Calgary, Alberta.

Chan Kwok B. "Coping with Aging and Managing Self-Identity: The Social World of the Elderly Chinese Women." *Canadian Ethnic Studies* 15.3 (1983): 36-50.

Chan Kwok Bun. *Smoke and Fire: The Chinese in Montreal.* Hong Kong, The Chinese University Press, 1991.

Chapman, Sherry Ann, Norah Keating, and Jacquie Eales. "Client-centred, Community-based Care for Frail Seniors." *Health and Social Care in the Community* 11.3 (May 2003): 253-61.

Chappell, Neena L. "Correcting Cross-Cultural Stereotypes: Aging in Shanghai and Canada." *Journal of Cross-Cultural Gerontology* 18 (2003): 127-147.

------. "Perceived Change in Quality of Life among Chinese Canadian Seniors: The Role of Involvement in Chinese Culture." *Journal of Happiness Studies* 6 (2005): 69-91.

------ and Karen Kusch. "The Gendered Nature of Filial Piety–A Study among Chinese Canadians." *Journal of Cross-Cultural Gerontology* 22 (2007): 29-45.

------ and David Lai. "Health Care Service by Chinese Seniors in British Columbia, Canada." *Journal of Cross-Cultural Gerontology* 13 (1998): 21-37.

Cheng, Sheung-Tak and Alfred C.M. Chan. "Filial Piety and Psychological Well-Being in Well Older Chinese." *Journal of Gerontology: PSYCHOLOGICAL SCIENCES* 61B.5 (2006): 262-269.

"Chieng's Adult Day Centre." *www.successbc.ca/eng/services/multi-level-care-society/chieng-s-adult-day-centre*, accessed 2014.10.04.

Chinese Christian Wing Kei Nursing Home Association 2005 Annual Report.

Chinese Christian Wing Kei Nursing Home Association 2006 Annual Report. Wing Kei website, *www.wingkeicarecentre.org/aboutus.htm,* accessed 2007.11.28.

Chinese Christian Wing Kei Nursing Home Association 2012 Annual Report. Wing Kei website, *www.wingkeicarecentre.org/images/AnnualReports/Wing Kei-AnnualReport2012.pdf,* accessed 2014.10.02.

"Community Services." Yee Hong website, *www.yeehong.com/centre/community_services.php*, accessed 2014.09.29.

Confucius. *The Analects.* Translated by D.C. Lau. London: Penguin, 1979.

Creighton, Judy. "Chinese Geriatric Centre Keeps Spouses Together." Canadian Press NewsWire, 1997.09.16.

Cruikshank, Sheila. "Chinese Families in Supportive Care." Master of Science dissertation, University of British Columbia, 1990.

Dawson, Brian. *Mooncakes in Gold Mountain: From China to the Canadian Plains*. Calgary: Detselig, 1991.

Debates of the Legislative Assembly (Hansard). Province of British Columbia. Fourth Session, 38th Parliament. 2008.02.19, Afternoon Sitting, 26.8.

Eales, Jacquie, Norah Keating, and Annita Damsma. "Seniors' Experiences of Client-centred Residential Care." *Ageing and Society* 21.3 (May 2001): 279-296.

"eBay Canada helps Yee Hong build caring." *communitypages.ebay.ca/community/aboutebay/releases/0303.html#2Ibid*, accessed 2014.09.30.

Edmonton Chinatown Care Centre website, *www.edmccc.net/*, accessed 2007.11.29.

"Edmonton Chinese Seniors Lodge (Seniors Lodge)." China Benevolent Association website, *www.edmccc.net/seniorslodge.htm*, accessed 2014.10.03.

The Gee How Oak Tin Benevolent Association of America, *www.ghot.org/history.html*, accessed 2007.10.07

Government of Canada. "Facts and figures 2011 – Immigration overview: Permanent and temporary residents." *www.cic.gc.ca/english/resources/statistics/facts2011/permanent/10.asp*, accessed 2014.11.06.

"Harmony House." S.U.C.C.E.S.S. website," *www.successbc.ca/eng/services/multi-level-care-society/harmony-house-assisted-living*, accessed 2014.10.04.

Health Canada. *Canada's Aging Population*. Minister of Public Works and Government Services Canada, 2002. 43 pages.

Historical Chinese Language Materials in British Columbia. *www.sfu.ca/davidlamcentre/hclmbc/*, accessed 2007.10.07.

"History." Montreal Chinese Hospital website, *www.montrealchinesehospital.ca/history.html*, accessed 2014.10.01.

"How it All Started." Yee Hong website, *www.yeehong.com/centre/story.php*, accessed 2014.09.29.

Kaimu tekan, Jianada Yaboda sheng, Kacheng Huafu Laoying Zongxin (Special Inauguration Publication, Grand Opening of the Calgary Chinatown Seniors' Centre, Alberta, Canada). Calgary, Calgary Chinese Elderly Citizens' Association, 1996.

Keshen, Jeff. *Construire Une Capitale: Ottawa*. Ottawa: University of Ottawa Press, 2001.

Kembhavi, Rohan. "Research Note – Canadian Seniors: A Demographic Profile." Elections Canada, Nov. 2012, *www.elections.ca/content.aspx?section=res&dir=rec/part/s en&document=index&lang=e*, accessed 2014.11.11.

Ikels, Charlotte. *Aging and Adaption: Chinese in Hong Kong and the United States*. Hamden, Connecticut: Archon, 1983.

Lai, Daniel W.L. and Shireen Surood. "Filial Piety in Chinese Canadian Family Caregivers." Version of paper presented to Western Social Science Association Conference 49th Annual, 2007.04.13, Calgary, Canada.

Lai, David Chuenyan. "Three Chinatowns." In *Edmonton the Life of a City*, edited by Bob Hesketh and Frances Swyripa, 256-66. Edmonton: NuWest Press, 1995.

Lee, Jik-Joen. "Asian American Elderly: A Neglected Minority Group." *Journal of Gerontological Social Work* 9.4 (1986): 103-116.

Legislative Assembly of Ontario. "Standing Committee on Social Policy, Local Health System Integration Act, 2006." In *Official Report of Debates [Hansard]*, 2006.02.06.

Leung, Ho Hon and Lynn McDonald. "Chinese Immigrant Women Who Care for Aging Parents." Joint Centre of Excellence on Immigration and Settlement, 2001. *www.ceris.metropolis.net/Virtual%20Library/RFPReports/RFPReports.htm*, accessed 2007.11.17.

Li, Peter. *The Chinese in Canada*. Second edition. Toronto: Oxford, 1998.

"Long Term Care." Yee Hong website, *www.yeehong.com/centre/long-term_care.php*, accessed 2014.09.29.

"Looking Back the Twenty Unforgettable Years . . . ." *Calgary Chinese Elderly Citizens' Association 20th Anniversary Supplement*, 49-57. Calgary, Calgary Chinese Elderly Citizens' Association, 2005.

Lum, Doman, Lucia Yim-San Cheung, Eric Ray Cho, Tze-Yee Tang, and How Bao Yau. "The Psychological Needs of the Chinese Elderly." *Social Casework: The Journal of Contemporary Social Work* 61.2 (1980): 100-106.

The McCreary Centre Society. "Silk Road to Health: A Journey to Understanding Chinese Youth in BC." 1998.

"Medical Services. " Yee Hong website, *www.yeehong.com/centre/medical_services.php#1*, accessed 2014.09.29.

Michael J. MacLean, Nancy Siew, Dawn Fowler, and Ian Graham. "Institutional Racism in Old Age: Theoretical Perspectives and a Case Study about Access to Social Services." *Canadian Journal on Aging* 6.2 (1987): 128-140.

"Mon Sheong Foundation–Profile." Mon Sheong Foundation website, *wwww.monsheong.org/msf2/eng/index.php/1-foundation/2-history*, accessed 2014.10.01

"Mon Sheong Long-term Care Centres." Mon Sheong website, *www.monsheong.org/msf2/eng/index.php/27-ltc/27-homeforaged*, accessed 2014.09.29.

Mon Sheong Foundation website, *www.monsheong.org/ltc.html*, accessed 2006.07.22

Naquin, Susan. "Funerals in North China: Uniformity and Variation." In *Death Ritual in Late Imperial and Modern China*, edited by James L. Watson and Evelyn S. Rawski, 37-70. Berkeley: University of California Press, 1988.

O'Hanley, Stephanie. "Kicked to curb." *Hour,* 2005.12.01. *www.hour.ca/news/news.aspx?iIDArticle=7879*, accessed 2007.12.11.

Ottawa Seniors website, *www.ottawaseniors.com/resview.php?srchqry=&query_id=10&offset=5*, accessed 2007.12.06.

"Our Mission." Montreal Chinese Hospital website, *www.montrealchinesehospital.ca/ourmission.html*, accessed 2014.10.01.

"Our Story." China Benevolent Association website, *www.edmccc.net/aboutus.htm*, accessed 2014.10.03.

"Our Story." Yee Hong website, *www.yeehong.com/centre/story.php,* accessed 2014.09.30.

Parker, David. "Facility Operates for the Love of Seniors." *Calgary Herald,* 2012.06.29, E.2.

Peel Community Information Database, *peel.cioc.ca/details.asp?RSN=18097*, accessed 2007.12.01

"A Review of Five Years Work of F.E.E.C.S.R." *Kaimu tekan, Jianada Yaboda sheng, Kacheng Huafu Laoying Zongxin* (Special Inauguration Publication, Grand Opening of the Calgary Chinatown Seniors' Centre, Alberta, Canada), 29-

38. Calgary, Calgary Chinese Elderly Citizens' Association, 1996.

Robb Kullman Engineering website, *www.robb-kullman.com/Residential.htm*, accessed 2007.12.12.

Senior Association of Greater Edmonton. "Seniors Housing Guide 2007." *www.mysage.ca/housingguide.cfm*, accessed 2007.12.12.

Services/Publications." S.U.C.C.E.S.S. website, *www.successbc.ca/eng/services/publications/evergreen-news*, accessed 2014.10.03.

"Simon K.Y. Lee Seniors Care Home." S.U.C.C.E.S.S. website, *www.successbc.ca/eng/services/multi-level-care-society/simon-k-y-lee-seniors-care-home*, accessed 2014.10.03.

Statistics Canada. "2011 National Household Survey: Immigration, Place of Birth, Citizenship, Ethnic Origin, Visible Minorities, Language and Religion." *www.statcan.gc.ca/daily-quotidien/130508/dq130508b-eng.htm*, accessed 2014.11.09.

"Subsidized Housing - Aw Chan Kam Chee Evergreen Manor." Yee Hong website, *www.yeehong.com/centre/subsidized_housing.php*, accessed 2014.09.29.

S.U.C.C.E.S.S (United Chinese Community Enrichment Services Society) website, www.successbc.ca/eng/, accessed 2014.10.03.

Turcotte, Huguette. "Hospitals for Chinese in Canada: Montreal (1918) and Vancouver (1921)." *Canadian Catholic Historical Association Historical Studies* 70 (2004): 131-142.

"Victoria Chinatown Care Centre." Victoria Chinatown Care Foundation, *chinatowncarefoundation.com/component/content/article/*

21-featured-news / 236-victoria-chinatown-care-centre, accessed 2014.10.04.

Villa Cathay Care Home website, *www.villacathay.ca/,* accessed 2008.06.06.

"Volunteer and Make a Difference." *www.yeehong.com / centre / volunteer.php,* accessed 2014.09.29.

"Wei Yikang chouhuo ershiwuwan yuan jingfei" [Raise $250,000 for Yee Hong]. *Singtao Community Pulse* (Toronto), 2003.03.05.

Wilson, Mary Elizabeth. "Family Caregiving to the Elderly in the Chinese Community." M.S.W. thesis, University of British Columbia, 1989.

Wing Kei Care Centre Grand Opening Publication. Calgary: Chinese Christian Wing Kei Nursing Home Association, 2005.

Whyte, Martin K. "Death in the People's Republic of China." In *Death Ritual in Late Imperial and Modern China,* edited by James L. Watson and Evelyn S. Rawski, 289-316. Berkeley: University of California Press, 1988.

Wong, Joseph. Interviews 2001.06.01 and 2002.05.02, Toronto, Ontario; and 2003.06.27, Calgary, Alberta.

------. Public lecture, 2001.05.05, Calgary Chinatown Senior's Centre in Calgary, Alberta.

"Yee Hong Centre for Geriatric Care." Yee Hong website, *www.yeehong.com /foundation /index.php,* accessed 2007.10.10.

"Yee Hong Centre for Geriatric Care" (pamphlet), post 2012. *www.yeehong.com /centre /pdf/ YHGenBro%28E%29.pdf,* accessed 2014.09.29.

"Yee Hong Centre for Geriatric Care: A Special Marketing Supplement Prepared for the Yee Hong Community Wellness Foundation." *The Globe and Mail*, 2001.04.23, Y1-Y6.

"Yee Hong Community Wellness Foundation." Yee Hong website, *www.yeehong.com/foundation/index.php*, accessed 2014.09.29.

Yee Hong Garden Terrace. *www.yeehong.com/centre/gardenterrace/index.html*, accessed 2007.10.19.

"Yee Hong Garden Terrace–Harmonious Living in Balance with Nature." Yee Hong website, *www.yeehong.com/centre/lifelease_housing.php*, accessed 2014.09. 29.

"Yee Hong Heights/Long Term Care/Our Services/Introduction to HKSR." Yee Hong website, *www.rehabsociety.org.hk/english.html*, accessed 2007.10.19.

"Yee Hong Provides Model for Other Groups." *The Globe and Mail,* 2001.04.23, Y2.

Yee, Paul. *Chinatown: An Illustrated History of the Chinese Communities of Victoria, Vancouver, Calgary, Winnipeg, Toronto, Ottawa, Montreal and Halifax.* Toronto: James Lorimer, 2005.

Yip, Christopher, Manager, Wah Ying Mansions, Calgary, Alberta. Interviewed 2006.09.08, Calgary, Alberta.

9. TRADITIONAL CHINESE MEDICINE - INTEGRATION IN CANADA[1]

1. Introduction

Traditional Chinese Medicine (TCM), arguably, is the most unusual manifestation of Chinese culture within Canada and a strong indication of the persistence of Chinese Canadians in preserving their ethnic culture. It also offers an interesting example of integration, as the Canadian public and medical system attempt to recognize and appropriate the benefits that TCM seems to offer. This chapter will present a general description of TCM, including the name's origin, its practices, and its underlying concepts and theory. Then, it will describe the benefits and detriments of TCM, followed by a demonstration of the current presence of TCM in China and a detailed portrayal of TCM in Canada. This latter portrayal will look at its institutionalization, testing, regulation, and the creation of self-regulating and teaching institutions. The chapter will close with a description of the achievements of Chinese Canadians with regard to the presence of TCM in Canada. The conclusion will show that Chinese Canadians have helped established the infrastructure for a system of alternative medicine that is proving viable and leading conventional medicine and organizations governing medicine to study its effects and create regulations to ensure its proper practice.

Arguably, the establishment of TCM has improved present medical care as many people are turning toward it for maintenance of good health and relief from suffering. Furthermore, with many Chinese Canadians now practising as care providers within the mainstream system and many non-Chinese becoming TCM practitioners, there is increasing potential to integrate conventional medicine and TCM. As the mainstream Canadian medical system incorporates practices from TCM, the role that Chinese Canadians have played in supporting TCM leading up to this integration becomes more apparent.

---

[1] The author would like to acknowledge the assistance of Ms. Betty Trinh in researching this topic.

One aspect of this chapter that should be noted is that it does not detail the role of Chinese Canadians in realizing the achievements described. To a large degree their role is assumed or evidence for it is presented generally. This is different from other chapters, such as that on the economic achievements of Chinese Canadians, where it was necessary to identify and link individual Chinese Canadians to the specific economic achievements described because to do otherwise could leave readers with the doubt that, for example, the investments in hotels described were done mostly by Chinese Canadian businesspeople.

The case for TCM is different. Although it is theoretically possible that Chinese Canadians have had an insignificant role in promoting it within Canada and integrating it into the mainstream medical system, it is highly unlikely that such is the case. If anything, this chapter will probably underestimate their role in order to ensure that its claims are not exaggerated. Unlike the claims for economic achievement, there are fewer grounds for doubting the claim that Chinese Canadians have been largely responsible for the establishment of TCM within Canada. One further point is that the benefit of certifying that Chinese Canadians are a major force in the promotion of TCM and its integration into the conventional medical system is hardly worth the effort. One would be proving a fact that on the basis of commonsense could have been reasonably assumed.

There are fewer grounds for doubt because the ability to promote and integrate TCM depends greatly on belief in a different paradigm of human health that a non-Chinese person is unlikely to have and there are general indications that Chinese Canadians are playing a major role in the promotion of this paradigm. The difference in paradigm is the result of Chinese cultural values that encourage people to think holistically, that is to consider their individual health as part of an environment, and at the same time to believe that they have the power to influence it. It is not just a matter of understanding the concept, but believing it, having it part of one's overall perspective on experience. On the basis of this belief one then has the confidence to promote TCM, which, in turn, leads to its integration with the mainstream medical system as more and more people recognize its benefits.

As for the general indications that Chinese Canadians are playing a major role in the promotion of TCM, in 2003 more than two thirds of the practitioners of TCM in British Columbia were Asian,[2] and it is likely that nearly all of these were Chinese Canadians. As well, the founders and instructors of TCM schools appear to be predominately Chinese Canadian based on their surnames. Similarly, the members of provincial regulatory bodies are also mostly Chinese Canadian, again judging from their surnames.

If one were to ascertain that Chinese Canadians were in fact a significant force in the promotion of TCM, it would require large expenditures of time and other resources when it is already fairly apparent that such is the case. The promotion and integration of TCM are part of a groundswell movement produced by the contribution of many different individuals: it comprises Chinese Canadians that practise eating functional food and promote the practice to their non-Chinese acquaintances; it is fostered by the small Chinese Canadian TCM clinics that operate across the country; and it is made up of the schools that teach the skills and transmit the knowledge. To survey and determine the ethnic origins of the agents of these actions would be huge tasks and one would only be ascertaining what is already fairly certain. For this reason, the role of Chinese Canadians in promoting TCM within the country is in large part assumed.

2. What is Traditional Chinese Medicine?

2.1 Consolidation of Practices and Creation of the Term "Traditional Chinese Medicine"

When the term "Traditional Chinese Medicine" is used in Canada, one is not usually aware of the political process that led to its creation. Indeed, the motivation for its coining and the irony that surround the term would also make one suspect that they were being misled. The Chinese government decided in the early 1950s to consolidate what was the diverse body of Chinese medicine–and to a large extent remains so today–in order to harness its benefits for the Chinese nation. Part of this process was to create a system and coherent body of knowledge that

---

[2] Asia Pacific Foundation, "Canada Begins to Assimilate Traditional Chinese Medicine," *Canada Asia Commentary* 32 (December 2003), 4.

438

could be integrated with the system of Western medicine that was being practised in China. As an extension of this goal, the English term "Traditional Chinese Medicine," was invented.[3] The first known use of the term was in 1955 in an article entitled "Why our Western-Trained Doctors Should Learn Traditional Chinese Medicine" by Fu Lianzhang, then President of the Chinese Medical Association and Deputy Minister of Health.[4]

The government, in order to create a coherent body of knowledge on Chinese medicine, set up four academies to organize Chinese medical knowledge, to compile textbooks, and to train teachers. It subsequently published standardized textbooks of TCM, then set about to establish TCM as a credible medical system within the national health care system. This consolidation of the diverse forms of medical knowledge then extant within China into a coherent body was also supposed to contribute to its ultimate integration with Western medicine.[5]

Arguably the coining of the term "Traditional Chinese Medicine" was an appeal to non-Chinese to view the result of the government's efforts as the creation of systemic body of knowledge that contained valuable medical information. The article within which the term is said to have first appeared promoted the value TCM to English readers, such as foreign doctors, medical schools, and churches, who had an impact on determining healthcare in China then but might otherwise be unaware of the efforts to strengthen the indigenous practices and knowledge. Furthermore, promoters of this cause would have been strongly motivated because the call to have Western trained doctors study Chinese medicine was said to have come from Mao Zedong.[6]

---

[3] Kim Taylor, *Chinese Medicine in Early Communist China, 1945-63: A Medicine of Revolution* (London: RoutledgeCurzon, 2005), 84-85, 87. Also Elisabeth Hsu, *The Transmission of Chinese Medicine*, (Cambridge, U.K.: Cambridge University Press, 1999), 8.

[4] In *Chinese Medical Journal* 73.5 (Sept.-Oct. 1955), front page; page reprinted in Taylor, 85.

[5] Taylor, 84, 87.

[6] Taylor, 87; citing Hua Zhongfu and Liang Jun, *Zhongguo Zhongyi Yanjiu Yuan yuanshi* (History of China's Research Academy of Traditional Chinese Medicine) (Beijing: Zhongyi guji chubanshe, 1995), 4; and Wang Zhipu and

The term comes with a large degree of irony, and, knowing this leads to a richer understanding of what is being created in Canada with the promotion of TCM. There is no equivalent term for TCM in Chinese; it seems to have been created primarily for communication with non-Chinese. The closest equivalent term in Chinese is "Chinese medicine" (*Zhongyi*), which is inclusive of TCM.[7] Furthermore, what is being called TCM is not traditional in the sense that much of it is the product of recent government action in China. The government has taken a diversity of practices and knowledges from shamanic, temple-based, divinatory, home-based herbal, and other practices, organized and standardized them, and placed them into institutional settings of colleges, hospitals, and clinics. The result is a construct that can be presented and seen as scientific and modernized.[8]

The construction of TCM by the government of China is relevant to its development in Canada because it is likely that the focused efforts of the Chinese government will produce a system that is attractive to Chinese and non-Chinese Canadians alike. One already finds the sophisticatedly prepared and packaged products of Chinese medicine producers on the shelves of TCM practitioners and health food stores across Canada. There will also be a tendency to integrate TCM and conventional Western medicine that accompanies the appeal of TCM. Arguably, this is the goal and what is occurring in China. The institutionalization of Chinese medicine mirrors the Western medical system in that the colleges, hospitals, and clinics within which it is taught and practised are modeled after those in the West. TCM and Western medicine are also practised side-by-side within the same premises. Ideally, the best of both systems can be extracted and they can complement each other.

One will also see in Canada some of the diversity that has historically been part of Chinese medicine. There will be

Cai Jingfeng, *Zhongguo Zhongyiyao, 50 nian, (1949-99)* (Fifty years of China's traditional Chinese medicine and pharmacology [1949–99]) (Fuzhou: Fujian kexue jishu chubanshe, 1999), 10.

[7] Hsu, 7.

[8] Hsu, 7-8.

practitioners and their methods that do not conform to the standards that the government in China has tried to apply in their creation of TCM. Because of these cases, the need for regulation of TCM on Canada's part is becoming more apparent. This too can be seen as part of the trend toward greater integration of TCM into Canadian society.

2.2 Underlying Concepts and Theories

At first blush, the potential for integration between TCM and Western conventional medicine seems weak. There are a number of concepts and theories within TCM that seem unscientific and lacking explicative power, which easily is grounds for dismissal. At best they seem exotic, especially to the non-initiated; at worst, they seem superstitious. However, this weakness is hardly pervasive. Furthermore, there are also within TCM concepts and theories that have strong intuitive appeal and the contrast of TCM to the Western conventional medical system offers a basis for deep reflection within the latter on ways to improve. These strengths support a trend toward greater integration.

There are a number of concepts essential to TCM and, to reiterate, some of them have strong intuitive appeal; for example, the concept of emphasizing maintenance of good health, as contrasted with the effective treatment of injury or cure of a disease. There is also the concept of balance, itself a metaphor, with its plasticity that subsumes a number of other concepts, particularly the quintessential concept of polar complementariness *yin-yang*. *Qi* is primal substance-energy that it said to permeate the universe. Its conceptualization is essential to explaining the need for and effects of TCM practices; for example, medicinal herbs contain *qi* that is extracted by the human digestive system and transferred to the human body. Another concept that is essential to TCM is the holistic perspective with which practitioners view health. All natural events are considered to be interrelated, including the state of health of individual human beings. An individual's health is not only a physical state, but comprises their psychological and spiritual states, and is dependent upon their physical environment and relationships. These various concepts have an immediate appeal that would motive further investigation, and, therefore, increase the potential for the integration of TCM with Western conventional medicine.

However, it should be acknowledged that not all concepts important to TCM have this appeal. The concept of five phases *(wuxing)* is used to explain the use of herbal remedies and other treatments on specific human organs; for example, a child that experiences chronic fear (an emotion linked to the water phase) and tends to wet the bed (urine is also linked to the water phase) probably has weak kidneys (the organ linked to the water phase) and should be treated with an appropriate remedy.[9] A counterpart in Western conventional medicine are scientifically proven descriptions of causal relationships between treatments and cures. Compared to the latter, the concept of "five phases" pales in appeal. A more detailed description of these concepts, both appealing and not, allows the reader to measure the benefits of TCM, thus the potential for its integration with Western conventional medicine.

2.2.1 Maintenance

The complexity of maintaining one's health does not immediately present itself when one considers the concept. Good health is taken to be the norm and as the norm it is, well, normal. One has to assume common sense and the moderation that accompanies it, but it seems that the average person should be able to expect a modicum of good health in their lives. Those who do not achieve the norm are considered to be misfortunate. In contrast, the norm of good health is not taken for granted in TCM; for example, TCM contains a large amount of advice on diet that promises the individual the opportunity to improve the probability of enjoying good health.

Two terms, "functional food" and "nutraceutical," used in the health products industry alert one to the potential of maintaining one's health through researched food consumption. "Functional food," as defined by Agriculture and Agri-Food Canada, "is similar in appearance to, or may be, a conventional food that is consumed as part of a usual diet, and is demonstrated to have physiological benefits and/or reduce the risk of chronic disease beyond basic nutritional functions, i.e.,

---

[9] Daniel P. Reid, *Chinese Herbal Medicine* (Boston: Shambhala, 1987), 33.

they contain bioactive compounds."[10] The key phrase in this definition for distinguishing functional food is "beyond basic nutritional functions." One is aware, of course, of the physical need for nourishment. However, the definition indicates a distinction, that foods can have specific functions that extend beyond those of basic nutrition and these functions are apparent in the decreased incidence of chronic disease. These foods contain ingredients that do more than fulfill an essential need; they actually initiate a process within the body that improves health, including the prevention of disease.

Linked to the concept of functional food is that of nutraceutical, which "is a product isolated or purified from foods that is generally sold in medicinal forms not usually associated with foods. A nutraceutical is demonstrated to have a physiological benefit or provide protection against chronic disease."[11] A nutraceutical is an isolation of the active ingredient in a functional food that is said to promote good health. For example, long chain omega-3 fatty acids, which are said to reduce the risk of cardiovascular disease and improve mental and visual functions, are extracted from fish oils and sold in capsules.[12][13]

---

[10] "What are Functional Foods and Nutraceuticals?", Agriculture and Agri-Food Canada website, "Agri-Industries > Functional Foods and Nutraceuticals," *www4.agr.gc.ca/AAFC-AAC/display-afficher.do?id=1171305207040&lang=e*, accessed 2009.12.03.

[11] *Ibid.*

[12] *Ibid.*

[13] It should be noted that Agriculture and Agri-Food Canada has since modified its terminology. Nutraceuticals are referred to as "natural health products" and defined as "extracts derived from natural sources and which have demonstrated health benefits." Functional foods are defined as "foods enhanced with bioactive ingredients and which have demonstrated health benefits. Examples are probiotic yogurt, or pea fibre-fortified breads and pasta." ("Functional Foods and Natural Health Products - Canadian Industry," *www.agr.gc.ca/eng/industry-markets-and-trade/statistics-and-market-information/by-product-sector/functional-foods-and-natural-health-products/functional-foods-and-natural-health-products-canadian-industry/?id=1170856376710*, accessed 2015.07.10)

Although the new definition does not include foods in their original form, the former definition did and, therefore, conformed to the Chinese concept. Furthermore, the former definition is still in current use; for example, see *Wikipedia, s.v.* "Functional food."

The concept of functional foods is well established in TCM and probably began there. Functional foods are consumed for the following purposes: "to maintain and improve health status; to prevent disease and help in treating disease; and to facilitate rehabilitation."[14] It is natural that the Chinese would link food and medicine because they consider them to both come from the same source. Historically, there are references to herbal medicine in China as early as the 1500 BCE.[15] *Shiliao bencao* (Dietotherapy of medical material) authored by Meng Xian in approximately 702 is one of the earliest extant monographs of dietetic treatment.[16] The term "medicinal food" *(yaoshi)* was used as early as the Later Jin (936-946) period[17] and it is claimed that it was frequently seen in the literature of the Han Dynasty (220 BCE 220 CE).[18] There were hundreds of functional foods and corresponding recipes documented in classical TCM publications running from before the common era until the sixteenth century. One example was the use of marine algae (kelp) to prevent and treat goiter that was described in Ge Hong's (283-343) *Handbook of Prescriptions for Emergencies.*[19] Other examples of functional foods include Chinese wolfberry *(gouqi)*, which is said to improve vision, and wheat, which is supposed to be good for the heart.[20]

---

[14] Weijian Weng and Junshi Chen, "The Eastern Perspective on Functional Foods Based on Traditional Chinese Medicine," *Nutrition Reviews* 54.11 (Nov. 1996): (II) S11. It should be noted that some researchers do not attribute therapeutic purposes to functional food and they cite various Chinese government offices as supporting this stipulation (Chunyan Yao, Ruiwen Hao, Shengli Pan, and Yin Wang, "Functional Foods Based on Traditional Chinese Medicine, *Nutrition, Well-being and Health,* ed. Jaouad Bouayed [Shanghai: InTech, 2012], 181).

[15] Reid, 19.

[16] Yao et al, 187.

[17] s.v. *"yaoshi"* (medicinal food), *Zhongwen da cidian* (The encyclopedic dictionary of the Chinese language), Vol. 29 (Taipei: Zhongguo wenhua xueyuan chubanbu). A more contemporary equivalent of *yaoshi* is *yaoshan.*

[18] Weng and Chen, S11.

[19] *Ibid.*

[20] Reid, 153 and 122.

There are other similar concepts found in TCM. *Buping* "are regular Chinese herbal medicines cooked in food and taken to cope with the stress and strain of life, with environmental changes, and to replenish a person's natural immunity. Preparations made from these plant products are often taken seasonally and occasionally for keeping the body in tone and for the prevention of diseases."[21] *Buping* are slightly different from functional foods in that they are consumed for special purposes rather than on a continual basis. Following from this, the preparation and consumption of *buping* are more deliberate. While both are consumed for the purposes of maintaining good health and have more medicinal effects than ordinary food, *buping* are less readily available. They are not part of the daily diet.

One can see that the practice of drawing medicinal benefit from one's diet is highly developed in Chinese thinking. The concepts of functional foods, medicinal foods, and *buping* are indications of this. This practice is also evidence of the importance given to maintenance of health in TCM. The immediate benefits and remedial effects of diet are limited; however, over the long term they can produce a proven benefit for human health. This is a goal and an important concept in the practice of TCM.

2.2.2 Balance

The concept of balance in TCM pays heed to the fact that human health benefits from the presence of a multitude of different influences, both within the human body and outside it. In TCM the norm, the state of good health that one naturally possesses, is a balanced relation among these forces. The intuitive appeal of this concept is obvious because it also exists outside of TCM; praising references to a balanced diet or life are common in English.

In TCM special attention is given to recognizing and balancing *opposing* influences. Human health benefits from heat and cold, activity and rest, struggle and ease, support and challenge, sweetness and saltiness, fats and plant juices,

---

[21] Shiu-ying Hu, *Food Plants of China* (Hong Kong, The Chinese University Press, 2005), 161.

depressants and stimulants, and so on. With the need for opposing forces in one's life also comes the need to keep these forces in equilibrium, so that one force does not exert excessive influence, which could cause harm to one's health. The concept of balance is embodied in the icons of *yin* and *yang* that are pervasive in both TCM and Chinese philosophy. Similarly to the concept of balance, *yin/yang* points to a need to keep the opposing forces within a dynamic entity in proper proportion in order to promote the viability of that entity. In TCM, this entity is human health.

There is a large diet regime in TCM that is based on the concept of maintaining or restoring the balance characterizing human health and is explained with the concepts of *yin* and *yang*. The balance may be of forces within the human body, such as when suffering a cold, one has an excess of yin forces, which can be counterbalanced with the consumption of foods boosting yang force; for example, drinks made from fresh ginger. The need for balance also holds for the relation of a human body to its environment. "Foods and herbal medicines redress yin-yang imbalances by supplementing the deficient element. One example of basic preventive care based on the yin-yang theory is to adjust the diet according to the season: in summer, cooling yin foods should be increased in the diet and overly hot yang foods avoided. In winter, plenty of warming yang foods should be included in the diet, and in extreme cold a few warming yang herbal medications should be consumed regularly as well."[22]

The concept of balance is utilized in the practice of acupuncture as well. Acupuncture is held to unblock obstructions of *qi* or energy within the body. This redirection of *qi* within the body by the use of acupuncture needles is described as restoring balance to the body.[23] In this case maintaining balance means facilitating the ongoing movement of forces within the body. The breadth of the use of the concept of balance is further indication of its importance in TCM.

---

[22] Reid, 31.

[23] Glenn S. Rothfeld, *The Acupuncture Response: Balance Energy and Restore Health–a Western Doctor Tells You How* (Chicago: Contemporary Books, 2002), 41.

2.2.3 *Qi*

Simply stated, *qi* is the omnipresent medium by which energy is transmitted and transmuted. It has substance, but one that is dynamic, and some of the terms used to translate it, such as "vital force," "primal substance-energy," and "life energy'" reflect its kinetic nature. The Chinese have historically conceptualized the universe to be an organic whole. Unlike in a mechanical model of the universe, in which relations among entities is straight forward and governed by laws of physics, relations among entities in an organic universe, such as the environment and one's body, are more complex and the results of their interactions are difficult to predict.

The Chinese concept of *qi* fits well with the concept of an organic universe. There has to be a substratum that underlies the connections among the different parts of the universe and that substratum is *qi*. It is also amorphous enough to account for the diversity of shapes, sizes, and materials in the universe that it is supposed to underlie.

Besides being the substratum that transmits energy among entities, *qi* also accounts for the change of form or transmutation that energy undergoes. For example, in maintaining a healthy body the most important factors are the food one eats and the air one breathes. Digestion extracts *qi* from food "and transfers it to the body; breathing extracts *qi* from air and transfers it to the lungs. When these two forms of *qi* meet in the bloodstream, they transmute to form human *qi*, which then circulates throughout the body as life energy."[24] Therefore, the concept of *qi* is not only able to account for the transmission of energy; it also accounts for the different forms that this energy takes.

The ability of *qi* to transmute is explained with the help of another concept. Entities are distinct or individual because of their particular embodiment of form or, as the Chinese term *"li"* is usually translated, "principle." For example, a tree would be composed of *qi*, just like any other entity and would be different from a frog because it embodied the principle of a tree. Acknowledgment of *qi's* ability to transmute is also seen in the different forms that it takes while still being identified as *qi*; for

---

[24] Reid, 28.

example, the organs of the human body have their own *qi,* the *qi* dwelling in the heart is *xinqi* (literally, the vital force of the heart), the *qi* of the liver is *ganqi,* and so on.[25]

The concept of *qi* is also closely connected to the concept of balance. The norm and ideal state of human health is one in which the various forms of *qi* are in balance, which means that there is ideal combination of quality and quantity of *qi* both within the body, such as a balance between the *qi* that nourishes (*yingqi*) and the *qi* that protects *(weiqi),*[26] and between various *qi* within the human body and those in the external environment, such as the need for a build-up of heat within the body to counteract cold weather. Another important dimension of the concept of the balance of *qi* is that an ideal state is often one of constant flow and transmutation.[27] Within the body, there are many processes, such as the circulation of the blood or the ongoing nourishment and cleansing of individual body parts, that require the synchronization of a number of different sub-processes. The maintenance of these processes in a norm that supports the optimal operation of the body is also a matter of balance, though one complicated by the ongoing changes in relations among the sub-processes. This reflects the complexity of the concept of balance and that of *qi* along with it.

2.2.4 Holism

In TCM all natural phenomena are believed to be mutually influencing. The universe is seen as an integrated whole with each part having an effect on every other part, however minuscule this effect may be. With regard to human health, this holistic view is manifested in treatment of the human subject as part of a whole, integrated system. In other words, one's environment including the air one breathes, the amount of sunlight one receives, and so on, are all considered to have an effect on one's health.

---

[25] Hsu, 82.

[26] Reid, 29.

[27] Hsu, 87.

There are important implications for TCM treatment arising from this view. For one, the features of one's environment have to be considered when attempting to promote health. An obvious example is the climatic conditions within which one lives having a large impact on one's health. There are more subtle examples, such as the emotional stress that may arise from one's work environment. Although the possibilities seem endless, the main focus seems to be to increase awareness of environmental factors in determining human health. Furthermore, there is an art, fengshui, that has organized the knowledge of creating an environment that is conducive to human viability.[28] Therefore, there is assistance available in attempting to predict and respond to environmental influences on human health. One need not refuse or despair of understanding these influences because of their complexity.

Besides viewing the human subject as integrated with and, therefore, affected by their environment, TCM also applies the concept of integration to the human body. All personal processes, whether physical or psychological, are considered mutually influencing; for example, an irregularity in one part of the body will have an influence in another. It may also be the case that one's emotional state will influence one's physical well being or vice versa.

This holistic view of how human health is constituted has apparent ramifications in TCM. Human health is not merely defined in terms of physical well being; rather it refers to the configuration of physical and psychological health and even has strong links to the well being of the environment. It follows that the goals of TCM will also be different from Western conventional medicine because TCM will be targeting more than the physical parts and structure of the body. In some cases, given the mutual influence between the physical and psychological processes, the latter and the external factors that influence them, may be among its targets.

This view contributes to three important differences between TCM and Western medical treatments. First, TCM relies much more on activating the psychological capacities in order produce beneficial effects in the body. For example,

[28] The belief that fengshui influences a number of human conditions, including wealth, emotional state, romance, as well as health, also reflects the holistic approach of TCM.

meditation will be used to relax and rest the body, or the emotions will be controlled so as not to disturb it. Second, TCM is much less injury centred than Western conventional medicine. Specific treatments may not be concentrated on the diseased or injured area. The underlying belief is that the disease or injury is often the result of causes originating elsewhere or it can be treated by applications to other parts of the body. For example, acupuncture applied to the elbow is held to be a treatment for sinusitis.[29]

The third important difference between TCM and Western medical treatments that results from embracing the concept of holism is that TCM emphasizes more long term treatment. Western conventional medicine has emphasized the development of expeditious treatments, such as surgery and strong pharmaceuticals, to achieve cures of illness, disease, or injury. These methods have been particularly effective, especially in treating emergencies. However, they have also contributed to the perception that scientific discovery and technological invention can create miracle cures and allow humans to overcome what are thought to be natural limitations.

In contrast, Chinese medical practitioners have sought to understand all aspects of a patient's state: physical, mental, ancestral, and even environmental, which has led to a strength of "sophisticated analysis of how functions were related on many levels, from the vital processes of the body to the emotions to the natural and social environment of the patient, always with therapy in mind."[30] Based on this approach, they have "tended to reject the idea of instant remedies, believing that most illnesses and debilitations were the result of deep-rooted problems and that without continuous long-range treatment the root problem would simply manifest itself again and again, in different forms and in different parts of the body."[31]

---

[29] Giovanni Maciocia, *The Practice of Chinese Medicine : the Treatment of Diseases with Acupuncture and Chinese Herbs*, second edition (Edinburgh: Churchill Livingstone Elsevier, 2008), 205 and 1013-14.

[30] Nathan Sivin, "Science and Medicine in Chinese History," *Heritage of China: Contemporary Perspectives on Chinese Civilization*, ed. Paul S. Ropp. (Berkeley: University of California Press , 1990), 186.

[31] Reid, 14.

2.2.5 Five Phases *(wuxing)*

Five phases is an explicative and mnemonic device for describing natural phenomena, which has been used in China since 200 BCE.[32] It subsequently became an important tool in Chinese science, including TCM. It uses generative and subjugative relations among five basic elements: earth, wood, metal, fire, and water (e.g., water extinguishes fire but nourishes wood) as analogies to explain natural phenomena. It is also known as "five elements," "five processes," and *"wuxing."*

The five phases can be aligned with specific organs, such as water with the kidneys. In diagnosing a problem with the heart, the practitioner of TCM will suspect a problem with the kidneys.[33] According to the model of the five phases, water, and its corresponding organ the kidneys, has a subjugative role over fire and its corresponding organ the heart. Therefore, the TCM practitioner will strengthen the kidneys as a way of curing the problem with the heart.[34]

There seems to be less use of five phases in explaining TCM treatments.[35] It could be that with increasing numbers of TCM practitioners trained in Western medicine, they are importing more efficient explicative devices from the latter. Also, as TCM seeks to integrate with Western conventional medicine, the benefit of having common forms of explanation becomes more apparent.

2.2.6 Being Proactive

Another concept that underlies TCM is the importance of its users being proactive. Because of this importance, users are not easily distinguished from practitioners. Effective use of TCM requires considerable

[32] A.C. Graham, *Disputers of the Tao: Philosophical Argument in Ancient China* (La Salle, Illinois: Open Court, 1989), 341.

[33] According to Bill Reid, heart failure is generally accompanied by renal complications, 36.

[34] Reid, 36.

[35] Maciocia's fifteen hundred page monograph only mentions the five phases on three pages, 1479 (index).

knowledge, effort, and time. This is mostly because of the maintenance that is an essential part of TCM. The demands of being holistic also mean that the user approaches the professional in the intensity of their involvement in the use of TCM. The simple and inexpensive techniques of TCM that one can implement themselves enable the nonprofessional to take a greater role in promoting their personal health.

Maintenance in TCM includes the use of functional foods, which is a daily activity that requires modification with changes to the individual's health and external conditions, such as the change of seasons. The use of functional foods also requires the user to acquire knowledge of the effects of the different foods, along with awareness of one's own health and external conditions, which again encourages their involvement in maintaining their health.

The emphasis on a holistic approach to health also encourages this involvement. It is impossible for the professional practitioner of TCM caring for a number of different patients to delve deeply into the personal lives of each in order to understand the myriad of factors that are affecting them. If a user of TCM is going to respond to external factors in order to promote their good health, they will have to rely mostly on their own efforts.

TCM facilitates being proactive because many of its techniques for maintaining good health are simple, inexpensive, and self-implemented. Planning one's diet, including adjusting it for one's bodily and environmental changes, can be done easily. While some of the ingredients in herbal medicines and functional foods can be expensive, many others are items of daily consumption that are not. One can also massage oneself, or have a nonprofessional do it, and many learn and practise *qigong*. These simple techniques combined with the quotidian and detailed efforts required by health maintenance and the holistic approach lead to the TCM user being proactive in managing their health.

In closing this discussion of the concepts underlying TCM, it is also important to emphasize the psychological benefits of being proactive, in other words, being able to actively participate in the process of promoting one's own health. Empowerment comes from control, which feeds upon itself to build even more power. As the TCM user is required to become more involved in promoting their own health, the benefits of doing so become more apparent and thereby serve as an impetus to continue and even increase involvement.

2.3 Practices

There are a number of different techniques or practices in TCM. Diet, of course, is a major one; others include the use of herbs as prescriptions, acupuncture, massage, and qigong. The uniqueness of some of these practices increases the potential benefit of integrating TCM with Western conventional medicine. There is a greater possibility that they will offer benefits that the latter does not possess.

2.3.1 Diet

Given that food comes from the same source as much of the medicine used in TCM, that food is consumed in order to produce similar effects as medicine, that food impedes as well as promotes the effects of medicinal herbs, and that food is consumed daily, diet has become an important, if not the most important practice in TCM.

One of the main features of the ideal TCM diet is its diversity. This feature is important to being able to meet the individual needs of each user, especially to maintain the balance that is an essential goal of TCM. Each person's physiology is different as is their physical and social environment. The diversity of food allows the individual to make a fine degree of differentiation in selecting the constituents of their diet so that they are best able to meet the demands of their physiology and environment. Chinese diet is well known for the variety of products consumed and the methods of preparation. Stories abound of exotic dishes such as monkey brains and swallows' nests, but even simple foods like buckwheat and various forms of soy bean, are indicative of the diversity in Chinese diet. As well, cooking methods vary from steaming to stir fry to fermentation, and these can have a major influence on health.[36] The variety of foods eaten and methods

---

[36] For example, baking can supply a heating effect to foods, so is a way for vegetarians to supply their bodies with this effect, which is especially useful given their large consumption of foods that tend to cool the body (Jöerg Kastner, *Chinese Nutrition Therapy: Dietetics in Traditional Chinese Medicine (TCM)* [Stuttgart: Thieme, 2004], 32).

used to prepare them align with the goal of TCM to provide diversity in the user's diet. With this wider choice they are then better able to meet their individual needs.

The diversity of a TCM diet also allows the user to maintain the balance that is essential in TCM. TCM assumes that the complexity of the human body requires that factors influencing health be kept in suitable relation. TCM's efforts to maintain balance through diet can be seen in description of two qualities, the thermal nature and flavour of food, that are of principal importance in Chinese nutritional therapy.[37]

Following the paradigm of *yin and yang,* foods are categorized according to their thermal natures and are used to maintain the body in balance. Certain foods, such as highly fatty ones (e.g., lamb or alcohol), are considered hot or *yang.* These foods warm the body and stimulate its *qi.* Other foods, such as watermelon and celery, are considered cold or *yin.* These cool the body and have a calming effect on it.[38] Depending on factors such as the time of day, the season, and an individual's constitution, the consumption of "hot" foods such as ginger and chilly can protect the body from catching a cold.[39] Likewise, the consumption of "cool" foods, such as apples, pears, and green tea, can be a remedy for hypertension.[40] The goal is to maintain or restore balance in the body.

Normally, an individual will be healthy, so food therapy will attempt to preserve the balance. If an individual consumes a meal rich in fat and spice (for example, one containing lamb, peanuts, and chilies), they can prevent excessive "heat" build-up by supplementing the meal with a few "cooling" foods, such as oranges.[41]

The second quality of value in nutritional therapy is flavour. In TCM there are five major flavours: sweet, acrid, salty, sour, and bitter. Each of these is related to an internal

---

[37] Kastner, 21.

[38] *Ibid.,* 23.

[39] *Ibid.,* 63.

[40] *Ibid.,* 205.

[41] Reid, 60.

organ through the explicative device of the five phases: sweet with the spleen and stomach, acrid with the lungs and large intestine, salty with the kidney and bladder, sour with the liver and gallbladder, and bitter with the heart and small intestine. The relations when adequate, not deficient or excessive, contribute to good health, sweetness strengthening the spleen, acridity the lungs, saltiness supplementing the kidneys, sourness "cooling the emotional 'heat' in the liver/gall bladder," and bitterness supporting the body's digestive and excretion functions.[42]

The importance of a diverse diet in the nutritional therapy of TCM is manifested in the analysis of the thermal natures and flavours of the various foods. The diversity allows for deployment across a wide spectrum of body states and the fulfilment of the needs of various internal organs. The goal of this deployment and fulfilment also reflects the underlying concept of balance. There is an attempt to maintain, through proper proportioning, an internal stability among the various forces within the dynamic entity that is the body and thereby support its viability.

2.3.2 Herbal medicine

Medicinal herbs are mostly derived from the same sources as the functional foods that make up diet in TCM. Therefore, they are characterized much the same. For instance, the individual thermal nature of each herb has to be considered and balance is an important norm to be maintained with their use. Nevertheless, herbal treatments are more specific than functional foods in their application; they are often aimed at preventing or curing specific ailments. Moreover, the use of herbal medicine is, as one would think, much more complex. More than eleven thousand different plant species are used in one hundred thousand TCM herbal prescriptions.[43] Thermal natures are also measured more finely; they are categorized into hot, warm, cool, and cold. The ingredients of prescriptions or formulae can include minerals as well as plant and animal

---

[42] Kastner, 26-27.

[43] Jane Qiu, "Traditional Medicine: a Culture in the Balance," *Nature* 448.7150 (2007.07.12), 127.

matter. Prescriptions are not necessarily taken internally and can also be applied externally as poultices. A herbal prescription is usually a mixture of many herbs that has been tailored to the individual patient and their state. Decoction is the most common method of extracting active ingredients from the herbs. Furthermore, herbs may be added as secondary ingredients to mitigate the toxicity or side-effects of the main ingredients.

Some of the specific functions served by herbal medicines include purgative, resuscitative, expectorant, tonic, etc.,[44] and these functions can be even more finely distinguished. For example, the purgative function can be fulfilled using herbs of different thermal natures and it is the responsibility of the herbalist or TCM doctor to know and prescribe the best one. For example, rhubarb *(rheum officinale)* and purging croton *(croton tiglium)* are both used as purgatives, but the former's thermal nature is cold and the latter's is hot. The former is used as a purgative, laxative, and astringent (e.g., diminishes discharges of blood) and can even be applied directly to burns.[45] The latter is the strongest of all purgatives and can be used as an external irritant to erupt abscesses and boils.[46] The practitioner has to keep in mind that herbal remedies, because of their potency, are potentially overbearing; therefore, weak and elderly patients should not be administered the stronger hot and cold remedies.[47] It is this complexity that distinguishes herbal medicine from functional foods.

A simple example of a herbal prescription is one for indigestion due to excess consumption of meats and fats. One combines the fruit of the hawthorn (fifteen g.), the rind of the mandarin orange (six g.), the unripened fruit of the trifoliate orange (eight g.), and the rhizomes of the mishmi bitter (four g.). Then one boils the mixture with three cups of water in a covered vessel until it decocts to one cup. After straining, take as one dose, sipping the brew gradually.[48] Although the

---

[44] Reid, 81-159.

[45] *Ibid.,* 88.

[46] *Ibid.,* 91.

[47] *Ibid.,* 46.

[48] *Ibid.,* 162.

prescription sounds simple enough, each of the ingredients still has a thermal nature that has to be taken into account as well as the individual patient's circumstances. Even a deceptively simple prescription is consumed within a complex configuration of circumstances that are part of the diagnosis making its selection far from simple.

The complexity of herbal medicine is further seen in one of its important theories, the principle of *jun-chen-zuo-shi*. These four terms designate four different functions that a herb can serve in a prescription. "The *jun* (emperor) herbs treat the main cause or primary symptoms of a disease. The *chen* (minister) herbs serve to augment or broaden the effects of *jun*, and relieve secondary symptoms. The *zuo* (assistant) herbs are used to modulate the effects of *jun* and *chen*, and to counteract the toxic or side effects of these herbs. The *shi* (courier) herbs are included in many formulae to ensure that all components in the prescription are well absorbed, and to help deliver or guide them to the target organs." To add to this complexity, the "*jun* and *chen* herbs in one formula may serve as *zuo* and *shi* herbs in another."[49] The varying function of an individual herb when combined with others in a prescription is but one example of the complexity of TCM herbal medicine.

2.3.3 Acupuncture

Acupuncture is used to treat ailments and provide local anesthesia by the insertion of thin steel needles at identified points on the human body. There are more than eight hundred acupuncture points; however, only about fifty are commonly used. A point is stimulated by rotating the needles until a tight, twisting sensation is felt there by the patient. These points are believed to be situated on channels, usually called "meridians." When an acupuncture point is stimulated, the movement of *qi* or vital force is experienced along the meridian. If a part of the body along this channel is diseased, the sensation will be directed to it.

There are said to be a total of fifty-nine meridians in the body, of which twelve are the main ones and dominate the

---

[49] Qiu, "Traditional," 127.

others. Each of the main meridians connects to one of twelve vital organs and *qi* flows from one meridian to another in a specific order until the entire network is covered, delivering vital force to every part of the body.[50] Stimulating one of the points has specific therapeutic effects on the related organ, specific effects on the body areas covered by the meridian, and a general effect on the body's vital force through the meridian complex. Therefore, acupuncture can be used to cure diseases of the internal organs as well as to relieve pain in bones, muscles, joints, and skin. Acupuncture and herbal prescriptions are commonly used together.[51] The meridians along which a sensation is created are different from the nerve, blood vessel, and lymphatic pathways, although there is some proximity to the nerve systems.

In North America the use of acupuncture that has received the most attention is the control of pain. "In the United States, acupuncture has its greatest success and acceptance in the treatment of musculoskeletal pain. Problems such as acute sprains and strains are most easily treated, while chronic pain patients make up the largest numbers of patients seeking acupuncture from US physicians."[52] In Canada, the first recorded use of acupuncture in medical surgery outside of dental surgery took place in 1996 in Alberta. Steven Aung, trained in both Western and TCM, applied acupuncture analgesia instead of anesthetic drugs to allow a noncancerous lump to be removed from the thigh of a patient.[53]

2.3.4 Massage

---

[50] Reid, 35.

[51] *Ibid.*, 57.

[52] Steven E. Braverman, "Medical Acupuncture Review: Safety, Efficacy, And Treatment Practices," *Medical Acupuncture* 15.3 (2004), *www.acupunctureadvocates.com/uploads/1/0/0/9/10094929/vol_15_3_-_medical_acupuncture_review__safety_efficacy_and_treatment_practices_-_steven_e.pdf*, accessed 2013.09.18.

[53] Robert Walker, "History Made with Acupuncture Operation," *Calgary Herald*, 1996.10.14, B2.

There are two basic forms of massage in TCM: *tuina* and acupressure. The theories of *qi*, acupuncture points, and meridians have strongly influenced the theories and techniques of both. *Tuina* is used to clear *qi* blockages along the meridians, and even indirectly treat internal organs, much the same way acupuncture works. It is also used to loosen muscles and joints so as to relieve strains much like standard forms of massage in the West. It can also be used to realign the position of bones and internal organs. Massage techniques vary from light stroking to pressing, kneading, and even pinching. Massage is often used in conjunction with herbal poultices.[54]

Acupressure is also called *zhiya* and can be likened to *shiatsu*, a Japanese derivative. Pressure is applied to the same points as in acupuncture, but employing sharp finger pressure instead of needles. The goal is, as in acupuncture and *tuina*, to stimulate the flow of energy. It is usually combined with *tuina* in therapy.[55]

2.3.5 *Qigong*

"*Qigong*" is the transliteration of two Chinese characters: the first one pronounced "*qi*" meaning "vital force," and "*gong*" meaning "work" or "benefits acquired through perseverance and practice." Together they mean "working with the life energy, learning how to control the flow and distribution of *qi* in order to improve the health and harmony of mind and body";[56] improving health includes curing illness and prolonging life. "*Qigong* is a wholistic system of self-healing exercise and meditation, an ancient, evolving practice that includes healing posture, movement, self-massage, breathing techniques, and meditation." "*Qigong* techniques are divided into two general categories: dynamic or active *qigong (donggong)* and tranquil or passive *qigong (jinggong)*. Dynamic *qigong* includes obvious movement. The entire body moves from one position to another, as though performing a dance, or a posture is held while the

---

[54] Reid, 58.

[55] *Ibid.*, 57.

[56] Kenneth Cohen, *The Way of Qigong: the Art and Science of Chinese Energy Healing* (New York: Ballantine Books, 1997), 3.

arms move through various positions . . . In tranquil *qigong* the entire body is still. The *qi* is controlled by mental concentration, visualization, and precise methods of breathing."[57] Advanced practitioners can also perform a form of healing through *qigong*. It is said that they are able to transmit healing *qi* to a sick person.[58]

The extraordinary claims made for *qigong* are open to query. It is not only a question of proving that its physical and mental exercises can achieve the results claimed, such as the healing of others; there is even doubt of the existence of *qi*.[59] These questions clearly reflect the divide between TCM and Western conventional medicine. The latter places great emphasis on having scientific evidence to support medical claims and those of TCM have often been found faulty in this regard.

Other unusual practices of TCM seem to raise similar questions and also contribute to the differences between it and Western conventional medicine. The primary reliance on diet is in strong contrast to the sophisticated technology that allows Western medical practitioners to intervene in even the most extreme injuries and illnesses. The consumption of natural herbs, animal parts, and minerals differs from the intake of highly refined pharmaceuticals. Acupuncture has no equivalent in Western conventional medicine, and, even though massage is common to both Western medicine and TCM, its affinity with acupuncture in TCM distinguishes it as well.

Nevertheless, against this background of different practices, beliefs, and standards for evidence, one finds substantial presence of TCM within Canada. There are reasons for this, which are mainly seen in the benefits offered by TCM and the efforts of Chinese Canadians to promote them.

3. Benefits of Traditional Chinese Medicine

3.1 Early Achievements

---

[57] Cohen, 4.

[58] *Ibid.*, 5.

[59] Reid, 77.

Historically, other civilizations have gained much from the early scientific achievements of the Chinese. Gunpowder, printing, the compass, and paper are Chinese inventions that have had major impacts in the world. Furthermore, the impacts are hardly limited to those issuing from these four. Robert Temple estimates that more than half of the basic inventions upon which the "modern world" rests come from China. He points out "modern agriculture, modern shipping, the modern oil industry, modern astronomical observatories, modern music, decimal mathematics, paper money, umbrellas, fishing reels, wheelbarrows, multistage rockets, guns, underwater mines, poison gas, parachutes, hot-air balloons, manned flight, brandy, whisky, the game of chess, printing, and even the essential design of the steam engine, all came from China."[60]

Chinese civilization also made global contributions in the field of medicine. For example, the Chinese were inoculating against smallpox as early as the eleventh century and were doing so widely in the sixteenth century. From China the method was transmitted to the Turkish regions where the British began to adopt it.[61] The Chinese were also precocious in the development of medical training and accreditation. Between 620 and 630, an Imperial Medical College was established along with medical colleges in all the main provincial cities, and medical degrees were awarded from that point on. Following two hundred years of Chinese-Arab contact through to 931, the first qualifying medical exams were held in Baghdad. Then in 1140 there were state examinations for physicians held in Sicily and in 1224 a school in Salerno began to graduate doctors of medicine.[62] The fact that the Chinese had already developed medical techniques and training by an early time that would

---

[60] The Genius of China: 3,000 Years of Science, Discovery, and Invention (New York: Simon & Schuster, 1986), 9.

[61] Joseph Needham with Lu Gwei-Djen, "Hygiene and Preventive Medicine in Ancient China," in Clerks and Craftsmen in China and the West (Cambridge, England: At the University Press, 1970), 375. Needham reports how the wife of British ambassador at Constantinople allowed the technique to be used on her own family in 1718 (ibid.).

[62] Needham with Lu Gwei-Djen, "Medicine," in Clerks and Craftsmen in China and the West (Cambridge, England: At the University Press, 1970), 276.

later be adopted by Western civilizations implies that these civilizations can still learn from Chinese accomplishments. Specifically, one should recognize the potential gain from exploring and developing TCM.

3.2 Benefits

China's historical medical achievements are indicators of the potential integration of TCM with the Western medical systems. In Canada, the presence of a large and active Chinese Canadian population has contributed to the use and promotion of TCM, which, in turn, has created an interest and even greater opportunities to use TCM among mainstream Canadians; however, ultimately it should be its effectiveness and lower cost that will contribute mostly to its integration. To those who would argue that the efficacy of TCM has not yet been proven, one can counter that historical and scientific evidence indicate otherwise. Moreover, one reason that this may be contested is that a major part of TCM's claimed effectiveness is in the prevention of health problems, which is both difficult to measure and not usually utilized as a criterion for medical effectiveness. However, with its greater exposure in the West and the adoption of Western scientific practices and technologies in China, one should see not only added evidence for its effectiveness, but also more ways to practise and new uses for TCM.

3.2.1 Effective[63]

China's history as a nation that has produced a high level of civilization and the largest population in the world is indirect evidence of the efficacy of its medicine. The development of civilization and extended growth of the population would require a high level and pervasiveness of medical expertise. As shown above in the overview of Chinese science and medicine, China created sophisticated medical means to sustain and grow its large population. Presently, even with a low standard of living, the Chinese person enjoys a

---

[63] This section should be read in conjunction with "4.2 Weak Evidence for Claims" below. Obviously, if the claims for TCM are weakly supported, there are grounds to question its efficacy.

relatively long life span.[64] This long life span is supported by the use of TCM, which makes up an estimated 40 percent of all health care delivered.[65] It is further estimated that TCM has "accounted for a quarter of the overall output value in China's medical industry."[66]

More proof of the effectiveness of TCM is in its adoption outside China. As documented above in the description of the spread of medical training and smallpox inoculation from China to the West, Western medicine has benefitted from the achievements of TCM. In present day, this has included the adoption of Chinese herbal medicines. For example, ephedrine, an amphetamine-like stimulant prescribed for the treatment of bronchial asthma, is derived from *mahuang (Ephedra sinica)* and was the first Chinese herbal remedy to enter the Western pharmacopoeia. Artemisinin, an antimalarial drug, is sourced from the herb *qinghao (Artemisia annua* or sweet wormwood).[67] Arsenic trioxide has also been adopted from Chinese medicine for the treatment of acute promyelocytic leukemia.[68]

Besides the evidence for the efficacy of TCM based on historical usage in China, present day researchers have also

---

[64] Chinese life expectancy is 70 years for males and 73 years for females (*National Geographic Atlas of China* [Washington, D.C.: National Geographic, 2008], 46). World life expectancy is 62.7 years for males and 66 years for females (Matt Rosenberg, "Life Expectancy: Overview of Life Expectancy," Aug. 19, 2007, *geography.about.com/od/populationgeography/a/lifeexpectancy.htm*, accessed 2009.01.19.). China's total per capita expenditure on health was 342 International Dollars in 2006 compared to 3672 International Dollars for Canada and 6714 International Dollars for United States in the same year taking into account purchasing power parity (World Health Organization Statistical Information System, *www.who.int/whosis/data/Search.jsp*, accessed 2009.01.19).

[65] "WHO [World Health Organization] Traditional Medicine Strategy 2002-2005," 1, *whqlibdoc.who.int/hq/2002/WHO_EDM_TRM_2002.1.pdf*, accessed 2009.05.28.

[66] "Traditional Chinese Medicine (TCM): In China and Worldwide 2005-2006-2010-2015," Helmut Kaiser Consultancy, *www.hkc22.com/chinesemedicine.html*, accessed 2009.05.28.

[67] Lisa Melton, "Chinese Medicine in Western Packaging," *Chemistry World* May 2007, 48.

[68] Jane Qiu, "Traditional," 127.

confirmed some of its claims by conducting scientific tests. For example, in 1997, a panel of experts assembled by the U.S. National Institutes of Health at the Consensus Development Conference analyzed studies and interviewed practitioners of acupuncture. They found, among other benefits, that acupuncture was "effective in treating painful disorders of the muscle and skeletal systems, such as fibromyalgia and tennis elbow—even more effective, in some cases, than conventional therapy."[69] The same conference also declared acupuncture to be "a proven effective treatment modality for nausea and vomiting" usually induced by chemotherapy.[70]

Chinese herbs have also been shown effective in the treatment of cancer. It has been found that blood supply and circulation are poor in most malignant tumors and that cancer cells in these conditions are more resistant to therapies. However, blood destagnation or detoxification herbs have been shown to potentiate conventional treatments. Herbs commonly used include *taoren (Prunus persica), honghua (Carthamus tinctorius), dang gui (Angelica sinersis), and danshen (Salvia miltiorrhiza)*.[71] The herb ginseng, commonly used in TCM, has also been proven to provide medical benefits. For example, three studies have reported a reduction in blood glucose in type 2 diabetes with the use of ginseng.[72]

Besides these examples of already proven TCM effectiveness, there are also many ongoing studies that are adding to the evidence. Given the complexity of TCM remedies and the emphasis on testing simple drug configurations in Western conventional pharmaceutical research, it is logical that much more of the testing of TCM herbal remedies would be at

---

[69] Dick Thompson, "Acupuncture Works," *Time*, 1997.11.17, 65.

[70] Cited by Siu Man Ng, "The Role of Chinese Medicine in Cancer Palliative Care," in *Death, Dying and Bereavement: A Hong Kong Chinese Experience*, ed. Cecilia Lai Wan Chan and Amy Yin Man Chow (Hong Kong: Hong Kong University Press, 2006), 202. Ng also cites three other studies in support of this claim (335n.28, 29, 30).

[71] Ng, 201; Ng cites three different studies.

[72] Theresa L. Charrois, Jessica Hrudey, and Sunita Vohra, "Ginseng: Practical Management of Adverse Effects and Drug Interactions," *Canadian Pharmacists Journal* 139.2 (Mar./Apr. 2006), 44.

the stage of mounting evidence rather than having produced conclusive results. Some examples of the mounting evidence include laboratory studies that "suggest that some herbs increase the effectiveness of conventional chemotherapy without increasing toxicity. A healthy immune system is necessary for control of malignant disease, and the immune suppression associated with cancer contributes to its progression. Many Chinese herbs contain glycoproteins and polysaccharides (among them, constituents of *Coriolus versicolor, Ganoderma lucidum, Grifola frondosa, Astragalus membranaceus, Panax ginseng,* and various other medicinal mushrooms) that can modulate metastatic potential and the innate immune system."[73]

In another example of testing, the U.S. National Cancer Institute tested COLD-FX, an extract of North American ginseng, during the 2008-09 cold and flu season for prevention of respiratory infections among patients who were being treated for chronic lymphocytic leukemia. Earlier trials had shown that COLD-FX could significantly reduce the risk of acute respiratory infection in older adults.[74] As TCM continues to be integrated with Western medicine, one can expect to see further evidence of its effectiveness appear.

3.2.2 Preventive

The benefit of prevention is closely tied to one of the main functions of TCM described earlier, maintenance of health. In maintaining one's health, one is preventing the illnesses, diseases, and injuries that damage their health. In surveying the low expenditure on health by Chinese—342 International dollars for China in 2006 compared to 3672 International dollars for Canada and 6714 International dollars for United States in the same year[75]—it stands to reason that prevention of illness would be a main strategy in preserving

---

[73] S.M. Sagar and R. K. Wong, "Chinese Medicine and Biomodulation in Cancer Patients—Part Two," *Current Oncology* 15.2 (2008), 9.

[74] "World's Top Cancer Research Body Sponsors Landmark COLD-FX Trial: NCI Study to Focus on Cold/Flu Fighting Potential for Leukemia Patients," *Marketwire*, 2008.11.17.

[75] World Health Organization Statistical Information System.

Chinese health. They seem not to have enough to pay for major interventions to solve health problems, so the longevity that they enjoy is largely due to maintenance. Furthermore, it seems that this prevention of health problems is largely due to the use of TCM.

The main TCM practice that contributes to prevention is diet. As mentioned earlier, Chinese diet incorporates the concept of "functional food," which means that one deliberately designs one's diet to contain foods that produce physiological benefits and/or reduce the risk of chronic disease. Functional foods are also supplemented with *buping* or tonics to preserve health and prevent disease. The use of functional foods and *buping* increase the effectiveness of the Chinese diet, making it a credible candidate for the main cause of their relatively good health

There is a supplementary benefit to the probable prevention of illness through diet in TCM, that of encouraging the individual to be proactive, that is deeply involved in maintaining their own health. The simplicity and inexpensiveness of diet allow the individual to control more their own health, which in turn encourages even more involvement in doing so. With a strong impetus to be proactive comes certain psychological benefits. One is able to feel empowered, which in turn creates even more impetus to maintain one's health and prevent illness.

3.2.3 Economical

China's low per capita expenditure on health is the most obvious indicator of the economy of TCM. The Chinese are able to enjoy life expectancy more than 10 percent higher than the world's average where their costs are 1/10 of those in Canada and 1/20 of what it costs Americans, whose life expectancies are approximately 25 percent and 21 percent respectively higher than the world average.[76] Furthermore,

---

[76] Canada's life expectancy in 2005 was 80.4 ("Life Expectancy Hits 80.4 Years: Statistics Canada," CBC News, 2008.01.14, *www.cbc.ca/canada/story/2008/01/14/death-stats.html*, accessed 2010.07.07) and American life expectancy was 77.9 in 2007 (Centers for Disease Control and Prevention, "Life Expectancy," *www.cdc.gov/nchs/fastats/lifexpec.htm*, accessed 2010.07.07).

TCM provides an estimated 40 percent of all health care delivered. Therefore, TCM is an important factor in keeping health costs low.

TCM has a number of features that contribute to its low cost. Foremost is that its knowledge and skills are relatively easily transferred from expert to learner. Although formal institutions for training practitioners were established early in Chinese history, much of the knowledge and many of the skills remained within family enterprises where one generation would teach the next. There was no great need for large infrastructures and systems for transmitting knowledge. Granted there has been a consolidation of TCM knowledge and skills in the last sixty years and accompanying this more systematic means of disseminating them; however, this has not led to extraordinary costs for doing so, even in the relatively expensive environment of North America.[77] Furthermore, the layperson is supposed to implement many of TCM's practices, such as eating functional food and be aware of and respond to environmental influences on their health, which also means that TCM's knowledge and skills are easily transferred.

The functional foods and medicines consumed in TCM, the herbal remedies, are also natural products, which makes their discovery and production generally inexpensive. They exist in nature and their effects can be experienced and observed through the simple process of consumption. They can even be domesticated, such as in the American ginseng and antler farms one finds in Canada. For plants this is especially easy and it is claimed that cultivated herbs make up more than 50

---

[77] For example, tuition for a four year intensive doctor of TCM program at the Alberta College of Acupuncture & Traditional Chinese Medicine in Calgary is thirty-six thousand Canadian dollars (Alberta College of Acupuncture & Traditional Chinese Medicine, *www.acatcm.com/*, accessed 2009.06.07). In comparison, tuition fees to be trained as a medical doctor at the University of Alberta normally require twenty-five thousand for a qualifying undergraduate degree, thirty-seven thousand dollars for three years of medical school, and the costs of two years of internship, for a total of at least sixty-two thousand dollars and nine years of education (University of Alberta, *www.ualberta.ca*, accessed 2009.06.07). It is should also be noted that the student tuition only covers 11 percent of post-secondary education costs at Canadian universities; the rest being subsidized by government and donations ("Tuition fees: The higher cost of higher education," CBC News, 2006.09.01, *www.cbc.ca/news/background/higher-education/*, citing the Government of Canada, accessed 2009.06.07).

percent of the quantity bought and sold in China.[78] Nor do the products usually require much refinement to make them suitable for consumption. The easy discovery, availability, and small need for refinement make the production of the foods and herbal remedies in TCM inexpensive.

Besides the natural products consumed in TCM, the technology employed in practising TCM also has been simple and little changed; therefore, it has not required much investment. Firstly, there is not much technology. Herbalists use very little equipment and masseurs and practitioners of *qigong* use even less. Acupuncture is more technologically sophisticated; however, much of it has remained the same for hundreds of years.

The simplicity and the large number of natural ingredients of TCM have also meant that it is viewed as requiring less regulation, which is also a cost saving. In 1999, TCM products in the U.S. were all sold as dietary supplements, like vitamins, which came under much less stringent rules.[79] Special health related claims can be made about highly refined and tested pharmaceutical products; however, the testing and manufacturing are costly. One can see the cost difference between the same medicine when regulated and non regulated. A New Jersey-based drug developer Covance had been hoping in 1998 to shepherd two traditional Chinese medicines used to treat cardiovascular diseases through the approval process of the U.S. Food and Drug Administration. Even though the cures are widely used in China, the company calculated that it would take eight years and forty to sixty million U.S. dollars to get even one of them approved as a prescription drug in the U.S.[80]

The facts that knowledge and skills are relatively easily transferred from expert to learner, that functional foods and medicines consumed in TCM are natural products, that the technology employed in practising TCM has been simple and little changed, and that TCM is viewed as requiring less regulation have combined to make TCM an economical practice.

---

[78] Nina Zhao-Seiler, "Sustainability of Chinese Medicinal Herbs: A Discussion," *Journal of Chinese Medicine* 101 (Feb. 2013), 43.

[79] Jonathon Sprague, "A Leaf for the Book of Life," *Asiaweek*, 1999.08.08.

[80] *Ibid.*

3.2.4 Enhancement When Combined with Western Conventional Medicine and New Technology

Another benefit that increases the likelihood of the integration of TCM with Western conventional medicine is its enhancement when it is used in combination with Western conventional medicine and new technology. In some cases, the benefits of integration are direct and clear. For example, some acupuncture practitioners utilize electrified needles (electroacupuncture) to increase the effectiveness of the practice.[81] Award winning TCM practitioner Tai Lahans in her book *Integrating Conventional and Chinese Medicine in Cancer Care: A Clinical Guide* has also documented many Western medical treatments that can be enhanced with the addition of herbal remedies.[82] She describes how herbal medicines are used with cytotoxic compounds, such as those targeting cancer cells, to increase their effect and also to ameliorate their harmful side effects. The goal is to allow the patient to remain as healthy as possible and to maintain the regime of cytotoxic intervention.[83]

Sometimes the enhancement comes about because new techniques lead to discoveries of new uses for TCM. Researchers at King's College, London have undertaken what is reported to be the biggest study yet of the main ingredients in TCM. They built a database of information on more than eight thousand phytochemical compounds from two hundred forty of the most commonly used herbs in Chinese medicine and then used computers to screen for their potential to treat HIV/Aids, cancer, Alzheimer's disease, arthritis, and other diseases.

---

[81] Results from a scientific study suggest that electroacpuncture may decrease the serum total cholesterol, triglyceride, and LDL cholesterol levels in obese women by increasing the serum beta endorphin level (Mehmet Tuğrul Cabioğlu and Nihon Eugene, "Electroacupuncture Therapy for Weight Loss Reduces Serum Total Cholesterol, Triglycerides, and LDL Cholesterol Levels in Obese Women," *The American Journal of Chinese Medicine* 33.4 [2005], 525).

[82] Tai Lahans was voted a *Seattle Magazine* Top Doc in 2003 (*Integrating Conventional and Chinese Medicine in Cancer Care: A Clinical Guide* [Philadelphia: Churchill Livingstone Elsevier, 2007], ii).

[83] *Ibid.*, 16.

Computer simulation allowed them to test TCM herbs against various drug targets–mostly enzymes associated with pathogens or chronic disease. "Of the 240 herbs sampled, 62 per cent had constituents that could be useful in treating one of the targets."[84]

Another advancement occurring from the combination of TCM and new technology is the widespread dissemination of knowledge about herbal medicine on the internet. A search of terms related to Chinese herbal medicine on the internet found 1.16 million results for "Chinese herbal medicine" and more than six hundred thousand for "Chinese herbal formula." Contributing to the large number of results is the fact that much of the knowledge of herbal medicine is easy to understand. The ingredients are often common items that most people are familiar with and the preparation of formula is simple enough for most people to duplicate. With this ease of understanding, people are comfortable posting prescriptions online and users are equally at ease in searching for and reading them. This creates a body of users who are willing to share their information, and the reach of the internet provides an efficient means to do so. The result is large body of information available on the internet, and greater use by the general public as they have access to this information.

In summary, TCM's has important benefits that should further its integration with Western conventional medicine. First, it has been shown to be effective in treating various illnesses and injuries. Second, TCM helps to prevent illness and injury in great part because it emphasizes the role of daily diet in doing so and because it encourages users of TCM to be proactive in caring for their health. Third, TCM is economical. Its knowledge and skills are easily transferred and implemented. There is smaller need for large organizations to do so. Much of its material, such as herbs, is natural, therefore, relatively inexpensive. Many of its tools are simple as well. Because of these latter two reasons, TCM has also required less regulation. The fourth benefit of TCM is the enhancement produced when it is combined with Western conventional medicine and new technology. The effectiveness of Western

---

[84] Lisa Melton, "Chinese Medicine in Western Packaging," *Chemistry World* 4.5 (May 2007), 49.

conventional medicine is improved when used in combination with TCM, such as in the case of cancer or pain treatment. Similarly, the effectiveness of TCM is increased with application of new technology. Probably, most interesting is the hope for unlocking even greater potential from herbal medicines as advanced research techniques are used to isolate and target the active ingredients within them. These benefits promise to foster the integration of TCM and Western medicine as users seek to take advantage of the merits of both and the synergies created when they are used in combination.

4. Detriments of Traditional Chinese Medicine

In evaluating the possibility of TCM's integration with Western conventional medicine, one should also consider its detriments that might militate against such integration. There are four main ones: it is difficult to standardize the strength of active ingredients in herbal formulae, the weak evidence for its claims, possible harmful effects, and its ecological insensitivity.

4.1 Difficult to Standardize

One main detriment of TCM is the difficulty of standardizing the potency of the active ingredients in herbal remedies either for the sake of treating an illness or for testing efficacy. To begin with Chinese herbal prescriptions can be very complex. As mentioned earlier, Chinese records show more than eleven thousand plant species used in more than one hundred thousand compound formulae.[85] Most herbal remedies are decoctions of compounds of up to twenty different herbs.[86]

Besides this plethora of factors, one has to consider the further complexity of when and where the ingredients were harvested. The chemical constitution of a plant varies accordingly, like fruit that is sweeter closer to its becoming ripe and grapes grown in France tasting different from those grown in Canada. The herbalist trying to determine the ideal

---

[85] Jane Qiu, "Traditional," 127.

[86] Robert Yuan and Yuan Lin, "Traditional Chinese Medicine: An Approach to Scientific Proof and Clinical Validation," *Pharmacology & Therapeutics* 86 (2000), 191.

prescription has to consider all these factors. They make it difficult to produce the same effect in their patients each time. It is difficult for the same reasons to duplicate the exact same chemical composition each time; therefore making it difficult to reach the level of standardization required to test a formula against Western pharmaceutical standards.

4.2 Weak Evidence for Claims

While one can look to the long history and health of the Chinese nation as proof of TCM's effectiveness, it has not been easy to translate this achievement into scientific evidence. R. Barker Baussell as a senior biostatistician and research methodologist at the University of Maryland directed its National Institutes of Health-funded Center for Integrative Medicine for five years.[87] This allowed him with to evaluate the common components of integrative medicine, including TCM and his evaluation is contained in the monograph *Snake Oil Science: The Truth About Complementary and Alternative Medicine.* In reviewing the clinical studies conducted on TCM he finds little evidence of superior efficacy in treating disease and illness when compared to a placebo.[88] Although Bausell's main criticism is directed toward the testing methods used, mainly that many of the tests have not tested efficacy against that produced with a placebo, he demonstrates that there are few tests that have shown superior results when a placebo is used.

Concerns for the lack of evidence of TCM's efficacy can even take on a sinister tone. It is claimed that "millions of taxpayers' dollars are being spent in the United States on seemingly ridiculous research projects" by the National Center for Complementary and Alternative Medicine and the Office of Cancer Complementary and Alternative Medicine and the "fact that they are supporting these projects is often used to lend an appearance of legitimacy to treatments and ideas that are not legitimate." This "diminishes the primacy of science in our

---

[87] Lawrence Charles Parish, review *Snake Oil Science: The Truth About Complementary and Alternative Medicine, The Journal of the American Medical Association* 301.3 (2009.01.21): 332-33.

[88] For example, see pages 254, 258-59.

health policy discourse and degrades our healthcare system," which in turn "lends dangerous and undue authority to pseudoscience, degrading respect for science in the public realm."[89]

Granting the persuasiveness of Bausell's argument, it still should not be the definitive judgment on the value of TCM for at least four reasons. First, arguably the biggest benefit of TCM is the prevention of illness and the longitudinal observation of the health of the Chinese population is evidence of this. The tests that Bausell cites were aimed at testing short-term efficacy.

The second reason that Bausell's argument should not be seen as the definitive judgment is that there is still belief among researchers that by using accepted scientific methods TCM can be proved to be effective. Scholars Arya Nielsen and Richard Hammerschlag offer three measures specifically related to acupuncture that they claim will lead to valid test outcomes: training acupuncturists in clinical research, involving acupuncturists in the design of clinical research, and a commitment by the health care community to improve its understanding of acupuncture.[90] Furthermore, one is seeing a trend toward the use of scientific methods in research on TCM, especially notable among Chinese researchers.[91] If this trend continues, one can reasonably expect that there will more likely be a basis for a more definitive judgment on the efficacy of TCM.

Third, there is a complexity in TCM that may not have been accounted for in past testing. Some of this complexity was described in the section above (2.3.2) on herbal medicine.

---

[89] Ben Kavoussi, "The Acupuncture and Fasciae Fallacy," 2010.12.30, Science-Based Medicine: Exploring Issues & Controversies in Science & Medicine website, www.sciencebasedmedicine.org/acupuncture-and-fascial-planes-junk-science-and-wasteful-research/, accessed 2014.12.10. Kavoussi cites the Centre for Inquiry in claiming that the 2010 budget of the National Center for Complementary and Alternative Medicine was $US 128.8 million— more than sixty times greater than its $US 2 million budget in 1992 and the budget of the Office of Cancer Complementary and Alternative Medicine was $US 121 million in 2008.

[90] *Ibid.*, 206.

[91] See bibliography Yao *et al.*, 194-200.

Another example is the conception of bodily organs in TCM. They should not be categorized in parallel to Western physiology "because the organs in East Asian medicine operate not as distinct entities but in contextual interrelationalship with the other organs, substances, and potentials of becoming and declining."[92] This description reflects the holistic view that TCM practitioners adopt, seeing the objects of their concern, body parts, as pieces of a process that cannot be isolated from what is taking place around them.

Fourth, it is not easy to attain the results that can be attained with a placebo. Those being tested have to believe that they could be receiving a *bona fide* treatment and with TCM it is much easier to perpetuate such a belief. Even if laboratory tests do not show any superior efficacy, the long history, different paradigms, and exotic tools, medicines, and methods give TCM an aura that could enhance its efficacy. Arguably, this psychological influence would be undermined if tests continue to show TCM's lack of efficacy; however, the reverse could be true as well and it is interesting to note that efforts to prove its efficacy have increased rather than diminished showing that belief in it remains strong.

4.3 Harmful Effects

Despite the natural origin of herbal remedies, they can produce harmful effects. There have been Health Canada's warnings about them. For example, in 2001, Bao Ji Wan pills and Chinese Modular Solution chest relief tablets were reported to contain substances that posed a serious health risk.[93] Likewise, in 2002, the agency warned not to consume any Longdan or Long Tan Xie Gan herbal medicine products as they contained aristolochic acid, which had been shown to cause mutations in human cells and end-stage kidney failure.[94] As well, some herbal products are known to interfere with the

---

[92] Nielsen and Hammerschlag, 189.

[93] "Health Canada Warns against Two Traditional Chinese Herbal Products," Canadian Press NewsWire, 2001.02.28.

[94] "Health Canada Warns Consumers against Cancer-Causing Herbal Products," Canadian Press NewsWire, 2002.05.16.

action of Western pharmaceuticals, either limiting their efficacy or amplifying undesirable effects, which results in increased toxicity.[95]

4.4. Ecologically Insensitive

Some of the ingredients used in TCM herbal medicine create the impression, if not the case, that Chinese herbal medicine is ecologically insensitive. This is to say that its practice does not take into consideration the serious damage that it inflicts upon the environment through the harvest of animals and plants that have become endangered. For example, rhinoceros and tigers are killed for their horns and bones respectively; bear bile, comes from a species under pressure and is harvested cruelly. One also hears of certain plants becoming scarce because their medicinal value leads to excessive harvesting.

Sometimes these species are large mammals and predators that have a major role in supporting the ecological structure. Therefore, for them to be destroyed, especially when they are in danger of extinction is clearly contradictory to the holistic principles of TCM. The same is true, albeit less obvious, for smaller animal and plant species that are in the same situation. The elimination from the ecosystem of these organisms could cause imbalances leading to disturbances that would eventually affect human beings in a negative way, thereby placing more pressure on human health.

A telling example of this argument is the case of sharks. These predators have been decimated in previous years, some species declining by more than 99 percent. The effect of this decimation has been described by Julia Baum, a marine ecologists at Dalhousie University in Halifax as "triggering changes that cascade through the food web." Sharks contribute to ocean sanitation by eating the carcasses of dead whales, they control the growth of species such as tuna and seals that have few other predators, and "they contribute to the long-term health of countless species by culling the ailing, deformed and

---

[95] Jean-Paul Collet, interview, "Clinical Research in the Assessment of Efficacy and Safety of Traditional Chinese Medicine," *Wellness Options* 33 (2007), 15.

unfit."[96] Their decline has also been linked to a twenty-fold increase to an estimated forty million cownose rays of the U.S. East Coast, which has, in turn, being linked to the disappearance of scallops along the same coast.[97]

The problem is that sharks are being decimated because their fins demand a high price in TCM, where their consumption is said to enhance human health. This, together with their ceremonious consumption at prestigious Chinese banquets seems to be one of the main drivers of the decimation of the world's shark population. This destruction of the ecological system essential to the health and survival of the human species and the production of other TCM ingredients undermines TCM's own principles and raises the question of how capable TCM is of modifying itself.

In answer to this latter question, TCM does seem to contain the ability to initiate change within itself. Within its own tradition of trial and error and in contact with Western conventional medicine, it has attempted to improve and test its efficacy. The use of ecological harming ingredients is also receiving more publicity and many practitioners are welcoming the regulation that would prevent their use.

5. Presence in China

The presence of TCM within Canada is dependent to a great extent on its presence within China. The magnitude and state of TCM in China have direct bearing on how it has and will develop in Canada. Most of the expertise and materials that have informed TCM in Canada have originated in China and it is there that the strongest efforts are being made to develop it further. The body of knowledge that underlies TCM was developed in China. Most of the practitioners have received their training directly or indirectly from Chinese sources. The ingredients were originally harvested in China and these sources continue to be tapped. Furthermore, with the decision to consolidate and promote TCM as a strong complement to Western medicine, China has poured resources into developing

---

[96] Joe Dupree, "The Most Important Fish in the Sea," *National Wildlife* 46.2 (Feb./Mar. 2008).

[97] *Ibid.*

it, particularly establishing standards and methods acceptable
to Western consumers. Also, emigrants from China arrive
steeped in the paradigms of TCM and naturally seek to
preserve and promote them in Canada. Therefore, the state of
TCM in China has been a major determinant of the state of
TCM in Canada.

The strong presence of TCM in China is evidenced by large
domestic use; promotion by the government, including for
foreign consumption; and a high level of exports. These three
major areas demonstrate the strength of TCM in China and
also forces that should continue to support its presence and
development.

5.1 Domestic Use

The reported figures on the use of TCM within China
indicate that the system is used widely. In 1996, traditional
treatments, including herbal remedies, acupuncture,
acupressure and massage, and moxibustion, were said to
account for around 40% of all health care delivered in China.
Furthermore, this figure does not include the large amount of
self medication with traditional herbs, which are used not only
to treat illness, but also to promote health.[98] In 1997, every city
had a hospital practising TCM and in nearly all hospitals
practising Western medicine there is a department of TCM.[99] In
2008 Chinese Vice Premier Wi Yi reported that China had
3,072 TCM hospitals with more than 330,000 beds.[100]

In 2005, the output value of TCM amounted to 110.3 billion
Renminbi (RMB, $C16 billion), about a quarter of the overall
output value of China's medical industry. Moreover, while this

---

[98] Terese Hesketh and Wei Xing Zhu, "Health in China: Traditional Chinese
Medicine: One Country, Two Systems," BMJ 315 (July 12, 1997), 115-117;
citing R. Chen and C. Martin, "Traditional Chinese Medicine in China Today,"
China Review 1966.3, 24-25.

[99] *Ibid.*

[100] "Vice Premier: Future of Traditional Chinese Medicine Is Bright," *People's
Daily Online*, 2008.01. 25, *english.people.com.cn*, accessed 2010.05.17.

value was predicted to rise 70% by 2015,[101] a 2007 report in the People's Daily Online citing the Information Office of the State Council stated that it had already reached 177.2 billion RMB ($C25.6 billion), a rise of 61%, and comprised more than one quarter of China's total pharmaceutical industrial output.[102] In fact, China had 1,500 TCM companies, manufacturing more than 9,000 kinds of Chinese medicine products.[103]

5.2 Government Promotion

Chinese government promotion is the second area that demonstrates the strength of TCM in China. The government has established a supportive regulatory environment and allocated funds for research and development. As early as 1992 the government issued the Regulation on the Protection of Traditional Chinese Medicines for the purpose of encouraging research and development of TCM.[104] Guidelines for identifying functional foods were promulgated in 2005 and improving these foods became part of the National Development Plan of Science and Technology for 2011-15.[105]

Besides developing TCM for domestic use, the Chinese government is planning to promote it abroad, even to globalize it by 2020. For this reason the government has been planning to boost standards, including conducting clinical research on the safety and efficacy of TCM remedies, encouraging international collaboration, improving manufacturing techniques, and

---

[101] Helmut Kaiser Consultancy, "Traditional Chinese Medicine (TCM): In China and Worldwide, 2005-2006-2010-2015," *www.hkc22.com/chinesemedicine.html*, accessed 2010.05.16.

[102] "Industrial Output of Traditional Chinese Medicine Reaches 177.2 Bln Yuan," *People's Daily Online*, 2008.07.18, *english.people.com.cn*, accessed 2010.05.17.

[103] "Vice Premier: Future of Traditional Chinese Medicine Is Bright," *People's Daily Online*, 2008.01.25, *english.people.com.cn*, accessed 2010.05.17.

[104] "Industrial Output."

[105] Yao *et al.*, 182.

bringing the drug regulatory system into line with international guidelines.[106]

These measures were part of a fifteen-year plan that was supported by sixteen government ministries and headed by the Ministry of Science and Technology, the Ministry of Health, and the State Administration of Traditional Chinese Medicine. The plan was supported by a budget of at least $US 480 million for research and development and $US 1.1 billion for the TCM-related part of the public healthcare system.[107]

One also sees the influence of the government in the amount of laboratory research that is being conducted in China on herbal products. Yao *et al.* describe three products, the Chinese forest frog, *Dendrobium officinale*, and pine-tree fungus, and list a large number of experiments, including on mice, that have been carried out with them. These experiments are documented in scientific journals, many of which should be government supported.[108]

5.3 Export

The large amount of TCM exports is also indicative of the strength of TCM within China. The world market for TCM products had doubled in the past decade (till 2007), with Europe and US as the biggest importers.[109] China's response to this demand has been to export a reported two hundred thousand tons of raw herbs annually.[110] It is estimated that exports of Traditional Chinese Medicine reached twenty-six billion U.S. dollars in 2013.[111]

---

[106] Jane Qiu, "China Plans to Modernize Traditional Medicine," *Nature* 446.7136 (2007.04.05), 590.

[107] *Ibid.*

[108] P. 183-86, 194-200.

[109] Qiu, "China Plans," 590.

[110] Helmut Kaiser Consultancy.

[111] "Herb Extracts Exports Maintain Growth," *ChinaDaily.com.cn*, 2012.05.08, accessed 2014.12.02. The figure of twenty-six billion U.S. dollars was arrived at by multiplying by four the total given in the article for herbal extracts for the first three months of the year to calculate an approximate value for the

In areas of export, government promotion, and large domestic use, TCM demonstrates that it has thriving base within China that is likely to contribute to its development in Canada.

6. Presence of TCM in Canada

To this point, the findings of this article support the supposition that TCM has a strong presence in Canada. It has a sophisticated theoretical underpinning and set of practices. It has a long history of contributing to supporting a large population in China and its benefits seem to outweigh its detriments by a large margin. Furthermore, it has a strong base in China, where the government is promoting it, including its export and use abroad.

This supposition is also supported by the evidence of the longevity of Chinese Canadians. Richmond residents, of whom 40 percent were ethnic Chinese, have been living an average of 83.4 years, longer than anywhere else in Canada.[112] A study of Alberta's population between 1995 and 2003 found that life expectancy at birth for ethnic Chinese resident males was 83.3 years compared 77 years for non-Chinese males. For ethnic Chinese female residents, life expectancy was 87.9 years compared to 82.5 years for non-Chinese.[113] Two of the factors that the authors of this latter study speculated might be the cause of Chinese Albertans' longer life expectancy were culture and health behaviours.[114]

One of the main health service providers in Alberta, the Calgary Health Region, reports that various chronic diseases and chronic disease risk factors such as obesity, diabetes, coronary artery disease, heart failure, peripheral vascular disease, and myocardial infarction have been found to be

year, then multiplying this figure by two as it is stated in the article that the export of herbal extracts is nearly half that of all TCM exports.

[112] Jane Armstrong, "Richmond, B.C., Holds the Secret to a Long Life," *The Globe and Mail*, 2005.02.02, A 3; citing Statistics Canada.

[113] Hude Quan, Fu-Lin Wang, Donald Schopflocher, and Carolyn De Coster, "Mortality, Cause of Death and Life Expectancy of Chinese Canadians in Alberta," *Canadian Journal of Public Health* 98.6 (Nov.-Dec. 2007), 500.
[114] *Ibid.*, 504.

significantly lower among Chinese Canadians compared to the general Canadian population. Older Chinese Canadians also reported better overall physical health compared to the general population, although they reported significantly worse mental health.[115]

It is possible, and arguably likely, that the use of TCM by Chinese Canadians has contributed to the longer life expectancies observed. One naturally assumes that they would be more frequent users of TCM and studies have shown that they often use some form of complementary or alternative medicine.[116] The likelihood that TCM would contribute to improved health, including longer life spans, and the actuality of the longer life spans among those most likely to use TCM, i.e., Chinese Canadians, leads one to conclude that TCM has a strong presence within Canada.

6.1 General Trend

The use of complementary and alternative medicine, which includes TCM, has been increasing. In the United States based on the 1999 National Health Interview Survey of 30,801 respondents, an estimated 28.9% of US adults had used at least one complementary or alternative therapy in the past year.[117] Another study of 1.5 to two thousand people showed that the use of at least one alternative therapy a year increased from 33.8% in 1990 to 42.1% in 1997, including a 380 percent increase in the use of herbal remedies.[118] This trend both

[115] Alberta Health Services, "Health and Chinese Canadians," 2009.03.09, www.calgaryhealthregion.ca/programs/diversity/diversity_resources/health_div_pops/chiinese_canadians.htm, accessed 2014.12.02.

[116] Marilyn A. Roth and Karen M. Kobayashi, "The Use of Complementary and Alternative Medicine among Chinese Canadians: Results from a National Survey," *Journal of Immigrant Minority Health* 10 (2008): 518.

[117] H. Ni , C. Simile, and A.M. Hardy AM, "Utilization of Complementary and Alternative Medicine by United States Adults: Results from the 1999 National Health Interview Survey," *Medical Care* 40 (2002), 353.

[118] D. M. Eisenberg, D. M., R. B. Davis, S. L. Ettner, S. Appel, S. Wilkey S. M. Van Rompay, *et al.*, "Trends in Alternative Medicine Use in the United States, 1990–1997: Results of a Follow-up National Survey," *The Journal of the American Medical Association* (JAMA) 280 (1998), 1569, 1572.

quickened and was shown to be even wider spread. In 2009 it was reported that "complementary and alternative medicines (CAMs) are used in more than 80% of the world's population and are becoming an increasing component of the US health care system, with more than 70% of the population using CAM at least once and annual spending reaching as much as $34 billion."[119]

The same trend is noted among Canadians as well. According to a 1997 poll, about 42 percent of them were trying some form of complementary health care, the most popular forms being chiropractics, herbal medicine, acupuncture, and homeopathy.[120] Furthermore, in 1999 the Canadian Health Food Association, a group representing herbal manufacturers and distributors, estimated that health supplements, including herbal derivatives, were a $2-billion industry in Canada, and growing.[121] A 2007 report confirmed this trend in stating that at least 50 percent of Canadian adults were using one or more natural medicines,[122] such as American ginseng and Chinese wolfberry. As would be expected, this trend is also reflected among Chinese Canadians. A study conducted in 1995, showed that approximately half of ethnic Chinese seniors used TCM for both minor and serious illnesses.[123]

6.2 Institutionalization

---

[119] Timothy Mainardi, Simi Kapoor, and Leonard Bielory, "Complementary and Alternative Medicine: Herbs, Phytochemicals and Vitamins and Their Immunologic Effects," *Journal of Allergy and Clinical Immunology* 123.2 (2009.02.10): 283.

[120] Yen Yip, "New Age Medicine Meets Western Science," *University Affairo*, October 1999, 17

[121] *Ibid.*

[122] Stuart MacLeod, "Maximizing Benefits from Traditional Chinese Medicine," A Canadian Health Research Series, *Wellness Options* 33 (2007), 14.

[123] Chappell, Neena L. and David Lai, "Health Care Service by Chinese Seniors in British Columbia, Canada," *Journal of Cross-Cultural Gerontology*, 13 (1998), 21. This article uses the term "traditional Chinese care"; however, from the term's description on page 26, it is apparent that TCM is meant.

Following from the general trend of increased use of complementary and alternative medicine, the strong presence of TCM within Canada is further confirmed and defined by its institutionalization within the country. "Institutionalization" is taken to mean having a strong presence within large medical institutions and widespread commercialization.

There are a number of noteworthy organizations practising acupuncture within or in association with Canadian hospitals; for example, the Acupuncture Clinic at St. John's Rehabilitation Hospital in Toronto. Mount Sinai Hospital in Toronto provides acupuncture treatment in both the Rebecca MacDonald Centre for Arthritis and Autoimmune Disease and the Rehab and Wellbeing Centre. HealthWorks, a rehabilitation clinic located in the Regina General Hospital, also provides acupuncture treatment.

For nearly seven years, from 1996 to 2003, there was also the Tzu Chi Institute for Complementary Medicine at Vancouver General Hospital that provided integrative health care using new and innovative models.[124] This institute was founded with a $2-million gift from the Buddhist Compassion Relief Tzu Chi Foundation Canada,[125] which itself was founded by Gary Ho in 1992 under the direction of Dharma Master Cheng Yen, a well known Taiwanese Buddhist nun.[126] However, it was unable to continue its operations when its operating grant was cut by the provincial government.

It is in the realm of commercialization that one sees clearly the widespread institutionalization of TCM in Canadian society. A passing search of the Yellow Pages directories for Toronto, Vancouver, and Calgary in 2014 uncovered respectively 495, 276, and 94 practitioners of acupuncture. The total is 865 and this number does not include those practitioners who would advertise solely through the Chinese language media. The same

---

[124] Andrea Mulkins, Marja Verhoef, Joanna Eng, Barbara Findlay, and Darlene Ramsum, "Evaluation of the Tzu Chi Institute for Complementary and Alternative Medicine Integrative Care Program," *The Journal of Alternative and Complementary Medicine* 9.4 (Aug 2003), 586.

[125] Brian Whitwham, "No Alternative to Closure for Complementary Medicine Centre," *Canadian Academic Journal* 168.7 (2003.04.01), 885.

[126] Tzu Chi Foundation Canada website, *en.tzuchi.ca/canada/home.nsf/about/index*, accessed 2010.05.24.

search for herbalist turns up 25, 20, and 8 in the respective cities for a total of 53. Similarly for practitioners of acupuncture, this total does not include the herbalists who would advertise solely through the Chinese language media. A 2005 report estimated that 650 stores in Canada featured traditional Chinese medicines.[127]

The institutionalization of TCM in commercial endeavours has more examples. Afexa Life Sciences was a large scale TCM manufacturer with headquarters in Calgary, Alberta until it was bought out by Valeant Pharmaceuticals International in 2011. It was capitalized for about fifty million dollars and its flagship product Cold-FX was said to be the top selling cold and flu remedy in Canada since 2004.[128] Other Afexa products are said to strengthen the immune system and improve memory and concentration. These functions, and the company's mission to discover, develop, and commercialize natural therapeuticals that prevent disease and maintain good health, fit with the emphasis in TCM to maintain human physical and mental capacities.

Besides the emphasis on natural therapeuticals and health maintenance that are already indicative of the influence of TCM, the company's former president and cofounder Jacqueline J. Shan has a doctorate in pharmacology from Peking Union Medical College, as well as another in physiology from the University of Alberta.[129] A main ingredient in the company's

---

[127] "Healthy Choices Impact Food Product Sales," *Plant* (Willowdale, Ontario), 64.11 (2005.11.14), 35; citing a study sponsored by the Canadian Health Food Association, in cooperation with the Canadian Natural Products Association and the Canadian Homeopathic Pharmaceutical Association.

[128] "Cold-fx® Chosen Canada's # 1 Pharmacist Recommended Natural Cold Remedy for Fourth Straight Year. Recommended by 73% of Pharmacists Nationally According to Leading Pharmacy Magazine Survey," news release on COLD-FX website, citing AC Nielsen's MarketTrack Drug Service for Cold Remedies, natural Supplements & Vitamins categories, *www.cold-fx.ca/news_may5_09.htm*, accessed 2010.05.25.

[129] Life Sciences Analytics, "CV Technologies Inc." (note Afexa Life Sciences was once named "CV Technologies"), *www.lsareports.com*, accessed 2010.05.25. Since the Valeant takeover Shan has founded and become the chief scientific officer for Afinix Life Sciences, a company developing natural health products for improving cardiovascular and cognitive health, as well as rheumatoid arthritis (Diane Jermyn, "Mind behind Cold-FX Launches Product Line for Aging Boomers," *The Globe and Mail*, 2013.10.11).

products is North American ginseng (*Panax quinquefolius*),[130] which is used extensively in Chinese herbal medicine and which Canada has exported to China for nearly three hundred years. The company also developed ChemBioPrint in order to standardize the active ingredients in its products leading to consistent effects when consumed. This is an example of the technological advancement that Chinese Canadians are fostering in TCM, the result being a successful company that has marketed Canadian produced Chinese medicine all over the world.

Two other significant areas of commercialization of TCM within Canada are in agriculture and medical insurance coverage. Agricultural production ranges from the more exotic antler ranches, to the more common ginseng farms. Ginseng has been exported to China from Canada since 1721 and in 2005 crop production was worth $70 million, a huge increase from 1980 when it was only worth $2.8 million.[131] From 1994 to 2003, North American ginseng was Ontario's fifth largest cash crop,[132] and the province has become the world's largest supplier exporting $140 million worth in 2012.[133]

The significant amount of medical insurance coverage given for TCM is also indicative of its commercialization and institutionalization. In the United States, as of 2004, 47 percent of Americans enrolled in employer health insurance plans were covered for acupuncture treatments.[134] In Canada, workers' compensation boards in B.C., Alberta, Manitoba, Yukon and Ontario, and some insurance companies, such as Pacific Blue Cross and Maritime Life, and even Veterans Affairs Canada

---

[130] This is a different species of ginseng from that grown in East Asia, whose species name is Panax ginseng (Reed, 66, 144).

[131] Statistics Canada, "Table 002-0001Farm cash receipts," n.d., *www5.statcan.gc.ca/cansim/a47*, accessed 2013.09.18.

[132] Asia Pacific Foundation, 6.

[133] Ann Hui, "Ontario Research Uprooting Myths about Ginseng's Health Benefits," *The Globe and Mail*, 2013.09.26.

[134] Gary Claxton, Isadora Gil, Ben Finder, Erin Holve, Jon Gabel, Jeremy Pickreighn, Heidi Whitmore, Samantha Hawkins, and Cheryl Fahlman. "The Kaiser Family Foundation and Health Research and Educational Trust Employer Health Benefits 2004 Annual Survey," 2004, 106–107.

have provided coverage for acupuncture for their clients.[135] At present, the Medical Service Plan of British Columbia covers ten acupuncture treatments per year up to a cost of $23 each for those needing assistance with payment of premiums.[136] The Insurance Corporation of British Columbia also covers the costs of acupuncture,[137] as does the Worker Safety and Insurance Board in Ontario.[138]

6.3 Testing

The testing of TCM treatments within North America is further indication of the integration of TCM into the Canadian medical system, and indirectly, the achievements of Chinese Canadians, such as Jacqueline Shan. The extensive testing of COLD-FX for prevention of respiratory infections among patients who are being treated for chronic lymphocytic leukemia–described above--by as important an institution as the U.S. National Cancer Institute highlights the potential of TCM and the efforts of those such as Shan to develop it. In addition, there have been a number of other tests that confirm the efficacy of COLD-FX.[139]

Part of the impetus for the testing of TCM is the suggestion by both the World Health Organization Traditional Medicine Strategy and the White House Commission on Complementary and Alternative Medicine Policy that clinical trials should be conducted in order to determine the efficacy of complementary

---

[135] Asia Pacific Foundation, 4.

[136] British Columbia Ministry of Health, "Information for Supplementary Benefit Practitioners," *www.health.gov bc.ca/map/infoprac/suppbilling/index.html*, accessed 2014.12.05.

[137] Insurance Corporation of British Columbia, "ICBCclaiminfo.com," *www.icbcclaiminfo.com/node/65*, accessed 2014.12.06.

[138] McMaster University Health Sciences, "Contemporary Medical Acupuncture Program," *www.acupunctureprogram.com/*, accessed 2014.12.06.

[139] "Clinical Trials," COLD-FX website, *cold-fx.ca/hcp/health_clinical.htm*, accessed 2014.12.06.

and alternative medicine.[140] Furthermore, research has suggested that TCM is one of the most frequently used forms of complementary and alternative medicine,[141] which would justify its being selected for testing.

This policy suggestion combined with the popularity of TCM has led to large research efforts to determine the chromatographic profile of individual TCM herbs. A chromatographic profile reveals the identity and quality of the bioactive components in raw herbs or their extracts. It is also accepted by the U.S. Food and Drug Administration as proof of such.[142] This is what Afexa Life Sciences accomplished when it developed the ChemBioPrint process to ensure that the chemical fingerprint and biological activity of COLD-FX matches that of the active ingredient used in clinical trials and scientific studies.[143]

6.4 Regulation

In Canada, because health policy is the mandate of provincial governments, so they have shouldered most of the responsibility for regulating TCM. This has created variations across the country where presently only four provinces formally regulate it. Nevertheless, a trend of following the lead of British Columbia seems to be developing, particularly in regulating the practice of herbal medicine and establishing industry self-regulation in the form of colleges. The federal government is also involved, mainly in attempting to regulate standards for the ingredients of herbal medicine. As regulation increases and

---

[140] Ian K..Y. Tsang, "Establishing the Efficacy of Traditional Chinese Medicine," *Nature Clinical Practice Rheumatology* 3.2 (2007), 60-61.

[141] Lyren Chiu, "Practising Traditional Chinese Medicine in a Canadian Context: The Roles of Immigration, Legislation, and Integration," *Journal of International Migration and Integration* 7.1 (Winter 2006), 96; Chiu cites various studies to support the claim.

[142] Yaw L. Siow, Yuewen Gong, Kathy K. W. Au-Yeung, Connie W. H. Woo, Patrick C. Choy, and Karmin O, "Emerging Issues in Traditional Chinese Medicine," *Canadian Journal of Physiology & Pharmacology* 83.4 (Apr. 2005), 323-24.

[143] "Standardization Process," COLD-FX website, *cold-fx.ca/hcp/standardization-process.htm*, accessed 2014.12.06.

federal legislation impacts the industry, there have been efforts to harmonize regulation across the nation.

6.4.1 British Columbia

In 1996 the B.C. Ministry of Health established the self-regulating College of Acupuncturists, which awarded licenses to practise acupuncture for the first time in 1999.[144] Its responsibilities were transferred to the newly formed College of Traditional Chinese Medicine Practitioners and Acupuncturists of British Columbia (CTCMA) in 2000 when the regulations surrounding TCM were broadened to cover the prescribing of Chinese herbal medicines. British Columbia was the first jurisdiction to bestow professional titles on those who practise TCM. The college grants four different certificates depending upon type of medicine practised and qualifications.[145] With the awarding of certificates to nine hundred thirty-three TCM practitioners in 2003, British Columbia became the first jurisdiction in North America to officially license the practice of herbal medicine.[146] The majority of CTCMA's board members and its staff are Chinese Canadian and its newsletters are partially written in Chinese.[147]

6.4.2 Ontario

The Government of Ontario passed the Traditional Chinese Medicine Act, Bill 50, regulating TCM, in 2006. This legislation led to the establishment of the Transitional Council of the College of Traditional Chinese Medicine Practitioners and Acupuncturists of Ontario in 2008. The council was charged with establishing the College of Traditional Chinese Medicine

---

[144] "BC Issues Acupuncture Licenses," Canadian Press NewsWire, 1999.12.13.

[145] Asia Pacific Foundation, 2. The four titles for qualified practitioners are Registered Acupuncturist (RAc), Registered Herbalist (RTCM-H), Registered Practitioner (RTCM-P), and Doctor of Traditional Chinese Medicine (Dr. TCM).

[146] Chiu, 99.

[147] College of Traditional Chinese Medicine Practitioners and Acupuncturists of British Columbia, www.ctcma.bc.ca/, accessed 2014.12.12.

Practitioners and Acupuncturists of Ontario, which began operations in 2013, and with developing the regulations and standards of practice in order to provide quality TCM to the Ontario public.

As in the case of the College of Traditional Chinese Medicine Practitioners & Acupuncturists of British Columbia, the majority of the council members are Chinese Canadian and much of the information, such as their newsletters and minutes of council meetings, is presented in Chinese.[148]

6.4.3 Quebec

The need to regulate acupuncture was recognized early in Quebec where in 1973 it was officially placed under the control of the *Corporation professionnelle des médecins du Québec* (Professional corporation of physicians of Quebec) (later to become *Collège des médecins du Québec* [Quebec College of Physicians]). The first accreditation exam for acupuncturists took place in 1986, having been preceded by several legal actions against acupuncturists for practising illegally. In 1995 the *Ordre des acupuncteurs du Québec* (Québec order of acupuncturists) was formed and charged with regulating the profession including attributing titles, creating exams, and discipline.[149]

6.4.4 Alberta

Acupuncture has been regulated in Alberta since 1988 under the Alberta's Health Disciplines Act – Acupuncture Regulation. In November 2006, an interim council of the College and Association of Acupuncturists of Alberta (CAAA) was created with collaboration of three professional associations, namely, the Acupuncture Society of Alberta, the Alberta Association of Traditional Chinese Medicine Doctors, and the Canadian Health Profession Acupuncture Society. The CAAA was designated to regulate the acupuncture profession as of

---

[148] College of Traditional Chinese Medicine Practitioners and Acupuncturists of Ontario, www.ctcmpao.on.ca/, accessed 2014.12.12.

[149] Ordre des Acupunctures du Québec, "Historique," *www.o-a-q.org/*, accessed 2010.06.06.

January 1, 2011. As the governing body, the CAAA is responsible for ensuring that its members have the proper education and training.[150]

6.4.5 Newfoundland and Labrador

Acupuncture became a regulated profession in Newfoundland and Labrador in October 2012. It is regulated by the College of Traditional Chinese Medicine Practitioners and Acupuncturists of Newfoundland and Labrador and only members of the college are considered eligible providers of acupuncture services in the province.[151]

6.4.6 Government of Canada

On a national level, one of the earliest moves to regulate TCM was the creation of the Office of Natural Health Products (later renamed Natural and Non-prescription Health Products Directorate) by Health Canada in 1999.[152] Its mandate is to oversee all aspects of natural health products, including safety, accuracy of health claims, standards, licensing, enforcement of standards, and research. The Natural Health Product Regulations came into effect in 2004 with a six-year transitional period for implementation. Under these regulations, all manufacturers were required to have site licenses and employ Good Manufacturing Practices by the end of 2005. By the end of 2007, manufacturers were required to provide evidence of their products' safety and effectiveness and to obtain a license and natural product numbers. Traditional natural health products are able to use "traditional references

---

[150] "About the CAAA," College and Association of Acupuncturists of Alberta website, *acupuncturealberta.ca/about-caaa/*, accessed 2014.12.06.

[151] College of Traditional Chinese Medicine Practitioners and Acupuncturists of Newfoundland and Labrador, www.ctcmpanl.ca/, accessed 2014.12.12.

[152] Gary Gnirss, "It's a Whole New Ball Game: Health Canada Is Set to Play a Brand New Role in its Approach to Defining and Regulating Natural Health Products in their own Environment," *Food in Canada* 59.5 (June 1999), 33.

in which folkloric use of a product is well documented" as evidence of safety and effectiveness.[153]

The government attempted to strengthen regulation of herbs and other natural health products with the proposed Food and Drugs Act Bill C-51, introduced in 2008. However, Bill C-51 met considerable opposition from the natural health products industry and users because it was seen as proposing excessively restrictive measures. After this, the bill was allowed to die when Parliament prorogued in 2008.

The debate surrounding Bill C-51 seems to be part of an effort to create a new paradigm for assessing natural health products, and the evaluation of herbal medicine within TCM is an example of this effort. Researchers recognize the intrinsic difficulties and limitations in using conventional research methods for assessing TCM.[154] The fact that the Natural Health Products Directorate would allow folkloric documentation instead of the results of clinical tests as evidence of safety and efficacy is recognition of these limitations. Another is the relaxation of guidelines for the approval of herbal formulae as medicine by the FDA in the United States. In 2004, it issued guidelines that such formulae were to be approved if shown to be safe and effective even if the active ingredients were unknown.[155]

One other measure implemented by the federal government was the creation of the Advisory Council on Traditional Chinese Medicine in 2012. The council comprises representatives of industry, consumers, health care professionals, and academics whose mandate is to provide the Government of Canada with advice on current and emerging issues related to TCM.[156]

Also taking place on a national level are efforts to standardize qualifications for TCM practitioners. There are two factors driving these efforts. The main one is the 1994

---

[153] Sandy Hutty, "Natural Health Products – Understanding the Regulations," *Pharmacy Practice* (Mississauga) 20.11 (November 2004), CE1-4.

[154] Chiu, 111.

[155] Collet, 15.

[156] "Harper Government Continues to Engage with Traditional Chinese Medicine Community in Canada," Health Canada website, *www.hc-sc.gc.ca/ahc-asc/media/nr-cp/_2013/2013-44-eng.php*, accessed 2014.12.06.

Agreement on Internal Trade signed by the Canadian federal, provincial, and territorial governments allowing for the movement of qualified workers across provincial and territorial boundaries. This has increased the likelihood that TCM practitioners recognized in one jurisdiction could practise in another, thus creating the need for common standards across jurisdictions. In response, the Canadian Alliance of Regulatory Bodies for Traditional Chinese Medicine Practitioners and Acupuncturists (CARB) has been established.

CARB is composed of the College of Traditional Chinese Medicine Practitioners and Acupuncturists of British-Columbia, the College of Traditional Chinese Medicine Practitioners and Acupuncturists of Ontario, the College and Association of Acupuncturists of Alberta, the College of Traditional Chinese Medicine Practitioners and Acupuncturists of Newfoundland and Labrador, and the *Ordre des acupuncteurs du Québec*. In 2009 CARB issued a list "Entry-Level Occupational Competencies for the Practice of Traditional Chinese Medicine in Canada" that was recommended to provincial authorities for their adoption.

The other factor that is encouraging standardization within Canada is occurring at the international level. The Standardization Administration of China (SAC) had contacted the Transitional Council of the College of Traditional Chinese Medicine and Acupuncturists of Ontario regarding the former's application to the International Organization for Standardization. SAC is attempting to develop new international standards on TCM and was seeking the Transitional Council's support. Also, China has created the World Federation of Chinese Medicine Societies that seeks to develop and publish international standards related to Chinese medicine, which would serve as a basis for international certification and to promote international exchange and cooperation among societies of Chinese medicine. Its membership consists of ninety-five Chinese medicine societies in twenty-three countries and regions.[157]

6.5 Self-Governing and Teaching Institutions

---

[157] World Federation of Chinese Medicine Societies' website, *www.wfcms.org/English/*, accessed 2010.07.10.

There are other types of organizations involved in the promotion of TCM besides those that have an official role in regulating it. Two apparent ones are operated solely by practitioners and have the roles of self-governance and teaching.

6.5.1 Self-governance

Compared to conventional medical practices, those of TCM have had considerably less regulation. Naturally, this has led to debate as to whether TCM should not be more regulated, and, thus, the establishment of the regulatory bodies described above. The debate has also been accompanied by efforts within the industry to establish its own regulation, perhaps in order to pre-empt what might be excessively interventionist, government regulation and to minimize the cost of outside intervention.
Whatever the reasons, some practitioners have recognized the need to govern themselves while fostering cooperation.

There are two national, the Chinese Medicine and Acupuncture Association of Canada (CMAAC) and the Canadian Society of Chinese Medicine & Acupuncture (CSCMA), and several provincial, industry associations that promote TCM within Canada. The CMAAC began in 1983 with a mandate to lobby for regulation of TCM. There are nine chapter offices and three hundred seventy-five members across Canada and it has been a member of the World Federation of Acupuncture-Moxibustion Societies since 1989. It lists among its objectives the establishment of high standards of education and training for TCM practitioners and it has been active in obtaining professional liability insurance for its members.[158]

The CSCMA was established in 1994. It too has a mandate to promote TCM regulation in Canada and claims to have twenty-three hundred members as of 2010. Its international linkages seem strong because its website contains news of TCM conferences outside Canada and meetings between CSCMA and Chinese government officials. Furthermore, their website has a

---

[158] Chinese Medicine and Acupuncture Association of Canada website, *www.cmaac.ca/*, accessed 2014.12.06.

nearly full Chinese language version and the association's newsletter is mostly in Chinese.[159]

One of the more active provincial organizations is the Traditional Chinese Medicine Association of BC (TCMABC), which was founded in 1992 with a mandate to serve TCM practitioners. It claims to have been one of the first associations to petition the BC government to regulate the practice of TCM. In 2010 it joined with British Columbia Qualified Acupuncturists and Traditional Chinese Medicine Practitioners Association in efforts to unify the profession and create a stronger voice. TCMABC maintains an active website including a public forum for classified ads and educational events.[160]

The presence of active self-governing TCM organizations both at national and provincial levels indicates a high level of achievement by Chinese Canadians in the promotion of TCM. They are important participants in the process of regulation as witnessed by the use of Chinese and their large membership and leadership roles in these organizations.

6.5.2 Teaching Institutions

The number and sophistication of institutions that teach the practice of TCM are high and they are found all over Canada. This again reflects the increasing importance of TCM and the achievements of Chinese Canadians. Generally, there are two types of teaching institutions: private schools that have developed quickly under the direction of Chinese Canadians and public institutions that have recognized the need for critical research of medical techniques that offer much promise while receiving strong popular support.

6.5.2.1 Private Schools

A 2010 survey of telephone directories for Toronto, Vancouver, and Calgary respectively found fourteen, four, and four TCM schools in each of these cities. An internet

---

[159] Canadian Society of Chinese Medicine & Acupuncture website, *www.tcmcanada.org*, accessed 2014.12.06.

[160] Traditional Chinese Medicine Association of BC website, *www.tcmabc.org/*, accessed 2010.06.24.

494

search uncovered a total of twenty-three schools in the three provinces: British Columbia with eleven schools, Ontario with eight, and Alberta with three.[161] There are examples of remarkable educational development among these schools. The International College of Traditional Chinese Medicine of Vancouver claims to have one hundred twenty students, fifteen faculty members, and occupy six hundred fifty square meters. It was established by Henry Lu in 1986–originally in Victoria–so it is one of the longest existing schools in British Columbia, if not Canada. The school offers the four diploma programs–a five-year program for Doctor of Traditional Chinese Medicine, a four-year program for Traditional Chinese Medicine Practitioner, a three-year program for Acupuncturist, and a three-year program for TCM Herbalist–permitted under provincial regulations. As well, it offers a short program in *tuina* and opportunities to intern abroad.[162]

---

[161] The eleven schools in British Columbia are Academy Of Classical Oriental Sciences (Nelson, *www.acos.org/*), Canadian College of Acupuncture and Oriental Medicine (Victoria, *www.ccaom.com/*), Central College (New Westminster, *www centralcollege.ca*), International College of Traditional Chinese Medicine of Vancouver (*www.tcm college.com/*), Merinol College (Surrey, *www.merinolcollege.ca*), Oshio College of Acupuncture & Herbology (Victoria, *www.oshiocollege.com/*), Pacific Rim College, School of Acupuncture and Oriental Medicine (Victoria, *www.pacificrimcollege.ca*), PCU College of Holistic Medicine (Burnaby, *www.pcucollege.ca/*), Shang Hai TCM College of B.C. (Burnaby, *www.acupuncture-college.com/home.asp*), Vancouver Beijing College of Chinese Medicine (Richmond, *www.tcmvbc.com/*), and Western Canadian Institute of TCM Practitioners (Richmond, *www.tcm.bc.ca*). The eight schools in Ontario are Acupuncture Foundation of Canada Institute (Scarborough, *www.afcinstitute.com/*), Acupuncture & Natural Healing Centre (Sarnia, *www.acupuncturesarnia.ca/*), Canadian College of Holistic Health (Richmond Hill, *www.cchh.org/*), College of Acupuncture & Therapeutics (Kitchener, *www.collegeofacupuncture.com/*), College of Traditional Chinese Medicine and Pharmacology Canada (Toronto, *www.ctcmpc.com*), International Academy of Traditional Chinese Medicine (Ottawa, *www.intlacademy.com/*), Ontario College of Traditional Chinese Medicine (Toronto, *www.octcm.com/*), and Toronto School of Traditional Chinese Medicine (*www.tstcm.com/*).The three schools in Alberta are Alberta College of Acupuncture & Traditional Chinese Medicine (Calgary, *www.acatcm.com/*), Calgary College of Traditional Chinese Medicine and Acupuncture (*www.cctcma.com/*), and Canadian Institute of Traditional Chinese Medicine (Calgary, *www.citcm.com/*).

[162] International College of Traditional Chinese Medicine of Vancouver website, *www.tcmcollege.com/*, accessed 2014.12.06.

The Alberta College of Acupuncture & Traditional Chinese Medicine in Calgary was founded in 1997 by Benny Xu and was the first TCM institution in Alberta. It offers a three-year acupuncture program and a four-year TCM program. It is also the Canadian Education Centre for Beijing University of Chinese Medicine allowing its students to pursue study there. Beijing University of Chinese Medicine was founded in 1956 and is included in the "211 Project" and the "985 Project Innovation" that channel government resources to key Chinese universities. The college also promotes student employment and relations by posting employment opportunities and alumni work positions as well as announcements of social and academic events.[163]

The Canadian Institute of Traditional Chinese Medicine in Calgary was established in 2004 by Xia Cheng. It teaches a variety of programs including a four-year acupuncture diploma program, a four-year doctor of TCM program, and a five-year bachelor degree in TCM with a one-year internship in a Chinese teaching hospital, as well as specialized programs in massage medicine.[164]

The Toronto School of Traditional Chinese Medicine was founded in 1995 by Mary Xiumei Wu. It offers diploma programs in Traditional Chinese Medicine, acupuncture, Chinese herbal medicine, and *tuina* massage. Wu has been active in efforts to regulate TCM in Canada.[165]

The World Chinese Medicine and Acupuncture College in Toronto was founded in 2011. It offers two to three year programs in acupuncture, herbal medicine, and massage. The college is unique in having a close connection to the development of TCM in China. It established an agreement with Beijing University of Chinese Medicine in 1996. In 2011 it signed an agreement with the World Federation of Chinese Medicine Societies (WFCMS) to become the first college of TCM outside China to offer a program designed specifically to

---

[163] Alberta College of Acupuncture & Traditional Chinese Medicine website, *www.acatcm.com/*, accessed 2014.12.06.

[164] Canadian Institute of Traditional Chinese Medicine website, *citcmacupuncture.com/*, accessed 2014.12.07.

[165] Toronto School of Traditional Chinese Medicine website, *www.tstcm.com/html/about_tstcm.html*, accessed 2014.12.07.

prepare students to write the International Qualification Examination for TCM Professionals, which is part of an effort by China to establish worldwide credentials for TCM practitioners. The college's programs are designed around WFCMS's qualification exams and TCM programs offered by well-known universities in China. Lecturers are either from the Beijing University of Chinese Medicine or recommended by the WFCMS.[166]

6.5.2.2 Public Education

The presence of instruction on TCM in the public education system shows further progress in the acceptance of TCM and, thus, the achievements of Chinese Canadians in promoting this acceptance. While private TCM schools may be more motivated by the profit accruing from tuition fees, public education often has to justify the use of public funds to conduct the research and offer the instruction that supports its curriculum. This justification requires critical examination, thus, any ensuing approval is added evidence for the acceptance of TCM.

As in the private sector, there are a surprisingly large number of initiatives to promote TCM within public education. In British Columbia, the provincial government announced in 2014 plans to establish the first public school of TCM at Kwantlen Polytechnic University.[167]

The University of Alberta has offered the Certificate Program in Medical Acupuncture from 1991 until 2013. The program entailed two hundred hours of instruction over an eight-month period. It is estimated that this course has contributed to about 15 percent of Alberta's dental students becoming proficient in acupuncture.[168] Furthermore, the Complementary and Alternative Research and Education

---

[166] World Chinese Medicine and Acupuncture College website, *wcmaac.com/about.html*, accessed 2014.12.07.

[167] "Kwantlen to Host Traditional Chinese Medicine School," British Columbia Newsroom, 2014.01.24, *www.newsroom.gov.bc.ca/2014/01/kwantlen-to-host-traditional-chinese-medicine-school.html*, accessed 2014.12.07.

[168] Heather Kent, "East Meets West in Busy Edmonton Practice," *Canadian Medical Association Journal* 163.4 (2000.08.22), 484.

(CARE) Program in the Department of Pediatrics in the University of Alberta has been conducting a number of research projects on TCM, such as the use of TCM to treat fatigue. Grant MacEwan University in Edmonton offers a three-year acupuncture program that prepares one to become a registered acupuncturist in Alberta.

The University of Manitoba opened the Richardson Centre for Functional Foods and Nutraceuticals in 2006, which is dedicated more to the development of functional foods and nutraceuticals rather than education about them. The centre envisions being able to produce foods that will improve the health and wellness of Canadians.[169]

In Ontario, McMaster University offers the Contemporary Medical Acupuncture Program, which began in 1998 after acupuncture was introduced to the university in 1984 as part of its Acupuncture/Pain Clinic. The program includes one hundred twenty-six hours of class instruction spread over five weekends, which are spread over four months, and one hundred seventy-four hours of assignments. The program is particularly suited to qualified medical professionals and is designed to offer them another tool or means by which to provide their patients the best medical care.[170]

In Quebec, the College de Rosemont (Montreal) offers a three-year program in acupuncture. Graduation from the program entitles students to write the examination of l'Ordre des acupuncteurs du Québec. Those who successfully complete this examination become registered acupuncturists and are granted a work permit in Quebec.[171]

The variety of TCM offerings within public education is also notable. There are major multi-year programs, initiation courses, and those targeting specific groups, such as McMaster's, which attracts many international students.

---

[169] University of Manitoba Richardson Centre for Functional Foods and Nutraceuticals *website, umanitoba.ca/centres/rcffn/aboutus.html*, accessed 2014.12.07.

[170] McMaster University Health Sciences Contemporary Medical Acupuncture Program website, *mcmasteracupuncture.com/*, accessed 2014.12.07.

[171] Collège de Rosemont website, *www.crosemont.qc.ca/public/bd6fad11-ee4c-4d0c-a5d7-c094a8a27d06/mes_documents/brochures/2015/acupuncture.pdf*, accessed 2014.12.11.

7. Achievements

The description above has covered a broad range of subjects many of which are only indirectly related to the achievements of Chinese Canadians with regard to TCM. The explanations of theory and concepts underlying TCM, along with its history and presence within China are offered to support the claim that TCM has a strong potential for acceptance within Canada, so that one should not be surprised at its actual presence there.

TCM's strong potential for a significant presence in Canada stems originally from a set of concepts and theories that offer a valid and rich explanation of human health and that has formed the basis of supporting the health of the Chinese people for thousands of years. These concepts and theories have included maintenance of good health; balancing a variety of forces, sometimes opposing, within the human body; *qi,* the vital energy present in all things and accounting for transmutation; holism, the view of the human subject and his or her environment forming an integrated system; the five phases, an explicative and mnemonic device for describing natural phenomena such as processes within the human body; and being proactive in practising TCM and maintaining one's health.

There are also a number of TCM practices that contribute to its fundamental attractiveness. Diet is practised on a daily basis and as such is mainly managed by the subject rather than the practitioner. It is also an important determiner of good health. Herbal medicine has a long history of being able to support the health of the Chinese people and some of its formulae have been adopted into Western conventional medicine. It offers inexpensive, usually milder, yet effective alternatives to conventional medical cures. Acupuncture is broadly used in North America, mainly as treatment for pain. Massage therapy and *qigong* are two other TCM practices that offer benefits to their users.

These benefits are seen in TCM's effectiveness, prevention of illness, economy, and enhancement when combined with Western conventional medicine and new technology. The general effectiveness of TCM is seen in Chinese civilization's ability to extend itself indefinitely while supporting a large population. The maintenance of good health that has contributed to these accomplishments has relied primarily upon TCM, which today still makes up an estimated 40 percent of all health care. This effectiveness has been recognized outside China's borders, an example of this being the early transmission of smallpox vaccination from China to the rest of the world. Further evidence is provided by modern testing methods; these have shown, for example, acupuncture effective in treating painful disorders of the muscle and skeletal systems. TCM's ability to prevent illness is demonstrated in the relatively long longevity of the Chinese despite the low levels of investment they have made in interventions to counter illness, injury, and disease. Maintenance of health mainly relies upon diet and the adoption of a proactive attitude toward doing so. While the Chinese have not invested heavily in interventions to correct health problems, the emphasis on maintenance has proved to be economically advantageous. The Chinese are able to enjoy a relatively long life, yet incurring very low health expenditures. The cost is further reduced because the means of disseminating medical knowledge and ingredients, and the tools used are all relatively inexpensive. Another benefit of TCM derives from its combination with Western conventional medicine and new technology. It is perhaps the greater integration of these two systems that is suggested with this combination that promises the biggest benefit of TCM. TCM has been shown to enhance the effects of Western medical treatments. New research methods are also able to increase confidence in the use of TCM by providing stronger evidence for its efficacy and the internet offers more efficient means to disseminate and organize information on TCM.

The actual and potential benefits of TCM are made more accessible by the strong presence of TCM in China, which is evidence of its effectiveness and is favorably manifested in the standardization and development that the government continues to promote.

7.1 Presence in Canada

The promotion within China and benefits of TCM have contributed to its considerable presence within Canada. The relatively long life of Chinese Canadians that is indicative of good health seems to stem, at least in part, from the use of TCM. Furthermore, it is likely that this phenomenon, along with evidence from China's experience, is contributing to the increasing use of complementary and alternative medicine within North America. This use is seen in consumer trends and the creation of large organizations, such as individual practitioners and major medical institutions, that offer TCM services. It is also seen in large commercial endeavours, such as the activities of Afexa Life Sciences and the large scale growing of American ginseng. It has also led to broad regulation of TCM by provincial and national governments. British Columbia, Alberta, Ontario, Quebec, and Newfoundland and Labrador, along with the federal government, all have regulations in place, with those of British Columbia being the most comprehensive because they include regulation of herbal medicine. The federal government has implemented the Natural Health Product Regulations in order to ensure product safety and effectiveness.

The TCM industry within Canada has also established self-governing and combined training and accreditation organizations. Nationwide, it has established the Canadian Alliance of Regulatory Bodies for Traditional Chinese Medicine Practitioners and Acupuncturists to standardize acceptable qualifications for TCM practitioners. There are two other national and several provincial associations that promote TCM within Canada. There are also a number of private institutions, universities, and colleges across the country that teach TCM in programs of up to five years.

8. Future Trend: Integration of TCM and Western Conventional Medicine

One should see continuing integration of TCM and Western conventional medicine. The general trends within TCM strongly support this. There is strong fundamental value in TCM as exemplified by its history and present status in China. Westerners are increasingly aware of and wanting to take advantage of this value. Chinese Canadians are contributing to this trend by maintaining TCM practices within Canada rather than replacing them completely with those from Western conventional medicine. They have been very proactive in doing so; through their creation of institutions for practising, teaching, and even regulating TCM within Canada, TCM has become well established there. This has created a platform upon which to foster greater integration.

Apart from these broad factors that have contributed to the establishment of TCM within Canada, there are a number of smaller ones that will also contribute to this trend, probably adding to the speed with which greater integration can be achieved. Taking the facts that 67 percent of those who were practising TCM professionally in British Columbia in 1996 were Asian and that many of these were previously practicing doctors from China and Asia[172] as generally indicative of the TCM industry in Canada, one can assume that many of the educated immigrants that Canada draws from China will seek to find work within the TCM industry. They will thus add resources to it, further contributing to its development and attractiveness.

The attractiveness, and thus trend toward integration, will be amplified because there is a need for economical alternatives in Canada's health system. Health costs demand large portions of provincial health budgets and the amounts are increasing. Randy Wong, a former hospital head, as registrar of the College of Traditional Chinese Medicine Practitioners and Acupuncturists of British Columbia, pointed out that it is more cost-effective to treat some ailments and chronic conditions with visits to a herbalist or acupuncturist that cost $50 or $100 than $500 to $1,500-a-day hospital admissions.[173]

It seems also that in North America, the potential cost savings, as well as the medical benefits, from using TCM have been recognized. Authorities have been willing to alter established standards in order to permit TCM treatments to be administered. For example, even if the active ingredients have not been known, herbal mixtures have been approved for dispensing since 2004 in the United States if they are shown to be safe and effective.[174] In Canada since 2004, Natural Health Product Regulations have allowed herbal manufacturers to use traditional references in which folkloric use of a product is well documented as evidence of safety and effectiveness.

---

[172] Asia Pacific Foundation, 4.

[173] Ken MacQueen, "The Best of Both Worlds," *Maclean's* 114.11 (2001.03.12).

[174] Qiu, "Traditional," 127.

The alteration of standards has also been applied to titles awarded to practitioners. Awarding the title "Doctor" to TCM practitioners in British Columbia was originally opposed by the government's Health Professions Council on the grounds that granting the title "Doctor" to practitioners would lower the status of this title. In response the TCM community argued that not granting the title would imply the inferiority of TCM to Western medicine and they were able to convince the government to confer the title "Doctor of Traditional Chinese Medicine " for approved practitioners with five or more years of training. This decision made it more likely for TCM and Western medical professionals to work together as equals, and, thus, contributed to the trend toward integration of the two systems.[175]

In fact, there have been some significant efforts to integrate the two systems. For example, the Tzu Chi Institute for Complementary and Alternative Medicine in Vancouver was able to open because of the reputation of one of its major supporters, Wah Jun Tze. Tze had headed the pediatric endocrinology division of the University of British Columbia's medical school and had been director of the metabolic investigation unit at British Columbia's Children's Hospital. He was awarded the Order of Canada in 1994 for his work promoting children's health around the world. Tze persuaded the Tzu Chi Foundation of Canada to provide six million dollars of seed money; the Vancouver Hospital to provide space, infrastructure support, and a partnership grant; and several major hospitals to become research partners. Tze offered two reasons for the need for Western medicine to pay closer attention to alternatives: first, the Western approach to medicine has shortcomings, such as the inability to manage chronic pain well; second, complementary medicine stresses maintaining wellness over attacking disease, which can save the health system much money.[176]

---

[175] Asia Pacific Foundation, 3.

[176] Rebecca Wigod, "East Meets West at Vancouver Hospital: a Respected Physician Has Convinced the Facility to Open a Privately Funded Institute to Research Treatments Such as Acupuncture and Homeopathy.: Acceptance of Eastern Medical Techniques Expected to Bring Standards, Regulation;" (sic.), *The Vancouver Sun*, 1996.06.13, A1.

The Tzu Chi Institute offered integrative care from 1998 to probably 2003 when it ceased operations. Its patients received care from a "multidisciplinary team of practitioners representing biomedicine, chiropractic, nursing, naturopathy, acupuncture, nutrition, Traditional Chinese Medicine, massage therapy, and mind-body healing." Patients mostly used acupuncture services and nearly 90 percent rated the service as excellent.[177]

Another significant example of integration of TCM and Western medical knowledge is in the work of Tai Lahans. Lahans was voted Faculty of the Year at Bastyr University in 1998 and was included in Seattle Magazine's "TopDocs" in 2003. She is the author of *Integrating Conventional and Chinese Medicine in Cancer Care: A Clinical Guide*. This text is described by its publisher as combining Chinese herbal medicine with Western medicine in order to enhance and improve medical care for patients with cancer. Each chapter covers a different type of cancer, first introducing the conventional medical understanding of that cancer, then the prospective Chinese medicine for it. Case studies show how the respective treatments can be integrated for each cancer type.[178] According to a review of this book, Lahans has been able to promote the use of Chinese herbal medicine to conventional medical oncologists and to numerous hospitals. Furthermore, clinical research has shown her correct, the integrated approach is more effective than either modality used separately.[179]

9. Conclusion

The integration of TCM and Western conventional medicine is strongly supported by the history and recent development of TCM within China. Moreover, arguably, this integration in Canada, both in its actual and potential form, is the

---

[177] Mulkins, 586, 590, and 589.

[178] Elsevier website, *www.elsevier.com/wps/find/bookdescription.cws_home/708303/description#description*, accessed 2010.07.19.

[179] Jake Paul Fratkin, Review of *Integrating Conventional and Chinese Medicine in Cancer Care: A Clinical Guide*, 2007, *www.drjakefratkin.com/pdf/LahansCancer.pdf*, accessed 2010.07.19.

achievement of Chinese Canadians. A large percentage of the
practitioners of TCM are Chinese Canadian and Chinese
Canadians who, more so than other Canadians, have access to
resources in China by which to promote TCM. They also
embody more the cultural values that underlie TCM. Their
sense of personal responsibility, awareness of environmental
and emotional influences, and deep understanding that good
health depends more on long term, daily practices than
extraordinary interventions reflect a culture that has proven
able to support good health over millennia. The desire to share
this means to attain good health while benefitting from the
advantages of modern science and technology follows from this
culture as well. It is within these conditions that Canada
witnesses the integration of TCM with Western conventional
medicine.

BIBLIOGRAPHY

"About the CAAA." College and Association of Acupuncturists of
    Alberta website, *acupuncturealberta.ca/about-caaa/*,
    accessed 2014.12.06.

Alberta College of Acupuncture & Traditional Chinese
    Medicine. *www.acatcm.com/*, accessed 2014.12.06.

Alberta Health Services. "Health and Chinese Canadians,"
    2009.03.09.
    *www.calgaryhealthregion.ca/programs/diversity/diversity
    _resources/health_div_pops/chiinese_canadians.htm*,
    accessed 2014.12.02.

Agriculture and Agri-Food Canada website. "Functional Foods
    and Natural Health Products - Canadian Industry."
    *www.agr.gc.ca/eng/industry-markets-and-trade/statistics-
    and-market-information/by-product-sector/functional-
    foods-and-natural-health-products/functional-foods-and-
    natural-health-products-canadian-
    industry/?id=1170856376710*, accessed 2015.07.10

------. "What Are Functional Foods and Nutraceuticals?". "Agri-Industries > Functional Foods and Nutraceuticals," *www.agr.gc.ca/*, accessed 2009.12.03.

Armstrong, Jane. "Richmond, B.C., Holds the Secret to a Long Life." *The Globe and Mail*, 2005.02.02, A 3.

Asia Pacific Foundation. "Canada Begins to Assimilate Traditional Chinese Medicine." *Canada Asia Commentary* 32 (December 2003): 1-7.

Bausell, R. Barker. *Snake Oil Science: The Truth About Complementary and Alternative Medicine*. New York: Oxford University Press, 2007.

"BC Issues Acupuncture Licenses." Canadian Press NewsWire, 1999.12.13.

Braverman, Steven E. "Medical Acupuncture Review: Safety, Efficacy, and Treatment Practices." *Medical Acupuncture* 15.3 (2004): 12-16.

British Columbia Ministry of Health. "Information for Supplementary Benefit Practitioners." *www.health.gov.bc.ca/msp/infoprac/suppbilling/index.html*, accessed 2014.12.05.

Cabioğlu, Mehmet Tuğrul and Nihon Ergene."Electroacupuncture Therapy for Weight Loss Reduces Serum Total Cholesterol, Triglycerides, and LDL Cholesterol Levels in Obese Women." *The American Journal of Chinese Medicine* 33.4 (2005): 525-533.

Canadian College of Acupuncture and Oriental Medicine website, *www.citcmacupuncture.com/*, accessed 2014.12.07.

Canadian Institute of Traditional Chinese Medicine website, *www.citcm.com/*, accessed 2010.07.03.

Canadian Society of Chinese Medicine & Acupuncture website, *www.tcmcanada.org*, accessed 2014.12.06.

Centers for Disease Control and Prevention. "Life Expectancy." *www.cdc.gov/nchs/fastats/lifexpec.htm*, accessed 2010.07.07

Chappell, Neena L. and David Lai. "Health Care Service by Chinese Seniors in British Columbia, Canada." *Journal of Cross-Cultural Gerontology* 13 (1998): 21-37.

Charrois, Theresa L., Jessica Hrudey, and Sunita Vohra. "Ginseng: Practical Management of Adverse Effects and Drug Interactions." *Canadian Pharmacists Journal* 139.2 (Mar./Apr. 2006): 44-46.

Chinese Medicine and Acupuncture Association of Canada website, www.cmaac.ca/, accessed 2014.12.06.

Chiu, Lyren. "Practising Traditional Chinese Medicine in a Canadian Context: The Roles of Immigration, Legislation, and Integration." *Journal of International Migration and Integration* 7.1 (Winter 2006): 95-115.

Claxton, Gary, Isadora Gil, Ben Finder, Erin Holve, Jon Gabel, Jeremy Pickreighn, Heidi Whitmore, Samantha Hawkins, and Cheryl Fahlman. *Employer Health Benefits 2004 Annual Survey*. Menlo Park, California: The Kaiser Family Foundation; and Chicago, Illinois: Health Research and Educational Trust. 164 pages.

"Clinical Trials." COLD-FX website, *cold-fx.ca/hcp/health_clinical.htm*, accessed 2014.12.06.

Cohen, Kenneth. *The Way of Qigong: the Art and Science of Chinese Energy Healing*. New York: Ballantine Books, 1997.

"Cold-fx® Chosen Canada's # 1 Pharmacist Recommended Natural Cold Remedy for Fourth Straight Year. Recommended by 73% of Pharmacists Nationally According to Leading Pharmacy Magazine Survey." COLD-FX website, *www.cold-fx.ca/news_may5_09.htm*, accessed 2010.05.25.

Collège de Rosemont website,
www.crosemont.qc.ca/public/bd6fad11-ee4c-4d0c-a5d7-c094a8a27d06/mes_documents/brochures/2015/acupunct ure.pdf, accessed 2014.12.11.

College of Traditional Chinese Medicine Practitioners and Acupuncturists of British Columbia. www.ctcma.bc.ca/, accessed 2014.12.12.

College of Traditional Chinese Medicine Practitioners and Acupuncturists of Newfoundland and Labrador. www.ctcmpanl.ca/, accessed 2014.12.12.

College of Traditional Chinese Medicine Practitioners and Acupuncturists of Ontario. www.ctcmpao.on.ca/, accessed 2014.12.12.

Collet, Jean-Pault, interview. "Clinical Research in the Assessment of Efficacy and Safety of Traditional Chinese Medicine." *Wellness Options* 33 (2007): 15-17.

Dubey, Anita. "Acupuncture Treatment Shows Promise, Research Review Finds: US Panel Endorses the Method for a Variety of Ailments." *The Journal – Addiction Research Foundation* (Toronto) 27.1 (Jan./Feb. 1998): 2.

Dupree, Joe. "The Most Important Fish in the Sea." *National Wildlife* 46.2 (Feb./Mar. 2008): 38-45.

Eisenberg, D. M., R. B. Davis, S. L. Ettner, S. Appel, S. Wilkey, S. M. Van Rompay, *et al.* "Trends in Alternative Medicine Use in the United States, 1990–1997: Results of a Follow-up National Survey." *The Journal of the American Medical Association* (JAMA) 280 (1998): 1569–75.

Elsevier website,
www.elsevier.com/wps/find/bookdescription.cws_home/70 8303/description#description, accessed 2010.07.19.

Fratkin, Jake Paul. Review of *Integrating Conventional and Chinese Medicine in Cancer Care: A Clinical Guide,* 2007.

www.drjakefratkin.com/pdf/LahansCancer.pdf, accessed 2010.07.19.

Gnirss, Gary. "It's a Whole New Ball Game: Health Canada Is Set to Play a Brand New Role in its Approach to Defining and Regulating Natural Health Products in their own Environment." *Food in Canada* 59.5 (June 1999): 33.

Graham, A.C. *Disputers of the Tao: Philosophical Argument in Ancient China.* La Salle, Illinois: Open Court, 1989.

Grant MacEwan University website, *www.macewan.ca/*, accessed 2010.07.04.

"Harper Government Continues to Engage with Traditional Chinese Medicine Community in Canada." Health Canada website, *www.hc-sc.gc.ca/ahc-asc/media/nr-cp/_2013/2013-44-eng.php*, accessed 2014.12.06.

"Health Canada Warns against Two Traditional Chinese Herbal Products." Canadian Press NewsWire, 2001.02.28.

"Health Canada Warns Consumers against Cancer-Causing Herbal Products." Canadian Press NewsWire, 2002.05.16.

"Healthy Choices Impact Food Product Sales." *Plant* (Willowdale, Ontario) 64.11 (2005.11.14): 35.

Helmut Kaiser Consultancy. "Traditional Chinese Medicine (TCM): In China and Worldwide, 2005-2006-2010-2015." *www.hkc22.com/chinesemedicine.html*, accessed 2009.02.23.

"Herb Extracts Exports Maintain Growth." *ChinaDaily.com.cn*, 2012.05.08, accessed 2014.12.02.

Hesketh, Terese and Wei Xing Zhu. "Health in China: Traditional Chinese Medicine: One Country, Two Systems." *BMJ* 315 (1997.07.12): 115-117.

Hui, Ann. "Ontario Research Uprooting Myths about Ginseng's Health Benefits." *The Globe and Mail*, 2013.09.26.

Hutty, Sandy. "Natural Health Products–Understanding the Regulations." *Pharmacy Practice* (Mississauga) 20.11 (November 2004): CE1-4.

Hsu, Elisabeth. *The Transmission of Chinese Medicine.* Cambridge, U.K.: Cambridge University Press, 1999.

Hu, Shiu-ying. *Food Plants of China.* Hong Kong, The Chinese University Press, 2005.

"Industrial Output of Traditional Chinese Medicine Reaches 177.2 Bln Yuan." *People's Daily Online*, 2008.07.18. *english.people.com.cn*, accessed 2010.05.17.

Insurance Corporation of British Columbia. "ICBCclaiminfo.com." *www.icbcclaiminfo.com/node/65*, accessed 2014.12.06.

International College of Traditional Chinese Medicine of Vancouver website, *www.tcmcollege.com/*, accessed 2014.12.06.

Jermyn, Diane. "Mind behind Cold-FX Launches Product Line for Aging Boomers." *The Globe and Mail*, 2013.10.11.

Kastner, Jöerg. *Chinese Nutrition Therapy: Dietetics in Traditional Chinese Medicine (TCM)*. Stuttgart: Thieme, 2004.

Kavoussi, Ben. "Acupuncture and Fasciae Fallacy," 2010.12.30. Science-Based Medicine: Exploring Issues & Controversies in Science & Medicine website, www.sciencebasedmedicine.org/acupuncture-and-fascial-planes-junk-science-and-wasteful-research/, accessed 2014.12.10.

Kent, Heather. "East Meets West in Busy Edmonton Practice." *Canadian Medical Association Journal* 163.4 (2000.08.22): 484.

"Kwantlen to Host Traditional Chinese Medicine School."
British Columbia Newsroom, 2014.01.24.
www.newsroom.gov.bc.ca/2014/01/kwantlen-to-host-traditional-chinese-medicine-school.html, accessed
2014.12.07.

Lahans, Tai. *Integrating Conventional and Chinese Medicine in Cancer Care: A Clinical Guide*. Philadelphia: Churchill
Livingstone Elsevier, 2007.

"Life Expectancy Hits 80.4 Years: Statistics Canada." CBC
News, 2008.01.14.
www.cbc.ca/canada/story/2008/01/14/death-stats.html,
accessed 2010.07.07.

Life Sciences Analytics. "CV Technologies Inc." (note Afexa Life
Sciences was once named "CV Technologies").
www.lsareports.co, accessed 2010.05.25.

Maciocia, Giovanni. *The Practice of Chinese Medicine: the Treatment of Diseases with Acupuncture and Chinese
Herbs*. Second edition. Edinburgh: Churchill Livingstone
Elsevier, 2008.

MacLeod, Stuart. "Maximizing Benefits from Traditional
Chinese Medicine," A Canadian Health Research Series.
Wellness Options 33 (2007): 14.

MacQueen, Ken. "The Best of Both Worlds." *Maclean's* 114.11
(2001.03.12): 44-46.

Mainardi, Timothy, Simi Kapoor, and Leonard Bielory.
"Complementary and Alternative Medicine: Herbs,
Phytochemicals and Vitamins and Their Immunologic
Effects." *Journal of Allergy and Clinical Immunology* 123.2
(2009.02.10): 283–294.

McMaster University Health Sciences. "Contemporary Medical
Acupuncture Program," *www.acupunctureprogram.com/*,
accessed 2014.12.06.

McMaster University Health Sciences Contemporary Medical Acupuncture Program website, *mcmasteracupuncture.com/*, accessed 2014.12.07.

Melton, Lisa. "Chinese Medicine in Western Packaging." *Chemistry World* (May 2007): 46-50.

Mulkins, Andrea, Marja Verhoef, Joanna Eng, Barbara Findlay, and Darlene Ramsum. "Evaluation of the Tzu Chi Institute for Complementary and Alternative Medicine Integrative Care Program." *The Journal of Alternative and Complementary Medicine* 9.4 (Aug 2003): 585-592.

Nielsen, Arya and Richard Hammerschlag. "Acupuncture and East Asian Medicine." In *Integrative Medicine: Principles for Practice,* edited by Benjamin Kligler and Roberta Lee, 177-217. New York: McGraw-Hill, 2004.

National Geographic Atlas of China. Washington, D.C.: National Geographic, 2008.

Ni H., C. Simile, and A.M. Hardy. "Utilization of Complementary and Alternative Medicine by United States Adults: Results from the 1999 National Health Interview Survey." *Medical Care* 40 (2002): 353-58.

Needham, Joseph with Lu Gwei-Djen. "Hygiene and Preventive Medicine in Ancient China." In *Clerks and Craftsmen in China and the West*, 340-78. Cambridge, England: At the University Press, 1970.

------. "Medicine and Chinese Culture." In *Clerks and Craftsmen in China and the West*, 263-93. Cambridge, England: At the University Press, 1970.

Ng, Siu Man. "The Role of Chinese Medicine in Cancer Palliative Care." In *Death, Dying and Bereavement: A Hong Kong Chinese Experience*, edited by Cecilia Lai Wan Chan and Amy Yin Man Chow, 195-208. Hong Kong: Hong Kong University Press, 2006.

Ordre des Acupunctures du Québec. "Historique." *www.o-a-q.org/*, accessed 2010.06.06.

Parish, Lawrence Charles. "Review *Snake Oil Science: The Truth About Complementary and Alternative Medicine.*" *The Journal of the American Medical Association* 301.3 (2009.01.21): 332-33.

Qiu, Jane. "China Plans to Modernize Traditional Medicine." *Nature* 446.7136 (2007.04.05): 590-591.

------."Traditional Medicine: a Culture in the Balance." *Nature* 448.7150 (2007.07.12): 126-28.

Quan, Hude, Fu-Lin Wang, Donald Schopflocher, and Carolyn De Coster. "Mortality, Cause of Death and Life Expectancy of Chinese Canadians in Alberta." *Canadian Journal of Public Health* 98.6 (Nov. -Dec. 2007): 500-05.

Reid, Daniel P. *Chinese Herbal Medicine*. Boston: Shambhala, 1987.

Rosenberg, Matt. "Life Expectancy: Overview of Life Expectancy," 2007.08.19. *geography.about.com/od/populationgeography/a/lifeexpectancy.htm*, accessed 2009.01.19.

Roth, Marilyn A. and Karen M. Kobayashi. "The Use of Complementary and Alternative Medicine among Chinese Canadians: Results from a National Survey." *Journal of Immigrant Minority Health* 10 (2008): 517-528.

Rothfeld, Glenn S. *The Acupuncture Response: Balance Energy and Restore Health–a Western Doctor Tells You How*. Chicago: Contemporary Books, 2002.

Sagar, S. M. and R. K. Wong. "Chinese Medicine and Biomodulation in Cancer Patients—Part Two." *Current Oncology* 15.2 (2008): 9-30.

Shufelt, Tim. "Eaten to Extinction." *The Globe and Mail*, 2009.11.17, M5.

Sivin, Nathan. "Science and Medicine in Chinese History." In *Heritage of China: Contemporary Perspectives on Chinese Civilization*, edited by Paul S. Ropp, 164-196. Berkeley: University of California Press, 1990.

Siow, Yaw L., Yuewen Gong, Kathy K. W. Au-Yeung, Connie W. H. Woo, Patrick C. Choy, and Karmin O. "Emerging Issues in Traditional Chinese Medicine." *Canadian Journal of Physiology & Pharmacology* 83.4 (Apr., 2005): 321-334.

Sprague, Jonathon. "A Leaf for the Book of Life." *Asiaweek*, 1999.08.08, 26-31.

"Standardization Process." COLD-FX website, *cold-fx.ca/hcp/standardization-process.htm*, accessed 2014.12.06.

Statistics Canada. "Table 002-0001, Farm cash receipts." *www5.statcan.gc.ca/cansim/a47*, accessed 2013.09.18.

Taylor, Kim. *Chinese Medicine in Early Communist China, 1945-63: A Medicine of Revolution*. London: RoutledgeCurzon, 2005.

Temple, Robert. *The Genius of China: 3,000 Years of Science, Discovery, and Invention*. New York: Simon & Schuster, 1986.

Thompson, Dick. "Acupuncture Works." *Time*, 1997.11.17, 84. Toronto School of Traditional Chinese Medicine website, *ww.tstcm.com/html/about_tstcm.html*, accessed 2014.12.07.

Traditional Chinese Medicine Association of BC website, *www.tcmabc.org/*, accessed 2010.06.24.

Tsang, Ian K..Y. "Establishing the Efficacy of Traditional Chinese Medicine." *Nature Clinical Practice Rheumatology* 3.2 (2007): 60-61.

514

"Tuition fees: The higher cost of higher education." CBC News, 2006.09.01. *www.cbc.ca/news/background/higher-education/*, accessed 2009.06.07.

Tzu Chi Foundation Canada website, *en.tzuchi.ca/canada/home.nsf/about/index*, accessed 2010.05.24.

University of Alberta website, *www.ualberta.ca*, accessed 2009.06.07 and 2010.07.04.

University of Manitoba Richardson Centre for Functional Foods and Nutraceuticals *website*, *umanitoba.ca/centres/rcffn/aboutus.html*, accessed 2014.12.07.

"Vice Premier: Future of Traditional Chinese Medicine Is Bright." *People's Daily Online,* 2008.01.25. *english.people.com.cn*, accessed 2010.05.17.

Walker, Robert, "History Made with Acupuncture Operation." *Calgary Herald*, 1996.10.14, B2.

Weng, Weijian and Junshi Chen. "The Eastern Perspective on Functional Foods Based on Traditional Chinese Medicine." *Nutrition Reviews* 54.11 (Nov. 1996): (II) S11-S16.

Whitwham, Brian. "No Alternative to Closure for Complementary Medicine Centre." *Canadian Medical Academic Journal* 168.7 (2003.04.01): 885.

"WHO [World Health Organization] Traditional Medicine Strategy 2002-2005." *whqlibdoc.who.int/hq/2002/WHO_EDM_TRM_2002.1.pdf* , accessed 2009.05.28.

Wigod, Rebecca. "East Meets West at Vancouver Hospital: a Respected Physician Has Convinced the Facility to Open a Privately Funded Institute to Research Treatments Such as Acupuncture and Homeopathy.: Acceptance of Eastern Medical Techniques Expected to Bring Standards, Regulation;" (sic.). *The Vancouver Sun*, 1996.06.13, A1.

World Federation of Chinese Medicine Societies' website, *www.wfcms.org/English/*, accessed 2010.07.10.

World Chinese Medicine and Acupuncture College website, *wcmaac.com/about.html,* accessed 2014.12.07.

World Health Organization Statistical Information System. *www.who.int/whosis/data/Search.jsp*, accessed 2009.01.19.

"World's Top Cancer Research Body Sponsors Landmark COLD-FX Trial: NCI Study to Focus on Cold/Flu Fighting Potential for Leukemia Patients." *Marketwire*, 2008.11.17.

Yao, Chunyan, Ruiwen Hao, Shengli Pan, and Yin Wang. Functional Foods Based on Traditional Chinese Medicine." In *Nutrition, Well-being and Health,* edited by Jaouad Bouayed, 179-200. Shanghai: InTech, 2012.

Yip, Yen. "New Age Medicine Meets Western Science." *University Affairs*, October 1999: 16-19.

Yuan, Robert and Yuan Lin. "Traditional Chinese Medicine: An Approach to Scientific Proof and Clinical Validation." *Pharmacology & Therapeutics* 86 (2000): 191-198.

Zhao-Seiler, Nina. "Sustainability of Chinese Medicinal Herbs: A Discussion." *Journal of Chinese Medicine* 101 (Feb. 2013): 42-46.

10. CONCLUSION

This final chapter summarizes the findings and consolidates the claims made in this book. Included are descriptions of significant sources of information about Chinese Canadians, the historical transformation of Chinatowns, the preservation and promotion of Chinese culture in Canada, the economic influence of Chinese Canadians, the presence of Chinese language media in Canada, the work of the Culture Regeneration Research Society, Chinese Canadian institutional eldercare, and the establishment of Traditional Chinese Medicine in Canada.

The claims reviewed are that the achievements of Chinese Canadians offer attractive alternatives to the Canadian mainstream; that Chinese culture has had a role in these achievements and, therefore, may be something that mainstream Canadians would want to study; and that, even though Chinese culture may have had a role in Chinese Canadian achievements, they still want to form a Canadian identity, but that there is some resistance on the part of mainstream Canadians to them doing so.

1. Sources of Information on Chinese Canadians

Information on Chinese Canadians can be found across a number of organizations, projects, and texts. Organizations that make this information available include the University of British Columbia, Simon Fraser University, the Asia Pacific Foundation of Canada, and the Chinese Canadian National Council. The collection of the University of British Columbia contains nearly ninety years of copies of one of the earliest Chinese language newspapers in Canada the *Dahan Gongbao (Chinese Times,* Vancouver) and personal papers, such as those of Alexander Cumyow the first Chinese born in Canada. The university also maintains an informational website: "The Chinese Experience in British Columbia: 1850-1950."

Simon Fraser University houses the David C. Lam Institute for East-West Studies that provides access to the database "Historical Chinese Language Materials in BC." It contains more than eleven thousand records. The Asia Pacific

Foundation of Canada has produced a number of reports documenting the achievements of Chinese Canadians as part of its mission to engage Canadians with Asia. The Chinese Canadian National Council is very active in disseminating information on contemporary popular activities among Chinese Canadians, particularly youth.

Projects that have gathered significant information about Chinese Canadians are the Multicultural Canada Project and the Chinese-Canadian Genealogy Project. The Multicultural Canada Project is noteworthy in its efforts to provide online access to primary sources of information, such as newspapers. The Chinese-Canadian Genealogy Project, besides offering resources that allow Chinese Canadians to discover their family history in Canada, also provides resources for researching their general history.

There are also a number of texts that include detailed bibliographies and consolidate information about Chinese Canadians. *From China to Canada: A History of the Chinese Communities in Canada* and *The Chinese in Vancouver, 1945-1980: The Pursuit of Identity and Power* have elaborate bibliographies of sources of information. *The Chinese in Canada* is one of the best overviews of contemporary Chinese Canadians. Also of value is *Chinatowns: Towns within Cities in Canada* for its history of early Chinese Canadian settlements.

Finally, there is the possibility of having access to the historical records of Chinese Canadian organizations that to this point have remained closed. As holders, such as the Chinese Freemasons (Hongmen hui), of these records, recognize the benefit of doing so, they will make them available for academic research.

2. Chinese Canadian Achievements

The establishment of Chinatowns was the earliest achievement of Chinese Canadians. They were established in the face of strong, sometimes violent opposition, and a lack of acceptance that lasted into the 1960s. In their more than one hundred fifty years of history Chinatowns have provided first for the needs of Chinese Canadians and now increasingly for the broader population as well. They provided goods and services not available elsewhere, physical protection, support for ethnic businesses and workers, and a platform for

developing the skills needed to enter mainstream society. As
Chinese Canadians needs evolved other functions also became
important: Chinatowns have become supporters and symbols of
Chinese culture. They hold cultural events, conduct language
schools, serve as a two-way gateway for participation in both
Chinese and mainstream society, and, as symbols of Chinese
culture, serve to fortify heritage values that Chinese Canadians
aspire to preserve.

The first Chinatown was established in Victoria in about
1860. At its peak it contained about one hundred fifty
businesses, theatres, Chinese schools, temples and shrines, a
hospital, then-legal opium factories, gambling dens, and
brothels. Today, depending on how one defines "Chinatown,"
there are nine to eighteen Chinatowns in Canada, a range that
does not include the Chinese themed shopping centres that are
drawing Chinese Canadians to reside in their vicinity. Of these
Chinatowns, those in Vancouver and Toronto stand out for
various reasons. Vancouver's population is nearly 20 percent
Chinese Canadian, and that of neighbouring Richmond about
45 percent. This large population, combined with a long history
of Chinese Canadian presence and a proximity to Asia, have led
to a vibrant historical Chinatown in Vancouver's center, with a
cultural centre, a museum, archives, the Dr. Sun Yat-sen
Classical Garden, as well as the social agency United Chinese
Community Enrichment Services Society (S.U.C.C.E.S.S.).
Richmond, in contrast, is highly commercialized with shopping
centres and restaurants catering to well-to-do Chinese
Canadian consumers.

Toronto is noted for having two designated Chinatowns, in
addition to more than sixty-five Chinese shopping centres. The
shopping centres are manifestations of the changing nature of
the concentrations of Chinese Canadian populations and the
economic contributions that they are making to the
communities in which they are situated.

Of course, Canada's Chinatowns have been faced with
many challenges. They were subjected to mob attacks early in
their history and to demolition as slums in the 1960s. Having
overcome these challenges, historical Chinatowns are facing
new ones. They are inadequate to meet Chinese Canadian
needs, so Chinese Canadians are conducting many of their
activities elsewhere, leaving the historical Chinatowns lacking
vitality. At the same time, the properties within Chinatown

have increased in value as the areas surrounding them have developed. This has encouraged the property owners to want to sell them for purposes outside the traditional ones in Chinatown, such as for office buildings and which would again undermine Chinatown's sustainability. Finally, as more and more elderly have made their homes in Chinatowns, it has led to a resident population that has less spending power as well as ability to support the community.

These challenges give rise to the question of whether Chinatowns will be able to survive. In answer to this question it should be pointed out that many organizations, both from inside and outside the Chinese Canadian community, believe there are practical benefits to preserving historical Chinatown and are taking measures to ensure their viability. Chinese Canadians also have a long history of defending, preserving, and promoting Chinatowns that leads them to continue to do so. Finally, there is the long term perspective that Chinatowns preserve a critical mass of traditional Chinese cultural values that should be preserved and promoted as resources for Chinese Canadians and alternative options for those outside this community.

The preservation and promotion of Chinese culture is another achievement of Chinese Canadians. Arguably, the most obvious manifestation of this achievement is the use of Chinese language within Canada. The 2011 Canadian census reported that there were 1,112,610 individuals using Chinese as their mother tongue—comprising about 84 percent of Chinese Canadians—and that Chinese was the third most used mother tongue in Canada. Chinese Canadians began formally educating the younger generations in the Chinese language and culture as early as the nineteenth century when the number of Chinese Canadian children in Victoria reached about one hundred. By the 1930s there were an estimated twenty-six Chinese schools in eleven locations across Canada. Present day estimates vary from thirty-five to three hundred schools in the two cities of Vancouver and Toronto alone.

The efforts of the language schools are augmented by the widespread presence of Chinese language media in Canada. Experts claim that there are at least two hundred outlets and that Canada has some of the richest Chinese-language media outside Greater China. These media not only provide widespread usage of Chinese, which emboldens the average speaker, but also specifically promote the language's use through employment opportunities and speech and writing contests.

Besides the promotion of Chinese language through the schools and media, there is the direct promotion of Chinese culture in cultural centres, artistic expression, and festivals. There are at least seven Chinese cultural centres in various Canadian cities, which offer presentations and instruction in Chinese arts, cooking, and language, as well as housing libraries. There is Chinese Canadian literature written in both English and Chinese. Chinese New Year celebrations attract thousands of participants in individual cities across Canada and the Dragon Boat Festival is widely celebrated.

Chinese food is deeply associated with the culture. From the medicinal qualities attached to it, through the evocative descriptions on Chinese menus, to the variety of fresh produce in Chinese grocery stores, one finds a rich cultural significance attached to Chinese food.

Arguably, the achievements of Chinese Canadians are most obvious in the economy. The impoverished status of early Chinese Canadians is easily seen from their wages being half that of the average and their large presence in low-profit ethnic industries. Yet, today, on average, they live in more expensive homes and have greater disposable income, and their economic activities encompass a broad range and are not restricted to enclaves. There are large economic organizations controlled by Chinese Canadians, such as Li Ka-shing's ownership of Husky Oil or the H.Y. Louie family's ownership of one of the largest grocery wholesale and distribution companies in British Columbia and London Drugs. Besides the large commercial operations, there are also large business associations that promote industry standards and progress, such as the Chinese Professionals Association of Canada.

The most apparent areas of Chinese Canadian economic achievement are in business investment and property development. Chinese investors have dominated the Canadian government's Business Immigration Program, investing billions of dollars in the country while creating tens of thousands of jobs. Chinese Canadian firms have also been prominent in developing residential and commercial property. Early notice of this occurred when what was described as "the biggest urban development on the continent" took place in 1988. Concord Pacific Developments Ltd. purchased the 82.5 hectares that comprised the former Expo 86 lands in downtown Vancouver for one hundred twenty-five-million dollars and proceeded to commit three billion dollars to building eight thousand five hundred housing units along with schools, daycare centres, hotels, parks, and theaters for twenty thousand residents. The company has followed with developments across Canada, most notably on former Toronto railway lands. Other Chinese Canadian residential development companies, such as the Hopewell Group of Companies, are also well known in the industry. Even Yee Hong Centre for Geriatric Care, the noted provider of culturally sensitive eldercare, has begun designing and building housing to suit their clients.

The main manifestation of Chinese Canadian commercial development is the large number of Chinese-themed shopping centres that have been built across Canada. The early versions were mostly developed by Chinese Canadians, but as mainstream developers realized their potential, they too began to build them. These shopping centres cater to Chinese Canadian shoppers with familiar products and service in Chinese, and they spared both Toronto and Vancouver the pain of deeper recessions as their construction buoyed their economies. There were more than sixty-five of them in Toronto as of 2006 and ten in Vancouver as of 1998. They are also found in Calgary and Montreal.

Given the apparency of Chinese Canadian economic achievements, it is a promising area for exploration of the reasons for these achievements, perhaps even for the reasons for Chinese Canadians achievements in general. There are academics who argue that the achievements of Chinese Canadians should primarily be attributed to factors external to the community, such as the economic restrictions that forced them to strive more than most to survive and improve themselves. On the other hand, there are also strong arguments for exploring the strength of Chinese culture in contributing to these achievements. This book claims that more weight should be given to it especially in face of evidence that Canada is generally under-estimating the potential contributions of Chinese Canadians. One of these potential contributions is to facilitate trade between Canada and China, an area that Canada has been weak in. Many Chinese Canadian entrepreneurs are transnationalists who travel and live in both

Canada and China. They are helping the country make inroads into the region.

The creation of a large scale Chinese language media in Canada—some of the most developed outside Greater China—is another remarkable achievement of Chinese Canadians. There are national television and newspaper networks, local newspapers, local radio and TV stations, and many forms of internet publication. Mainstream media organizations, such as the Canadian Broadcasting Corporation, have also recognized the demand so are disseminating some of their content in Chinese.

Again, after looking at early Chinese Canadians, this achievement seems even more remarkable. Most of the early immigrants were illiterate and poor; there would have been little need for and few resources to support Chinese language media. Yet, by the early twentieth century there were daily Chinese newspapers circulating in Vancouver and Toronto. Large numbers of educated, and sometimes wealthy Chinese immigrants, arriving in the 1980s and onward, gave a further boost to Chinese language media. Their investments, expertise, and demand led to the creation of national newspaper and television networks and many local Chinese language media.

Chinese Canadians have three main accomplishments with regard to Chinese language media. The development itself has reached a remarkable level and it is said that "Chinese language television and radio programming in Canada has arguably become the richest and most sophisticated outside China, Hong Kong and Taiwan."[1] A second accomplishment is the amount of advertising that Chinese language media attracts. A third are the media's efforts to encourage Chinese Canadians to involve themselves in the Canadian mainstream. In a little more than a hundred years since Chinese language media were established in Canada, Chinese Canadians have developed a vast and complex network that not only spans the nation but also reaches into niche markets, with newspapers, television and radio programming, and internet sites devoted to business, human health, entertainment, and other areas.

---

[1] Zhou Min, Wenhong Chen, and Guoxuan Cai, "Chinese-language Media and Immigrant Life in the United States and Canada," in *Media and the Chinese Diaspora: Community, Communications, and Commerce,* ed. Wanning Sun (London: Routledge, 2006), 66.

The quantity of and revenue from advertising in Chinese language media is substantial. Some newspapers contain more than 50 percent advertising. The total advertising revenue for Toronto's three main Chinese dailies in 1996 was a total of 34.5 million dollars, which can be compared to advertising revenues of 215 million dollars in the Toronto Star in 2001, which had a target audience twelve times greater and a circulation seven times that of all the Chinese language dailies together. Chinese language media have also been promoting Chinese Canadian participation in the Canadian mainstream. They support mainstream charities, such as children's hospitals, cancer societies, and major art groups. They also do major reporting on important national events, such as elections.

In spite of these efforts to involve Chinese Canadians in mainstream activities, Chinese language media is still criticized for contributing to the isolation of Chinese Canadians by sourcing large portions of their content from Greater China. Nevertheless, there has been a significant change in focus away from China and toward Canada starting in the 1960s with the English language *Chinatown News* and later the radio program "Pender Guy." Since then, major media have made it their mandate to foster a Canadian identity for their consumers.

The mandate of the Culture Regeneration Research Society (CRRS) is to promote the exchange between and mutual enhancement of Chinese and Western cultures. The reason for its location on Canada's West Coast seems obvious, with the latter's large Chinese Canadian population and cultural influence. Founded in 1994 and led by an active scholar Thomas Leung, CRRS has focused on education as the main means by which to achieve its goals. Headquartered in Burnaby, CRRS has six offices around the world. Revenue for the Vancouver, Hong Kong, and U.S. offices all together has been about $1.8 million annually in recent years. One of CRRS's main programs is to provide basic education in poor areas of China. It began in rural areas then expanded to the children of migrant workers in Shanghai. It has now taken up educating Canadian youth about the needs of China.

As part of its mission, CRRS also publishes extensively. The journal *Wenhua Zhongguo (Cultural China)*, has published quarterly since 1994, researches Chinese culture and compares it to Western counterparts. CRRS also produces books and video and audio recordings that introduce Chinese culture to overseas Chinese and organizes conferences around the theme of developing Chinese culture.

Regarding the CRRS achievements, it has been innovative in fostering interaction and mutual learning between Chinese and Western cultures. It has also retained a neutral position in dealing with the different political entities in Greater China, which has allowed it to present a variety of perspectives in its various fora. It has also gained access to high ranking Chinese government officials, allowing it to assist more than eight thousand economically-disadvantaged Chinese students complete their education, many of them female.

CRRS has two distinct characteristics: the altruistic nature of its mission and its promotion of Christianity, which are obviously related. The altruism is fortified with strong idealism, such as to infuse the Chinese community with the highest ideals of ethics and spiritual discipline from the West, and tempered with the practical endeavour of providing basic education in poorer regions in China. The president and founder Thomas Leung holds that the Christian spirit of unconditional love, self-sacrifice, and forgiveness could have a positive influence in China. This thinking has led to CRRS partnering with Lanzhou University to establish the Research Centre for Christianity Studies and assisting Sichuan University in launching the first doctoral programme in Christian studies in China.

In spite of CRRS' lofty ideals, it does face two issues that will complicate its future. One, its resources, reflecting demand, are overwhelmingly devoted to promoting the development of China, compared to the development of the West, particularly Canada, where it is resident and securing major support. Two, CRRS relies heavily upon Leung's leadership. Canadians, in general, do not seem open to learning from Chinese culture, which has led the organization to focus its efforts more on China. Leung is CRRS' founder and his activities garner most of its support. He is very much the "face" of the organization. While his efforts have been largely successful, at this point it would be difficult for CRRS to continue if he were unable to take the leading role.

The provision of care for elders is not only an achievement, it is also an area within which Chinese Canadians have excelled, establishing standards that surpass those of the mainstream, particularly at a time when there are serious concerns about the viability of the mainstream system. The senior population, which requires more care, is increasing as are health costs, which is leading governments to look for alternative ways of caring for the elderly. Chinese Canadians, after much lobbying, have been able to persuade governments that they can provide such alternatives, with culturally-sensitive care that is client-centered and community-based.

Chinese Canadians have developed two types of organizations for the care of their seniors: nursing homes and facilities that work to allow seniors to remain independent longer. The much-awarded Yee Hong Centre for Geriatric Care is an example of the first type. It has been managing more than eight hundred long term care beds in four different centres in the Toronto area. Besides in-house services for residents of the centres, Yee Hong also provides community services, such as daycare programs, visitation, and transportation. Yee Hong also manages subsidized housing along with independent living housing linked to a long term care facilities. Yee Hong is required to raise 2.5 million dollars a year to cover operation expenses and accumulate capital to construct new centres. It also relies on the services of more than one thousand volunteers.

Yee Hong's achievements have been closely followed by other organizations wanting to duplicate them. They too have raised general standards for Chinese Canadian eldercare, promoted culturally-sensitive eldercare, and fostered innovation in the industry. There are, at least, thirteen of these Chinese Canadian operated organizations that support the elderly with a range of services and individual care. Apart from them, housing societies, that manage apartment buildings such as the Wah Ying Mansions in Edmonton and the Chinese Community Building in Ottawa, support Chinese elders who are then able to live independently longer.

While examining Chinese Canadian achievements in establishing culturally sensitive eldercare for their seniors, there are also four issues that should be considered. It is questionable whether the underlying value of filial piety can be sustained. The second issue is whether the Chinese Canadian elderly need, or even want, the resources that have been provided for their care. Also an issue is the fact that Chinese Canadians had to make such an effort in order to provide adequate care for their elderly. The fourth issue is the viability of maintaining this achievement given the attractiveness of the service to non-Chinese. In spite of the existence of these issues, Chinese Canadian eldercare remains a model that the mainstream can learn from.

Another achievement of Chinese Canadians, the establishment of Traditional Chinese Medicine (TCM) in Canada, is unusual in that it has already become a common practice and not just a model. What is known as TCM, ironically, owes much of its existence to the efforts of early Chinese Communist leaders who choose to consolidate and systematize the myriad of practices that comprised native Chinese medicine in order to create and preserve a coherent body of knowledge as well as to articulate its merits for practitioners of Western medicine. TCM's popularity outside of China can be attributed, in part, to its underlying concepts and theories. Its emphasis on maintaining good health; a balance in the influences on one's health; its holistic consideration of one's health, environment, and psychological state; and the importance of one being proactive in maintaining one's health; all resonate with users. The practices within TCM also contribute to its acceptance. Diet is a major one, which manifests many of TCM's underlying concepts. Herbal medicine, acupuncture, and massage are also widely practised.

These concepts, theories, and practices contributed to China having one of the earliest medical systems in the world and to the benefits apparent today. One benefit is its effectiveness; it has historically supported a large Chinese population and continues to do so today, making up an estimated 40 percent of all health care delivered in China. It can be argued that TCM contributes largely to the prevention of illnesses, disease, and injury. The low per capita expenditure on medical interventions means that TCM is also economical. The simplicity of and use of natural ingredients in TCM contribute to this.

TCM's use and promotion by China have created a basis for its acceptance around the world, including in Canada. Besides developing TCM for domestic use, the government is boosting standards, including conducting clinical research on the safety and efficacy of TCM remedies, encouraging international collaboration, improving manufacturing techniques, and bringing the drug regulatory system into line with international guidelines. These have contributed to the institutionalization of

TCM within Canada. A number of hospitals provide acupuncture treatment, there are many commercial practitioners and herbal remedy producers, including for Cold-FX, claimed to be the top selling cold and flu remedy in Canada since 2004. TCM is also regulated by legislation in five provinces and by the federal government. This legislation includes the establishment of colleges to oversee accreditation. Accompanying this legislation, TCM practitioners have established their own organizations for self-governance and schools to teach related knowledge and skills.

As TCM practice in Canada adopts a structure similar to that in place for Western conventional medicine, it appears likely that Canada will see more integration of the two systems. Rising health costs will make alternatives available through TCM more attractive. Furthermore, TCM practitioners often have a deep knowledge of Western medicine; therefore, are able to balance the limitations of and integrate the merits of the two systems.

In reviewing the achievements of Chinese Canadians, there are a number that stand out. There are the preservation and promotion of Canada's Chinatowns, the preservation and promotion of Chinese culture, Chinese Canadians' widespread economic influence, the development of Chinese language media, the promotion of Western and Chinese cultural interaction, the establishment of eldercare for Chinese Canadian seniors, and the integration of TCM with the mainstream medical system.

3. Alternatives for the Mainstream

In reviewing the achievements of Chinese Canadians, of particular note are the alternatives that they have established for the mainstream. The fact that Chinese Canadians have proven themselves to be pioneers in heritage education, founders of culturally sensitive eldercare, and developers of an alternative system of medicine within Canada are more obvious examples. Other examples are not that much less apparent. Canada Chinatowns, all nine to eighteen of them, offer a myriad of alternatives, whether it is in celebration of traditional holidays, or education in another language, or even a meal on Christmas Eve. The cultural idioms of Chinese Canadians also offer alternatives to the Canadian mainstream. Chinese orchestras abound; Chinese Canadian authors present a different, less-known perspective; martial arts are based on a different paradigm of self-development; and so on. Chinese cuisine is particularly different, with its communally shared dishes, the use of chopsticks, and de-emphasization of consumption of animal products. Chinese Canadian economic achievement has brought variety in shopping experience and products, as well as different commercial ownership models, such as strata titles. Chinese Canadian eldercare facilities have set high standards for eldercare and established a precedent for providing culturally-sensitive eldercare. Traditional Chinese Medicine offers a credible complement or alternative to treatment with Western medicine, especially in its emphasis on maintaining good health.

In providing these alternatives Chinese Canadians highlight the value of the policy of multiculturalism in Canada. Chinese Canadians have established actual alternatives, values in practice, rather than formulating mere ideas. Furthermore, many of them have a critical mass, e.g., culturally-sensitive eldercare or Chinese food, that give them a higher profile in Canadian society and make them more viable. With a critical mass, the implementation of the values underlying these alternatives can be studied more thoroughly and, if chosen, further adopted by the mainstream and supported by resources already in place within the Canadian Chinese community.

The measure of success for multiculturalism should not only be mutual tolerance and support for other cultures. It should also be a measure of how open a mainstream culture is to adopting the values or methods of other cultures if those values and methods prove superior. Arguably, Chinese Canadians have provided examples where there are values and methods outside those commonly used in the mainstream that are superior, which should be sufficient to make them attractive to the mainstream. Probably, the most successful example is found in Traditional Chinese Medicine. When one sees the long life spans of Chinese Canadians, as seen in Alberta and Richmond, one naturally is curious about the possible reasons for it. When one cannot find satisfaction within the mainstream medical system, TCM is one of the more obvious alternatives. Anecdotally, practitioners of TCM will tell you that the majority of their patients are not Chinese Canadians. Assuming these observations are accurate and these patients are receiving relief for their ills, TCM is an alternative that is being integrated with the mainstream system and, therefore, is evidence of the further value of multiculturalism.

4. The Role of Chinese Culture

Arguably, Chinese culture has had a significant role in producing the achievements of Chinese Canadians. There is firstly the contribution it has made in uniting Chinese Canadians. While this is a role that any strong culture can play, in the case of Chinese Canadians, Chinese culture has helped overcome particularly difficult barriers, which were the restrictions placed on Chinese Canadians for the first near hundred years of their presence in Canada. In other words, the support provided by their culture had to be especially fortifying in order to allow Chinese Canadians to survive and eventually prosper in spite of those restrictions. The value of mutual support enabled them to live and work together for survival and protection, while the value of perseverance allowed them to overcome institutional racism to become equal and one of the more successful segments of Canadian society.

The argument is that culture was likely a necessary support that allowed Chinese Canadian identity to survive the physical attacks, the restrictions on their employment, the prevention of their early immigration, and to emerge strong enough to preserve their culture, their communities, and even assist the mainstream in an exemplary way during WW II. If this culture had not been strong, there would have been little or no Chinese Canadian identity for new immigrants to build upon when they arrived after 1947 and, subsequently, their achievements would have been very different. For example, how likely would it have been for *Sing Tao* to establish itself in Canada if there had not already been a number of Chinese language daily newspapers published there for more than fifty years?

Moreover, the role of Chinese culture goes beyond creating an identity and thereby unifying the community. This may not be easy to see in early Chinese Canadian history when the role of creating an identity was essential to their survival and even though the role exemplified extraordinary strength because this identity had to be forged facing very strong opposition. However, in the present age, one finds examples of a strong link between Chinese culture and other Chinese Canadian achievements. The establishment of superior eldercare is motivated by the filial piety and general respect for the elderly important in Chinese thinking. In a Canadian setting it has been translated into devoted caregiving, successful fund raising, and large volunteer efforts. There is a strong synergy between widespread Chinese language use and the highly-developed Chinese-language media. The former enables and creates a demand for the latter and the latter encourages even more use of the former. The production of Chinese literature creates quality writers, who, in turn, can turn their skills to enhance the content of the media. A confidence in and the practice of Traditional Chinese Medicine has enabled Chinese Canadians not only to maintain a higher level of health, but also to establish a complementary medical system to the mainstream one. In understanding the economic achievements of Chinese Canadians, one should also acknowledge the important contribution that Chinese culture has made to them. The pursuit of education, the willingness to persevere, the prominence of mutual support, the value of personal responsibility, and efforts to maintain harmony in society and business dealings, all contribute to better economic outcomes, ones that are found among Chinese Canadians.

It is also these economic outcomes that are the most apparent examples of Chinese Canadian achievements. Economic indicators are some of the most objective, broadest, and easiest to measure in determining success and thus achievement. Chinese Canadians have progressed from been one of the most disadvantaged—and discriminated—groups in Canada to one of the richest. It is even the case that by the third generation Chinese Canadians have become the highest average employment-income-earning group in Canada, surpassing all other third generation groups, including White Canadians.[2] Furthermore, research has shown that later generations of Chinese Canadians tend to retain Chinese cultural values, similar to the way that those born abroad do.[3]

[2] Jack Jedwab, "The Changing Vertical Mosaic: Intergenerational Comparisons in Income on the Basis of Visible Minority Status in Canada, 2006" (Montreal: The Association for Canadian Studies, 2008), 2.

[3] Ai-Lan Chia and Catherine Costigan, "Understanding the Multidimensionality of Acculturation Among Chinese Canadians," *Canadian*

This is not surprising, given that the Canadian policy of multiculturalism encourages a diversity of identities, a claim also supported in the research.[4]

5. Pursuit of a Canadian Identity

5.1 Creating a Canadian Identity

While highlighting the role of Chinese culture in the achievements of Chinese Canadians, it is also important to keep in mind Chinese Canadian efforts to establish an identity, and thus culture, that is accepted within Canada. There is a long history to these efforts. As early as 1914 Chinese Canadians were referring to themselves as such, i.e., "Chinese Canadians." In the 1970s Vancouver's Chinese population were expressing a desire to establish an identity grounded in their Canadian residency. Media had a role in awakening this will. In 1974, a tabloid called *Gum Sam Po* challenged the ethnic Chinese in Vancouver to make their concept of a Chinese-Canadian community a viable one. The radio program Pender Guy, running from 1976 to 1981, featured descriptions of Chinese-Canadian experiences.

Present day media have picked up this mandate. Fairchild Media Group seeks to foster a local identity for ethnic Chinese, and encourage them to participate in mainstream society. *Ming Pao* envisioned constructing a new identity for Chinese in Canada when it entered Canada in 1993 with more depth, breadth, and amount of Canadian news.

This trend was subsequently reflected in the Ethnic Diversity Survey in 2002. "The survey revealed that 84 percent of ethnic Chinese has assumed Canadian citizenship, 53 percent expressed a sense of belonging to Canada (just below the average for all ethnic groups), while 40.5 percent had a sense of Canadian identity (above other visible minorities, but below whites)."[5] Furthermore, a *Ming Pao* survey revealed "the

---

Journal of Behavioural Science 38.4 (Oct. 2006), 321.

[4] *Ibid.*, 320.

[5] David Ley, *Millionaire Migrants: Trans-Pacific Life Lines*, (Chichester, U.K.: Wiley-Blackwell, 2010), 222-23, citing J. Reitz and R. Banerjee, "Racial Inequality, Social Cohesion and Policy Issues in Canada," in *Belonging?*

same steady incorporation of Canadian identity over time, with the respondents describing themselves as Canadian or Chinese-Canadian rising from 29 percent for those resident five years or less to 43 percent among those resident more than ten years, with an equivalent decline in the numbers self-identifying as Chinese or Canadian-Chinese."[6]

5.2 Barriers to Creating a Canadian Identity

In spite of Chinese Canadian achievements and their desire and efforts to forge a Canadian identity, suspicion lingers that they are still subject to deliberate neglect or even racism. Part of the reason for this is that not only are newly arriving Chinese immigrants finding it difficult to make an adequate living in spite of the high levels of education and expertise they possess, they also seem to be encountering discrimination in their efforts to improve themselves. Many find it difficult to find work commensurate with their credentials and experience and find their abilities underutilized. For this reason, some return to Greater China to develop their futures there.

This phenomenon would be easier to explain if it were restricted to individuals and their inability to find suitable employment; however, it also occurs in the lack of development of foreign trade. Canadian companies refuse opportunities to develop trade with China when Chinese Canadians with suitable experience approach them. Michael Chan is Chairman of Café de Coral, one of the world's largest Chinese fast food restaurant groups and owner and operator of Manchu Wok in North America. As a Canadian who studied and worked there, he thought that his company could have strong business ties with the country, but instead Canadian companies do not approach them. He gives the example of their buying beef from

---

Diversity, Recognition and Shared Citizenship in Canada, ed. K. Banting, T. Courchene, and F. L. Seidle (Montreal, Institute for Research on Public Policy, 2007), 489-545. , and *Ming Pao,* "Telephone Survey for *Ming Pao:* Recognition of Identity among Ethnic Chinese and Cross–Cultural Marriage," 1997.12.24, A1.

[6] *Ibid.,* citing *Ming Pao,* "Telephone Survey for *Ming Pao:* Recognition of Identity among Ethnic Chinese and Cross–Cultural Marriage," 1997.12.24, A1.

Australia instead of Canada, in part because Canadian producers are unwilling to tailor their cuts to Asian standards.[7]

The sociologist Peter Li offers further insight into the phenomenon with a description of the integration of immigrants to Canada. He argues that Canada, in promoting the value of integration, should be more open to its immigrants, but is not:

> If integration is meant to be a two-way street as officially endorsed, the integration discourse has only succeeded in insisting upon a report card to show how immigrants have been changing or not changing in Canada, and not a similar report care to indicate the degree of institutional openness with which Canadian society is accepting newcomers as equal partners to shape the future of the nation.[8]

On an institutional level, Canada has not succeeded in being open to the benefits that immigrants have presented to the country.

6. Conclusion

In closing, one should note that this book is not comprehensive. There are other Chinese Canadian achievements that have not been described. For example, Chinese Canadians have made significant contributions to the diversification and support of religious practices. The spread of and the construction of Buddhist temples has largely been supported by Chinese Canadians. There are also large congregations of Chinese Christians and their similarly large churches. Their existence creates another avenue for further integration of Chinese Canadians with the mainstream. Chinese Canadians also comprise a large proportion of the practitioners in the medical and science professions. This positions them to make further contributions to Canadian society.

---

[7] Andrea Mandel-Campbell, "Leaving Canada Behind," *Maclean's* 120.13 (2007.04.09).

[8] Peter Li, "Deconstructing Canada's Discourse of Immigrant Immigration," Working Paper No. WP04-03 (Prairie Centre of Excellence for Research on Immigration and Integration, August 2003), 11.

Another theme that deserves more attention is the integration, both actual and potential, of Chinese culture with its mainstream Canadian counterpart. It can be found in the complementary use that "consumers" make of TCM and mainstream medicine, e..g., Tai Lahans descriptions of how TCM can enhance treatment for cancer. It is found in the enjoyment and celebration by all Canadians of the Chinatowns that were once considered a scourge. It is likely in the future that Canadians of all ilks will want to understand more of China and look to Chinese Canadians to provide some of this understanding. Maybe then the Culture Regeneration Research Society will be able to fulfill a more balanced mandate by promoting the merits of Chinese culture to the Western mainstream.

This is not to say that Chinese Canadian achievements have not been recognized. To a certain extent they have been, albeit in a limited way. From 1967 through 2010 fifty-three Chinese Canadians were appointed to the Order of Canada.[9] Moreover, popular interest in Chinese Canadians has increased in step with the rising influence of China. The talents and culture of Chinese Canadians are now seen as convenient channels into understanding and taking advantage of the strengths of China. At the same time, Chinese Canadians have developed sufficient resources to promote their causes, such as culturally-sensitive care for their elders, leading not only to effective venues for doing so, but also to even greater interest in Chinese Canadians on the part of the Canadian mainstream.

BIBLIOGRAPHY

Chia, Ai-Lan and Catherine Costigan. "Understanding the Multidimensionality of Acculturation Among Chinese Canadians." *Canadian Journal of Behavioural Science* 38.4 (Oct. 2006): 311-324.

Jedwab, Jack. "The Changing Vertical Mosaic: Intergenerational Comparisons in Income on the Basis of

---

[9] Simon Fraser University, David See-Chai Lam Centre for Communication website, *www.sfu.ca/chinese-canadian-history/chart_en.html#*, accessed 2015.03.24.

Visible Minority Status in Canada, 2006." Montreal: The Association for Canadian Studies, 2008. 9 pages.

Ley, David. *Millionaire Migrants: Trans-Pacific Life Lines.* Chichester, U.K.: Wiley-Blackwell, 2010.

Li, Peter. "Deconstructing Canada's Discourse of Immigrant Immigration." Working Paper No. WP04-03. Prairie Centre of Excellence for Research on Immigration and Integration, August 2003. 16 pages

Mandel-Campbell, Andrea. "Leaving Canada Behind." *Maclean's* 120.13 (2007.04.09): 24-27.

Simon Fraser University. David See-Chai Lam Centre for Communication website, *www.sfu.ca/chinese-canadian-history/chart_en.html#*, accessed 2015.03.24.

Zhou, Min, Wenhong Chen, and Guoxuan Cai. "Chinese-language Media and Immigrant Life in the United States and Canada." In *Media and the Chinese Diaspora: Community, Communications, and Commerce,* 42-74, edited by Wanning Sun. London: Routledge, 2006.

ABOUT THE AUTHOR

Lloyd Sciban is semi-retired professor of East Asian Studies at the University of Calgary in Calgary, Alberta, Canada. He studied in Taiwan for ten years. His research interests are Confucian ethics and the influence of Chinese culture in Canada. Since finishing this manuscript, he has begun research on the Chinese philosopher Wang Yangming (1472-1529) and his theory of the unity of knowing and acting and how it can be applied in environmental ethics.

CPSIA information can be obtained
at www.ICGtesting.com
Printed in the USA
LVHW091627020321
680381LV00001B/27

9 780978 424503